The Rough Guide to

Romania

written and researched by

Tim Burford and Norm Longley

with additional contributions by

Thomas Brown

D1302049

NEW YORK • LONDON • DELHI

www.roughguides.com

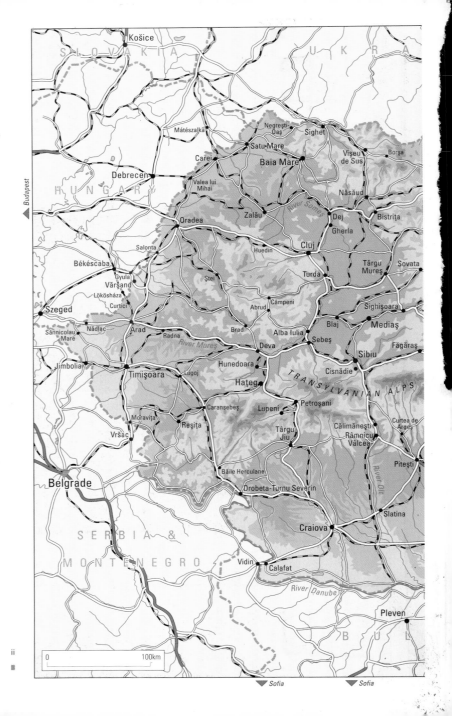

U K R A I N E

Chernovtsy

M O L D O V A

Metres
2000
1500
1000
500
200
100
0

Putna
Moldoviţa
Suceviţa
Rădăuţi
Botoşani
Suceava
Gura Humorului
Câmpulung
Moldovenesc
Paşcani
Vatra
Dornei
Târgu
Neamţ
Iaşi
River Prut
Chişinău
River Dnister
Toplita
Piatra
Neamţ
Roman
River Siret
Gheorgheni
Praid
Bacău
Vaslui
Huşi
Miercurea Ciuc
Bârlad
Odorheiu
Secuiesc
Adjud
UKRAINE
Mărăşeşti
Tecuci
Focşani
Braşov
Săcele
Galaţi
Chilia Veche
Periprava
Râşnov
Bran
Predeal
Brăila
Sulina
Sinaia
Tulcea
Murighiol
Câmpulung
Muscel
Buzău
R. Danube
Babadag
St Gheorghe
Ploieşti
Fǎurei
Târgovişte
Urziceni
Hârşova
EASTERN CARPATHIANS
Slobozia
Bucharest
Cernavodă
Medgidia
Mamaia
Oltenita
Călăraşi
Constanţa
Roşiorii de Vede
Silistra
Adamclisi
BLACK
Negru
Vodă
Giurgiu
Ruse
Mangalia
SEA
Kardam
Dobrich
Balčik
G   A   R   I   A
Varna
N

△ Town house, Sibiu

Introduction to

Romania

Travel in Romania is as rewarding as it is challenging. The country's fantastic mountain scenery and great diversity of wildlife, its cultures and people, and a way of life that at times seems little changed since the Middle Ages, leave few who visit unaffected. Rather than expecting an easy ride, try to accept whatever happens as an adventure – encounters with Gypsies, wild bears and oafish officials are likely to be far more interesting than anything purveyed by the tourist board.

As fascinating as the major cities are – such as the capital, Bucharest, Braşov, Cluj and Timişoara – Romania's charm essentially lies in the remoter, less-visited regions. Almost any exploration of the **villages** of rural Romania will be rewarding, with sights as diverse as the log houses in Oltenia, Delta villages built of reeds, and the magnificent wooden churches, with their sky-scraping Gothic steeples, of Maramureş, not to mention the country's abundance of more traditional churches, which reflect a history of competing communities and faiths. Romanians trace their **ancestry** back to the Romans, and have a noticeable Latin character – warm, spontaneous, anarchic, and appreciative of style and life's pleasures. In addition to ethnic Romanians, one and a half million Magyars pursue a traditional lifestyle long since vanished in Hungary, while dwindling numbers of Transylvanian Germans (Saxons) reside around the fortified towns and churches their ancestors built in the Middle Ages to guard the mountain passes. Along the coast, in the Delta and in the Banat, there's a rich mixture of Russians, Ukrainians, Serbs, Slovaks, Bulgars, Gypsies, Turks and Tatars.

The regime of **Nicolae Ceauşescu** drove the country to the brink of bankruptcy, and Ion Iliescu's efforts to provide tangible fruit of

Fact file

- Occupying an **area** of some 237,000 square kilometres, and with a **population** of around twenty-three million, Romania is one of central-eastern Europe's largest nations. Its capital, Bucharest, lies in the far south of the country on the plains of Wallachia, located between the Danube and the mountainous region of Transylvania to the north. The highest peak is Moldoveanu (2544m), in the Carpathian mountains.

- The constitution sets in place a **parliamentary system of government**, elected every four years, with the prime minister at its head – the president is head of state. Having been admitted to NATO in April 2004, Romania is set to become a full member of the European Union in 2007.

- **Tourism** is one of the fastest growing sectors of the Romanian economy, with mountain, coastal and health spa resorts absorbing the bulk of the country's tourist traffic. Romania's most important **exports** are textiles and footwear, metal products, and machinery and equipment, and its main trading partners are Italy and Germany.

- Romania's most famous **historical figure** is Vlad Țepeș (c1431–76), also known as Vlad the Impaler and, more familiarly, as Dracula.

1989's revolution further disrupted the economy; as a consequence, Emil Constantinescu's government had to embark on a savage austerity programme that has led to big cuts in real earnings. Although Romania remains one of Europe's poorer cousins, the country is at last on a firmer footing, and remains firmly on course for full European Union membership in 2007.

Where to go

The first point of arrival for many visitors to Romania is the capital, **Bucharest**. Whilst far from alluring – its wide nineteenth-century Parisian-style boulevards are choked with traffic, once-grand fin-de-siècle buildings are crumbling and the suburbs are dominated by grim

△ Lacu Roșu

apartment blocks – it remains the centre of the country's commercial and cultural life.

From the capital, most visitors make a beeline for the province of **Transylvania** to the north, setting for the country's most thrilling scenery and home to its finest cities: the gateway to Transylvania is **Braşov**, whose medieval old town is a good introduction to the Saxon architecture of the region, which reaches its peak in the fortified town of **Sibiu** and the jagged skyline of **Sighişoara**, Romania's most atmospherically sited town and the birthplace of Vlad the Impaler (Dracula). Further north and west, the great Magyar cities of **Târgu Mureş**, **Cluj** and **Oradea** have retained a wealth of medieval churches and streets, as well as impressive Baroque and Secession edifices. To the southwest of the country, near the border with Serbia, is **Timişoara**, source of the 1989 Revolution and a fine place to spend a day or two.

▽ Bucegi cable car

The best of Romania, though, is its countryside, and in particular the wonderful mountain scenery. The wild **Carpathians**, forming the frontier between Transylvania and, to the east and

Churches

Romania's abundance of **churches** testifies to its history of competing faiths, a religious mix that together with the frequency of invasions accounts for the country's extraordinary diversity of church **architecture**, ranging from the inspired wooden *biserici de lemn* in Maramureş villages to the austere fortified Kirchenburgen raised by the Saxons around Braşov and Sibiu. Having absorbed the Byzantine style of architecture in Moldavia and Wallachia, masons and architects ran riot with colour and mouldings (as at Curtea de Argeş) before producing wonderful ornamental stone facades – most notably at Iaşi's Church of the Three Hierarchs, and in Wallachia, where the Brâncoveanu style flourished, with its porticoes and stone carving derived from native woodwork motifs.

The **frescoes** so characteristic of medieval Orthodox churches achieved their ultimate sophistication in Maramureş, at the hands of largely unknown artists, and were boldly executed on the exterior walls of Suceviţa, Voroneţ and the other **Painted Monasteries** of Bucovina, in northern Moldavia. The Orthodox Church maintains dozens of monasteries, including Snagov, where Vlad the Impaler is buried, and Horez, Brâncoveanu's masterpiece.

south, Moldavia and Wallachia, shelter bears, stags, chamois and eagles; while the Bucegi, Făgăraş and Retezat ranges and the Padiş plateau offer some of the most undisturbed and spectacular hiking opportunities in Europe. In contrast to the crowded **Black Sea beaches** along Romania's east coast, the waterlogged **Danube Delta** is a place set apart from the rest of the country, where life has hardly changed for centuries and where boats are the only way to reach many of the settlements. During spring and autumn, especially, hundreds of species of birds from all over the Old World migrate through this area or come to breed. Whilst not quite as remote, the northern region of **Maramureş**, bordering the Ukraine, retains an almost medieval-like feel, its villages renowned for their fabulous wooden churches. Close by, sprinkled amidst the soft, rolling hills of **Bucovina**, are the wonderful Painted Monasteries, whose specimens of religious art are amongst some of the most outstanding in Europe.

△ Statue of Mátyás Corvinus, Cluj

When to go

The **climate** is pretty crucial in deciding where and when to go. Romanian **winters** can be fairly brutal – snow blankets much of the country, temperatures of minus fifteen to twenty degrees are not uncommon, and a strong, icy wind (the *crivaţ*) sweeps down from Russia. Conditions improve with **spring**, bringing rain and wildflowers to the mountains and the softest of blue skies over Bucharest, and

△ Sighet train station

OUTDOOR ACTIVITIES

Criss-crossed by an intricate nexus of forestry tracks and paths, many of them waymarked, the beautiful and unspoilt Romanian countryside offers some of the most enjoyable **hiking** anywhere in Europe, with trails to suit walkers of all abilities. Moreover, you're more likely to encounter local shepherds and foresters, or, if you're less lucky, brown bear, than you are other hikers. Cutting right across the country are the Carpathian mountains, whose best known range is the Făgăraş, between Braşov and Sibiu in the south of Transylvania, harbouring over seventy lakes and Romania's highest peaks. However, it's the Retezat and Piatra Craiului mountains, located respectively to the west and east of the Făgăraş, which present Romania's most challenging and scenically rewarding hikes. Close by, just south of Braşov, is the Bucegi massif, offering shorter and easier hikes (especially if you take advantage of the cable-cars to get you up the mountains). Less well known, and consequently much less visited, options include the remote and lovely Rodna mountains, near the Ukrainian border in Maramureş; the more modest Bucovina hills – studded with glorious Painted Monasteries – immediately east; and, closing off the western end of the Transylvanian plateau, the Apuseni mountains, which offer comparatively undemanding hikes but great karstic phenomena such as limestone caves, potholes and gorges. Hiking aside, Romania's mountains are also well disposed to **skiing**, with resorts such as Sinaia and Poiana Braşov in the Carpathians, and Borşa, in Maramureş, catering to a growing number of both domestic and foreign visitors.

△ Barbershop, Constanța

prompting the great migration of birds through the Delta. By May, the lowlands are warming up and you might well find strong sunshine on the coast before the season starts in July. Although by far the hottest time of the year, **summer** or **early autumn** is the perfect time to investigate Transylvania's festivals and hiking trails (though brief but violent thunderstorms are common in the Carpathians during this period), and to see the Painted Monasteries of Bucovina, while flocks of birds again pass through the Delta towards the **end of autumn**.

△ Rural transport

Average monthly temperature °C (°F)

	Braşov (The mountains)		Bucharest		Constanţa (The coast)		Timişoara (The Banat)	
	°C	°F	°C	°F	°C	°F	°C	°F
January	1	34	-3	26	-1	31	-2	28
February	1	34	-1	31	1	34	1	34
March	6	42	4	40	3	39	5	41
April	11	52	11	52	13	55	11	52
May	16	61	17	62	19	66	16	61
June	19	66	21	69	24	75	20	67
July	21	69	23	71	26	79	20	67
August	21	69	22	70	26	79	18	65
September	18	65	18	65	22	70	18	65
October	13	55	12	53	17	62	12	53
November	7	45	5	41	11	52	6	43
December	2	36	1	34	6	43	1	34

things not to miss

It's not possible to see everything Romania has to offer in one trip – and we don't suggest you try. What follows is a selective and subjective taste of the country's highlights: outstanding architecture, natural wonders, spectacular hikes and unforgettable festivals. They're arranged in five colour-coded categories, so you can browse through to find the very best things to see, do, buy and experience. All highlights have a page reference to take you straight into the guide, where you can find out more.

01 Prahova valley Page **134** • Riddled with impressive karstic formations, the Prahova valley is a suitably dramatic introduction to Transylvania.

02 **Timişoara** Page **335** • The crucible of the 1989 Revolution, Timişoara is one of Romania's most vibrant and engaging cities.

03 **Ceahlău massif** Page **253** • Teeming with wildlife, and swathed in beech, fir and pine, the weirdly shaped outcrops of the Ceahlău massif are yet another hiker's paradise.

04 **Pageant of the Juni**
Page **147** • Dancing, costumes and brass regiments constitute Braşov's liveliest event.

05 **Braşov** Page 142 • Shadowed by mountains and containing a fine Baroque centre, Braşov is one of Transylvania's most appealing cities.

06 **Black Sea** Page 364 • Strewn with brash resorts, the Black Sea coast offers opportunities aplenty for swimming, sailing or windsurfing.

07 **Constantin Brâncuşi**
Page **116** • Romania's greatest sculptor has bequeathed an impressive legacy of striking, yet simple, works of art, such as the *Endless Column* in Târgu Jiu.

08 Merry Cemetery, Sapânţa Page **309** • True to its name, the Merry Cemetery is a riot of beautifully carved and brightly coloured headstones.

09 Painted Monasteries Page **274** • Nestled behind huge walls, the monasteries of southern Bucovina are renowned for their magnificent exterior frescoes.

10 Measurement of the Milk Festival Page **229** • Enjoyable and unusual spectacle in which shepherds vie to see who has the most productive animals.

11 Peleş Castle, Sinaia Page **137** • Once a refuge for Ceauşescu and visiting dignitaries, Peleş remains the country's most opulent palace.

12 **Girl Fair of Muntele Găina** Page **225** • Taking place atop Mount Găina, this feverish spectacle of music, song and dance is one of the most anticipated festivals on the Romanian calendar.

14 **Dracula** Page **162** • The tomb at Snagov, old castle ruins at Poienari, and the birthplace in Sighişoara (below) – the Dracula legend is alive and kicking.

13 **Village homestay** Page **28** • Wonderful rural retreats offering cheap and relaxing accommodation and great home-cooked food.

15 **Wooden churches of Maramureş** Page **299** • The villages of this remote northern region are dominated by marvellous wooden churches, characterized by their magnificent Gothic spires.

16 **Vişeu de Sus train ride** Page **314** • Jump aboard the early morning logging train for a slow, meandering ride up the picturesque Vaser valley.

17 **Fǎgǎraş mountains** Page **154** • The spectacular snow-dusted peaks of the Fǎgǎraş are amongst the highest in Romania, providing access to some of the Carpathian's most challenging hikes.

18 Danube Delta Page **350** • Bordering the Ukraine, this remote and beautiful landscape has an abundant array of wildlife, and offers some of the finest bird-watching in Europe.

19 Spa visit
Page **342** •
Wallow in
temperatures
of 30 degrees C
at one of the
country's
many spa
resorts, such
as elegant
Băile Herculane.

20 Sheep's cheese Page **165** • Fresh from the highland pastures, a sample of tasty sheep's cheese is a must.

21 **Bicaz gorges** Page **255** • Take a drive through the majestic Bicaz gorges, bisected by sheer, three-hundred-metre-high limestone cliffs.

22 **Palace of Parliament, Bucharest** Page **71** • Formerly known as the "Madman's House", this monumental edifice is Ceauşescu's most conspicuous legacy.

23 Folk and Gypsy music

Page **230** • Don't miss the chance to experience the wild, irrepressible sounds of Romanian folk and Gypsy music.

24 Bear and wolf tracking

Page **153** • This excellent ecotourism project offers a rare chance to get close to Romania's most feared and revered creatures.

25 Hiking in the Carpathians

Page **40** • One of Europe's most stunning and least spoilt mountain ranges, the Carpathians are a first-class hiking region.

26 **Sighişoara** Page **159** • A brooding skyline of ramparts, towers and spires marks Sighişoara out as Transylvania's most atmospheric medieval town.

27 **Ţuică** Page **32** • A typically powerful Balkan brandy, Romania's national drink should be tried at least once.

Contents

Using this Rough Guide

We've tried to make this Rough Guide a good read and easy to use. The book is divided into six main sections, and you should be able to find whatever you want in one of them.

Colour section

The front colour section offers a quick tour of Romania. The **introduction** aims to give you a feel for the place, with suggestions on where to go. We also tell you what the weather is like and include a basic fact file.

Next, our authors round up their favourite aspects of Romania in the **things not to miss** section – whether it's great food, amazing sights or a special hotel. Right after this comes a full **contents** list.

Basics

The Basics section covers all the **pre-departure** nitty-gritty to help you plan your trip. This is where to find out which airlines fly to your destination, what paperwork you'll need, what to do about money and insurance, about Internet access, food, security, public transport, car rental – in fact just about every piece of **general practical information** you might need.

Guide

This is the heart of the Rough Guide, divided into user-friendly chapters, each of which covers a specific region. Every chapter starts with a list of **highlights** and an **introduction** that helps you to decide where to go, depending on your time and budget. Likewise, introductions to the various towns and smaller regions within each chapter should help you plan your itinerary. We start most town accounts

with information on arrival and accommodation, followed by a tour of the sights, and finally reviews of places to eat and drink, and details of nightlife. Longer accounts also have a directory of practical listings. Each chapter concludes with **public transport details** for that region.

Contexts

Read Contexts to get a deeper understanding of what makes Romania tick. We include a brief **history**, articles about **religion**, **wildlife**, **music** and **Dracula**, and a detailed further reading section that reviews dozens of **books** relating to the country.

Language

The **language** section gives useful guidance for speaking Romanian and pulls together all the vocabulary you might need on your trip, including a comprehensive **menu reader** and some words of German and Hungarian. Here, you'll also find a **glossary** of terms peculiar to the country.

small print + Index

Apart from a **full index**, which includes maps as well as places, this section covers publishing information, credits and acknowledgements, and also has our contact details in case you want to send in updates and corrections to the book – or suggestions as to how we might improve it.

Chapter list and map

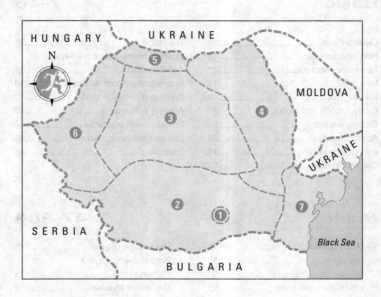

Contents

Colour section

Basics

Guide

Contexts

Language

small print and Index

Basics

Basics

Getting there

Flying is the easiest way to reach Romania, with TAROM and British Airways offering direct flights to Bucharest from the UK, although there are presently no direct flights from North America or Australasia. Travelling overland from the UK takes around a day and a half by train and two days by bus. If you are planning on including Romania as part of a wider trip, you may wish to consider an InterRail pass, which covers travel to and around Romania and is more economical than a return train ticket. The other option is driving, a journey of some 2000km from Britain; an absorbing trip but one best covered slowly over a couple of days.

Airfares always depend on the **season**, with the highest being around June to August; fares drop during the "shoulder" seasons – March to May and September to October – and you'll get the best prices during the low season, from November to February (excluding Christmas and New Year when prices are hiked up and seats are at a premium).

You can often cut costs by going through a **specialist flight agent**, who in addition to dealing with discounted flights may also offer student and youth fares and travel insurance, rail passes, car rentals, tours and the like. Some agents specialize in **charter flights**, which may be cheaper than scheduled flights, but again departure dates are fixed and withdrawal penalties are high.

Booking online

Many websites offer tickets, hotels and holiday packages online, cutting out the costs of agents and middlemen; these are worth going for, as long as you don't mind the inflexibility of the deals. There are bargains to be had on auction sites, too.

Useful websites

ⓦ www.cheapflights.co.uk Flight deals, travel agents, plus links to other travel sites.

ⓦ www.cheaptickets.com Discount flight specialists (US only). Also at ☏ 1-888/922-8849.

ⓦ www.ebookers.com Efficient, easy to use flight finder, with competitive fares.

ⓦ www.etn.nl/discount A hub of consolidator and discount agent links, maintained by the non-profit European Travel Network.

ⓦ www.expedia.co.uk Discount airfares, all-airline search engine and daily deals.

ⓦ www.flyaow.com "Airlines of the Web" – online air travel info and reservations.

ⓦ www.gaytravel.com US gay travel agent, offering accommodation, cruises, tours and more. Also at ☏ 1-800/GAY-TRAVEL.

ⓦ www.geocities.com/thavery2000 An extensive list of airline websites and US toll-free numbers.

ⓦ www.kelkoo.co.uk Useful UK-only price-comparison site, checking several sources of low-cost flights (and other goods & services) according to specific criteria.

ⓦ www.lastminute.com

ⓦ www.opodo.co.uk Popular and reliable source of low UK airfares. Owned by, and run in conjunction with, nine major European airlines.

ⓦ www.priceline.co.uk Name-your-own-price website that has deals at around forty percent off standard fares.

ⓦ www.skyauction.com Bookings from the US only. Auctions tickets and travel packages to destinations worldwide.

ⓦ www.travelocity.co.uk

ⓦ www.travelshop.com.au Australian site offering discounted flights, packages and insurance. Also on ☏ 1800/108 108.

ⓦ www.travel.yahoo.com Incorporates some Rough Guides material in its coverage of destination countries and cities across the world, with information about places to eat and sleep.

ⓦ www.zuji.com.au Australian site detailing destination guides, hot fares and great deals for car rental, accommodation and lodging.

From the UK and Ireland

Flying to Bucharest from the UK takes approximately three hours. Both British Airways (BA) and TAROM, the Romanian national carrier, run direct daily flights **from London Heathrow to Bucharest Otopeni** airport. The cheapest Apex return fares with both airlines in the summer start at around £170, including tax, though seats at these fares are usually limited, so you will have to book early. Apex tickets usually have to be booked and paid for at least fourteen days in advance; in addition, you are required to stay at least one Saturday night, while the maximum stay is two months and any changes to the booking are subject to a fee of around £40.

Most **other British airports** offer connecting flights to Heathrow. BA has add-on fares starting at around £75 on top of the return fare from London, but it may also be worth taking advantage of special offers to London, and getting a regular ticket from there. From regional airports served by Air France, KLM or Lufthansa, you can avoid London completely, changing planes in Europe instead. Tickets to Bucharest cost upwards of £260 return, and can be bought direct from the airlines or through specialist agents (see opposite).

Indirect flights with other airlines, such as Air Austria, Air France and Lufthansa, are also worth looking into – they do take longer and connections times are often very tight, but they can be competitive in price, with tickets from around £220.

Another possibility is to **fly to Budapest**, in neighbouring Hungary, with easyjet or Sky Europe – from where there are good, and cheap, onward connections by bus or train to Romania; depending on when you go, and how far in advance you book, tickets can be obtained for as little as £40 return, including tax.

There are no direct scheduled flights from **Dublin or Belfast**, so you'll have to take a flight to London and an onwards connection.

Airlines

Aer Lingus UK ☎0845/084 4444, Republic of Ireland ☎0818/365 000, ⊛www.aerlingus.ie.
Air France UK ☎0845/359 1000, Republic of Ireland ☎01/605 0383, ⊛www.airfrance.com.
Austrian Airlines UK ☎0845/601 0948, Republic of Ireland ☎1800/509 142, ⊛www.aua.com.
British Airways UK ☎0870/850 9850, Republic of Ireland ☎1800/626 747, ⊛www.ba.com.
easyJet UK ☎0871/750 0100, ⊛www.easyjet.com. Low-cost flights London to Budapest.

Lufthansa UK ☎0845/773 7747, Republic of Ireland ☎01/844 5544, ⊛www.lufthansa.com.
Malev Hungarian Airlines UK ☎0870/909 0577, Republic of Ireland ☎01/844 4303, ⊛www.malev.hu.
SkyEurope UK ☎020/7365 0365, ⊛www.skyeurope.com. Low-cost flights London to Budapest.
Swiss UK ☎0845/601 0956, Republic of Ireland ☎1890/200 515, ⊛www.swiss.com.
Tarom UK ☎020/7224 3693, ⊛www.tarom.ro.

Travel agents

Flightcentre UK ☎0870/890 8099, ⊛www.flightcentre.co.uk. Rock-bottom fares worldwide.
Flights4Less UK ☎0871/222 3423, ⊛www.flights4less.co.uk. Good discount airfares. Part of Lastminute.com.
Holidays4Less UK ☎0871/222 3423, ⊛www.holidays4less.co.uk. Discounted package deals worldwide. Part of Lastminute.com.
Joe Walsh Tours Republic of Ireland ☎01/676 0991, ⊛www.joewalshtours.ie. Long-established general budget fares and holidays agent.
McCarthys Travel Republic of Ireland ☎021/427 0127, ⊛www.mccarthystravel.ie. Reputable Irish travel agent now part of the Worldchoice chain of travel shops. Featuring flights, short breaks, pilgrimages and group holidays.
North South Travel UK ☎01245/608 291, ⊛www.northsouthtravel.co.uk. Friendly, competitive travel agency, offering discounted fares worldwide. Profits are used to support projects in the developing world, especially the promotion of sustainable tourism.
Premier Travel UK ☎028/7126 3333, ⊛www.premiertravel.uk.com. Discount flight specialists.
STA Travel UK ☎0870/160 0599, ⊛www.statravel.co.uk. Worldwide specialists in low-cost flights, overland and holiday deals. Good discounts for students and under-26s.
Top Deck UK ☎020/7244 8000, ⊛www.topdecktravel.co.uk. Experienced agent dealing in discount flights and tours.
Trailfinders UK ☎020/7938 3939, ⊛www.trailfinders.com, Republic of Ireland ☎01/677 7888, ⊛www.trailfinders.ie. One of the best-informed and most efficient agents for independent travellers.
Travel Bag UK ☎0870/890 1456, ⊛www.travelbag.co.uk. Discount deals worldwide.
USIT Northern Ireland ☎028/9032 7111, ⊛www.usitnow.com, Republic of Ireland

⊕0818/200 020, ⓦwww.usit.ie. Specialists in student, youth and independent travel – flights, trains, study tours, TEFL, visas and more.

Specialist operators

There is no shortage of tour operators in the UK offering package and specialist-interest tours to Romania – from the standard ski and coastal resort holidays to more specialized cultural, hiking, and wildlife and conservation trips. For fanatics, there are even Dracula-themed tours. In Romania, there are several more agencies offering ready-made and tailor-made tours – these are detailed in the relevant parts of the guide.

Avian Adventures ⊕01384/372 013, ⓦwww.avianadventures.co.uk. Ten-day birding tours in the Danube Delta; £1155.

Balkan Holidays UK ⊕0845/130 1114, ⓦwww.balkanholidays.co.uk. Two-country holidays on the Romanian and Bulgarian Black Sea Coast, and ski packages in Poiana Braşov, from around £300.

Exodus UK ⊕020/8675 5550, ⓦwww.exodus.co.uk. Nine-day hiking and conservation tours – including wolf tracking – in the Carpathians, with accommodation in local guesthouses; all tours (May–Oct & Dec–March), from £595 excluding flights. In Republic of Ireland, contact Worldwide Adventures ⊕01/679 5700.

Explore Worldwide UK ⊕01252/760 000, ⓦwww.explore.co.uk. Eleven-day guided tour (with some hiking) of the Maramureş villages, the painted monasteries of Bucovina, and the Danube Delta; £620.

High Places ⊕0114/275 7500, ⓦwww.highplaces.co.uk. Two-week treks in the Carpathians, including a four-day traverse across the Fagaraş ridge – Aug–Sept; £890.

Inghams ⊕020/8780 4433, ⓦwww.inghams.co.uk. Ski packages in Poiana Braşov from around £325 for seven nights.

Limosa Holidays ⊕01263/578 143, ⓦwww.limosaholidays.co.uk. Four- to twelve-day nature trips in the Danube Delta and Transylvania.

Martin Randall Travel ⊕020/8742 3355, ⓦwww.martinrandall.com. One-week tour in June of Bucovina's painted monasteries, with accommodation in comfortable three- and four-star hotels; £1380.

Naturetrek ⊕01962/733 051, ⓦwww.naturetrek .co.uk. Ten-day wildlife tour – by boat and foot – in the Carpathians, coast and Delta in May and August; £1095.

Ride World Wide ⊕01837/82544, ⓦwww.rideworldwide.co.uk. Six- (£595) and eleven-day (£995) riding holidays in the Carpathians between April and October; four to six hours riding each day and accommodation in local guesthouses.

Romania Travel Centre ⊕01892/516 901, ⓦwww.romaniatravelcentre.com. Romania specialists offering a comprehensive programme including Bucharest city breaks, coastal, ski and spa holidays, wildlife eco tours, and biking trips. Flights and tailor-made accommodation deals too.

Transylvan ⊕020/8568 4499, ⓦwww.transylvan.co.uk. Six-day Treasures of Transylvania tour (£870), and eight-day Best of Romania tour (£990), plus Bucharest city tours.

Transylvania Uncovered ⊕01482/350 216, ⓦwww.beyondtheforest.com. One of the UK's best and most comprehensive Romania specialists; package and special interest tours (wilderness, wine and culture, riding, spas, Dracula), flights, accommodation, car hire and rail tickets.

Travelling Naturalist ⊕01305/267 994, ⓦwww.naturalist.co.uk. Eight-day bird watching trips to the Danube Delta/Transylvania in May and September; £1175.

Wildwings ⊕0117/965 8333, ⓦwww .wildwings. co.uk. Ten-day birding tours on the Black Sea Coast, Danube Delta and Transylvanian Alps from £840.

By rail

Travelling **by train** is likely to be considerably more expensive than flying, and the shortest journey takes about 36 hours. However, stopovers are possible, and prices are more attractive if you're a student, under 26 or over 60. If you have an InterRail pass, you can take in Romania as part of a wider trip around Europe (see the "Getting around" section on p.23 for details.

A standard second-class **return ticket**, incorporating Eurostar, will cost around £350. Arriving in Paris, you take a train to either Munich or Vienna and change there for the next leg to Budapest. In Budapest, you need to change again for the last leg to Bucharest. Tickets are usually valid for two to three months and allow for unlimited stopovers.

Rail agents in the UK and Ireland

Eurostar UK ⊕0870/160 6600, ⓦwww.eurostar.com. Trains depart more or less hourly (roughly 6am–7.30pm) from London Waterloo through the Channel Tunnel to Paris Gare du Nord (2hr 40min) or Brussels-Midi/Zuid (2hr 20min). The cheapest return ticket is currently £59, though restrictions apply. You can get through-ticketing from stations around Britain from Eurostar, many travel agents and mainline stations. Inter-Rail, Eurail, Britrail and Eurodomino passes give discounts on Eurostar trains.

International Rail UK ☎0870/751 5000, ⊛www.international-rail.com. Offers a wide variety of rail options, including Eurostar, all European passes and tickets, Motorail, international sleepers, ferry crossings and more.

Rail Europe UK ☎0870/584 8848, ⊛www .raileurope.co.uk. Broad range of mainstream rail options, including Eurostar, tickets for major destinations in Europe. Also national passes for all European countries. Motorail, and InterRail and Eurodomino passes. Eurail must normally be bought outside Europe, but people resident outside the EU can go to Rail Europe's central London office and buy a Eurail pass over the counter on production of a non-EU passport.

Trainseurope UK ☎0900/195 0101 (60p per min, refundable against a booking), ⊛www .trainseurope.co.uk. Useful selection of rail options, for travel all across Europe (including many parts of Eastern Europe). Point-to-point tickets, passes, Motorail, Eurotunnel, national passes, InterRail, Eurodomino, and more.

By bus

Eurolines (UK ☎08705/808 808, ⊛www .eurolines.co.uk, Republic of Ireland ☎01/836 6111, ⊛www.eurolines.ie) operates a service from **London to Bucharest**, though the journey time is a stamina-sapping forty-nine hours, with one change in Brussels; departing London at 9.30pm, four days a week (Mon, Thurs, Fri & Sat). The bus also stops in Arad, Timişoara, Deva, Sibiu, Braşov and Ploieşti, before reaching Bucharest – the same service then continues to Constanţa. A standard return fare costs around £210 (valid for six months), though look out for promotional fares. Eurolines is a brand name under which 30+ companies operate international buses all around Europe; **National Express** (☎0870/580 8080, ⊛www.nationalexpress.com) is the UK operator, **Bus Éireann** (⊛www.bus

eireann.ie) is the Republic of Ireland operator.

By car

Driving to Romania, a distance of 2000km from London, can be a pleasant proposition. However, it's really only worth considering if you are planning to travel around Romania extensively or want to make various stopovers en route.

Once across the channel (see p.13), the best **route** (around thirty hours at a leisurely pace with plenty of stops) is through France, Germany, Austria and Hungary, passing Frankfurt, Nuremberg, Regensburg, Linz, Vienna and Budapest, and then taking the E60 down to the Borş frontier crossing near Oradea or the E75/E68 to Nădlac near Arad. With the difficulty of travelling through Serbia, these borders are now very busy with trucks heading for Bulgaria and Turkey. New **border crossings** have opened for cars and buses only, the most useful of which is from Battonya to Turnu, just west of Arad. Most trucks use the main crossing at Arad, so this is best avoided; the surface of the route from Oradea to Cluj, to the north, is in better condition and far more scenic. There are lesser crossing points, particularly from northern Hungary towards Satu Mare, but these are more accustomed to local travellers. Major border crossings are open 24 hours a day. Detailed printouts of the route can be obtained from the websites of the AA (⊛www.theaa.com), or RAC (⊛www.rac.co.uk). See p.26 for details of driving within Romania.

There are numerous **ferry** services between Ireland and Britain, and between the British Isles and the European mainland. Ferries from the southeast of Ireland and the south coast of England connect with northern France and Spain; those from Kent in the southeast of England reach northern France and Belgium; those from the east coast and northeast of England cross the North Sea to the Netherlands, Germany and Scandinavia.

Ferry prices vary dramatically according to the time of year, time of day, length of stay and, for motorists, the size of your car.

Whilst the Hoverspeed to Calais is more expensive, the journey time is half that of the ferry. Look out for frequent special offers on the Hoverspeed and other ferries.

Via the Channel Tunnel

Eurotunnel UK ☎0870/535 3535, ⓦwww.eurotunnel.com. Operates drive-on drive-off shuttle trains for vehicles and their passengers only. Fares for the journey between Folkestone and Coquelles near Calais (35min, 45min for some night departure times) vary; it's cheaper to travel between 10pm and 6am, during the week, and outside July and August.

Ferry companies in the UK and Ireland

Hoverspeed UK ☎0870/240 8070, ⓦwww.hoverspeed.co.uk. Dover to Calais.
P&O Ferries UK ☎0870/520 2020, ⓦwww.poferries.com. Dover to Calais; Portsmouth to Bilbao/Caen/Cherbourg/Le Havre; Hull to Rotterdam/Zeebrugge
SeaFrance UK ☎0870/571 1711, ⓦwww.seafrance.com. Dover to Calais.
Stena Line Britain ☎0870/570 7070, Northern Ireland ☎028/9074 7747, ⓦwww .stenaline.co.uk, Republic of Ireland ☎01/204 7777, ⓦwww.stenaline.ie. Harwich to Hook of Holland.

From the USA and Canada

There are **no direct flights** from either **Canada** or the **USA** to Romania, so you'll have to rely on using one of the bigger European airlines to fly you into their home hub, from where you can continue the journey – expect to pay around US$650/CA$1300 low season and US$1000/CA$1700 high season. Another, possibly cheaper, alternative is to fly into the capital city of one of the neighbouring countries, such as Budapest, in Hungary, from where there are good onward bus and train connections into Romania. Malev, the Hungarian carrier, flies direct from New York's JFK to Budapest, with fares from around US$550 low season and US$700 high season, whilst they also schedule direct flights from Toronto, with fares from around CA$900 low season and CA$1300 high season.

Airlines

Air Canada ☎1-888/247-2262, ⓦwww.aircanada.com.
Air France US ☎1-800/237-2747, Canada ☎1-800/667-2747, ⓦwww.airfrance.com.
American Airlines ☎1-800/624-6262, ⓦwww.aa.com.
Austrian Airlines ☎1-800/843-0002, ⓦwww.aua.com.
British Airways ☎1-800/AIRWAYS, ⓦwww.ba.com.
Lufthansa US ☎1-800/645-3880, Canada ☎1-800/563-5954, ⓦwww.lufthansa.com.
Malev Hungarian Airlines ☎1-800/223-6884 or 212/566-9944, ⓦwww.malev.hu.
Northwest/KLM International ☎1-800/447-4747, ⓦwww.nwa.com, ⓦww.klm.com.
United Airlines ☎1-800/538-2929, ⓦwww.united.com.

Travel agents

Airtech ☎212/219-7000, ⓦwww.airtech.com. Standby seat broker; also deals in consolidator fares.
Educational Travel Center ☎1-800/747-5551 or 608/256-5551, ⓦwww.edtrav.com. Low-cost fares worldwide, student/youth discount offers, and Eurail passes, car rental and tours.
Flightcentre US ☎1-866/WORLD-51, ⓦwww .flightcentre.us, Canada ☎1-888/WORLD-55, ⓦwww.flightcentre.ca. Rock-bottom fares worldwide.
New Frontiers US ☎1-800/677-0720, ⓦwww.newfrontiers.com. Discount firm, specializing in travel from the US to Europe, with hotels, package deals and especially good offers to France.
STA Travel US ☎1-800/329-9537, Canada ☎1-888/427-5639, ⓦwww.statravel.com. Worldwide specialists in independent travel; also student IDs, travel insurance, car rental, rail passes, and more.
Student Flights ☎1-800/255-8000 or 480 /951-1177, ⓦwww.isecard.com/studentflights. Student/youth fares, plus student IDs and European rail and bus passes.
TFI Tours ☎1-800/745-8000 or 212/736-1140, ⓦwww.lowestairprice.com. Well-established consolidator with a wide variety of global fares; less competitive on the US domestic market.
Travel Avenue ☎1-800/333-3335, ⓦwww.travelavenue.com. Full-service travel agent that offers discounts in the form of rebates.

B

Travel Cuts US ☎1-800/592-CUTS, Canada
☎1-888/246-9762, ⊛www.travelcuts.com.
Popular, long-established student-travel organization,
with worldwide offers.
Travelers Advantage ☎1-877/259-2691,
⊛www.travelersadvantage.com. Travel club, with
cash-back deals and cut price car rental.
Membership required (US$1 for 3 months' trial).
Travelosophy US ☎1-800/332-2687,
⊛www.itravelosophy.com. Good range of
discounted and student fares worldwide.
Worldtek Travel ☎1-800/243-1723,
⊛www.worldtek.com. Discount travel agency for
worldwide travel.

Specialist operators

Adventures Abroad ☎1-800/665-3998,
⊛www.adventures-abroad.com. Eight-day
countrywide tour, including Transylvania and the
painted monasteries, as well as multi-country
tours (Romania/Hungary/Bulgaria/Ukraine and so
on) tours.
Adventure Center ☎1-800/228-8747 or
510/654-1879, ⊛www.adventurecenter.com.
Five-day Bucharest and Bears tour (US$430), and
eleven-day village folklore and Danube Delta tour
(US$850).
Contiki Tours ☎1-888/CONTIKI,
⊛www.contiki.com. 18- to 35-year-olds-only tour
operator. Extensive European tours, some of which
incorporate Romania in the itinerary.
Dream Tours International ☎818/956-8397,
http://dreamtourist.com. Three- and eight-day tours
of Transylvania and the Bucovina monasteries,
between US$495 and US$895.
Elderhostel ☎1-877/426-8056. Multi-country tour
(Slovakia, Hungary and Romania) taking In Cluj and
Sibiu on the Romanian leg.
Real Traveller ☎1-866/REAL-TVL,
⊛www.realtraveller.com. Canadian agent offering
nine-day Romanian wildlife trekking tours including
wolf and bear-tracking (US$1450).
Quest Tours and Adventures ☎1-800
/621-8687, ⊛www.romtour.com. Wide range of set
tours and fully customized packages, including Jewish
Heritage and Dracula tours, as well as Bucharest city
packages.

From Australia and New Zealand

There are **no direct flights** to Romania
from Australia or New Zealand so you'll
have to change airlines, either in Asia or
Europe, although the best option is to fly to
a Western European gateway city and get
a connecting flight from there. A standard
return fare from eastern **Australia** to
Bucharest, via London, with Quantas, is
around AU$2100 low season and
AU$2600 high season. Most flights typi-
cally require a stop in London, Paris or
Frankfurt, continuing onwards from there.
The same routings apply for flights from
New Zealand, with a standard return fare
from around NZ$2800.

Airlines

Aeroflot Australia ☎02/9262 2233,
⊛www.aeroflot.com.au.
Air France Australia ☎1300/361 400, New
Zealand ☎09/308 3352, ⊛www.airfrance.com.
Air New Zealand Australia ☎13 24 76,
⊛www.airnz.com.au, New Zealand ☎0800
/737 000, ⊛www.airnz.co.nz.
Austrian Airlines Australia ☎1800/642 438 or
02/9251 6155, New Zealand ☎09/522 5948,
⊛www.aua.com.
British Airways Australia ☎1300/767 177, New
Zealand ☎0800/274 847, ⊛www.ba.com.
Lufthansa Australia ☎1300/655 727, New
Zealand ☎0800/945 220, ⊛www.lufthansa.com.
Qantas Australia ☎13 13 13, New Zealand
☎0800/808 767 or 09/357 8900,
⊛www.qantas.com.

Travel agents

Flight Centre Australia ☎13 31 33, ⊛www
.flightcentre.com.au, New Zealand ☎0800 243
544, ⊛www.flightcentre.co.nz. Rock-bottom fares
worldwide.
Holiday Shoppe New Zealand ☎0800/808 480,
⊛www.holidayshoppe.co.nz. Great deals on flights,
hotels and holidays.
OTC Australia ☎1300/855 118, ⊛www.otctravel
.com.au. Flight and accommodation deals.
STA Travel Australia ☎1300/733 035, New Zealand
☎0508/782 872, ⊛www.statravel.com. Worldwide
specialists in low-cost flights, overlands and holiday
deals. Good discounts for students and under-26s.
Student Uni Travel Australia ☎02/9232 8444,
⊛www.sut.com.au. Great deals for students.
Trailfinders Australia ☎02/9247 7666,
⊛www.trailfinders.com.au. One of the best-
informed and most efficient agents for independent
travellers.
travel.com.au and travel.co.nz Australia
☎1300/130 482 or 02/9249 5444,

Ⓦ www.travel.com.au, New Zealand ☎ 0800/468 332, Ⓦ www.travel.co.nz. Comprehensive online travel company, with discounted fares.

Specialist operators

Adventure World Australia ☎ 02/8913 0755, Ⓦ www.adventureworld.com.au, New Zealand ☎ 09/524 5118, Ⓦ www.adventureworld.co.nz. Agents for Explore's ten-day escorted tours

through the Maramureş and Danube Delta regions.
Eastern Eurotours Australia ☎ 1800/242 353 or 07/5526 2855, Ⓦ www.easterneurotours.com.au. Transylvanian ski and snowboarding holidays, and five-day Danube Delta (AU$1095) and seven-day Dracula (AU$1399) tours.
High Places ☎ 03/540 3208, Ⓦ www.highplaces .co.nz. Fourteen-day hikes – moderate to difficult – in the Carpathians (NZ$2540).

Red tape and visas

EU, US and Canadian citizens can enter Romania with just a passport and may stay in the country for up to ninety days. Similarly, most other European citizens can enter the country without a visa, though can only stay for thirty days. Australians and New Zealanders must procure a visa prior to arriving in Romania. However, visa requirements do change, so it's always advisable to check the current situation before leaving home.

Visa applications can be made to any Romanian consulate abroad in person, or by post. A tourist visa is valid for ninety days within six months of issue and costs AU$50/NZ$50. Transit visas, valid for three days' stay within one month of issue, cost AU$35/NZ$40. Overstaying is an offence generally solved by paying a fine to the border police, but it is preferable, and slightly cheaper, to obtain a **visa extension** from any county (*judeţ*) police headquarters or the office at Str. Luigi Cazzavillan 11, Bucharest (Mon, Thurs & Fri 8.30am–1pm, Tues 8.30am–1pm & 5.30–7pm; ☎ 021/650 3050).

Romanian embassies and consulates

Australia 4 Dalman Crescent, O'Malley, Canberra ACT 2606 ☎ 02/6290 2442.

Britain 4 Palace Green, Kensington Gardens, London W8 4QD ☎ 020/7376 0683 or ☎ 020/7937 9667.
Canada 655 Rideau St, Ottawa ON, K1N 6A3 ☎ 613/789-4037; 111 Peter St, Suite 530, Toronto ON, M5V 2H1 ☎ 416/585-5802); 1111 St Urbain, Suite M-01, Montreal PQ, H2Z 1Y6 ☎ 514/876-1793.
Ireland 47 Ailesbury Rd, Ballsbridge, Dublin 4 ☎ 01/269 2852.
USA 1607 23rd St NW, Washington DC 20008-2809 ☎ 202/232-3694 or 332-4846; 200 East 38th St, New York, NY 10016 ☎ 212/682-9122; 11766 Wiltshire Blvd, Los Angeles, CA 90025 ☎ 310/444-0043.

Information and maps

Ensure that you pick up as much information as possible before you leave your own country, as getting hold of it in Romania is nigh on impossible. Incredibly, Bucharest doesn't have a tourist office, though a few towns are slowly cottoning on to the fact that providing information for visitors might actually be a worthwhile venture; otherwise, most places should have an agency (usually more concerned with selling package trips) where you might be able to extract some basic advice, and possibly a map.

Information offices abroad

UK 22 New Cavendish St, London W1G 8TT
℡ 020/7224 3692, ℮ romaniatravel
@btconnect.com.
USA 14 East 38th St, 12th Floor, New York, NY
10016 ℡ 212/545-8484, ⓦ www
.romaniatourism.com.

Governmental travel advisories

Australian Department of Foreign Affairs
ⓦ www.dfat.gov.au.
British Foreign & Commonwealth Office
ⓦ www.fco.gov.uk.
Canadian Department of Foreign Affairs
ⓦ www.dfait-maeci.gc.ca.
Irish Department of Foreign Affairs
ⓦ www.irlgov.ie/iveagh.
New Zealand Ministry of Foreign Affairs
ⓦ www.mft.govt.nz.
US State Department ⓦ travel.state.gov.

Useful websites

ⓦ www.antrec.ro Website of the national homestay organization.
ⓦ www.inyourpocket.com/romania /Bucharest/en Online version of the excellent magazine, *Bucharest In Your Pocket*, with exhaustive listings – worth consulting before any trip to the capital.
ⓦ www.cimec.ro Site of the Institute for Cultural Memory with good links to archaeological sites, monuments and museums.
ⓦ www.cfr.ro The Romanian Railways site, with full timetable.
ⓦ www.hihostels-romania.ro The Romanian Youth Hostels site.
ⓦ www.MTRomania.ro Official website of the Romanian Ministry of Tourism.

ⓦ www.romaniatravel.com General tourist information site with tips on getting around, services, and good coverage of towns and cities and all major attractions.
ⓦ www.rotravel.com Best and most comprehensive travel site – practical info, hotels, agencies and attractions – together with extensive coverage of Romanian and regional history.
ⓦ www.ruraltourism.ro Listings of rural homestays throughout the country.
ⓦ www.spas.ro National organization of spas, with links to all Romania's spa resorts.

Maps

Nearly all the best **maps** of Romania are published outside the country, but they are available through most good map outlets, including a few shops in Romania itself. The country map published by the ADAC (the German motorists' association) is very detailed (at 1:500,000), as is the Szarvas/Kárpátia/Top-O-Gráf atlas (including city plans), which can be bought at Shell fuel stations in Romania (and through Stanfords in the UK). Other quality maps are produced by Falk (1:1,000,000), Cartographia (1:750,000), and Szarvas/Kárpátia/DIMAP (1:700,000), along with a Kümmerley & Frey map of Romania and Bulgaria (1:1,000,000), and The GeoCenter Euromap (1:800,000), which includes Moldova. Cartographia and Falk also publish good maps of **Bucharest**, while Top-O-Gráf/Freytag & Berndt produce maps of Transylvanian cities such as Cluj. DIMAP also publishes maps of most tourist areas.

The maps produced by the national tourist offices are fairly poor, but just about adequate for **motoring**, but the campsite and cabana maps are useful for hikers. There are also good **hiking maps** of the major mountain massifs, by Editura pentru Turism and Abeona in Bucharest and Editura Focul Viu in Cluj, (available from bookstores as well as tourist offices). Hikers should also look out for the booklet *Invitaţie Ón Carpaţi*; the text is Romanian, but it contains detailed maps of the region's 24 main hiking areas, showing trail markings, huts, peaks, etc (reproduced in *The Mountains of Romania* – see p.426). See p.40 for more information on hiking. In Bucharest, the best place for maps is the Librăria Noi bookshop at B-dul Bălcescu 18 (see p.16).

Map outlets

In the UK and Ireland

Blackwell's Map Centre 50 Broad St, Oxford OX1 3BQ ☎01865/793 550, ✆maps.blackwell .co.uk. Branches in Bristol, Cambridge, Cardiff, Leeds, Liverpool, Newcastle, Reading and Sheffield.
The Map Shop 30a Belvoir St, Leicester LE1 6QH ☎0116/247 1400, ✆www.mapshopleicester.co.uk.
National Map Centre 22–24 Caxton St, London SW1H 0QU ☎020/7222 2466, ✆www.mapsnmc.co.uk.
National Map Centre Ireland 34 Aungier St, Dublin ☎01/476 0471, ✆www.mapcentre.ie.
Stanfords 12–14 Long Acre, London WC2E 9LP ☎020/7836 1321, ✆www.stanfords.co.uk. Also at 39 Spring Gardens, Manchester ☎0161/831 0250, and 29 Corn St, Bristol ☎0117/929 9966. 13–15 Blenheim Crescent, London W11 2EE ☎020/7229 5260, ✆www.thetravelbookshop .co.uk.
Traveller 55 Grey St, Newcastle-upon-Tyne NE1 6EF ☎0191/261 5622, ✆www.newtraveller.com.

In the US and Canada

110 North Latitude US ☎336/369-4171, ✆www.110nlatitude.com.
Book Passage 51 Tamal Vista Blvd, Corte Madera, CA 94925 and in the San Francisco Ferry Building ☎1-800/999-7909 or ☎415/927-0960, ✆www.bookpassage.com.
Distant Lands 56 S Raymond Ave, Pasadena, CA 91105 ☎1-800/310-3220, ✆www.distantlands.com.
Globe Corner Bookstore 28 Church St, Cambridge, MA 02138 ☎1-800/358-6013, ✆www.globecorner.com.
Longitude Books 115 W 30th St #1206, New York, NY 10001 ☎1-800/342-2164, ✆www.longitudebooks.com.
Map Town 400 5 Ave SW #100, Calgary, AB, T2P 0L6 ☎1-877/921-6277 or ☎403/266-2241, ✆www.maptown.com.
Travel Bug Bookstore 3065 W Broadway, Vancouver, BC, V6K 2G9 ☎604/737-1122, ✆www.travelbugbooks.ca.
World of Maps 1235 Wellington St, Ottawa, ON, K1Y 3A3 ☎1-800/214-8524 or ☎613/724-6776, ✆www.worldofmaps.com.

In Australia and New Zealand

Mapland 372 Little Bourke St, Melbourne, VC ☎03/9670 4383, ✆www.mapland.com.au.
Map Shop 6–10 Peel St, Adelaide, SA ☎08/8231 2033, ✆www.mapshop.net.au.
Map World 371 Pitt St, Sydney, NSW ☎02/9261 3601, ✆www.mapworld.net.au. Also at 900 Hay St, Perth, WA ☎08/9322 5733, Jolimont Centre, Canberra, ACT ☎02/6230 4097 and 1981 Logan Road, Brisbane, QLD ☎07/3349 6633.
Map World 173 Gloucester St, Christchurch ☎0800/627 967, ✆www.mapworld.co.nz.

Insurance

Even though EU health care privileges apply in Romania, you'd do well to take out an insurance policy before travelling to cover against theft, loss, and illness or injury. Before paying for a new policy, check whether you are already covered by your home insurance policy or private medical scheme. In Canada, provincial health plans usually provide partial cover for medical mishaps overseas, while holders of official student/teacher/youth cards in Canada and the US are entitled to meagre accident coverage and hospital in-patient benefits. Students will often find that their student health coverage extends during the vacations and for one term beyond the date of last enrollment.

A typical travel insurance policy usually provides cover for the loss of baggage, tickets and – up to a certain limit – cash or cheques, as well as cancellation or curtailment of your journey. Most of them exclude dangerous sports unless an extra premium is paid: in Romania, this could mean, for example, trekking. If you do take medical coverage, ascertain whether benefits will be paid as treatment proceeds or only after you return home, and if there is a 24-hour medical emergency number. When securing baggage cover, make sure that the per-article limit – typically under £500/US$750/CA$1235 /AU$1260 and sometimes as little as £250/US$400/CA$610/AU$630 – will cover your most valuable possession. If you need to make a claim, you should keep receipts for medicines and medical treatment, and in the event you have anything stolen, you must obtain an official statement from the police (called a *declaratie*).

Rough Guides travel insurance

Rough Guides Ltd offers a low-cost travel insurance policy, especially customized for our statistically low-risk readers by a leading British broker, provided by the American International Group (AIG) and registered with the British regulatory body, GISC (the General Insurance Standards Council). There are five main Rough Guides insurance plans: **No Frills** for the bare minimum for secure travel; **Essential**, which provides decent all-round cover; **Premier** for comprehensive cover with a wide range of benefits; **Extended Stay** for cover lasting four months to a year; and **Annual multi-trip**, a cost-effective way of getting Premier cover if you travel more than once a year. Premier, Annual Multi-Trip and Extended Stay policies can be supplemented by a "Hazardous Pursuits Extension" if you plan to indulge in sports considered dangerous, such as scuba-diving or trekking. For a policy quote, call the Rough Guide Insurance Line: toll-free in the UK ☏0800/015 09 06 or ☏+44 1392 314 665 from elsewhere. Alternatively, get an online quote at www.roughguides.com/insurance.

Health

No vaccinations are required for Romania, although having hepatitis A, polio and typhoid boosters would be wise if you're planning to stay in remote areas where hygiene can sometimes be an issue. There's a reciprocal health agreement between Romania and western countries (including the UK, USA, Canada, Australia and New Zealand), so emergency treatment (excluding drugs) is free.

Summers can be blisteringly hot, particularly in the coastal region, so make sure you take a high-factor **sun cream**, and very strong **insect repellent** if visiting the Danube Delta. Conversely, inclement weather in the mountainous regions, particularly at higher altitudes, can present potential dangers – take appropriate clothing, sufficient provisions and equipment, and keep an eye on the weather. **Tap water** is safe to drink practically everywhere, though bottled water (apă minerala) is widely available. **Diarrhoea**, though, can

be a problem, so stock up with Lomotil before you leave (remember that this treats only symptoms, not causes), besides any specific medication required. Avoid any contact with **stray dogs**, as there's a very slight risk of rabies.

In case of minor complaints, go to a **pharmacy** (*farmacie*), where the staff are usually well trained and have the authority to prescribe drugs, and – in the big towns at least – may understand English, French or German. There should be at least one pharmacy in each town open 24 hours – failing

Spas

Spa holidays are much favoured by Romanians, following the Habsburg tradition, and the country boasts one third of all Europe's mineral springs, and 160 spa resorts (băile). The theory is that you stay in a resort for about eighteen days, following a prescribed course of treatment, and ideally return regularly over the next few years. However, if you can get cheap accommodation (best booked at a Romanian travel agency) a spa can make a good base for a holiday. In any case, it's worth bearing in mind that even the smallest spas have campsites and restaurants.

The basic treatment naturally involves drinking the **waters**, which come in an amazing variety: alkaline, chlorinated, carbogaseous, and sodium-, iodine-, magnesium-, sulphate- or iron-bearing. In addition, you can bathe in hot springs or sapropelic muds, breath in foul fumes at mofettes, or indulge in a new generation of complementary **therapies** such as ultrasound and aerosol treatment, ultraviolet light baths, acupuncture and electrotherapy. A great deal of work has been done to put a scientific gloss on spa treatment, and drugs such as Pellamar, Gerovital H3 and Aslavital, said to stop and even reverse the ageing process, have been developed here.

The spas all have their own areas of specialization: Sovata is the best place for **gynaecological problems**; Covasna, Vatra Dornei and Buziaş deal with **cardiovascular complaints**; Călimăneşti-Căciulata, Slănic Moldova, Sângeorz-Băi and Băile Olăneşti with **digestion**; and others (notably Băile Herculane and Băile Felix) with a range of **locomotive and rheumatic ailments**. Mountain resorts such as Sinaia, Băile Tuşnad and Moneasa treat **nervous complaints** with fresh air, which has an ideal balance of ozone and ions.

that, dial the emergency number displayed in the pharmacy window.

In Bucharest, the British and American embassies can supply the address of an English-speaking **doctor or dentist**, and there's a special clinic for treating foreigners. In **emergencies**, dial ☎961 or ask someone to contact the local casualty (*staţia de salvare*) or first aid (*prim ajutor*) station, which should have ambulances. Each county capital has a fairly well-equipped county hospital (*spital judeţean*), but **hospitals** and health centres (policlinics) in smaller towns can be poor. Foreigners are likely to receive preferential treatment, but Romanians routinely pay large tips to doctors and nurses to ensure that they're well cared for.

Medical resources for travellers

General

ⓦ http://health.yahoo.com Information on specific diseases and conditions, drugs and herbal remedies, as well as advice from health experts.

ⓦ www.fitfortravel.scot.nhs.uk Scottish NHS website carrying information about travel-related diseases and how to avoid them.

ⓦ www.istm.org The website of the International Society for Travel Medicine, with a full list of clinics specializing in international travel health. Publishes outbreak warnings, suggested inoculations, precautions and other background information for travellers.

ⓦ www.tripprep.com Travel Health Online provides an online-only comprehensive database of necessary vaccinations for most countries, as well as destination and medical service provider information.

In the UK and Ireland

British Airways Travel Clinics 156 Regent St, London (Mon–Fri 9.30am–6pm, Sat 10am–5pm, no appointment necessary; ☎0845/600 2236); 101 Cheapside, London (Mon–Fri 9am–4.45pm, appointment required; ☎0845/600 2236); ⓦ www.britishairways.com/travel/healthclinintro. Vaccinations, tailored advice from an online database and a complete range of travel healthcare products.

Dun Laoghaire Medical Centre 5 Northumberland Ave, Dun Laoghaire, County Dublin ☎01/280 4996, ⒻF01/280 5603. Advice on medical matters abroad.

MASTA (Medical Advisory Service for Travellers Abroad) Forty regional clinics (call ☎0870/6062782 for the nearest). Also operates a pre-recorded 24hr Travellers' Health Line (UK ☎0906/822 4100, 60p per min), giving written information tailored to your journey by return of post.

Travel Health Centre Department of International Health and Tropical Medicine, Royal College of Surgeons in Ireland, Mercers Medical Centre, Stephen's St Lower, Dublin 2 ☎01/402 2337. Expert pre-trip advice and inoculations.

In the US and Canada

Canadian Society for International Health 1 Nicholas St, Suite 1105, Ottawa, ON K1N 7B7 ☎613/241-5785, ⓦ www.csih.org. Distributes a free pamphlet, *Health Information for Canadian Travellers*, containing an extensive list of travel health centres in Canada.

International SOS Assistance Eight Neshaminy Interplex Suite 207, Trevose, PA, USA 19053-6956 ☎1-800/523-8930, ⓦ www.intsos.com. Members receive pre-trip medical referral info, as well as overseas emergency services designed to complement travel insurance coverage.

MEDJET Assistance ☎1-800/963-3538 or ☎205/595-6658, ⓦ www.medjetassistance.com. Annual membership program for travellers that, in the event of illness or injury, will fly members home or to the hospital of their choice in a medically equipped and staffed jet.

Travel Medicine ☎1-800/872-8633, ⓦ www.travmed.com. Sells first-aid kits, mosquito netting, water filters, reference books and other health-related travel products.

In Australia and New Zealand

Travellers' Medical and Vaccination Centres 27–29 Gilbert Place, Adelaide, SA 5000 ☎08/8212 7522, 1/170 Queen St, Auckland ☎09/373 3531; 5/247 Adelaide St, Brisbane, QLD 4000 ☎07/3221 9066; 5/8–10 Hobart Place, Canberra, ACT 2600 ☎02/6257 7156; 270 Sandy Bay Rd, Sandy Bay, Hobart TAS 7005 ☎03/6223 7577; 2/393 Little Bourke St, Melbourne, VIC 3000 ☎03/9602 5788; Level 7, Dymocks Bldg, 428 George St, Sydney, NSW 2000 ☎02/9221 7133; Shop 15, Grand Arcade, 14–16 Willis St, Wellington ☎04/473 0991. ⓦ www.tmvc.com.au

Costs, money and banks

Romania continues to be one of Europe's few bargain destinations, and travellers will find costs, accommodation aside, considerably lower than they would at home. Because the Romanian currency, the leu, remains relatively unstable, all costs in the guide have been given in pound sterling/euro. The more expensive hotels, flights, car rental and excursions are sometimes priced in euros, but must usually be paid for in lei.

Average costs

Your biggest expenditure in Romania is likely to be **accommodation.** Outside Bucharest and the coast, the average three-star hotel can cost anything between £25/€35 and £40/€56 for a double room. Budget travellers have a choice between private rooms/homestay accommodation (£5–7/€7–10 per bed), hostels (£5.50–7/€8–10 per bed), cabanas (£2/€2.80 per bed) and campsites (£2/€2.80 per person). **Eating out**, even in the better restaurants, remains very affordable – you should be able to get a decent two-course meal, with a glass of wine or beer, for between £4–7/€5.50–10 (a more basic meal costs around half this price). **Public transport** is extremely cheap – a one-hundred-kilometre train trip (second class) is around £1/€1.40, a similar length bus/maxitaxi journey around £2/€2.80. Car rental, however, is on a par with most other European countries, and you can expect to pay around £50/€75 a day for an economy model. **Museum** admission charges are almost negligible; with the exception of a handful of places in Bucharest, very few museums and galleries charge more than around £0.50p/€0.70 – which is why we have omitted listing prices (unless over this amount) throughout the guide. Curiously, some of the major attractions levy a fee (often twice the amount it costs to actually get in) for the use of cameras/camcorders.

Youth and student discounts

Full-time students are eligible for the **International Student ID Card** (ISIC, ⓦwww.isiccard.com), which entitles the bearer to special air, rail and bus fares and discounts at museums, theatres and other attractions. For Americans, there's also a health benefit, providing up to US$3000 in emergency medical coverage and US$100 a day for 60 days in hospital, plus a 24-hour hotline to call in the event of a medical, legal or financial emergency. The card costs $22 in the USA; CA$16 in Canada; AU$18 in Australia; NZ$20 in New Zealand; £7 in the UK; and €13 in the Republic of Ireland.

Teachers qualify for the **International Teacher Card**, offering similar discounts and costing £7, €13, US$22, CA$16, AU$18 and NZ$20. All these cards are available in the US from Council Travel, STA, Travel CUTS and, in Canada, Hostelling International (see p.29 for addresses); in Australia and New Zealand from STA or Campus Travel; in Ireland from USIT or STA and in the UK from STA.

Several other travel organizations and accommodation groups also sell their own cards, good for various discounts.

Currency and exchange rates

Romania's unit of **currency** is the leu (meaning "lion"; plural **lei**). Coins come in denominations of 500, 1000 and 5000 lei; and there are notes (which are either paper or, bizarrely, plastic) of 2000, 10,000, 50,000, 100,000 and 500,000 lei. The exchange rate is currently around L55,000 to the pound sterling (L32,000 to the US dollar). Although the rate is more stable than it has been for a number of years, the leu remains unpredictable – for current rates, check the websites ⓦwww.xe.net/currency or ⓦwww.oanda.com/converter.

Banks and changing money

It is best to **change money** at one of the private exchange offices (*casa de schimb valuta*) found in most towns; in Bucharest and several other major cities, some are open 24 hours. Expect long queues when changing money in banks (*banca*) – which are generally open Monday to Friday between 9am and 3 or 4pm. As a rule, neither exchange offices nor banks charge commission. Although not as ubiquitous as it was a few years ago, the **black market** is still alive and kicking, but there's now little profit to be made by changing money this way – the exchange rate at the street kiosks is almost as good, and it's a *much* safer deal. Make sure that you get rid of any unwanted lei before you leave the country, as it's unlikely you'll be able to change them once outside Romania.

Cash and travellers' cheques

If taking **cash**, a modest denomination of US dollar bills is advisable, though euros and pound sterling are also accepted in most places. By far the most recognized **travellers' cheques** are American Express, either sterling or dollars. Although it may not be required in all instances, make sure you have your passport when changing either cash or travellers' cheques. Also note that, in some banks, you may have to show the receipt from the issuing bank, or another cheque to prove continuity of serial numbers.

The usual fee for travellers' cheque sales is one or two percent, though this may be waived if you buy them through a bank where you have an account. Make sure to keep the purchase agreement and a record of cheque serial numbers safe and separate from the cheques themselves. In the event that cheques are lost or stolen, report the loss to the American Express office in Bucharest, which is at Marshal Turism, B-dul Magheru 43 (Mon–Fri 9am–6pm, Sat 9am–1pm; ☎021/223 1204); lost or stolen cheques can usually be replaced within 24 hours.

Credit and debit cards

Credit cards are a very handy backup source of funds, and can be used either in ATMs or over the counter. Mastercard, Visa and American Express are accepted just about everywhere, but other cards may not be recognized in Romania. **Cash machines** (Bancomats) are ubiquitous, even in the smallest towns (including many railway stations), whilst most of the better hotels, restaurants and shops accept plastic.

Remember that all cash advances are treated as loans, with interest accruing daily from the date of withdrawal; there may be a transaction fee on top of this. However, you may be able to make withdrawals from ATMs in Romania using your **debit card**, and the flat transaction fee is usually quite small – your bank will be able to advise on this. Make sure you have a personal identification number (PIN).

Wiring money

Having money wired from home using one of the companies listed below is never convenient or cheap, and should be considered a last resort. It's also possible to have money wired directly from a bank in your home country to a bank in Romania, although this is somewhat less reliable because it involves two separate institutions. Your home bank will need the address of the branch bank where you want to pick up the money and the address and telex number of the Bucharest head office, which will act as the clearing house; money wired this way normally takes two working days to arrive, and costs around £25/US$40/CA$54/AU$52/NZ$59 per transaction.

Money-wiring companies

Travelers Express/MoneyGram
UK, Republic of Ireland and New Zealand ☎00800/6663 9472, Australia ☎0011800 /6663 9472, US ☎1-800/444-3010, Canada ☎1-800/933-3278, ⓦwww.moneygram.com.
Western Union UK ☎0800/833 833, Republic of Ireland ☎66/947 5603, US and Canada ☎1-800/CALL-CASH, Australia ☎1800/501 500, New Zealand ☎0800/005 253, ⓦwww.westernunion.com (customers in the US and Canada can send money online).

Getting around

Most Romanian towns are easily reached by train, and although not the fastest or cleanest system in the world, travelling this way is remarkably cheap and reliable. In the absence of a coordinated bus network, maxitaxis (minibuses) are everywhere, linking many of the larger centres and often providing a more direct and frequent mode of transport than trains. Driving is another attractive proposition, enabling you to visit anywhere you please, and in your own time.

Trains

The SNCFR (Societatea Naţională a Căilor Ferate Române, generally known as the **CFR**, or ChéFéRé) network covers most of the country. Tickets are amazingly cheap, though this is offset by the habitually derelict carriages, bizarre timetable and sweltering/freezing conditions – the (often crowded) trains frequently lack light and water, making long journeys somewhat purgatorial. Those who use the trains regularly, however, often end up very much in sympathy with their rough-and-ready spirit and the generally excellent timekeeping. Moreover, many routes are wonderfully scenic, particularly in Transylvania.

There are several types of train: **Intercity** ("IC") and **Rapid** ("R") services, halting only at major towns, are the most comfortable and expensive types of train, while **Accelerats** ("A") are only slightly slower, with more frequent stops, and are the standard means of inter-urban travel. The painfully slow **Personal** ("P") trains should be avoided as a rule, unless you're heading for some tiny destination. **EuroCity** ("EC") and

EuroNight ("EN") trains have final destinations abroad.

Trains generally conform to the **timetables** (*orar trenurilor*) displayed in stations and CFR offices; arrivals are often on a white board, departures on a yellow one. For key terms, see p.436. Watch out for services that run only during certain months (*circulă numai*, eg *Óntre 9.V ši 8.IX* – May 9 and Sept 8), or only on particular days (1 represents Mon, 2 represents Tues; *nu circula Sâmbata ši Duminica* means the service doesn't run on Sat or Sun). If you're planning to travel a lot by train, try to get hold of the notoriously elusive national **CFR timetable**, the *Mersul Trenurilor*, issued each December. Otherwise, you could check out the web version ⓦ www.cfr.ro. In any case, you should always check at the station. Details of main **routes** are given in the text, and summarized at the end of each chapter.

Tickets

Fares (calculated by distance travelled) are extremely low; a journey of 100km, for

---

Useful timetable publications

The red-covered *Thomas Cook European Timetables* details schedules of the main Romanian **train** services, as well as timings of **ferry** routes and **rail-connecting bus services**. It's updated and issued every month; main changes are in the June edition (published middle-end of May), which has details of the summer European schedules, and the October one, (published middle-end of Sept), which includes winter schedules; some have advance summer/winter timings also. The book can be purchased online (for a ten-percent discount) at ⓦ www.thomascookpublishing.com or from branches of Thomas Cook (see ⓦ www.thomascook.co.uk for your nearest branch), and costs £10.50. Their useful *Rail Map of Europe* can also be purchased online for 25 percent off the normal retail price of £7.95.

example, will cost around £1/€1.40 second class, and around £1.50/€2.10 first class, which makes travelling first-class a bargain. Supplements are required on Intercity and Rapid services, costing around £2/€2.80 and £1.50/€2.10 respectively for a 100km journey. **Advance bookings** for fast services are recommended, and on most such trains you're required to have a seat reservation, although if you board at a relatively minor stop you may have to take potluck. Thus, your ticket (*bilet*) will usually be accompanied by a second piece of card, indicating the service (*nr. trenului*), your carriage (*vagon*) and reserved seat (*loc*); in Bucharest, tickets are computerized, with all information on one paper ticket. Return tickets (*bilet dus întors*) are rarely issued except for international services. Many long-distance overnight trains have **sleeping cars** (*vagon de dormit*) and **couchettes** (*cuşete*), for which a surcharge of around £5–10/€7–14 and £2.50/€3.50 respectively is levied.

With the exception of Personal trains, **tickets** are sold at stations only an hour before departure time, and usually at specific windows for each train; these are not always clearly marked, so buying a ticket can lead to a bit of a scrum. Far easier, (though costing a little extra), is to book tickets a day ahead at the local **Agenţia CFR** – allow seven days for services to the coast during summer. Addresses of offices are given in the guide, and in the CFR timetable. Should you fall victim to double-booking, ticket collectors are notoriously corrupt and a small tip can work wonders. Indeed, some people never buy tickets, simply paying off the conductor instead.

Rail passes

There are a number of rail passes available for travelling in Romania, all of which can be found on Rail Europe (ⓦ www.raileurope.com), the umbrella company for all national and international rail purchases – its comprehensive website is the most useful source of information on which rail passes are available; it also gives all current prices. Those presently available for travel within Romania are the **Inter-Rail** (see.opposite) and **Euro Domino** passes (see opposite). There is also

a Romanian pass, but given how cheap train travel is here, it's a waste of money (£55/€77 for three days travel within fifteen days).

Inter-Rail pass

Inter-Rail passes are only available to European residents, and you will be asked to provide proof of residency before being allowed to purchase one. They come in over-26 and (cheaper) under-26 versions, and cover 28 countries grouped together in zones:

  A Republic of Ireland/Britain
  B Norway, Sweden, Finland
  C Germany, Austria, Switzerland, Denmark
  D Czech and Slovak Republics, Poland, Hungary, Croatia
  E France, Belgium, Netherlands, Luxembourg
  F Spain, Portugal, Morocco
  G Italy, Greece, Turkey, Slovenia plus some ferry services between Italy and Greece
  H Bulgaria, **Romania**, Serbia and Montenegro, Macedonia

Passes are available for one zone for twelve days (£125 for people under the age of 26/£182 for those older or €182/ €266) and 22 days (£149/£219 or €219/€318); two zones in one month (£195/£275 or €285/€402); three zones in one month (£225/£320 or €329/€468); or a global pass covering all zones (£265/£379 or €389/€552). Inter-Rail passes do not include travel between Britain and the continent, although holders are eligible for discounts on rail travel in Britain and Northern Ireland and cross-Channel ferries, as well as reduced rates on the London–Paris Eurostar service.

Euro Domino passes

Only available to European residents of six months or longer, the range of individual country passes available from **Euro Domino** (ⓦ www.b-rail.be/internat/E/passes /eurodomino) provide unlimited travel in 28 European and North African countries. The passes are available for first or second class for between three and eight days' travel within a one-month period; prices vary depending on the country, but include most high-speed train supplements. You can buy as many separate country passes as you want. There is a discounted price for under 26s and children aged 4–11.

Rail contacts

In the UK and Ireland

Rail Europe UK ☎0870/5848 848, ⓦwww.raileurope.co.uk. Discounted rail fares for under-26s on a variety of European routes; also agents for Inter-Rail, Eurostar and Euro Domino.

In the US and Canada

CIT Rail US ☎1-800/CIT-TOUR, ⓦwww .cit-rail.com.
DER Travel US ☎1-800/283-2424, ⓦwww.der.com/rail.
Europrail International Canada ☎1-888 /667-9734, ⓦwww.europrail.net.
Rail Europe US ☎1-877/257-2887, Canada ☎1-800/361-RAIL, ⓦwww.raileurope.com/us.
ScanTours US ☎1-800/223-7226 or 310 /636-4656, ⓦwww.scantours.com.

In Australia and New Zealand

CIT World Travel Australia ☎02/9267 1255 or 03/9650 5510, ⓦwww.cittravel.com.au.
Rail Plus Australia ☎1300/555 003 or 03 /9642 8644, ⓦwww.railplus.com.au.
Trailfinders Australia ☎02/9247 7666 or ☎03/9600 3022, ⓦwww.trailfinder.com.au.

Planes

Romania has a well integrated **plane** network, serving most of the larger cities. **TAROM**'s domestic **services** depart most days from Bucharest's Otopeni airport to Arad, Baia Mare, Cluj, Constanţa, Iaşi, Oradea, Satu Mare, Sibiu, Suceava, Timişoara and Târgu Mureş. In addition, there are a couple of excellent private airlines: **Carpatair** (ⓦwww.carpatair.ro) operates flights from Timişoara to Bacau, Cluj, Iaşi, Oradea and Sibiu; **Angel Airlines** (ⓦwww.angelairlines.ro) operates regular flights out of Bucharest's Băneasa airport to Arad, Iaşi, Suceava and Timişoara. A single **fare** for any destination within the country is typically £35–45/€50–65; bookings should be made at least 36 hours in advance.

Buses and maxitaxis

Romania's **bus** network consists of a confusing and poorly coordinated array of private companies, and is really only useful if you're planning to visit some local village not served by train. In the countryside, knowing when and where to wait for the bus is a local art form, and on Sundays many regions have no local buses at all.

An increasingly popular mode of road transport are minibuses, or **maxitaxis**. The advantage they have over trains is the frequency and speed with which they can get you to your chosen destination. That said, passengers are usually crammed aboard with scant regard for comfort, and there's usually very little luggage space available. Moreover, the speed and recklessness with which many drivers go about getting to their destination leaves a lot to be desired. Prices are slightly more than trains – expect to pay around £2/€2.80 from Bucharest to Piteşti (100km), or £4/€5.60 from Bucharest to Sibiu (250km). Maxitaxis often begin and end their journeys from the local bus or train station. Main bus and maxitaxi routes are listed in the travel details section at the end of each chapter.

All towns have **local bus services**, and in the main cities you'll also find **trams** (*tramvai*) and **trolley buses** (*troleibuz*). Tickets are normally sold in pairs (around £0.15/€0.20) from street kiosks. Validate them yourself aboard the vehicle, but be prepared to fight your way to the machine through the crush.

Bicycles

Given the mountainous terrain and the poor state of many of the country roads, you'll need to be fit and self-reliant to **cycle** around Romania. Cycle shops are few and far between, although most village mechanics can manage basic repairs. Carry a spare tyre and a few spokes, and check carrier nuts regularly, as the potholes and corrugations will rapidly shake them loose. A touring bike is better than a mountain bike unless you want to go off road; with the immense network of forestry roads (Drum Forestiere) and free access to the hills, genuine mountain biking is wonderful here. If you do bring your own bike, avoid cycling in **Bucharest**, where the roads are so hazardous that few people ever cycle there and drivers will have little idea how of to avoid you. Carrying your bike by train is easiest on personal services, where you can simply put it in the carriage, though you should stay with it at all times and will probably have to tip the conductor; on accelerats, it'll have to be carried in the baggage van (this should be indicated on the timetable) and a good tip is necessary to ensure that it's properly guarded.

Cars and motorbikes

Driving in Romania is, on the whole, an attractive proposition. Outside the major towns and cities, you'll find the roads relatively traffic-free, and many routes, particularly through Transylvania, are wonderfully scenic. The main roads (Drum Naţional or DN) are, generally speaking, in good condition. County roads (Drum Judeţean) are poor, however, whilst many of the local roads are disintegrating – potholes are a particularly nasty hazard. It is also a big country, and long distances are best covered at a steady pace, especially if driving in the more mountainous regions where greater powers of concentration are required.

Romania makes a fine country for motorcycling, except that the speed limit for **motorbikes** is ludicrously low: 40kph in built up areas and only 50kph (30mph) on the open road. Helmets are compulsory and you should bring vital spares, as well as a tool kit.

Petrol stations (*benzarie*) can be found almost everywhere, even in the most rural backwaters – the best and most common are those run by OMV (Austrian), MOL (Hungarian) and Shell, many of which have good refreshment and toilet facilities, while the Romanian-run PETROM is perfectly adequate; you should avoid the small, private stations, where fuel may be dirty or diluted. Most cars just use regular **benzină**, but super and lead-free petrol (*fără plomb*) and diesel are widely available – expect to pay around £0.50/€0.70 per litre of unleaded. Credit cards are accepted at most stations. Whilst most service stations open from around 7am to 8 or 9pm, there are quite a few 24-hour ones, usually located on the outskirts of larger towns and cities.

Rules and regulations

Driving regulations in Romania are fairly standard. The most important rules are to **drive on the right** and overtake on the left side, and for traffic on a roundabout to give way to traffic entering from the left. Seat belts are required outside towns. **Speed limits** for cars are 50kph in built-up areas, 90kph on the open road, and 120kph on the motorway. Drinking and driving is absolutely prohibited and severely punished.

Police (*poliţia*) are no longer empowered to levy on-the-spot **fines** for road traffic offences (eg speeding), and instead you'll be issued with a ticket (typically €40–80); if you settle up within 48 hours – at one of the CEC banks found in most towns – then you'll only have to pay half the fine.

Make sure you have a national driving licence and third party insurance.

Accidents and breakdowns

If you have an **accident**, you're legally obliged to await the arrival of the police. You can get **technical assistance** and motoring **information** from ACR (Romanian Automobile Club), whose main Bucharest offices are at Str. Tache Ionescu 27 (☏021/315 5510) and şos. Colentina 1 (☏021/635 4140). In the event of a breakdown, call ACR's 24-hour **breakdown service** on ☏222 2222, whereupon an English-speaking operator will direct you to the nearest point of assistance. In rural areas, the danger isn't so much other motorized traffic as the risk of hitting horses and carts, drunks on bicycles and various animals that have yet to accept the impact of the motor age – squashed dogs lying on the side of the road are an all too common sight. For these reasons, it's best to **avoid driving after dark** wherever possible. The usual precautions apply when it comes to the potential for **theft**: never leave valuables inside the car and always lock it, even if you're just popping into a shop for five minutes.

Motoring organizations

UK & Ireland AA UK ☏0870/600 0371, ⓦwww.theaa.com; AA Ireland Dublin ☏01/617 9999, ⓦwww.aaireland.ie; RAC UK ☏0800/550 055, ⓦwww.rac.co.uk.

US & Canada AAA ☎1-800/AAA-HELP,
🌐www.aaa.com; CAA ☎613/247-0117,
🌐www.caa.ca.
Australia & New Zealand AAA Australia
☎02/6247 7311, 🌐www.aaa.asn.au.

Car rental

Renting a car is simple enough, provided you are 21 or older, and hold a valid national driving licence. You can order a car through rental agencies in your own country (see below), which sometimes works out cheaper, particularly if you book online. Most of the major car rental companies have branches in Bucharest (and Otopeni airport) and the other major cities. Car rental **costs** are not especially cheap; expect to pay around £50/€75 for a day's hire (unlimited mileage) and £40/€55 per day for seven days hire or more. You may find that local companies offer better deals. Credit cards are usually required for a deposit. Before signing, **check** on any mileage limits or other restrictions and extras, as well as what you're covered for in the event of an accident. You may be able to take the car into neighbouring countries, although some companies may charge you more.

Agencies in Britain

Avis ☎0870/606 0100, 🌐www.avis.co.uk.
Budget ☎01442/276 266, 🌐www.budget.co.uk.
Europcar ☎0870/607 5000,
🌐www.europcar.co.uk.
Hertz ☎0870/844 8844, 🌐www.hertz.co.uk.
Holiday Autos ☎0870/400 0099,
🌐www.holidayautos.co.uk.
National ☎0870/536 5365,
🌐www.nationalcar.co.uk.

Agencies in Ireland

Atlas Republic of Ireland ☎01/844 4859,
🌐www.atlascarhire.com.
Avis Northern Ireland ☎028/9024 0404, Republic of Ireland ☎021/428 1111, 🌐www.avis.ie.
Budget Republic of Ireland ☎09/0662 7711,
🌐www.budget.ie.
Europcar Northern Ireland ☎028/9442 3444,
Republic of Ireland ☎01/614 2888,
🌐www.europcar.ie.
Hertz Republic of Ireland ☎01/676 7476,
🌐www.hertz.ie.
Holiday Autos Republic of Ireland
☎01/872 9366, 🌐www.holidayautos.ie.

Agencies in the US and Canada

Auto Europe US and Canada ☎1-888/223-5555,
🌐www.autoeurope.com.
Avis US ☎1-800/230-4898, Canada
☎1-800/272-5871, 🌐www.avis.com.
Budget US ☎1-800/527-0700, Canada
☎1-800/472-3325, 🌐www.budget.com.
Europcar US & Canada ☎1-877/940 6900,
🌐www.europcar.com.
Hertz US ☎1-800/654-3131, Canada
☎1-800/263-0600, 🌐www.hertz.com.
National ☎1-800/962-7070,
🌐www.nationalcar.com.

Agencies in Australia

Avis ☎13 63 33 or 02/9353 9000,
🌐www.avis.com.au.
Budget ☎1300/362 848, 🌐www.budget.com.au.
Europcar ☎1300/131 390,
🌐www.deltaeuropcar.com.au.
Hertz ☎13 30 39 or 03/9698 2555,
🌐www.hertz.com.au.
Holiday Autos ☎1300/554 432,
🌐www.holidayautos.com.au.
National ☎13 10 45, 🌐www.nationalcar.com.au.

Agencies in New Zealand

Avis ☎09/526 2847 or 0800/655 111,
🌐www.avis.co.nz.
Budget ☎09/976 2222 or ☎0800/652-227,
🌐www.budget.co.nz.
Hertz ☎0800/654 321, 🌐www.hertz.co.nz.
Holiday Autos ☎0800/144 040,
🌐www.holidayautos.co.nz.
National ☎0800/800 115 or ☎03/366-5574,
🌐www.nationalcar.co.nz.

Hitchhiking

Hitchhiking (*autostop* or *occasie*) is an integral part of the Romanian transport system to supplement patchy or nonexistent services on backroads – it's even common (although illegal) on the autostrada. It's accepted practice to pay for lifts; although this is often waived for foreigners, make sure you've got some small change to hand if you think it would be good to give the driver some money. Hitchhiking, however, is a risky business in any country, and if you decide to travel this way, take all sensible precautions. It goes without saying that women should never hitch alone, nor is hitching at night advisable.

Accommodation

You should have little trouble finding a bed in Romania, whatever the season. Hotels run the full gamut from plush, top-end establishments, to flea-pit dives with an intermittent water supply. There are also a reasonable number of youth hostels, in addition to a good spread of private rooms and village homestays, the last of which typically offer wonderfully peaceful retreats.

If you're keen to save money on accommodation and you're travelling around a lot, you can use the **trains** to your advantage. On the long overnight journeys by Rapid or Accelerat train, it only costs a little more to book a comfortable sleeping car or couchette.

Hotels

Hotels use the traditional five-star grading system for classification, although in many cases this often gives only the vaguest idea of prices, which can fluctuate wildly according to the locality and season. Moreover, the ratings are not always indicative of the quality of a place, particularly at the lower end of the scale, where standards can, and do, vary tremendously. The plushest four- and five-star hotels (mostly confined to Bucharest, the coast, and the major cities) offer all the luxuries one would expect of such establishments, while three-star hotels can be unpredictable in terms of both quality and cost; you should, however, expect a reasonable standard of comfort, as well as private bathroom and TV, in most.

In some of the most basic places you may find that hot water is only available for a few hours a day (*cu program*), so check before deciding to take a room. It's not unusual, either, to find some hotels in smaller towns doubling up as the local nightclub.

There are a growing number of **pensions**, too, many of which offer much better value than hotels of a similar price. In summer, it's safer, though only really essential on the coast, to make advance hotel reservations.

Another option is **motels**, which often have similar facilities and prices to the mid-range hotels, but since they're situated along main highways or beyond urban ring roads, are not much use unless you have your own transport. You may also come across **sport hotels** (an old East European institution), which were traditionally intended for visiting teams and school groups, but which now admit tourists too. Although often very basic, they invariably offer a clean and cheap place to bed down for the night.

Village homestays and private rooms

Village homestays (*agroturism*) – rural farmhouse-style accommodation – is an increasingly thriving sector, and offers visitors the opportunity to spend some time with a Romanian family (not all of whom will speak English) in often lovely surrounds. The downside is that many places are in fairly

---

Accommodation prices

Hotels listed in this guide have been price-coded according to the scale below. Prices given are for the cheapest **double room** available during peak season. Price codes are expressed in euros as the Romanian leu is still a relatively unstable currency, but you will generally pay for your room in leu.

① Under €12
② €12–17
③ €17–23
④ €23–30
⑤ €30–40
⑥ €40–50
⑦ €50–65
⑧ €65–80
⑨ Over €80

remote locations, and are therefore difficult to reach unless you have your own transport. Homestays are **graded** according to a daisy classification system; four or five daisies (of which there are few) denotes a house with large, well-furnished rooms with private bathroom or shower/toilet, while one or two daisies represents a more basic place offering shared shower and toilet facilities. Expect to pay between €7–20 per person per night depending upon the category; many places also offer breakfast (around €2.80) and dinner (€5.60) upon request.

In addition to the schemes listed below, you should also look out for signs reading "cazare la particular" or "camere de inchiriat" (**private rooms**) in traditional resorts and more touristed areas. In the countryside, where there is a strong custom of hospitality, people may take you in and refuse payment, but you should offer something anyway, or come armed with a few packets of coffee, which make welcome presents.

The official nationwide body for homestays is **ANTREC** (the National Association of Rural, Ecological and Cultural Tourism) Str. Maica Alexandra 7, Bucharest (☎021/223 7024, ⓦwww.antrec.ro); their Bucharest reservations office is at Str. Washington 32 (☎021/231 0955, Ⓔrezervari@antrec.ro). The other two options are also based outside Romania: the offices of **OVR** (Opération Villages Roumains) are in Charleroi, Belgium (☎+32/071/284082, Ⓔovr@win.be), but bookings can be made in Romania through PanTravel, Str. Grozăvescu 13, 3400 Cluj (☎0264/420 516, Ⓔmail@pantravel.ro); while the Amsterdam-based **ECEAT** (the European Centre for Eco-Agro Tourism; ☎+31/20/668 1030, ⓦwww.eceat.org), with a less structured network in Alba, Mureş, Harghita and Bucovina counties, is coordinated by the Focus Eco-Center in Târgu Mureş (OP 6, PO Box 620, Str. Crinului 22; ☎0265/163 692, Ⓔzoli@netsoft.ro). In addition, there's a network of **Gästehäuser** in the Saxon villages; although these aren't homestays, they still provide village accommodation, coordinated by Kilian Dörr, Evangelisches Pfarrhaus, Piaţa Huet 1, 2400 Sibiu (☎ & ℻0269/211 203) and Hugo Schneider, Str. Gh. Doja 23, Mediaş (☎0269/828 605). A guidebook to the Gästehäuser is available in English from

The Mihai Eminescu Trust, 63 Hillgate Place, London W8 7SS, UK (☎020/7792 9998, ⓦwww.mihaieminescutrust.org).

Hostels

Although Romania doesn't have an extensive network of **youth hostels**, there are now a reasonable number of places dotted around the country. Aside from half a dozen in Bucharest, most places are confined to the larger cities or more tourist-oriented towns such as Sighişoara. Expect to pay around £7/€10 for a dorm bed, with a very basic breakfast included. Whilst student accommodation is largely in short supply, you may find the odd student residence willing to let out a bed, though these are likely to be available only in July and August – however, these are unlikely to be advertised, so ask for details at the local tourist office or town agency.

Youth hostel associations

In England and Wales

Youth Hostel Association (YHA) ☎0870 /770 8868, ⓦwww.yha.org.uk. Annual membership £13.50; under-18s £6.70; lifetime £195.

In Scotland

Scottish Youth Hostel Association ☎0870 /155 3255, ⓦwww.syha.org.uk. Annual membership £6, under-18s £2.50.

In Ireland

Irish Youth Hostel Association ☎01/830 4555, ⓦwww.irelandyha.org. Annual membership €25; under-18s €10.50; family €50; lifetime €75.

In Northern Ireland

Hostelling International Northern Ireland ☎028/9032 4733, ⓦwww.hini.org.uk. Annual membership £13; under-18s £6; family £25; life £75.

In the US

Hostelling International-American Youth Hostels ☎301/495-1240, ⓦwww.hiayh.org. Annual membership US$28; seniors (55 or over) US$18; under-18s and groups of ten or more, free; life US$250.

In Canada

Hostelling International Canada ☎1-800 /663 5777 or 613/237 7884, ⓦwww.hihostels.ca.

Adult membership (16–20 months) CA$35+tax; under-18s free; life CA$175.

In Australia

Australia Youth Hostels Association
☎02/9261 1111, ⊛www.yha.com.au. Annual membership AU$52 (under-18s, AUS$19) for first twelve months, then AU$37 each year after.

In New Zealand

Youth Hostelling Association New Zealand
☎0800/278 299 or 03/379 9970, ⊛www.yha .co.nz. Adult membership NZ$40 for one year, NZ$60 for two and NZ$80 for three; under-18s free; life NZ$300.

Cabanas

In the countryside, particularly in the mountainous areas favoured by hikers, there are well over a hundred **cabanas** or hikers' huts, ranging from chic alpine villas with dozens of bedrooms to fairly primitive chalets with bunk beds and cold running water. The hikers' cabanas are generally friendly and serve as useful places to pick up information about trails and the weather. Some (mainly in the Bucegi range) can be easily reached by cable car, while others are situated on roads just a few miles from towns; however, the majority are fairly isolated and accessible only by mountain tracks or footpaths. The location of the cabanas is shown rather vaguely on an ONT map, *Cabane Turistice*, but more precisely on hiking maps. Cabanas are supposed not to turn hikers away, but in the Făgăraş mountains, in particular, it might be wise to **book in advance**, by phone or through a local agency. Beds in remoter areas cost about £2/€2.80, but a little more if in a private room or in one of the more comfortable cabanas.

Camping

Romania has well over a hundred **campsites**, situated all over the country. You'll generally pay about £2/€2.80 per person per night, though an ISIC student card may secure a thirty- to fifty-percent reduction. Second-class campsites are rudimentary, usually with filthy toilets, but first-class sites often have **cabins** or bungalows (*căsuţe*) for rent (about £3/€4.20 for a two-bed cabin), hot showers and even a restaurant. However, water shortages hit campsites especially hard, while along the coast over-crowding is a major drawback.

In the mountains, certain areas may be designated as a camping area (*loc de cam-pare*), these are few and far between. However, providing you don't light fires in forests, leave litter or damage nature reserves, officialdom turns a blind eye to tourists **camping wild**, or, at the worst, may tell you to move along.

International camping carnet

If you're planning to do a lot of camping, an **international camping carnet** is a good investment. The carnet gives discounts at member sites and serves as useful identification. Many campsites will take it as an alternative to deposit your passport during your stay, and it covers you for third-party insurance when camping.

In the **UK and Ireland**, the carnet costs £4.50/€10, and is available to members of the AA or the RAC (see p.12), or the **Camping and Caravanning Club** (☎024/7669 4995, ⊛www.campingand caravanningclub.co.uk, the **CTC** (☎0870/873 0061, ⊛www.ctc.org.uk, or the **Carefree Travel Service** (☎024/7642 2024), which provides the carnet free if you take out insurance with them.

In the **US and Canada**, the carnet is available for US$10 from home motoring organizations, or from **Family Campers and FCRVers** (FCRV; ☎1-800/245-9755 or ☎716/668-6242, ⊛www.fcrv.org).

Eating and drinking

Romanian cuisine tends to be filling and wholesome rather than particularly tasty or imaginative. That said, the range and quality of restaurants is steadily improving, particularly in the capital and the bigger cities, where it's now possible to enjoy cooking from a number of different countries. For a glossary of food and drink terms, see p.442.

Breakfasts, snacks and sandwiches

If you're staying in a hotel, **breakfast** typically consists of a light meal of bread rolls and butter (sometimes known as *ceai complet*), to which an omelette, salty cheese or long, unappealing-looking skinless sausages can be added. This is washed down with a large white coffee or a cup of tea.

For **snacks**, known as *gustări* (also the Romanian word for hors d'oeuvres), look out for flaky pastries (*pateuri*) filled with cheese or meat, often dispensed through hatches in the walls of bakeries; brioche, a Moldavian speciality; sandwiches (*sandvici*); a variety of spicy grilled sausages and meatballs, normally sold by street vendors and in beer gardens; and small pizzas topped with cheese, salami and ketchup. Note that a "snack bar" serves only drinks. Ice cream, however, is sold on the streets almost all year round.

Main meals and desserts

Wherever you eat, it's best to go upmarket if you can, since the choice of dishes in cheaper **restaurants** is limited to cutlet (*cotlet*) and chips, and they tend to be thinly disguised beer halls. At least the grisly selfservice Autoservire canteens that Ceauşescu intended to make the mainstay of Romanian catering have largely vanished; unfortunately, they've been replaced for the most part by burger bars. Lacto-Vegetarian restaurants are also vanishing; although not particularly vegetarian, where they still exist they offer affordable food in reasonably congenial surroundings. Whatever you settle on, always enquire *Care feluri le serviţi astazi, ve rog?* ("What do you have today?") or *Ce Óhmi recomandaţi?* ("What do you

recommend?") before studying the menu too seriously, for sometimes the only thing going is the set menu (*un meniu fix*), usually dominated by pork.

However, at smarter restaurants, there's a fair chance of finding **authentic Romanian dishes**, which can be delicious. The best known is *sarmale* – cabbage leaves stuffed with rice, meat and herbs, usually served (or sometimes baked) with sour cream or horseradish; they are sometimes also made with vine leaves (*sărmăluţe in foi de viţă*) or, in Maramureş, with corn (*sarmale cu pasat*). *Mămăligă*, maize mush or polenta, often served with sour cream, is authentic country fare. Stews (*tocane*) and other dishes often feature a combination of meat and dairy products. *Muşchi ciobanesc* (shepherd's sirloin) is pork stuffed with ham, covered in cheese and served with mayonnaise, cucumber and herbs; while *muşchi poiana* (meadow sirloin) is beef stuffed with mushrooms, bacon, pepper and paprika, served in a vegetable purée and tomato sauce.

Keep an eye out for **regional specialities** (*specialităţile regiunii*). Moldavian cooking is reputedly the best in Romania, featuring rissoles (*pârjoale*), and more elaborate dishes such as *rasol moldovenesc cu hrean* (boiled pork, chicken or beef, with a sour cream and horseradish sauce), *tochitură moldovenească* (a pork stew, with cheese, *mămăligă*, and a fried egg on top), *rulade de pui* (chicken roulade), and *pui Câmpulungean* (chicken stuffed with smoked bacon, sausage, garlic and vegetables). Because of Romania's Turkish past, you may come across moussaka and varieties of pilaf, while the German and Hungarian minorities have contributed such dishes as smoked pork with sauerkraut and Transylvanian hotpot.

Cakes and desserts are sticky and very sweet. Romanians enjoy pancakes and pies with various fillings, as well as Turkish-influenced baclava and savarină (crisp pastry soaked in syrup and filled with whipped cream).

Inevitably, standards of **service** vary depending upon the type of establishment you are dining in, but generally speaking, don't expect anything but the most perfunctory of service. By and large, waiting staff in Romania, some of whom may speak English, remain largely indifferent to the concept of customer service.

Vegetarian food

Vegetarians will have a dull time in a country where voluntarily doing without meat is simply beyond comprehension. You could try asking for *ghiveci* (mixed stewed veg); *ardei umpluți* (stuffed peppers); *ouă umpluțe picante* or *ouă umpluțe cu ciuperci* (eggs with a spicy filling or mushroom stuffing); *ouă românești* (poached eggs); or vegetables and salads (see p.442). However, in practice, you're likely to end up with omelette, *mămăligă* (maize mush or polenta) or *cașcaval pané* (cheese fried in breadcrumbs). You can try asking for something *fără carne, vă rog* ("without meat, please"), or check *este cu carne?* ("does it contain meat?"), but you're unlikely to get very far.

Drinking

Café establishments called *cofetărie* serve coffee, soft drinks, cakes, ice cream, and beer. Romanians usually take their coffee black and sweet in the Turkish fashion; ask for *cafea cu lapte* if you prefer it with milk, or *fără zahăr* without sugar. The instant varieties are called Ness. **Bars**, meanwhile, are generally men-only places and range from dark rough-and-ready dives to places with a rather chintzy ice-cream-parlour atmosphere. They're all usually open well into the small hours, except in smaller towns. A *crama* is a wine cellar, while a *gradina de vară* is a terrace or garden, usually offering *mititei* (spicy sausages) as well as beer.

The **national drink** is *țuică*, a tasty, powerful brandy usually made of plums, taken neat. In rural areas, home-made spirits can be fearsome stuff, often twice distilled (to over 50 percent strength, even when diluted) to yield *palincă*, much rougher than grape brandy (*rachiu* or *coniac*). All spirits are alarmingly cheap (and served in large measures, usually 10cl; ask for a *mic*, 5cl, if you want less), except for whisky, which retails for around €12 a bottle.

Most **beer** is European-style lager (*bere blondă*). Silva (from Reghin), Valea Prahova (from Azuga), Ciucaș (from Brașov), Ursus (from Cluj), Ciuc (from Miercurea Ciuc), Timișoreana (from Timișoara), and Hațeg are probably the best regional brews, while Bergenbier and Eggenburger are acceptable mass-produced brands; you will also occasionally find brown ale (*bere neagră* or *brună*). Beer is usually sold by the bottle, so a request for *o sticlă* will normally get you one of whatever's available; draught beer is known as *halbă*.

Romania's best **wines** – and they are good – are the white Grasa from Cotnari, near Iașl; Tamaioasa, a luscious, late-harvested Moldavian dessert wine; Fetească Neagră, the blackberryish reds from Dealu Mare, east of Ploiești; and the sweet dessert wines from Murfatlar (notably Merlot and Cabernet Sauvignon, and white Muscat Ottonel). They can be obtained in most restaurants, while some places may just offer you a choice of red or white. Sparkling (*spumos*) wines from Alba Iulia and Panciu (north of Focșani) are very acceptable. Wine is rarely sold by the glass, but it does no harm to ask – *Serviți vin la pahar?*

Coca-Cola, Pepsi and Romanian mineral water are omnipresent; Romanian **soft drinks**, such as Cappy or Frutti Fresh, are good thirst-quenchers, but only severe dehydration justifies resorting to the indigenous *sirop*.

Self catering

Most **shops** have a good choice of foodstuffs; supermarkets are ubiquitous and have a wider range of imported foods but these are relatively expensive. There are also kiosks almost everywhere, selling biscuits and chocolate as well as their mainstays of booze and cigarettes. The basics are sardines, meat paste, pickled fruit and vegetables, pasta, jam, processed cheese and biscuits. Fresh cheese, eggs and meat are sold in the general foodstores (*alimentară*), while fruit and veg should be bought in the market (*piaţa*), where honey is also a good buy – in smaller towns and villages,

you may be expected to bring your own bag. Most **bread** is white, and not unpleasant, but it's worth asking for wholemeal bread (pâine graham or pâine diatetică).

Communications

Most post offices are open Monday to Friday from 7am to 8pm, and on Saturdays from 8am to noon; like the red-painted mail boxes, they are marked "Poştă". Stamps (timbru) and prepaid envelopes (plic) can be bought here; there may be long queues, but they're almost certainly not for stamps, which are often huge and, as several are normally needed, should be stuck on before writing your card. Sending mail home from Romania is relatively pricey – around €0.70 to overseas destinations – and takes about five days to Britain, two weeks to North America and Australasia.

Letters can be sent **poste restante** to main post offices in Romania: make sure they're addressed Officiul Poştal *no. 1, poşte restante*, followed by the name of the town, and that the recipient's last name is underlined. To collect letters, you'll have to show your passport and pay a small fee. Important messages should be sent by postcard, as letters from abroad can go missing if they look as if they might contain dollars. American Express also offer their cheque/cardholders a poste restante service at their office in Bucharest.

Telephones

Most public phones are orange **card-phones**, used both for internal and international calls. **Phone-cards** (*cartelă telefonică*) currently cost L80,000 (€2) and L135,000 (€3.50); insert them with the gold lozenge foremost and facing upwards, and after a few seconds you should get a sign indicating that you can start dialling; at the end, wait until the message *scoateţi cartela* indicates you can remove the card. Calls are most expensive from 7am to 7pm Monday to Friday and 7am to 3pm on Saturday, and cheapest from 11pm to 7am daily. All towns and many villages have a

Romtelecom office (usually open weekdays 6.30am–10pm, sometimes seven days a week), where the staff will connect your call. You'll normally pay the three-minute minimum in advance, and the balance afterwards.

Calling home from Romania

International calls can be made from cardphones, from Romtelcom offices (with a wait of ten minutes or so, as a rule), or by dialling ☎951 for the international operator from domestic phones and the better hotels (though the costs from hotels can be extortionate). Calls to Britain from Romtelcom offices cost about €1 a minute, and to North America and Australasia €2; from cardphones, they cost a bit more, so the cards don't last long. In Bucharest, discounted international calls can also be made at NexCom, at Str. Academiei 35-37.

Telephone charge cards

However, one of the most convenient ways of phoning home from Romania is via a **telephone charge card** from your phone company back home. Using a PIN number, you can make calls from most hotels, public and private phones that will be charged to your account. Since most major charge cards are free to obtain, it's certainly worth getting one at least for emergencies; enquire first, though whether Romania is covered, and bear in mind that rates aren't necessarily cheaper than calling from a public phone.

In **the UK and Ireland**, British Telecom (☎0800/345 144, ⓦwww.payphones.bt .com/2001/phone_cards/chargecard/charge card.) will issue free to all BT customers the BT Charge Card, which can be used in Romania; while NTL (☎0500/100 505) issues its own Global Calling Card, which can be used in more than sixty countries abroad, though the fees cannot be charged to a normal phone bill.

In the **US and Canada**, long-distance companies all enable their customers to make credit-card calls while overseas, billed to your home number. Call your company's customer service line to find out if they provide service from Romania, and if so, what the toll-free access code is.

To call **Australia and New Zealand** from Romania, telephone charge cards such as Telstra Telecard (☎1800/038 000), or Optus Calling Card (Australia; ☎1300/300 937) and Telecom NZ's Calling Card (☎04/801 9000) can be used, which are charged back to a domestic account or credit card.

Mobile phones

The main **mobile phone** providers in Romania are Connex, Cosmorom and Orange, although all mobile numbers are designated by a phone code beginning with ☎07. Calling a mobile from within Romania, you must dial all the numbers; calling from abroad, you need to drop the "0". If you want to use your mobile phone in Romania,

you'll need to check with your phone provider whether it will work abroad, and what the call charges are. You may get charged extra for this, depending on your existing package, as you are going to get charged for incoming calls while in Romania, with the people calling you paying their usual rate. If you want to retrieve messages while you're away, you'll have to ask your provider for a new access code, as your home one is unlikely to work abroad. For further information about using your phone in Romania, check out ⓦwww.telecomsadvice.org .uk/features/using_your_mobile_abroad.

Unless you have a tri-band phone, it is unlikely that a mobile bought for use inside the **US** will work outside the States. They tend to be very expensive to own in the US, too, as users are billed for both incoming and outgoing calls. For details of which mobiles will work outside the US, contact your mobile service provider.

Email

One of the best (and cheapest) ways to keep in touch while travelling is to sign up for a **free Internet email address** that can be accessed from anywhere, for example Yahoo! (ⓦwww.mail.yahoo.com) or Hotmail (ⓦwww.hotmail.com). **Internet access** is readily available in just about every town in Romania, although connections in most places are dreadfully slow, meaning it can take an hour just to read your mail; it is cheap, though, costing around £0.50p/€0.70 per hour or less.

For more information, ⓦwww.kropla .com is a useful website giving details of how to plug your lap-top in when abroad, phone country codes around the world, and information about electrical systems in different countries.

International dialling codes

Note that the initial zero is omitted from the area code when dialling the UK, Ireland, Australia and New Zealand from abroad.

USA and Canada 001 + area code.

Australia 0061 + city code.

New Zealand 0064 + city code.

UK 0044 + city code.

Republic of Ireland 00353 + city code.

The media

Most of Romania's newspaper offices are in the Casa Presei Libere, north of central Bucharest. There are supposedly some 1600 titles nationwide, many of them local, and very few of any real worth. Nationalist papers have a total circulation of around a million, but the biggest sellers are the sensationalist tabloid Tineretul Liber (Free Youth) and the most useful, România Liberă (Free Romania).

Most of the very few **English-language** publications that exist in Romania are found in Bucharest; *Nine O'Clock* (Ⓦwww .nineoclock.ro), a reasonably informed, though not particularly well-written, daily news sheet available free in hotels, and *Bucharest Business Week* (Ⓦwww.bbw.ro), a standard business weekly with the occasionally enlightening article, are useful. Of the listings magazines, *Bucharest In Your Pocket* (Ⓦwww.inyourpocket.com) is by far the most informative and up-to-date, while *Bucharest – What, Where, When*, has local editions for Braşov, Cluj, Iaşi and Timişoara. Western newspapers can be difficult to track down, though the classier hotels usually have a small kiosk selling same-day or previous day's editions, while you can read week-old newspapers (and monthly magazines) at the British, American, French and German libraries in Bucharest.

Television and radio

Romanian **television** offers the standard diet of news, soaps and gameshows, and is rarely turned off in many homes and bars. Once restricted to two hours a day, with half of that devoted to Ceauşescu's feats – ironically, it was TV that played a crucial role in his overthrow (see p.64) – these days there is no shortage of programming. The state channel TVR isn't too bad, offering a reasonable mix of independent news and documentaries, while commercial channels such as ProTV and Antena 1 do the soap/quiz/sport thing to varying degrees of success. Many people also now have access to cable TV, offering the standard foreign channels – BBC World, CNN, MTV, and so on. Any decent hotel should have TV with cable or satellite TV. Like many of the foreign-language programmes on Romanian TV, films at the cinema are shown in their original language with Romanian subtitles.

There are plenty of private **radio** stations, but for news most listeners tune into foreign stations, especially the BBC World Service (Ⓦwww.bbc.co.uk/worldservice), Radio Canada (Ⓦwww.rcinet.ca) and Voice of America (Ⓦwww.voa.gov).

Opening hours, public holidays and festivals

Opening hours in Romania are notoriously unreliable and weekends can be like the grave, with a surprising number of restaurants and cinemas closing mid-afternoon or not opening at all. Shops are generally open from 9 or 10am to 6 or 8pm on weekdays, with department stores (magazin universal) and some food stores opening from 8am to 8pm Monday to Saturday and from 8.30am to 1pm on Sunday. If you're trying to sort out flights, visas or car rental, be aware that most offices are closed by 4pm. Post offices (poşta) in the majority of places are open Monday to Friday from 7 or 8am to 6 or 7pm, and Saturdays 8am–noon; and banks (banca) are generally open Monday to Friday between 9am and 3 or 4pm. Although pharmacies (farmacie) are typically open Monday to Saturday and from 9am to 6pm, most towns should have at least one place that's open 24 hours.

Museums (*muzeu*) are generally open Tuesday to Sunday from 9am to 5pm or 10am to 6pm, though some do also close on Tuesdays. For visitors, museums can soon pall thanks to the lack of information in any language but Romanian, not to mention the uniform approach to national history. **Village museums** (mostly closed in the winter), however, are interesting even without the benefit of captions, containing peasant houses filled with artefacts, huge oil presses, watermills and other structures rescued from the agrarian past, laid out as if in a real community.

Public holidays and festivals

Romanian festivals fall into four groups: those linked to the Orthodox religion, with its twelve Great Feasts and hosts of lesser festivals; those marking events such as birth, marriage and death; those marking stages in the agricultural cycle; and secular anniversaries. While the last are **public holidays**, and never change their date, other festivals are less predictable. The Orthodox Easter is a moveable feast and still reckoned according to the Julian calendar, rather than the Gregorian calendar that's used in the West and for secular purposes in Romania. Rural festivals take place on a particular day of a month, the actual date varying from year to year, and they can also be advanced or delayed depending on the progress of the crops. Check dates at the **cultural office** in the county prefecture.

Festivals specific to particular places are listed at the appropriate point in the guide; the following is an overview.

Public holidays

January 1 & 2 New Year
Easter Monday/Good Friday is not a holiday, but women are usually given the day off to shop and cook
May 1 Labour Day
December 1 National Day
December 25 & 26 Christmas

Winter festivals

Christmas (Crăciun) and **New Year** (Revelion) celebrations are spread over the period from December 24 to January 7, and preparations often begin as early as December 6 (St Nicholas' Day) while on December 20, pigs are slaughtered for the forthcoming feasts. Groups of youths and children meet to prepare the festival costumes and masks, and to rehearse the *colinde* – allegorical songs wishing good health and prosperity for the coming year that are sung outside each household on **Christmas Eve** (Ajun), when the faithful exchange pastries called *turte*.

In Moldavia and Bucovina, processions follow the Capră, a goat-costumed dancer whose mask has a moveable lower jaw which he clacks in time with the music (to represent the death pangs of the old year). The masked carnival on December 27 in the

Maramureş town of Sighet has similar shamanistic origins.

On **New Year's Eve**, groups of *plugăraşi* (ploughmen) pull a plough festooned with green leaves from house to house in rural areas, cutting a symbolic furrow in each yard while a *doină* (an ancient song) calling for good health and fecundity is recited, accompanied in Transylvania by carolling, for example at Arpaş and şercaia in Braşov county. In Tudora and the villages around Suceava, and in Maramureş, New Year's greetings are delivered by the *buhai*, a friction drum which imitates the bellowing of a bull when horse hair is drawn through a hole in the membrane. This accompanies the *pluguşor*, a mime play featuring people masked as goats, horses and bears.

Although the official holidays end on January 2, villagers may keep celebrating through to **Epiphany** (Bobotează) on the 6th, when water is blessed in church and taken home in bottles for medicinal purposes, and horse races are staged in areas like the Wallachian plain and Dobrogea. The Huţuls and Lipovani, who follow the Julian calendar, celebrate Christmas on January 6. The final festivity in January is **Three Hierarchs' Day** on the 30th, celebrated with great pomp in Iaşi's Three Hierarchs' Church, which is dedicated to the saintly trio.

A review of Gorj county's folk ensembles and miners' brass bands – the **Enchanted Water Springs** or Izvoare fermecate – is held on the third Sunday of February in Târgu Jiu, winter conditions permitting. March is the time of **Lent**, and though few Romanians are nowadays devout enough to observe the fast, some rural folk still bake twisted loaves (*colaci*) on March 9, **Forty Saints' Day,** and take them to the village church to be blessed and distributed as alms. On one weekend during the month (decided at fairly short notice) an early spring festival, the **Kiss Fair**, takes place at Hălmagiu, providing the opportunity for villagers from the Apuseni and Banat regions to socialize and trade crafts.

Spring festivals

With the onset of spring in April and May, agricultural work begins in earnest.

Urbanization and collectivization have both affected the nature of **spring festivals**, so that Reşiţa's **Spring Parade** (Alaiul primaverii) features firefighters and engineers as well as folklore ensembles in its parade of floats (first week in April). Village festivals have tended to conglomerate, so that perhaps a dozen smallish fetes have been replaced by a single large event drawing participants and visitors from across the region – for example, the **Flowers of the Olt** (Florile Oltului) at Avrig on the second Sunday of April, attended by dozens of communities around Sibiu, some of whom wear the traditional Saxon jewellery of velvet and paste. Similarly, the Girl Fair at Gurghiu, on the second Sunday in May, is an occasion for villagers from the Gurghiul, Beica and Mureş valleys to make merry. For pomp and crowds on a larger scale, the **Pageant of the Juni** (see p.147) is held in Braşov on the first Sunday of May.

Though its exact dates vary, the Orthodox **Easter** (Paşte), the holiest festival of the Christian year, also falls in April or May. From Palm Sunday (Floriile), through the **Week of Sufferings** (Săptămâna patimilor) – during which, it's believed, souls will ascend directly to heaven – the devout fast, clean their houses, and attend church services, culminating in the resurrection celebration at midnight on Easter Saturday. The cry *Hristos o-nviat* ("Christ has risen") and the reply *Adevărat c-o-nviat* ("Truly he has risen") resound through the candlelit churches, overflowing with worshippers. Hard-boiled eggs are hand-painted on **Maundy** ("Great") Thursday with red dyes obtained from onion skin, to be given to friends and relatives on Easter Sunday and kept by the family icons; it's said that the devil cannot win as long as people go on singing carols at Christmas and painting eggs at Easter. With the exception of Pentecost or **Whitsun** (Rosalia), fifty days after Easter Sunday, other Orthodox festivals are nowadays less widely observed.

In southern Romania, there's a traditional belief still held by a minority that groups of mimes and dancers could work magic, and to this end selected young men were initiated into the **ritual of Căluş**. On **Whit Sunday**, an odd-numbered group of these

Călușari began their ritual dance from house to house, accompanied by a flag-bearer and a masked Mut (a mute who traditionally wore a red phallus beneath his robe and muttered sexual invocations), thus ensuring that each household was blessed with children and a bountiful harvest, and, if need be, exorcizing anyone possessed by the spirits of departed friends and family. Căluș rites are still enacted in some Oltenian villages, and the Călușari meet to celebrate their dancing and musical prowess at Whitsun, starting with a parade in Slatina and then two days of performances in Caracal. There's a similar festival, the **Festival of the Călușari** (Călușarul Transilvanean), in Deva during the second week of January, which doesn't have any particular magical significance, being nowhere near the heartland of Căluș culture, but is nevertheless impressive. The Roman Catholic Székely hold their Whitsun pilgrimage to Csíksomlyó (near Miercurea Ciuc) on a date set by the Gregorian calendar. Once common practice, the ritual garlanding of the plough is now rare, although the **Festival of the First Ploughman** or Tânjaua (first Sunday of May) at Hoteni, in Maramureș, is similar.

The age-old pastoral rites and feasts marking the sorting, milking and departure of the flocks to the hills are still widespread throughout Maramureș and the Apuseni mountains during late April or early May, depending on local tradition and climatic factors. The best-known **Measuring of the Milk** festivals (Sâmbra oilor) occur on the first or second Sunday of May, at the Huta pass into Oaș and on the ridge of Măgura Priei; lingering snows, however, can delay the smaller festivals until early July.

Summer and Autumn festivals

The **Cherry Fair** at Brâncovenești on the first Sunday of June anticipates other harvest festivals later in the month, and the round of great **summer fairs** known as Târg or Nedeias. In the days before all-weather roads, these events provided the people of remote highland villages with an annual opportunity to arrange deals and marriages. On the second Sunday of June, folk from some thirty Banat settlements attend the Nedeia of Tălcălșele at Avram Iancu; another village with the same name is the base for the famous **Girl Fair of Mount Găina** (see p.225), held on the Sunday before July 20. The highlanders of Oltenia gather for the similar **Polovragi Fair** on July 15 or 20.

Other summer festivals perpetuate Romania's old customs and folklore: the light-hearted **Buying Back of the Wives** at Hodac, near Târgu Mureș, and the funereal declamation of *boccas* during **The King of the Fir Trees** (see p.235) at Tiha Bârgăului in the heart of fictional Dracula country (on the second and third Sundays of June). Various "summer folk holidays" occur between June 21 (**Midsummer Day**) and June 29 (**St Peter's Day**); Drăgaica, the pagan pre-harvest celebration in the fields on Midsummer Day, is only practised in a few districts of southern Wallachia. The most widespread, however, is the feast of **St John the Baptist** (Sânziene) on June 24, celebrated with bonfires and wreathes of yellow flowers that are thrown over the houses. The regional diversity of folk costumes and music can be appreciated at events like șomcuta Mare's pastoral **The Oak Tree** (Stejarul), or the larger **Rarău Mountain festival** at Ilișești, held on the first and second Sundays of July respectively.

August is probably the best month for music, with four major festivals. During the first week of the month, the **Songs of the Olt** at Călimănești in Wallachia draws musicians and folklore ensembles from all over Oltenia. On the first Sunday, people from Maramureș, Transylvania and Moldavia meet for the great **Horă** at the Prislop Pass in their finest costumes; a week later, the **Festival of the Ceahlău Mountain** is held at Durău near the shores of Lake Bicaz. The music of pan pipes and the bands of Gorj county characterize another festival, **Tismana Garden festival** where you can also find a wide range of handicrafts. This is held on August 15, the Feast of the Assumption or Dormition of the Virgin Mary (known as **Great St Mary's**), when there are many church festivals and pilgrimages across the country, notably at Moisei in Maramureș and Nicula, north of Cluj. Fundata's **Nedeia of the Mountains**, on the last Sunday of August, is the traditional gathering for the highlanders of the Braşov, Argeş and Dâmboviţa regions.

Reaping preoccupies many villages during September, giving rise to **harvest festivals**, although the custom is gradually declining. The timing of these varies with the crop, and from year to year, but you can usually rely upon **At the Vintage** at Odobeşti in the eastern Carpathians being held on the last Sunday. On the second Saturday of September, the remaining Saxons gather for the **Sachsentreffen** at Biertan. Earlier in the month, on the first Sunday, you can hear the pan-pipers of the northwest perform the **Rhapsody of the Trişcaşi** at Leşu, in Bistriţa-Năsăud county. Many of the musicians here are shepherds, who compete with each other at **The Vrancea Shepherd's Long Pipe**, a festival held at Odobeşti on the third Sunday of November. Finally, December 1 is Romania's **national day**, celebrated above all in Alba Iulia, scene of the declaration of union between Transylvania and the rest of Romania.

Sports and outdoor activities

Romania's sporting pedigree is surprisingly strong, thanks largely to the exploits of the tennis player Ilie Nastase and the legendary gymnast Nadia Comaneci, both of whom achieved significant success and fame during the 1970s. Sporting triumph in the 1980s and 1990s came on the football field, with notable achievements by both the country's leading club side, Steaua Bucharest, and the national team, led by the mercurial Gheorghe Hagi. Romania's present day sporting superstar is the women's World and Olympic 5000m champion, Gabriel Szabo. The Romanian countryside lends itself perfectly to a multitude of outdoor activities, from hiking, skiing and cycling in the Carpathians to bird-watching in the Danube Delta – activities which can be done either individually or as part of a group tour.

Football

The 1994 World Cup brought the Romanian football team to international attention but many had been aware of their ability since 1986, when **Steaua Bucharest** became the first team from behind the Iron Curtain to lift the **European Cup** (the Champions' League), defeating Barcelona on penalties. Although Inter Milan allegedly offered to build a Fiat car plant in Romania in order to get their hands on Gheorghe Hagi, players were only able to move freely to West European clubs after 1990: by 1992, nine of the national team were playing abroad, from Red Star Belgrade to Real Madrid.

Romania progressed to the quarterfinals of the **1994 World Cup**, a tournament at which **Gheorghe Hagi** was arguably the best player. Dubbed the "Maradona of the Carpathians" – as much for his temperament as for his magical left foot – Hagi is a legend in Romania; born in Constanţa, he played for the local side before transferring to Steaua Bucharest on the orders of Ceauşescu's son Valentin, who effectively ran the team. After the revolution, he moved to Real Madrid for £1.8m, and after the 1994 World Cup to Barcelona, before flitting around a succession of lesser European clubs.

Romania's involvement in both the **1998 World Cup** and the **Euro 2000**

Championships ended at the second round stage, their defeat to Italy in the latter marking the end of Hagi's international career – ignominiously, and somewhat predictably, with a sending off. The national team has had a rather more frustrating time of it in recent years, failing to qualify for both the 2002 World Cup and the 2004 European Championships, despite the efforts of a talented young team featuring the likes of Adrian Ilie, Cristian Chivu and Adrian Mutu, who tied up a lucrative move to Chelsea In 2003.

The **domestic game** is dominated by the three big Bucharest clubs, **Steaua** (traditonally the army team), **Dinamo** (the police and Securitate), and **Rapid** (rail workers), who regularly carve up the championship between them. Although few other clubs in Romania have the financial muscle to put a stop to this hegemony, the big three have still to make an impression in European club competition, though this is hardly surprising when their best players are continually sold abroad. Every town has its stadium (*stadion*), and you should have no problem catching a game. **Matches** are usually played on Saturdays from August to May, with a break from November to February, and **tickets** for league games cost roughly €1–3.

Outdoor activities

Although two-thirds of Romania is either plains or hills and plateaux, the country's geography is dominated by mountains, which almost enclose the "Carpathian redoubt" of Transylvania, and merge with lesser ranges bordering Moldavia and Maramureş. Throughout these areas, there are opportunities to pursue several outdoor activities – hiking, skiing, caving and even shooting rapids. The Danube Delta is a totally different environment, unique for its topograhy – of which only one tenth is dry land – and as a wildlife habitat that attracts some three hundred species of bird during the spring and autumn migrations. If you don't fancy going it alone, there are now a wide variety of tours and trips offered by a host of agencies in the UK (see p.11), and to a lesser degree, in North America (see p.14) and Australasia (see p.15).

Hiking

The **Carpathians** – a continuation of the Alps – are the most sinuous chain of mountains in Europe, in Romania forming a natural barrier between Transylvania and the old Regat provinces, interrupted by a few narrow passes or wide depressions. Though few of its peaks are higher than 2500m, with the majority ranging between 1000m and 2000m, lack of altitude is more than compensated for by the variety of geological formations and rockscapes, with mighty **gorges** (*cheile*) at Turda and Bicaz, and spectacular **valleys** cut by the Olt and Prahova rivers. Bizarrely-eroded **rock formations** characterize Mount Ceahlău and karstic areas such as the Padiş plateau and the "Valley of Hell" in the Apuseni mountains, while the Bucegi range is famous for the Babele Sphinx, and the sheer walls overhanging Buşteni in the Prahova valley.

Dozens of **hiking trails** – signposted with red triangles, blue stripes or other markings – are shown on *Hartă Turistică* maps, and several good walks are detailed in the text of the guide. The **Bucegi massif** is perfect for short hikes within a limited time, for it offers dramatic crags, caves and waterfalls within a few hours' walk of the cable car, which

Useful hiking terms

cabana	mountain hut
cota	altitude
stăna	sheepfold
artă	map
potecă/traseu	path/route
nerecomandabil iarna	unsafe during winter
refugiu (salvamont)	refuge (with first aid)
şau	col (saddle)
stânca	rock
colţ	cliff
aven	doline
poiana	glade
izvor	spring
cascada	waterfall
telecabina	cable car
teleschi	ski-drag
telescaun	chairlift
vârf	peak

ascends from the valley just an hour's train ride from Braşov or two from the capital. To the southwest, the Făgăraş, Retezat and Parâng mountains offer the chance of longer hikes crossing several ranges.

Some tour operators organize all-inclusive **walking holidays** in the Carpathians. Independent hikers should bring camping gear and food, since accommodation in mountain cabanas can't be guaranteed, and some huts don't serve meals. These **cabanas** (marked on hiking maps) are convivial places where you can learn much about the mountains; but many Romanians simply pitch camp by rivers, and provided you're not in a nature reserve, you can do the same.

Skiing

Skiing is popular from November or December through until March, or even April, at the country's nine resorts. Foreign package operators favour Poiana Braşov for its superior slopes and facilities, but by going through local agencies or turning up on the spot you can also ski at Predeal, Buşteni and Sinaia, Borşa in Maramureş (for beginners), Păltiniş south of Sibiu, Semenic in southwestern Transylvania or Durău/Ceahlău on the edge of Moldavia. The majority of **pistes** are rated "medium" or "easy" (colour-coded red or blue), but each of the major resorts has at least one difficult (black) run, and the descents from Coştila and Caraiman to Buşteni are positively hazardous.

Bird-watching

The best place for seeing **birdlife** is without doubt the **Danube Delta** in late May and early June. Millions of birds winter here, or stop over during the spring (March–May) and autumn (Aug–Oct) migrations – a unique concentration of different species, including Europe's largest colonies of pelicans. Agencies can arrange boat **tours** down the main Sulina channel of the Delta, and their Tulcea or Crişan offices may sometimes rent small boats, which are the only means to penetrate the backwaters, where most of the birds nest. Canoes, kayaks or rowing boats are best for exploration, since boats with motors scare the wildlife and get caught up in vegetation.

You may also be able to negotiate with a local fisherman for a boat (*Pot să închiriez o barcă?*), bearing in mind that he'll probably act as rower and guide. Doing it this way, however, lessens your freedom of movement and is likely to be fairly time-consuming. For more on birds and bird-watching, see p.403.

Caving

Though a number of **large caves** (*peşteri*) with magnificent stalactites are easily accessible, most of Romania's **mountain caves** are known only to a dedicated band of potholers.

The science and practice of caving owes much to a Romanian, Emil Racoviţa, who founded the world's first speleological institute at Cluj University, near the karst zone of the Apuseni mountains. This region offers the greatest range of possibilities, from easy strolling passages to vertical shafts and flooded tunnels: there are **tourist caves** such as Chişcău and Meziad; big river caves such as Humpleu, Magura and Cetaţile Ponorului; and any number of crevices that should only be attempted by experts. The second main area is the southern Banat and the Mehedinţi massif, which has river caves such as Topolniţa, Cloşani and Comarnic.

Interested groups or individuals should write several months in advance to the **Racoviţa Institute** (Str. Clinicilor 5, 3400 Cluj, ☎0264/195 954, or Str. Frumoasă 11, 78114 Bucureşti, ☎021/211 3874), stating their experience. An offer to contribute gear and a share of the costs should increase your chances of acceptance by a local club.

Canoeing

The Racoviţa Institute can also put you in touch with **canoeing** enthusiasts devoted to shooting the rapids: an exciting sport practised on rivers like the Vaser in Maramureş and the Bistriţa Aurie in Bucovina, which descend steeply from their highland sources. Some local agencies may have kayaks to rent for fairly large groups. Otherwise, you'll need to bring your own equipment.

Crime and personal safety

Romania remains generally safe, despite the rise in violent crime, usually blamed on Gypsies, but in fact more to do with alcohol abuse and the demise of the police state. However, robbery with violence is rare, and a few commonsense precautions should minimize the risk of theft.

The police

Since the revolution, the **police** (*poliția*) have been reformed to a certain extent, and are generally regarded as honest if ineffectual, though they continue to attract Western disapproval by abusing the rights of Gypsies, homosexuals and other citizens. Unfortunately, the **Romanian Information Service** (the SRI, still generally known as the **Securitate**) is still on the scene, although an obsession with anti-socialist activities long ago changed to a commitment to keeping the ruling elite in power. Environmental and human rights activists may still be harassed, but the SRI doesn't normally concern themselves with tourists. Be aware of the self-styled **tourist police** who prey on tourists on the streets of Bucharest (see p.55); someone (or more usually, two, people) will approach you, flash fake ID and demand to see a passport or some other such document; never hand anything to these people – just walk away. The (real) police are generally approachable, though unlikely to speak much English.

Specific offences and emergencies

Watch out for **pickpockets**, in particular on public transport in Bucharest, where thieves are adept at relieving tourists of their belongings; wearing a (hidden) money-belt is advisable. Take care on overnight trains, shutting the door of your sleeper compartment as securely as you can (there are no locks). If your **passport** goes missing while in Bucharest, telephone your consulate immediately; anywhere else, contact the police. Guard your **traveller's cheques** fanatically, as they can be very difficult to replace in Romania. Thefts and other losses can be reported to the police who will issue the paperwork required for insurance claims back home, though only slowly and with painstaking bureaucratic thoroughness.

Foreigners are sometimes stopped and asked for **identification** (which should be carried at all times). However, this should be the extent of your dealings with the police, unless you have something stolen or break the law. Firstly, it's obviously safer not to become involved with the black market (see p.22). **Photography** is permitted everywhere except in areas designated by a sign (showing a crossed-out camera), usually near barracks, no matter how unimportant; while **nudism** and **topless bathing** are forbidden except on a few beaches (although offenders are more likely to be cautioned than punished). **Camping wild** is not allowed in nature reserves and forests. **Sleeping rough** in towns is risky and will attract the *poliția's* displeasure unless you do so in a train station and claim to be waiting for a train departing in the small hours. Should you be arrested, identify yourself, be polite and stay cool; try to avoid making a statement unless the officer speaks your language fluently; and demand to contact your consulate. **To call the police** dial ☎955.

Women Travellers

It's rare for Romanian men to subject women tourists to **sexual harassment**. As independent women travellers are few and far between, they're likely to be accorded some respect but also viewed with amazement, particularly in rural areas. Romanians (both male and female) are highly tactile, so you may find yourself being prodded more than you care for. Most trouble is alcohol-fuelled, so it's best to avoid going alone to any but the classiest bars, especially on weekend evenings. Within earshot of other people, you should be able to scare away any local pest by shouting *lasaţi-ma in pace!* ("Leave me alone!") or calling for the *poliţia*.

Working in Romania

Opportunities for working in Romania are relatively few. The most traditional form of work abroad, teaching English, is one option, while there are a few opportunities for participation or you could get involved in one of the country's summer work camps, with projects such as an archaeological dig or work in an orphanage.

Teaching English

Teaching English – often abbreviated as **ELT** (English Language Teaching) – is a good way of earning a living in Romania; you can get a **CELTA** (Certificate in English Language Teaching to Adults), a **TEFL** (Teaching English as a Foreign Language) or a **TESOL** (Teaching English to Speakers of Other Languages) qualification before you leave home or while you're in Romania – **International House** (ⓦwww.ihworld.com) has a branch in Bucharest, at B-dul Dimitrie Cantemir 2 (Ⓣ021/335 4490, ⒺOffice@ih .ro). You don't need a degree to do the course, but you'll certainly find it easier to get a job with the degree/certificate combination. Certified by the RSA, the courses are very demanding and cost about £1025/US$2500/CA$1440/AU$2550/NZ$3720 for the month's full-time tuition; you'll be thrown in at the deep end and expected to teach right away. The **British Council's** website, ⓦwww.britishcouncil.org/work/job, and the **TEFL** website, ⓦwww.tefl.com, both have a list of English-teaching vacancies.

Useful resources

Another pre-planning strategy for working in Romania, whether teaching English or otherwise, is to get hold of one of the books on summer jobs published by Vacation Work; call Ⓣ01865/241 978 or visit ⓦwww .vacationwork.co.uk. Travel magazines like the reliable *Wanderlust* (every two months;

€5) have a Job Shop section that often advertises opportunities with tour companies. ⓦwww.studyabroad.com has listings and links to study and work programmes, including many in Romania.

Study and work programs

From the UK and Ireland

British Council Ⓣ020/7930 8466, ⓦwww.britishcouncil.org. Produces a free leaflet detailing study opportunities in Romania, recruits TEFL teachers, and provides information about teacher development programmes in Romania.
BTCV (British Trust for Conservation Volunteers) Ⓣ01302/572 244, ⓦwww.btcv.org.uk. One of the largest environmental charities in Britain, it also has a programme of national and international working holidays (as a paying volunteer).
Earthwatch Institute Ⓣ01865/318 838, ⓦwww.uk.earthwatch.org. Long-established international charity with environmental and archeological research projects in Romania.
Field Studies Council Overseas Ⓣ01743 /852 150 or Ⓣ0845/852 150, ⓦwww.fscoverseas.org.uk. Respected educational charity with over 20 years' experience of organizing specialized holidays with study tours visits in Romania.
International House Ⓣ020/7518 6999, ⓦwww.ihlondon.com. Offers TEFL training leading to the award of a CELTA, and recruits for teaching positions in Romania.

From the US and Canada

Bernan Associates ☎1-800/274-4888, ⓦwww.bernan.com. Distributes UNESCO's encyclopaedic *Study Abroad*.
Earthwatch Institute ☎1-800/776-0188 or 978/461-0081, ⓦwww.earthwatch.org. International non-profit organization whose members volunteer to work on field research projects – in Romania, this involves archaeological digs.

Volunteers for Peace ☎802/259-2759, ⓦwww.vfp.org. Non-profit organization offering summer "workcamps" in Transylvania, including work in Romanian orphanages.

From Australia and New Zealand

Australians Studying Abroad ☎03/9509 1955 or ☎1800/645 755, ⓦwww.asatravinfo.com.au. Study tours focusing on art and culture.

Travellers with disabilities

Very little attention has been paid to the needs of the disabled in Romania, and there's no sign of any change in attitude. Getting around is a major problem, as public transport is often inaccessible while cars with hand controls are not available from the car rental companies. The only place where facilities for disabled persons are likely to be anything like comprehensive are In some of the classier hotels, and perhaps the best solution is to book a stay in a spa (see p.19), where there should be a degree of level access and some awareness of the needs of wheelchair users.

Read your **travel insurance** carefully to make sure that people with a pre-existing medical condition are not excluded, and use your travel agent or tour operator to make your journey simpler: airlines or bus companies can cope better if they are expecting you. A **medical certificate** of your fitness to travel, provided by your doctor, is also extremely useful; some airlines or insurance companies may insist on it. Make sure you carry a **prescription** for any drugs you need, including the generic name in case of emergency, and spares of any special clothing or equipment, as it's unlikely you'll find them in Romania.

Contacts for travellers with disabilities

In the UK and Ireland

Irish Wheelchair Association Blackheath Drive, Clontarf, Dublin 3 ☎01/818 6400, ⓦwww.iwa.ie. Useful information about travelling abroad with a wheelchair.

Tripscope Alexandra House, Albany Rd, Brentford, Middlesex TW8 0NE ☎08457/585 641, ⓦwww.tripscope.org.uk. Telephone information service offering free advice on international transport for those with a mobility problem.

In the US and Canada

Access-Able ⓦwww.access-able.com. Online resource for travellers with disabilities.
Directions Unlimited 123 Green Lane, Bedford Hills, NY 10507 ☎1-800/533-5343 or 914 /241-1700. Travel agency specializing in bookings for people with disabilities.
Mobility International USA 451 Broadway, Eugene, OR 97401 ☎541/343-1284, ⓦwww.miusa.org. Information and referral services, access guides, tours and exchange programmes.
Society for the Advancement of Travelers with Handicaps 347 5th Ave, New York, NY 10016 ☎212/447-7284, ⓦwww.sath.org. Non-profit educational organization representing travellers with disabilities.
Wheels Up! ☎1-888/389-4335, ⓦwww.wheelsup.com. Provides discounted airfare,

tour and cruise prices for disabled travellers, and publishes a free monthly newsletter.

In Australia and New Zealand

ACROD (Australian Council for Rehabilitation of the Disabled) PO Box 60, Curtin ACT 2605; ☎02/6282 4333 (also TTY), ⓦwww.acrod.org.au.

Provides lists of travel agencies and tour operators for people with disabilities.
Disabled Persons Assembly 4/173–175 Victoria St, Wellington, New Zealand ☎04/801 9100 (also TTY), ⓦwww.dpa.org.nz. Resource centre with listings agencies and operators for people with disabilities.

Gay and lesbian travellers

The communist regime was relentlessly homophobic. Sexual relations between consenting adults of the same sex were illegal; offenders were jailed or forced to submit to "voluntary treatment", including electric shocks, drugs or even castration, unless they agreed to become an informer for the Securitate, a bait for other victims. The Constantinescu government, however, committed to adhering to international norms such as the European Convention on Human Rights, finally repealed the law against homosexuality in July 2000, despite church opposition.

The majority of the population remains largely **unsympathetic** towards the gay and lesbian community, and there are very few manifestations of gay life, even in Bucharest. To find out more, contact Accept (PO Box 34–56, Bucharest, ☎021/252 1637, ⓦwww .accept-romania.ro), a Bucharest-based organisation involved in the promotion of gay and lesbian activities in Romania, and who also offer counselling and HIV testing services.

Contacts for gay and lesbian travellers

In the UK

ⓦwww.gaytravel.co.uk Online gay and lesbian travel agent, offering good deals on all types of holiday. Also lists gay- and lesbian-friendly hotels.
Dream Waves Holidays ☎0870/042 2475, ⓦwww.gayholidaysdirect.com. Specializes in exclusively gay holidays, including skiing trips and summer sun packages.
Madison Travel ☎01273/202 532, ⓦwww.madisontravel.co.uk. Established travel

agents specializing in packages to gay- and lesbian-friendly mainstream destinations, and also to gay/lesbian destinations.

In the US and Canada

gaytravel.com ☎1-800/GAY-TRAVEL, ⓦwww.gaytravel.com. The premier site for trip planning, bookings, and general information about international gay and lesbian travel.
International Gay & Lesbian Travel Association ☎1-800/448-8550 or 954 /776-2626, ⓦwww.iglta.org. Trade group that can provide a list of gay- and lesbian-owned or -friendly travel agents, accommodation and other travel businesses.

In Australia and New Zealand

Silke's Travel ☎1800/807 860 or 02/8347 2000, ⓦwww.silkes.com.au. Long-established gay and lesbian specialist, with an emphasis on women's travel.
Tearaway Travel ☎1800/664 440 or 03/9510 6644, ⓦwww.tearaway.com. Gay-specific business dealing with international travel.

Directory

Addresses Written as Str. Eroilor 24, III/36 in the case of apartment buildings, ie Street (Strada) of Heroes, number 24, third floor, apartment 36. Some blocks have several entrances, in which case this is also given, eg *scara B*. Each district of Bucharest has a *sector* number, while in some towns each district (*cartier*) is named. In small villages, houses simply have a number and no street name. Streets, boulevards (*bulevardul*), avenues (*calea* or *şoseaua*) and squares (*piaţa*) are commonly named after national heroes like Stephen the Great – Ştefan cel Mare – or Michael the Brave – Mihai Viteazul – or the date of an important event, such as December 1, 1918, when Transylvania was united with the Old Kingdom.

Camera film Major brands of colour print are widely available, as well as instant processing facilities. Note that it is forbidden to take pictures near military or government buildings.

Children Kids qualify for various reductions, depending on their age. Rail transport is free for under-5s, and half-price for under-10s. On TAROM flights, children under two pay only ten percent, and those up to the age of 12 receive a 33-percent discount. In hotels, children under ten may often share an adult's bed for free, or pay half of the adult cost for an extra bed in the room. In big coastal resorts and at Poiana Braşov there are kindergartens for the benefit of holidaymakers. A few train stations have a specially heated room for mothers with babies (*camera mama şi copilul*). For travellers with children, the big problems are shortages of nappies (diapers) and baby food. Local milk is not to be trusted – bring supplies with you. Mamaia and Poiana Braşov offer the best entertainments for kids, but most large towns have a puppet theatre (Teatrul de Păpuşi).

Cigarettes Romanian cigarettes are generally unappealing. Mărăşeşti and Carpaţi, (the cheapest at about €0.25 a pack), are of rough black tobacco; Snagov are milder and cost slightly more. The most common Western brands are Hollywood, L&M and Monte Carlo. Kent is the most expensive at about €1 a pack. Matches are called *chibrit*, while a light is a *foc* and a lighter a *brichetă*. On trains, smoking is allowed only in corridors or vestibules; buses are smoke-free.

Electric power 220 volts; a standard continental adaptor enables the use of 13 amp, square-pin plugs.

Laundries There are several in Bucharest, but elsewhere they can be difficult to find; it's usually a choice between washing clothes yourself or paying a hotel to do it.

Left luggage Offices (*bagaje de mână*) exist in most train stations, where you'll usually have to pay around €1; there may also be lockers, but it's best to avoid these, as the locks have a tendency to jam.

Time Romania is two hours ahead of GMT, seven hours ahead of Eastern Standard Time and ten ahead of Western Standard Time: clocks go forward one hour for the summer at the same time as other European countries (from the last Sunday of March to the last Sunday of September).

Tipping Although not obligatory, it's appreciated if you round the bill up for good service.

Toilets In public places, these are generally awful; in larger train stations, you'll have to pay for regularly cleaned facilities. Elsewhere, a few clean private toilets are appearing. In any case, you should carry a supply of paper. "Barbaţi" means men and "Femei" means women.

Guide

Guide

Bucharest

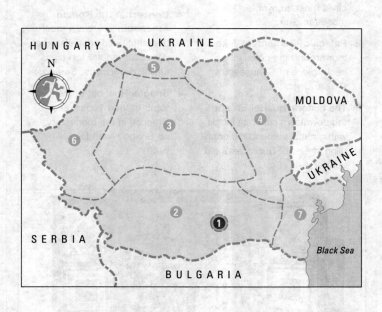

CHAPTER 1 # Highlights

* **National Art Museum** The country's biggest and best collection, the highlight of which is the spectacular gallery of Romanian Medieval art. See p.66

* **Museum of the Romanian Peasant** A superb collection of traditional textiles, ceramics, carvings and icons in the city's most enjoyable museum. See p.70

* **Palace of Parliament** Take a tour around the colossal centrepiece of Ceauşescu's Centru Civic. See p.71

* **The historic quarter** Escape the downtown concrete jungle with a ramble around the crumbling streets of Bucharest's old quarter. See p.75

* **Herăstrău Park** Combine a leisurely stroll through Bucharest's largest, greenest park with a cruise on the adjoining lake. See p.78

* **Village Museum** A wonderful assemblage of dwellings, churches, barns and other structures from all over Romania. See p.79

* **Concert at the Roman Atheneum** The city's most beautiful building is also the venue for regular top-class classical concerts. See p.84

* **Snagov** Row out to the tomb of Vlad Ţepeş, aka Dracula, in the monastery on Snagov Island. See p.89

△ Bucharest Village Museum

Bucharest

For many people, initial impressions of **BUCHAREST** (Bucureşti), a sprawling, dusty city of some two million people, are less than favourable. As Romania's centre of government and commerce and site of its main airport, most visitors to the country will find themselves passing through the city at some point, but it's chaotic jumble of traffic-choked streets, ugly concrete apartment blocks and monumental but mostly unfinished communist developments are often enough to send the majority of travellers scurrying off to the more obvious attractions further north. Yet it's a city that rewards patience: behind the congested arteries lies a tangle of backstreets where concrete is softened by abundant greenery and the inhabitants – a cosmopolitan mixture of Romanians, Gypsies, Turks, Arabs, Africans and Chinese – manage to rise above the bureaucratic obstructions and inadequacies of the city's infrastructure.

The architecture of the old city, with its cosmopolitan air, was notoriously scarred by Ceauşescu's redevelopment project in the 1980s, which demolished an immense swathe of the historic centre – including many religious buildings and thousands of homes – and replaced it with a concrete jungle, named the **Centru Civic**. The centrepiece of this development was an enormous new palace for the communist leader, now known as the **Palace of Parliament**, which currently lays claim to being Bucharest's premier tourist attraction. The palace aside, other sites that can on their own justify a visit to the city include the superbly renovated **National Art Museum**, housing a particularly fine collection of Romanian medieval art, and the **Village Museum**, a wonderful assemblage of vernacular buildings garnered from Romania's multifarious regions. Once you've tired of the museums, there's plenty of greenery to explore – most obviously the **Cişmigiu Gardens** in the heart of the city, or the more expansive **Herăstrău Park** to the north – as well as a generous sprinkling of cafés, bars and restaurants to sample.

From Bucharest, there are excellent train and road connections to the rest of the country, but local services to the towns and villages in the immediate vicinity are often limited or tortuous. There are, however, some enjoyable visits to be had outside the capital, most notably the lake and monastery at **Snagov** (see p.89), the palace at **Mogoşoaia** (see p.89) and the village of **Clejani** (see p.91), home to some outstanding Gypsy music.

Some history

According to legend, Bucharest was founded by a shepherd called **Bucur**, who built a settlement amid the Vlăsia forest. It was recorded as a nameless "citadel on the Dâmboviţa" in 1368, and named as Bucharest in an edict from the time of Vlad the Impaler. Over the centuries, both Târgovişte (see p.102) and

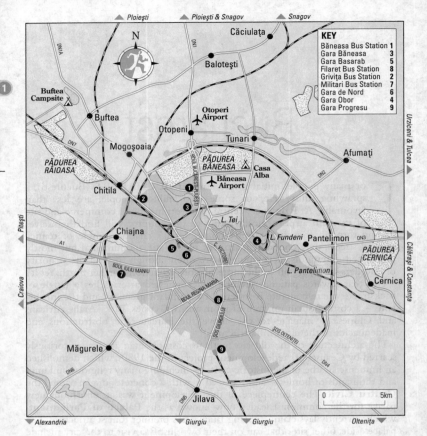

The map shows Bucharest and surroundings with a KEY:

KEY

Băneasa Bus Station	1
Gara Băneasa	3
Gara Basarab	5
Filaret Bus Station	8
Grivița Bus Station	2
Militari Bus Station	7
Gara de Nord	6
Gara Obor	4
Gara Progresu	9

Bucharest have served as the **Wallachian capital**, but the latter finally secured its claim in 1659 – its position at the convergence of the trading routes to Istanbul outweighing the defensive advantages of Târgoviște's location in the Carpathian foothills.

As the boyars (nobles) moved into the city they built **palaces** and **churches** on the main streets radiating from the centre; these streets were surfaced with timber baulks and known as "bridges" (*pod*). Despite earthquakes and periodic attacks by Turks, Tatars, Austrians and Russians over the course of its history, the city continued to grow and to modernize. New **boulevards** were driven through the existing street pattern in the 1890s, after the style of Haussmann's Paris, and they still form a ring road and the main north–south and east–west axes of the city today. Most of the major buildings, such as the **Romanian Atheneum** and the **Cercul Militar**, were designed by French or French-trained architects and built in the years before World War I.

It was around this time that the city was dubbed the "Paris of the East", as much for its hectic and cosmopolitan social scene as for its architecture. The Romanian aristocracy was among the richest and most extravagant in Europe, but this lifestyle depended on the exploitation of the poor, and in Bucharest the two coexisted in what Ferdinand Lasalle described as "a savage hotchpotch", with beggars waiting outside the best restaurants, and appalling slums within a few steps of the elegant boulevards.

By 1918, the city's population had grown to 380,000 and roads such as Podul Mogoșoaiei, Podul de Pământ and Podul Calacilor were widened, paved and renamed as the Calea Victoriei, Calea Plevnei and Calea Rahovei respectively, in honour of the battles of the 1877–78 War of Independence from Turkey. After World War II, the city was ringed with ugly apartment buildings, first in areas such as "Red Grivița", which the Allies had bombed flat (aiming for the rail yards), then expanding into the surrounding countryside; the population doubled from one to two million.

A massive **earthquake** in 1977 reduced large parts of the city to rubble and left over 1500 people dead. Whilst this prompted the construction of several major city projects, including a brand new metro system and an airport (Otopeni), it also provided Ceaușescu with the perfect excuse to implement his megalomaniac vision for the city. In 1984, and in order to create a new **Centru Civic**, Ceaușescu had most of the area south of the centre levelled, which entailed the demolition of thousands of homes, as well as churches, a monastery and a hospital. To this day, scores of unfinished projects litter the landscape and seem likely to scar the city for many years to come.

In December 1989, the city found itself at the centre of the most violent of the popular **revolutions** sweeping across Eastern Europe that year, when nearly three hundred people were killed in the uprising. Ceaușescu's execution did not, however, mark a complete end to the violence, and the following summer similar scenes erupted when miners from the Jiu Valley were brought in to stamp out student protests over the government, resulting in a further seventy deaths.

Whilst the post-communist era has brought back a conspicuous consumption to the city, manifest in the proliferation of luxury hotels, glossy shops full of designer clothes, and restaurants, bars and clubs, few Bucharestians can afford to indulge in them.

Arrival

While city transport, at least round the centre, is pretty good during the day, it's almost non-existent at night, and street lighting throughout Bucharest leaves much to be desired. It is therefore best to avoid arriving late at night, unless you're willing to take a taxi to your hotel (for more on which, see p.57). Both of Bucharest's **airports** are on the main road north of the city and linked to the centre by express bus; the main **train station** is a little way out of the centre to the northwest, but is well connected to the downtown area by both bus and metro. There are six **bus stations** scattered around the city, all in the suburbs and mainly serving the local villages, so it's unlikely that you'll need to use any of them. In any case, you're more likely to use one of the many maxitaxis (minibuses), which serve both short and long distance destinations; there are two main departure points for these located near the Garas de Nord and Obor.

By air

International air passengers arrive at the completely renovated **Otopeni airport**, 16km north of the centre. There are several exchange counters (with poor rates) and a cash machine here, as well as half a dozen car rental outlets (see listings, p.87). Sky Services (℡021/204 1002; 24hr) provides **transfers** to any point in the city centre (€8 one-way, €12 return); alternatively, express bus #783 (5.30am–11.15pm Mon–Fri every 15min, Sat & Sun every 30min; journey time 30–40min; around €1.25, return ticket only) departs for Piaţa Unirii, stopping at Piaţa Victoriei, Piaţa Romană and Universităţii along the way. Buses leave from outside the domestic arrivals hall, one floor below international arrivals – buy your ticket from the booth by the stop.

Whilst not as bad as they used to be, the waiting mob of taxi drivers outside are still a nuisance. If you do decide to take a taxi make sure you use a reputable company (see p.57); moreover, and as the various signs dotted around the arrivals hall indicate, you shouldn't pay more than €4 for a ride into the city centre.

Some internal flights (and those of Angel Airlines, Carpatair, and Ukrainian Airlines) land at **Băneasa** airport, from where you can catch bus #131 or #783 or tram #5 into the centre, or bus #205 to the Gara de Nord, until around 11.30pm.

By train

Virtually all international and domestic services terminate at the **Gara de Nord**, a chaotic place, but which is now much cleaner and less intimidating than it used to be, thanks to a heavy security presence and a negligible entrance fee (payable if you don't possess a ticket). Outside, however, you are still likely to be accosted by any number of oddball (but generally harmless and easily ignored) characters, variously offering transport, accommodation or some other service. Luggage can be stored at the bagaje de mână (roughly €1; open 24hr) on the concourse opposite platforms 4 and 5. Local trains (mostly Personals, the very slow ones) terminate at the **Gara Basarab** (700m northwest of Gara de Nord or one metro stop towards 1 Mai), **Gara Obor**, northeast of the centre at the end of B-dul Ferdinand I (trolley buses #69 and #85), and **Gara Progresu**, on the southern outskirts (bus #116). **Gara Băneasa**, north of Piaţa Presei Libere, is used mainly by a handful of summer trains to the coast.

It's a thirty-minute walk from the Gara de Nord to the city centre; head right along Calea Griviţei to reach Calea Victoriei, the city's main north–south axis. Alternatively, you could take the metro to Piaţa Victoriei, where you can change onto line M2 to reach Piaţa Universităţii, the nearest stop to the heart of the city, or catch a taxi, which shouldn't cost more than a couple of euros. Buses and trams from the Gara de Nord run around the centre rather than straight through it.

By road

Driving in Bucharest is not recommended for those of a nervous disposition, but if you are arriving **by road**, beware of potholes, cyclists and horses and carts. Approaching from Transylvania on the DN1 you'll pass both airports before reaching the şoseaua Kiseleff, an avenue which leads directly to the centre. The approach from Giurgiu (the point of entry from Bulgaria) on the DN5 is less inspiring, with a long run through high-rise suburbs until Bulevardul Dimitrie Cantemir finally reaches the Piaţa Unirii; likewise, the A1 motorway from Piteşti and the west brings you in through serried ranks of apartment blocks before reaching the Cotroceni Palace. The DN3 from the coast leads through the modern suburb of Pantelimon before reaching the older districts along Bulevardul Carol I.

Bucharest doesn't possess a central **bus station**, which makes locating buses for specific destinations tricky. Instead, it has a smattering of stations on the edge of town which primarily serve the local villages: Filaret, on Piaţa Filaret (in the station built in 1869 for Bucharest's first rail line), which sends buses south and southeast towards Giurgiu and Olteniţa; Băneasa, on B-dul Ionescu de la Brad 1, serving Snagov, and Ploieşti to the north; Militari, B-dul Păcii (Metro Păcii or bus #785), for points west; and Griviţa, şos. Chitilei 221 (at the Mezeş terminal of tram #45), serving Târgovişte. Maxitaxis (for Braşov, Piteşti, Sibiu and other destinations) depart from a small bay opposite Gara de Nord, whilst there's another departure point at Str. Ritmului 35, to the northeast of town near Gara Obor.

Information and tours

Getting **information** in Bucharest is, quite simply, a nightmare. Incredibly, the city is without a tourist office, a situation that looks unlikely to change in the near future. Your best bet is the highly informative, entertaining and on-the-ball *Bucharest In Your Pocket* (€2), available from hotels and bookshops, and published bi-monthly. Otherwise, there is a stack of other, more straightforward business-orientated **listings magazines**, none of which particularly excel. The best **maps** of Bucharest are those published by Amco Press, which incorporates a separate public transport map, and AGC, which also covers some of the outlying areas, such as Mogoşoaia. *Nine O Clock*, the main English-language newspaper, is available free from major hotels and airline offices.

The best of the city's **sightseeing tours** is run by the concierge department in the *Athénée Palace Hotel* (☎021/303 3777); three-hour trips (Mon–Sat at 9.30am; €20) include entrance fees to the Museum of the Romanian Peasant and Village Museum, transport and refreshments – longer tours can be arranged upon request.

> ## Bucharest hassles
>
> There are a couple of hassles in Bucharest that it's as well to be aware of during your stay. If at some stage you're approached by two or three men demanding to see your **passport**, don't be too alarmed. Ignore their demands and don't give them anything – simply saying that all your documents are at the hotel should be enough to put them off – and walk off confidently; these self-styled tourist police are nothing more than con men. If they persist, insist that they accompany you to your hotel or the nearest police station, which should put them off.
>
> You should also be extremely vigilant where your **belongings** are concerned, in particular at the Gara de Nord, where bags can suddenly disappear, and on the buses, where a standard trick is to slit bags open, thus emptying some of the contents. Keep your bag close to your chest and eyes peeled.
>
> Another, albeit minor, hassle, are **stray dogs**. During Ceauşescu's systematization programme of the 1980s, many houses were bulldozed and owners had little choice but to kick their beloved canines out onto the street; this resulted in the little beasts multiplying like nobody's business, roaming the streets scavenging around rubbish tips, and generally making a nuisance of themselves. If at any time you feel threatened, either walk on slowly and confidently or mime throwing a stone and they'll back off; do not run. Whilst the chances of a nip on the ankles are slim, confrontations with these dogs can be unpleasant and intimidating.

City transport

Public transport is a little chaotic, but has improved over recent years, and remains extremely cheap. Apart from some express buses on the main axes, most **bus** and **tram** routes avoid the central zone, though this is covered by the **metro system**. However, you may still find yourself walking a lot – no great hardship in this city of green, picturesque backwaters. Beyond the downtown thoroughfares, roads are still so poor that buses and trams seem set to rattle themselves to pieces, and trolley buses frequently slip from the wires and stall.

Buses and trams

There is a flat fare of about €0.25 on **trolley buses** (*troleibuz*), **trams** (*tramvai*), and most **buses** (*autobuz*), all of which run from around 5am until 11.30pm. You need to buy tickets in advance from street kiosks (roughly Mon–Fri 6am–8/9pm, Sat 7am–7pm, Sun 7am–2.30pm), and "validate" them once aboard – they are not transferable. Day passes cost €1.25 and weekly passes €2.50, both representing excellent value. It costs about double the standard fare to travel on the city's express buses, using tickets with a magnetic strip, also bought in advance from the kiosks (day and weekly passes not valid). In addition, private **minibuses** (*maxitaxis*) operate along the major arteries; these too charge about double the standard bus fare, the current rate being posted in the window. Ticket inspectors are ubiquitous, and travelling without a valid ticket will earn you a fine of €8.

The metro

Looking much older than its twenty-five years, the Bucharest **metro** is not the most user-friendly system in the world – maps and signposting are somewhat confusing, lighting is poor and announcements are barely audible, but it is clean, cheap and safe. Trains run from 5.30am until 11.30pm, with magnetic tickets costing around €1 for two rides to €1.25 for ten. Running east–west, the M1 line (shown in red on maps) was built to serve the new working-class suburbs; the second line, the M2 (blue), runs north–south straight through the centre; and the third, M3 (yellow), does a complete loop to and from the Gara de Nord; the M4 (green) links Gara de Nord with 1 Mai in the northwest, although you'll have little reason to use this line.

Key bus and trolleybus routes	
North–south	along B-duls Magheru and Bălcescu: #783 (express)
	along Calea Dorobanţilor: #131 and #301
East–west	(north of the centre)
	from Gara de Nord along B-dul Dacia (via Piaţa Romană): #79 and #86
	along B-dul Dacia: #133
	along B-duls Regina Elisabeta and Carol I (via the university): #66 (Metro Obor), #69 (Gara Obor).
	from Gara de Nord to Strada Baicului (Gara Obor): #85
East–west	(south of the centre)
	along Splaiul Independenţei and B-dul Unirii: #104 (Opera–National Stadium), #123 (Gara de Nord–Vitan).
East	from Piaţa Rosetti: #63 (to Metro Obor).

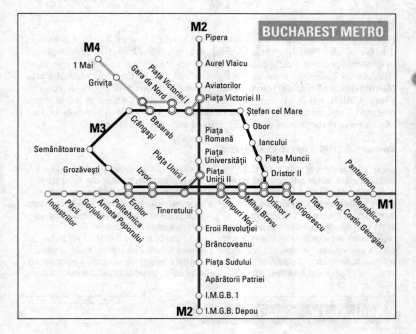

Taxis

Bucharest's **taxi** drivers have something of a reputation for harassing and ripping off foreigners, and though the situation is not nearly as bad as it once was, you should still be wary – stick to one of the following companies: Cristaxi (☎021/9461), Meridian (☎021/9444) and Perozzi (☎021/9631), each of which should have an operator who speaks English. The same can't be said for the majority of drivers, so have the address written down just in case. Avoid any driver who approaches you at the airport or train station, and on no account get into an unmarked taxi; also, give any taxi not displaying the fare a wide berth. Although price rises are common, taxis are still remarkably cheap, and you can expect to pay around €0.20 per kilometre.

Accommodation

Bucharest is well stocked with **hotels**, a good number of which have undergone extensive renovation in recent years. Whilst this has meant higher standards of comfort all round, it has also led to many hotels demanding unrealistic prices. Meanwhile, the few budget places that do exist are generally located in the worst area of town, near the Gara de Nord. In addition to the ever-expanding **hostel** scene, there are a growing selection of **private rooms** and **apartments** available. Bucharest has just one **campsite**, though this is located way out to the north of the city between the two airports.

Hotels

Hotels are found in four main areas of the city: the cheapest location is around the **Gara de Nord**, which, despite the recent addition of a couple of new hotels, remains a rather seedy (though generally safe) area. The city's most characterful hotels are sited in the heart of the city, in the areas around **Piața Revoluției** and the university, with a handful more further south towards **Piața Unirii**. Most of the hotels to the **north** of the centre are business oriented, but you can find the best of the city's privately run places here, too. Most of the better hotels now offer airport pick-ups and transfers.

Around the Gara de Nord

Bucegi Str. Witing 2 ☏ 021/212 7154, ℱ 212 6641. Reasonable budget option smack-bang next to the station, offering small, and slightly musty, one- to four-bed rooms, some with bathrooms. ❸
Cerna B-dul D. Golescu 29 ☏ 021/311 0535, ℱ 311 0721. Directly opposite the *Bucegi*, but with larger, cleaner and brighter rooms (sinks in rooms), this is a good-value budget hotel, with both singles and doubles. Breakfast not included. ❹
Elizeu Str. Elizeu 11–13 ☏ 021/212 6931, ⓦ www.hotelelizeu.ro. This bright new hotel is a very pleasant, and affordable, alternative to the other places hereabouts; spotless rooms with appealing furnishings, comfy leather sofas and a/c. Located just off B-dul Golescu, midway between Gara de Nord and Gara Basarab. ❻
IBIS Calea Griviței 143 ☏ 021/222 2722 ⓦ www.ibishotel.com. Injecting a dash of colour into this otherwise grim area, this is much like any other IBIS in the world; respectably neat, clean and

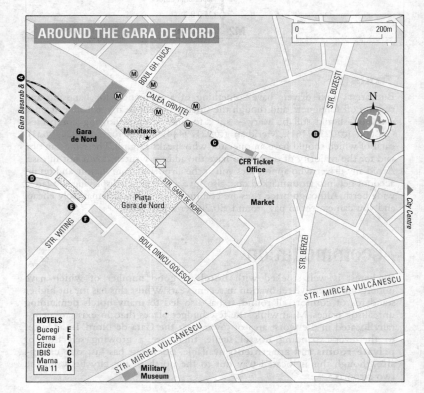

AROUND THE GARA DE NORD

0   200m

Gara Basarab & Ⓐ

BDUL GH. DUCA

Ⓜ Ⓜ

CALEA GRIVIȚEI

Ⓜ Ⓜ

STR. BUZEȘTI

Gara de Nord

Maxitaxis ★

Ⓜ

Ⓒ

Ⓑ

N

Ⓓ

CFR Ticket Office

✉

STR. GARA DE NORD

Market

City Centre ▶

Piața Gara de Nord

Ⓔ

Ⓕ

STR. WITING

BDUL DINICU GOLESCU

STR. BERZEI

STR. MIRCEA VULCĂNESCU

STR. MIRCEA VULCĂNESCU

HOTELS	
Bucegi	E
Cerna	F
Elizeu	A
IBIS	C
Marna	B
Vila 11	D

Military Museum

functional rooms with standard TV and mini-bar facilities. Breakfast is extra. ⑦
Marna Str. Buzeşti 3 ☎021/212 8366, ℻312 9455. One of the better options in this area, both price and cleanliness wise. Singles and doubles, with and without bathrooms, at a range of prices, but with trams rattling by, it's fairly noisy. Breakfast included. ③–④

Around Piaţa Revoluţiei and the university

Athénée Palace Hilton Str. Episcopiei 1–3, on the northern side of Piaţa Revoluţiei ☎021/303 3777, ⓦwww.hilton.com). This remains the most opulent hotel in the city, with first-rate facilities, including rooms for disabled guests and three no-smoking floors. It's already the most famous hotel in Romania, with a long history of intrigue and espionage (see p.67). ⑨

Capitol Calea Victoriei 29 ☎021/315 8030, ⓦwww.hotelcapitol.ro. A fine nineteenth-century building near the central post office, though the rooms are disappointing, as are the broom-cupboard sized bathrooms. There's little to distinguish between the two- and three-star rooms (in terms of both quality and price), so you may as well opt for the former. Triples available too. ⑧

Capşa Calea Victoriei 36 ☎021/313 4038, ⓦwww.capsa.home.ro. This splendid building dating from 1852 has been beautifully restored to accommodate one of the city's premier hotels; magnificently furnished rooms (the suites are something else altogether) and first-class service. ⑨

Carpaţi Str. Matei Millo 16 ☎021/315 0140, ℻312 1857. The best-value budget hotel in town, and a great central location to boot; singles and doubles with and without bathrooms and TVs. Unusually welcoming staff, too. ④–⑤

Continental Calea Victoriei 56 ☎021/313 4114, ⓦwww.continentalhotels.ro. Dating from 1860, the *Continental* occupies a lovely building on this venerable old street. Its large, old-style, rooms are rather soulless, however, and the hotel retains a pretty downbeat atmosphere. ⑨

Intercontinental B-dul N. Bălcescu 4 ☎021/310 2020, ⓦwww.intercontinental.com. This towering city landmark remains the businessmans' and journalists' hotel of choice, with all the class you'd expect of a five-star – immaculate rooms, marble-tiled bathrooms and top-notch facilities, including sauna, gym and rooftop pool; the citywide views are unbeatable. ⑨

Lido B-dul General Magheru 5–7 ☎021/314 4930, ✉lido_hotel@hotmail.com. Located on a busy downtown thoroughfare, this stylish 1930s art-deco hotel offers large, bright and light rooms furnished in classical style. Sauna, gym, pool and jacuzzi. ⑨

Majestic Str. Academiei 11 ☎021/310 2720, ⓦwww.majestic.ro. Magnificent building, renovated at last to live up to its name, though the rooms are surprisingly modest given that it's one of the most expensive places in town. The main entrance is by the Odeon theatre on Calea Victoriei. ⑨

Muntenia Str. Academiei 19–21 ☎021/314 6010, ℻314 1782. The most centrally located budget hotel, south of Piaţa Revoluţiei. Spartan but clean singles, doubles, triples and quads, some with showers. Breakfast not included. ④

Opera Str. Ion Brezoianu 37 ☎021/312 4855, ✉hopera@kappa.ro. Completely renovated hotel near the Cişmigiu Gardens. Attractive, originally furnished rooms incorporating some nice touches, such as tea- and coffee-making facilities, neat desk lamps, and pictures of old Bucharest on the walls. Moreover, the staff are wonderfully attentive, though the operatic-style get-up is a bit much. ⑨

Between the University and Piaţa Unirii

Central Str. Brezoianu 13 ☎021/315 5636, ℻315 5637. Just behind McDonalds, off the busy B-dul Regina Elisabeta. Sister hotel to the *Opera*, though far less character – clean, modern and supremely ordinary rooms. Overpriced, too. ⑨

Hanul lui Manuc Str. Franceză 62 ☎021/313 1415, ⓦwww.hanulmanuc.ro. Simple, agreeable and good-value rooms in a famous old *caravanserai* just off Piaţa Unirii. Reservations advisable as this is a popular place. However, avoid the restaurant here. ⑤

Horoscop B-dul Dimitrie Cantemir 2 ☎021/335 4031, ✉horoscop@rdsnet.ro. Modern and shiny, if a little uninspiring, new place on the south side of Piaţa Unirii. ⑨

Hostel Miorita Str. Lipscani 12 ☎021/312 0361, ℻312 0328. Not really a hostel at all, this very pleasant and unassuming pension-style establishment has six homely en-suite rooms, and is terrifically located in this famous old street just off Calea Victoriei. Extremely good value with breakfast included. ⑤

Marriott Grand Hotel Calea 13 Septembrie 90 ☎021/403 1000, ⓦwww.marriotthotels.com. Originally conceived by Ceauşescu as a hotel for communist party hacks, this is now one of the most sumptuous establishments in town. Over 400 rooms of unbridled luxury, each with a separate bath and shower; also boasts a couple of high-class restaurants, a sports bar (see p.83) and a small shopping precinct. Bus #385. ⑨

North of the centre

Casa Victor Str. Emanoil Porumbaru 44 ☎021/222 5723, ✉victor@mediasat.ro. A pleasant private hotel with twenty tastefully decorated rooms in a quiet area north of the centre (metro Aviatorilor). ⑦

Crowne Plaza Flora Str. Poligrafiei 1 ☎021/224 0034, ⓦwww.bucharest.crowneplaza.com. Top-drawer hotel in the no-man's land to the north beyond Piaţa Presei Libere; superb facilities including pool, fitness suite, sauna and tennis courts. Bus #331 from Piaţa Lahovari. ⑨

Floreta de Aur Str. Aviator Popa Marin 2 ☎021/230 6496. Great-value place frequented in the main by athletic types using the adjoining sports facilities; big square rooms (singles, doubles and triples), each with fridge, phone and TV. Hidden away behind the swimming pool. ⑤

Helveţia Piaţa Charles de Gaulle 13 ☎021/223 0566, ✉helvetia@ines.ro. Not far from Casa Victor out by the Aviatorilor metro, this colourful, tidy place is of similar size and quality, though more expensive. ⑥

Minerva Str. Gh. Manu 24 ☎021/311 1550, ⓦwww.minerva.ro. Another of the city's top business hotels, though the modestly sized, average-looking rooms don't warrant the price. Also houses Bucharest's longest-established Chinese restaurant (see p.83). ⑨

Residence Str. Clucerului 19 ☎021/223-1978, ⓦwww.residence.com.ro. Located in a pleasant, leafy street running parallel to Şos. Kiseleff (near the Arc de Triumf), this is one of Bucharest's best small hotels. Elegantly furnished with wrought iron beds, desks and chairs, wood-carved cupboards, wall pictures and plants. Delightful. ⑧

Sky Gate Otopeni Şos. Bucureşti-Ploieşti ☎021/203 6500, ⓦwww.skygatehotel.ro. Typically sterile and very expensive airport hotel, almost exclusively geared towards business folk. Convenient if flying in late or stopping over for the night. ⑨

Sofitel B-dul Expoziţiei 2 ☎021/224 3000, ⓦwww.sofitel.com. Catering largely to conference members from the Exhibition Centre nearby, this is the best of the top end hotels in this rather anonymous part of the city. ⑨

Triumf Şos. Kiseleff 12 ☎021/222 3172, ⓕ223 2411. A huge red-brick building in the indigenous neo-Brâncovenesc style, set in parkland (with tennis courts) just off this main boulevard. There's still a whiff of the state-owned about this place, manifest in the phenomenally dull rooms – singles and twins, all with showers – and antiquated bathrooms, but the location is lovely and there are few cheaper options in this part of town. ⑦

Hostels

From just one a couple of years back, there are now a number of excellent small **hostels** in the city, all of which are open year-round. Booking ahead is advisable, particularly in the summer months. Pretty much all of these hostels offer a discount for stays of longer than a week.

Backpacker's Lodge Str. Radu Beller 9 ☎021/231 3438 Neat little hostel with three six-bed dorms in the well-heeled Dorobanţi neighbourhood a short way north of the centre. Breakfast not included but kitchen available for use. There are some excellent cafés and restaurants, as well as a 24hr supermarket, close by. Bus #282 from Gara de Nord to Piaţa Dorobanţilor, or a ten-minute walk from Piaţa Victoriei metro. €10 for a dorm bed.

Elvis' Hostel Str. Avram Iancu 5 ☎021/312 1653, ⓦwww.elvisvilla.ro. Bright, colourful and well-run hostel east of Universităţii, with a/c dorms sleeping between five and twelve; laundry, Internet access and breakfast included in the price. Take bus #85

from the station to the junction of B-dul Carol I and Piaţa Protopopescu, from where it's two-minute walk. €10

Funky Chicken Str. General Berthelot 63 ☎021/312 1425, ✉funkychickenhostel @hotmail.com. Cracking central location just fifteen minutes' walk from Gara de Nord, near the Cişmigiu Gardens. This friendly, informal place (the sister hostel to the Villa Helga) has four-, six- and eight-bed dorms, some multi-sex. Breakfast not included, but self-catering facilities are available. €8 for dorm bed.

Vila 11 Str. Institutul Medico Militar 11 ☎072/2495 900, ✉vila11bb@hotmail.com.

Welcoming and quiet family-run bed-and-breakfast style place in a peaceful back street just five minutes' walk from the station. Doubles as well as three- and four-bed rooms. Transfers available upon request. Exit Gara de Nord by platform one, head north along B-dul Golescu for 200m, turn left up Str. Vespasian, and it's your first left again. €12.50 per person in dorms, €27.50 for a double room. Price includes a pancake breakfast.
Villa Helga Str. Salcâmilor 2 ⊙021/610 2214, ©helga@rotravel.com. The original Bucharest hostel (run by the owners of the *Funky Chicken*, see p.60) is still going strong; small, clean and cosy, with five dorms (sleeping four to six) and one double. Internet, laundry and cooking facilities are available. Bus #79, #86 or #133 from Gara de Nord to Piața Gemini (along Bulevard Dacia) – from here, take the first right, Str. Vitorului, and it's across the road on the left. A word of warning: if anyone approaches you at the Gara de Nord claiming to be from the hostel and offers you a lift, decline – the *Villa Helga* does not meet people. €9.50 for dorm bed (IYHF members), €10 (non-members), including a basic breakfast.

Private accommodation and homestays

In recent years, numerous agencies have emerged offering **private rooms** and **apartments**, and these generally represent good value. Two of the better ones are Bucharest Comfort Suites, at B-dul Nicolae Balcescu (⊙021/310 2884) and Adrian Accommodation (⊙021/460 3053, ⓦwww.bucharest-accommodation.ro), both of which have centrally located rooms and apartments from around €40 per day. You may be approached at the Gara de Nord by locals offering a room, but exercise caution if you decide to take up this option.

The rural tourism agency Antrec, at Str. Washington 32 (Mon–Fri 9am–5pm; ⊙021/231 0955, rezervari@antrec.ro), may be able to find **homestay** accommodation (around €10 including breakfast) in a village outside the city. It's also possible to book accommodation here for other homestay schemes throughout the country.

Camping

Bucharest's one **campsite**, the Casa Alba (⊙021/230 5203, ⓦwww.casaalba.ro; year-round), is situated out towards Otopeni airport in the Pădurea Băneasa woods at Aleea Privghetorilor 1–3. It's a large, well-guarded site with excellent facilities, including a wide range of cabins, some with showers (❸–❹), cooking amenities, phone and postal services; there's also a snack bar on site, and a restaurant (the *Casa Alba*) nearby. To get there, take bus #301 from Piața Romană (or #783 if coming from Otopeni); get off at the Băneasa restaurant stop, the fifth one after Băneasa airport.

The City

The heart of the city is the **Piața Revoluției**, site of the old Royal Palace and the scene of Ceaușescu's downfall. It lies halfway along Bucharest's historic north-south axis, the **Calea Victoriei**, which is still the main artery of city life. Buses heading north and south, however, use the scruffy boulevards east of Calea Victoriei; the main junction along them is the **Piața Universității**, scene of major events immediately after the 1989 revolution.

The majority of sights are within walking distance of these two Piațas. Just to the south lies the **historic centre** of the city, a pleasant antidote to the noisy, modern surrounds, and which holds the remains of the original **citadel**. Beyond this, across the River Dâmbovița, is the contrasting cityscape of

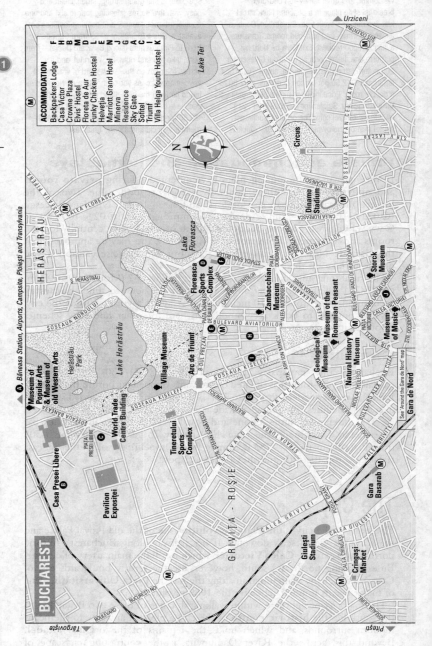

BUCHAREST

▲ Urziceni

ACCOMMODATION
Backpackers Lodge	F
Casa Victor	H
Crowne Plaza	B
Elvis' Hostel	M
Floreta de Aur	D
Funky Chicken Hostel	L
Helvetia	E
Marriott Grand Hotel	N
Minerva	J
Residence	G
Sky Gate	A
Sofitel	C
Triumf	I
Villa Helga Youth Hostel	K

▲ Băneasa Station, Airports, Campsite, Ploiești and Transylvania

Lake Tei

HERĂSTRĂU

Museum of Popular Arts & Museum of old Western Arts

Casa Presei Libere

Pavilion Expoziței

Herăstrău Park

Lake Herăstrău

World Trade Centre Building

Village Museum

Arc de Triumf

Tineretului Sports Complex

GRIVIȚA - ROȘIE

Gara Basarab

Giulești Stadium

Crîngași Market

Floreasca Sports Complex

Lake Floreasca

Dinamo Stadium

Circus

Zambacchian Museum

Geological Museum

Natural History Museum

Museum of the Romanian Peasant

Museum of Music

Storck Museum

See Around the Gara de Nord map

Gara de Nord

▲ Târgoviște

▲ Pitești

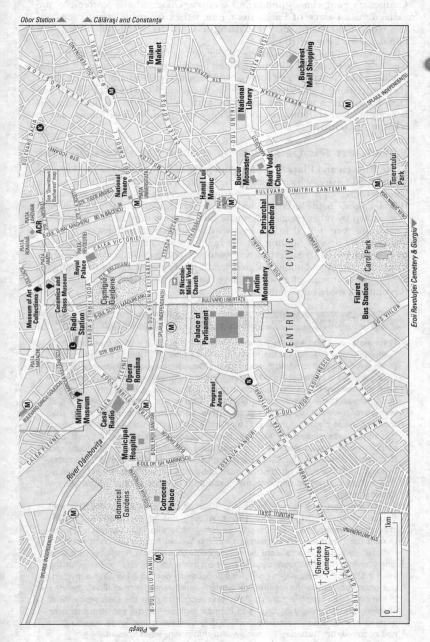

Obor Station ▲   ▲ Călăraşi and Constanţa

Eroii Revoluţiei Cemetery & Giurgiu ▼

▲ Piteşti

Traian Market

Bucharest Mall Shopping

National Library

Bucur Monastery

Radu Vodă Church

Tineretului Park

Hanul Lui Manuc

BULEVARD DIMITRIE CANTEMIR

Patriarchal Cathedral

National Theatre

CENTRU CIVIC

ACR

Royal Palace

Museum of Art Collections

Ceramics and Glass Museum

Cişmigiu Gardens

St Nicolai-Mihai Vodă Church

Antim Monastery

BULEVARD LIBERTĂŢII

Carol Park

Radio Station

Palace of Parliament

Filaret Bus Station

CENTRU CIVIC

Military Museum

Opera Română

Casa Radio

Progresul Arena

River Dâmboviţa

Municipal Hospital

Botanical Gardens

Cotroceni Palace

Ghencea Cemetery

See Downtown Bucharest map

0   1km

63

Ceauşescu's compellingly monstrous **Centru Civic**, whose centrepiece, the extraordinary **Palace of Parliament**, is now the city's main tourist attraction. Just west of the centre are the **Cişmigiu Gardens**, a tranquil space and a popular place for assignations.

For a taste of the old atmosphere of the city, you need to wander north and west of the gardens past the vine-covered facades, to suburbs where life retains a village-like slowness and intimacy. Alternatively, head north from Piaţa Revoluţiei along Calea Victoriei and Şoseaua Kiseleff to **Herăstrău Park**, the city's largest green space and site of a superb collection of buildings brought here from all over Romania and assembled to form an area known as the **Village Museum**.

Western Piaţa Enescu and Piaţa Revoluţiei

Piaţa Enescu and **Piaţa Revoluţiei** (Square of Revolution) are two irregularly shaped squares which break up the southern end and Calea Victoriei. The latter was created in the 1930s to ensure a protective field of fire around the Royal Palace, in the event of revolution. While Romania's monarchy was overthrown by other means, the square fulfilled its destiny in 1989, when the Ceauşescus were forced to flee by crowds besieging communist party headquarters; two days of fighting left the buildings around the square burnt out or pockmarked with bullet holes – with the conspicuous exception of the Central Committee building, which was at the centre of the storm. Many of the edifices around the square have since been restored, giving Piaţa Revoluţiei a more purposeful air.

The fall of the Ceauşescus

Romania's revolution was the most dramatic of the popular revolts that convulsed Eastern Europe in 1989. On the morning of December 21, 1989, a staged demonstration – organized to show support for the **Ceauşescu** regime following days of rioting against it in Timişoara – backfired. Eight minutes into Ceauşescu's speech from the balcony of the Central Committee building, part of the eighty-thousand-strong crowd began chanting "Ti-mi-şoa-ra, Ti-mi-şoa-ra"; the leader's shock and fear were televised across Romania before transmissions ceased. From that moment, it was clear that the end of the Ceauşescu regime was inevitable. Though the square was cleared by nightfall, larger crowds poured back the next day, emboldened by news that the army was siding with the people in Timişoara and Bucharest. Strangely, the Ceauşescus remained inside the Central Committee building until midday, when they scrambled aboard a helicopter on the roof, beginning a flight that would end with their **execution** in a barracks in Târgovişte, on Christmas Day.

The revolution was tainted by having been stage-managed by the **National Salvation Front (FSN)** that took power in the name of the people. The FSN consisted of veteran communists, one of whom later let slip to a journalist that plans to oust the Ceauşescus had been laid months before. Among the oddities of the "official" version of events were Iliescu's speech on the Piaţa Revoluţiei at a time when "terrorist" snipers were causing mayhem in the square, and the battle for the Interior Ministry, during which both sides supposedly ceased firing after a mysterious phone call. Given the hundreds of genuine "martyrs of the revolution", the idea that it had been simply a ploy by Party bureaucrats to oust the Ceauşescus was shocking and potentially damaging to the new regime – so the secret police were ordered to mount an investigation, which duly concluded that while manipulation had occurred, the Russians, Americans and Hungarians were to blame.

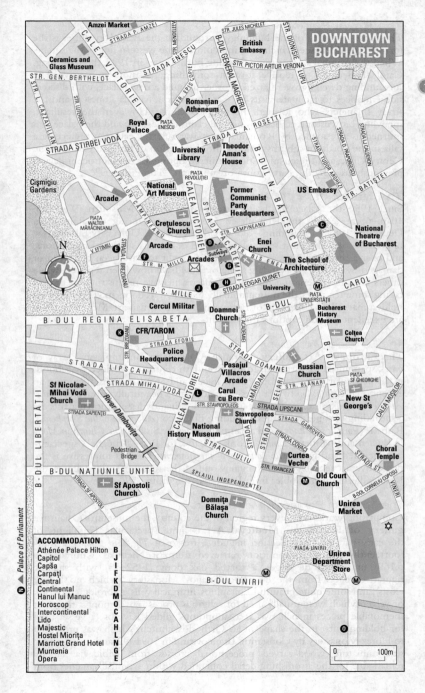

DOWNTOWN BUCHAREST

Amzei Market

Ceramics and
Glass Museum

British
Embassy

Romanian
Atheneum

Royal
Palace

University
Library

Theodor
Aman's
House

Cişmigiu
Gardens

Arcade

National
Art Museum

Former
Communist
Party
Headquarters

US Embassy

Cretulescu
Church

Arcade

Enei
Church

National
Theatre
of Bucharest

Arcades

The School of
Architecture

Subways

University

Cercul Militar

Doamnei
Church

Bucharest
History
Museum

CFR/TAROM

Coltea
Church

Police
Headquarters

Pasajul
Villacros
Arcade

Russian
Church

Sf Nicolae-
Mihai Vodă
Church

Carul
cu Bere

New St
George's

Stavropoleos
Church

National
History Museum

Choral
Temple

Pedestrian
Bridge

Curtea
Veche

Old Court
Church

Sf Apostoli
Church

Domniţa
Bălaşa
Church

Unirea
Market

Unirea
Department
Store

Unirea Department Store

Palace of Parliament

ACCOMMODATION

Athénée Palace Hilton	B
Capitol	J
Capşa	I
Carpaţi	F
Central	K
Continental	D
Hanul lui Manuc	M
Horoscop	O
Intercontinental	C
Lido	A
Majestic	H
Hostel Miorita	L
Marriott Grand Hotel	N
Muntenia	G
Opera	E

0   100m

The Royal Palace

The most imposing of the buildings surrounding the Piaţa Revoluţiei is the former **Royal Palace**, which consumes most of the western side of the square. When the original single-storey dwelling burnt down in 1927, the then king, Carol II, decided to replace it with something far more impressive. The surrounding dwellings were razed in order to build a new palace, with discreet side entrances to facilitate visits by Carol's mistress, Magda Lupescu, and the shady financiers who formed the couple's clique. However, the resultant, sprawling brownstone edifice has no real claim to elegance and the palace was spurned as a residence by Romania's post-war rulers, Ceauşescu preferring a villa in the northern suburbs pending the completion of his own palace in the Centru Civic, and Iliescu and Constantinescu opting for the Cotroceni Palace, previously used by the Party youth organization, "The Pioneers".

The National Art Museum

Since 1950, the palace has housed the **National Art Museum** (Wed–Sun 10am–6pm; €3) in the Kretzulescu (south) wing. During the fighting in December 1989, this building – along with the Central University Library (see opposite) – was the most seriously damaged of the city's cultural institutions, and over a thousand pieces of work were thought to have been destroyed or damaged by gunfire and vandals; some of these have now been repaired, while others are still undergoing restoration. After a massive reconstruction project taking some ten years, the museum finally reopened its doors in 2000, and now holds a marvellous collection of European and Romanian art. Moreover, there are excellent English captions throughout.

The European Art gallery

The **European Art gallery** (entrance A1) contains an impressive array of work spanning the fourteenth to the twentieth centuries. Divided by schools, it has particularly fine paintings from Italian and Spanish artists, including an exceptional *Crucifixion* by Da Messina, and Cano's beautifully mournful *Christ At The Column*. Amongst the line-up of predominantly lesser-known artists are a sprinkling of superstar names, including El Greco (*Adoration of the Shepherds*), Rubens (*Portrait of a Lady*), and a painting apiece by Sisley (*The Church in Moret in Winter*) and Monet (*Camille*). Look out, too, for Peter Brueghel's spectacularly detailed and gruesome *Massacre of the Innocents*. No less impressive is the decorative art section, which contains one of the museum's oldest items, the Reichsadlerhumpen Goblet from Bavaria, dating from 1596.

The gallery of Romanian Medieval Art

Comprising works from every region of the country, the museum's exhaustive **gallery of Romanian Medieval Art** is quite spectacular. Highlights of the early part of the collection include a fresco of *The Last Supper*, a mid-fourteenth-century composition retrieved from St Nicholas' Church (see p.169) in Curtea de Argeş, a carved oak door (1452–53) with shallow figurative reliefs from the chapel of Snagov Monastery (which no longer exists), and some quite beautiful Epitaphios, liturgical veils embroidered on silk or velvet which were usually used for religious processions. Amongst the most memorable pieces in hall two is a sumptuous gilded Kivotos (a vessel used for holding gifts) in the shape of an Orthodox church, which was presented to Horez Monastery by Constantin Brâncoveanu in 1691–92, and some exquisite, miniature wood-carved processional crosses from Moldavia, chiefly remarkable for the astonishing detail contained within – typically, scenes from the life of Christ. The standout items from the latter part of the collection are an enormous iconostasis retrieved from Cotroceni Palace (see p.76) when Ceaușescu had the monastery demolished in 1986, and a wood-carved iconostasis by Brâncoveanu from Arnota Monastery.

The gallery of Romanian Modern Art

Up on the second floor, the **gallery of Romanian Modern Art** features the best of the country's nineteenth- and twentieth-century painters, including Aman, Andreescu and Pallady, and the Romania's most revered painter, Nicolae Grigorescu (see p.101) – look out for his brilliant character paintings, *The Turk* and *Gypsy Girl from Ghergham*, and the dramatic *The Spy*. Moreover, there's a terrific assemblage of sculpture, by Storck, Paciurea and Constantin Brâncuși, Romania's one truly world-renowned artist (see p.116). Using various mediums, Brâncuși's versatility is manifest in a sublime body of work, including the beautiful white marble head of a sleeping woman (*Sleep*), a bronze, weeping nude (*The Prayer*), and the limestone-carved *Wisdom of the Earth*.

Eastern Piața Enescu and Piața Revoluției

The north side of Piața Enescu is filled by the **Athénée Palace Hilton Hotel**, which, since it was built in 1912, has been one of the most prestigious hotels in Bucharest. For decades the hotel was also a notorious hotbed of espionage, beginning in the 1930s when the liveried staff and almost all the characters who populated the lobby spied for Carol's police chief, for the Gestapo or for British Intelligence. Symbolic of that fevered, corrupt era, Bucharest's elite partied here through the night while police were shooting strikers in the "Red" Grivița district only a mile away. During the early 1950s the hotel was extensively refurbished as an "intelligence factory", with bugged rooms and tapped phones, to reinforce the reports of its informers and prostitutes.

To the east stands the **Romanian Atheneum**, a magnificent Neoclassical structure built in 1888 almost entirely from funds generated from the city's citizens, after the original patrons ran out of money. Take a look inside at the rampantly *fin-de-siècle* dome decorated with lyres or, better still, try and catch a concert by the resident George Enescu Philharmonic Orchestra (see p.84). To the south is the **University Library**, totally gutted in December 1989 but now rebuilt. Just behind this, at Str. Rosetti 8, is **Theodor Aman's House** (Tues–Sun 9am–5pm), one of many "memorial houses" of noble artists dotted around the city. Aman (1831–91) trained in Paris before returning to be the first director of the Bucharest Art College. A somewhat academic painter, he was a leading member of the group of Francophile intellectuals (with fellow Romanians, the painter Gheorghe Tattarescu and the sculptor Karl Storck) that dominated Bucharest's cultural life in the late nineteenth century. The house, now badly in need of renovation, was built in 1868 to Aman's own designs and decorated by himself and Storck. It contains a number of rather gloomy family portraits as well as some finely sculpted pieces, wooden chests and tables.

The southeastern corner of Piața Revoluției is dominated by the **former Communist Party Headquarters**, a Stalinist monolith that now houses government offices. The famous balcony where Ceaușescu delivered his last speech is surprisingly near ground level, and quite unmarked by bullet holes. Ironically, it was from the same spot, two decades earlier, that Ceaușescu had drawn cheers of approval for his denunciation of the Soviet invasion of Czechoslovakia, and made his vow that Romania would defend its own independence – casting himself as a "maverick communist" whom Western leaders could embrace. It was a delusion that persisted almost until the end; as Romanian's point out, the honorary knighthood bestowed on Ceauşescu by Buckingham Palace in 1978 was only revoked after the revolution began. Directly in front of the headquarters is a marble **memorial** with the inscription *Glorie Martirilor Nostri* ("Glory to our Martyrs"), dedicated to those who died during the revolution.

Southern Calea Victoriei

Calea Victoriei (Avenue of Victory), on the site of the wood-paved Podul Mogoşoaiei, has been Bucharest's most fashionable street since wealthy boyars first built their residences along it. The arrival of the boyars encouraged Bucharest's most prestigious shops to open along the avenue and, after it was repaved and took its present name in 1918, strolling along the avenue became de rigueur, causing the writer Hector Bolitho to remark that "to drive down the Calea Victoriei between twelve and one o'clock will prove you a provincial or a stranger". Along the street were "huddles of low, open-fronted shops where Lyons silk and Shiraz carpets were piled in the half-darkness beside Siberian furs, English guns and Meissen porcelain", while lurking in the side streets were starving groups of unemployed, lupus-disfigured beggars and dispossessed peasants seeking justice in the capital's courts.

The avenue still displays marked contrasts: at its northern end near the Piaţa Victoriei, it seems verdant and sleepy with touches of old-world elegance, while to the south it becomes an eclectic jumble of old apartment buildings, glass and steel facades, and shops selling cakes and Western couture – still the setting for a promenade around noon and in the early evening. To the east and west lies the busy Piaţa Amzei, site of one of the city's busiest food markets.

A short walk south along the avenue from Piaţa Revoluţiei, the **Creţulescu Church** fronts a tangle of streets which wend west towards Cişmigiu Gardens. The church – high and narrow with mock arches, bricks laid in saw-toothed patterns around the towers and elaborate carvings over the entrance – is built in the style created by Constantin Brâncoveanu, a seventeenth-century ruler of Wallachia who set out to forge a distinctive national genre of architecture. It was paid for in 1720 by the boyar Iordache Creţulescu and his wife Safta, Brâncoveanu's daughter. Sadly, little remains of its frescoes by Tattarescu, or of the one on the porch, which features scenes from the apocalypse. Seriously damaged during the fighting in December 1989, the church exterior has now been restored, unlike the Humanitas building next to it, whose walls have been left heavily pockmarked as a permanent reminder of the events.

Further south, just beyond the *Continental* hotel, the **Pasajul Victoriei** (Victory Passage) sneaks one block further east to Strada Academiei and the smoke-blackened **Enei Church**, built in 1702; the church is also known as the Dintr-o zi or "(Made) In One Day" church, as that's precisely how long it took to erect. Back on Calei Victoriei, the street continues down past a couple of upmarket hotels and shops to the noisy junction with Bulevardul Regina Elisabeta, Bucharest's main east–west axis. Dominating the area is the Neoclassical **Cercul Militar** (Army House), which replaced the previous monastery church of Sărindar in 1912. Crossing Bulevardul Regina Elisabeta, an alleyway just beyond *Pizza Hut* slips off to the courtyard of the picturesque **Doamnei Church**, built in 1683 and now undergoing extensive renovation, though you can still pop in to view the frescoes amidst the gloom.

Bucharest's **police headquarters**, a short walk further down Calea Victoriei, is now screened by a tall fence, after it was stormed by a mob in 1990, an attack

Iliescu used as his pretext for calling in the miners to smash the student opponents. Directly opposite the headquarters, an inconspicuous portal leads into the **Pasajul Villacros** (Villacrosse Passage), whose glass roof and gracefully curved arcade of shops gives an idea of why Bucharest once claimed to be the "Paris of the East", although its grandeur has faded badly over the years. East off the Calea, on Strada Stavropoleos, is the diminutive **Stavropoleos Church** that gives the street its name. Built between 1724 and 1730 for the first Phanariot ruler, Nicolae Mavrocordat, the church has a gorgeous, almost arabesque, facade, with a columned portico carved with delicate tracery. On this same street, at no. 3, you'll also find the *Carul cu Bere* (*The Beer Cart*), an ornately decorated tavern dating from 1875 (see p.82).

Returning to Calea Victoriei, the **National History Museum** (Wed–Sun 9am–5pm; €1) is housed in the former Post Office building of 1900, just north of the river at no. 12. A much-needed overhaul of the museum is now under way, though this is not expected to be complete until 2006 at the earliest. In the meantime, and in addition to the regular schedule of temporary exhibitions held in the capacious foyer, there's still a reasonable amount to see: the modern lapidarium, in the courtyard, houses plaster casts from Trajan's Column covered with depictions of his Dacian campaigns, as well as Greek, Roman and medieval tombstones and carvings. Better still, a basement vault displays Romania's national treasures: a dazzling display of gold and jewellery, from prehistoric finds (see particularly the elaborate Coţofeneşti helmet) to Queen Marie's crown and the casket said to hold her heart, to the sceptres of Ferdinand I and Carol II. When the remainder of this huge museum reopens, expect to see a comprehensive overview of Romanian history from the earliest times to the present, including anthropomorphic figures moulded in clay by the Neolithic Cucuteni and Hamangia cultures (including a "Thinker", possibly the model for Rodin's statue), Bronze Age Thracian tools, Geto-Dacian coins, Celtic weapons, Roman tools and glassware, and medieval clothing and manuscripts. Previously closed to the public, you may also get to see the voluminous display of gifts presented to Ceauşescu on his sixtieth birthday.

From the National History Museum, it's a short walk to the **River Dâmboviţa**. An old saying has it that whoever drinks the "sweet waters" of the Dâmboviţa will never wish to be parted from Bucharest, to which one nineteenth-century traveller retorted that anyone who ever did "would be incapable of leaving the city for ever afterwards". Always prone to flooding, the Dâmboviţa was canalized in the 1880s and now passes underground at Piaţa Unirii. The river marks the abrupt transition from the organic fabric of the old city to the arbitrarily imposed pattern of the Centru Civic.

Northern Calea Victoriei

Heading north from Piaţa Revoluţiei towards Piaţa Victoriei along the quieter, northern end of Calea Victoriei, you'll pass three museums of interest – though at the time of writing, these first two were closed for renovation. At no. 107, in the former Ştirbey Palace (built in 1856), is the **Ceramics and Glass Museum**. The collection is small and varied – in rooms furnished with splendid mirrors, carpets, chandeliers and tiled stoves, you can see eighteenth- and nineteenth-century Turkish and Iranian tiles, European, Japanese and Chinese porcelain, and lovely Art Deco pieces, including a Tiffany lamp. The early nineteenth-century Ghica Palace at no. 111 houses the **Museum of Art Collections** – an assortment of paintings, furniture, icons on glass and other antiques "donated to" (confiscated by) the communist state. At no. 141, a superb, early twentieth-century, clamshell-shaped porte-cochere topped with fluttering cherubs shades the entrance to the Cantacuzino Palace, one-time residence of Romania's national composer, George Enescu (1881–1955). It now houses the small **George Enescu Museum of Music** (Tues–Sun 10am–5pm), a handful of rooms packed with memorabilia and personal effects – photos of Enescu with his peers, batons, manuscripts, concert programmes and suchlike. For more on Enescu, see the box on p.409.

Continuing north along Calea Victoriei, you eventually reach Piaţa Victoriei, a vast circular space, around which crazed drivers manically jockey for position. On the east side of the square stands the main government building, the hulking Palaţul Victoria, completed in 1944 but even then already showing a chilly Stalinist influence in its design. On the north side, along Şos. Kiseleff, there is a cluster of museums: at no. 1 is the **Grigore Antipa Natural History Museum** (Tues–Sun 10am–6pm), named after the eponymous conservationist and founder of Romanian icthyology. The museum's collection of 300,000 items includes a 4.5-metre-high skeleton of a dinosaur unearthed in Moldavia, over 80,000 butterflies and moths, and the obligatory selection of stuffed animals.

Next door, at no.3, is Bucharest's finest museum, the **Museum of the Romanian Peasant** (Muzeu Ţăranului Român; Tues–Sun 10am–6pm; €1.20). The premises were occupied by the Museum of Communist Party History until 1990, and there are still remnants from this time in the basement, which contains a curious collection of paintings and busts of former communist leaders. The main reason for coming here, though, is the wonderful display of traditional peasant artifacts garnered from Romania's multifarious regions: colourfully woven linen and textiles, carvings, ceramics, and a superb collection of wood and glass-painted icons. In 1992, the museum purchased several churches, two of which are on display here; the one inside is an incomplete timber church, around which lie some of its furnishings – altar doors, a holy table, church bells and so on – while the second, a wooden church typical of those found in Maramureş, stands on a neat patch of grass at the rear of the museum. Located here, too, is the museum shop, which sells a beautiful assortment of rugs, costumes and other folksy objects. Directly opposite at Şos. Kiseleff 2, the **Geological Museum** (Mon–Fri 10am–4pm) contains an exhaustive collection pertaining to Romania's great mineral riches; although undeniably an impressive hoard, the dusty cabinets and absence of English captions are not exactly conducive to an entertaining visit, though the collection of luminescent rocks in an otherwise unlit basement room is worth a look.

Southeast of here, in between B-dul Lascăr Catargiu and B-dul Iancu de Hunedoara at Str. V. Alecsandri 16, the fabulous **Storck Museum** (Tues–Sun 9am–5pm) is one of Bucharest's lesser known delights. Inside is a superb collection of sculpted works by Frederic Storck (whose father, Karl, was the first Romanian teacher of sculpture), as well as a prolific number of paintings and murals by his wife Cecilia. They actually lived in the house next door; the museum building was originally built as a workshop.

The Centru Civic

In 1971, Ceauşescu visited North Korea and returned full of admiration for the grandiose avenues of Kim II Sung's capital, Pyongyang. Thirteen years later, inspired by what he had seen in Pyongyang, Ceauşescu set out to remodel Bucharest as "the first socialist capital for the new socialist man", and to create a new administrative centre which was to be "a symbolic representation of the two decades of enlightenment we have just lived through". In truth, of course, this **Centru Civic** was meant to embody the state's authority and that of Ceauşescu himself. Implementing this megalomaniac vision entailed the demolition of a quarter of Bucharest's historic centre (about five square kilometres), said to be slums damaged by the 1977 earthquake, but in fact containing 9000 largely undamaged nineteenth-century houses, whose 40,000 inhabitants were relocated in new developments on the outskirts of the city. There was worldwide condemnation of this vandalism, particularly since many old churches were to be swept away. Though some of the churches were in the end reprieved, they are now surrounded by huge modern apartment blocks and are separated from the urban context that gave them meaning. The core of the complex was largely completed by 1989, just in time for the dictator's overthrow.

Uniting the two halves of the Centru Civic is **Bulevardul Unirii**, at 4km long and 120m wide, slightly larger – intentionally so – than the Champs-Élyseés after which it was modelled. The western end of the development, which extends from Piaţa Unirii to the Palace of Parliament, remains eerily desolate, its vacant shops and apartments and bone-dry fountains rendering the area a virtual ghost town. Although the longer eastern extension is still blighted with unfinished projects, most notably a colossal building that was to have been a cultural centre (a wasteland now referred to by the locals as "Hiroshima"), the area does at least seem human, thanks to the presence of a few shops and banks, and a heavy stream of traffic.

The Palace of Parliament

Dominating the entire project from the western end of Bulevardul Unirii is the colossal **Palace of Parliament** (Palatul Parliamentului; daily 10am–4pm; €2.50, plus €2 for use of cameras), claimed to be the second largest administrative building in the world – after the Pentagon – measuring 270m by 240m, and 86m high. It epitomizes the megalomania that overtook Ceauşescu in the 1980s; here he intended to house ministries, Communist Party offices and the apartments of high functionaries. Built on the site of the former Spirei Hill, which was razed for this project, the sheer size of the building can only be grasped by comparison with the toy-like cars scuttling past below. It has twelve storeys, four underground levels (including a nuclear bunker), a one-hundred-metre-long lobby and 1100 rooms, around half of which are used as offices while the remainder are redundant. The interiors are lavishly decorated with marble and gold leaf, and there are 4500 chandeliers (11,000 were planned), the largest of which weighs 1.5 tonnes, but the decoration was never finished due to the Ceauşescus' ever-changing whims; they were demanding patrons, allowing little more than a technical role to the architects, of which there were around 700 – one staircase was rebuilt three times before they were satisfied. Meanwhile, the floor pattern – which mirrors the layout of the building itself – was, apparently, designed that way so Ceauşescu wouldn't get lost.

This huge white elephant was officially known as the Casa Republicii, then as the Casa Poporului, but more generally as the Casa Nebunului (Madman's House), before taking on its present name. The new government spent a long time agonizing about an acceptable use for it, and in 1994 it was finally decided to house the Senate and Parliament; it is now also used for international conferences. You can visit from entrance A1 (left-hand side as you face it), although you may have to wait until there are enough people to make up a tour group. The 45-minute tour takes you through ten of the most dazzling, most representative or simply the hugest of the halls, such as the extraordinary, glass-ceilinged **Sala Unirii** (Unification Hall), where legendary Romanian gymnast Nadia Comaneci was married in 1996. One of the last rooms you're led to is the Alexandru Ioan Cuza room, whose balcony offers defining views of the city. Although Izvor is the nearest metro stop, the approach along Piaţa Unirii gives you the most impressive view of the building.

Hidden away among the rows of new buildings that make up the Centru Civic are numerous tiny Orthodox churches thankfully reprieved from demolition. In Bucharest, you'll frequently find churches in inappropriate places – such as the courtyards of apartment buildings – where the city planners have built around them, but here the churches seem even more disregarded and incongruous than elsewhere. The most striking example of this is the **Sf Nicolai-Mihai Vodă Church**, built by Michael the Brave in 1591; to make way for the Centru Civic development, the church was moved 279m east on rails to Str. Sapienţei 4, which entailed the demolition of the church's medieval cloisters and ancillary buildings. What's more, as it's now standing on a concrete platform, the church will probably collapse when the next major earthquake hits Bucharest. A similar fate probably awaits the wretched-looking **Sf Apostoli Church**, five minutes south of here at Str. Sf Apostoli 33A; this grey, largely seventeenth-century structure was embellished in 1715 with a fine little steeple by Stefan Cantacuzino, a portrait of whom is just about visible inside the almost pitch-black interior. Located in slightly more civilized surrounds a further five minutes' west, at Calea Rahovei 3, is the late-nineteenth-century **Domniţa Bălaşa Church**, one of the most popular churches in the city. Named after Constantin Brâncoveanu's sixth daughter, Doamna – a statue of whom stands in the garden in front of the church – this orange brick edifice is actually the third church on this site, the previous two having burnt down in the eighteenth century. The interior, one of the most complete in the city, features a beautiful wooden cross-shaped chandelier.

On the southern side of Bulevardul Unirii, at Str. Justiţiei 64, is the **Antim Monastery**, a surprisingly large, walled complex dating from 1715 with a high-domed church and a small chapel, but minus half its eastern wing. At the top of Dealul Mitropoliei stands the colourless **Patriarchal Cathedral**, built in 1655–68 and seat of the Romanian Orthodox Church. The interior contains the most dazzling of the city's iconostasis, as well as a couple of exquisitely carved side altars. Completing the set of buildings here is the Brâncoveanu-commissioned campanile, the Patriarchal Palace (built in 1875), and the former Palace of the Chamber of Deputies (1907). East of the cathedral, on the other side of Bulevardul Dimitrie Cantemir, a couple of other churches lie in wait: at Strada Radu Vodă 24A, the **Radu Vodă Church** (also known as Holy Trinity, or Sf Treime) was founded in 1568 and once laid claim to being the richest monastery in the country with 8342 properties, whilst directly opposite, wedged between an apartment block and a glass high-rise on a mound above a high wall, is the forlorn-looking **Bucur Monastery** (1743).

Piaţa Unirii and south

Midway along Bulevardul Unirii, **Piaţa Unirii** (Square of Union) is an oversized expanse of concrete dominated by traffic, notable only as a key metro interchange, as the site of the city's main department store – the slicked-up Unirea – and as the best place to view the Palace of Parliament. From the square, Bulevardul Dimitrie Cantemir runs south about 1km to the much older Calea Şerban Vodă. The two roads cover the site of Podul Şerban Vodă, destroyed by a fire in 1825. This was the route taken by merchant Turkish officials heading for the Sublime Porte of Constantinople, Sultan's Court. The two roads meet at the north end of **Tineretului** (Youth Park), which contains a fairground and a lake, as well as the crematorium, a strange, rather Masonic chapel filled with caskets of ashes. To the west is the more popular and formal **Carol I Park**; its tatty southern end, site of an ugly monument which once held the remains of Gheorghiu-Dej and other communist leaders, gives way to a lovely green space bisected by a long promenade and a smaller lake; about half way down, two soldiers guard the grave of the unknown soldier. Not far from the lake is the **Museum of Technology** (Tues–Sun 9am–5pm), an oddball place intended to assert Romania's technological fecundity, particularly several "firsts", such as the metal-bodied aeroplane (1912) and the streamlined motor car (1923). Ironically, it's the names of British, French and German firms that dominate the collection.

Ten minutes' walk south along Calea Şerban Vodă, at the junction of the highways to Olteniţa and Giurgiu and opposite the Eroii Revoluţiei metro, is the **Eroii Revoluţiei Cemetery**; buried here, in neat rows of identical white marble graves, are more than 280 "Heroes of the Revolution", gunned down by "terrorists" in 1989 – despite the traffic roaring by, it's an affecting place, and even more poignant given that some of the victims were as young as fourteen. To the left of the cemetery stands the Church of the Martyr Heroes. From here, you can see the minaret of Bucharest's working mosque, at Str. C. Mănescu 4. Next to the Eroii Revoluţiei Cemetery is the **Bellu Cemetery**, resting place of Romania's greatest writers, including Mihai Eminescu (see p.262), and opposite, on the Şoseaua Giurgiului, is the **Sephardic Jewish Cemetery** (closed on Saturdays) and the **Lutheran Cemetery**.

The Ceauşescus are buried in **Ghencea cemetery**, southwest of the city along Drumul Sării; you can get here by bus from Eroii Revoluţiei metro station (#173, Mon–Fri only) and from Piaţa Unirii (#385; nearest stop at the junction of Drumul Sării and Calea 13 Septembrie). They were originally buried under pseudonyms, but their graves are now marked with their own names. Nicolae's, surrounded by a small black fence, is on the left side of the central alley before the chapel; Elena's trashed grave is in the alley on the opposite side, and that of their playboy son, Nicu, is on the left side opposite the church. Ask one of the guards to show you if you can't find them. Next door is a Military Cemetery, a surreal forest of propeller blades marking the graves of airmen.

Piaţa Unirii to Piaţa Universităţii

Immediately to the east of Piaţa Unirii, behind the department store, stands the large, domed hall of **Unirea market** (Mon–Sat 6am–8pm, Sun 6am–noon), a good place to stock up on meat, dairy produce, fruit and veg. You'll also find intriguing wooden, ceramic and enamel household items here.

From the market, continue up B-dul Corneliu Coposu to the junction of Str. Sf Vineri; a few paces along to the left, at no. 9, is the **Jewish Choral Temple**, a red-brick structure built in 1857 and which still serves the local community (services Sat 8.30am & 6pm). A five-minute walk to the right along Str. Sf Vineri brings you to the **Great Synagogue**, Str. Mămulari 3, which now houses a **museum of Jewish history** (Mon, Wed & Sun 9am–1pm, Thurs 10am–6pm). There are still around four thousand Jews in Bucharest, but it is an ageing population and declining by several hundred a year.

△ Palace of Parliament, Bucharest

Just north of Piaţa Unirii, Strada Franceză leads west off Bulevardul I. C. Brătianu into the maze of streets and pleasantly decrepit houses that surround the oldest part of Bucharest. Mercifully, this picturesque little quarter was spared Ceausescu's bulldozers, and it now offers a welcome respite from the concrete monotony of the Centru Civic. It was here that Prince Vlad Ţepeş ("Vlad the Impaler", otherwise known as Dracula – see p.421) built a **citadel** in the fifteenth century. The building was severely damaged during Ţepeş' attempt to regain the throne in 1476 (in which he succeeded, only to be murdered a few months later), and was further damaged by various earthquakes and fires over the following centuries; it was subsequently auctioned off as wasteland. Thus, little remains of the ancient citadel – just some of the walls, arches and shattered columns of the **Curtea Veche** (Old Court), at Str. Franceză 60 (Tues–Sun 9am–5pm). If you wish to understand what you're looking at – there is nothing in the way of explanation – it is best to have a guide, included in the entrance fee, show you around; you can find one at the entrance gate. The adjoining **Old Court Church**, established by Mircea the Shepherd in 1546–58, is the oldest church in Bucharest. It is a typical example of sixteenth-century Wallachian church architecture, with its horizontal bands of brick facing and rows of small niches beneath the cornice. The interior frescoes, sadly, are almost blackened beyond recognition. A few doors east from the Curtea Veche, at Str. Franceză 62, an austere white wall with barred windows conceals Bucharest's most famous hostelry, **Hanul lui Manuc** (Manuc's Inn). It was built as a *caravanserai* in 1808 by a wealthy Armenian, Manuc-bey Mirzaian, and now houses a hotel (see p.59), and a *cramă* or wine cellar (daily 7am–11pm).

From Str. Franceză, pick your way through a warren of small streets to Strada Lipscani, a narrow thoroughfare named after the merchants from Leipzig who traded here in the eighteenth century. It now holds a lively Gypsy street market (Mon–Sat 8am–4pm), selling Turkish jeans, pirated cassettes and all manner of other goodies. This whole area is a labyrinth of little shops and cafés, interspersed with arcades, such as the Hanul cu tei at no. 63. Beware of pickpockets in this area.

A couple of streets further north, on Strada Doamnei, stands the brazenly colourful, corkscrew-domed **Russian Church** (1905–09). The church, faced with yellow brick, Art Nouveau green tiling and pixie-faced nymphs, has a small interior, with frescoes, blackened with age and smoke.

Piaţa Universităţii and around
Piaţa Universităţii is the focus of city life and traffic, and was one of the key sites of the 1989 revolution, as evinced by the numerous memorials (note the ten stone crosses in the road island) to those killed at Christmas 1989 and in June 1990. The latter marks the date on which miners, under Iliescu's orders, drove out students who had been on hunger strike since April 30, causing the square to be nicknamed Piaţa Tiananmen. The most poignant of the memorials is the black cross and wall plaque at B-dul Bălcescu 18, some 200m north of the *Intercontinental* – this marks the spot where the first victim, Mihai Gătlan, fell, at 5.30pm on December 21.

West of the square is **Bucharest University**. Occupying the first block on Bulevardul Republicii, its frontage is lined with statues of illustrious pedagogues and statesmen, as well as a regular crop of bookstalls. Established in 1859 after the union of Wallachia and Moldavia, the university equipped the sons of bourgeois families to become lawyers and men of letters until the communists took over in 1949. Technical skills and education for women were subsequently given top priority, but since the revolution business studies and foreign languages have overtaken them in popularity. The university continues to have an excellent reputation.

Just north of the square, adjacent to the *Intercontinental* hotel, is the **National Theatre of Bucharest** (TNB), which resembles an Islamicized reworking of the Colosseum; it was a pet project of Elena Ceauşescu, who had the facade rebuilt twice, and the roof once, before she was satisfied. Opposite is the **School of Architecture**, built between 1912–27 in the neo-Brâncovenesc style – ornate pillars, prominent, richly carved eaves and a multitude of arches. On the southwest corner of Piaţa Universităţii, the **Bucharest History Museum** (Tues–Sun 9am–5pm) traces the city's evolution over the course of 150,000 years, with a dull collection of old documents, coins, photographs and prints. The neo-Gothic building was built as the Suţu Palace in 1833–34; its superb *porte-cochère* was added later in the century.

Across the road from the museum lie two ancient and much-loved churches: in front of the hospital of the same name and period is the **Colţea Church** (1700–15), and, a few paces further south, the **New St George's Church** (1575), which holds the tomb of Constantin Brâncoveanu, reburied here in 1720 after his wife brought him back from Istanbul. A suitably grand bronze statue, completed by Karl Storck (see p.70), stands in the grubby garden in front of the church.

Cişmigiu Gardens

West of Piaţa Universităţii, midway along Bulevardul Regina Elisabeta, the lovely **Cişmigiu Gardens** were laid out as a park on land bequeathed to the city in 1845. Originally belonging to a Turkish water inspector, the gardens now fittingly contain a serpentine lake upon which small rowing boats and pedalos glide, rented by couples seeking solitude among the swans and weeping willows (rental daily 8am–8pm in summer; about €1.20 per hour, plus €1.20 deposit, from a kiosk by the waterside). The gardens provide a tranquil space, with workers snoozing beneath the trees at lunch times in summer and pensioners meeting for games of chess.

Opera Română and Casa Radio

A few hundred metres beyond, on Bulevardul Kogălniceanu, stands the mint-green **Opera Română**, a drab 1950s building containing a collection of operatic costumes, scores, photographs and posters – although these are not particularly interesting, do try and catch a performance here if you get the chance (see p.84). Looming over the Opera building is the monstrous **Casa Radio** (Radio House), another of Ceauşescu's unfinished projects. Initially intended to house the National History, Army and Communist Party museums, as well as Ceauşescu's tomb, it has long been rumoured that it will become, as the name implies, a radio centre. However, given the speed (or rather lack of) at which things move round here, this is highly unlikely, and the building seems destined to remain in architectural limbo for many years to come.

Cotroceni Palace and the Botanical Gardens

From the Opera Română, buses and trolley buses trundle south across the river along Bulevardul Eroilor Sanitari to the Cotroceni Palace and the Botanical Gardens, passing an area of lovely bourgeois villas, each one individually designed. The **Cotroceni Palace** was built as a monastery by Şerban Cantacuzino between 1679–82 and served as base for the Austrian army in 1737, the Russian army in 1806, and Tudor Vladimirescu's rebels in 1821. Damaged by numerous fires and earthquakes over the course of its history, the original building was demolished in 1863 and the palace rebuilt in 1893–95 to provide a home for the newly wed Prince Ferdinand and Princess Marie. Under communism, it served as the Palace of the Pioneers – the Soviet-bloc equivalent of the Boy Scouts. A new south wing was added during restoration following the 1977 earthquake, and this is now the presidential residence. In 1986, Ceaușescu had the church demolished, apparently because it spoilt the view. Enter the palace by a small door in the north wall at Şos. Cotroceni 37 (Tues–Sun 9am–5.30pm; €2.50; advance booking necessary on ☏021/221 1200). Tours pass first through the remains of the monastery, where the Cantacuzino family gravestones are kept, then through the new rooms from the 1893–95 rebuild, decorated in an eclectic variety of Western styles.

On the other side of Şoseaua Cotroceni lie the university's well-tended **Botanical Gardens** (daily 8am–7pm), which keep pine trees and lily ponds, as well as glasshouses and a museum of botany (Tues, Thurs & Sun 9am–1pm).

The National Military Museum and around

A short way north of the Opera Română, in a former army barracks at Str. Mircea Vulcănescu 125, is the **National Military Museum** (Tues–Sun 9am–5pm). The first part of the museum is an intermittently interesting trawl through Romania's eventful military history, featuring an impressive array of weapons, banners and uniforms. The one section of the museum that really merits a visit, however, is the exhibition on the 1989 revolution, which is comprised mainly of personal belongings donated by families of soldiers and civilians killed during the fighting – from glasses, watches and medals to more sobering items such as blood-splattered jumpers and bullet casings. The main exhibit is the pistol, walkie-talkie and blood-soaked uniform of General Vasile Milea, Minister of Defence at the time of the revolution, who was executed for refusing to carry out orders to shoot upon the civilians. Despite the voluminous display of memorabilia on view in the remainder of the museum, Romania has rarely gone in for martial adventures; indeed from 1958, it was the only Warsaw Pact country without Soviet troops on its soil. Ceaușescu called vociferously for disarmament, announcing peace proposals and cuts in the defence budget. Post-communist Romania has become more involved in international concerns, contributing a chemical-warfare unit to the Gulf War forces, a military hospital to the UN in Somalia, and peace-keeping troops to Albania and the former Yugoslavia. In 1999, Romania allowed NATO – of which it is now a member – to use its air space to fly bombing missions across Serbia.

North of the museum, towards the Gara de Nord, is a village-like neigh-bourhood of tiny street-corner churches and dimly lit workshops. Ivy and creepers cloak the residential houses – all outwardly run-down, but often concealing parquet-floored apartments with elegant antique furniture and other relics of pre-war bourgeois life.

The northern suburbs

The **Şoseaua Kiseleff**, a long, elegant avenue lined with lime trees, extends north from Piața Victoriei towards the Herăstrău Park and the Village Museum (see p.79), the best of Romania's open-air museums of vernacular architecture,

The Skopți

The Skopți coachmen, who worked along the Șoseaua Kiseleff until the 1940s, were one of the curiosities – or grotesqueries – of Bucharest. Members of a dissident religious sect founded in Russia during the seventeenth century – and related to the Lipovani of the Danube Delta – the Skopți ritually castrated themselves in the belief that the "generative organs are the seat of all iniquities", interpreting literally Christ's words on eunuchs in the Gospel of St Matthew. This was done after two years of normal married life – a period necessary to ensure the conception of future Skopți. Driving *droshkys* pulled by black Orloff horses, the coachmen wore caftans sprouting two cords, which passengers tugged to indicate that the driver should turn left or right.

before heading out towards the airports and the main road to Transylvania. Modelled on the Parisian chausses – though named after a Russian general – Șoseaua Kiseleff is a product of the Francophilia that swept Romania's educated classes during the nineteenth century; it even has its own Arc de Triumf.

East of Șoseaua Kiseleff, beyond B-dul Aviatorilor at Str. Muzeul Zambaccian 21, the **Zambaccian Museum** (Wed–Sun 10am–6pm) is another little gem. This little-known museum houses a small but terrific collection of art accumulated by wealthy businessman Krikor H. Zambaccian (1889–1962), and is notable for its paintings by established Romanian artists such as Grigorescu, Andreescu and Lucian, and French artists Renoir and Matisse; it is also home to the only painting in the country by Cézanne, as well as a few pieces of sculpture from Brâncuși and Storck.

About 1km north along Șos. Kiseleff you'll come to the **Arc de Triumf**, built in 1878 for an independence parade, and patched together in 1922 for another procession to celebrate Romania's participation on the winning side in World War I and the gains achieved at the Versailles peace conference. Originally made of wood, it was more fittingly rebuilt in stone in 1935–36, in the style of the Arc de Triomphe in Paris.

Immediately beyond the Arc is **Herăstrău Park**, which is best reached by metro – the Aviatorilor stop is at its southeastern corner. Paths run past formal flowerbeds to the shore of **Lake Herăstrău**, one of the largest of a dozen lakes strung along the River Colentina. These lakes were created by Carol II to drain the unhealthy marshes that surrounded Bucharest and form a continuous line

The Băneasa bridge

The bridge immediately north of the Băneasa station, where the DN1 crosses the River Colentina, was the scene of a **crucial battle** in August 1944. The success of the August 23 coup against Marshal Antonescu (see p.390) meant that Hitler's oil supplies were more than halved, which is reckoned to have shortened the war in Europe by at least six months. However, at the time just 2800 Romanian troops faced between 20,000 and 30,000 Germans, mostly at Băneasa and Otopeni, but without orders due to the cutting of phone lines. King Mihai offered the Germans safe passage out of Romania, but they responded by bombing Bucharest. The bridge was held by a Romanian lieutenant and a handful of men until August 25, when Romanian reinforcements began to arrive from Craiova. Allied help finally came the following day when four hundred American planes bombed the German positions, and by August 27 Bucharest had been cleared of German forces (only to be occupied by the Red Army four days later).

across the northern suburbs. Arched bridges lead via the small and fragrant Island of Roses to numerous lakeside snack bars and restaurants, from where rowing boats can be rented (€1.20 per hour). Alternatively, you can take a thirty-minute lake cruise (€0.75); tickets for both must be bought from the windows opposite the departure point (May–Sept for both boats and lake cruise). Also located within the park is the Expo-market, a vast indoor shopping arena, and a creaky old fairground.

The residential area east of the park is one of Bucharest's most exclusive neighbourhoods. It is where the communist elite once lived, cordoned off from the masses they governed; the Ceauşescus lived in the Vila Primavera, at the east end of Bulevardul Primăverii. The area is still inhabited by technocrats, favoured artists and other members of the ruling elite.

The Village Museum

Another of Bucharest's worthwhile sights is the **Village Museum** (Muzeul Satului: April–Sept Mon 9am–5pm, Tues–Sun 9am–8pm; Oct–March daily 9am–5pm; €1) on the shores of Lake Herăstrău – the entrance is on Şos. Kiseleff, just up from the Arc de Triumf. Established in 1936, this wonderful ensemble of over three hundred dwellings, workshops, churches, windmills, presses and other structures from every region in the country illustrates the extreme diversity of Romania's folk architecture.

The most interesting are the oaken houses from Maramureş with their rope-motif carvings and shingled roofing, and their beamed gateways carved with animals and hunting scenes, Adam and Eve and the Tree of Life, and suns and moons. Other highlights are the heavily thatched dwellings from Sălciua de Jos in Alba county; dug-out homes, or "pit" houses (with vegetables growing on the roof) from Drăghiceni and Castranova in Oltenia; colourfully-furnished homesteads from Moldavia; and windmills from Tulcea county in the Delta. Keep an eye out, too, for the beautiful wooden church from the village of Dragomireşti in Maramureş. Mud-brick dwellings from the fertile plains iron-ically appear poorer than the homes of peasants in the less fertile highlands where timber and stone abound; while the importance of livestock to the Székely people of Harghita county can be seen by their barns, which are taller than their houses.

The museum has had a pretty rough time of it in recent years, suffering two serious incidents of fire: the first, when several houses were subject to an arson attack by an embittered ex-employee; and the second time, in 2002, when more than a dozen houses burnt down in somewhat less suspicious circum-stances. Understandably, this is a no-smoking museum.

Piaţa Presei Libere

Şoseaua Kiseleff ends at **Piaţa Presei Libere** (Free Press Square), in front of **Casa Presei Libere** (Free Press House), a vast, white Stalinist building, which was once the centre of the state propaganda industry; little seems to have changed, as the free publishing industry is still largely corralled into this one building. Romania's Commodities Exchange is also based here. Until 1989, the pedestal in front of the building once accommodated a huge statue of Lenin, before he was carted off to Mogoşoaia Palace (see p.89) and uncere-moniously dumped.

Some 500m further north of here, by the Băneasa train station just off the Bucureşti–Ploieşti Highway, are Bucharest's two least known museums. Both of these eccentric buildings on Str. Dr Minovici were built in the early twentieth century, specifically to hold the private collections of the oil-rich Minovici family. Built in 1905 in the style of a fortified manor house, the **Museum of Popular Arts** (Tues–Sun 9am–5pm) at no. 2 exhibits woven blankets, Transylvanian blue pottery, painted Easter eggs, spinning wheels, musical instruments, furniture and beautiful peasant garments – there's also a tiny Orthodox chapel with eighteenth-century icons. Next door at no. 3, constructed in 1910 in a bizarre fusion of English Tudor and Italian Renaissance styles, the **Minovici Museum of Old Western Arts** (Thurs–Sun 9am–5pm) is filled with hunting trophies and weapons, Flemish tapestries, Florentine furniture, German and Swiss stained-glass windows, and a fine rug from Mosul in Iraq.

Eating, nightlife and entertainment

Between the wars Bucharest was famed for its bacchanals, its gourmet cuisine and its Gypsy music – but all this ended with the puritanical postwar regime of communism. However, the situation has improved distinctly in recent years, with a burgeoning, and still remarkably cheap, **restaurant** scene. The city's nightlife is also on the up, and there are now some terrific **bars** and **clubs** scattered around town.

The best places for **snacks** are the street stalls, pizzerias, kebab and burger bars on the main avenues, around the Gara de Nord and in the Piaţa Universităţii underpass; these are generally open Monday to Saturday from 9am until around 7pm, though many of those near the station are open around the clock. **Patisseries** are also a good bet for a quick snack; most of them dispense freshly baked sweet and savoury pastries, cakes and confectionery. Look out, too, for the kiosks doling out *gogoş*, large, elongated doughnuts that come with a choice of fillings.

There are at least half a dozen **markets** (see shopping, p.86) in the city, where you can select from a huge and colourful selection of fruit and vegetables, which vary depending on the season. For **self-catering**, see p.86.

Cafés and patisseries

After years of providing little more than uninspiring, dusty old joints, Bucharest is now home to some genuinely enjoyable and idiosyncratic **cafés**, an increasing number of which offer sandwiches and snacks. Many also sell alcoholic beverages. Note that a lot of the **patisseries** often have stand-up counters instead of seats.

Alpi Blanche Str. Stirbei Vodă 152 (at the corner of B-dul D. Golescu). This fabulous place has been doling out the city's best ice-cream for over a decade – cones or tubs to eat in or takeaway.

Brit C@fe Calea Dorobanţilor 14. Busy little café inside the grounds of the British Council, with (old) English newspapers and Internet access; there's also an outlet of the *Sandwich Factory* here (see opposite).

Casandra B-dul Magheru 32. A friendly sit-down place serving fancy cakes and biscuits.

Caffe and Latte B-dul Schitu Măgureanu 35. In a lovely leafy location across from the Cişmigiu Gardens, this is one of the city's most enjoyable new cafés; excellent coffees, fruit and chocolate shakes, and pastries, run by happy smiling staff.

Café Molinari Str. N. Golescu 14–16. Ultra-stylish, if a little too pretentious, joint just behind the *Atheneum*, with squishy chairs and mellow background tunes.

Nova Brasilia Str. Radu Beller 6. Upmarket café with the town's best (and most expensive) range of coffees, as well as hot and cold sandwiches, croissants and pancakes.

Panipat B-dul Bălcescu 24 (24hr), Gara de Nord (24hr), Str. M Rosetti 15, B-dul Brătianu 44, Şos. Ştefan cel Mare 48 and B-dul Kogălniceanu 55. Thoroughly modern franchise patisserie with good takeaway buns, pizzas and cakes, including strudel.

Patisserie Parisienne B-dul Magheru 29 and Piaţa Romană 9. Hot and cold snacks and a delicious selection of cakes.

Picasso Café Str. Franceza 2–4. Cool, relaxing and beautifully lit café, the perfect coffee stop after trooping around the National History Museum just up the road.
Café Royal Bistro Str. Episcopiei 1–3. The

Athénée Palace's coffee house is as classy – though not as expensive – as you'd expect.
Scala B-dul Bălcescu 36 (at Str. Rosetti). Small shop but with a huge choice of chocolates and cakes; the baklava is especially good.

Sandwich bars and fast food

Gregory's B-dul Magheru 32–34 and Str. Lipscani 27. Fairly decent sandwich and deli outlets, though not in the same league as the Sandwich Factory.
Pizza Hut Calea Dorobanţilor 1 and B-dul Regina Elisabeta 17. Reliably the same as anywhere else in the world, smoking and no-smoking sections.
Sandwich Factory Piaţa Dorobanţi, Calea Victoriei

222, Str. Ion Câmpineanu 10, and Str. Amzei 7–9. Bright and fashionable outlets serving the freshest and tastiest sandwiches, salads and soups in town.
Spring Time B-dul N. Titulescu 6, Str. Academiei 35, and Calea Floreasca 131. Lebanese-run fast-food chain with a wide range of foods to take away or eat in.

Restaurants

Bucharest's **restaurant** scene is changing fast, and for the better. In recent years, there's been a welcome diversification in the types of cuisines available, from Belgian and French, to Lebanese and Fusion, though it's still very difficult to find, for example, decent Asian or South–Central American food. Whilst restaurants in Bucharest are marginally more expensive than elsewhere in the country, dining out remains a fantastically cheap pastime. As a general rule, expect to pay around €6 for a two-course meal with wine, around a third more for the very best establishments. Although it's now rare for restaurants to **overcharge** tourists, there are still one or two places that will try and get away with it, so study the bill assiduously and if you think the waiter has got it wrong (deliberately or otherwise), don't be afraid to question. Although by no means widespread, an increasing number of restaurants – and certainly the better ones – now provide **no-smoking** sections. **Credit cards** are also now widely accepted. Telephone numbers have also been given where it's best to reserve a table. Note that many of the restaurants listed here can be quite tricky to find, as they tend to be secreted away down leafy side streets in residential areas or in anonymous-looking buildings.

Around Piaţa Revoluţiei and Piaţa Universităţii

Bistro Atheneu Str. Episcopiei 3 ☏ 021/313 4900. Across from the Atheneum concert hall, this homely little restaurant has been keeping pre- and post-concert punters happy for over a decade with its tasty Romanian and continental food. Daily noon–midnight.
Burebista Str. Batiştei 14. Named after the great Dacian ruler, you can eat as cheaply or as expensively as you wish in this convivial place located 200m east of the Intercontinental hotel; a prodigious menu offering some of the best-value Romanian food in town – the White Bean soup and Sarmalute (Moldavian Stuffed Cabbage) are especially recommended. Daily noon–midnight.
Café de la Joie Str. Ion Nistor 4. Delightful and intimate little French restaurant serving

sensational fondues. Tricky to find as there is no sign indicating the place; it's behind the Bucharest History Museum next to the Bluezone Café sign. Mon–Sat 6pm–1am.
Casă Veche Str. Enescu 15. Large and attractive stone-cobbled terrace/garden with a huge selection of wood-oven-baked pizzas and salads alongside some choice Belgian beers. The service, however, can be achingly slow. Daily 11am–1am.
La Mama Str. Episcopiei 9 (☏ 021/312-9797), Str. Barbu Văcărescu 3 (☏ 212 4086), and Str. Delea Veche 51 (☏ 320 5213). With every good reason, La Mama is absurdly popular; mammoth portions of wholesome Romanian food (grills, stews and cabbage dishes), a bustling atmosphere, and cracking prices. They also do take-outs. No shorts

allowed inside after 6pm, but, in summer, the terrace is equally as enjoyable. Book ahead. Daily 10am–2am, Fri & Sat till 4am.

La Taifas Str. Clemenceau 6. The smells wafting out on to the street should be enough to tempt you into this wonderfully cosy place just around the corner from its sister restaurant, the *Bistro Atheneu*. Delicious grilled and fried meats (the lamb mix is very good) rustled up on the patio area before your very eyes. Daily 6pm–1am.

East of Bulevardul G. Magheru and Bulevardul N. Bălcescu

Balthazar Str. Dumbrava Rosie 2 ☏021/212 1460. Superb contemporary fusion restaurant offering a French menu that changes weekly, and an Asian menu that changes daily (Japanese, Thai, Vietnamese, Chinese). The classy surrounds, warm atmosphere and impeccable service make the not inconsiderable expense worth it. Daily noon–12.30am.

Chelsea Bistro Str. Jules Michelet 9. Fairly cheap and simple eatery opposite the British embassy, serving light meals such as salads, spaghettis and omelettes; there's also a stylish café in the same building. Mon–Fri 9am–midnight, Sat & Sun 3pm–midnight.

Cyprus Taverna Str. Calderon 41. Quiet, simple and friendly little taverna with a wide range of charcoal-cooked Greek and Cypriot dishes (souvlaki, cotlets and moussaka) and *meze* plates. Mon–Sat 12.30–3pm & 4pm–midnight. Sun noon–3.30pm.

Mediterraneo Str. Icoanei 20 ☏021/211 5308. Cramped, but warm and hospitable restaurant whose mainly Italian menu is complimented by some interesting Turkish dishes. They also do an excellent three-course lunch menu for €5. Immensely popular, so get there early. Daily 10am–2am.

Mesogios Str. Calderon 49 ☏021/313 4951. A few paces along from the *Cyprus Taverna*, this beautifully turned-out restaurant is *the* place to come for seafood – cuttlefish, octopus, red snapper and squid are just a few of the dishes on offer – but it's not cheap. Reasonably smart dress required. Daily 12.30pm–12.30am.

Nicorești Str. Maria Rosetti 40. Solid, unfussy and cheap Romanian fare under a straw-covered terrace near the *Villa Helga* hostel. Located at the corner of Str. M Rosetti and Str. Toamnei. Daily 11am–11pm.

Smarts Str. Al. Donici 14 ☏021/211 9035. Just around the corner from *Mediterraneo*, this romantic little restaurant features an accomplished and comprehensive western European menu, but with a major slant towards Belgian – their steaks are amongst the best in the city, while the freshwater-fish pancakes make for an unusual entrée. Neat little inn-style bar downstairs, too, where you can sample Belgian beers. Daily noon–3am.

South of Piața Universității

Carul cu Bere Str. Stavropoleos 3. Along with the *Hanul lui Manuc* (to be avoided at all costs), the *Beer Cart* is the city's premier tourist hang out. Its attractive surrounds, featuring splendid neo-Tannhauser décor, just about compensates for the rather average food – the *mititei* (grilled sausages) are good though – and sloppy service. Beware of the tendency to overcharge tourists. Daily 10am–midnight.

Count Dracula Club Spl. Independenței 8a, 200m west of Calea Victoriei. You'll not be surprised to learn that everything here is themed: the furniture, the food, even the waiters, but it's not as tacky as it sounds; solid Romanian food at good prices. Daily 12.30pm–1am.

Taj Calea 13 Septembrie 127–131. Fine Indian establishment offering some of the most authentic ethnic food in the city; the resident Indian chef cooks up a feast of fantastically tasty meat and sauce based dishes using the freshest ingredients, and vegetarians are well catered for, too. Despite its poor location out near the *Grand Marriott* hotel, it's well worth the effort to get to. Bus #385 to the corner of Str. Vladimirescu. Daily noon–2am.

Whispers Str. Ion Brezoianu 4. Upscale, yet informal, American-style diner, serving burgers, hot sandwiches and salads. Suffices equally for a lunch stop-off or a more hearty evening meal. Daily 10am–midnight.

North of the centre

Barka Saffron Str. Av. Sănătescu 1 ☏021/224 1004. Awkwardly located, but brilliantly original and enchanting Indian–Fusion restaurant with a different menu for each day. Great little bar playing Cuban–Latino music. Daily noon–1am.

Casa Doina Şos. Kiseleff 4 ☎ 021/222 3179. Occupying a prime location on the edge of a wooded park, this late-nineteenth-century building accommodates an elegant and formal (no shorts allowed inside) restaurant serving an upscale, and expensive, take on Romanian dishes; good vegetarian options, too. Live music each night from 6pm. Daily noon–midnight.

Die Deutsche Kneipe Str. Stockholm 9. Terrific, family-run restaurant in a quiet residential street off Calea Dorobanţilor; gut-busting portions of succulent German sausages served with lashings of sauerkraut and washed down with German Pils or keg beer. Mon–Sat 5pm–midnight.

Lobb's B-dul Expozitiei 2. A long way out and in an anonymous location (inside the World Trade Centre), but worth the trek for the very accomplished, and not-too-expensive, pasta and fish dishes. There's top-class jazz here, too, on Friday evenings. Daily 8am–2am.

Nan-Jing Str. Gh. Manu 2, in the *Hotel Minerva* ☎ 021/311 1550. Whilst nothing out of the ordinary, Bucharest's oldest oriental restaurant remains the best place to go for Chinese food, though it's patronized mainly by businessmen staying at the hotel. Daily noon–midnight.

Piccolo Mondo Str. Clucerului 16. One of a handful of terrific Lebanese eateries to have established themselves in Bucharest recently, this handsome restaurant lists a long menu of salads, kebabs (including a good choice for vegetarians), yoghurt-based dishes, and cured meats. Post-meal, enjoy a smoke on a hookah pipe. A good place for al fresco dining in the summer. Daily noon–1am.

Uptown Bar and Grill Str. Rabat 2. Another pleasantly secluded place just off B-dul Aviatorilor (or a ten-minute walk from Piaţa Dorobanţilor). Delicious crêpes, salads, pastas, risottos and grilled meats – try and grab a table in the elegant horseshoe-shaped conservatory. Daily 11am–1am.

Bars and clubs

Bucharest does not immediately strike visitors as a place where **nightlife** abounds, but this is partly because, like the best of the city's restaurants, many places are discreetly tucked away or concentrated in unlikely areas of the city. Indeed, Bucharest is currently experiencing a new vibrancy, with **bars** springing up all over the city on a regular basis, coming and going according to the latest trends. The **club** scene, too, is fast improving, and in addition to the growing number of bars that double up as clubs there are now some choice venues scattered around town, increasingly catering to a more discerning range of musical tastes. Bucharestians, however, have long been starved of decent **live music**, a situation reflected in the dearth of venues.

Amsterdam Grand Café Str. Covaci 6. This classy café-bar in the old historic quarter is a great spot either for a daytime coffee chill-out (flick through the magazines at the smart reading table, or just observe the passing locals through the big bay windows) or a convivial evening beer; there's also a very commendable kitchen here, which serves the best breakfasts and brunches in town. Daily 11am–1am. *Exit*, the café's basement club, roars into life on Fridays and Saturdays (9pm–4am).

Backstage Str. Gabroveni 14. An old hand on the local disco scene, you can count on a relaxed vibe and a good mix of retro tunes at this perennially popular club. Daily 9pm–5am.

Becker Brau Calea Rahovei 155. Located behind the Palace of Parliament, this outstanding German bar has ale brewed on the premises and waitresses in Bavarian costume scuttling around at optimum speed. Daily noon–2am.

Champions Sports Bar Calea 13 Septembrie 90, on the first floor of the *Grand Marriott* hotel.

Thoughtfully designed, American-style bar and diner adorned with an impressive array of superstar memorabilia, including George Foreman's gloves and Dan Marino's helmet, as well as items belonging to local heroes, Ilie Nastase, Gheorghe Hagi and Nadia Comaneci. Large plasma screens for all your sporting kicks. Daily 1pm–midnight.

Club A Str. Blănari 14. The Young Architects Club is something of a Bucharest institution; an energetic, pro-active venue with good music, cheap drinks and a happy youthful crowd. Occasionally features drama, foreign films and jazz.

Dubliner B-dul N. Titulescu 18. The original expat hang out ten minutes' walk west of Piaţa Victoriei, but now showing its age. However, it's the only place in town where you can watch live English football. Daily 9am–2am.

Green Hours 22 Club Calea Victoriei 120. Intimate cellar bar with live jazz most evenings – in summer, gigs take place in the leafy courtyard, a lovely place to kick back and sup a beer. Daily until 3am.

The Harp Str. Bibescu Voda 1, on the south side of Piața Unrii. The *Dubliners'* sister pub, but larger and more lively, and attracting a predominantly Romanian crowd. Serves the usual expensive Irish beers: Guinness, Murphy's and Kilkenny. Daily 9am–2am.

Jukebox Str. Şepcari 22. Loud, sweaty and smoky cellar bar near *Hanul lui Manuc*, with frequent live music – featuring local groups and the resident house band – and karaoke evenings. Mon–Sat 11am–2am.

Lăptăria Enache on the 4th floor of the National Theatre, B-dul Bălcescu 2. Massive outdoor terrace bar invariably packed to the gills, and which occasionally has live jazz and film screenings on the huge projector. Daily noon–2am, Fri & Sat till 4am.

The Office Str. Tache Ionescu 2. One of the hottest club venues in town, with banging tunes, good-time atmosphere, and a hip crowd. Drinks are not cheap though. Daily 7.30pm–2am.

Salsa II Str. Luterană 9. Fabulous party place where the locals indulge in a more sophisticated mode of dancing – Latino and Salsa. Mon–Sat 10pm–4am.

Terminus Str. G. Enescu 5. Well-established downtown bar just around the corner from *Planter's*, with English pub-style furnishings and a gloomy cellar. Daily until 5am.

Tipsy B-dul Schitu Măgureanu 13. A three-in-one pub, club (a "plub", apparently) and restaurant; have a bite in the very good restaurant before moving on to the busy pub, or, at weekends (Thurs–Sat), the cellar club, which hosts one of the best discos in town. Restaurant and pub open daily 6pm–4am.

Yellow Bar Str. Edgar Quinet 10. Funky café/bar with plush leather sofas, loud tunes and a good-looking crowd. Daily 10am–3am, Sat & Sun till 5am.

Entertainment

Bucharest's cultural forte is undoubtedly **classical music**, and it's possible to catch some top-drawer, and incredibly cheap, concerts in several locations around town. Operatic and ballet performances, too, are invariably excellent, with fantastically ostentatious sets and huge casts. The highlight of the city's cultural offerings is the bi-annual **George Enescu Festival** (ⓦ www.festival enescu.ro; €5–12 depending on performance) in September, which features three weeks of concerts by some of the world's finest musicians – recent participants have included the London Philharmonic and the Moscow Philharmonic orchestras. A festival of piano music, named after Romania's greatest pianist, Dinu Lipatti, takes place in early May. Note that many **theatres** and **concert halls** close during the summer, but over the rest of the year check *Bucharest In Your Pocket* (see p.55) for the most up-to-date listings.

Classical music, opera and ballet

Several internationally acclaimed musicians have cut their teeth with the **George Enescu Philharmonic Orchestra**, which plays in the architecturally and acoustically superb Romanian Atheneum at Str. Franklin 1 near Piața Enescu (box office Tues–Sat noon–7pm, Sun 6–7pm; ☎021/315 6875). The **Opera Română**, at B-dul Kogălniceanu 70 (box office Tues–Sat

---

Casinos

There's a rash of **casinos** in Bucharest, which pander unashamedly to the pretensions of travelling businessman and the city's nouveau riche, with overpriced drinks and underclad hostesses. Some of them are in very beautiful historical buildings, and they often have genuinely good restaurants, open well into the early hours. The most attractive are the Palace Casino, incorporating the *Casa Vernescu* restaurant, in the Lenș-Vernescu palace at Calea Victoriei 133 (☎021/231 0220), the Grand Casino (☎021/659 4913) in the basement of the *Athénée Palace Hilton Hotel* at Str. Episcopiei 1, and the Casino Bucharest (☎021/310 2020) in the *Intercontinental* hotel at B-dul N. Bălcescu 4. In general, you can gamble with US dollars or lei.

10am–1pm & 2–7pm; tickets €1–4; ☎021/314 6980), is the principal venue for operatic and ballet performances, with other productions taking place at the Teatrul Operetă (☎021/313 6348) next to the National Theatre, at B-dul Bălcescu 2. There are also high-quality concerts at the **Sala Radio**, Str. Berthelot 62 (box office daily 10am–6pm; tickets €0.50–2; ☎021 /314 6800), which is home to the National Radio Orchestra. Occasional **outdoor concerts** are held in Cişmigiu Gardens and Tineretului Park during the summer.

Drama

The huge **National Theatre**, B-dul Bălcescu 2 (☎021/314 7171), with its three auditoriums, is the premier venue for both domestic and foreign theatre productions. Other venues with productions that might just surmount linguistic barriers are the Tăndărică Puppet Theatre, Str. E. Grigorescu 24; the two music halls at Calea Victoriei 33 and 174; the Comedy Theatre at Str. Măndineşti 2, and the State Jewish Theatre, Str. I. Barasch 15. In the second week of November, the Ion Luca Caragiale Festival, named after Romania's best-known playwright, brings to town the best of the year's drama from the provincial theatres. The **circus** is at Aleea Circului 15 (metro Ştefan cel Mare; ☎021/211 4195), but is usually closed through the summer months.

Cinemas

Cinemas are plentiful, both in the centre and the suburbs, showing films from all over the world, though, predictably, subtitled Hollywood flicks are the most popular fare. Prices are very cheap; expect to pay around €1.50–3. The modern, ten-screen Hollywood Complex in the Bucharest Mall at Calea Vitan 55–59, has the most varied programme, as well as late screenings; the best of the city centre cinemas (where films are slightly cheaper) are Patria and Scala, on Bulevardul Magheru, and Corso on Bulevardul Elisabeta. The Elvira Popesco Hall, in the French Institute at B-dul Dacia 77 (☎021/210 0224), has an excellent programme of world films and is usually the place to catch what few film **festivals** take place in Bucharest, while the Cinematecă, at Str. Eforie 2 (☎021/313 0483), shows a good selection of screen classics – programmes are posted outside.

Sports and activities

Bucharest's only major spectator sport is **football**, with four clubs residing in the city: the most popular and famous is the army team, **Steaua** Bucureşti (B-dul Ghencea 35; tram #8 or #47, trolley bus #69), closely followed by the rail-workers team, **Rapid** (Şos. Giuleşti 18; Metro Cringaşi), and the one-time Securitate team, **Dinamo** (Şos. Ştefan cel Mare 9; Metro Ştefan cel Mare). Bucharest's fourth side, **Naţional**, play at the Cotroceni stadium, behind the *Grand Marriott* hotel. Tickets (between €1–3) can be bought at the respective stadiums before each game.

The best of the city's relatively few **sporting facilities** are the Herăstrău complex, Şos. Nordului 5–7 (tennis, €4 for 1hr fitness, sauna and massage facilities), and Club Floreasca/Pit Gym Club, B-dul Mircea Eliade 1 (tennis, basketball, gym, ice skating). In the summer, Strandul Tineretului, Aleea Ştrandului 1 offers water sports and tennis. For swimming, the Lucian Grigorescu Hall, Str. Aviator Popa Marin 2; and the Naţional and Dinamo stadia have pools, as do hotels such as the *Intercontinental* and *Athénée Palace*. You can also **swim** in the city lakes – Floreasca (Metro Aurel Vlaicu), Strauleşti (western terminus of trolley bus #97) and Băneasa (bus #131 or #205). The students' swimming pool is at Ştrandul Tei, off B-dul Lacul Tei.

❶ Shopping

Bucharest's range of **shops** has expanded considerably in recent years, with many international names appearing in the city's handful of new and refurbished shopping malls. The main **shopping complex** is the enormous Unirea department store at Piaţa Unirii 1 (Mon–Sat 9am–9pm, Sun 9am–3pm), followed by the rather soulless Bucureşti Mall, south of the centre at Calea Vitan 55–59 (daily 10am–10pm), and the World Trade Plaza, inside the World Trade Centre building at B-dul Expoziţiei 2 (daily 8am–8pm). The posh Grand Avenue (daily 10am–8pm) is a small precinct inside the *Grand Marriott* hotel (see p.59) housing a few designer and boutique shops. For **antiques**, try the streets around the historic quarter, and in particular Str. Lipscani and Str. Covaci; two of the best places are Craii de Curtea Veche, Str. Covaci 14 (Mon–Fri 10am–6pm, Sat 10am–3pm), and the Hanul cu Tei bazaar, Str. Lipscani 63–65 (same times). For craftwork and traditional **souvenirs**, head out to the Museum of the Romanian Peasant or the Village Museum; and for Romanian **music**, try the Sony Music Centre on the third floor of the Unirea department store (see p.73), or Muzica, Calea Victoriei 43 (Mon–Fri 9.30am–7pm, Sat 9.30am–2.30pm).

The best place to get hold of English-language **books** – including Romanian history and politics, fiction and non-fiction, and some excellent children's books – is Salinger's (Mon–Sat noon–9pm, Sun 10am–9pm), located in the small shopping precinct inside the *Grand Marriott* hotel, with another, much smaller branch inside the *Athénée Palace* hotel (see p.59). The much larger Librăria Noi, at B-dul Bălcescu 18 (Mon–Sat 10am–8pm, Sun 11am–7pm), also carries a decent range of English-language books, translated Romanian literature, and CDs – it's also the best place to pick up **maps**. Humanitas, next to the Creţulescu church at Calea Victoriei 45, has a varied selection of titles on Romania, while there are secondhand bookshops at B-dul Carol I no. 62 and at B-dul Iuliu Maniu 54, as well as lots of stalls in the Piaţa Universităţii underpass that occasionally have foreign books. Foreign newspapers and magazines are tricky to come by, but the kiosks in the *Athénée Palace*, *Grand Marriott* and *Intercontinental* hotels usually have same-day foreign editions.

For food, the best **supermarkets** are La Fourmi in the Unirea department store (Mon–Sat 8.30am–9pm, Sun 9am–4pm) and at B-dul 1 Mai (Mon–Sat 9.30am–8.30pm); Mega Image at B-dul N. Titulescu 39–49 (Mon–Sat 8.30am–9.30pm, Sun 8.30am–6pm), and at Şos. Ştefan cel Mare 226; and Nic, on Piaţa Amzei (Mon–Sat 9am–9pm, Sun 9am–6pm) and at Str. Radu Beller 6 (24hr). All of these have good deli counters. The 24-hour grocery store at Calea Griviţei 142, opposite the Gara de Nord station, is a useful place to stock up on foodstuffs before embarking on a long journey.

The best of the city's many **markets** – where you can pick up fresh produce and a variety of other knick-knacks – are Unirii (behind the Unirea department store), the huge Obor market east of town, Amzei, just south of Piaţa Română, and Matache (behind the CFR office near the Gara de Nord). There's also a vast Sunday morning **flea market** (Trgul Vitan) on Calea Vitan, fifteen minutes' walk south of the Dristor I metro station, alongside the Dâmboviţa embankment. Beware of pickpockets at all these places.

Listings

Airlines The main Tarom office is at Spl. Independenţei 17 (Mon–Fri 9am–7pm, Sat 9am–1pm; ☎021/337 0400, ⊛www.tarom.ro), with additional offices at Str. Buzeşti 59, just off Piaţa Victoriei (Mon–Fri 9am–7.30pm, Sat 9am–1pm; ☎021/204 6464); and Str. Brezoianu 10 (Mon–Fri 9am–7.30pm, Sat 9am–noon; ☎021/314 4295). Angel Airlines ☎021/201 1701, ⊛www.angelairlines.ro) is based at Băneasa airport and Carpatair is at Str. Vasile Conta 3 (☎021/314 7975). Air France, Str. G-ral Praporgescu 1–5 (☎021/312 0085); Austrian Airlines, B-dul Magheru 16–18 (☎021/312 0545); British Airways, Calea Victoriei 15 (☎021/303 2222, ⊛www.british airways.com); KLM, Aleea Alexandru 9a (☎021/231 5619); Lufthansa, B-dul Magheru 18 (☎021/315 7575); Malev, Calea Victoriei 26 (☎021/312 0427); Swissair, B-dul Magheru 18 (☎021/312 0238).

Airport information Otopeni ☎021/204 1000; Băneasa ☎021/232 0020.

American Express At Marshal Turism, B-dul Magheru 43 (Mon–Fri 9am–6pm, Sat 9am–1pm; ☎021/223 1204, ⊛www.marshal.ro) and B-dul Unirii 20 (same hours; ☎021/335 1224).

Banks and exchange There are many exchange counters all over the city, with a good spread along B-dul Magheru and B-dul N. Bălcescu – two of the better ones are Alliance Exchange, at B-dul N. Bălcescu 30, and O.K. at no. 20, both of which are open 24hr. Changing travellers' cheques is a relatively painless process; amongst the quickest and most efficient places is the Bank Austria Creditanstalt on Piaţa Revoluţiei, and the BCR at B-dul Regina Elisabeta 5.

Buses Atlassib, B-dul Gh. Duca 4 (☎021/222 4735); Eurolines Touring, B-dul Al. Ioan Cuza (☎021/210 0890) for buses to Germany; Murat, B-dul D. Golescu 31 (☎021/222 7307) or Toros, Calea Griviţiei 136–138 (☎021/223 1898) for buses to Istanbul; Anesis, Str. Poteraşi 20–22 (☎021/330 9176) for buses to Athens.

Car rental Avis, Str. Mihail Moxa 9 (☎021/210 4345, ⊛www.avis.ro) and at the *Intercontinental* hotel (☎021/314 1837); Budget, Str. Polonă 35 (☎021/210 2867, ⊛www.budgetro.ro); Europcar, Calea Calarasi 46 (☎021/320 8554); and Hertz, Str. Ion Bianu 47 (☎021/222 1256, ⊛www.hertz.com.ro) and the *Grand Marriott* hotel (☎021/403 2956). All these companies have outlets at Otopeni airport.

Car repairs ACR has its head office at Str. Tache Ionescu 27 (☎021/315 5510, eacr@acr.ro) and technical assistance centres at Calea Dorobanţilor 85 (☎021/211 1835) and Spl. Independenţiei 204 (☎021/212 6433). These should be open 24hr. Automecanica, Calea Floreasca 43 (☎021/230 0196; Mon–Fri 8am–8pm, Sat 8am–4pm, Sun 8am–2pm), is a private company that may be able to help with foreign cars.

Embassies and consulates Australia, B-dul Unirii 74 ☎021/320 9826, ⊛www.romaniaaustralia.ro; Bulgaria, Str. Rabat 5 ☎021/230 2150, ⊜bulembassy@pcnet.ro; Canada, Str. N. Iorga 36 (☎021/307 5000, ⊛www.dfait-maeci.gc.ca /bucharest); Hungary, Str. Calderon 63–65 ☎021/312 0073; Moldova, Aleea Alexandru 40 ☎021/230 0474, ⊜moldova@customers .digiro.net; Serbia and Montenegro, Calea Dorobanţilor 34 ☎021/211 9871; UK, Str. J. Michelet 24 ☎021/312 0303, ⊛www .britishembassy.gov.uk/romania; Ukraine, Calea Dorobanţilor 16 ☎021/211 6986, ⊜emb.ukr@itcnet.ro; USA, Str. Filipescu 26 ☎021/210 4042, ⊛www.usembassy.ro

Emergencies Ambulance ☎961; police ☎955; fire service ☎981.

Hospitals For emergency treatment, you should go to the Emergency Clinic Hospital (Spital Clinic de Urgenţa), at Calea Floreasca 8 (Metro Ştefan cel Mare; ☎021/230 0106), or the private Biomedica International Medical Centre, Str. M. Eminescu 42 (Mon–Sat 8am–8pm; ☎021/211 9674, for emergencies, ☎230 8001). Your embassy can recommend doctors speaking your language. There's excellent, Western-standard dental treatment at the German-run B.B. Clinic, Str. Ionescu Gion 4 (☎021/320 0151).

Internet access New places offering online services are popping up all the time, but the best of the current bunch are: Acces Internet, B-dul Catargiu 6 (daily 24hr); Biblioteca GDS, Calea Victoriei (daily 24hr); Brit C@fé, inside the British Council at Calea Dorobanţilor 14 (Mon–Thurs 8.30am–5pm, Fri 8.30am–1pm); Cyber Espace, inside the French Institute at Dacia 77 (Mon–Sat 10am–8pm); Cyber Club, B-dul Carol I 25 (daily 10am–10pm); PC Net, Calea Victoriei 136 (daily 24hr); Sweet Internet Café, Str. Maria Rosetti 79 (daily 24hr). Expect to pay around €1 for an hour online, and around half that after 9/10pm.

Laundry Immaculate Cleaners, Str. Polonă 107a (Mon–Fri 7.30am–8.30pm, Sat 9am–4pm; ☎021/211 4413); Nufărul, Calea Moşilor 276 (Mon–Fri 7am–8pm, Sat 9am–1pm; ☎021/210 1441); Nuf Nuf, Calea Şerban Vodă 76–78 (☎021/335 0168; 24hr) and Ştefan Cel Mare 24.

Pharmacies There is at least one 24hr pharmacy in each sector of the city. Sensiblu have a number of pharmacies throughout the city, including central outlets at Calea Dorobanților 65, Str. G. Enescu 36–40, B-dul Titulescu 39–49, B-dul Bălcescu 7 (there's a good optician here, too), and in the Unirea department store. In addition, Farmadex have a 24hr pharmacy at Calea Moșilor 280.

Photography The best places for buying and processing films are Kodak and the Fujifilm Image Centre, both on the ground floor of the Unirea department store on Piața Unirii; both can develop prints in one hour. Otherwise, most hotels sell film. If you need passport photos, there are booths in the Gara de Nord station and in the Piața Universității underpass.

Police Each sector has its own police station, but the most central is at B-dul Lascăr Catargiu 20 (entrance on Str. Daniel; ☎021/659 2046). Traffic accidents (with damage) should be dealt with at Str. Logofăt Udriște (☎021/323 3030).

Post office The main post office is at Str. Matei Millo 10 (Mon–Fri 7.30am–8pm, Sat 8am–2pm).

To receive mail here, make sure it is addressed c/o Officiul PTTR no. 1, Bucureşti.

Trains Agenție CFR's advance booking offices are at Str. Domnița Anastasia 10–14 (Mon–Fri 7.30am–7.30pm, Sat 8am–noon; ☎021/313 2642), and next to the IBIS hotel at Calea Grivței 139 (same times; ☎021/212 8947); to be sure of a seat in summer, you should book tickets one day in advance. You can also buy national and international tickets from Wasteels in the Gara de Nord (Mon–Fri 8am–7pm, Sat 8am–2pm; ☎021/222 7844, ⊛www.wasteelstravel.ro); foreign currencies are accepted here.

Travel agents Atlantic Tours, Calea Victoriei 202 (☎021/212 9232); Dacia Tour, B-dul Magheru 1–3 (☎021/310 2547); European Travel Services, Str. Orzari 5 (t021/323 6187, ⊛www.european-travel-services.com); J'Info Tours, Str. Jules Michelet 1 (☎021/222 5010); SimpaTurism, Str. Puțu cu Plopi 18 (☎021/312 7495, ⊛www.simpaturism.ro) and at Str. Calderon 1 (☎021/314 0323) for city tours; Paralela 45, B-dul Regina Elisabeta 29–31 (☎021/311 1958, ⊛www.paralela45.ro) for ski and spa bookings.

Around Bucharest

There's a fine selection of places to visit in Bucharest's immediate surroundings. The city is ringed by some superb monasteries, such as **Căldăruşani** and **Snagov**, country houses – most notably **Mogoşoaia** – and interesting villages, such as Clejani, which is home to some of the country's finest Gypsy music. However, without your own transport, many of these places are quite hard to reach, the only option in most cases a painfully slow and crowded bus ride.

North of Bucharest

If you travel to Snagov by road, you'll pass through the area most notoriously affected by Ceauşescu's **systematization** programme (see box on p.90). **Baloteşti**, just north of Otopeni airport, consists of stark modern apartment buildings housing people displaced from villages, such as Dimieni, which lay just east of the airport. Vlădiceasca and Cioflinceni, just off the DN1 on the road to Snagov, were bulldozed in 1988, and the inhabitants resettled in Ghermăneşti, on the western outskirts of Snagov.

Four kilometres east of Baloteşti is **CĂCIULAŢI**, built as a planned estate village by the Ghica family, whose villa – now the property of the Romanian Academy – was occupied by the Securitate; over 300 bodies, unrecorded victims of the communist police state, were found buried in its run-down park in the mid-1990s. Seven **trains** a day from Bucharest (to Urziceni) stop here and, of these, five continue on to **GRECI**, another 10km east. A couple of kilometres south of Greci is the **Căldăruşani Monastery**, which is beyond the reach of public transport from Bucharest. This inconvenience didn't stop the world press from mobbing it when tennis stars Mariana Simionescu and Bjorn Borg were married here in 1980. The church where the wedding took place was built in 1638 by Matei Basarab and is noted for its school of icon painting, established in 1787. Among the many icons on display here are eight by the juvenile Grigorescu (see box on p.101), who studied at the school from 1854 to 1855. The monastery is now home to some thirty monks and over 150 boys attending the priest school. Father Calinic may be able to give you a short guided-tour of the church and also take you down to the ossuary, where a large number of monks' skulls are held.

Snagov

SNAGOV, a small sprawling village 40km north of Bucharest, is the most popular weekend destination for Bucharestians: its beautiful sixteen-kilometre-long lake comes complete with watersports facilities and a reserve for water plants, such as Indian waterlily, arrowhead, and also oriental beech. In the centre of the lake is an island occupied by a **monastery** built in 1519. King Mihai and later Ceauşescu and other high functionaries had their weekend villas around the shore, and the lake was also the scene of the summit which saw Yugoslavia's expulsion from the Warsaw Pact in 1948. Bălcescu and other revolutionaries of 1848 were held in the monastery's prison, as was the Hungarian leader Imre Nagy following the Soviet invasion of 1956.

Visitors now come here principally to seek the **tomb of Dracula**, sited in front of the church altar. Though lacking identifying inscriptions, its likely that this is indeed the burial place of Vlad the Impaler: the richly dressed corpse exhumed in 1935 had been decapitated, as had Vlad, whose head was supposedly dispatched, wrapped and perfumed, as a gift to the Sultan. Vlad's murder is believed to have occurred in the forests nearby, and the monks would have been predisposed to take the body, since both Vlad and his father had given money to the monastery. Indeed, Vlad is thought to have had quite a hand in its development, insisting that several features be added, including, appropriately enough, a prison and torture chamber. To get across to the island, you can hire a rowing boat (€3) from the jetty on the southern shore of the lake, just past the Complex Astoria (see below); follow the reeds round to the left until the monastery comes into view – give yourself a good couple of hours to make the trip over and back. Note that you must be appropriately dressed to gain admittance to the monastery.

Nine **buses** a day make the rather long-winded trip from the Băneasa bus station – located 500m west of Băneasa airport on B-dul Ionescu de la Brad 1 – to Snagov. Get the driver to drop you off at the fork in the road 1km beyond the village, and walk the remaining half a kilometre or so to the **Complex Astoria**, a large and crowded leisure park on the lake's southern shore; there's a small entrance fee payable to enter the complex (€0.50 per person and €2.50 for cars). Although it's unlikely you'll need, or want, to stay here, the complex contains the overpriced *Snagov Minihotel* (☎021/313 6782; ⑥), and an unofficial **campsite** with the most basic facilities. There's better accommodation in the village of **Ghermăneşti**, 2km south of Snagov, namely the roadside *Pension Galanton* at Ghermăneşti 18 (☎0722/222 353; ⑤), which has a dozen smartly furnished rooms, restaurant and pool – the bus to Snagov stops in the village.

Mogoşoaia

The lovely palace at **MOGOŞOAIA** (Tues–Sun 10am–6pm), 10km northwest of Bucharest along the DN1, is perhaps Wallachia's most important non-religious monument. Designed by Constantin Brâncoveanu in 1698–1702, it's

Systematization

Systematization was Ceauşescu's policy to do away with up to half the country's villages and move the rural population into larger centres. The concept was first developed by Nikita Krushchev in the Soviet Union in 1951, to combat the move-ment of younger people to the towns by **amalgamating villages** to raise the standard of rural life. Similar plans were put forward in Hungary, and in 1967 Ceauşescu reorganized Romania's local government system and announced a scheme to get rid of up to 6300 villages and replace them with 120 new towns and 558 agro-industrial centres.

His declared aim (based on an original idea in Marx and Engels' *Communist Manifesto*) was "to wipe out radically the major differences between towns and villages; to bring the working and living conditions of the working people in the countryside closer to those in the towns", by herding people together into apartment buildings so that "the community fully dominates and controls the individual", and thus produce Romania's "new socialist man". Thankfully, the project was forgotten while Ceauşescu was preoccupied by other prestige projects such as the Danube–Black Sea Canal and Bucharest's Centru Civic, but he relaunched it in March 1988, when he was becoming obsessed with increasing exports and paying off the national debt.

Since collectivization, Romania's agricultural output had declined steadily, and this on fertile land with one of the longest growing seasons in Europe. In 1985, the minuscule private sector produced 29 percent of the country's fruit, 14 percent of its meat and almost 20 percent of its milk. Ceauşescu was determined to **revolution-ize agriculture** by increasing the growing area, while also further increasing centralization and reducing the scope and incentive for individual initiative. While the peasants had previously been able to support themselves with their own livestock, there was to be no accommodation for animals in the new blocks. To add insult to injury, the peasants were to receive derisory compensation for their demolished homes and then be charged rent.

The model development was to be the **Ilfov Agricultural Sector**, immediately north of Bucharest, where the first evictions and demolitions took place in August

a two-storey building of red brick with a Venetian-style loggia overlooking a lake. After Brâncoveanu's execution, the palace became an inn, then, after a fire destroyed the interior, a warehouse. Towards the end of the nineteenth century, the palace was passed to the Bibescu family (descendants of Brâncoveanu), before finally being handed over to the state in 1956.

At the end of the long drive, which extends from the main road up to the palace, you pass the small St George's Chapel (1688) before entering the com-plex proper through the entry tower; to the left is the L-shaped great house, to the right, the old kitchen, and straight in front, the main palace building. Its interior is now given over to a series of rather dull, furniture-less (thanks to Ceauşescu, who requisitioned it all) rooms, occasionally brightened up with tapestries, vestments and icons, whilst the fine vaulted cellar to the left of the entrance contains a stack of stoneworks. The lush gardens, and the lake behind the main building, do, however, make a visit worthwhile, and there's some good rambling to be had in the nearby woods. Hidden away on waste ground behind the old kitchen wall is a mammoth statue of Lenin, removed from Piaţa Presei Liberă and dumped here after the 1989 revolution; next to the prostrate Russian leader is the statue of the former communist prime minister Petru Groza. The easiest way to get to Mogoşoaia is by **maxitaxi** (heading for Buftea), or **bus** #460 from the Laromet tram terminus. A less enticing option

1988; only two or three days notice was given before shops were closed down and bus services stopped, forcing the people into the designated villages. Entire communities were removed to blocks in Otopeni and Ghermăneşti, where up to ten families had to share one kitchen and the sewage system had not been completed. At the same time, the villagers of Buda and Ordoreanu, just south of Bucharest on the River Argeş, were relocated to Bragadiru to make way for a reservoir for the proposed Bucharest–Danube Canal. In other villages across the nation – including, fittingly, Scorniceşti, Ceauşescu's birthplace in Wallachia – ugly **concrete Civic Centre buildings** began to appear in the centres of the planned New Towns.

Repairs were banned in all the doomed villages and on all single-storey buildings, but these regulations were interpreted differently by the various counties. In Maramureş, the authorities, aware that greater distances to the agricultural land would be a disadvantage, allowed repair work on outlying farms and also permitted attics to count as a second storey. In the Banat, efforts were made to attract migrants to houses left by emigrating Schwabs, although these should have been demolished.

There was widespread condemnation of this scheme that was set to uproot half of the rural populace; in August 1988, the Cluj academic **Doina Cornea**, one of the country's few open dissidents, wrote an open letter (published in the West) in protest, pointing out that the villages, with their unbroken folk culture, are the spiritual centre of Romanian life, and that to demolish them would be to "strike at the very soul of the people". She was soon placed under house arrest, but the campaign abroad gathered pace. Although the Hungarian view that the plan was an attack on their community was widely accepted, It does seem clear that Ceauşescu's aim was indeed a wholesale assault on the rural way of life.

Approximately eighteen villages had suffered major demolitions by the end of 1989, when the scheme was at once cancelled by the FSN, the new ruling party following the revolution; new buildings are going up all over the country, and those people uprooted by Ceauşescu's scheme are returning to the sites of their villages and starting all over again.

is to take one of the five daily local **trains** (to Urziceni), although this entails a 3km walk back along the tracks into the village.

Clejani

Some 40km southwest of Bucharest is the small village of **CLEJANI**, renowned throughout the region as a centre for **Gypsy music**; the world-famous band Taraf de Haidouks (see p.413) live here when they're not touring, as well as a number of other tremendously talented musicians. If you're a fan of such music, or if you're just interested in experiencing Gypsy culture close up, then take half a day to visit the village – and if you're lucky, you may get to hear some of the spellbinding music first-hand.

The village itself is unremarkable, but the Gypsy settlement – little more than a dusty, mud-dried street lined with crumbling, one-roomed homes – is easily found; upon arriving at the village from Vadu Lat (see below), take the first left, continue walking for 400m and you'll find the Gypsy settlement on your right. Strangers are few and far between here, and you may initially feel a little intimidated, but for every pair of eyes fixed on you there will be a bare-footed, grinning child tagging along, eager to have their photo taken. Whilst it's doubtful that you'll even find the Taraf de Haidouks (likely to be away touring), let alone afford to pay for them, you may well find another group who will be

ore than happy to put on an impromptu **performance**; ask around for
ndin Marin, also known as Zis Tagoia, who should be able to gather together
the Taraf de Plugări band. It's expected that you'll offer some money in return
for the band's efforts (€10–15 would be appropriate), and a few bottles of beer
wouldn't go amiss either. Whilst at the settlement, take the opportunity to
wander around; it's likely you'll get invited into someone's house, which will
give you the opportunity to witness first-hand the paucity of Gypsy life.

To get to Clejani from Bucharest, take one of the five daily **trains** from the
Gara Basarab to Vadu Lat (the last train back to Bucharest is at 10pm). From
the station, it's a 3km walk: turn right and continue along the tracks for 100m
until you come to some steps set into an embankment; from here, walk along
the path across the field until you come to the main road, then turn left and
carry on walking for 2km – there's also a good chance you'll be able to hitch
a ride.

Travel details

Trains

Bucharest to: Baia Mare (2 daily; 11hr–13hr);
Braşov (23 daily; 2hr 30min–4hr 45min); Cluj (6
daily; 7hr–11hr 15min); Constanţa (10–15 daily;
2hr 30min–5hr 30min); Craiova (17 daily; 2hr
30min–4hr 45min); Galaţi (5 daily; 3hr 30min–5hr
15min); Giurgiu Nord (8 daily; 1hr 30min); Iaşi (6
daily; 5hr 30min–7hr 45min); Mangalia (4–7 daily;
3hr 45min–5hr 15min); Oradea (2 daily; 11hr);
Piteşti (10 daily; 1hr 30min–3hr); Ploieşti (every
20–60min; 45min–1hr 45min); Satu Mare (2 daily;
13–14hr); Sibiu (5 daily; 4hr 45min–11hr 30min);
Sighişoara (10 daily; 4hr–7hr 30min); Suceava (5
daily; 5hr 30min–6hr 30min); Târgovişte (5 daily;
1hr 15min–2hr 15min); Timişoara (7 daily; 7hr
30min–10hr 30min); Tulcea (2 daily; 5hr
45min–6hr 45min).

Buses and maxitaxis

Bucharest (Băneasa) to: Snagov (9 daily).
Bucharest to: Bacau (10 daily); Braşov (every
30min); Craiova (every 30min); Piatra Neamţ (10
daily); Piteşti (every 45min); Sibiu (2 daily); Sinaia
(every 30min); Târgu Mureş (7 daily).

Planes

Bucharest (Băneasa airport) to: Arad (12
weekly); Iaşi (20 weekly); Satu Mare (3 weekly);
Suceava (20 weekly); Timişoara (6 weekly).
Bucharest (Otopeni airport) to: Cluj (9 weekly);
Constanţa (4 weekly); Oradea (6 weekly); Satu
Mare (3 weekly); Timişoara (10 weekly).

International trains

Bucharest to: Belgrade, Serbia (1 daily; 12hr
30min); Budapest, Hungary (4 daily; 12–13hr);
Chişinău, Moldova (1 daily; 12hr 30min); Kiev,
Ukraine (1 daily; 30hr); Moscow, Russia (1 daily;
45hr); Prague, Czech Republic (2 daily; 23hr);
Ruse, Bulgaria (3 daily; 2hr 30min–3hr); Sofia,
Bulgaria (2 daily; 10hr 30min); Thessaloniki,
Greece (1 daily; 23hr); Vienna, Austria (2 daily;
17hr).

International buses

Bucharest to: Athens, Greece (Tues & Fri);
Chişinău (1 daily); Istanbul, Turkey (3 daily).

2

Wallachia

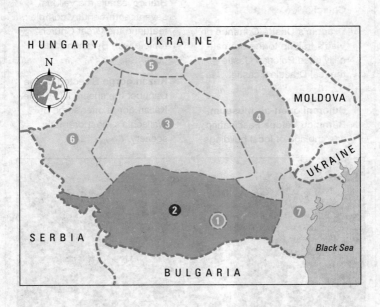

CHAPTER 2

Highlights

* **Princely Court, Târgovişte**
Survey the ruins of the Princely Court, from where Vlad the Impaler once ruled the Wallachian lands. See p.102

* **Curtea de Argeş** Attractive small town with two of the region's most striking ecclesiastical monuments – the Princely Church and Episcopal Church. See p.109

* **Dracula's Castle** Continue on Vlad's trail up to the dramatically sited Poienari Castle – the real Dracula's castle. See p.110

* **Bujoreni open-air museum, Râmnicu Vâlcea** Fascinating assemblage of local buildings and other structures from the Olt valley region. See p.112

* **Brâncuşi's sculptures, Târgu Jiu** Outdoor collection of some of the great Romanian's most famous sculptures, including the *Endless Column*. See p.114

* **Horezu Monastery** Brâncoveanu's marvellous seventeenth-century complex, featuring the Great Church replete with Byzantine frescoes. See p.117

* **Kazan gorge** Bisected by the Danube, the sheer cliffs of the Kazan gorge offer some of Wallachia's most dramatic scenery. See p.122

△ Kazan gorge

2

Wallachia

Centuries before the name "Romania" appeared on maps of Europe, foreign merchants and rulers had heard of **Wallachia**, the land of the Vlachs or Wallachs, known in Romanian as Ţară Romaneasca (Land of the Romanians). A distant outpost of Christendom, it succumbed to the Turks in 1417 and was then largely forgotten until the nineteenth century. Occasional travellers reported on the region's backwardness and the corruption of its ruling boyars, but few predicted its sudden union with Moldavia in 1859 – the first step in the creation of modern Romania. Today, in the highlands and on the Bărăgan Steppe – where pagan rites such as the festivals of Ariet and Căluş are still practiced – peasant life largely follows the ancient pastoral cycle, but industrialization and collective farming have wrought huge changes to the plains around **Ploieşti**, **Piteşti**, **Craiova** and the Jiu Valley, all places that now have little to recommend them. The region is mainly comprised of flat and featureless agricultural land, and is in many ways the least interesting of Romania's three principal provinces, but as it is home to the nation's capital, Bucharest, people will invariably find themselves passing through en route to Transylvania, the coast, or Bulgaria.

The most rewarding part of Wallachia is its western half, known (after its chief river) as Oltenia, which stretches from Bucharest via Târgovişte and Curtea de Argeş to the Iron Gates on the Danube. Here, the foothills of the Carpathians are largely scenic and unspoilt, and possessed of the region's most attractive and historically interesting towns, such as Sinaia (see p.135) and **Curtea de Argeş**. Moreover, both **Poienari castle**, north of Curtea de Argeş, and the town of **Târgovişte**, have strong connections with Vlad Ţepeş, better known as Dracula, who was once ruler of Wallachia even though modern myth links him with Transylvania. In addition, a string of fine monasteries, such as **Horezu** and **Arnota**, runs along the foothills; most were raised at the behest of "progressive" despots (who otherwise spent their time fighting the Turks and repressing their own peasantry), but were rebuilt in the late seventeenth century in the distinctively Romanian style developed by Constantin Brâncoveanu. The remainder of the region is dominated by large industrialized centres, such as **Ploieşti**, **Piteşti**, **Craiova** and **Târgu Jiu**, the last of which does at least have the work of Romania's world renowned sculptor Constantin Brâncuşi as a major inducement to visit. Otherwise, there's a fine excursion to be had up along the **Kazan gorge**, near the Danube's Iron Gates that mark the border with Serbia.

Wallachia is renowned for its **festivals**. During the third week in February, folk musicians gather for the Izvoare fermecate festival at Târgu Jiu, while Polovragi to the east is the setting for a big fair between July 15 and 20. Another fair, devoted to pottery, coincides with the Songs of the Olt festival at

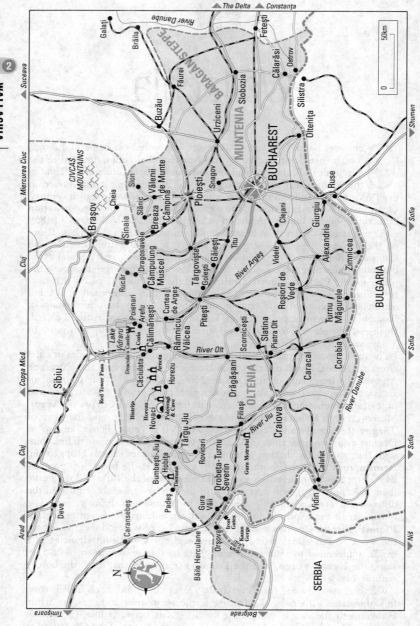

Calimăneşti during the first week in August; and on August 15, pan-pipers congregate at Tismana. **Getting around** the region is easy enough: trains fan out from Bucharest in all directions, serving most place listed here, whilst regular maxitaxis shuttle between the capital and the larger towns, including more distant destinations such as Craiova and Târgu Jiu.

Ploieşti, Târgovişte and Piteşti

The large industrial towns of **Ploieşti** and **Piteşti** are typical of much of Wallachia as a whole, but though neither is very attractive nor possesses much in the way of sights, they do serve as useful springboards for more enticing destinations in the region. Ploieşti lies on the principal road and rail line between Bucharest and Transylvania, with a couple of sites of interest to the north, while Piteşti is situated astride the main routes from Bucharest to Câmpulung and the Argeş and Olt valleys. The most worthwhile of the three major towns north and northwest of Bucharest is **Târgovişte**, the old capital of Wallachia, boasting several ancient churches and the ruins of Vlad Ţepeş's court.

Ploieşti and around

An oily smell and the eerie nighttime flare of vented gases proclaim **PLOIEŞTI** as Romania's biggest oil town. In 1857, the world's first oil wells were sunk here and in Petrolia, Ontario; the first ever refinery was built in Ploieşti, and Bucharest became the first city in the world to be lit by oil lamps. By the outbreak of World War I, there were ten refineries in the town, all owned by foreign oil companies; these were wrecked in 1916 by British agents to deny them to the Germans, and patched together again only to be destroyed once more, this time by the retreating German forces in 1918. However, it was the townsfolk who really paid the price, when Allied aircraft carpet-bombed Ploieşti in 1944 – hence, the town centre's almost total concrete uniformity today. The main reason to come to Ploieşti is to take advantage of the excellent **train links** to the more interesting parts of Wallachia.

Arrival and information

Generally speaking, trains to and from Transylvania use Ploieşti's Vest station, southwest of town at the end of Strada Maraşeşti, while those to and from Moldavia use Ploieşti Sud, 1km south of town on Piaţa 1 Decembrie 1918; trains from Bucharest may arrive at either. The two stations are linked by bus #2, both of which pass close to the centre of the town. There are two **bus stations**, the Nord on Strada Dragolina, fifteen minutes' walk north of the centre and served by the occasional bus #4 (Mon–Fri), and the grubby Sud, 200m west of the **train station** of the same name. **TAROM** has an office next to the department store at B-dul Republicii 17 (☎0244/195 620), with the **CFR** office in the same building.

The Town

There's little to detain you in Ploieşti, though the town does have several moderately interesting museums. In the huge Neoclassical Palace of Culture at Str. Catalin 1, the natural sciences museum has been transformed into the **Museum of Human Biology** (Tues–Fri 9am–5pm, Sat & Sun 9am–1pm), whose eye-catching displays on evolution, anatomy and ecology make it one of the most striking museums of its kind in Romania. In the same building, the

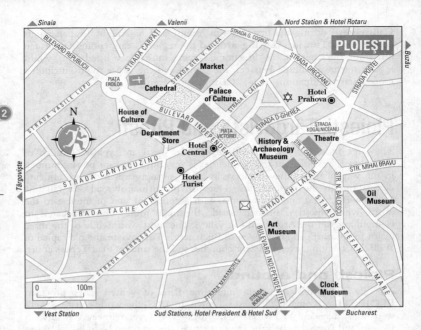

Ethnography Museum (Tues–Fri 8am–4pm, Sat & Sun 9am–1pm) houses more conventional displays of peasant costumes and artefacts, mostly from the Carpathian foothills. The intermittently interesting **Oil Museum** at Str. Bagdascar 10 (Tues–Sun 9am–5pm) has a comprehensive account of its origins in Romania, whilst the **History and Archaeology Museum**, nearby at Str. Toma Caragiu 10 (Tues–Sun 9am–5pm), records the wartime destruction of the town and also dedicates two rooms to Romanian sporting achievements, particularly Olympic and footballing feats. The town's most enjoyable museum, however, is the **Art Museum** at B-dul Independenţei 1 (Tues–Sun 10am–6pm), a fine, recently restored neo-Baroque building holding a healthy collection of paintings by several of Romania's foremost artists, including Aman, Pallady and Grigorescu, as well as some impressive Orthodox icons from Greece and Russia. Ploieşti's most unusual museum is the **Clock Museum** (Tues–Sun 9am–5pm) at Str. Simache 1, where you can view (and listen to) an engagingly varied collection of clocks and timepieces.

Accommodation

For a town of such limited tourist appeal, there's an unfeasibly large amount of **accommodation** here. The two best options – both of which are convenient for the Sud train and bus stations – are the clean, cheap and modern *Hotel Sud* (☎0244/597 411; ❸) in between the two stations at Str. Depoului 4; and, a little further west at Str. Bobâlna 88, the *Hotel President* (☎0244/596 376, Ⓦwww.restaurant-president.ro; ❼), whose six garishly coloured and eccentrically furnished rooms wouldn't look out of place in an *Austin Powers* movie – believe it or not, the mini-bar is free. A good third option is the comely *Rotaru*, a ten-minute walk north of the centre at Str. Patriei 8 (☎0244/594 255; ❻), which is a small, rustic pension with ornate, but boxy, wood-furnished rooms; from the Palace of Culture, head up Strada E. Cătălin, cross Strada G. Coşbuc,

The Ploieşti ploy

In 1940, it was feared that Germany would occupy Romania – as it had in World War I – to guarantee oil supplies from what was then Europe's second largest producer (after the Soviet Union). There was tacit support from the neutral Romanian government for Anglo–French plans to **sabotage the oil wells**, thus making a German invasion pointless, but technical problems and bad luck meant that these never went ahead. The back-up plan, to stop the oil barges reaching Germany along the Danube by sinking barges in the Iron Gates gorge and blocking the navigable channel, was a greater fiasco: the Germans soon found out about the British barges making their way upstream from Galaţi, supposedly in secret, and forced the Romanian authorities to expel the crews (naval ratings ill-disguised as art students).

A third plan involved the RAF bombing the oil wells from its bases around Larissa in Greece. However, the 660km route would have taken the early Wellington bombers over Musala, the highest peak in southeastern Europe, to an altitude that would be at the extreme limits of their range. Following severe maintenance problems, the plan was abandoned. It wasn't long after this that the Allies were driven out of Greece, allowing the Axis powers access to Romania's oil wells, from which it subsequently obtained a third of its aviation fuel. On August 1, 1943, 178 new American Liberator B-24Ds took off from bases in North Africa and launched a surprise attack on **Ploieşti** in what was then the longest-range bombing raid; although at least 360 crew were lost, a heavy blow was dealt to the Nazi war machine. By 1944, further raids had succeeded in halving oil production, despite terrible Allied losses.

---

then up Strada Romană – Strada Patriei is the next street on the right. Otherwise, there's little to distinguish between the three other hotels, all of which are rather dated: the *Turist*, at Str. Tache Ionescu 6 (℡0244/150 441; ⑥), which has a/c rooms; the *Central*, Str. Tache Ionescu 2 (℡0244/126 641; ⑤–⑥); and the *Prahova*, a grim high-rise block at Str. Dobrogeanu-Gherea 11 (℡0244/126 850, ℻126 302; ④–⑦). Without your own transport it's almost impossible to reach the **campsites**: *Româneşti* (11km south on the DN1 towards Bucharest at km49), *Pădurea Păuleşti* (8km north on the DN1 to km68.5 and 3km east) and *Paralela 45* (with rooms, 19km north on the DN1 at km79).

Eating and drinking

Choices for **eating** in Ploieşti are limited to the very good restaurant in the *President* hotel, which has a surprisingly eclectic mix of Indian and Mexican cuisine; the *Pelican* restaurant, a ten-minute walk south along Bulevard Independenţei at Str. Bobâlna 9, whose rustically attired waitresses serve up wholesome Romanian fare; and, across the road at Ana Ipătescu 7, the *Vienna Café*, which covers the whole gamut of soups, salads, pastas and grilled meat dishes – they've also got a great little bar menu available until 4pm. This also happens to be just about the liveliest **drinking** venue in town. For quick snacks, try the market behind the Palace of Culture or the several stand-up places (pizza and *gogoş*) next to the post office.

Around Ploieşti

From Ploieşti, the DN1 and the DN1A head north towards Braşov, the gateway into Transylvania. The DN1 is the main route, passing through the small towns of **Câmpina**, **Breaza**, Sinaia (see p.135) and Buşteni (see p.139), and the rail line follows the road closely right through to Braşov. The DN1A, a much quieter and more relaxing route, runs along the lovely **Teleajen valley** into the foothills of the Carpathian mountains; public transport along this route is poor, but it is well worth considering if you have your own car or bike.

Câmpina

CÂMPINA, another of Romania's key oil towns, lies on the DN1, 32km north of Ploieşti, just before the mountains of the Prahova valley begin. Like Ploieşti, Câmpina was heavily bombed during the war and hence is not an attractive place, though it does have two tourist sights that just about make a stop-off worthwhile. Around 1km north of the centre, across the rail tracks and up by the bend in the road, the unassuming **Nicolae Grigorescu memorial house** at B-dul Carol I no. 166, was where the eponymous artist spent the last years of his life (see box on p.101); it's a modest, yet enjoyable collection of his oeuvre, including a self-portrait and the painting he was completing when he died. Five minutes' walk further along the road, at no. 145, is **Hasdeu Castle** (Tues–Sun 9am–5pm), an odd cruciform structure with battlements and buttresses, built in 1894–96 by historian and linguist Bogdan Petriceico Hasdeu (1838–1907), one of the progenitors of the nationalist and anti-semitic philosophy that infected Romanian politics throughout the twentieth century. He built the castle as a memorial to his daughter Julia, to plans he claims were transmitted by her in séances. After finishing high school, Julia went to study in Paris, and would have been the first Romanian woman to receive a doctorate from the Sorbonne had she not died of tuberculosis in 1888, aged just nineteen. Amongst the many items retained within the castle is the desk she used in France. She also left three volumes of plays and poetry, all of which were published after her death.

The **train** station is 3km west of Câmpina but is connected to the centre by maxitaxis, whilst the **bus** station is south of town on Str. N. Bălcescu. If you're really desperate to stay, then the two unappealing choices are the *Casa Tineretului* youth hotel, next to the bus station at Str. N. Bălcescu 50 (T0244/334 540; ❷), and the thoroughly depressing and absurdly overpriced *Muntenia* hotel at B-dul Carol I no. 62 (T0244/333 090, F333 092; ❻).

Breaza

The small town of **BREAZA**, just a few kilometres north of Câmpina on a loop road off the DN1, is a good place to break-up a journey en-route to Sinaia and also offers the possibility of a quiet stopover. The town provides some excellent examples of the local architectural style – with many houses having carved wooden verandas – but Breaza's one real sight is the small Orthodox **church** of Sf Nicolae, a short walk south of the centre of town. Finished in 1777, the church's interior is totally covered in paintings; of special note is that of the *Last Judgement* in the porch.

Arriving by **train** entails an arduous two-kilometre-long walk uphill into town, which is little more than one long street; maxitaxis to Bucharest leave from the park. The best of the several pensions in town is the *Tudor house* at Str. Morii 7 (T0244/341 321; ❹), which has a handful of funkily designed en-suite rooms; it's a little tricky to find – walk north of the park for 400m, head down Str. Morii for 200m, then turn left down the path by the lamp post. There's also **accommodation** – double rooms (❺–❻), studio apartments (❻) and suites (❽–❾) – at the Lac de Verde **golf club** (T0244/343850, Wwww.lacdeverde.ro), 1.5km west of town at Str. Caraiman 57 (it's signposted). The short but very scenic nine-hole course (€20 for 9-holes, €30 for 18-holes) is one of the few courses in Romania.

Nicolae Grigorescu

Romania's most famous painter, **Nicolae Grigorescu**, was born in 1838 and came to Bucharest at the age of ten to train as a church painter; his earliest signed works, dating from 1853, are in the church of Sf Constantine and Helena in Baicoi (near Ploieşti). Grigorescu subsequently worked in Căldăruşani (1854–55), in Zamfira (1856–58), and in Agapia (1858–60), where his work represents the high point of Romanian classicism. Here, he met Kogălniceanu, who arranged a grant for him to study in Paris, where he became a friend of Millet, joining the Barbizon group and beginning to paint *en plein air*. In 1869, he returned to Romania, where he painted society portraits, but also toured the Prahova, Dâmboviţa and Muscel counties painting local characters in a mobile studio in an adapted coach. In 1877–78, he accompanied the army in the War of Independence, producing, among others, major works of the battle of Griviţa. Grigorescu held his first solo exhibition in 1881, which was a great success, and from 1881 to 1884 he lived in Paris. He kept a studio here until 1894, although from 1890 he spent increasing amounts of his time with his companion Maria Danciu in **Câmpina**, where he died in 1907.

For **food**, there's a mini supermarket, a pizzeria and the *Temperanţa* restaurant – possibly the only temperance restaurant in Romania – all clustered together in the centre.

Continuing northwards from here takes you to Sinaia and Buşteni in the magnificent Prahova valley (see p.134) and on into Transylvania.

The Teleajen valley

The main place to stop along the DN1A route to Braşov is **VĂLENII DE MUNTE**, served by trains from Ploieşti 30km to the south; the town's train and bus station are just south of its two **hotels**, both located on the main thoroughfare, B-dul N. Iorga – the smart hotel *Capitol* at no. 50 (☎0244/281 965; ❹) and the grim but cheap *Ciucaş* hotel at no. 77 (☎0244/280 425; ❸). A few hundred metres north of the *Ciucaş*, at B-dul Iorga 90, is a fine **memorial house** (Tues–Sun 9am–5pm) dedicated to the great historian and former prime minister Nicolae Iorga, who lived here from 1910 until his murder by the Iron Guard in 1940; ironically, Iorga founded the National Democratic Party, a predecessor of the Guard. As well as some beautiful furniture, many of Iorga's personal effects – books, handwritten letters, family photos and portraits – have been neatly preserved. There's also a lovely little ethnographic collection here, featuring some superb glass- and wood-painted Orthodox icons.

From Vălenii, a minor road heads west for 11km to **SLĂNIC** (sometimes known as Slănic Prahova, to distinguish it from Slănic Moldova, to the north). Here, the Muntele de Sare, or Salt Mountains – a product of the salt mining that has taken place in the area since at least 1532 – stand between two lakes in which you can swim in summer. The town's salt-working heritage is displayed in the tiny **Museum of Salt** (daily 9am–7pm), housed in the Casa Cămărăşiei (the former Salt Chancellery built in 1800) at Str. 23 August no. 9. More worthwhile is the **Unirea Mine Complex** (Tues–Sun 9am–3pm), a ten-minute walk east of town across the bridge, which displays scenes from Romanian history carved in salt. Slănic lies at the end of a rail line from Ploieşti Sud via Ploieşti Vest; some of the six daily trains do the distance in an hour and a quarter, but others stop for 45 minutes in Plopeni. The only **accommodation** in Slănic is the run-of-the-mill hotel *Slanic* at Str. 13 Decembrie 15 (☎0244/240 131; ❹).

North of Vălenii, a minor road forks east off the DN1A, and about 7km along that another minor road strikes off north, running parallel to the DN1A and ending at the small village of **SLON**, 22km north of Vălenii. Five buses a day run from Ploieşti via Vălenii to this woodworking centre, which produces barrels, spindles, spoons and shingles; it is very much a working village, but you may be able to invite yourself into one of the workshops.

The DN1A continues north along the Teleajen valley past Suzana nunnery (built in the eighteenth century and rebuilt in 1835–38 with icons by Tattarescu) to the pleasantly relaxed resort of **CHEIA**, 35km north of Vălenii, at the foot of the Ciucaş mountains; minibuses to the resort meet trains at Măneciu, 17km north of Vălenii. As part of the Antrec scheme, Cheia has a good stock of guest and farmhouses that make useful bases for exploring the surrounding area; you can either take potluck by wandering around looking for somewhere (places to stay are indicated), or book ahead through the Prahova branch of Antrec (☎0244/192 915, ✆prahova@antrec.ro). From Cheia, the DN1A continues due north into the **Ciucaş mountains**, a compact range of weirdly eroded conglomerate outcrops and pillars, with fine open walking country all around. The Bratocea Pass is away to the northwest, between the Roşu and Ciucaş mountains. Seven kilometres from Cheia, at the foot of the mountains, is the *Muntele Roşu* cabana (❶), from where it's a two-hour walk up to the friendly but basic *Ciucaş* cabana (❶). From the Bratocea Pass, the road leads downhill all the way past the *Babarunca* cabana (❶) into Săcele and Braşov.

Târgovişte

TÂRGOVIŞTE, 50km west of Ploieşti on the DN72, was the capital of Wallachia for more than two centuries, vestiges of which can be seen in the old Princely Court complex, the town's principal attraction and the one major reason for coming here. In recent times, the town has been best known as an industrial centre, producing equipment for the oil industry, but gained notoriety when Nicolae and Elena Ceauşescu were executed in its army barracks on Christmas Day, 1989.

The Town and around

The **Princely Court** (Curtea Domneasca; Tues–Sun 9am–5pm, summer until 7pm), lies north of the centre on Calea Domneasca (on some maps this is still shown as Strada Nicolae Bălcescu). Now a mass of crumbling ramparts, with a few well-preserved sections, it was once the royal seat of Wallachia (1415–1659), from where more than forty voivodes exercised their rule – all of whom are denoted on the inside wall of the southern gate, the entrance to the complex. The Princely Court figured large in the life of **Vlad the Impaler** (see p.421), who spent his early years here, until he and his brother Radu were sent by their father to Anatolia as hostages. Following the murder of his father and his eldest brother, Mircea, who was buried alive by Wallachia's boyars, Vlad returned to be enthroned here in 1456, and waited three years before taking his revenge. Invited with their families to feast at court on Easter Sunday, the boyars were half-drunk when guards suddenly grabbed them and impaled them forthwith upon stakes around town, sparing only the fittest who were marched off to labour on Vlad's castle at Poienari (see p.110). Dominating the complex is the twenty-seven-metre-high **Sunset Tower** (Turnul Chindiei), raised during the fifteenth century and originally used as a watchtower for Vlad's soldiers. It now houses an exhibition, albeit in

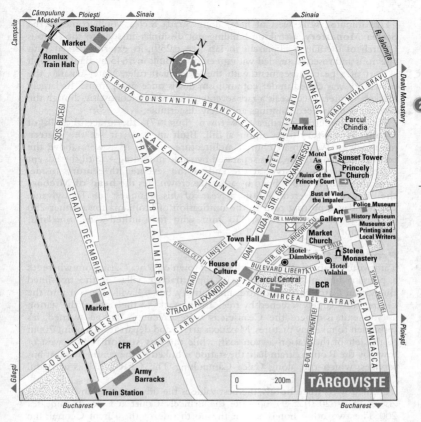

Romanian, charting his life and times; there are also some terrific views of the complex and the rest of the town from the top of the tower. Nearby stands the sixteenth-century **Princely Church**, where Vlad's successors used to attend services, sitting upstairs in a special section screened from the congregation. The interior contains a vast iconostasis, as well as dozens of wall painted frescoes of Wallachian princes, such as Basarab, Catacuzino and Brâncoveanu.

Due south of the Princely Court, along Calea Domneasca, are a triple-header of museums, the first two of which are the **Art Gallery** (Tues–Sun 9am–5pm) and **History Museum** (Tues–Sun: winter 9am–5pm; summer 10am–6pm). The latter was set up in the former Law Courts by Ceauşescu in 1986, and the first floor, now used for temporary art shows, was devoted to his achievements. At the same time, he removed the heating from the art gallery, housed in the former prefecture opposite, which, as a consequence, is now in a terrible condition – at the time of writing, it was closed pending extensive renovation. Across the way is the unlikely sounding **Museum of Romanian Police** (daily 9am–5pm), not surprisingly the only one of its kind in the country. As well as charting the history and evolution of the Romanian police, it also exhibits costumes garnered from numerous forces from around the world, including an old-fashioned British bobby's uniform.

Five minutes' walk west of here, along Strada Stelea, you'll come to the **Stelea Monastery**, a striking building not dissimilar in style to the famous Church of the Three Hierarchs in Iaşi (see p.259), its exterior carved with chevrons and rosettes studded with green discs. Built in 1645 by Basil the Wolf as part of a peace agreement with the Wallachian ruler, Matei Basarab, the monastery was closed under communism but is once more in use. Its largely blackened interior conceals a rare seventeenth-century iconostasis, though the Byzantine-influenced paintings are barely discernible.

Three kilometres northeast of town (bus #7), the graceful bulk of **Dealu Monastery** rises upon a hill. Built in 1501, it set the pattern for much of Wallachian church architecture – with its towers above the pronaos and cornice arcades separated by cable moulding – until the advent of the Brâncovenesc style at the end of the seventeenth century. Inside, beneath a marble slab topped by a bronze crown, lies the **head of Michael the Brave** – severed within a year of his conquest of Transylvania and Moldavia, putting paid to the unification of Romania for another 250 years. The inscription reads: "To him who first united our homeland, eternal glory".

Practicalities

Târgovişte's **train station** is southwest of town on Piaţa Garii, from where it's a pleasant fifteen-minute walk past the attractive villas of the tree-lined Bulevardul Carol I to the centre; alternatively, bus #4 will take you into the centre. Now largely screened by trees, the barracks to the right of the station as you exit is where the Ceauşescus were executed, but be warned, it's forbidden to take any pictures. Maxitaxis arrive and depart from a point 200m to the left of the station as you exit, while the **bus station** is 1km west of town by the Romlux train halt; the station is linked to the centre by most bus services, which run along Calea Câmpulung. The **CFR** office is at B-dul Carol I no. 2.

Of the town's three **hotels**, the best value is the tidy, seven-room *Motel Club As* (☎0245/620 012; ❷), opposite the Princely Court at Calea Domneasca 200. The two other hotels are on the north side of the Parcul Central: the *Dâmboviţa*, at B-dul Libertăţii 1 (☎0245/613 961, ⊛www.hoteldambovita.ro; ❺) has smart rooms overlooking the park; and 200m further along at B-dul Libertăţii 7 (☎0245/634 491, ⓕ615 658; ❸), is the cheaper *Valahia*, which is fine, if a little dull. The Priseaca **campsite** is 7km out along the Câmpulung road, reached by bus #18. The best of the very few **places to eat** in town is the *Crama Voievozilor* (just behind the *Hotel Valahia*), a neat little cellar restaurant serving up salads, spaghettis and schnitzels.

Piteşti and around

Situated at the end of Romania's only completed highway, some 100km northwest of Bucharest, **PITEŞTI** is another of Wallachia's dour industrial towns, though it does make a useful base for forays up into the Argeş valley. Much of the town's architectural appeal has been wrecked by earthquakes and subsequent re-buildings, and these days it's dominated by the Renault (formerly Dacia) factory – origin of most of Romania's cars – and the wood-working and petrochemical industries and their pollution. If you are planning to stop here en route to western Wallachia, come on a Friday or Saturday, when Piteşti fulfils its traditional role as a **market** town for the country folk of the Argeş valley.

For many Romanians, the town of Piteşti is synonymous with its **prison**, the scene under the early Stalinist regime of some of the most brutal psychiatric abuse anywhere in the Soviet bloc. In May 1948, there were mass arrests of dissident students, and from December 1949 about a thousand of them were brought here, to the "Student Re-education Centre", for a programme aimed at "re-adjusting the students to communist life" and eliminating the possibility of any new opposition developing. In fact, it simply set out to destroy the personality of the individual: by starvation, isolation, and above all by forcing prisoners to torture each other, breaking down all distinctions between prisoner and torturer, and thus between individual and state. "United by the evil they have both perpetrated and endured, the victim and the torturer thus become a single person. In fact, there is no longer a victim, ultimately no longer a witness", as Paul Goma put it in his book *The Dogs of Death*. Sixteen students died during this atrocious **"experiment"**.

The programme was extended to Gherla and other prisons and the Danube–Black Sea Canal labour camps, but security was looser here and the torture stopped when word got out. The experiment was abandoned in 1952, when the Stalinist leader Ana Pauker was purged; it was claimed that the authorities had not been involved, and in 1954, those running the Piteşti prison were tried secretly for murder and torture. The leader of the "Organization of Prisoners with Communist Convictions", Eugen Ţurcanu, was executed along with several of his henchmen, while others were sentenced to forced labour for life. Nevertheless, because of the guilt of all involved, both prisoners and guards, there followed a conspiracy of silence, which only began to break in 1989.

The Town

The heart of the town is Strada Victoriei, a broad pedestrianized throughfare variously lined with shops, cafés and hotels, with a couple of minor sights located at either end. Standing on a solitary patch of grass at its eastern end is the seventeenth-century **Princely Church** of Constantin Şerban, and at the opposite end, on Pasajul Victoriei, is the **Naïf Art Gallery** (Tues–Sun 9am–5pm), featuring a typically exuberant collection of works by local naïve painters. Fifty metres south of the Naïf, through the park at B-dul Republicii 33, is the town's main **Art Gallery** (Tues–Sun 9am–5pm), which houses a good sample of works by some of Romania's finest painters – Grigorescu, Pallady and Iser – as well as some intriguing wooden pieces by Gheorge Calineşti, one of the country's foremost sculptors.

South of B-dul Republicii on the parallel Strada Călinescu, the **County Museum** (Tues–Sun 10am–6pm), housed in the turn-of-the-century prefecture building, offers a standard review of the region's history, as well as a dull natural history section. A synagogue survives nearby at B-dul Noiembrie 1. The seventeenth-century **Trivale Hermitage**, southwest of the centre in Trivale Park, is nothing special, but it's a lovely twenty-minute, traffic-free walk to it up Strada Trivale through fine oak woods. Alternatively, buses #2A, #5 and #8 run up Strada Smeurei just to the east, leaving you in the midst of modern apartment blocks immediately above the hermitage. The **Ştrandului Argeş Park**, on the bank of the Argeş at the end of Strada Rurilor, contains a sports centre, outdoor pool and small beach area, all of which get very crowded in the warmer months.

Practicalities

The town's main **train station** is Piteşti Sud, linked to the centre by buses #2, #8 and #19 and frequent maxitaxis, although trains serving Curtea de

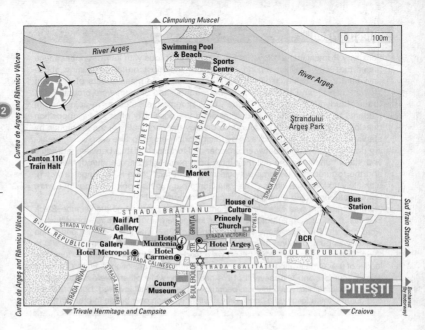

Arges also call at the Canton 110 halt (no ticket office) and at Piteşti Nord, in the northern suburbs. Piteşti's filthy **bus station** is located on Strada Târgul din Vale, to the northwest of the train station. The best source of **information** on the town and the region is the Muntenia tourist agency (Mon–Fri 8am–7pm, Sat 9am–1pm; ℡0248/625 463), next to the hotel of the same name on Piaţa Muntenia.

There's plentiful **accommodation** in town, all of it very central. Easily the best-value hotel is the colourful and modern *Metropol* (℡ & ℻0248/222 207; ❸), just off B-dul Republicii at Str. Panselelor 1, followed by the *Carmen* at B-dul Republicii 84 (℡0248/222 699, ℻290 433; ❹), which has a mix of older and newer rooms (❸), some of which overlook the park. Facing each other across Piaţa Muntenia are two state-run hotels, the very cheap and very basic *Arges* at no. 3 (℡0248/625 450, ℻214 556; ❷), which has singles and doubles with and without bathrooms; and, at no.1, the *Muntenia* (℡0248/625 450, ℻214 556; ❺–❼), an ugly concrete mass with a range of rooms of varying quality. There are also chalets (❷) in the Trivale Park **campsite** (℡0248/634 190).

There are a couple of highly commendable **restaurants** in town: the *Calabria*, across from the County Museum at Str. Eroilor 5, is an atmospheric Italian place dishing up steaming plates of pasta and spaghetti, and just around the corner, at Str. Primăverii 11, is *Athina*, a classy little Greek establishment serving the standard Greek staples. There's simpler fare at the *Sicilia in bocca* pizzeria and *cofetaria* at B-dul Republicii 41, which also has a great selection of cakes and ice cream. The liveliest **drinking** spots are *La Ureche*, next to *Sicilia*, and the *Garden Pub* on Strada Victoriei. **Internet access** is available at the *IQ Club* (daily 9am–1am), on the corner of Strada Victoriei and Strada Justiţiei.

Golești

The village of **GOLEȘTI**, 8km east of Pitești on the Bucharest rail line and just off route 7 (the road running parallel to the Bucharest–Ploiești highway), was once the fiefdom of the Golescus, one of the leading liberal families of nineteenth-century Wallachia – not only were they active members of both the 1821 and 1848 revolutions, but they also militated in favour of Romanian union in 1859 and Romanian independence in 1877. Their home – now at the heart of a very enjoyable open-air **Museum of Fruit and Vine Growing** (May–Sept; Tues–Sun 9am–5pm) – is in fact a *conac* or summer residence (winters would be spent in Bucharest or Paris), and is beautifully cool, with authentic furnishings and historical displays. The museum itself is behind the house, settled amongst plum and pear orchards, and comprising over one hundred structures from Romania's fruit- and vine-growing communities, mainly dwellings (including dug-out homes, or "pit houses"), but also churches, wine presses and wells – the oldest structure is the wooden church of Drăgutești, built in 1814. Over the gateway is the immaculately restored foișor or watchtower of Tudor Vladimirescu, leader of the 1821 peasant revolt, who was captured here and taken to Târgoviște where he was killed. Beside this stands an early nineteenth-century schoolhouse, which still retains some original fixtures and fittings, including German, Greek and Latin teaching books, and a sandbox that was used for practising writing. There's also an interesting little **Ethnographic Museum** (same times) in the grounds, exhibiting various viticultural implements, peasant costumes and craftworks. The village church, across the road from the museum's main gate, dates from 1646; if you want to look around, you'll need to ask in the village for the caretaker who will let you in to the church.

Câmpulung Muscel and north to Transylvania

Câmpulung, or **CÂMPULUNG MUSCEL** (as it is properly known), 55km north of Pitești, is overshadowed by mountains to the north, and begrimed by pollution from its factories. However, the town, which dates back to pre-Roman times, has played an important role in Wallachia's history, including a stint as the region's first capital after the voivodate was forged around 1300. Today, there are a couple of minor attractions to while away an hour or two, and it's a convenient place to break-up a journey en route to Transylvania. About 500m north of the train station on Strada Negru Vodă, Câmpulung's main drag, is the town's major sight, the **Negru Vodă Monastery**, attributed to its name-sake, Romania's legendary thirteenth-century Black Prince, but largely rebuilt following several earthquakes. The present building was completed in 1837 and incorporates stonework from the original; the infirmary chapel to its rear dates from 1718. The monastery's most striking feature is the massive seventeenth-century gate tower, with its heavy beech gates and twelfth-century stone carving of a doe to the left as you enter; this was brought from a nearby Dominican monastery and is remarkably Western European in style.

Continuing north along Strada Negru Vodă, brings you to Strada Republicii, which forms the southbound stretch of the centre's one-way system (Strada Negru Vodă forms the northbound). Housed in a fine seventeenth-century building at Str. Republicii 5 is a fabulous little Ethnographic Museum (Tues–Sun 9am–5pm), containing some exquisitely crafted furniture, colourful regional costumes, and a stock collection of farming and cooking implements. Beyond here is the town centre, with the wonderful neo-Brâncovenesc buildings on the west side of Strada Negru Vodă, and the town hall and the main hotel, the *Muscelul*, to the east. The fourteenth-century Roman Catholic **Bărăției Church** is at Str. Negru Vodă 116, and the **History Museum** (Tues–Sun 9am–5pm) at no. 119, opposite the *Muscelul*. The museum offers a fairly standard overview of the region's history, albeit without English captions, in addition to a dusty collection of artwork by the likes of Grigorescu and Lucian, as well as a couple of sketches by Pallady. There's also coverage of the **Roman fort**, or castrum, of Jidava, part of the Limes Transalutanus defensive line, which was destroyed by the Goths in 244 AD; the fort's remains, by the Pescăreasa rail halt 6km south of town en route to Pitești, have been preserved and can be visited Tues–Sun 9am–5pm) – there's also a small museum here housing a few fragments excavated from the site and a mock construction of how the camp would have looked.

Practicalities

Most **trains** from Pitești terminate at Câmpulung station, 2km south of town, and are met by maxitaxis. Otherwise, there are regular maxitaxis to and from Pitești from the main bus station, located to the east of town across the river at Strada I.C. Frimu.

The town's only central **hotel** is the *Muscelul* at Str. Negru Vodă 117 (☎0248/812 400, ☎219 249; ❺), a drab 1970s-style place with dated, plastic furniture. A better, but more distant, alternative, is the *Motel Flora* (☎0744/520 709; ❷), 3km north of town on the road to Brașov, just before the Lerești turn-off. There are also several agrotourism programmes in the area, the oldest of which centres on the village of **Lerești**, 8km north of town. **Homestays** here (and in equally attractive villages such as Rucăr, Dâmbovicioara and Dragoslavele) can be booked through the local Antrec office in Rucăr (☎0248/542 230, ✉arges@antrec.ro). Lerești is served by regular maxitaxis from Câmpulung's **bus station**. Just about the only decent **place to eat** here is the *Brâncovenesc* restaurant, behind the Bărăției church at Str. C. Brâncoveanu 39, while there's a good little patisserie opposite the *Hotel Muscelul*.

North to Transylvania

The scenery becomes increasingly dramatic on the road north from Câmpulung into Transylvania. Eight kilometres beyond Câmpulung, a road branches off to the left (the Târgoviște road forks right) to the village of **Nămăești** (bus #4), site of a gorgeous little rock church complete with an ancient and miraculous icon and cells hewn from sandstone by sixteenth-century monks. Today, the small monastery complex is inhabited by a handful of nuns.

Some 3km further along the road to Brașov, the austere, lighthouse-shaped **Mateias Mausoleum** marks the spot where Romanian troops managed to repel a major German offensive for forty-five days in 1916. In the event, more than two thousand Romanians lost their lives, the remains of whom are kept in a large glass chest in the ossuary. The walls and ceiling of the mausoleum, meanwhile, are beautifully decorated with mosaics, depicting soldiers at war as well as some of Romania's most prominent historical figures, including Mircea the Old, Constantin Brâncoveanu and Vlad Țepeș. There's also a small **museum** (daily 9am–5pm) half way up the steps containing artefacts, photographs and a working diorama relaying the events of the afore-mentioned battle.

Beyond the monument, the road continues to the villages of **Dragoslavele** and **Rucăr**, with their traditional wooden houses and verandas. Dragoslavele also has an eighteenth-century wooden church, and there's a campsite just beyond Rucăr; homestays are available at both villages. From Rucăr, the road continues up in a series of hairpin bends towards the Bran (or Giuvala) Pass, encountering the **Bridge of the Dâmboviţa**, a spectacular passage between the Dâmboviciorei and Plaiu gorges to the north and the yet narrower Dâmboviţei gorges to the south (see p.151 for the continuation of the route beyond the Bran Pass).

Curtea de Argeş, Arefu and Poienari Castle

After the Old Courts of Bucharest and Târgovişte (see p.75 and p.102 respectively), Wallachia's Dracula trail continues west via the small town of **Curtea de Argeş**, another former princely capital, to the remains of **Dracula's Castle** at **Poienari**. Selling Dracula as hard as it can, the tourist industry concentrates its efforts on Bran castle in Transylvania (see p.151), which has almost no connection to either the historical Dracula or Bram Stoker's fictional character. Yet the castle at Poienari exudes a far more authentic atmosphere, and its location in the foothills of the Făgăraş mountains makes for a wonderfully dramatic setting.

Curtea de Argeş

CURTEA DE ARGEŞ, Wallachia's second capital (after Câmpulung and before Târgovişte), lies some 36km northwest of Piteşti, and is easily accessible by road or rail. Not far north of the centre, enclosed by a wall of river boulders, is the **Court of Argeş** and the oldest church in Wallachia. The complex (Tues–Sun 10am–6pm) was rebuilt in the fourteenth century by Radu Negru, otherwise known as Basarab I, the founder of Wallachia. Its **Princely Church** was constructed in 1352 and its interior decorated with frescoes in 1384; later restoration work has now been largely removed to reveal the original frescoes, which are fully in the Byzantine tradition but wonderfully alive and individual, reminiscent of Giotto rather than the frozen poses of the Greek masters. Across the square, in the blue and white painted villa, the **town museum** (Tues–Sun 9am–4pm) displays a rather mundane collection of local artefacts.

More visually impressive is the monastery, or **Episcopal Church** (daily 8am–7pm), sited a good kilometre north of the court along the main through road, B-dul Basarabilor, reached by bus #2 from the town centre. Resembling the creation of an inspired confectioner, it's a boxy structure enlivened by whorls, rosettes and fancy trimmings, rising into two twisted, octagonal belfries, each festooned with little spheres and the three-armed cross of Orthodoxy. **Manole's Well**, in the park across the road, next to the restaurant of the same name, is a spring said to have been created by the death of **Manole**, the Master Builder of Curtea de Argeş. Legend has it that Manole was marooned on the rooftop of his creation, the Episcopal Church, when Prince Neagoe Basarab, the ruler who had commissioned him to build it, ordered the scaffolding to be removed, in an attempt to ensure that the builder could not repeat his masterwork for anyone else. Manole tried to escape with the aid of wings made from roofing shingles – only to crash to his death on the ground below, whereupon a spring gushed forth immediately. The story is perhaps that of a crude form of justice, for legend also has it that Manole had immured his wife within the walls of the monastery – at the time it was believed that *stafia* or ghosts were needed to keep buildings from collapse.

The current Episcopal Church is not Manole's original creation of 1512–17 but a re-creation of 1875–85 by the Frenchman Lecomte de Noy, who grafted on all the Venetian mosaics and Parisian woodwork; he wanted to do the same to the Princely Church, but the historian Nicolae Iorga managed to get legal backing to stop him doing so. Inside the garish red, green and gold painted interior lie the tombs of the church founder and kings Carol I (1866–1914), and Ferdinand (1914–27).

Practicalities

It's just five minutes to the old town centre from the ornate Mughal-style **train station** and the adjacent **bus station** – turn left out of the stations and then right up Strada Castanilor. Unusually, all the town's sights are exceptionally well signposted, starting at the station, so you'll have no trouble finding your way around. Moving on by train, your only option is one of the five daily services to Piteşti; there's more choice at the bus station, with services to Arefu, Bucharest, Câmpulung, Braşov, Râmnicu Vâlcea and Sibiu; whilst maxitaxis run from outside the Princely Church as far as Bracov – get another maxitaxi there on to Piteşti, 10km to the south.

All the town's amenities are on or just off Bulevardul Basarabilor, including the one **hotel** here, the dowdy but reasonably good-value *Hotel Posada*, south of the monastery at B-dul Basarabilor 27 (☎0248/721 451, ⓕ721 109; ❷–❸). There's also the *San Nicoară* **campsite** at Str. Plopiş 13 (☎0248/722 126; open all year), which has a few two-bed huts (❶) and three-room apartments (❸); to get there, head up the steep Strada San Nicoară, and the site is opposite the ruined seventeenth-century Potters Church.

There are precious few places to **eat and drink** in town: *Matrix*, near the Episcopal Church, offers little more than snacks and light meals, while *Curtea Veche* and *My Club*, side-by-side opposite the Princely Church, should suffice for a drink.

Arefu and Poienari Castle

Twenty-five kilometres north of Curtea de Argeş is **AREFU**, a long, ramshackle village 3km west of the valley road – note that, if you're travelling by car, it's a very rough surface from the main road to the village. It was to here, in 1457, that the survivors of Vlad the Impaler's massacre in Târgovişte (see p.421) were marched to begin work on his castle. This is the real Dracula's Castle – his only connection with the better-known one at Bran is that he may have attacked it once (see p.151). Situated on a crag north of the village, the moody **POIENARI CASTLE** (daily 9am–5pm) can only be reached by climbing 1400 steps (about a 30min walk) from the hydroelectric power station (and a kiosk selling refreshments) 4km north on the road from Arefu, which proves a powerful disincentive to most visitors. Note that buses only go as far as Arefu, so you'll need your own transport (or walk) to go beyond there. Struggle to the top and you'll find that the citadel is surprisingly small, one third having collapsed down the mountainside in 1888. Entering by a narrow wooden bridge, come across the crumbling remains of two towers within; the prism-shaped one was the old keep, Vlad's residential quarters, from where, according to one legend, the Impaler's wife flung herself out of the window, declaring that she "would rather have her body rot and be eaten by the fish of the Argeş" than be captured by the Turks, who were then besieging the castle. Legend has it that Vlad himself escaped over the mountains on horseback, fooling his pursuers by shoeing his mount backwards – or, according to some versions, by affixing horseshoes that left the impression of cow prints. Seven buses a day (two at weekends) head up the Argeş valley from Curtea de Argeş to Arefu. Simple **private rooms** (❶) are available both here – contact Gheorghe Tomescu on ☎0248/730 102 – and in the two villages preceeding Arefu, Corbeni and Căpăţânenii Pământeni, where you can try places (advertising *camere* or *cazare*) at random.

If you have your own transport, you can continue from Poienari up the twisting road to **Lake Vidraru**, and a spectacular dam (165m). Four hundred metres beyond the dam is the *Casa Argeşeana* cabana (☎0248/730 315; ❶), essentially a **restaurant** but with a limited number of **beds** available too. A further eight kilometres on, above the main road beside the lake, is the *Cabana de Pesti* (☎0248/730 250; ❻), an attractive hotel popular at weekends with local fishermen; comfortable rooms are complimented by an outstanding fish restaurant. Beyond the lake, the road continues along the **Transfăgărașan Highway** to the **Făgăraş mountains** in Transylvania (see p.154).

The Olt valley

The **River Olt** runs south from its source in Transylvania through the Red Tower Pass below Sibiu, carving a stupendous 50km gorge through the Carpathians down into Wallachia, where it passes through **Râmnicu Vâlcea**, 34km west of Curtea de Argeş, and continues south to the Danube. In Wallachia, the valley can best be approached by road from Piteşti and Curtea de Argeş or from Târgu Jiu further to the west. From Târgu Jiu, the route is long but very scenic, while the one from the autostradă at Piteşti is very busy, as the difficulty of travelling through Serbia has made this the main truck route between Turkey and Western Europe. **Trains** from Piatra Olt, midway along the Piteşti–Craiova line, head north up the valley to Podu Olt and Sibiu, with slower services stopping at the villages in between.

Râmnicu Vâlcea

There are more interesting places further north up the Olt valley but it's worth pausing in **RÂMNICU VÂLCEA**, west of Piteşti, to buy food, get local information and check festival dates for the surrounding area. Sprawling across successive terraces above the River Olt, it's a typically systematized town, with many modern apartment blocks, but there are several attractive old churches as well as an excellent open-air museum here.

The town's main street, Calea lui Traian, runs along the western side of Piaţa Mircea cel Bătrân; to the south of this square lies the daily fruit and veg market, and to the north, opposite the *Alutus* hotel, is the sixteenth-century **Church of the Annunciation** (Buna Vestire), established in 1545–49 by Mircea the Shepherd and rebuilt in 1747 by the citizens of Sibiu. Heading north along Calea lui Traian you'll pass two more old churches: **St Paraschiva**, built in 1557–87, and **All Saints**, built in 1762–64 in a post-Brâncovenesc style with distinctive oblique cable mouldings that make the towers seem twisted. A few paces further north you'll come to the **County Museum** at Calea lui Traian 157 (Tues–Sun 10am–6pm), which holds a better than average hoard of local archaeological finds. Behind All Saints, at the corner of Strada Carol I and Strada Căpitan Negoescu, is a modern villa housing the **Art Gallery** (Wed–Sun 10am–6pm), with works by the customary Romanian artists, Grigorescu and Pallady. Another five minutes north, at Str. Carol I no. 53, is the **Bishopric** (Episcopiei), a wonderfully tranquil complex, with three small churches set in well-kept lawns. It dates from the sixteenth century, although the main church, with its Tattarescu paintings, was only built in 1856, after a fire destroyed the original. Further north, at Calea lui Traian 351, the **Citadel church** (1529) still stands amid the remains of its fortifications.

At the northern town limits is the superb **Bujoreni open-air museum** (Tues–Sun 10am–6pm), a fine ensemble of some eighty structures laid out as per a typical village from the Vâlcea region. It's possible to enter a good cross-section of these units, including a splendidly preserved inn (1899), one of the largest buildings in the village and the focal point for social life, a perfectly furnished village school (1904), complete with period books and maps, and a *cula*, or watchtower, dating from 1802. The oldest building is the church (1785), complete with a candelabrum featuring wooden eggs hanging below wooden birds, and some original icons. To get here, take a **maxitaxi** from town and get the driver to set you down on the main road right outside the museum; otherwise, it's a fifteen-minute walk south of the Bujoreni train station.

Practicalities

The **train station** is east of the centre on Strada V. Popescu, from where it's a ten-minute walk along Strada Regina Maria (50m to the left of the station as you exit) to Piaţa Mircea cel Bătrân and Calea lui Traian. From the **bus station**, south of the river on Strada G. Coşbuc, it's a short walk along Strada Dacia and across the bridge into the centre. Your best bet for **information** is the Vâlcea Tourism Association at Strada Regina Maria 7 (℡0250/733 449). The **CFR** office is at Calea Traian, by Piaţa Mircea cel Bătrân (Mon–Fri 7am–8pm).

The town's three **hotels** are uniformly dull, and neither do they represent particularly good value for money: the most central is the *Alutus* at Strada G-ral Praporgescu 10 (℡0250/737 740, ℻737 760; ❹), while more restful alternatives are located on the slopes of the hills immediately west of town: the *Capela* (℡0250/738 906; ❹), which also has chalets (❷), is a good twenty-minute walk from the centre along Calea Lui Traian, past the County Museum and left at the top of Aleea Castanilor; while the slightly more expensive *Gemina* (℡0250/735 101, ℻731 949; ❹), a ten-minute walk past the art gallery to the top of Strada Pinului, is basic but acceptable, with lumpy beds compensated for by good views. Located on the southern outskirts is the *Popas Ostroveni*, a basic **campsite** with chalets (❶). Save for the cracking *Boromir* patisserie on the southeastern corner of Piaţa Mircea cel Bătrân (opposite the Galerille Romanta), and a handful of run-of-the-mill pizzerias dotted around town, there's nowhere particularly interesting to **eat** and you're just as well buying your food at the central **market** on Strada Regina Maria.

Călimăneşti–Căciulata

The twin settlements of **CĂLIMĂNEŞTI–CĂCIULATA** mark the entrance to the Olt valley, a deep, sinuously twisting gorge of great beauty and the site of several monasteries, most notable of which are **Cozia** and **Turnul**. Although the river was notoriously wild and dangerous here, it has now been tamed, with a project to build a series of dams; viaducts carry the road in places. While the main road runs along the Olt's west bank, a lesser road (as far as Cozia) and the rail line follow the other side of the defile.

The dormant village of **CĂLIMĂNEȘTI**, 15km north of Râmnicu Vâlcea, is home to the renowned **Songs of the Olt folklore festival** and a **pottery fair**, both of which usually take place during the first week in August. The nearest **train** station to this spa town is actually in the neighbouring village of Jiblea just to the south, although the station itself takes Călimănești's name; buses run roughly every two hours from here into Călimănești, then to its twin town of Căciulata and onwards as far as Cozia monastery. However, the station is only 1km from Călimănești, and it takes just ten minutes, walking beside the train tracks, then turning left along Strada Vlahuță, to reach the dam which carries the main road across the Olt into town. The municipal park, **Ostrov island**, at the point where the Olt emerges from the mountains, is the site of a tiny **hermitage**, built in 1520–22 for Despina, wife of Neagoe Basarab, with painted frescoes dating from 1752–60 – the hideous green-faced women in the porch are no indication of the beautiful paintings inside. The only **accommodation** in Călimănești itself is the *Hotel Central* (☎0250/750 990, ⓕ 751 138; ➋), a classic, and ridiculously cheap, spa hotel at Calea lui Traian 398 towards the northern end of town. The *Pensiune Călimănești Varianta* (☎0250/751 179; ➍), at a filling station 1km south of the town, is worth considering, as is the *Seaca* **campsite**, on the main road north of the centre.

There's stacks more accommodation immediately to the north of Călimănești in **CĂCIULATA**, a one-street spa town lined with dilapidated villas, many of which advertise *cazare* or *camera* (rooms). The most prominent hotel here is the *Traian* (☎0250/750 780; ➋), whose clean and amazingly good-value rooms belie the spectacularly grim exterior; just behind it there's the *Vila Flora* (☎0250/750 164; ➍), a small villa complete with treatment facilities. At the village's northern extremes, beyond the triumvirate of ghastly hotels, are two more excellent possibilities: the *Vila Lilicul* (☎0250/750 440; ➍), which has refreshingly clean and colourful rooms, and the similarly bright *Hotel Pension International* (☎0722/176 892; ➍), a few metres along. There is also a **campsite**, the *Ștrand*, immediately north of the *Traian* hotel.

Cozia and Turnul

Beautifully pitched amidst elegant pine trees and fragrant rose bushes, **Cozia Monastery**, 1km north of Căciulata (4km from the centre of Călimănești), is the earliest example of Byzantine architecture in Wallachia. Built by Serbian architects in 1388 – thanks to the patronage of Vlad Tepeș' grandfather, Mircea the Old (who is buried within the monastery) – the church's principal architectural features include alternating bands of brick and stone, filigree latticework and fluted, false pillars. The church portico was added by Constantin Brâncoveanu in the early eighteenth century, although it's not a particularly striking example of the Brâncovenesc style. The monastery also houses a small **museum of religious art**, exhibiting a dazzling collection of church treasures – mostly seventeenth- to nineteenth-century icons. Across the road is the impossibly slender Bolnița, or **Infirmary Church**, built in 1542–43, with murals dating from the same period. Immediately south stands the *Hanul Cozia* motel (☎0250/751 909; ➋), where buses from the train station terminate; just to the north, the Olt is spanned by a dam, leading to the reconstructed Arutela *castrum*, built in 137 AD as part of the Limes Alutanus, the Romans defensive line along the Olt.

About 3km north of Cozia Monastery, on the east bank of the River Olt near the Mânăstirea Turnu train halt, is **Turnul Monastery**, based around rock cells hewn by hermits from Cozia at the end of the sixteenth century. From here, it's a five- to six-hour walk up a steep trail marked by red stripes to the *Cozia* cabana (❶), situated near the summit of the **Cozia massif**. Sheltered from northeasterly winds by the Făgăraş mountains, this has the mildest climate of all Romania's ranges, enabling oak, walnut and wild roses to grow at altitudes of up to 1300m.

Târgu Jiu and around

Forewarned about **TÂRGU JIU** and the surrounding **Jiu valley**, visitors often decide to ignore them completely but the town does merit a visit on the strength of it's association with Romania's foremost sculptor, Constantin Brâncuşi. Ranged along the valley, from Petroşani (see p.192) to Rovinari, are the **coal and lignite mines** that support all the country's other industries. For the most part, this is a bleak landscape, made grimmer by slag heaps, pylons and the mining towns themselves, while the sandbanks in the river are almost solid coal dust. Under communism, the miners were lauded as the aristocrats of the proletariat, but had to be placed under **martial law** in 1985, when Ceauşescu demanded ever higher output and docked pay by fifty percent when quotas weren't achieved. After the revolution of 1989, the **miners** were used as Iliescu's shock troops, being rushed on special trains to Bucharest to terrorize the opposition as required, and even to precipitate the resignation of prime minister Petre Roman himself (see p.395). Târgu Jiu is known for its great winter music gathering, the **Festival of Enchanted Water Springs** (Izvoare Fermecate), normally staged during the third week of February – a pretty uninviting time of year.

The Town

Although Târgu Jiu has no links with coal mining, it still suffered the gross "modernization" imposed by Ceauşescu on Romania's coal-mining centres. Nevertheless, this busy, dusty town, dominated by windswept, concrete buildings, does hold one singularly important attraction (or attractions), namely the monumental sculptures that **Constantin Brâncuşi** (see box on p.116) created in the late 1930s as a war memorial for the town of his boyhood. His most famous piece of work, at the eastern end of Calea Eroilor, is the recently restored **Endless Column** (*Coloană Infinita*), a vast thirty-metre-high totem pole of smooth rhomboidal blocks, whose rippling form is emulated on many of the verandas of the old wooden houses throughout the region. Brâncuşi actually began working on variations of the column in 1918, though this structure wasn't installed until 1937, following a request from the local authorities to create a memorial for those killed during World War I.

Brâncuşi's other sculptures lie at the opposite end of Calea Eroilor, which runs 1.7km west from the *Endless Column* to the park on the banks of the Jiu river: the **Gate of the Kiss** (*Poarta Sărutului*) at the entrance to the park opens onto the **Avenue of Seats** (*Aleea Scaunilor*), flanked by twenty-seven stone chairs (which you are forbidden to sit on), which in turn leads to the **Table of Silence** (*Masa Tăcerii*), surrounded by twelve stools representing the continuity of the months and the traditional number of seats at a funeral feast. Brâncuşi had originally proposed a series of twelve sculptures in Târgu Jiu, but completed only these four before he died. To the north of the park, in a villa

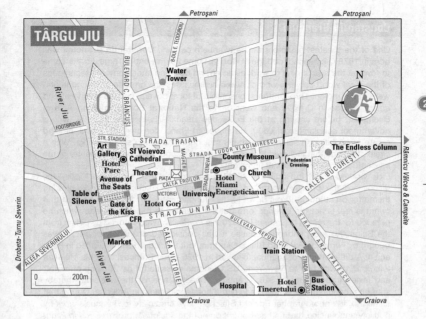

purpose-built for Ceaușescu, is the modern **Art Gallery** (Tues–Sun 9am–5pm); surprisingly, there's nothing of Brâncuși's work here, just a clutch of rather ordinary contemporary paintings and some eighteenth- and nineteenth-century icons, including one from Mount Athos in Greece.

Cutting through the centre of town, Calea Eroilor is a surprisingly narrow street, and the vista east from the park to the *Endless Column* is blocked by a modern, and ugly, church. However, there are some striking architectural pieces amid the concrete, most notably around the pedestrianized Piața Victoriei, where you will find the neo-Brâncovenesc prefecture and the tiny **Cathedral of St Voievozi**, built in 1749–64. The **County Museum** at Str. Geneva 8 (Tues–Sun 9am–5pm), is unremarkable, offering the standard view of Romanian history and, 3km north of the town centre on the main road to Petroșani, at B-dul Ecaterina Teodoroiu 270 (Wed–Sun 9am–4pm), is the birthplace of **Ecaterina Teodoroiu** Romania's answer to Joan of Arc; she was only 23 when she died in August 1917, fighting disguised as a man in the crucial battle of Mărășești (see p.244).

Practicalities

The **train** and **bus stations** are just a stone's throw apart on Strada Titulescu, a twenty-minute walk east of town. Târgu Jiu is on the Simeria–Petroșani–Craiova train line, with some trains continuing to Arad, Cluj, Deva and Bucharest. From Târgu Jiu, there are bus services to Bucharest, Râmnicu Vâlcea, Drobeta-Turnu Severin, Sibiu, and several of the surrounding villages, while maxitaxis run to Craiova. Rail bookings can be made at the CFR office at Bloc 2, Strada Unirii (Mon–Fri 7am–8pm).

The town's four **hotels** are nothing special, but they all offer reasonable value for money: the bizarrely named *Miami Energeticianul* at Calea Eroilor 27 (℡0253/218 407, ℻213 449; ④) is the most modern, with large, a/c rooms;

Constantin Brâncusi

One of the greatest sculptors of the twentieth century, **Constantin Brâncuşi** was born in 1876 in a peasant cottage at Hobiţa, some 28km west of Târgu Jiu. He came to town at the age of nine to work as an errand boy, and later learnt the techniques of the local wood carvers, who chiselled sinuous designs on rafters, verandas and wells in the region. Through the sponsorship of local boyars, he was able to attend an art college in Craiova and went on to the **National School of Fine Arts** in Bucharest, before arriving at the Ecole des Beaux Arts in Paris in 1904, with a government scholarship of L600. He stayed in France for over fifty years, helping create a revolution in sculpture with his strikingly strong and simple works. With a circle of friends that included Picasso, Gide and Pound, he was at the centre of the intellectual ferment of Paris at its height.

He worked briefly in Rodin's studio, then, in company with Amadeo Modigliani, discovered the primitive forms of African masks and sculptures, concentrating thereafter on stripping forms down to their fundamentals. In 1907, he claimed that "what is real is not the exterior form but the essence of things", a credo which he pursued for the rest of his career. In 1920, his *Prinţesa X* was removed by police from the Salon des Independents because it was considered obscenely phallic; it was bought by Fernand Leger and Blaise Cendrars, but Brâncuşi never exhibited in Paris again. A different sort of scandal followed in 1926 when Brâncuşi took his *Măiastra* (*Magic Bird*) with him to New York. US Customs classified it as "a piece of metal" and levied import duty of $10; Brâncuşi appealed against the decision, thereby starting a critical furore which made him a household name in America. During that same trip, the photographer Edward Steichen gave credibility to Brâncuşis work by publicly announcing that he had bought one of the sculptor's bronze *Birds in Flight* for $600 – by 1967, it was worth $175,000. Brâncuşi died in 1957, with his series of sculptures for Târgu Jiu unfinished, and is buried in Montparnasse cemetery in Paris. You'll find examples of his work in Craiova and Bucharest as well as Târgu Jiu, and also in London, New York and Philadelphia; his last studio is preserved in Paris.

the *Parc*, B-dul C. Brâncuşi 10 (℡0253/215 981, Ⓕ 211 167; ❺), has tidy, albeit gaudily decorated, rooms; while the grim-looking *Gorj* at Calea Eroilor 6 (℡ & Ⓕ0253/217 817; ❺) has dank rooms. Cheapest of the lot is the grubby *Tineretului*, one block south of the bus station at Str. Titulescu 26 (℡0253/238 353; ❷). There's also a motel with **campsite** 10km east of the town on the DN67 at Drăgoeni (℡0253/218 827; ❶). **Homestay accommodation** in the area (❶) can be arranged through the Guardo Tours agency, just behind the cathedral at Str. Tudor Vladimirescu 17 (℡0253/223 081, ✉gorj@antrec.ro).

There's a paucity of **places to eat** in town. The *Lider*, opposite the *Hotel Gorj* on Calea Eroilor and serving a good range of standard Romanian dishes, is about as good as it gets, while the *Deli Pat* patisserie close by suffices for quick snacks. For **drinking**, try the *Simigerie*, a decent little bar with a busy outdoor garden on the west (older) side of Piaţa Victoriei, or *Enigma*, next to the *Lider* restaurant. There's **Internet** access in the building next to the theatre.

East of Târgu Jiu

Away from the industry of the Jiu valley, there are plenty of tranquil villages where traditional customs and dress are still a part of everyday life. The area east of town has particularly impressive **cave formations** and important **monasteries**, notably those at Horezu. Unfortunately, the more remote sights are poorly served by buses from Târgu Jiu and Râmnicu Vâlcea. There are also several mountain hikes north into Transylvania.

Polovragi and around

POLOVRAGI, 48km east of Târgu Jiu and dominated by the Căpăţânii mountains, is home to one of the great Wallachian **fairs**. An occasion for highlanders to dress up, dance and do deals in the old fashion, the *Nedeia* usually occurs on the Sunday between July 14 and 20. If your visit doesn't coincide with the fair, the main sights of interest are north of the village, where a forestry road runs into the 1.6-kilometre-long **Olteţu gorges**, along which, after 1km, you'll find the **Polovragi Monastery and cave**. The small monastery was originally built in 1470, then rebuilt by Brâncoveanu in 1647; the later **Bolniţa Church** (1736), on the same site, is definitely worth the trip for its fine frescoes. Further on, lurking behind the eastern rockface at the mouth of the gorge, is the Polovragi cave, once believed to be the abode of Zalmoxis, the Dacians' chief deity. Now fully illuminated and open for guided tours (daily 9am–5pm), it was first explored in 1860 by the French naturalist Lancelot, and is renowned for the stalactites in its "Candlesticks Gallery".

From Baia de Fier, 7km west of Polovragi, a road leads 3km north to a beautiful grotto in the smaller **Galbenul gorges**. Although only two passages out of the ten kilometres of convolutions that make up the so-called **Women's Cave** (Peştera Muierii; daily 9am–5pm) have been illuminated, it's an impressive sight nonetheless; halfway in, multicoloured stone columns resemble petrified wood, while in the lower passage the skeletons of 183 cave bears have been discovered. The cave gets its name from the human skeletons – mainly those of women and children, and dating from prehistoric times – found on its upper levels. From the cave and nearby *cabana*, a footpath leads up to the **Rânca tourist complex** (☏0244/461 542; ❸) 15km away in the Parâng mountains in Transylvania; the basic accommodation is useful mainly for hikers in the summer. The next settlement west, **NOVACI**, marks the start of the forestry road to Rânca (18km) and on to Sebeş (see p.178). There are two ordinary motels in Novaci, on Strada Tudor Vladimirescu.

Horezu and the monasteries

Set amid apple and plum orchards, sweet chestnut trees and wild lilac, 16km east of Polovragi on the main road to Râmnicu Vâlcea, is the small town of **HOREZU** – so-called after the numerous owls (*huhurezi*) who reside here (the town is also shown as Hurez on some maps). Although wooden furniture and wrought-iron objects are also produced here, Horezu is best known for its **pottery**, especially its plates, which by tradition are given as keepsakes during funeral wakes. The Cocoşul de Horezu pottery fair, held on the first Sunday of June, is one of the year's biggest events in the area – otherwise, you'll see many wares displayed outside houses along the roadside. Four kilometres south in **Măldăreşti** stand two *culas* or tower houses, built in the eighteenth and nineteenth centuries, when punitive raids by Turkish troops were still a possibility.

The real attraction, however, lies around 3km northeast of town, off the main road near the village of Romanii de Jos. Built between 1691 and 1697, and now a UNESCO World Heritage Site, **Horezu Monastery** is the largest and finest of Wallachia's Brâncoveanu complexes, and is the site of the school which established the Brâncovenesc style. The complex is centred around the **Great Church**, built in 1693 and entered via a marvellous ten-pillared porchway and doors of carved pearwood. Inside, the frescoes, once tarnished by the smoke from fires lit by Turkish slaves who camped here, are in the painstaking process of being restored, but you can still make out portraits of Brâncoveanu and his family, Catacuzino and Basarab, as well as scenes from Mount Athos and the Orthodox calendar. To the right of the church as you enter is a vacant tomb, which was the intended resting place of Brâncoveanu – as it is, he is buried in St George's Church in Bucharest (see p.76).

Opposite the church is the Nuns' Refectory, which contains some more but poorly preserved frescoes and, to the left, another Brâncoveanu porch, featuring a splendid stone balustrade carved with animal motifs. Set apart to the north and west are the small hermitages of the Holy Apostles and of St Stephen, built in 1700 and 1703 respectively. The chapel of St Michael outside the gates was built by Brâncoveanu for the local villagers.

There's **accommodation** in Horezu at the *Horezu* motel (☎0250/861 040; ❷), in the centre of the village where buses stop, and the *Stejarii* camp-site, at the very beginning of the village; they've also got tiny, bunker-like huts sleeping two (☎0250/860 570; ❶). Six kilometres on towards Râmnicu Vâlcea on the DN67, a left turn at Costeşti leads another 6km north to **Bistriţa Monastery**, funded by the boyars of Craiova in the fifteenth century. You will, however, need your own transport, as bus services no longer run here. As well as three churches, dating from the sixteenth and seventeenth centuries, there is a cave containing two more chapels, in one of which the relics of St Gregory the Decapolite were hidden during the Turkish wars; a nun from the monastery can lead you to the cave along the precipitous cliff-side path. The seventeenth-century **Arnota Monastery** stands on a hill, 4km north of Bistriţa beyond a large quarry; by financing the construction of this monastery, voivode Matei Basarab guaranteed himself a tasteful burial place within its church surrounded by his chattels and murals of his wife, of which only fragments remain. As is so often the case in this area, the porch is the work of Brâncoveanu.

West of Târgu Jiu

The small scenic towns and villages to the west of Târgu Jiu are a complete contrast to the flat, grimy mining areas to the east and south. Buses run from Târgu Jiu along the DN67d, stopping close to most of the sites of interest. The small village of **HOBIŢA**, 24km west of Târgu Jiu just off the DN67d, is the birthplace of Constantin Brâncuşi (see p.116). From the main road at Peştişani, it's a 3km walk south to the village and the sculptor's childhood home, which has been turned into a small **museum** (Wed–Sun 9am–5pm) – if it's closed, you can ask in the shop at the crossroads for the custodian of the museum to let you in. The birthplace is an attractive, traditional cottage, surrounded by plum and cherry trees, in which you'll learn relatively little about Brâncuşi, but it's worth seeing the ceramics and textiles displayed inside, and the intricate spiral motifs on the veranda posts. One hundred metres away on the same road is the *Popas* pension, where you can sleep in *căsuţe* (summer only; ❶), by a ford which leads into a wood dotted with sub-Brâncuşi sculptures left by a 1981 summer-school group. Further south, at the edge of the same wood, but reached by the main road through the village, is the village cemetery, with a tiny wooden chapel; even if it's closed, it's possible to enter the chapel's roof space by a ladder from the open porch to admire the skill of the local carpenters.

TISMANA, another 10km west on the DN67d, harks back to the region's traditional pastoral ways. **Tismana Monastery**, 5km to the north of the village, is the oldest in Romania, founded in 1375; surrounded by a high wall during the reign of Matei Basarab, the monastery served as a meeting place for rebels in the 1821 rising led by Tudor Vladimirescu. Tismana is the setting for the annual **Tismana Garden Festival** of music and crafts on

August 15, where the most popular instrument is the *nai* or shepherds' pan-pipes. You'll find wooden utensils, sculptures, embroidered clothing and Oltenian rugs on sale during the festival, but the quality and range of goods has declined in recent years. Tismana has some good **homestay** possibilties – scout around the village or contact the Guardo Tours Agency in Târgu Jiu (see p.116).

Buses for Călugăreni and Cloșani turn north off the main road about 12km west of Tismana, stopping after 5km in **PADEȘ,** where the 1821 peasant revolt, led by Tudor Vladimirescu, began. Some village men still wear folk costume – narrow white homespun trousers piped with braid and voluminous cloaks – which resemble the uniforms worn by Vladimirescu's soldiers. Picturesque karst formations abound in the region, particularly around Cloșani and Ponoarele, 7km south of the main road just west of Baia de Aramă; here, the **Giant's Bridge**, 25m wide by 50m long, was formed when the ceiling of a large cave collapsed.

Drobeta-Turnu Severin and the Danube

Drobeta-Turnu Severin lies in the far west of the region, on the north side of the **River Danube**, the country's natural border with Serbia and Bulgaria. The river narrows below Moldova Veche before surging through the **Kazan gorge** towards Orșova, only to be tamed and harnessed by the dam at the mighty **Iron Gates**, before reaching the town. Motorists driving down from Moldova Veche can see something of this magnificent panorama (the rail journey is less scenic); but if you're coming from Târgu Jiu, the real landscape feast doesn't start until you reach Drobeta-Turnu Severin. The shortest route from Târgu Jiu is via the badly surfaced DN67, usually crowded with trucks. By train, you'll have to travel down to the unappealing town of **FILIAȘI** to join the Craiova–Drobeta-Turnu Severin line. The only **place to stay** is the basic but very cheap *Filiași Hotel*, at Str. Racoteanu 15 (☎0251/441 201; ❷); it's located at the far end of Strada Gării, the street leading away from the station.

Drobeta-Turnu Severin

Dubbed the "town of roses" for its beautiful parks, **DROBETA-TURNU SEVERIN**'s modern appearance belies its origins as the Dacian settlement of *Drobeta*, more than two thousand years ago. Its Roman conquerors left more enduring landmarks, however, notably the ruins of **Trajan's bridge**, which Apollodorus of Damascus built to span the Danube at the order of the emperor in 103–105 AD. As the travel writer Patrick Leigh Fermor put it, "two great stumps of his conglomerate masonry still cumbered the Romanian side", and these can be seen from the train or from the grounds of the **Museum of the Iron Gates** (Porţile de Fier; Tues–Sun 9am–5pm) at the southern end of Strada Independenţei on the east side of town. Nearby, also within the museum precincts, are the remains of a Roman bath, and the foundations of the fourteenth-century **Metropolitan's Basilica** and of the Roman fort guarding Trajan's bridge. The museum itself is divided up into several sections which, overall, are a bit hit-and-miss: the most enjoyable is the ethnographic section, featuring a lovely assortment of rugs, costumes, ceramics and painted chests, whilst the aquarium, with tanks full of weird and wonderful species from the Danube, will keep kids happy. Otherwise, the natural science,

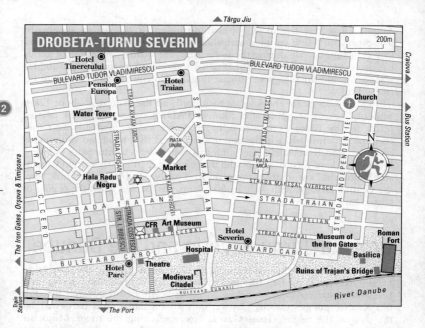

archaeological and historical departments are eminently missable, if only because, all captions are in Romanian. The small **art museum** (Tues–Sun 9am–5pm) at Str. Rahovei 3 holds a few works by important Romanian painters, including several stills and nudes by Pallady.

A five-minute walk south of the art museum, across Bulevardul Carol I and down past the hospital, stand the remains of a **medieval citadel**. Heading back north, on Piaţa Unirii, is the lively daily market, while, to the west of here, is a dilapidated **synagogue** and the site for a new Orthodox cathedral, and the Hala Radu Negru Market, now a huge furniture store.

Practicalities

Drobeta-Turnu Severin's main **bus station** is on Strada D. Ghiaţa, to the east of the centre just off Bulevardul Tudor Vladimirescu (bus #9 every 30min), with services to Băile Herculane and Timişoara in the Banat and east to Târgu Jiu and Râmnicu Vâlcea. From the **train station** west of town, it's a fifteen–minute walk along Bulevardul Carol I to the centre; train tickets can be booked at the **CFR** office at Str. Decebal 43. The best source of **information** on the area is the *Parc* hotel's tourist agency, who can also arrange riverboat trips upstream from Orşova (see opposite) to Moldova Veche (see p.122).

Easily the best of the four **hotels** in town is the smart *Pension Europa* at B-dul Tudor Vladimirescu 66 (☎0252/333 737, ⓕ325 845; ❺–❻), which has comfortable, a/c rooms and apartments. The alternatives, none very exciting, consist of the *Parc*, down by the river at B-dul Carol I no. 2 (☎0252/312 851, ⓔparc@drobeta.expert.ro; ❻), the very ordinary *Severin* at Str. Eminescu 1 (☎0252/312 074, ⓕ306 017; ❸), and the supremely tatty *Traian*, at B-dul Tudor Vladimirescu 74 (☎0252/311 760, ⓕ310 290; ❹). Cheapest of all is the *Tineretului* youth hotel, just north of the *Europa* at Str. Crişan 25

(☎ & 🖷0252/317 999; ❶). The *Vatra Haiducilor* (Outlaws' Hearth) **campsite** is 3km north along Strada Crişan in the Crihala forest. Antrec, at Str. Avram Iancu 38 (☎0252/318 076, 🄴mehedinti@antrec.ro), can arrange **homestay accommodation** in the county. The classy little restaurant in the *Pension Europa* serves upscale Romanian fare and is without doubt the best place to **eat**.

The Iron Gates

The **Iron Gates** have a formidable reputation owing to the navigational hazards (eddies, whirlpools and rocks) on this stretch of the River Danube, which formerly restricted safe passage during the two hundred days of the year when the river was in spate, and meant that boats had to take aboard a pilot at Moldova. The blasting of a channel in 1896 obviated these terrors, and the building of the largest hydroelectric dam in Europe (excluding the former Soviet Union) at Gura Văii, 8km upstream of Drobeta-Turnu Severin, finally tamed the river.

Conceived in 1956, the hydroelectric project was undertaken as a joint venture; Romania and Yugoslavia (as it was then) each built a 1000MW turbine plant and locks for shipping on their respective banks, linked by a slipway dam and an international road crossing, a task that took from 1960 until 1972 and raised the river level by 33m. Romantics have deplored the results, which, in the words of Leigh Fermor, "has turned 130 miles of the Danube into a vast pond which has swollen and blurred the course of the river beyond recognition", turning "beetling crags into mild hills". The damming has submerged two places worthy of footnotes in history – the island of **Ada Kaleh** and old **Orşova** – and has reduced the Danube's peak flow, so that the pollution of Central Europe is no longer flushed out to sea but gathers here, killing fish and flora.

Ada Kaleh

Legend has it that the Argonauts discovered the olive tree on **ADA KALEH**, an island that was famous at the beginning of the twentieth century for its Turkish community, complete with mosques, bazaars and fortresses. Their presence here at so late a date arose from a diplomatic oversight, for at the conference where the Ottoman withdrawal from the region was negotiated in 1878, Ada Kaleh was forgotten about, enabling it to remain Turkish territory until the Trianon Treaty officially made it part of Romania in 1920. Before Ada Kaleh's submersion, along with the mosque, in the Danube, Eugene of Savoy's citadel was removed and reconstructed on the **island of Ostrov Şimian**, 5km east of Turnu Severin. Unfortunately, owing to its current use as a military base, the island is no longer accessible. Close to the dam, 12km from Drobeta-Turnu Severin on the E70 (DN6), is the *Continental Motel Porţile de Fier* (☎0252/342 144, 🖰www.continentalhotels.ro; ❼), whose comfortable rooms mirror those of the other hotels in the *Continental* chain – they've also got a swimming pool and tennis courts.

Orsova

Before 1918, **ORŞOVA**, 23km upstream from Drobeta-Turnu Severin, was the frontier crossing into the Magyar-ruled Banat, and it was nearby that Kossuth buried the Crown of St Stephen on his way into exile after the failure of the 1848–49 revolt in Hungary. However, the town was flooded by the dam, and replaced by the new Orşova, 3km east of its train station.

There's nothing particularly worth stopping off for, but if for some reason you do want to stay, there are a couple of good value **hotels** available: the modern and bright *Hotel Meridian*, just across from the bus station at Str. Eroilor 12 (T0252/362 800, F362 810; ●), and the marginally cheaper *Hostel Flora*, close by at B-dul Porţile de Fier 26 (T & F0252/362 081; ●).

The Kazan gorge, Moldova Veche and Moldova Nouă

Sixteen kilometres beyond Orşova, on both sides of the village of **DUBOVA**, the sheer cliffs of the **Kazan gorge** (Cazanele Dunării) fall 600m into the tortuous river. Rather than attempt to cut a path through the rock, the Romans built a road by boring holes in to the side of the cliff to hold beams upon which they laid planks, roofing over the road to discourage Dacian ambushes. The first proper road was created on the northern side of the gorge on the initiative of the nineteenth-century Hungarian statesman Count Szechenyi, but had not long been finished when the 1920 Trianon Treaty transferred it to Romania, whereupon it was neglected and finally submerged by the rising waters. Since the building of the dam, modern roads have been built on both sides of the river, and the dramatic landscape makes this an excursion not to be missed. The river continues west for 77km to the small port of **MOLDOVA VECHE**. Its old quarter is largely inhabited by Serbs, while the high-rise blocks to the west are dominated by Romanians brought in during the Communist period, when the port was developed to serve the copper and molybdenum mines inland. There is, though, nothing of interest here now. Similarly, the new town, **MOLDOVA NOUĂ**, a mining community 4km inland from the port, is in a state of terminal decline, with both its hotel and museum now closed.

Before Moldova Veche, within sight of the port, the river divides around an island near the isolated **rock of Babakai**. According to legend, the Turkish governor of Moldova marooned Zuleika, one of his seven wives, here because she had attempted to elope with a Hungarian noble. Admonished to "Repent of thy sin!" (*Ba-ba-kai*) and left to die, Zuleika was rescued by her lover, who later had the joy of taunting the mortally wounded governor with the news that Zuleika was alive and had become a Christian. Another legend refers to the caves near the ruined fortress of **Golubac**, just downstream on the Serbian bank of the river, where St George is said to have slain the dragon. Thereafter, its carcass has reputedly fed the swarms of bugs that infest the town of the same name.

Southern Wallachia

In many respects, **southern Wallachia** is tedious, uninviting terrain, for while the Subcarpathians provide varied scenery and picturesque villages, below them stretch miles of featureless plains, dusty or muddy according to the season, with state farms lost amid vast fields of corn or sunflowers. Although the large industrial town of **Craiova** has a few rewarding museums, the only conceivable reason for venturing into this region is to cross the **border to Bulgaria**: there are crossing points at Calafat, 87km southwest of Craiova, and Giurgiu, some 60km south of Bucharest.

The Răscoala

Despite its rich soil, the southern plain has traditionally been one of Romania's poorest areas, as the boyars – and worse still, their estate managers – squeezed the peasants mercilessly with extortionate land taxes. The amount of available land diminished as the peasant population, taxes and rural unemployment increased, building up to the explosive **1907 uprising**, the *Răscoala*. Triggered near Vaslui in Moldavia where Jews, believed to prey upon peasants, were the first targets, the uprising raged southwards into Wallachia. Panic-stricken boyars flooded into Bucharest, demanding vengeance for the burning of their property – and the army obliged, quelling the ill-armed peasantry with cannon fire, and then executing "ringleaders" by the thousand. Though there's a **Museum of the Uprising** at Str. Dunării 54 (Tues–Sun 10am–5pm) in Roşiori de Vede (Teleorman county), the English translation of Liviu Rebreanu's novel *Uprising* (see Books, p.426) is a more gripping exposition of the subject.

Craiova

Almost every locomotive on the tracks of Romania originally emerged from the Electroputere workshops of **CRAIOVA**, which also exports to Hungary, Bulgaria, China and even Britain. It is also a centre for the Romanian automobile industry, with the Oltcit works (now Rodae, a joint venture with the Korean Daewoo conglomerate) producing many of the country's cars. These industries are here because of the ready availability of oil, whose presence is attested to by the derricks surrounding what is now the chief city of Oltenia and capital of Dolj county. Craiova does have a longer history than it might appear from its industrialized heritage, **Michael the Brave** having begun his career here as deputy governor. Now, it's a sprawling and polluted place, but you may find yourself breaking a journey to or from Bulgaria here, in which case there are a cluster of impressive museums to while away the time.

The Town

Built in 1900–08 by a French architect for one of Romania's richest men, the elegant neo-Baroque **Mihail Palace**, at Calea Unirii 10, was home to Nicolae Ceauşescu in the early 1950s when he was local party secretary, and since 1954 has housed the excellent **Art Gallery** (Tues–Sun 9am–5pm). At the core of the museum's collection are two rooms housing half a dozen pieces by Brâncuşi, including versions of *Mlle Pogany* and *The Kiss*, a room of paintings by local artist Theodor Aman (1831–91), and two dozen paintings by Grigorescu. There's also plenty of French decorative art, including Svres porcelain, and some Italian paintings, including works by Bassano and Bellotto.

Continuing south, Calea Unirii becomes the pedestrianized axis of the modern city centre; immediately to the right on the main plaza, at Str. Popa Şapcă 4, is the **Natural History Museum** (Tues–Sun 9am–5pm), offering the usual grim assortment of stuffed animals. Southwest of the museum, on Strada Madona–Dudu, is the **Madona Dudu church**, built in 1936 to house an icon of the Virgin, opposite which is the **History Museum** (Tues–Sun 9am–5pm). As well as displaying the oldest archaeological remains of Oltenia, medieval ornaments and frescoes, and some Brâncovenesc art, there's also coverage of the events in the city during the 1989 revolution, including photographs of the 24 (it's argued there were more) people killed during the fighting here.

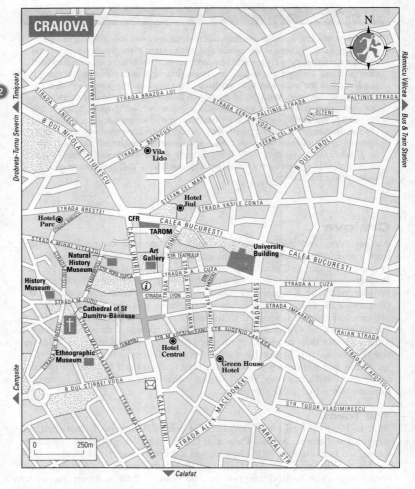

Immediately to the south on Strada Matei Basarab is the cathedral of **Sf Dumitru-Băneasa**, built in 1652 but thoroughly transformed in 1889 by Lecomte de Noy – it's less gloomy than most Orthodox churches, with a gorgeous golden glow to its frescoes. Occupying the former governor's residence, or *Casa Băniei* (dating from 1699), at Str. Matei Basarab 14, is the very worthwhile **Ethnographic Museum** (Tues–Sun 9am–5pm), which keeps a fabulous assortment of local costumes, ceramics from Horezu, porch pillars and some exquisitely carved staffs; the stunning cellar holds a superb assemblage of agricultural and viticultural implements, all with accompanying English captions.

Practicalities

Craiova's **train** and **bus stations** are located side by side northeast of the centre on Strada Dacia, from where it's a twenty-minute walk along Bulevardul

Carol I (or buses #1, #5, #12 and #29) to the main through road, Calea Bucureşti. There are two train lines between Craiova and Bucharest: one route crosses the southern plains by way of Caracal, Roşiori de Vede and Videle, on which ply stopping trains and several express trains; the second goes further north, via Piteşti (see p.104) on a non-electrified line. There are through-trains from Craiova to Iaşi via Braşov, but it's far quicker if you change trains in Bucharest. The **CFR** (Mon–Fri 7am–7.30pm) and **TAROM** (Mon–Fri 9am–5pm; ☎0251/411 049;) offices are at Calea Bucureşti 2, in the Unirea shopping complex opposite the *Hotel Jiul*. The only place to get **information** is the friendly Mapamond tourist agency, just off Calea Unirii at Str. Lyon 2 (Mon–Fri 8am–5pm, Sat 8am–1pm; ☎0251/415 071, ✉travel @mapamond.ro); they also act as an Antrec agent and can organize **homestay accommodation** (●) in the surrounding villages.

Craiova has a reasonable mix of **hotels**: the cheapest is the hostel-like *Hotel Central* at Str. M. Kogălniceanu 12 (☎0251/534 895, ⓦwww.rhp.ro/gemacon; ❸), and the best-value is the tidy *Vila Lido*, in a quiet, pleasant location at Str. C. Brâncuşi 10 (☎0251/590 332, ☏595 799; ❺). Otherwise, there's the *Green House Hotel*, Str. F. Buzeşti 25 (☎ & ☏0251/411 352; ●), which has comfortable, sunny rooms, and the very ordinary *Jiul*, at Calea Bucureşti 1 (☎0251/414 166, ☏412 462; ❺), and *Parc*, west of the centre at Str. Bibescu 16 (☎0251/417 257, ☏418 623; ❺). Both **campsites** are situated a long way out along the

Crossing into Bulgaria: Calafat and Giurgiu

The neat, orderly town of **Calafat**, 70km southwest of Craiova by road and rail, is one of the two major border crossings into Bulgaria. It's less than ten minutes' walk straight ahead from the train station to the centre of town, marked by a war memorial; to the right is the market, and to the left is the House of Culture (Casa de Cultură), surrounded by a couple of cafés and snack bars. The *Hotel Calafat* (☎0246/931 111; ❸), on Strada 22 Decembrie, is located near the port (*Vama*), and therefore convenient for the ferries to Bulgaria; turn left a block before the war memorial for Strada 22 Decembrie and head towards the obvious dockside cranes. Ferries depart hourly for the thirty-minute journey to **Vidin** in Bulgaria (winter daily 5.30am–midnight; 24hr in summer); fares are around €3 for pedestrians and €12 per car.

The second major crossing point into Bulgaria, and more convenient if travelling from Bucharest, is at **Giurgiu**, 64km due south of the capital, on the Danube. So-called rapid trains for Bulgaria take an hour and a half to crawl the 85km from Bucharest's Gara de Nord to Giurgiu Nord station just outside the town; slow trains run from Bucharest's Progresu station and continue from Giurgiu Nord to Giurgiu station, in the town next to the bus terminal. Built in 1954, to carry both road and rail traffic between Romania and Bulgaria, the three-kilometre-long **Danube Bridge** is open 24 hours a day, and with most people preferring to enter Bulgaria from Romania rather than through Serbia, it can get very congested.

If you need to stay here before pushing on, or if you don't want to arrive in Bucharest after dark, there are a few **hotels** in the town: the small and basic *Hotel Victoria* (☎0246/212 569, ☏213 453; ❸) is just five minutes from Giurgiu station at Str. Gării 1, hidden behind a block of flats to the right. For something more comfortable, try the *Vlaşca* at Str. Portului 12 (☎0246/215 321, ☏213 453; ❺), or the *Steaua Dunării*, a vaguely post-modern pile at Str. Mihai Viteazul 1 (☎0246/217 270, ☏213 453; ●), in the eastern outskirts near the bridge. You'll also find a **campsite** nearby on the Danube meadow (Lunca Dunării); plenty of buses run out this way from the town centre.

For those needing them, **visas** should be obtained either from the embassy in Bucharest (see p.87), or from home before you leave.

DN6: the *Lunca Jiului* is to the west of town on the Bucovaţ road, beyond the Ethnographic Museum, and the *Terasa Baniei* is out to the east.

There's a dire shortage of **places to eat** in Craiova, though *Sale and Pepe*, a simple restaurant serving hearty Romanian grub (it's located under the tangle of concrete next to the Mercur shopping centre), and the restaurant in the *Green House Hotel* are both better than average places. There's **Internet access** at Mama Café on the corner of Str. F. Buzeşti and Str. M. Kogălniceanu.

Travel details

Trains

Câmpulung to: Goleşti (5 daily; 1hr 30min).

Craiova to: Bucharest (15 daily; 2hr 45min–4hr 30min); Calafat (5 daily; 2hr 45min–3hr); Drobeta-Turnu Severin (12 daily; 1hr 45min–3hr); Filiaşi (24 daily; 25min–1hr); Piatra Olt (12 daily; 45min–1hr 30min); Piteşti (4 daily; 2hr 30min–4hr 30min); Sibiu (2 daily; 4hr 15min–7hr); Târgu Jiu (4 daily; 2hr–3hr); Timişoara (6 daily; 4hr 45min–6hr).

Curtea de Argeş to: Piteşti (6 daily; 1hr).

Drobeta-Turnu Severin to: Băile Herculane (8 daily; 45min–1hr 15min); Caransebeş (8 daily; 2hr–3hr 30min); Craiova (11 daily; 1hr 45min–3hr); Orşova (8 daily; 30min–45min); Timişoara (7 daily; 3hr–6hr).

Piatra Olt to: Călimăneşti (3 daily; 1hr 45min–3hr); Lotru (3 daily; 2hr–3hr 30min); Râmnicu Vâlcea (8 daily; 1hr–2hr 30min); Sibiu (6 daily; 3hr 30min–5hr 30min); Turnu Monastery (3 daily; 3hr–3hr 30min).

Piteşti to: Bucharest (9 daily; 1hr 30min–2hr 45min); Curtea de Argeş (6 daily; 1hr); Goleşti (9 daily; 10min); Titu (6 daily; 1hr–1hr 30min).

Ploieşti to: Braşov (every 30min–1hr; 1hr 45min–3hr 15min); Bucharest (every 20min–1hr; 45min–1hr 45min); Iaşi (4 daily; 4hr 30min–6hr); Slănic Prahova (6 daily; 1hr 20min–1hr 50min); Suceava (3 daily; 5hr–6hr); Târgovişte (4 daily; 2hr); Văleni (4 daily; 1hr 20min).

Râmnicu Vâlcea to: Călimăneşti (10 daily; 20–30min); Craiova (4 daily; 2hr–4hr); Lotru (8 daily; 40min–1hr); Piatra Olt (6 daily; 1hr 20min–2hr 45min); Podu Olt (4 daily; 1hr 30min–2hr 15min); Sibiu (5 daily; 2hr–3hr).

Târgovişte to: Bucharest (9 daily; 1hr 15min–2hr 15min); Ploieşti (4 daily; 2hr); Titu (9 daily; 30–45min).

Târgu Jiu to: Filiaşi (12 daily; 1hr–2hr); Petroşani (7 daily; 1hr–1hr 30min); Simeria (5 daily; 2hr 50min); Subcetate (4 daily; 2hr 15min).

Titu to: Târgovişte (9 daily; 30min–50min).

Buses and maxitaxis

Călimăneşti to: Bucharest (1 daily); Curtea de Argeş (1 daily); Polovragi (1 daily); Sibiu (3 daily); Târgu Jiu (1 daily); Voineasa (6 daily).

Câmpulung to: Braşov (4 daily); Bucharest (4 daily); Craiova (1 daily); Curtea de Argeş (2 daily); Lereşti (hourly); Piteşti (hourly); Ploieşti (2 daily); Râmnicu Vlcea (2 daily); Rucăr (10 daily); Târgovişte (4 daily).

Craiova to: Bucharest (every 45min); Drobeta-Turnu Severin (4 daily); Porţile de Fier (1 daily); Râmnicu Vâlcea (5 daily); Târgu Jiu (4 daily).

Curtea de Argeş to: Arefu (up to 7 daily); Braşov (Mon, Thurs, Fri & Sun 1 daily); Bucharest (2 daily); Câmpulung (Mon–Fri 1 daily); Piteşti (hourly); Râmnicu Vâlcea (Mon–Fri 2 daily); Sibiu (Mon & Fri 1 daily).

Drobeta-Turnu Severin to: Baia de Aramă (1 daily); Baile Herculane (5 daily); Calafat (5 daily); Craiova (4 daily); Orşova (6 daily); Râmnicu Vâlcea (1 daily); Târgu Jiu (3 daily); Timişoara (5 daily.)

Piteşti to: Braşov (3 daily); Bucharest (hourly); Câmpulung (every 30min); Craiova (3 daily); Rmnicu Vlcea (1 daily); Târgovişte (1 daily).

Ploieşti to: Câmpina (12 daily); Câmpulung via Târgovişte (2 daily); Slanic Prahova (up to 4 daily); Slon (4 daily).

Râmnicu Vâlcea to: Braşov (2 daily); Bucharest (12 daily); Câmpulung (3 daily); Cozia (9 daily); Craiova (7 daily); Curtea de Argeş (up to 3 daily); Drobeta-Turnu Severin (3 daily); Horezu (9 daily); Piteşti (12 daily); Sibiu (5 daily); Târgovişte (1 daily); Târgu Jiu (5 daily); Voineasa (3 daily).

Târgovişte to: Braşov (2 daily); Bucharest (9 daily); Câmpulung (4 daily); Piteşti (1 daily); Ploieşti (3 daily).

Târgu Jiu to: Baia de Aramă (2 daily); Baia de Fier (3 daily); Craiova (5 daily); Drobeta-Turnu Severin (3 daily); Râmnicu Vâlcea (2 daily); Reşiţa (1 daily);

Sibiu (2 daily); Timişoara (5 daily); Tismana (3 daily).

International trains

Craiova to: Belgrade (1 daily; 9hr 30min); Budapest (1 daily; 11hr 30min).
Drobeta-Turnu Severin to: Belgrade (1 daily; 7hr 30min).

Giurgiu Nord to: Istanbul (1 daily; 15hr 30min); Kiev (1 daily; 33hr); Moscow (1 daily; 48hr); Ruse (4 daily; 30min); Sofia (2 daily; 8hr 30min–9hr); Thessaloniki (1 daily; 21hr).

International ferries

Calafat to: Vidin, Bulgaria (roughly hourly).

Transylvania

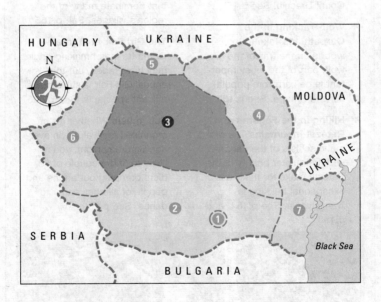

CHAPTER 3 # Highlights

* **Braşov** Wander the beautiful Baroque streets of Braşov's old town, whose medieval ramparts contain a variety of modern restaurants and bars. See p.142

* **Bran Castle** Stunningly located on a wooded outcrop, gothic Bran Castle looks every bit the vampire's lair, despite its tenuous links with the "real" Count Dracula. See p.151

* **Wolf-tracking in the Carpathians** Take to the woods on the trail of the grey wolf, part of the most important large carnivore populations in Europe. See p.153

* **Hiking in the Făgăraş and Retezat mountains** The dramatic schists of the Făgăraş and the quieter beauty of the Retezat make for the most exceptional trekking in Transylvania. See p.154 and p.190

* **Sighişoara** With its spikey skyline and quintessentially medieval old town, Sighişoara is a befitting birthplace for Vlad the Impaler. See p.159

* **Saxon fortified churches** Set high up on a hill, Biertan's Saxon church is the most prominent of the massive and austerely fortified churches that dominate many of the region's villages. See p.165

* **The Girl Fair at Muntele Găina** Its matchmaking origins may have faded, but the annual Girl Fair is still a magnificent spectacle. See p.225

* **Folk music** Whether it's an organised festival, or an average Saturday night, you're likely to find a couple of fiddlers pumping out a tune and people of all ages eager to dance. See p.230

△ Bran Castle

Transylvania

hanks to Bram Stoker and Hollywood, **Transylvania** (from the Latin for "beyond the forest") is famed abroad as the homeland of Dracula, a mountainous place where storms lash medieval hamlets, while wolves – or werewolves – howl from the surrounding woods. The fictitious image is accurate up to a point: the scenery is breathtakingly dramatic, especially in the Prahova valley, the Turda and Bicaz gorges and around the high passes; there are spooky Gothic citadels, around Braşov and at Sibiu, Sighişoara and Bran; and there was a Vlad, born in Sighişoara, who earned the grim nickname "The Impaler" and later became known as **Dracula** (see p.421).

But the Dracula image is just one element of Transylvania, whose near 100,000 square kilometres take in alpine meadows and peaks, caves and dense forests sheltering bears and wild boars, and lowland valleys where buffalo cool off in the rivers. The **population** is an ethnic jigsaw of Romanians, Magyars, Germans and Gypsies, among others, formed over centuries of migration and colonization, with high feelings in both Hungary and Romania routinely exploited by politicians. Most Hungarians view Erdély ("the forest land", their name for Transylvania) as a land first settled by them but "stolen" in 1920 (with the signing of the Trianon Treaty) by the Romanians, who continue to oppress some two million Magyars. Romanians, who call it Ardeal, assert that they appeared first in Transylvania and that for centuries it was the Magyar minority who oppressed them. Since 1920, the Romanian majority has been boosted by peasants brought in from Moldavia and Wallachia to form a new industrial proletariat. The revolution of 1989 enabled Transylvania's German population to return to their ancestral homeland, leaving the Hungarians as the region's main minority group. Meanwhile, Transylvania's Gypsies (Ţigani) still go their own way, largely unconcerned by growing prejudice against them. The result is an intoxicating brew of characters, customs and places that is best taken in slowly.

For the visitor, most striking of all are the Stuhls, the former seats of Saxon power, with their medieval streets, defensive towers and fortified churches. **Sighişoara**, the most picturesque, is their greatest legacy and an ideal introduction to Transylvania, followed by the citadels and churches of **Braşov** and **Sibiu**, and smaller settlements like **Cisnădioara**, **Hărman**, **Prejmer**, **Viscri** and **Biertan**. The other highlight of this southeastern corner is the castle at **Bran**, which looks just how a vampire count's castle should: a grim facade, perched high on a rock bluff, its turrets and ramparts rising in tiers against a dramatic mountain background. Travelling west, routes towards the Banat and Hungary pass through southwestern Transylvania, a region of peaks and moorland peppered with the citadels of the Dacians, rulers of much of Romania before the Roman conquest. To the north and east, Transylvania has a more

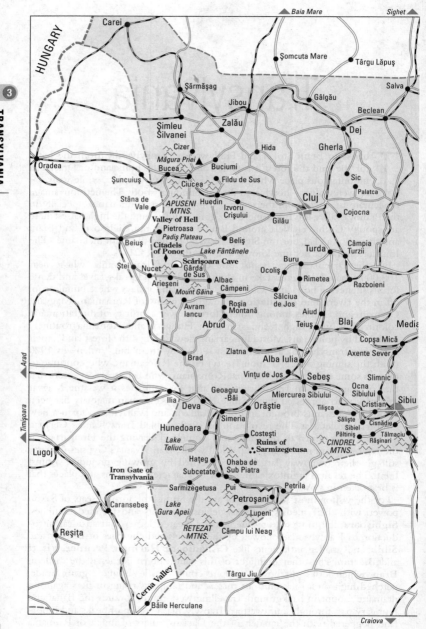

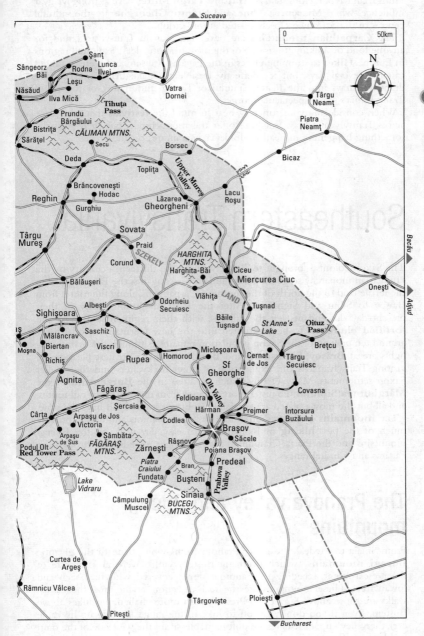

Hungarian flavour: cities such as **Cluj** and **Târgu Mureş** have a strong Magyar influence, while **Miercurea Ciuc** and **Sfântu Gheorghe** are the cultural centres of the Székely, a closely related ethnic group.

The **Carpathian mountains** are never far away in Transylvania, and for anyone fond of walking this is one of the most beautiful, least exploited regions in Europe. **Hikes** to stunning places in the Făgăraş, Apuseni and Retezat ranges can last several days, but it's perfectly feasible to make briefer yet equally dramatic forays into the Piatra Craiului or Bucegi mountains, or to one of Transylvania's many spectacular gorges.

When considering your itinerary, bear in mind the **festivals** that take place across Transylvania: May and June offer the most choice, but there's usually something happening in nearby Moldavia, Maramureş or the Banat.

Southeastern Transylvania

The Saxon colonists, brought to Transylvania in the thirteenth century by the Hungarian monarchy to guard the mountain passes against the Tatars, settled in the fertile land to the north of the southern Carpathians, along the routes from Braşov to Sibiu and Sighişoara. After the 1989 revolution, many of their present-day descendants left the villages, with their regimented layouts and **fortified churches**, to be repatriated into the new Germany – today, only around ten percent of the Saxon population remains. Although the main highlights are at **Braşov**, **Sighişoara** and **Bran**, one of the greatest pleasures of visiting Transylvania is the exploration of quiet backwaters and the smaller Saxon settlements. Many of these, such as those in the **Burzenland** or the **Mărginimea Sibiului**, lie just a short distance from major road or rail routes, and all but the most isolated are accessible by bus or train if you have the time.

The **mountains** in this region, home to bears, chamois and eagles, provide much of the best **hiking** in Romania, with easy day-walks in the Bucegi mountains and the Piatra Craiului, as well as longer expeditions through the Făgăraş and Cindrel ranges.

The Prahova valley and Bucegi mountains

From Sinaia to Predeal, the River Prahova froths white beneath the gigantic **Bucegi mountains**, which overhang Buşteni with a vertical kilometre of sheer escarpment, receding in grandiose slopes covered with fir, beech and rowan trees. These mountains are the real attraction of the area: the easiest walks are those above Sinaia and Predeal, with more challenging hikes above Buşteni. Even if you don't stop off to hike in the range (or ride up by cable car), the valley's upper reaches are unforgettable: sit on the west side of the train for the best views.

The stunning **Prahova valley**, dotted with fantastic caves and other karstic phenomena, is shadowed by the DN1 (E60) highway and the Bucharest–Braşov **rail line**: express services take two and a half hours to Braşov, stopping en route at Ploieşti (see p.97) and the resorts of **Sinaia**, in northern Wallachia, and **Predeal**, in Transylvania proper. There are also plenty of slower trains that stop at the smaller towns and villages – change at either Sinaia or Predeal for a Personal train to **Buşteni**, also served by some Accelerats. The DN1 has been largely modernised in recent years, and construction of a Bucharest–Braşov–Târgu Mureş–Cluj–Oradea motorway was scheduled to start in 2004. Frequent local buses and maxitaxis link Ploieşti, Sinaia, Buşteni and Azuga.

Sinaia

SINAIA, 122km from Bucharest, is famed for its magnificent mountain scenery and royal castle. Though technically in the province of Wallachia, it has much in common with the neighbouring Transylvanian towns and has been included in this chapter for convenience. Originally the preserve of a few hermits and shepherds, then an exclusive aristocratic resort, it is nowadays full of holidaymakers here to walk or ski in the dramatic Bucegi mountains.

Arrival and information

Steps lead up from Sinaia **train station** to the main street, Bulevardul Carol I, and beyond it the Dimitrie Ghica Park; turn left along the boulevard for the town centre. There's a **tourist information centre** in front of the town hall at B-dul Carol I no. 47 (☎0244/315 656, ⓦwww.infosinaia.ro; 9am–8pm daily), which gives free information but cannot help with accommodation. In addition to the plentiful buses and maxitaxis along the DN1, local minibuses run up to the hillside areas of Platoul Izvor and Furnica, and occasionally to Cota 1400, the roadhead at the mid-station of the Bucegi cable car.

Car rental is possible through Hertz (☎0244/310 426), at the *Hotel Palace*, and there are two **Internet** places opposite the *Hotel New Montana*. For **tours**, go to the Agencia de Turism Sinaia at B-dul Carol I no. 8 (☎0244/311 551, ⓦwww.mmc.ro/sinaia). **Ski gear** can be bought or rented in the *Hotel New Montana* and at Snow, located by the cable car terminal at Str. Cuza Vodă 2.

Hiking in the Bucegi mountains

The Romanian-language **maps** of the Munţii Bucegi are invaluable for hiking – they shouldn't be hard to understand if you refer to our vocabulary on p.40. Most walks in the region are easy day-walks, with cable cars an alternative on the steeper sections. There are plenty of **mountain cabanas**, which in theory aren't allowed to turn hikers away, and if you're really stuck, the maps also locate refuges and sheepfolds (*refugiu* and *stână*), where you may find shelter.

Snow covers **Mount Omu**, the highest point of the Bucegi (2505m), for two hundred or more days a year, but elsewhere retreats during April, leaving the meadows to a wealth of **wildflowers** such as ladies' gloves, grape-ferns and edelweiss. The forests shelter woodcock, hazel grouse and nightingales from the circling golden eagles, while other **wildlife** includes the Carpathian stag (around Bran) and wild boar. The last, like wolves and bears, are only a potential threat during the winter (when food is scarce) or if their litters are endangered. Above the forest, on the cliffs to the north of the massif, you may well see chamois.

Campsites, DN1 and Braşov

Peleş

Pelişor

STRADA PELEŞULUI

Peleşului Stream

ALEEA CARMEN SILVA

WWI Cemetery

Petrom Service Station

STRADA GĂRII

Casino

Dimitrie Ghica Park

Museum

BULEVARD CAROL I

STRADA GĂRII

River Prahova

Sinaia Monastery

STRADA FURNICA

STRADA MĂNĂSTIRII

STRADA OCTAVIAN GOGA

Train Station

ALEEA SFÂNTA ANA

ALEEA BRADULUI

STR DA LUCHIAN

STRADA MIHAIL CANTACUZINO

STRADA SĂNIŞULUI

STRADA CAZĂRMII

STRADA FURNICA

STRAD A ZĂGII

STRADA VÂRFUL CU DOR

BULEVARD CAROL I

STRADA GĂRII

STRADA SCHIORILOR

STRADA AOSTA

STRADA FURNICA

STRADA AOSTA

STEFAN CEL MARE

STRADA SION

STRADA AOSTA

STRADA GHEORGHE ŞINCĂ

VALEA REA

STIR GHEORGHE DOJA

COSTULUI IBIS

STRADA THEODOR AMAN

STRADA KOGĂLNICEANU

STIR DRUM

AL COTEI

STRADA SOIMUL

STRADA PUSTNICULUI

ALEEA SEREI

Căşeriei Stream

STRADA GĂRII

River Prahova

STRADA PUSTNICULUI

STRADA PINULUI

STR. TELECABINEI

STRADA KOGĂLNICEANU

I

STR. CUZA VODA

Primaria

PIAŢA UNIRII

J

STRADA PUSTNICULUI

STRADA CERBUL

STRADA KOGĂLNICEANU

STRADA CUZA VODA

BULEVARD CAROL I

Market

STRADA CALEA PRAHOVEI

VALEA REA

Piscu Câinelui Cabana

N

STRADA AVRAM IANCU

K

L

M

0   100m

Ploieşti and Bucharest

Furnica Hotel, Schiorilor Cabana and Cota 1400

Cota 1400

Accommodation

The town is well served with **hotels**, the prices of which vary greatly; there's a five-percent resort tax payable on the first night, which can sometimes be avoided by paying cash. The best **villas** are inside Peleş Park (℡0244/310 353, ℻311 150; ⑥) – avoid those in the upper town – while touts at the station and on the way into town offer **private rooms** (①). There are two **campsites** north of Sinaia; *Izvorul Rece*, at km118 and, 8km further on, *Vadul Cerbului*. Finally, the **cabanas** at the *Piscu Câinelui* (℡0244/315 492; ①) and *Schiorilor* (℡0244/313 655, ℻315 025 ①) at Drumul Cotei 7 are small but right on the outskirts of town.

3

Anda B-dul Carol I no. 30 ℡0244/306 020, ℇ hotel.anda@excelnet.ro. Less grandiose than the huge ski hotels but modern and comfortable. ⑦

Caraiman B-dul Carol I no. 4, in Dimitrie Ghica Park ℡0244/313 551, ℻310 625. Sinaia's first hotel, opened in 1881, remains very classy, with large, comfortable rooms and helpful staff. ②

Cerbul B-dul Carol I no. 19 ℡0244/312 391, ℇ hotelcerbul@hotmail.com. Renovated, affordable rooms, some with communal showers. ④

Economat Str. Aleea Peleşului 2 ℡0244/311 151. Benefiting from a great location inside Peleş Park, the *Economat* has a good restaurant as well. ⑥–⑦

El Dorado Str. Avram Iancu 14 ℡0244/312 667. This youth hostel, mainly dealing with groups but also welcoming individual travellers (aged under 25, in theory), has en-suite twin rooms and a full restaurant. ②

Furnica Strada Furnica 50 ℡0244/311 850, ℻311 853. A mock-Jacobean pile with cable TV and a disco. ④

Intim Strada Furnica 1 ℡0244/315 557. A cheaper, atmospheric place with excellent views over and into the monastery, the semi-privatized *Intim* offers good value, though hot water is available at set times only. ③

Marami Str. Furnica 52 ℡0244/315 560, ⓦ www.marami.ro. A stylish new hotel with sauna, jacuzzi, gym, and a good bar-pizzeria. ⑦–⑧

New Montana B-dul Carol I no. 24 ℡0244 /312 751, ⓦ www.newmontana.ro. This modern ski hotel, with pool, sauna and gym, attracts lots of tour groups. ⑨

Casa Noastră B-dul Republicii 9 ℡0244/314 556. An amazing high-rise wooden construction, which also houses a restaurant and deli. ②

Palace Str. Octavian Goga 11 ℡0244/312 051, ℇ scpalacesa@fx.ro. In the park by the casino, this gem of a hotel opened in 1912 retains the Edwardian style and consistently good service that made it famous, although it now also has a distinctly tacky nightclub. ⑦

Păltiniş B-dul Carol I no. 67 ℡0244/311 022. Pleasantly traditional neo-Brâncovenesc pile built atop two floors of treatment rooms, with innovations such as a non-smoking floor and real curtains. ③–⑤

Sinaia B-dul Carol I no. 8 ℡0244/311 551, ⓦ http://mmc.ro/sinaia. The main ski hotel in town, this has all the comforts but can get very busy in season. ⑥

The Town

Sinaia's train station is a historical site in itself; here, the Iron Guard murdered the Liberal leader Ion Duca in 1933, only three weeks after he had taken office as prime minister. Steps lead to **Dimitrie Ghica Park**, which contains a museum (daily 9am–7pm), with a basic natural history display and several fine buildings in neo-Brâncovenesc style. Beyond the park, a World War I military cemetery also houses a poetic memorial to the US airmen killed over Romania in World War II; from here, a footpath leads off Strada Mănăstirii up to **Sinaia Monastery** (daylight hours; €1), built in 1690–95 on the site of an earlier hermitage. The original church, decorated with a fine Last Judgement soon after it was built, is not the one before you as you enter (which was built in 1842–46), but hides through a passageway to the left.

Just behind the monastery, a path leads up to one of the most popular destinations in Romania, **Peleş Castle** (Tues 11am–5pm, Wed–Sun 9am–5pm; €3, park free; ⓦ www.peles.ro). Set in a large park landscaped in the English fashion, the castle outwardly resembles a Bavarian Schloss. Built in 1875–83 for

Carol I, and largely decorated by his eccentric wife Elisabeta (better known as the popular novelist Carmen Sylva), it contains 160 rooms, richly decorated in ebony, mother of pearl, walnut and leather – all totally alien to the traditional styles of Romanian art – and stuffed solid with antiques and copies of paintings housed in Bucharest's National Art Museum. There are two Venetian-style rooms, with kitschy Murano chandeliers, and a Moorish hall based on the Alhambra; one Louis XIV room (with paintings by a young Gustav Klimt) houses Romania's first cinema. How a man of such reputedly austere tastes as Carol managed to live here is something of a mystery, and indeed it hasn't been lived in since his death in 1914.

To visit the palace, follow signs to a ticket window and then to the separate entry hall where you wait for a guide to take you on a tour of sixteen rooms on the ground floor only, as the stairs and floors are in poor condition. Note that there are no toilets available.

Following the monarchy's demise, Peleş was opened to the public in 1953, with a temporary interruption when the Ceauşescus appropriated it as a "state palace". They actually preferred to stay in the **Pelişor Palace** (Little Peleş; Wed–Sun 9.30am–5pm; €1.50), a few hundred metres up the hill, built in 1899–1903 for Ferdinand and Marie, Carol I's heirs. Although its exterior is also in the German Renaissance style, the interior is Art Nouveau, with Viennese furniture and Tiffany and Lalique vases. **Foişor Lodge**, a little above Pelişor, was finished in 1878 and was home to Queen Elisabeta from 1914, and then to Prince Carol (later King Carol II) and Princess Helen from 1921; here, Carol met the Jewish Magda Lupescu, who for thirty years remained his mistress and the power behind the throne, outraging Romanian society, which tended towards anti-Semitism. Foişor park is open to the public (Wed–Sun 9am–4pm), but the lodge isn't.

Across the DN1 from the lower gate of the Peleş park, signs lead to the **George Enescu Memorial House** (Tues–Sun 9am–3pm; €1), in Cumpătu, 2km north of the town centre. Known as the Vila Luminiş (Sunshine House), it was built for the great composer-violinist in 1921–26 in the style of a *conac* (Turkish administrator's house); he spent his summers here until 1946. In 1995 it was handed over to the European Cultural Center, set up at the suggestion of Yehudi Menuhin, Enescu's favourite pupil. The ground floor contains Oriental, Biedermeyer and traditional Romanian furnishings, and Enescu's Ibert piano; upstairs are his near monastically simple bedroom (as well as Menuhin's more conventional room), and his workroom, looking west to the peaks of the Bucegi mountains, and home to photos, posters and scores of his works. Tours of Enescu's house are accompanied by his lushly romantic music, CDs of which are sold at the ticket desk.

Eating and drinking

There's fine **dining** to be had in the restaurants of the *Palace* and *New Montana* hotels in particular, but the most interesting food in Sinaia, as long as you're not a vegetarian, is the traditional Serbian fare served at the *Taverna Sârbului* (☎0244/314 400), a taxi ride away up Calea Codrului. In the centre of town, the *Bucegi* at B-dul Carol I no. 22 has very good pizza, game and excellent aubergine salad; there's a large *terasa* set back from the road. Next door at no. 18, the *Irish House* (✆www.irishhouse.ro) offers dishes such as Dublin chicken's liver, Irish breakfast, and "Irish salad" as well as Romanian dishes and pizza and pasta. To the south of the centre at B-dul Republicii 9, the *Casa Noastră* (see above) has an excellent *crama*, *terasa* and deli. The *Gaucho Steakhouse* (which actually serves Romanian dishes) opposite the *Hotel*

Furnica, and the *Restaurant Snow*, by the cable car terminal at Str. Cuza Vodă 2, are also both worth trying out.

For a **drink**, try the *Old Nick Pub*, B-dul Carol I no. 22 or the *Irish House* at no. 18, with draught Guinness and Sheridans, and Jameson's whisky (there's also an Irish pub in the *Hotel New Montana*). For later orders, try the *Blue Angel* at B-dul Carol I no. 41, where there's a disco until 4am, as well as billiards and table tennis; the *Disco Diana*, under the *Hotel Sinaia*, is also active until 4am. The only **cinema** is the Perla, opposite the *Sinaia*.

Around Sinaia

From its terminal on Strada Cuza Vodă (behind the *Hotel New Montana*), a cable car (summer Tues–Sun 8.30am–5pm; €1.50) whisks you aloft to an altitude of 1400m (**Cota 1400**) at the roadhead halfway up the hill, site of the *Alpin* hotel and numerous cabanas. From here, there's another cable car (Tues–Sun 8.30am–5pm; €1.50) to **Cota 2000**, and a chairlift (Wed–Mon 9am–5pm) to **Cota 1950**, both just a five-minute walk from the *Miorița* cabana on Mount Furnica. This is the start of the taxing Papagul ski run back down to Cota 1400. To the south, below Cota 1950, is the *Valea Dorului* cabana (☎0244/313 531; ➊), from where there's a three-hour circular walk down the Dorului valley to the beautiful tarns of **La Lacuri**, following a path marked with yellow crosses and red stripes.

Heading north, an attractive and easy half-hour walk takes you from Mount Furnica to *Piatra Arsă*, behind Mount Jepi Mari, where the cabana (➊) has been joined by the National Centre For Sports Training at Altitude. Here, blue triangles indicate the route downwards to Bușteni (2hr maximum) via **La Scari**, a spectacular "stairway" hewn into rock, while another path (marked with blue stripes) drops westwards into the central depression of the Bucegi, reaching the *Peştera* hotel (☎0245/311 094; ➋) and monastery in about an hour (for routes north of the *Peştera*, see p.141). Just west of the *Peştera*, past the **Ialomiţa cave** – a 400-metre long grotto with a walkway in awful condition (bring a flashlight) – is an unmarked path leading up through the Batrâna valley past several waterfalls, the "Gorge of the Bear" and two natural bridges. Half an hour to the south lies the *Padina* cabana (☎0244/314 331; ➊), from where a very rough road leads further south past more caves and gorges to a camping spot near **Lake Bolboci**, eventually emerging from the Izvoraşu valley just south of Sinaia.

Bușteni

Ten kilometres up the valley from Sinaia is **BUȘTENI**, a small resort overshadowed by the sheer peaks of Caraiman (2384m) and Coştila (2498m), separated from each other by the dark Alba valley and the highest conglomerate cliffs in Europe. Caraiman is identified by a huge cross, a war memorial erected in the 1920s, and Coştila by a TV tower that looks like a space rocket. There's nothing much to Bușteni itself, other than the house of writer Cezar Petrescu and a church founded by Carol I and Queen Elisabeta in 1889, but it's a good base for the excellent walking to be had in the surrounding mountains.

From the **train station**, which more or less defines the town centre, it's just a few hundred metres south on the main DN1 to the *Caraiman* **hotel** at B-dul Libertății 89 (☎0244/320 156; ➋), which caters to the youth market with a disco, table tennis and swimming pool; several hundred metres further south (past the Café-internet Gallaxy and to the right at the country's oldest paper

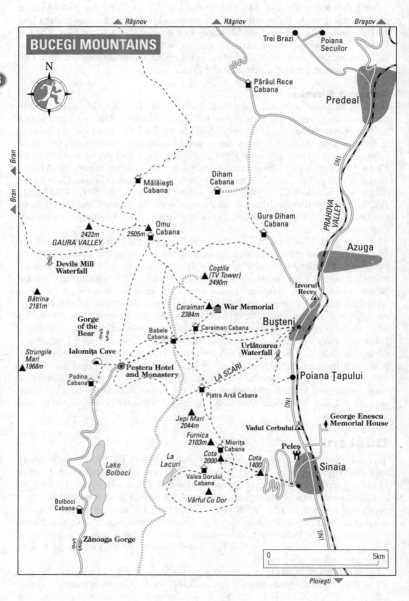

BUCEGI MOUNTAINS

N

Râşnov
Râşnov
Braşov

Trei Brazi
Poiana
Secuilor

Pârâul Rece
Cabana

Predeal

Bran
Bran

Mălăieşti
Cabana

Diham
Cabana

Gura Diham
Cabana

PRAHOVA VALLEY

Azuga

2422m
GAURA VALLEY

2505m
Omu
Cabana

DN1

Devils Mill
Waterfall

Coştila
(TV Tower)
2490m

Izvorul
Recei

Bătrina
2181m

Caraiman
2384m
War Memorial

Buşteni

Gorge
of the
Bear

Babele
Cabana
Caraiman Cabana

Urlătoarea
Waterfall

Strungile
Mari
1968m

Ialomiţa Cave

Peştera Hotel
and Monastery

LA SCARI

Poiana Ţapului

Padina
Cabana

Piatra Arsă Cabana

DN1

Jepi Mari
2044m

Vadul Cerbului

George Enescu
Memorial House

Furnica
2103m
Mioriţa
Cabana

Peleş

Lake
Bolboci

La
Lacuri

Cota
2000

Cota
1400

Sinaia

Valea Dorului
Cabana

Bolboci
Cabana

Vârful Cu Dor

Zănoaga Gorge

0   5km

Ploieşti

mill), at Str. Telecabiniei 36, is the *Silva* (📞0244/322 151, 🌐www.hotelsilva.ro; ⑤), Buşteni's best hotel, although it has no single rooms. On the same road, at no. 22, the *Villa Laura* guesthouse (📞0241/552 858, 🌐www.paradistours.ro; ④) offers discounts to Hostelling International members. To the north, at B-dul Libertăţii 153, the *Hotel Alexandros* (📞0244/320 138, ✉savinex@fx.ro; ⑦) has a lively disco and sports facilities. The friendly and informal *Motel Maximilian* is across the tracks to the southeast (in the Zamora quarter), at Str. Pescariei 8 (📞0244/323 297; ①); it's most easily reached by car (take the first turning on the left south of Str. Telecabinei). Strada Valea Albă, just north of the station, leads to the *Hotel-restaurant Marietta* (Str. Buştenilor 32, 📞0244/322 224, ✉alam.lembang@digicom.ro; ④). Strada Valea Albă also leads to the new Calinderu ski slope and quad chairlift. It's also worth enquiring at the **tourist office** (Mon–Fri 9am–4pm, Sat 9am–noon; 📞244/320 027) at B-dul Libertăţii 202, 150m north of the train station, about **villas** and **private rooms** (①); you'll also see *Oferim cazare* signs on houses that offer accommodation. The *Popasul Azuga* **campsite**, (📞0244/320 502/9), is about 1km north at km133 of the main DN1, but is close to the train line and so very noisy.

The best **restaurant** is in the *Hotel Silva*; other options are the *Crama The King*, B-dul Libertăţii 109, offering the usual pork, chicken, pizza and spaghetti, and the *Hotel Caraiman*, which serves good-value lunches on its *terasa*. The *Cofetăria Roza*, opposite the train station, sells snack-sized pizzas as well as coffee and cakes. You may find **events** taking place at the Casa de Cultura, or the Maison Franco-Roumaine opposite at B-dul Libertăţii 158.

Around Buşteni

From the *Hotel Silva* on Strada Telecabiniei, 1.5km south of the train station, an easy path marked with red dots leads to the **Urlătoarea waterfall** and back to the road at Poiana Ţapului (2hr), while a harder footpath, marked with blue crosses, and a **cable car** (Wed–Mon 8am–4.45pm in summer; €2), ascend the Jepi valley to the **cabanas** at *Caraiman* (📞0244/320 817; ①) and *Babele* (📞0244/314 450; ①). The latter offers a panoramic view, and is only five minutes' walk from an impressive skull-like rock formation, the **Babele Sphinx**. From here, you can walk (1hr) or ride the cable car (daily 8am–4pm) down to the *Peştera* hotel and monastery (see p.139). North of the *Babele* cabana, a path marked by yellow stripes leads to Mount Omu (4hr); alternatively, from *Peştera*, a blue-striped path takes you up the Ialomiţa valley to Omu (1–2hr). There's a small hut here (📞0244/320 677; closed winter), without running water; many hikers prefer to stay (unofficially) in the Omu meteorological station.

Though completely cloudless days are rare in the vicinity of **Mount Omu**, it is possible to see the Burzenland, the ridge of the Piatra Craiului, to the west and the Făgăraş range beyond. From Omu, a path marked with blue stripes descends a glacial valley past eroded rock "chimneys" to the *Mălăieşti* chalet (2–3hr); two other paths lead down **to Bran** in about six hours – the route indicated by yellow triangles is easier going, while the path marked with red crosses drops down the superb Gaura valley past the **Cascada Moara Dracului** (Devil's Mill waterfall), a fitting approach to "Dracula's Castle" in the village below (see p.110).

Mountain **bikes** can be rented in the village of **AZUGA**, a couple of kilometres north of Buşteni, which is known mainly for its brewery and bottle factory but also has a ski run and some accommodation. The best is the Hotel Azuga, Str. Victoriei 87 (📞 & 📠0244/327 406; ⑤); Pensiunea Căprioara, Valea Azugii 38 (📞0244/326 318/9) and Pensiunea Flora, Florilor 50 (📞0722/354 718; ②) are cheaper alternatives. The British winemakers Halewood have plans for a tasting hall in Azuga to promote their Dealu Mare wines (made just to the south of the Prahova valley) and especially sparkling champenoise.

Predeal

PREDEAL, sitting on the 1038-metre pass of the same name and marking the official border of Transylvania, is further from the more spectacular peaks that dominate Sinaia and Buşteni to the south, but is a popular centre for winter sports and easy strolls.

There's a reasonable choice of **accommodation** in town, which can be booked through the **tourist office** (☏0268/455 330, ⓦ www.predeal.ro; daily 8am–8pm) in a striking modern building outside the station, itself a decent piece of communist modernism. Private rooms and villas can be booked at SC Cristianul Braşov's office in the train station (☏ & ⓕ0268/455 042), though you're likely to be offered a room while near the station anyway. The *Carmen*, a good private hotel just south of the station at B-dul Săulescu 121 (☏0268/456 656, ⓕ455 426; ⑥) has a sauna, massage, gym and Internet, and can also provide slightly cheaper rooms in a villa. North of the station at B-dul Săulescu 129, the *Hotel Bulevard*, is a neo-Brâncovenesc pile with an attractive stair- and lift-well. Further north, on Strada Trei Brazi, are the *Cirus*, an old-style ski chalet (☏0268/456 035; ②), and the *Orizont* (☏0268/455 150, ⓕ455 472; ⑤), a good modern hotel with a swimming pool.

There are a few good **restaurants**, such as *Casa Ana*, B-dul Săulescu 2 bis (☏0268/456 572) and *Căprioara*, Str Libertăţii 90 (☏0268/456 964), which both serve Italian food, and *Mama Maria*, Str. Eminescu 28 (☏0268/456 650; closed Tues), which despite its name, serves not Italian but good Romanian fare. For those who prefer to cater for themselves, there's a grocery **shop** opposite the *Hotel Carmen*. The *Fulg de Neà* at Str. Teleferic 1 (☏0268/456 089, 455 413), on the way to the Clăbucet chairlift, has the best **bar** in town, and good food too; there's also good beer at the Green Club (or Guinness Pub), B-dul Săulescu 32 (☏0268/456 636), and there are **clubs** in most accommodation places. Decent **ski equipment** can be rented at the *Orizont* and *Cioplea* hotels, at the *Fulg de Neà* (which also has mountain bikes), or the Clăbucet-Sosire chairlift terminal.

Around Predeal

There's good **walking** in these hills, not as dramatic as in the Bucegi but with fine views to the high peaks and cliffs, and plenty of **cabanas** to aim for. *Gârbova* (☏0788/609 348) and *Susai* (☏0268/456 258) are within a few kilometres of Clăbucet-Plecare, and there are others northwest of Predeal in the foothills of the Bucegi massif: these include *Trei Brazi* (☏0268/608 971; ②), with a campsite nearby, *Pârâu Rece* (☏0268/456 491; ①) and *Poiana Secuilor* (☏0268/846 061; ①) – four buses a day run to the *Pârâu Rece*, within 2km of the others. The *Diham* cabana (☏0788/608 161) is higher up and further south, with a slalom run nearby.

Braşov

The medieval Saxons, with an eye for trade and invasion routes, sited their largest settlements within a day's journey of the Carpathian passes. **BRAŞOV** (Kronstadt to the Saxons and Brassó to the Hungarians) was one of the best placed and grew prosperous and fortified as a result, and for many centuries the

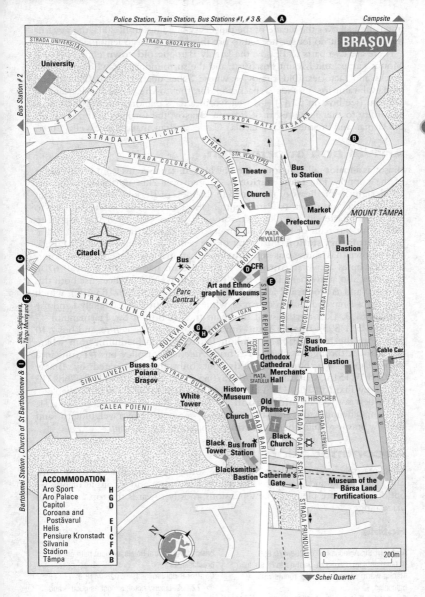

BRAȘOV

STRADA UNIVERSITĂȚII

STRADA GROZĂVESCU

University

STRADA SITEI

Bus Station # 2 ▲

STRADA ALEX. I. CUZA

STRADA MATEI BASARAB

B

3

TRANSYLVANIA | Brașov

STRADA COLONEL BUZOIANU

STR. VLAD ȚEPEȘ

STRADA IULIU MANIU

Theatre

Bus to Station

Church

Market

Prefecture

MOUNT TÂMPA

PIAȚA REVOLUȚIEI

STRADA N. IORGA

Citadel

Bus

CFR **D**

EROILOR

Bastion

Sibiu, Sighișoara, Târgu Mureș and ▲ **F** ◄ **C**

STRADA LUNGĂ

Parc Central

Art and Ethno-graphic Museums

E

STRADA REPUBLICII

STRADA POȘTĂVARULUI

STRADA NICOLAE BĂLCESCU

STRADA CASTELULUI

STRADA T. BREDICEANU

BULEVARD

LIVADA POȘTEI

STRADA SF. IOAN

G **H**

STR. MUREȘENILOR

PIAȚA ENESCU

Bus to Station

Bastion

Cable Car

Bartolomei Station, Church of St Bartholomew & ▲ **I**

SIRUL LIVEZII

STRADA DUPĂ ZIDURI

Buses to Poiana Brașov

Orthodox Cathedral

Merchants' Hall

PIAȚA SFATULUI

History Museum

White Tower

Old Phamacy

STR. HIRSCHER

CALEA POIENII

Church

STRADA BARIȚIU

Black Church

STRADA POARTA SCHEI

STRADA CERBULUI

Black Tower

Bus from Station

Blacksmiths' Bastion

Catherine's Gate

Museum of the Bârsa Land Fortifications

STRADA PRUNDULUI

ACCOMMODATION

Aro Sport	H
Aro Palace	G
Capitol	D
Coroana and Postăvarul	E I
Helis	C
Pensiure Kronstadt	F
Silvania	A
Stadion	B
Tâmpa	B

N

0   200m

▼ *Schei Quarter*

Saxons there constituted an elite whose economic power long outlasted its feudal privileges. During the 1960s, the communist regime drafted thousands of Moldavian villagers to Brașov's new factories, making it Transylvania's second largest city. The economic collapse in the 1980s led to the **riots of November 15, 1987** and again in **December 1989**, the casualties of which were claimed as martyrs by the new regime; as such, bullet holes were deliberately left

143

unrepaired all over the facade of the university buildings until 2003, the government decided it no longer needed to use them as a claim to legitimacy.

There are two parts to Braşov: the largely Baroque **old town** coiled beneath Mount Tâmpa and Mount Postăvaru; and the surrounding sprawl of apartment blocks and factories. Old Braşov – whose Schei quarter, Black Church and medieval ramparts provide a backdrop for the town's colourful Pageant of the Juni (see box on p.147) – is well worth a day's exploration; and the town's proximity to the alpine resort of **Poiana Braşov**, the fortified Saxon churches of Hărman and Prejmer, and "Dracula's Castle" at Bran, make it an excellent base.

Arrival and information

Braşov is a major rail junction, served by long-distance trains from every corner of the country. The **train station** is situated over 2km northeast of the old town, right in the heart of the concrete drabness of Braşov's new suburbs. Bus #4 will take you down to Parc Central (also known as Titulescu), and on to the Schei quarter in the old town. Buy a day pass (€0.50) if you expect to make four bus trips or more. Local trains from Zărneşti and Sibiu also call at the **Bartolomei station**, northwest of the centre at the end of Strada Lungă.

The town has three **bus stations**: international services and most long-distance buses arrive at **Autogară 1**, by the train station (☎0268/150 670); maxitaxis also arrive here. Buses from Piteşti and Râmnicu Vâlcea use both this terminal and **Autogară 2** at Str. Avram Iancu 114 (☎0268/163 192), which also serves Bran and Curtea de Argeş, while services from the Székely Land use **Autogară 3**, 1km northeast of the main train station at Str. Harmanului 47 (☎0268/311 595). **Bus #12** runs from *Autogară 2* to the centre, and bus #10 runs from the train station to Stadion Tineret (Youth Stadium), from where you can cut through to *Autogară 2*; from *Autogară 3*, trolley bus #1 runs into town. Braşov has hordes of **taxis**, but only those operated by Bratax (☎0268/311515), Cod (☎940, ☎0745/055 599), Martax (☎944, ☎0268/313 040), Rey Taxi (☎0268/411 111) or RoTaxi (☎0744/377 999) are reliable.

The best sources of **information** are Roving Romania (☎0268/326 271, ⓔroving@deltanet.ro) and the websites ⓦwww.brasovtravelguide.ro and ⓦwww.brasov.ro, plus there's a **listings** magazine, *Zile şi Nopţi*.

Accommodation

Most reasonably priced places to stay are some way from the old town, with just a few bland and overpriced **hotels** in the centre and a couple of budget options. There are plenty of new pensions, mostly towards the top end of the price range.

Hotels

Ambient Str. Aninoasa 5 ☎0268/470 856, ⓔhotelambient1@xnet.ro. Just north of Str. Iuliu Maniu; warm personal service, rooms with balconies. ❻

Aro Palace B-dul Eroilor 9 ☎0268/478 800, 142 840, ⓔaro.palace@rdslink.ro. Also known as the *Carpaţi*, this is the best hotel in Braşov, with all mod cons and a fine restaurant, but ludicrously mafioso. ❾

Aro Sport Str. Sfântu Ioan 3 ☎0268/478 800, 542 840. Hidden away on a side street, this is the most basic of the central hotels, without bath or breakfast. ❸

Capitol B-dul Eroilor 19 ☎0268/418 920, ⓕ472 999. Luxury hotel; almost as good – and as expensive – as the *Aro Palace*. ❼

Coroana Str. Republicii 62 ☎0268/544 330, ⓕ541 505. The only place in town with real character, this hotel is set in an atmospheric building and has a pleasant restaurant from where you can watch the city's main street. ❻

Heliş Memorandumului 29 ☏ 0268/410 223, 415 019, ✉ helis@deltanet.ro. Hungarian-run hotel out of the centre, not luxurious but well equipped and English-speaking. ❼

Pensiunea Kronstadt Str. de Mijloc 67 ☏ 0268/471 737, 471 295. Very warm and helpful, and more affordable than comparable places in Braşov. ❻

Pension Montana Stejeris 2A ☏ 0268/472 731. Excellent bed and breakfast (no other meals available), on the road up to Poiana Braşov, with views over the city. ❼

Silvania Str. Căprioarei 27 ☏ 0268/415 556, ✆ 551 739. A pleasant and comfy guesthouse on a dirt road north of the centre (take bus #14). ❻

Stadion Str. Cocorului 12 ☏ 0268/587 435. Just 100m from the Autocamion bus terminal (see below), with good, simple rooms, and tennis courts. Easily the best value in Braşov. ❷

Stejeriş Str Stejerişului 15 ☏ 0268/476 249. Very comfortable guesthouse 2km along the Poiana Braşov road; shared bathrooms. ❸

Tâmpa Str. Matei Basarab 68 ☏ & ✆ 0268 /415 180. A bit of a hike up a cobbled road and through the arch above no.66; a concrete block but pleasant enough inside. ❷

Tineret ADABelle Str. Pieţei 5 ☏ 0268/411080; ✉ adabelleh@msn.com. Across the road from the theatre, a modern place, almost hostel-style but with en-suite rooms and prices that include breakfast and dinner. ❹

Hostels, private rooms, camping and cabanas

The *Kismet Dao Villa*, an offshoot of Bucharest's *Elvis Villa*, is a backpackers' **hostel** at Str. Democratiei 2b (☏ 0268/514 296, 478 930, ⓦ www .kismetdao.com; ❷–❸); it's located in Schei, near the last stop on bus #4's route from the train station, or €1 by taxi. You'll find their gofer at the station until 4pm and 5.30–9.30pm daily. Something of a party scene, the hostel has dorms, private rooms and laundry facilities, and the price includes breakfast, a free beer and an hour's Internet time daily.

Closer to the centre or the station, your best option may be a **private room** (❶), likely to be in a modern apartment block; there are many people offering these on arrival at the train station: try the knowledgeable and characterful Maria Bolea and her husband Grig (☏ 0744/816 970; ❶); the helpful Eugene (☏ 0722/542 581, ✉ ejrr68@yahoo.com); the Beke family (☏ 0268/461 888); the Babes family (☏ 0268/543 728); Gigi and Diana Borcea (☏ 0268/416 243); and Gabriel Ivan (☏ 0744/844 223). Most can arrange local excursions.

The *Dârste* **campsite** (☏ 0268/339 462, ⓦ www.campingdirste.ro) is about 7km from Braşov's centre, on the Bucharest highway, the DN1. Take trolley #3 or bus #6 from the centre, or tram #101 from the train station, to the Saturn/Autocamion terminus (also known as Roman or IABV) on Calea Bucureşti, and then bus #21 (for Săcele, every 10min) out along the main highway until it turns off; the campsite is ten minutes' walk further south along the DN1. The site has reasonable facilities plus chalets, bungalows and rooms (❶) with 24-hour hot water.

The Town

The bus from the train station will set you down either at **Parc Central**, on the edge of the old town, or on **Piaţa Sfatului**, at the heart of a Baroque townscape that is quintessentially Germanic. The hub of Braşov's social and commercial life is the pedestrianized **Strada Republicii** (Purzengasse) leading from the main square towards the new town and the train station. It's a popular place for a stroll at lunchtime and in the early evening at its north-eastern end, there is still some bullet damage from the 1989 revolution to be seen on the circular Volksbank building; turning right along Eroilor here, you'll come to the theatre, department store and **market**, from where you can catch bus #4 (beware of pickpockets here) back to the train station.

Piaţa Sfatului

Local legend has it that when the Pied Piper enticed the children from Hamelin in Germany, they vanished underground and emerged in Transylvania near the site of Braşov's main square, now called the **Piaţa Sfatului** (Council Square). It is lined with sturdy merchants' houses, their red roof tiles tilted rakishly, presenting their shop fronts to the Casa Sfatului (Council House) in the centre of the square, which was built by 1420, rebuilt in the eighteenth century, and now houses the **History Museum** (Tues–Sun 10am–6pm). The exhibits tell the story of the Saxon guilds, who dominated Braşov and met in the Hirscher Haus or **Merchants' Hall** (Casa Negustorilor; 1539–45) opposite. Built in the "Transylvanian Renaissance" style, this now contains craft shops, a wine cellar and the *Cerbul Carpatin* restaurant. Through an archway at Piaţa Sfatului 3, you'll find the Orthodox cathedral, built in Byzantine style in 1896; on the opposite side of the square, the eighteenth-century Sf Treime (Holy Trinity) church, also Orthodox, is similarly hidden away down an alley at Str. Bariţiu 12.

To the southwest, the square is dominated by the pinnacles of the town's most famous landmark, the **Black Church** (Biserica Neagră; Mon–Sat 10am–5pm; €1), stabbing upwards like a series of daggers. The church took almost a century to complete (1383–1477) and is so-called for its once soot-blackened walls – the result of a great fire, started by the Austrian army that occupied Braşov in 1689. Inside, however, the church is startlingly white, with Turkish prayer mats hung in isolated splashes of colour along the walls of the nave – a superb collection built up from the gifts of local merchants returning from the east. **Organ recitals** on the four-thousand-pipe instrument are held on Tuesdays at 6pm. The main altarpiece is nothing too special, but there's an older triptych on the north wall, and a fine tympanum of the Virgin and Child with two saints in the inside of the south porch. To the south and west of the church are the buildings of the Honterus Gymnasium, the still-prestigious Saxon school named after the apostle of Luther's Reformation in Transylvania. On the far side of Strada Poarta Schei, Braşov's **synagogue**, built in 1901, has been beautifully restored and is in use again.

Dwarfed by the mighty Black Church, the Old Pharmacy nearby at Piaţa Sfatului 16 is slowly being restored to house the **Ethnographic Museum** (Ⓦwww.etnobrasov.ro), presently housed next to the Art Museum at B-dul Eroilor 21 (both Tues–Sun: summer 10am–6pm; winter 9am–5pm). For the time being, the only display is on the regional textile industry and local costume, although other craftworks are for sale, together with books and CDs. The **Art Museum** itself (Ⓦwww.mab.ro) has temporary shows on the ground floor and a decorative arts collection in the basement; upstairs, there's a large selection of canvases by Grigorescu, Aman and Tattarescu, as well as works by Braşov-born **János Máttis-Teutsch** (1884–1960), one of the most influential of modern Romanian artists. Maáttis-Teutsch was a painter, sculptor, writer and teacher who exhibited with avant-garde groups in Berlin, Budapest and Bucharest, before returning to figurative art.

The fortifications and Mount Tâmpa

With the threat of Turkish expansion in the fifteenth century, Braşov began to fortify itself, assigning the defence of each bastion or rampart to a particular guild. A length of **fortress wall** runs along the foot of Mount Tâmpa, beneath a maze of paths and a cable car running up to the summit – good **views** of the old town can be had from Strada Brediceanu, the semi-pedestrianized promenade past the lower cable car terminal, but the best views are from the forested heights of **Mount Tâmpa** (967m), accessible by cable car (Tues–Sun 9.30am–9pm) or by the various paths which wind up to its summit.

Of the original seven **bastions**, the best preserved is that of the Weavers (Bastionul Țesătorilor), on Strada Coșbuc, which has three tiers of wooden galleries and meal-rooms in which the townsfolk stocked bread, meat and other provisions in case of siege. Built in 1421–36, this now contains the **Museum of the Bârsa Land Fortifications** (Tues–Sun 10am–4pm), where displays recall the bad old days when the surrounding region was repeatedly raided by Tatars, Turks and, on a couple of occasions, by Vlad Țepeș; next door, the **Transylvanian Sport Museum** (Tues & Wed 11am–3pm, Fri noon–5pm) is a limp collection of medals and photos. The **Blacksmiths' Bastion** (Bastionul Fierarilor) and the **Black and the White Towers** (1494) on Calea Poienii (best seen from Strada Dupa Ziduri, squeezed between stream and walls) all managed to survive these onslaughts, but the inhabitants didn't always fare so well. When Țepeș attacked Brașov in 1460, he burnt the suburbs and impaled hundreds of captives along the heights of St Jacob's Hill to the north of the city. Referring to allegations that Vlad dined off a holy icon surrounded by his suffering victims, his hagiographer Stoicescu wrote that "being on campaign … the terrible Prince may not have had the time to take his meals otherwise".

The Schei quarter

During the heyday of Saxon rule, the Romanian-speaking population was compelled to live beyond the citadel walls, in the southwestern district of **Schei**. They could only enter the centre at certain times, and had to pay a toll at the gate for the privilege of selling their produce to their neighbours. The Poarta Schei, the gate on the street of the same name, was built in 1825 by Emperor Franz I, next to the splendid **Catherine's Gate** (Poarta Ecaterinei) of 1559, which bears the city's coat of arms. Today, Schei is a peaceful residential dead-end whose main sight is the **Church of St Nicholas**, on Piața Unirii, ten minutes' walk from Poarta Schei, which was the first Orthodox church to be built in Transylvania by the voivodes of Wallachia, between 1493 and 1564; it was extended and the clocktower added in 1751. On the left as

The Pageant of the Juni

The **Pageant of the Juni** (Sărbătoarea Junilor) is held on the first Sunday of May, traditionally the only day of the year that Romanians could freely enter the Saxon city. The name derives from the Latin for "young men", and on this day the town's youths dress up in costumes and, accompanied by brass bands, ride through town in groups named after famous regiments – the Dorobanți, or the Roșiori – while the married men, or Old Juni, bring up the rear. Some of the elaborate Juni costumes (now in the Schei Church Museum) are over 150 years old, while one of the Roșiori wears a shirt sewn with 44,000 spangles that weighs 9kg – the product of four months' work by Brașov's women each year.

The parade assembles in the morning on the **Piața Unirii**, which forms the historic heart of Schei. It then marches to Piața Sfatului, returns to the Schei backstreets, and finally climbs a narrow valley northwest to the **Gorges of Pietrele lui Solomon**. Here, spectators settle down to watch the Round Dances (Horăs), which for the dancers are something of an endurance test. The Horă, which still has the power to draw onlookers into its rhythmically stepping, swaying and stamping circles, used to serve as a sanction in village society – local miscreants seeking to enter the circle (and so re-enter society) were shamed when the dancing immediately ceased, resuming only when they withdrew.

you enter the churchyard is the first Romanian-language school (established in the fourteenth century and rebuilt in 1760–1), now a museum (daily 10am–6pm) exhibiting the first Romanian-language textbooks.

North of the centre

North of Bulevardul Eroilor and the Parc Central is a lowish hill crowned by the overgrown **citadel ruins**, with a touristy restaurant (the *Cetate*) hidden inside. To the west, Strada Lungă stretches for 3km to the **Church of St Bartholomew**, an early Gothic edifice built by 1260 by the hill where Vlad impaled his victims. It stands at the junction of Strada Lungă and the DN1 to Sibiu; the Bartolomei station and *Autogară* 2 are just west and east, respectively.

Eating and drinking

Braşov has a decent selection of places to **eat and drink**, with excellent **restaurants** in the main hotels; they're not cheap by Romanian standards, but service is good, with English spoken in most. For **fast food**, try *Casablanca* at the corner of B-dul 15 Noiembrie and Str. Blaga or the smokey *Mado* at Str. Republicii 10.

The **cafés** around Piaţa Sfatului serve a wide range of cakes and buns, and terraces to enable you to watch the comings and goings on this lively square; the best are the *Opium Bar* at Str. Republicii 2 and *Casata* at Piaţa Sfatului 13. *Vatra Ardealului*, Str. Bariţiu 14, has the creamiest cakes in town; in addition, Braşov's kiosks sell what is certainly the best apple strudel in Romania. Good **ice cream** can be had at *Mamma Mia*, Str. Mureşenilor 25.

Restaurants

Bistro de l'Arte Piaţa Enescu 11 bis ☎0268/473 994. A limited menu of excellent French-influenced food, worth a visit for its delicious fondu alone.

Blue Corner Piaţa Enescu 13 ☎0268/573 338. One of the nicest places in town (but with prices to match), the *Bistro Corner* serves French and Scandinavian cuisine in a pleasant atmosphere.

Ceasu' Rău Str. Iuliu Maniu 56 ☎0268/476 670. Known for its barbecued ribs, the *Ceasu' Rău*'s Romanian dishes, such as pastrami with *mămăliga*, are also good.

Intim Str. Mureşenilor 4. An unpretentious little place specialising in authentic Romanian fare – the excellent *mămăligă* is especially worth trying.

La Pizza Str. Republicii 17. Good Italian food and friendly service.

Pizza Roma Str. Hirscher 2. This friendly Italian place serves up decent pizzas on its genial street-side *terasa*.

Şirul Vămii Str. Mureşenilor 18 ☎0268/477 725, ✉rezervari@sirulvamii.ro. The best restaurant (and service) in town, offering a great choice of reasonably priced dishes.

Sergiana Str Mureşenilor 22. Set in an attractive maze of cellars, the *Sergiana* has a large menu of traditional and modern Romanian dishes.

Stradivari Piaţa Sfatului 1. This pizzeria has a wider wine and beer list than other places on the square, which can be sampled on its pleasant *terasa*.

Taverna Str. Politechnicii 6 ☎0268/474 618. An excellent if pricey restaurant that serves a better-than-average range of vegetarian dishes.

Bear-watching

Răcădău, a housing area on the edge of town, often sees **wild bears** scavenging from local rubbish skips and some hostels and tour guides now run "bear-watching excursions". Do not be tempted: as people's confidence grows (some have been photographed feeding biscuits to the bears), so does the likelihood of something very nasty happening – not only that, but if (or when) someone is savaged, the bears will be shot.

Drinking

For **drinking**, the *Groapa cu Bere*, Bulevardul Eroilor (till 10.30pm, closed Mon), is cheap and friendly; the pub-like *Britannia*, in the cellar at Str. Republicii 57, is less pleasant but still affordable. *Festival 39*, at Str. Mureșenilor 23, boasts a long cocktail list and weird decor, but can be pricey; nearby, the big, open-fronted *Saloon* at Str. Mureșenilor 13 has more seating (and bar food) and stays open till 2am, but is rather bland. The *For Sale Pub*, B-dul 15 Noiembrie 24 has bargain beer and unusual cocktails, but its eccentricity is rather forced. The *Formula Pub* at B-dul Eroilor 29 (look for the Guinness umbrellas) makes a good alternative to waiting for a bus at Livada Postei.

Nightlife and entertainment

The best places to **dance** are the Hacienda at Str. Carpaților 17, and the Club Sir Arthur, B-dul Eroilor 27, which is a lively **club** at weekends but a dead bar during the week, with rather alarming crossbows and axes on the wall. Avoid the Scotch Club at Str. Dinicu 14, across the road from the Grenadier, which hosts so-called erotic shows.

Classical concerts are held at the Gh. Dima Philharmonic at Str. Hirscher 10 (℡0268/141 378); tickets are inexpensive but usually sell out well in advance. Tickets for the municipal **theatre** on Piața Teatrului, at the east end of Bulevardul Eroilor, the less appealing **Lyric Theatre** (Str. Biserici Române 51), which mainly stages operettas and musicals, and the **puppet theatre** (Str. Hirscher 8) are sold at Str. Republicii 4 (℡0268/471 889). From mid-June to mid-September, there's unlikely to be much happening at any of these. There are no **cinemas** near the city centre; the main ones are the Patria (B-dul 15 Noiembrie), Cosmos (Str. Uranus 1) and Bulevard (B-dul Griviței 47).

The **Springtime Jazz and Blues Festival** takes place in early May in the municipal theatre; there's an **International Chamber Music Festival** in the first week of July; the **Golden Stag** pop music extravaganza takes over Piața Sfatului in late August or early September; and the **Beer Festival** brings a range of near-identical lagers to town in early October.

Shopping

Brașov is a good place to buy books and outdoor gear, and the food markets are fine, but it's hardly a shopper's dream. The STAR **department store** is at Str. Bălcescu 62 (Mon–Fri 9am–8pm, Sat 9am–5pm), and there are some fascinating **antique** and **junk** shops on Strada Coresi. English-language books can be found at the Coșbuc bookshop, Str. Republicii 29, and Aldus, Piața Sfatului 17, while the Șt. O. Iosif bookshop, Str. Mureșenilor 14, sells some useful **maps**. Ascent, also at Piața Sfatului 17, is the best **mountain-gear** shop outside Bucharest. The central food **market** is near the theatre on Str. Nicolae Bălcescu, and there's another behind the apartment blocks opposite the train station; both are open daily. Also near the station, on B-dul Victoriei, is the Rapid **supermarket** (24hr). For the greatest selection, head to one of the two big hypermarkets – Selgros, at Calea București 231 and Metro, 8km west at km174 of the DN1 towards Sibiu; show your passport on arrival to get the temporary membership form needed to shop here.

Listings

Banks and exchange There are plenty of ATMs around the centre, and private exchange offices at the junction of Piața Sfatului and Str. Mureșenilor that accept travellers' cheques; others on B-dul

Eroilor and at the top of Str. Barițiu charge commission. You can also change money at the CEC offices (Mon–Fri 8am–3pm) in the police headquarters at Str. Titulescu 28 and at the corner of Piața Sfatului and Republicii, or at the Banca Commerciala Romană at Str. Republicii 45 (Mon–Fri 8.30am–noon).

Car rental Avis, through Sun Tours, Piața Sfatului 19 ☏0268/417 639, ⓦwww.suntours.ro; Budget, *Hotel Aro Palace* ☏0268/474 564; CarpaTour, B-dul 15 Noiembrie 1 ☏0268/471 057, ⓦwww.carpatour.ro; Europcar through Astra Tours, Str. Barițiu 26 ☏0268/151 461; Hertz, Str. 15 Noiembrie 50A ☏ & ⓕ0268/471 485; Sixt, through Contempo, Dârste DN1 km160; ☏0268/339 446, ⓦwww.e-sixt.com.

Football FC Brașov play at Stadion Tineret on Strada Stadionului (€1).

Hospitals County Hospital, Calea București 45 ☏0268/135 080; Emergency Military Hospital, Pietei 9 ☏0268/416 393; Clinica Romano Americana, Str. Traian 10 ☏0268/332 023.

International bus tickets Amad Turistik, c/o Sun Tours (see above), & Str. Vlahuță 32 ☏0268 /329 364; Armin-Meyer Reisen, Str. M. Weiss 2 ☏0268/143 131; AtlasSib, Str. Lungă 1; Civic Trans, at the station ☏ & ⓕ0268/472 498, 152 774; Double-T, Piața Sfatului 25 ☏0268/410 466; Kaiser, Republicii 25 ☏0268/416 871, brasov.rep@eurolines.ro; Kessler, c/o Dialect Tour, Str. Toamnei 9 ☏0268/327 041; MegaSoy, Str. Mureșenilor ☏0268/470 816; Micomis, Str. Republicii 53 ☏0268/470 472, ⓦwww.canad.ro/~micomis; Mihu Reisen, Str. Cerbului 34 ☏0268/142 257; Pletl, Piața Teatrului 4 ☏0268/150 387; Simpa Turism (see below);

Tavi Reisen, Str. Vlahuță 38 ☏0268/416 378; Touring-Eurolines, Piața Sfatului 18 ☏0268 /474 008, ⓔbrasov@eurolines.ro; Wasteels, at the train station ☏ 0268/424 313, ⓦwww.wasteelstravel.ro. Budapest tickets can be bought from *Autogară* 1.

Internet access Club Internet, Str. Toamnei 17; Hip Internet C@fe, Str. 15 Noiembrie no. 1; Internet Café, Str. Agrișelor 25; Internet Caffé aslpls, Str. Republicii 41 (24hr); Internet Club, B-dul Victoriei 10; Prosum, Str. Republicii 48; and on the mezzanine floor of the train station.

Laundry ID Group Self-Lavoir, Calea București 73.

Library British Council, B-dul Eroilor 33; ☏0268/474 214, ⓦwww.britishcouncil.ro.

Pharmacy Eurofarm, Str. Republicii 27 ☏0268/143 560, is open 24 hours.

Police The county police headquarters are at Str. Titulescu 28 ☏0268/407 500. This is also the place to go for visa extensions.

Post office Str. Iorga 1. Poste restante available. Mon–Fri 7am–8pm, Sat 8am–2pm.

Telephone office B-dul Eroilor 23 (Mon–Fri 7am–9pm).

Tour and travel agents Tarom, B-dul Eroilor 27 ☏0268/142 840; KronTour, Str. Barițiu 12 ☏0268/410 515, ⓦwww.krontour.ro; Simpa Turism, Piața Sfatului 3 ☏0268/475 677, ⓦwww.simpaturism.ro; Air Training Transilvania, Str. Republicii 53; Paralela 45, Str. Mureșenilor 20 ☏473 399, ⓦwww.rotravel.com/agencies /paralela; and J'Info Tours, Str. Hirscher 2 ☏0268/414 421.

Train tickets CFR, Str. Republicii 53 ☏0268 /142 912; Wasteels (see above); and Civic Trans, on the station mezzanine.

Around Brașov

Brașov sits right at the foot of the mountains, and there are opportunities for hiking and skiing just a few kilometres from the city at **Poiana Brașov**. The most popular bus excursion is to the castle of **Bran**, and in spite of the crowds it's well worth a visit. Further to the south, the Bucegi mountains (see p.135) are within easy reach, and to the west the Făgăraș range (see p.154), containing Romania's highest peaks, can be accessed by train. Between these two ranges lies the very distinctive ridge of the **Piatra Craiului**, a single block of limestone that offers a marvellous, if tiring, day's walking.

Poiana Brașov and around

The rustic resort of **POIANA BRAȘOV** is set at an altitude of 1000m, on a shoulder of the spectacular Mount Postăvaru, 12km south of Brașov (20min by bus #20, every half-hour from Livada Postei, by the Parc Central). There is **skiing** here from December to March, and while it's a great place to learn to ski, with lots of English-speaking instructors, the experienced are likely to get bored; lessons are organized by the **tourist office** (daily 8am–8pm) in the Complex Favorit, who can also arrange guides for year-round **hiking** (as can Roving Romania, in Braşov; see p.144). **Skiing equipment** can be rented at several places, as can **mountain bikes**; **horse-riding** is also available.

The town's **hotels** are usually filled by package groups, but they may have space outside of the season, and the tourist office can try to find you a cheap room in a villa. The *Alpin* (☏0268/262 343, ⓦwww.hotelalpin.ro; ◉), has the best facilities and serves a heavy buffet breakfast, but the most attractive place, and ideally located for the slopes, is the *Sport* (☏0268/262 111, ⓕ262 154; ◉); the *Poiana Ursului* (☏0268/262 216; ◉) is a youth hotel that's open to all ages and offers simple facilities.

The resort's **restaurants** go in for folk architecture and local cuisine, as you'd expect with names like *Şura Dacilor* (Dacians' Barn) and *Coliba Haiducilor* (Outlaws' Hut), both open from 11am until midnight and offering pretty authentic pork-heavy cuisine.

Half an hour from Braşov by bus or train, and 12km west of Poiana Braşov by a back road, is **RÂŞNOV** (Rosenau), where a ruined **fort** (Tues–Sun 10am–6pm), founded around 1225 by the Teutonic Knights, crowns the fir-covered hill that overlooks the town, affording fantastic mountain **views**. To get there on foot, head through the archway and up the steps opposite the BCR bank on Piaţa Unirii, just south of the Lutheran church. There's also a road up to the castle, starting at the *Râşnov* cabana (☏0268/230 266; ◉), a decent **restaurant** with **rooms**, and a relatively good **campsite**; to get there, take Strada Cetăţii (the Poiana Braşov road) from the south end of Piaţa Unirii.

Bran and around

The small town of **BRAN** (Törzburg) is one of the most popular sites in Romania. Situated 28km southwest of Braşov, the town commands the entrance to the pass of the same name, once the main route into Wallachia. The Saxons of Kronstadt (Braşov) built a castle here in 1377–82 to safeguard this vital trade artery, and although what's now billed on every tourist brochure as **Dracula's Castle** (Tues–Sun 9am–6pm; €2) has only tenuous associations with Vlad the Impaler – it's likely he laid siege to it in 1460 when he attacked the Burzenland – Bran does look rather like a vampire count's residence, perched on a rocky bluff and rising in tiers of towers and ramparts from the woods against a glorious mountain backdrop. Aside from its castle, Bran is a good base for **hikes** into the Bucegi mountains to the east (see p.135) and onto the narrow ridge of the **Piatra Craiului**, the eastern extremity of the Făgăraş mountains, to the west (see p.153).

After lengthy restoration, the castle now looks much as it would have done in the time of its most famous resident, **Queen Marie of Romania**. A granddaughter of Queen Victoria and married to Prince Ferdinand in 1893, Queen Marie soon rebelled against the confines of court life in Bucharest – riding unattended through the streets, pelting citizens with roses during the carnival, and appointing herself a colonel of the Red Hussars. Her popularity soared after she organized cholera camps in the Balkan war and appeared at the Paris peace conference in 1919, announcing that "Romania needs a face, and I have come to show mine". Marie called Bran a "pugnacious little fortress", but whether because of her spirit pervading the rooms or the profusion of flowers in the yard, it seems a welcoming place, at odds with its forbidding exterior. A warren of spiral stairs, ghostly nooks and secret chambers filled with elaborately carved four-poster beds and throne-like chairs overhangs the courtyard. Not surprisingly, it can get horribly crowded: the trick is to arrive as the castle opens – the bus parties will be arriving as you leave.

In the grounds, the **Village Museum** (same hours and ticket as castle) comprises some fine examples of local architecture, including a fulling mill, and by the road south, the **Ancient Customs House Museum** (same hours and ticket), in the former *vama*, predictably stresses the trade links from the earliest times between the Vlachs on either side of the Carpathians, and displays examples of foreign goods, including an English clock and a Canadian travelling trunk. There's a hectic **crafts market** at the castle gate, but sadly in the last few years the quality has fallen, with lots of trash such as Dracula masks on sale instead. Bran holds its village **festival** on August 9 (the Feast of St Pantelimon).

Practicalities

Buses run from Braşov's *Autogară* 2 south via Râşnov and Bran to Moeciu de Jos, 3km south of Bran (Mon–Fri 24 daily, 12 on Sat & Sun – pay the driver); the few buses from Braşov south to Piteşti and Câmpulung Muscel will also stop off at Bran. Tourist **information** is available from Antrec at Str. Bologa 10 (July & Aug daily 9am–8pm; rest of year variable; ☎0268/236 884, ⒻF 152 598); there are also good map boards in the village.

The best **hotel**, complete with pool, is the *Popasul Reginei* on Strada Stoian (☎0268/236 134; ❸), across the main road from the castle and beyond a tiny park. A little further down Strada Stoian, a track leads left to a footbridge and the *Castelul Bran* cabana, only worth going to for its restaurant (see below). The *Han Turistic Bran* motel, just north of the centre at Str. Principală 363 (☎0268/236 556; ❶), is old-fashioned but adequate; there's also the pleasant *Villa Bran*, Sohodol no. 271A (☎0268/236 866; ❷), 100m to the east off the Braşov road, 1km from the centre.

Private rooms (❷, plus meals) are big business here, with over a hundred homes in the area offering agroturism accommodation: most of these are in fact mini-hotels in a rural setting. Book through Bran IMEX at Str. Stoian 395 (☎0268/236 642); or through Eurogites, or through Ovi-Tours, Str. Bologa 15 (☎0268/236 666), which also offers mountain bikes, sleigh rides, ski rental and excursions. There are better independent **guesthouses**, such as Veronica Cojanu's, nearby at Bologa 20 (☎0268/236 96; ❷); others are *Casa Laura* (☎0268/236 684; ❷), 1km to the left after the bridge 1.5km south of Bran, with a large garden; and British-run *Villa Jo* (☎0745 /179 475; Ⓔjocomp@deltanet.ro), opposite the *Han Turistic Bran* (the sign reads *Jo & Co*).

Of the hotel **restaurants**, the *Popasul Reginei*'s is good, as is that at the *Castelul Bran*, where you can try the local specialities *bulz* (polenta balls with cheese) and *pastrama de oaie* (dried pressed mutton pastrami). Otherwise, there's the decent *Cheile Castelului* for pizza, below the castle near the *vama*. Just beyond the *vama* is the atmospheric pub-like *Volanul de Aur*.

Fundata

In **MOECIU**, immediately south of Bran, there are plenty of pensions, all very clean with lots of stripped pine and big breakfasts, but all rather samey. **Buses** terminate just beyond the junction at km105; there's a group of three good guesthouses 2.5km up the Moeciu de Sus road, at Cheia 427A

(☎0268/237 234; ❶), 433 (☎0268/237 233; ❷) and 436 (☎0268/236 233, ✉golteanu@just.ro; ❶); call in advance and they'll pick you up. In Moeciu de Sus (Upper Moeciu) itself, 8km south of the junction, the best **place to stay** is the *Casa Orleanu*, also known as the *Centru de Ecologie Montană*, at no. 125 (☎0745/978 023, ⊕www.cem.ro; ❷), in the centre of the village; you can get information on local wildlife here.

Fourteen kilometres south of Bran, **FUNDATA**, one of the highest villages in Romania, sits atop the spectacular **Bran** or **Giuvala Pass** (1290m) and is served only by occasional Brașov–Câmpulung buses. Little more than a scattering of small farm houses, it is host to the popular **Mountain Festival** (Nedeia Muntelui) on the last Sunday of August. The underlying purpose is to transact business: exchanges of handicrafts, livestock and (formerly) of pledges of marriage. As Fundata straddles the border between Transylvania and Wallachia, the festival was important as a means of maintaining contacts between ethnic Romanians in the two provinces.

Zărneşti and the Piatra Craiului

Mountains dominate the skyline around Bran. To the east is the almost sheer wall of the **Bucegi range** – it takes about eight hours to climb the path from Bran to Mount Omu, where there's a cabana (see p.135). To the west, gentler slopes run up to the national park of **Piatra Craiului**, a narrow ridge at the eastern extremity of the Făgăraş mountains, the forested hills around which were the setting for 2003's Hollywood blockbuster *Cold Mountain*. This twenty-kilometre-long limestone ridge, punctured with karst caves along its eastern face, is known as the Royal Rock, and is home to Carpathian bears, lynx and chamois, as well as the endemic Piatra Craiului pink.

The **park headquarters** is at Str. Râului 27 in **ZĂRNEŞTI** (☎0268/223 008, ⊕www.pcrai.ro), a fairly mundane place but a good starting point for **hikes**. For information and activities such as wolf-tracking, horse riding and bike hire contact **Carpathian Nature Tours** (☎0268/223 098, ⊕www.cntours.de), Roving Romania (see p.144), or Mihai Zotta, the park's tourism officer (☎0723/330 474, ✉mzotta@pcrai.ro). There's a **visitor centre** (Mon–Fri 9am–5pm, Sat 8am–4pm) near the post office. Zărneşti is accessible from Brașov via Râşnov by **bus** and **train**; **guesthouses** include the *Guesthouse Elena*, Str. Piatra Craiului 43 (☎0268/223 0703; ❸) and the *Pensiunea Mosorel*, Str. Dr Şenchea 162 (☎0745/024 472; ❷).

From Zărneşti, it's under three hours' walk up the Bârsa Mare valley to the *Plaiul Foii* cabana (❶), the main centre for **hiking** in this area. The hut has hostel-style rooms with bunkbeds; note, though, that the water isn't safe to drink. The best day hike from here leads to the *Curmătura* cabana (1470m; ❶); it begins with a stiff climb (3–4hr, following red cross markings, and using fixed cables in places) to the main ridge 1400m above, and continues north along its knife-edge (following red dots), finally descending (following yellow stripes) to the right to the *Curmătura* cabana or to the left to Zărneşti. The route is demanding and you should be properly equipped with boots, waterproofs and plenty of water. The ridge offers fantastic **views** west towards the Făgăraş range and east towards the Bucegi.

In the foothills southwest of Zărneşti, between the Piatra Craiului and the Bran-Fundata road, hide tiny settlements where new agrotourism pensions are beginning to appear. The pick of the bunch is the *Montana* cabana in Măgura (☎0268/238 084; ❶) – phone ahead and they'll meet you off the bus in Zărneşti.

Făgăraş and around

FĂGĂRAŞ (Fogarasch), 54km west of Braşov, is scarred by chemical works and communist attempts at town planning. Nevertheless, it's a good jumping-off point for hikes in the mountains to the south, and for exploring the Saxon villages just north – thanks to a wide range of small, cheap hotels – and it does have some small-town charm in places. Founded by Hungarians and Saxons, from 1366 it and the surrounding duchy of Amlaş were under Wallachian rule; when Vlad the Impaler was deposed in 1460, he set out on a murderous rampage from the Olt Valley towards the Burzenland, razing the citadel of Făgăraş en route. The sturdy **fortress** that dominates the town centre today was built in the late sixteenth century on its ashes.

From the **train station** 1km south of the centre, turn left along Stradă Negoiu, and you'll pass between the market and an abandoned synagogue to reach the modern town centre and the fortress, which today houses a moderately good **museum** of local history (Tues–Fri 9am–4pm, Sat & Sun 9am–3pm) in its cellars. One block west is Piaţa Republicii, the old town centre; this is the heart of social life in the town.

Local **buses** run from next to the train station to and from Agnita, Ucea and Sâmbata de Jos. For **information**, the local NGO Fundaţia Culturală Negru Vodă (☏0268/211 193) is very helpful. The best **hotel** is the new *Montana*, just

---

Hiking in the Făgăraş mountains

The **Făgăraş mountains** are composed mainly of crystalline schists with occasional limestone outcrops, a series of pyramidal crests, linked by narrow ridges, that harbours more than seventy **lakes** at heights of 1800–2250m. Up to about 2000m the mountainsides are covered with spruce forests sheltering deer, bears, chamois and other **wildlife**; above this level there may still be snow as late as June.

Most **hiking routes** are well marked and fairly simple to follow with a *Hartă Turistică Munţii Făgăraşului* map, which can be bought in Braşov, Bran, Făgăraş or Sibiu, or in the cabanas in the mountains. It's useful, but rarely essential, to **reserve accommodation**. Always carry ample food and water, and wear boots and waterproofs – the weather is very changeable on the ridge.

Almost invariably, the starting point is one of the settlements along the Olt valley, where marked routes lead from the train stations to the mountains. All trains stop at **Ucea**, where passengers clamber onto buses south to **Victoria**, a town dominated by its chemical works, the siren of which is audible on the main ridge of the Făgăraş. From the bus station, follow the main road uphill to the works gates and then the route marked with red triangles round to the right (west). A forestry track bypasses the *Arpaş* cabana (☏0268/241 433; ❶) and continues as a steep trail past the *Turnuri* cabana (☏0269/438 405; ❶) and up to the basic *Podragu* cabana (☏0269/430 766; ❶) at 2136m, reached in 8–10 hours. From the *Podragu*, follow the **ridge path** marked with red stripes, either eastwards past Romania's highest peak, **Moldoveanu** (2544m), descending by the Sâmbăta valley to the friendly *Valea Sâmbetei* cabana (☏0722/760 840; ❶) and the *Complex Turistic Sâmbăta* (with a monastery and accommodation; ❶), from where occasional buses head to Făgăraş and Victoria, 11km west; or west to **Bâlea Lake** (2034m); the *Bâlea Lac* hotel (☏0745/072 602; ❸) also has dorms, a decent (but slowish) restaurant-bar, and an attractive *terasa* by the lake. From *Bâlea Lac*, you can descend either by the Trans-Făgăraş Highway (usually June–Sept) or by a cable car to the *Bâlea Cascada* cabana (☏0269/524 255; ❶), and from there to the *Vama Cucului* cabana (☏0269/524 717; ❶), Cârtişoara and the Cârţa rail halt.

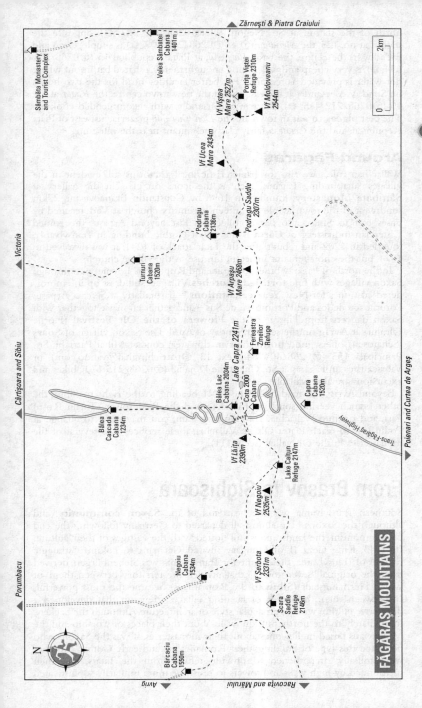

Zărneşti & Piatra Craiului

Valea Sâmbătei
Cabana
1401m

Sâmbăta Monastery
and Tourist Complex

Portiţa Viştei
Refuge 2310m

Vf Viştea
Mare 2527m

Vf Moldoveanu
2544m

Vf Ucea
Mare 2434m

Victoria

Podragu Saddle
2307m

Podragu
Cabana
2136m

Turnuri
Cabana
1520m

Cârtişoara and Sibiu

Vf Arpaşu
Mare 2468m

Fereastra
Zmeilor
Refuge

Lake Capra 2241m

Cota 2000
Cabana

Bâlea Lac
Cabana 2034m

Capra
Cabana
1520m

Bâlea
Cascada
Cabana
1234m

Poienari and Curtea de Argeş

Trans-Fǎgǎraş Highway

Vf Lǎiţa
2390m

Lake Caltun
Refuge 2147m

Vf Negoiu
2535m

Negoiu
Cabana
1534m

Vf Şerbota
2331m

Scara Saddle
Refuge 2146m

Porumbacu

Bârcaciu
Cabana
1550m

Avrig

Racoviţa and Mǎrului

N

FĂGĂRAŞ MOUNTAINS

0   2km

north of the station at Str. Negoiu 98 (℡0268/212 327; ➌); opposite the station at no. 125, the *Meridian* (℡ & ℻0268/212 409; ➊) is simple, clean and friendly. In the centre, the basic *Progresul*, at Piaţa Republicii 15 (℡0268/211 634; ➊), is very cheap and welcoming enough; there's a shared bathroom where hot water is provided as required. For better facilities, head for the two hotels on Strada V. Alecsandri at the east end of the new town centre: the *Roata*, at no. 10 (℡0268/212 415; ➊), is warm and friendly, with recommended cooking. The best **places to eat** in town are the *Don Giovanni* pizzeria, just east of Piaţa Republicii, and the *Cetate*, a fairly classy restaurant near the museum.

Around Făgăraş

Wallachian rule gave rise to characteristic local art forms still evident in the villages surrounding Făgăraş, such as the icons on glass in the gallery at **Sâmbata Monastery**, founded in 1696 by Constantin Brâncoveanu, 27km southwest of the town, while the fifteenth-century church at **Vad**, reached by buses east to Şinca, also has a collection. Just beyond Arpaşu, the ruined Cistercian monastery of **Cârţa** is the oldest Gothic building in Transylvania, founded in 1202 and rebuilt after the Tatar attack of 1241; it was dissolved in 1474, but the choir remains intact and in use, as the village church.

To the north of Făgăraş, buses to Agnita and Rupea (via Lovnic) pass through Saxon villages with fine **fortified churches**. Villagers still dress up in embroidered costumes for **New Year celebrations** – particularly at Şercaia, Arpaşu, Porumbacu de Jos and Porumbacu de Sus – and gather en masse together with Saxon dancers from Tilişca for the **Flowers of the Olt Festival** (Florile Oltului) at **Avrig** on the second Sunday of April. The Saxon village of **Şoarş** (Scharosch) offers good **homestays** in this area; contact Mihai Patrichi, Str. Principală 155 (℡0268/404 848, ext 13, ✉patrichimihai@yahoo.com), or Viorica Bica, in Făgăraş at Str. Gheorghe Doja 53 (℡0268/215 170); bikes and excursions are also available.

Beyond Avrig, the road forks: the DN1 heading to the right to Sibiu, the other branch veering south to Tălmaciu and the Red Tower (Turnu Roşu) Pass, and on into Wallachia. Travelling by train, you may need to change at Podul Olt to reach Piatra Olt in Wallachia; these services pass several of the monasteries in the Olt valley (see p.111).

From Braşov to Sighişoara

Southern Transylvania was the heartland of the **Saxon community**, and although the Saxons have almost all departed to Germany following the end of communism, the landscape is still dotted with the vestiges of their culture. In 1143, King Géza II of Hungary invited Germans to colonize strategic regions of Transylvania; their name for Transylvania was Siebenbürgen, derived from the original "seven towns" that divided the territory between them, of which Hermannstadt (**Sibiu** to the Romanians) became the most powerful. In-between them, hundreds of farming villages grew up that developed a distinctive culture with a vernacular style of architecture. Although the Székely, immediately to the north, put low walls about their places of worship and the Moldavians raised higher ones about their monasteries, it was the Saxons who perfected this type of building; their Romanesque and early Gothic churches were initially strengthened to provide refuge from the Tatars, and then surrounded by high walls and towers to resist the more militarily sophisticated

Turks. These **fortified churches**, some of which house warrens of storerooms to hold stocks of food sufficient to survive a siege, are highly individual.

Alas, for the Saxons, their citadels were no protection against the tide of history, which steadily eroded their influence from the eighteenth century on and put them in a difficult position during World War II. Although many bitterly resented Hitler's carving-up of Transylvania in 1940, which gave its northern half to Hungary, there were others who, relishing their new status as Volksdeutsche, embraced Nazism and joined the German army. As a collective punishment after the war, all fit Saxon men between the ages of 17 and 45, and women between 18 and 30 (30,000 in all) were deported to the Soviet Union for between three and seven years of slave labour; many did not return, and those who did found that much of their property had been confiscated.

Though **road** and **rail** routes diverge in places, it's fairly easy to reach the settlements along the Olt valley in particular; however, there are many more in the side valleys, which are well worth discovering and can only be reached by occasional buses, by car, bike or on foot. In summer, many Saxons return from Germany to their home villages, but at other times you're likely to be the only visitor.

Hărman

Visiting the Saxon villages around Braşov on the eve of World War II, the writer Elizabeth Kyle found churches prepared for siege as in the times of Sultan Süleyman and Vlad the Impaler. **HĂRMAN** (Honigberg), 12km north-east of Braşov, still looks much as she described it, situated "in a wide and lovely valley, its houses arranged in tidy squares off the main street which sweeps towards the grim fortress that closes the vista". The fascinating **church** (Tues–Sun 9am–noon & 1–5pm) dates from 1293 (with clear Cistercian influence), with later defensive walls and fifteenth-century frescoes in the chapel.

Hărman is served by six **buses** a day (Mon–Fri) from Braşov's *Autogară* 3; in addition, buses from *Autogară* 1 towards Târgu Secuiesc and Sfântu Gheorghe, and maxitaxis to Prejmer, will drop you by Hărman **train** station, 1.5km from the centre along Strada Gării and served by the same five trains a day that go on to Prejmer. **Accommodation** can be found at the unmarked *Country Hotel* at Mihai Viteazul 441 (⊤0268/367 051, ⓔmcosnean@yahoo.com; ⑤), with a small swimming pool; the *Motel Dynasty* is only a restaurant, and rather mafioso at that.

Prejmer

PREJMER (Tartlau), 7km to the east, and off the main road (but on the railway) has an even more spectacular **church** (Tues–Fri 9am–5pm, Sat 9am–3pm, Sun 11am–5pm), which is the easiest of all the Saxon ones to visit, with a concierge's lodge in the entrance passage. It was originally built in the form of a Greek cross (completed by 1225), but from the mid-thirteenth century was adapted to the Cistercian style. The crossing and choir are old, with splendidly worn rough stone, while the nave has late-Gothic vaulting, and there's a fine Gothic altarpiece depicting the Passion (1450–60). The church was surrounded after the Turkish campaign of 1421 by a five-towered wall, 12m high, lined two centuries later with four tiers of meal rooms. Now, two of the four towers on the exterior of the outer wall have been demolished, and, as at Hărman, the moat has been filled in. There is even a small **museum** (same hours – ask the caretaker if closed), boasting fine examples of Saxon costume and a view of the inner wall gateway's portcullis, up the covered stairs in the first court.

Prejmer is served by frequent **maxitaxis** from Braşov's Strada Harmanului, at the east end of Bulevardul Gării, and by **buses** from *Autogară* 3 to Vama Buzaului (6–8 daily). There are also five **trains** a day in each direction; note that the Ilieni train stop is closer to the town centre than Prejmer station proper (and nowhere near the village of Ilieni). Prejmer's Lutheran parish has a rather clinical **hostel** at Str. Mică 6, across the main road from the church – call ahead to check if it's open (☎0268/482 042, @ebbe@deuroconsult.ro; ➊). There are no restaurants or cafés here.

The Olt valley

Further north, towards Sighişoara along the River Olt, there are many more Saxon villages with fortified churches; Personal **trains** between Braşov and Sighişoara (four daily) stop at most, including **FELDIOARA** (Marienburg), where the Teutonic Knights built a citadel, refashioned into a basilica after 1241, **ROTBAV** (Rothbach), **MAIERUŞ** (Nussbach) and **APAŢA**, just across the Olt from **AITA MARE** (Nagyajta). The DN13 (E60) now bypasses Maieruş, swinging left across the wooded Perşani mountains.

North of Aita Mare, the sixteenth-century castle of the Kálnoky family in **MICLOŞOARA** (Miklósvar) is a rare example in Romania of the Italian Renaissance style. Count Kálnoky's three **guesthouses** here (☎0745/921 891, @kalnoky@transylvaniancastle.com; ➒), are beautifully furnished in Székely style; prices include meals, wine and excursions, such as wolf- and bear-tracking. Around 17km north is the Almaş cave in the gorge of the Vârghis (Vargyas) river, a system that continues for a total of 7.5km on four levels and where the **Pied Piper** legendarily surfaced with the children of Hamelin (who became the Saxon colonists of Transylvania). Guests are collected from Braşov or Otopeni; Micloşoara is also reached by daily **buses** from Sfântu Gheorghe and Braşov to Baraolt.

Almost 40km north of Apaţa is **RUPEA** (Reps), a small industrial town, and 15km kilometres north of here is the tiny Saxon village of **Roadeş** (Radeln), with an attractive church. It's another couple of kilometres north to **Buneşti** (Bodendorf), where the church's Speckturm (Bacon Tower) is still in use as a bacon store; 7km south from here along an unmade road is **VISCRI** (Deutsch-Weisskirch), one of the most impressive of all the Romanian **citadels**, set, gleaming white, upon a hill and now on UNESCO's World Heritage List. **Homestays** (➊) here, mostly on Strada Principală, are co-ordinated by the mayor, Caroline Fernolend (☎0788/608 679, ext 313); transfers to Viscri are

---

The Mihai Eminescu Trust

Established during Ceauşescu's dictatorship to give dissidents a lifeline to literary civilisation, the **Mihai Eminescu Trust** (☎020/7603 1113, ⓦwww .mihaieminescutrust.org), named after Romania's national poet, also helped save hundreds of towns and villages from destruction by alerting the West to his plans to bulldoze Romania's rural architecture. Since then, the Trust has continued to play a prominent role in the country's cultural rebirth, one aspect of which is evident in the Saxon villages of Transylvania, where they have renovated over a hundred medieval buildings using traditional methods, in order to help resurrect local income after the country's agricultural collapse, and revive a sense of community. Already, over a thousand Saxons have returned, with incoming Romanians and gypsies being integrated into the communities. These successes are influencing regional conservation policy and serving as a model for threatened communities elsewhere in Romania.

available from Rupea and Sighişoara. The Mihai Eminescu Trust (see box on opposite), which has done some sensitive restoration of village houses, also has accommodation in the area. The **church** key is available from Frau Fernolend at no. 13 Strada Principală, or her mother Frau Dootz at no. 141; it's largely thirteenth-century Gothic, with fortified walls added in 1525, and an assortment of towers from the fifteenth, seventeenth and eighteenth centuries. From the tower, there's a great **view** of the village.

ALBEŞTI (Fehéregyháza/Weisskirch bei Schässburg), reached by buses and trains from Sighişoara has a small **museum** that commemorates the life of Hungary's national poet **Petőfi Sándor**, killed nearby in battle against the Russians in 1849. The *Hotel Europa* (☎0265/778 822, 0721/250 000, ⓔinfo@hotel-kokeltal.com) sits on a hill south of the DN1 at km107.5, a couple of kilometres east of Albeşti; it has a decent **restaurant**, but is better set up for groups than independent tourists.

Sighişoara

A forbidding silhouette of battlements and needle spires looms over **SIGHI-ŞOARA** (Schässburg to the Saxons and Segesvár to the Hungarians) as the sun descends behind the hills of the Târnava Mare valley, and it seems fitting that this was the birthplace of Vlad Ţepeş, "The Impaler" – the man known to so many as **Dracula**. Visually archaic even by Romanian standards, Sighişoara is on UNESCO's World Heritage List and makes the perfect introduction to Transylvania, especially as the eastbound Dacia and Pannonia express trains stop here, making a convenient break in the long journey between Budapest and Bucharest.

A **Medieval Arts Festival** takes over the streets for the last weekend of July, sometimes later; it's a lively event, with costumed musicians and street performers. There's also an Inter-ethnic Cultural Festival in August. On **national holidays** a brass band often performs in Piaţa Cetăţii.

Arrival, information and accommodation

The **train station** is north of the centre, across the Târnave Mare river; outside, you'll see an antique locomotive which once ran on the Sibiu-

---

Draculaland

One of the juiciest scandals of the last few years in Romania has been the project to build a **Draculaland theme park**, on the southwest edge of Sighişoara – complete with blood-red candyfloss, garlic-flavoured ices, amusement rides and a centre for vampirology research – with a kilometre-long chairlift linking it to the citadel. The project received immediate opposition and UNESCO sent a team to investigate the park's impact on the citadel and concluded that it was a thoroughly bad idea. Even the Transylvanian Society of Dracula, which manages to tread the tightrope between academic accuracy and sensationalism, backtracked on its initial support and came out against the project. To make matters worse, it turned out that Greenpeace Romania, which supported the project, was fake and that foreign investors were nothing more than paper front companies. Above all, it was obvious that the sums were wrong and the project was a scam, though the park may yet be built at Snagov, which after all is Vlad Ţepeş's burial place.

Agnita-Sighişoara line. Immediately to the east is the **bus station**; most other services are grouped on Strada 1 Decembrie, in the lower town, including the **post office**. There's non-smoking **Internet** access in the Catacombe (Mon–Fri 10am–9pm, Sat 11am–3pm), in the basement of the House on the Rock.

Tours of the town (led by high school students) can be booked at the House on the Rock (℡0265/777 844; €2 donation) at Piaţa Cetăţii 8; they also offer an Off the Beaten Track tour, taking in the Roma areas on the outskirts of town (€4), and rent out **bikes**. Information is also available at ⓦwww.sighisoara.com.

Accommodation

In a welcome development over the last couple of years, a clutch of **hotels** has appeared in restored buildings in the citadel. **Private rooms** cost about €10 per person in the upper town, while near the station you might find a double for €12; on Strada Libertăţii, the friendly *Casa Costea* at no. 27 (℡0265/771 237, Ⓔraviczki@elsig.ro) has private and shared bathrooms; and *Gia House*, at no. 41 (℡0265/772 486; Ⓔgia.house@home.ro) has en-suites for up to four. In the upper town, Cristina Faur, Str. Cojocarilor 1 (℡0744/119 211, Ⓔcristinafaur2003@yahoo.de) and Marinella Kula, Str. Tâmplarilor 40 (℡0265/777 907), have rooms in typically Romanian homes; both are very friendly and speak good English. The *Dealul Gării* **campsite** (with cabanas and a restaurant; ℡0265/771 046, Ⓕ164 149) is on the hilltop overlooking the train station: turn left from the station, cross the tracks by a bridge, and then follow Strada Dealul Gării up the hill. In summer, there's also camping at the swimming pool off Strada Gării (℡ & Ⓕ0265/775 614), and at *Camping Tineret*, Str. 1 Decembrie 8 (℡0265/469 434), and *Camping Club Copiilor*, Str. 1 Decembrie 30A (℡0265/771 946). Lastly, the teenagers hawking accommodation at the train station are particularly friendly and are useful if you've got nowhere to stay.

Burg Hostel Str. Bastionului 4-6 ℡0265/772 234, Ⓔburghostel@ibz.org.ro. Located in the citadel, this good-value place has a range of rooms, from dorms with shared facilities to double and triple en-suites. ❷–❸

Casa cu Cerb Str. Scolii 1 ℡0265/774 625, ⓦwww.ar-messerschmitt-s.ro. Named after the painting on its corner, the *Casa cu Cerb* is a pleasantly rambling hotel, with a ground floor that doubles as a cellar bar. ❻

Chic Str. Libertăţii 44, ℡0265/771 046, Ⓕ164 149. A simple place opposite the station, the *Chic* has a small, pleasant bar and restaurant. ❷

Claudiu Str Ilarie Chendi 28 ℡ 0265/779 882, ⓦwww.hotel-claudiu.com. South of the citadel and not as central as the town's other hotels, but with guarded parking. ❺

Motel Dracula ℡0265/772 211, Ⓔdracula.danes@email.ro. Six kilometres to the west of town, this motel is better than the name might lead you to imagine, with a swimming pool and horse-riding on offer. ❸

Casa Legenda Str. Bastionului 8 bis ℡0744/632 775, ⓦwww.legenda.ro. Along an alley just north of Piaţia Cetăţii, this pension offers five very pleasant rooms. ❹

Poeniţa Str. D. Cantemir 24 ℡0265/772 739. *Poeniţa* is in a lovely location on the edge of town, 2km from the centre, but its service is variable. ❹

Rex Str. Dumbravei 18 ℡0265/777 431. A good hotel 1km east of the centre, along the Braşov road. ❹

Sighisoara Str. Scolii 4 ℡0265/771 000, Ⓔhotelsighisoara@sighisoara.com. Located in the former Bishop's Palace, the *Sighişoara* has a good restaurant and also a *terasa* at the rear. ❻

Steaua Str. 1 Decembrie 12 ℡0265/771 930, Ⓕ771 932. Slightly east of the Clocktower, the *Steaua* is the town's longest-established hotel. It's tatty but affordable. ❷

Casa Wagner Piaţa Cetăţii 7 ℡0265/506 014, ⓦwww.casa-wagner.com. A nicely restored hotel with antique décor – the rooms are comfortable, but the restaurant is let down by erratic service and a poor vegetarian choice. ❻

The Town

The old town or **citadel** dominates the newer quarters from a rocky massif whose slopes support a jumble of ancient, leaning houses, their windows overlooking the steps leading up from Piaţa Hermann Oberth to the main gateway. Above rises the mighty **Clock Tower**, where each night as the bell chimes midnight one of seven wooden figures emerges from the belfry to gaze over the lower town; two figures, representing day and night, face the upper town. The tower was raised in the thirteenth and fourteenth centuries when Sighişoara became a free town controlled by craft guilds, each of which had to finance the construction of an eponymous bastion and defend it during wartime. It was subsequently rebuilt after earthquakes and a fire in 1676.

Originally a Saxon town known as Castrum Sex (Fort Six), Sighişoara grew rich on the proceeds of trade with Moldavia and Wallachia, as the **history museum** in the tower attests (Mon 10am–3.30pm, Tues–Fri 9am–6.30pm, Sat & Sun 9am–3.30pm; €1). Most of the burghers were Magyar or Saxon, and

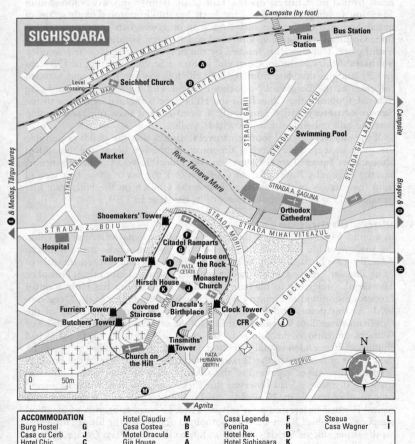

the Romanians – or Vlachs as they were then called – became inferior citizens in Transylvanian towns following edicts passed in 1540. The museum's best presented display, with text in English as well as Romanian, is on **Hermann Oberth**, one of the fathers of space travel, born in Sighişoara in 1894. In 1923, his book *The Rocket into Interplanetary Space* introduced the notions of a space station and a cosmic mirror. He worked in Berlin – launching his first rocket there in 1931 and teaching Werner von Braun – and at Peenemünde, on the V2 rocket, and in the 1950s and 1960s on the American equivalent.

To the north of the Clock Tower stands the Dominican or **Monastery Church** (Mon–Sat 10am–6pm, Sun 11.15am–6pm), now Lutheran, which has a stark, whitewashed interior hung with colourful carpets similar to those in the Black Church at Braşov, and an altar that resembles a wooden carpet-beater. The church was established by 1298, but was progressively rebuilt between 1484 and 1680. In summer, there's also an organ recital on Fridays at 6pm.

The main Saxon church dominates the hill at the southern end of the citadel. Aptly named the **Church on the Hill** (daily 10am–6pm), it was founded in 1345 and finished in 1525, and has been beautifully restored, with scraps of murals and memorial stones surviving in an otherwise bare interior, as well as three Gothic altars. Massively buttressed and with few windows, it is a cool and restful place. The church is reached by the impressive, steep, covered wooden **Scholars' Stairs** at the southern end of Strada Şcolii, consisting of 175 steps and 29 landings that date from 1642. At the top, the fine murals and wooden balconies of the Bergschule, or School on the Hill, built in 1619, are being restored. Opposite the Church on the Hill's door is the main entrance to the **Saxon cemetery** (daily 9am–4pm), a weed-choked mass of graves spilling over the hilltop beside the ruined citadel walls.

Of the citadel's original fourteen **towers**, named after the guilds responsible for their upkeep, nine survive, the most impressive being the hexagonal Shoemakers' Tower (Turnul Cizmarilor), the Tailors' Tower (Turnul Croitorilor) and the Tinsmiths' Tower (Turnul Cositorarilor); the last of these, best viewed from the gateway of the Pfarrhaus, below the Church on the Hill, has a fine wooden gallery and still shows traces of its last siege in 1704.

Vlad's birthplace

In around 1431, in or near a three-storey house at Piaţa Muzeului 6, within the shadow of the old town's Clock Tower, a woman whose name is lost to posterity gave birth to a son called Vlad, who in later life earned the title of "The Impaler". Abroad, he's better known as **Dracula**, derived from Dracul or The Devil – referring to his father, **Vlad Dracul**, whom the Holy Roman Emperor Sigismund of Hungary made a knight of the Order of the Dragon in 1431. At this point, Vlad Dracul was merely the guard commander of the mountain passes into Wallachia, but in 1436 he secured the princely throne of Wallachia and moved his family to the court at Târgovişte. Vlad's privileged childhood there ended several years later, when he and his brother were sent by their father as hostages to the Turkish Sultan in Anatolia; there, as the brothers lived in daily fear of rape and of the silken cord with which the Ottomans strangled dignitaries, Vlad observed the Turks' use of terror, which he would later turn against them. Nowadays, his birthplace contains a restaurant with typical Romanian fare and poor service. There's a small **museum** of medieval weapons (Tues–Sun 10am–3.30pm; combined ticket with the history museum) on the other side of Strada Cositarilor. Just to the west, Piaţa Cetăţii (Citadel Square) is the heart of the upper town, surrounded by recently restored sixteenth-century buildings, such as the **Hirsch House** and the House on the Rock opposite it.

The lower town

The **lower town** is less picturesque than the citadel, but there's a nice ambience around **Piaţa Hermann Oberth**, where townsfolk gather to consume coffee, beer or pizza, conversing in Romanian, Magyar and, occasionally, antiquated German. **Strada 1 Decembrie** has a fine array of Baroque facades, and there's a striking synagogue at Tache Ionescu 13.

The **Mill quarter**, between the citadel and the river, was partially cleared before 1989 for redevelopment as a Civic Centre, and the area is still in limbo. Taking the footbridge over the Târnave Mare river, you come to the Romanian **Orthodox Cathedral**, built in the Byzantine style in 1937. Its gleaming white, multifaceted facade is in striking contrast to the dark interior.

The **market**, off Strada Târnavei, sells food daily but is particularly recommended on Wednesdays and Saturdays, when crafts such as carved wooden spoons are sold for far less than in the citadel's stalls.

Eating, drinking and entertainment

The **restaurants** in the *Casa cu Cerb* and *Sighişoara* hotels are the best dining options in the citadel, while in the lower town *Jo*, overlooking the field at Str. Goga 12, and *La Strada*, Str. Morii 7, have good pizzas and outdoor seating. *Pani Toya Rom*, Str. Morii 11, has tasty Turkish snacks including baklava; more filling are the homemade cookies, cakes and quiches in the *International Café* in the House on the Rock, Piaţa Cetăţii 8. *Rustic*, Str. 1 Decembrie 1918 no. 5, offers fairly good Romanian food and becomes a popular **bar** at night. For more drinking, try the *Crama* at Str. Morii 17, a little locals' bar; the *Culture Pub* in the basement of the *Burg Hostel* has **live music** and stays open until 3am, while *No Limits*, beneath the clock tower, is the most central **club**.

From Sighişoara to Sibiu

The main approach to Sibiu is to follow the Târnave Mare river west from Sighişoara. From the train or the DN14, you'll see water buffalo pulling wagons or wallowing in the river, watched by their drovers, and glimpse the towers of fortified Saxon churches in villages situated off the main road. The area south and west of Sighişoara is particularly good for leisurely exploration, its villages all accessible by bus from Sighişoara.

Biertan

Following the route west from Sighişoara along the main DN14, a side road heads south through Laslea to **Mălâncrav** (Malmkrog), where a Saxon church nestles in a narrow wooded valley. It was built in the late fourteenth century and surrounded by low walls in the fifteenth century; it is noted for its altar-piece (c1520) and lovely frescoes from the late fourteenth century the second half of the fifteenth century. There's still a substantial Saxon population here, with hordes of summer visitors tearing around on trailbikes. The Mihai Eminescu Trust has a guesthouse opposite the church (see p.158 for booking details) and an organic orchard with ancient varieties of apple, pear, plum and walnut, producing wonderful apple juice.

△ Biertan fortified church

The Kirchenburgenschutzverein

The Kirchenburgenschutzverein (the Union for Protection of the Fortified Churches) is a group dedicated to the preservation of the **fortified churches** and associated aspects of Saxon culture; in addition to raising money among the Saxon diaspora in Germany, it has set up a network of Gästehäuser or small **guesthouses** (①), so that those interested in seeing the churches can contribute financially to the cause, and vice versa. These generally charge for a bunk or a bed and a basic bathroom; breakfast may be available by arrangement, but you shouldn't rely on it. The caretakers tend to be elderly and prefer pre-booked groups, rather than independent travellers. The **coordinators** are Kilian Dörr, at the Lutheran parish house (Evangelisches Pfarrhaus) in Sibiu at Piaţa Huet 1 (☎0269/213 141, ✉evang.kirche@logon.ro), and Hugo Schneider, at Str. Gh. Doja 23 in Mediaş (☎0269/828 605); there are also local contacts, listed with the villages in question. An excellent and inexpensive **guide** to the Gästehäuser and to walks in the area south of Mediaş can be bought at the parish houses of Sibiu and Mediaş.

Continuing west, a turning at **Şaros pe Târnave**, 26km from Sighişoara, leads to **BIERTAN** (Birthälm); if you're travelling by train, you'll need to get off at Mediaş for a local bus to Biertan; otherwise, it should cost no more than €8 to take a taxi from Sighişoara. The best approach to the village, however, is the four-hour hike through fields and wooded ridges from Brateiu (Pretai), the first rail halt east of Mediaş, via the tiny villages of Aţel (Hetzeldorf) and Dupuş (Tobsdorf), both with fortified churches; Aţel has a functional Gästehaus (☎0269/204 865, ext 114; ①) should you want to stop over. Biertan itself contains the best known of all the Saxon **fortified churches** (Tues–Sat 9am–noon 1–7pm, Sun 9–11am, 2–7pm), set high on a hill within two and a half rings of walls linked by a splendid covered staircase. Completed as late as 1522, and recently restored and added to UNESCO's World Heritage List, this was the seat of the Lutheran bishops from 1572 to 1867, and their fine gravestones can be seen inside the Bishops' Tower. Other notable features are the altarpiece (a classic polyptych dated 1483–1515), the sacristy door (from 1515 and with no fewer than nineteen locks), and a room where couples wanting to divorce were supposedly shut up together for two weeks.

The *Gambrinus* **restaurant** is between the church walls; **accommodation** in the *Gästehaus* (①) can be organized here or by contacting Martin Ohnweiler (☎0269/214 877) or the *Pfarrhaus* (☎0269/204 867). There are guesthouses on Strada Aurel Vlaicu and Strada 1 Decembrie. Home-made cheese can be bought at the private dairy (*lăptărie*) on the Copşa Mare road, while good white wine costs next to nothing at the factory set back from the Richiş road. The village is the site of the Sachsentreffen or Saxon Meeting, when many Saxons return from Germany to meet up, drink and dance on the second or third Saturday of September.

Mediaş

The main town between Sighişoara and Sibiu is **MEDIAŞ** (Mediasch), which despite being home to the tanneries and chemical works fed by the Târnava Mare valley's methane reserves, gets more attractive the further in you venture. Originally an Iron Age and then a Roman settlement, Mediaş was a predominantly Saxon town for many centuries, walled and with gate towers, two of which remain on Strada Cloşca, east of the bus station. After 1918, it began to develop an industrial and Romanian character, stemming from political changes after World War I and the construction here of Transylvania's first gas pipeline.

From the **train station** on Strada Unirii, turn right to reach the **bus station**, a few minutes walk away, opposite the synagogue; from here, head left up Strada Pompierilor and then take a right down Strada Roth to the town centre, **Piaţa Regele Ferdinand I**. This is dominated by the fifteenth-century **Evangelical Church of St. Margaret**, its seventy-metre bell tower slightly askew; the church (Mon–Sat 10am–7pm, Sun 11am–7pm) is a true citadel, surrounded by store rooms, high ramparts and towers (one of which, the Tailors' Tower, served as a jail for Vlad the Impaler in 1467). Inside, there are Anatolian carpets, frescoes, a colourful Baroque organ (used for recitals at 7pm on Mondays from June to Sept), and two superb Gothic altarpieces, including a Crucifixion with a view of Vienna painted in 1474–79. The **Schullerhaus**, on the same square at no. 25, was built in 1588 and once housed the Transylvanian Diet but now serves as a hotel (see below). For a limited insight into the history of the town, and a better wildlife display, visit the **town museum** (Tues–Sun 9am–5pm) in a former monastery east of the centre at Str. Mihai Viteazul 46.

Mediaş's oldest and largest **hotel** is the ugly *Central* (℡0269/841 787, ℻831 722; ❸), at Piaţa Corneliu Coposu 2, at the top of Strada Pompierilor; the private *Select*, at Str. Petőfi 3 (℡0269/834 874, ℻835 743; ❸), is much more comfortable, and there's also a new guesthouse, the *Schullerhaus*, at Piaţa Regele Ferdinand I no.25 (℡0269/831 347, ℻832 390; ❷). **Internet** access is available in the *Hotel Central*. Buses run from the bus station to Agnita, Sibiu and Târgu Mureş, and to all the surrounding villages. Some especially picturesque villages with fortified churches lie along the road to Agnita, notably **Moşna** (Meschen), whose church, built in 1491, has a fifty-metre tower.

Copşa Mică and Ocna Sibiului

Filthy **COPŞA MICĂ** (Kleinkopisch), 13km west of Mediaş, is probably Romania's most polluted town – and if you're unlucky with connections you may have to change trains for Sibiu here rather than in Mediaş. Life expectancy here is nine years below the national average.

There are good fortified churches in **Valea Viilor** (Wurmloch, 4km south of Copşa Mică), **Axente Sever** (Frauendorf) and **Agârbiciu** (Arbegen) – both visible just east of their rail halts. It's possible to follow easy hiking trails from Agârbiciu to Valea Viilor and Moşna to Biertan. Otherwise, there's little worth stopping for en route to Sibiu other than **OCNA SIBIULUI** (Salzburg), a bathing resort with fizzy, salty water, which bubbles up in four lakes formed in abandoned salt-workings. The grand fin-de-siècle spa building is very slowly being restored. The nearest train stop to the spa is Băile Ocna Sibiului, 2km north of Ocna Sibiului station proper, with a decent **campsite** adjacent.

Sibiu

"I rubbed my eyes in amazement," wrote Walter Starkie of **SIBIU** in 1929. "The town where I found myself did not seem to be in Transylvania, for it had no Romanian or Hungarian characteristics: the narrow streets and old gabled houses made me think of Nuremberg." Nowadays, the illusion is harder to sustain, in a city surrounded by high-rise suburbs and virtually abandoned by the Saxons themselves, but the old town is still a startling sight, with many of its houses painted sky blue, red, apricot or pea green, and home to some of Romania's best museums. Split into a **historic centre** and a lower **new town**, Sibiu has many fine old **churches**, as well as the remains of the original **Saxon Bastions** that formed the town's fortifications. The town's **pottery fair** is held on the first weekend of September.

Some history

Sibiu, known in German as Hermannstadt and in Hungarian as Nagyszeben, was founded in the 1190s and grew to be the chief city of the **Transylvanian Saxons**. Clannish, hard working and thrifty, its merchants dominated trade between Transylvania and Wallachia by the Olt gorge route, and by 1367 formed exclusive guilds under royal charter. They were envied by others and knew it; their literature and proverbs are marked by admonitions to beware of outsiders, and Sibiu's plethora of fortifications testifies to their historical caution. As early as 1241 their first citadel was destroyed by the Tatars, leaving only a hundred survivors; the townsfolk surrounded themselves with three rings of walls by 1350 and a fourth (which included the new lower town) in 1452. Behind these defences, mighty enough to repel the Turks three times, the people of Sibiu linked their buildings and streets with tunnels and gateways, and set heavily grated windows to cover the stairways and corners where they might ambush intruders. Parts of the walls were demolished, and new gateways opened up in the nineteenth century, but much remains. Now, the wheel has turned, and Sibiu has stronger trading links with Germany than any other Transylvanian town, and has even elected a Saxon mayor.

Arrival and information

Sibiu's **bus terminal** and **train station** are on the northeast side of town. The rail service is poor, but bus services are increasingly taking up the strain, reaching as far afield as Bucharest, Cluj, Constanța and Timișoara. To reach the centre, cross Piața 1 Decembrie 1918 (still generally known as Piața Gării) and follow Strada General Magheru up the hill. The **airport** is on the western edge of town, served by a bus to and from the TAROM office at Str. Bălcescu 10 (Mon–Fri 9am–12.30, 1.30-6pm; ☎0269/211 157, ⓦwww.tarom.ro); alternatively, you can take bus #11, #20 or trolley bus #T8, or a taxi for €2.

Tourist information is available in the Schiller bookshop, Piața Mare 7 (☎0269/211 110, ⓦwww.sibiu.ro/index-en), which also sells maps and hands out the *Sibiu Live* and *Șapte Seri* **listings magazines**. The **Lutheran Pfarrhaus**, Piața Huet 1 (☎0269/211 203), sells a leaflet (currently in German only, with summaries in English) describing the town's new Kulturweg circuit of information signs, as well as a book listing accommodation and walks in the Saxon villages to the north.

Accommodation

There is an increasingly wide range of **hotels** in Sibiu; alongside the state-run options, a new generation of small **private hotels** have opened up, spanning the range from cheap backpackers' places to bases for foreign businessmen. There is also a good-quality **campsite** (☎0269/214 022, Ⓕ228 777) in the Dumbrava forest 4km to the south (trolley bus #T1 from the train station), with the *Parc Dumbrava* **motel** next door (same tel; ❹), and a former **han**, now upgraded to the three-star *Palace Dumbrava* (☎0269/242 222, Ⓕ242 232; ❺), nearby. In the same direction (bus #5) is the *Valea Aurie* cabana (☎0269/242 696; ❸), well run and with a good restaurant.

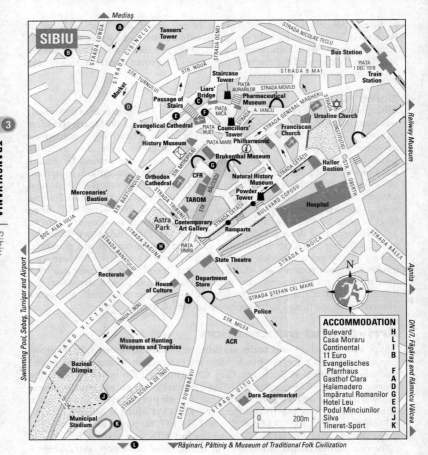

ACCOMMODATION

Bulevard	H
Casa Moraru	L
Continental	I
11 Euro	B
Evangelisches Pfarrhaus	F
Gasthof Clara	A
Halemadero	D
Împăratul Romanilor	G
Hotel Leu	E
Podul Minciunilor	C
Silva	J
Tineret-Sport	K

0   200m

▼ Răşinari, Păltiniş & Museum of Traditional Folk Civilization

Bulevard Piaţa Unirii 10 ☎0269/216 060, ℻215 175. Recently refurbished, with a glitzy new foyer and wheelchair access. **6**

Casa Moraru, Str. A. Vlahuţă 11A ☎0269 /216 291, ℻215 490. A private hotel with good facilities, including fitted hair dryers and alarm clocks in all rooms, a good restaurant and bar, plus a sauna and pool. **7**

Continental Calea Dumbrăvii 2 ☎0269/218 100, ℮conti.sb@directnet.ro, reservation @continentalhotels.ro. Luxurious (rooms come complete with cable TV and minibar) but over-priced chain hotel. **7**

11 Euro Tudor Vladimirescu 2 ☎0269/222 041, 214 221, ⊛www.11euro.net. So called because it costs €22 for a double room, there's an odd mix of basic and stylish touches here; spacious

en-suite rooms with awful curtains and no restaurant. **3**

Evangelisches Pfarrhaus Piaţa Huet 1 ☎0269/0269/211 203, ℮evang .kirche@logon.ro. The Lutheran parish house provides clean, simple hostel-style accommodation; arrive by 3pm or phone ahead so a key can be left for you. **2**

Gasthof Clara Str. Răului 24 ☎0269/222 914, ℻224 003. Across the Cibin River from the market, identifiable by its fake half-timbering, this is a pleasant new hotel with a good terrace-restaurant (noon–11pm). **6**

Halemadero Str. Măsarilor 10 (at Croitorilor) ☎0269/212 509. Pricey for a place with erratic hot water, but surprisingly popular, the *Halemadero* has no singles and only one bathroom for every two rooms, but there is a pleasant outside bar. **②**

Împăratul Romanilor Str. Bălcescu 4 ☎0269/216 500, ✉hir@verena.ro. By far and away the best place in the centre of town, this traditional hotel is comfortable and benefits from a great location. **❼**

Hotel Leu Str. Moș Ion Roată 6 ☎0269/218 392, ☎213 975. A tiny simple place, with communal showers; popular with backpackers, the rooms sleep up to four **②**

Podul Minciunilor Str. Azilului 1 ☎0269 /217 259. The "Liars' Bridge" guesthouse is quiet

and friendly, with permanent hot water, and no room sharing. **②**

Silva Aleea Eminescu 1 ☎0269/442 141, ✉silva@xnet.ro. A standard hotel, partially renovated, with a good terrace overlooking the Parc sub Arini; no singles. **❻**

Tineret-Sport at Str. Octavian Goga 2 ☎0269/233 673. Once a bargain-basement option with a reputation for overcharging foreigners, this has now been thoroughly renovated, with sixteen bright en-suite rooms, but no restaurant. **❸**

The Old Town

The old town centres on three squares – the **Piața Mare** (Grosser Ring), the **Piața Mică** (Kleiner Ring) and the **Piața Huet** (Huetplatz). Strada General Magheru (Sporergasse) leads south from the train station, on Piața 1 Decembrie 1918, to Piața Mare, the traditional hub of public life. Heading along Strada Magheru, you'll pass old **synagogue** (which is still used in the summer by Sibiu's remaining two-dozen Jews) and the **Ursuline church** at the junction with Strada Avram Iancu, dating from 1474–78 and now shared by Greco-Catholic and Roman Catholic congregations. One block south, on Strada Șelarilor, is the **Franciscan church**, also dating from the fifteenth century, although it was rebuilt in the Baroque style after its roof collapsed in 1776. Forking right onto Strada Avram Iancu, no. 16 is one of the oldest houses in town, built in the first half of the fourteenth century and now being restored.

  Piața Mare is surrounded by the renovated premises of sixteenth- and seventeenth-century merchants, whose acumen and thrift were proverbial. Its north side is dominated by a Roman Catholic church built in 1726-33; to its left, at Piața Mare 5, the eighteenth-century Brukenthal Palace, was the home of Samuel von Brukenthal, the imperial governor of Transylvania from 1777 to 1787. Built in 1778-85 by a Viennese architect in a refined Late Baroque style, the palace now houses Transylvania's finest art collection, partly assembled by von Brukenthal himself and opened to the public in 1817, three years before the Louvre in Paris. As well as an extensive array of Romanian and Western art, the **Brukenthal Museum** (Tues–Sun 9am–5pm, winter 10am–6pm; ⓦwww.brukenthalmuseum.ro/en) includes fifteenth- and sixteenth-century Transylvanian wooden religious sculptures and eighteenth-century Romanian icons. Heading from here into Piața Huet, you'll pass near the **History Museum** (same hours), housed in the Old City Hall (*Primăria Veche*; 1470-91) at Str. Mitropoliei 2 (Fleischergasse); the arcaded courtyard is worth a look even if you choose not to go inside to view the interesting exhibits on local history or the collection of silverware.

  In the **Piața Huet**, the massive **Evangelical Cathedral** (Mon–Sat 9am–6pm, Sun 10am-6pm), built in three phases between 1320 and 1520, dominates its neighbours, the Saxons' Brukenthal Gymnasium (Grammar School; 1782) and Pfarrhaus (Parish house; 1502) – confirming the town's pre-eminence as a centre of the Lutheran faith. The cathedral houses Romania's largest church organ, and in summer there are recitals on Wednesday evenings at 6pm. There's a fresco of the Crucifixion (1445) by Johannes von Rosenau on the north wall of the choir, showing Italian and Flemish influences, and the **tomb of Mihnea the Bad**, Dracula's son, is in the crypt; Mihnea was voivode of Wallachia for just three years before being stabbed to death in 1510 outside the cathedral after attending Mass (the building was still a Catholic place of worship at that time). There's also a fine collection of funerary monuments here, including a well-tended memorial to the dead of World War I. The cathedral **tower** (visits Mon–Sat noon & 4pm) is worth the climb for the expansive views it gives over the city. By the cathedral, an alley leads to the thirteenth-century **Passage of Stairs** (Pasajul Scărilor), which descends into the lower town overshadowed by arches and the medieval citadel wall.

Alternatively, head north into **Piaţa Mică**, where a miniature urban canyon runs down from the northwest corner under the elegant wrought-iron Iron Bridge (Podul de Fier). Dating from 1859, this bridge is nicknamed the **Liars' Bridge** (Podul Minciunilor), the story being that if someone tells a lie while standing on it the bridge will collapse. Ceauşescu managed to give a speech from it and survive, although he disliked the town and never returned.

By the bridge, at Piaţa Mică 21, stands the arcaded **House of the Butchers' Guild** (Fleischerhalle), now the Casa Artelor, hosting temporary art exhibitions. Also on the square are the **Pharmaceutical Museum** at no. 26 (Tues–Sun 10am–6pm), which preserves the fittings of an ancient pharmacy and also commemorates Samuel Hahnemann, founder of homeopathy, who lived in Sibiu in the 1770s (see box below); and the Casa Hermes (Hermeshaus) at no. 11, which houses both temporary art shows and the **Binder Museum of Ethnology** (same opening hours), based on the collection of Franz Binder (1820–75), who spent thirty years in Africa as a merchant and plant collector. At the rear of the Casa Hermes, the **Emil Sigerus Museum of Saxon Ethnography** on Piaţa Huet (same opening hours) has a rather limited collection of household goods. To get back to Piaţa Mare from Piaţa Mică, cut through the gate below the **Councillors' Tower** (Turnul Sfatului), built in the early thirteenth century as part of the city's second ring of fortifications, and rebuilt in 1588; open 10am–6pm daily, it gives fine **views** of the city.

The roots of homeopathy

Baron **Samuel von Brukenthal**'s achievements in his time as governor of Transylvania were many, but his role in the development of **homeopathy** was the widest-ranging and ultimately most important of these.

It was Brukenthal who paid for **Samuel Hahnemann** (1755–1843) to complete his medical degree in Germany and who then brought him to Sibiu to be his private doctor. In recompense, Hahnemann spent the best part of two years (1777–79) cataloguing Brukenthal's immense library of 280,000 books, including a large collection of rare manuscripts and books by medieval alchemists and physicians such as Paracelsus and Rumelius; it was his study of these authors that laid the basis of his lifetime's work.

In 1779, Hahnemann returned to Germany, married and had children – although desperately poor, he pursued his studies, driven on by his dissatisfaction with the conventional medicine that he was obliged to practise at the time, while gradually formulating his own theories. Although homeopathy was eventually marginalised by conventional (allopathic) medicine, by the 1870s this had itself absorbed key homeopathic principles, such as the abandonment of complex mixtures of drugs and the adoption of theories of disease based upon infectious agents.

In recent times, Romania was one of the first countries to legitimize homeopathy, due to the shortage of medicines and medical equipment under Ceauşescu, and from 1995 only qualified doctors were allowed to practice homeopathy (although those already registered as homeopaths are permitted to continue).

Alternatively, a passageway leads down through the **Staircase Tower** (Fingerlingsstiege) at Piața Mică 24 via Piața Aurarilor to Strada Movilei, a street pock-marked with medieval windows, doorways and turrets. Down in the rambling lower town northwest of the squares are the octagonal brick **Tanners' Tower** (Turnul Pielarilor), on Strada Pulberăriei, reached via Strada Valea Mare, and a busy food **market** beside the river on Piața Cibin – the site of the first settlement in Sibiu.

Over to the east, near the train station, the enjoyable **Railway Museum** (open daylight hours) is an open-air collection of over thirty steam locomotives, as well as snow ploughs and steam cranes – rail enthusiasts will love it. To get there, turn left from the station, ascend to the road bridge, cross the tracks and descend the steps to the right, turning left along Strada Dorobanților at the bottom; after 300m or so (at house no. 26), turn sharp right to the rail tracks and go through the arch to the left.

The New Town

In Saxon times, Sibiu's promenade was the Heltauergasse, now **Strada Bălcescu**, which heads south from Piața Mare to Piața Unirii, and this is still the heart of the modern city. At the northern end of the street is Sibiu's oldest hotel, the **Împăratul Romanilor**, still recognizable as the grand establishment once patronized by the likes of Liszt, Johann Strauss and Eminescu. The design of the hotel, which dates from 1895, was a reaction against the militaristic architecture that had previously dominated the town; this can be seen to the southeast in the three rows of **ramparts and bastions** on either side of Bulevardul Coposu, where three mighty **towers** were built in the late fourteenth century and manned by contingents of the Carpenters', Potters' and Arquebusiers' (later the Drapers') guilds. To the east, the **Powder Tower** (Pulverturm) was converted to a theatre in 1788 and is slowly being restored to this role. Just beyond it, at Strada Cetății 1, the **Natural History Museum** (Tues–Sun 9am–5pm) has the standard collection of stuffed wildlife. The **Haller Bastion** (1552) at the northern end of Strada Cetății, and the Soldisch or **Mercenaries' Bastion** (the last to be built, in 1627) further west on Strada Bastionului also survive.

Sibiu developed as a centre of intellectual and cultural life during the nineteenth century, and the first congress of **ASTRA** – The Association for the Propagation of Romanian Culture in Transylvania – was held in October 1861 on **Strada Mitropoliei**, a street east of the Mercenaries' Bastion that is full of significance for Romanian nationalists. No. 19 was the home of Zaharia Boiu (1834–1903), poet and founder of the first Romanian-language school in Sibiu, while Avram Iancu and Mihai Eminescu both stayed in houses here. Furthermore, opposite the **post office** is the **Orthodox Cathedral** (1902–06), which was based on the Aya Sofya in Istanbul and is embellished with all manner of neo-Byzantine flourishes and frescoes, plus mosaics from Munich. South of the cathedral is the **ASTRA Park**, lined with busts of Romanian worthies. In 1905, ASTRA opened a library and museum overlooking the park in a fine building at Str. Lupaş 5; from here, Strada Lupaş takes you east to Piața Unirii. A block east, from the park, at Tribunei 12, is the Brukenthal Museum's **Contemporary Art Gallery**.

Two blocks southwest of Piața Unirii, at Str. Şcoala de Înot 4, is the **Museum of Hunting Weapons and Trophies** (Tues–Sun 10am–5pm). Once the home of a Hapsburg general, it still shelters his collection of weapons, medals and stuffed animals, and is worth a brief visit.

Southwest of the centre along Calea Dumbrăvii (trolley bus #T1 from the train station), near the **Zoological Gardens** in the Dumbrava forest, is the excellent **Museum of Traditional Folk Civilization** (Tues–Sun 9am–5pm), one of the best open-air museums in Romania. Set against a mountain back-drop, it offers a fantastic insight into Romanian rural life, with authentic wooden houses and churches, all lovingly tended to; information, however, is only available in Romanian.

Bus #8, from the bridge south of the train station on Bulevardul Coposu, takes you to **TURNIŞOR**, where it will drop you outside the *Pfarrhaus* at Str. Bielz 62 (Kirchgasse). To Romanians, Turnişor is simply a suburb of Sibiu, but to its German populace it's a distinct village, Neppendorf. Originally Saxon, its population was boosted in the eighteenth century by an infusion of Austrian Protestants, expelled by their Catholic neighbours. Although the two groups never mixed in other villages throughout the region, here the Saxons and Landler intermarried – yet they are still seated separately in the church, with Landler women on one side of the nave and Saxon women on the other. The **church** was never fortified – the villagers fled to Sibiu when the Turks came to burn their settlement in 1493 – but the interior is typical of Saxon village churches, with lovely paintings on the gallery, and a Turkish rug; ask at the *Pfarrhaus* for the key. There's also an excellent **museum** in the north transept, mapping the history of the village, with lots of old photos and plenty of text (all in German). Today, there are only about 200 Germans in Turnişor, com-pared to some 4000 before World War II. Visible from trains to the north of Turnişor station is an amazing gypsy palace, like a Japanese castle with multi-ple Gothic spikes.

Eating, drinking and entertainment

Places to eat cluster along Strada Bălcescu and around Piaţa Mare and Piaţa Unirii, and some of the best are in the main hotels; the restaurant in the *Împăr-atul Romanilor*, for example, is noted for the quality of its Romanian cuisine. *Sibiul Vechi*, at Str. Papiu Ilarian 3, off Strada Bălcescu, serves excellent tradi-tional food, often with good Romanian folk music, too, and the *Turn*, by the Councillors' Tower at Piaţa Mare 1, also offers good local fare. Once you get down the dark corridor behind the *rotiserie* at Piaţa Mică 23, *Ciao Italia* is a tasteful Italian restaurant (closed Sun). To the north in the lower town, the *Pizzeria Michelangelo*, Str. Turnului 3, is slightly pricey but very good, especially for vegetarians; across the river, *Gasthof Clara* has a range of Romanian, German, Italian and even Thai dishes. For delicious traditional food, it's well worth heading out to the *Hanul Rustic* (☎0269/426 291), part of the Museum of Traditional Folk Civilization (see above) but with a separate entrance at km5 on the Răşinari road.

For faster food, there are several *rotiseries* in Sibiu, serving roast chicken. You could also try the **cafés** on Piaţa Mare, such as the refurbished *Perla* or the *Intim*, a good coffee, cake and pizza joint. The cafés on Piaţa Mica – *Dolly* at no. 14, and *Dori's* at no. 3 – are better value, with fine, freshly-baked fare, while west of the centre, the *Cofetăria Universităţii*, at the corner of Bulevardul Victoriei and Strada Banatului, has a good range of pastries and a lively student atmosphere. The richest, creamiest cakes in town are those at the *cofetărie* of the *Hotel Bulevard*, while for **breakfast**, your best bet is the non-smoking *Patiseria Aroma* at Str. Bălcescu 1 (Mon-Fri 8am-9pm, Sat & Sun 10am-8pm). *Teea*, at Magheru 10, is a stylish new teahouse.

The southern end of Strada Bălcescu is lined with *terasas* for pleasant daytime drinking, but Sibiu pretty much closes down by 9pm. **Bars** which stay open later include the cheap and very cheerful *Crama Naţional*, Piaţa Mică 17 (daily till 1am), *Chill Out*, Piaţa Mică 23 (playing house and techno music to a partly gay crowd until 6am, *Spielplatz*, Piaţa Mică 17 (a café with music until at least 1am), and the smoky *Art Café*, beneath the Philharmonic at Str. Filarmonicii 2 (daily till 2am), which has occasional jazz gigs. These are all cellar-bars which empty in summer, when it's more pleasant to drink outdoors: try the *Turn* (see opposite), which serves Guinness, or the *Trei Stejari* on Strada Bâlea, attached to a brewery, which has a *terasa* that's open until 11pm. The Tineretului **cinema**, at Str. Odobescu 4, sometimes doubles as a disco; there's also the Pacea cinema, Str. Bălcescu 29. **Classical concerts** are held in the House of Culture on Str. Şaguna and the adjacent Army House (Cercul Militar; B-dul Victoriei 3), as well as in the **state theatre**; tickets can be bought at Str. Bălcescu 17 or at the theatre, and details of what's showing are displayed on posters around town.

A **Jazz Festival** is held in the spring (between March and July), and the **International Theatre Festival** takes place between March and June. Ask at the county's Cultural Inspectorate, Str. Şaguna 10 (☎0269/210 531), for up-to-date information on festival dates.

Shopping

While not as good as Braşov or Cluj, Sibiu can meet most shoppers' needs, usually on Str. Bălcescu: the best for imported foodstuffs is Nic at no. 30; slide film is available at Foto Universal, no. 17. The main department store, the Dumbrava, is on the far side of Piaţa Unirii, opposite the *Continental* hotel. There are two **markets**, Piaţa Cibin, by the river on Strada Turnului, and Piaţa Teatrului, by the theatre on B-dul Coposu. For outdoor gear, go to Action Sports, Str. Avram Iancu 25; for crafts, it's best to head out to the open-air museum south of town. The Metro cash-and-carry is at Şoseaua Alba Iulia 79A (Mon–Sat 6am-9pm, Sun 8am–6pm).

The Librăria Freidrich Schiller, Piaţa Mare 7 (Mon–Fri 9am–5pm, Sat 10am–1pm) houses the tourist information centre and sells **maps and guides** (including the authoritative Fabini series on Saxon churches), postcards, calendars, and books (many in German) on Transylvanian architecture and culture. ThauSib, Piaţa Mică 3 has some English-language books, and Libreria Noica, Bălcescu 16 some maps.

Listings

Banks and exchange Prima, at Str. Cetăţii 1, and Olt Vegas and TransEuropa, on Str. Bălcescu, offer good rates for cash. IDM, at Str. Papiu Ilarian 12 (off Str. Bălcescu) and at Piaţa Mică 9, accepts credit cards and travellers' cheques, but at poor rates.

Buses Services to Germany and elsewhere in Western Europe are operated by: AtlasSib, Str. Tractorului 14 ☎0269/229 209, 224 101, ⓦwww.atlassib.ro and c/o the agency at the *Hotel Bulevard* ☎ & ⓕ0269/218 125; Amad Turistik, Calea Poplăcii 58 ☎0269/212 227, ⓕ233 127 and Piaţa Mare 6 ☎0269/216 997; Andronik Reisen, Str. Blănarilor 2 (at Str. 9 Mai, opposite the station); Double-T, Str. Bălcescu 1 ☎0269

/217 497; Kessler, Str. Bieltz 22 ☎0269/228 118, ⓕ229 011 and Str. Bălcescu 6 ☎243 820; Mihu Reisen, Şelimbăr ☎0269/560 127; Pletl, Str. Brukenthal ☎0269/228 007; Touring-Eurolines, B-dul Milea 13 ☎0269/212 248, ⓔsibiu @eurolines.ro; and TransEuropa, Str. Bălcescu 19 ☎0269/211 296, ⓔrezervari@transeuropa.ro & Str. Fraţii Grachi 5 ☎0269/431123. Tickets to Italy with Ognivia can be booked at the Prima agency, Str. Cetăţii 1.

Car rental Elite, Bălcescu 22, ☎ & ⓕ0269 /228 826, 0721/219 196; Toro, Str. Filarmonicii 5 ☎0269/232 237, 0745/514 441, ⓦwww.tororent.ro.

Hospital On B-dul Spitalelor, opposite the Haller Bastion.

Internet access Internet Verena, Str. Pann 12; Meridian, Tribunei 12; PowerNet, Str. Brukenthal 3.

Libraries The British Council library is in the university's Faculty of Letters (B-dul Victoriei 5–7 ☎ & ☏ 0269/211 056); it's also home to the American, French and German libraries.

Pharmacy Farmasib at Str. Bălcescu 53 is open to 11pm (Sat & Sun 10pm); there's night service at Farmacia San Marco, Complex Cedonia.

Police Str. Revoluţiei 4 ☎ 0269/430 929.

Post office Str. Mitropoliei 14 Mon–Fri 7am–8pm, Sat 8am–1pm.

Sport Facilities are clustered around the open-air swimming pool, the Ştrand, on Şos. Alba Iulia, while there's an indoor, Olympic-size swimming pool on B-dul Victoriei; at Str. Şaguna 2, the Baia Neptun (Tues-Sun 8am-8pm) has a 20m pool and sauna and massage. Sibiu's football team, FC InterSibiu, play in the Municipal Stadium in the Parc sub Arini.

Train tickets The CFR office is at Str. Bălcescu 6 (Mon–Fri 7.30am–7.30pm).

Travel agencies Eximtur, Str. Bălcescu 6 ☎ 0269/245 508, ☏ sibiu@eximtur.ro; Paralela 45, Calea Dumbrăvii 12 (at the rear of the Hotel Continental; ☎ 0269/216 096, 216 109, ☏ paralela45sibiu@hotmail.com).

Around Sibiu

Buses from the terminal by the train station serve many of the **old Saxon settlements** around Sibiu. Many of these villages have sizeable Romanian and Gypsy populations, now far outnumbering the Germans, but most have fortified churches and rows of houses presenting a solid wall to the street – hallmarks of their Saxon origins. "They have existed for seven hundred years, a mere handful, surrounded by races that have nothing in common with them, and yet they have not lost those customs that attach them to their fatherland", observed Walter Starkie in the 1920s. This remained largely true of the Saxon communities until 1989 – for example **Cisnădioara**, where the sight and feel of the place suggested Bavaria two hundred years ago – but the Saxons are disappearing fast, and it won't be long before their culture too has vanished from the area.

The villages south of Sibiu lie in the foothills of the **Cindrel** (or **Cibin**) mountains, where enjoyable day walks and longer hikes can be taken from the small ski resort of Păltiniş. To the east and north of Sibiu, there are more Saxon villages with doughty fortress-churches, including Vurpăr (Burgberg), Şura Mare and Şura Mică (Gross-Scheuern and Klein-Scheuern) and Slimnic (Stolzenburg), all accessible by bus, a pretty excursion through rolling hills and orchards. **Slimnic** is particularly interesting because the church, begun in 1450, was never finished, but the ruins of a substantial fortress around it survive.

Cisnădie and Cisnădioara

Two or three buses an hour (roughly one an hour at weekends) leave Sibiu's bus station for **CISNĂDIE** (Heltau), 12km to the south. Cisnădie's modern outskirts quickly give way to the old Red Town (so called by the Turks both for the colour of its walls and the blood that was shed attempting to breach them) – a long square leading to the largely Romanesque **church**, protected by a double wall and a moat. If you ask a warden, you may be taken up the massive thirteenth-century **tower**; the climb takes you up a succession of lofty vaults linked by creaking ladders and narrow stairways to the four turrets, medieval symbols of civic status, which crown the tower. From the belfry, the view of Cisnădie's angular courtyards and red rooftops is superb, while just visible in the distance below the Cindrel mountains is the conical rock that overlooks the village of Cisnădioara. At the rear of the church you can also call in at the **Textile Museum** (Mon–Sat 8am–4pm), which has comprehensive coverage of the local household industry.

If you're keen to stay in Cisnădie, ask at the museum about **private rooms** (❶–❷). The *Casa Blanca*, at Str. Țesătorilor 80 (☎0269/561 275; ❶), is another option; to get there from the central Piața Revoluției, head down Str. Podului (by the *Capșa* restaurant) and turn left at the end. The best option by far, however, is to head 2.5km south along Strada Cetății towards Sadu, to the *Cerbul Carpatin* (☎0269/562 937; ❹), which is comfortable and very friendly.

From central Cisnădie, it's a three-kilometre walk west along Strada Măgurii and the valley road, lined with poplars and orchards, towards the striking seventy-metre-high rock that looms over **CISNĂDIOARA** (Michelsburg), also reached by bus #32 from Sibiu every few hours. The tiny **Romanesque church** built in 1223 on the summit of this rock frequently withstood Tatar attacks; the villagers defended it by hurling down rocks which had previously been carried into the citadel by aspiring husbands, the custom being that no young man could marry until he had carried a heavy rock from the riverbed up the steep track (the villagers were anxious to prevent weaklings from marrying in case they spoiled the hardy race). Ask for the church key at the **ethnographic museum**, next to the lower church in the village; both are supposedly open Tuesday to Sunday from 10am to 5pm, but you may have to ask around to find the curator.

Follow the main road down through the village and you will pass a few shops and rows of neat, unmistakably German houses, now used as holiday homes. This road continues for half a kilometre to the village swimming pool, where the *Ştrand* **campsite** has been renovated. The best **accommodation** in the village is the centrally heated *Elimheim*, on the Rășinari road a few hundred metres from the village centre (☎0269/566 499; ❶), and Ioan Salistean's guesthouse at Str. Valea de Argint 105 (☎0744/978 308, 0745/937 078, Ⓔantobizna@yahoo.com; ❶). Alternatively, beyond the museum, at Cisnădioara 30, there's a Saxon *Gästehaus* advance bookings only through Max Herzberg, DFDR, Str. Gen. Magheru 1–3, 2400 Sibiu; ☎0269/215 417; ❶), with a wood fire, an outdoor toilet and water drawn from a well; or there are cabins at the *Hanul Pinul* at the edge of the village (☎0269/561 636, 0744/193 238; ❶).

Rășinari and Păltiniș

RĂȘINARI lies 12km from Sibiu on the road to Păltiniș. It's a tight-packed village with a painted Orthodox church built in 1752, and an **ethnographic museum** (Tues–Sun 10am–5pm), showing the usual range of local costumes and pottery. However, it's more noteworthy for the annual **Pastoral Album Folklore Festival**, held on the third Sunday of April, as well as the large gypsy population at the southern end of town. Maxitaxis leave from opposite Sibiu's swimming pool on B-dul Victoriei and run to the southern end of Rășinari. There are several **guesthouses** on Strada Octavian Goga, including the *Badiu* (☎0269/557 359), *Cristea* (☎0269/557 185) and *Phoenix* (☎0745/308 034); 2km east of the village along the Păltiniș road, it's possible to stay at the *Casa Mai* (☎0269/572 693; ❽), an Austrian-style pension with nice rooms, a good restaurant and a swimming pool. Rășinari is also connected to Păltiniș by a path (marked with red stripes) leading over the mountains in six to seven hours. About an hour before Păltiniș, near Mount Tomnaticu, a path marked with blue triangles turns right to the *Şanta* cabana (❶), a few kilometres east of the resort.

Ambiguous philosophers

Răşinari was the birthplace not only of the anti-Semitic prime minister and poet Octavian Goga, but also, in 1911, of the philosopher **Emil Cioran**. In 1934, he published *Pe Culmile Disperarii* (*On the Heights of Despair*), setting out the **nihilist anti-philosophy** that the only valid thing to do with one's life is to end it. He continued, with a total lack of humour, to expound this view in a succession of books, but never quite managed to actually do away with himself, dying only in 1995. In the 1930s, he supported the Legion of the Archangel Michael, better known as the Iron Guard, but, after moving to Paris in 1937, became less extreme in his views.

Another philosopher, **Constantin Noica** (1908–87), spent the last years of his life in nearby **Păltiniş**. In the 1930s, he too was a supporter of the Iron Guard, although he later retreated to the mountains to translate detective stories; in 1949, he was arrested (supposedly for writing a study of Goethe) and exiled to Câmpulung Muscel, and from 1958 to 1964 he was imprisoned (for writing to Cioran, and in effect for *Letters to a Distant Friend*, which Cioran published as a reply in Paris) – this case contributed to the founding of Amnesty International in 1961. He made his name with *Romanian Philosophical Speech* in 1970, and *The Romanian Sense of Being* in 1978. In 1974 he settled in a one-room cabin (Thurs–Sat 10am–6pm) in Păltiniş.

Noica remains an ambivalent figure. With a Platonic distrust of democracy and a fascination with "the Romanian soul" and with "pure" intellectual rigour, he preferred to criticize Western decadence rather than Ceauşescu's dictatorship, and his admirers included both prominent supporters and opponents of the regime. A romantic nationalist, he was opposed to materialist ideologies and saw culture as the only means of survival for a people's soul. Since 1989, his influence has been generally positive, but Romanian intellectual life in the twentieth century was by anti-Semitism, and he said little to help counter this.

PĂLTINIŞ (Hohe Rinne; 1442m), 22km from Răşinari, is primarily a minor (and overpriced) **ski resort**, but also attracts summer hikers. Three **buses** a day (#22) come here from Strada 9 Mai, near the train station in Sibiu. The Păltiniş travel agency has an office in Sibiu at Str. Tribuniei 3 (℗0269/223 860, ℗paltinis@bmfms.ro; Mon–Fri 8am–4pm) and can book villa **accommodation** (❶) in Păltiniş; backpackers should ask for a bed at the *Kloster Schitu*. You should phone directly to book a bed at the *Pensiunea Bufniţa* (℗0744/494 440), the central *Casa Turistilor* cabana (℗0269/216 001; ❸), which has a DJ, or the *Hotel Cindrel* (℗ & ℗0269/574 057; ❹), with decent rooms and **Internet** access.

The Cindrel and Lotrului mountains

Păltiniş makes a good starting point for walks into the **Cindrel and Lotrului mountains**, one of the lesser-known sections of the Transylvanian Alps; the mountains offer high open hikes on quiet trails, and easier terrain than the **Parâng range** to the west. It's only two or three hours' walk north from Păltiniş, predominantly downhill, through the **Cibin gorges** (Cheile Cibinului), past Lake Cibin, to the *Fântânele* cabana (❶), following the red dots beyond the *Casa Turistilor*. From here, you can push on in a couple of hours either to **Sibiel** village (see opposite) following blue dots, or direct to Sibiel rail halt following blue crosses.

However, the route barely takes you above the tree line, so it's worth trying some **longer hikes** of two or three days. A two-day route, marked with red triangles, leads south via the *Gâtu Berbecului* cabana (●; 2–3hr) and a forestry road along the Sadu valley and the Negovanu Mare (2135m) in the Lotrului mountains to Voineasa in the Lotru valley. If you take this route, you will need to camp, but the more popular route is to the west, into the Parâng mountains, east of **Petroşani** (see p.192), which has well-spaced cabana accommodation. This second route, indicated by red stripes, follows a mountain ridge to the *Cânaia* refuge (●; 5–6hr) and then continues over open moorland (poorly marked with red stripes and red crosses – be careful not to lose your way) to the *Obârşia Lotrului* cabana (●; another 9–10hr), at the junction of the north–south DN67C and the east–west DN7A, both unsurfaced and open only to forestry traffic. This is the gateway to the **Parâng mountains**, an alpine area with beautiful lakes; the red crosses continue up to the main ridge, from where red stripes lead you west to Petroşani.

The Mărginimea Sibiului and Sebeş

West of Sibiu, the DN1/7 (E68/E81) and the rail line pass through the **Mărginimea Sibiului** (Borders of Sibiu) towards Sebeş. This area is fairly densely populated, mostly by Romanians rather than Saxons, with a lively folklore recorded in small ethnographic museums in most villages. There are many sheep-raising communities here, and you'll see flocks on the move, with donkeys carrying the shepherds' belongings. Personal trains between Sibiu and Vinţu de Jos (a few kilometres beyond Sebeş) halt a short distance from several settlements en route.

The first of the accessible villages, reached from Sibiu by Personal trains and bus #20 (hourly), is **CRISTIAN**, where a double wall protects the fifteenth-century Saxon church of Grossau, with its massive towers. Since 1752, the village has in fact been largely dominated by an Austrian Protestant population, who fled here to avoid Catholic oppression. The *Spack* (☎0269/579 262; ●), just north of the train station at Str. II 9, is a good, clean hotel owned by a Saxon family; however, it has no restaurant.

The main road passes to the north of all of the villages after Cristian, and some of the train stations – notably those for Sălişte and Tilişca – are several kilometres north of the villages they serve, which makes using public transport slightly problematical here; however, there are good guesthouses in every village. **ORLAT**, with its medieval castle ruins, is about 6km south of Cristian, and is served by buses (to Gura Râului) ten times a day (just twice at weekends) as well as by the Personal trains; there's a **guesthouse** here at Str. Noua 771 (☎ & ⓕ0269/571 036, 0744/542 365) which charges €7 per person, or €2.50 for a two-person tent, plus meals.

It's 2km west to the Sibiel train station, from where an even smaller road leads west past Fântenele (an attractive hamlet with a charming little museum) and, 3km from its station, the village of **SIBIEL**, a sheep-raising community with a strong tradition of **witchcraft**. Perhaps understandably, witches and ghosts are more feared for their attacks on livestock than on people. The villagers blow horns to prevent witches (*strigoi*) from stealing their ewes' milk on St George's Day, but also credit witches with occasional good deeds, such as magically shutting the jaws of wolves intent on ravaging their flocks. The rather good **Museum of Icons Painted on Glass**, next to the eighteenth-century Orthodox church, has a display of over 700 icons on various religious themes; from here, a footpath leads uphill past a ruined citadel to the *Fântânele* cabana (●) and through the Cibin gorges to Păltiniş in eight hours (see opposite).

Continuing north from Sibiel, the road meets the route east back to the main DN1/7 at **SĂLIŞTE**, famous for its peasant **choir**, which performs occasionally in the community centre, and for its co-operative, which produces carpets and embroidered costumes, the latter worn during Sălişte's **Meeting of the Youth Festival** (December 24–31). From a distance, the village church could almost be Saxon, but it is in fact firmly Orthodox. Just beyond it, on Piaţa Eroilor, is the **ethnographic museum**, which can only be visited by booking a day in advance (☏0269/553 086); it houses costumes and artefacts specific to the area. Near a watermill in excellent condition ten minutes' walk along the Tilişca road, lives Radu Ilies, who makes the distinctive black felt hats worn by men in this area and lets visitors watch him as he works.

Costumes are more likely to appear during the course of everyday life at **TILIŞCA**, about 3km west; this is a less spoilt settlement than Sălişte and one which can trace its origins back to Dacian times. There are OVR **homestay** schemes in both Sălişte (contact Maria Cazan, Str. I. Moga 1266; ☏0269/553 357) and Tilişca (contact Elena Iuga, Str. Principală 561; ☏0269/554 012, ✉horeacazan@hotmail.com); alternatively, there's the *Pensiune Raceu*, Str Scolii 535 (☏0269/554 009, 0744/313 102, ✉irinaraceu@hotmail.com; ❸), or the unmodernized Sălişte **motel** (❷), 6km west of the village on the DN1/7.

North of Sălişte, the main road takes a direct route west through the attractive village of **Apoldu de Sus** (Grosspold), settled by Austrian Landlers in 1752 and maintaining its traditional architecture, while the railway crawls through beautiful oakwoods, loops south around Apoldu de Sus, and passes through the Hungarian village of **Apoldu de Jos** (Kisapold). Road and rail are reunited at **MIERCUREA SIBIULUI** (Reussmarkt), a village whose name derives from the Romanian word for Wednesday, the traditional market day – there is still a market here on this day. In the centre of the village is a small, well-preserved thirteenth-century basilica, fortified during the fifteenth century like other Saxon churches, with food stores on the inside of its oval ring wall. Trains and buses also stop 5km further on at **BĂILE MIERCUREA**, a modest spa resort with a run-down campsite, tourist cabana (❶) and a new hotel-restaurant on the main road. A few kilometres west, a handful of cabins (❶) stand at the junction to **CÂLNIC** (Kelling/Kelnek), 3km south of the DN1/7, where a massive keep, built around 1300, and a very simple Romanesque chapel of the same period, are enclosed within one and a half rings of walls that resisted several Turkish sieges. The castle has recently been restored and opened to visitors; local trains halt at Cut, just northwest of the road junction.

Sebeş

The town of **SEBEŞ** grew up on the proceeds of the leather-working industry, trading mainly with Wallachia; as Mühlbach, it was the capital of the Unterwald, the westernmost zone of Saxon settlement. The German street names have recently been resurrected, but Italian influence is now dominant. In 1438, a Turkish army arrived, demanding that the town surrender; a number of inhabitants refused, barricading themselves in one of the towers of the **citadel**, which the Turks stormed and burned. The only survivor, a student aged 16, was then sold as a slave, but escaped twenty years later to write a best-selling exposé of the bogeymen of fifteenth-century Europe. The **Student's Tower** (also known as the Tailors' Tower), at Str. Traian (or Parkgasse) 6, is thus one of the main sights of Sebeş, although it's not open. Heading west brings you to the large **Evangelical Church**, built in Romanesque style between 1240 and 1270, with a disproportionately large and grand Gothic choir added by 1382, followed by the upper part of the tower in 1664. The choir boasts the best Parleresque statues in Transylvania, as well as a large polychrome altar, dating from 1518. Just to the north stands the cemetery chapel, built in 1400 and now used by the Uniates. A **museum** (Tues–Fri 8.30am–3.30pm, Sat & Sun 11am–6pm) featuring the standard ethnographic displays is housed on the north side of the square in the late fifteenth-century **House of the Voivodes**.

Practicalities

The **train station** (Sebeş Alba) and **bus station** are to the east, in the new town. From the stations, a pleasant route into town heads right on Strada Mărăşeşti, crossing the road to Daia Romană – with a view of the dramatic Red Cliffs (Râpa Roşie) to the north of town – and along Strada Mihai Viteazul to the main square. There's little incentive to linger, but should you need to **stay** overnight, the *Motel Dacia* (℡ & ℻ 0258/732 743; ➌) just east on the DN1, has been well renovated and offers a good view of the Red Cliffs. Note that if you're travelling the few kilometres north to Alba Iulia, you're best off catching one of the frequent buses from Sebeş, saving the lengthy wait for a train connection at Vinţu de Jos.

Southwestern Transylvania

Heading west from Mediaş or Sibiu, you soon leave the Saxon part of Transylvania and move into an area where Hungarian influence is more apparent. However, while a Hungarian ruling class lived here for centuries, the peasantry has always been Romanian. Over the course of millennia, the stone-age tribes that once huddled around the caves and hot springs of the Carpathian foothills developed into a cohesive society, whose evolution was largely determined by events in **the southwest** of the region. The stronghold of the Dacian kingdom lay here, in the hills south of **Orăştie**, and these were ultimately conquered by Roman legions marching up from the Danube through the narrow passes known today as the Eastern Gate (Poarta Orientală) and the Iron Gate (Poarta de Fier) of Transylvania. The conquerors founded their new capital, **Sarmizegetusa**, in the Haţeg depression, and the area became one of the earliest centres of Romanian culture in Transylvania; it's now known for the *haţegana*, a quick dance (and the name of the local beer), and some of Romania's oldest and most charming churches can be found here. To the north, Hungarian churches and castles dominate the main route along the Mureş valley to and from Hungary – **Hunedoara** is the site of the greatest medieval fortress in Romania. **Alba Iulia**, one of the most important towns in this region has been a centre of Romania's wine industry since the first century BC. By contrast, the smoggy mining towns at the feet of the **Retezat mountains**, in the far southwest of Transylvania, belie the beauty of the range, whose peaks feed dozens of alpine lakes, making this one of the most beautiful of the Carpathian ranges and deservedly popular with hikers.

Alba Iulia and around

The tension between the Hungarian and Romanian communities is symbolized in **ALBA IULIA**, 14km north of Sebeş, by the juxtaposition of the Roman Catholic and Orthodox cathedrals in the heart of its citadel. This hill top was fortified by the Romans and then by the Romanians, before the Hungarian ruler, István I, occupied it and created the bishopric of Gyulafehérvár – the Magyar name for Alba Iulia – in the early part of the eleventh century, to consolidate his hold on Transylvania. Only after World War I did the Romanians take over the levers of power here and build their own cathedral. The town is dominated by its huge **citadel**, in effect the **upper town**, laid out in the shape of a star; east of this, the **lower town** has been tidied up since it was partly cleared for "rationalization" in Ceauşescu's last years, and is home to a scattering of low-key Art Deco buildings.

Arrival and information

Alba Iulia's **bus and train stations** are both 1.5km south of the centre on B-dul Ferdinand I (DN1), reached by buses #3 and #4, looping via the lower town and the Cetate quarter every 10 minutes (10–20min at weekends), one in each direction. Strada Iaşilor, parallel to the DN1, makes a pleasant walk

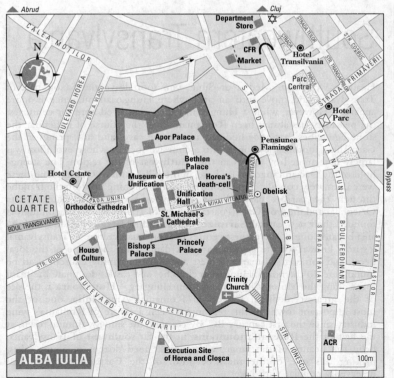

ALBA IULIA

Train & Bus Stations, Sebeş, Motel Dintre Sălcii and Hanul cu Berze ▼

from the stations into town; turn left at the police station and Romtelecom (which also houses the **post office**) for the citadel. Albena Tours, Str. Parcului 2 (☎0258/812 140, ✉albenatours@rdslink.ro) and Silvana Tour, opposite the *Hotel Transilvania*, sell **bus tickets**, as does Aero Transilvania, at Tudor Vladimirescu 3 (☎ & ☏0258/819 853), who also sells **flights**. The CFR agency, for **train tickets**, is at Str. Moţilor 1. **Internet** is available at Parc Net opposite the *Hotel Parc*, Easy PC at the market (not very customer-friendly), Domino, B-dul Horea 42, and a couple of places on Bulevardul Transilvaniei. **Bike repairs** are possible at Str. Moţilor 21 (☎0745/880 744).

Accommodation

Accommodation in Alba Iulia is limited and pricey, except for the *Pensiunea Flamingo* and a couple of places by the river 4km south of the centre on the DN1 (bus#12 or #13). There's also a small new **motel** to the north of town at km384.

Cetate Str. Unirii 3, ☎0258/811 780, ✉cetate@cristalsoft.ro. The best hotel in Alba Iulia, with some triples available, the *Cetate* is west of the centre, in the new town. ❺

Hanul cu Berze Str. Republicii 179, ☎ & ☏0258/810 129. A friendly, family-run place, on the north side of the river 2km south of the bus and train stations. ❷

Motel Dintre Sălcii, ☎0258/812 137. Just over the bridge from the *Hanul cu Berze* (and almost as nice), this is a very cheap but pleasant motel. ❶

Parc Str. Primăverii 4, ☎0258/811 723, ☏812 130. A communist-era place on the Parc Central, with cable TV. ❺

Pensiunea Flamingo Str. Mihai Viteazu 6, ☎0258/816 354. The only central budget option, with seven simple rooms (two en-suite and four with cable TV) and a bar serving basic meals. ❷

Transilvania Piaţa Iuliu Maniu 21, ☎0258/812 052, ☏811 195. Similar in style to the *Parc*, this hotel only has twin rooms. ❹

The Town

Between 1715 and 1738, twenty thousand serfs, under the direction of the Italian architect Visconti, built the Vauban-style **citadel**, which was named Karlsburg in honour of the reigning Hapsburg monarch. Imperial levies on the countryside did much to embitter the Romanian peasants, who turned on their (mainly Hungarian) landlords in the 1784 uprising led by Horea, Cloşca and Crişan. After the uprising had been crushed, Horea and Cloşca were tortured to death, a martyrdom commemorated both at the execution site south of the citadel walls, and by an obelisk standing before the richly carved Baroque main gateway (above which is Horea's death-cell). Crişan cheated the excecutioner by committing suicide. From the gateway, the road leads down to the lower town; the first and third gateways are being restored, but only the pillars of the gate, between them remain. To the south of the gateway, the **Trinity church** is a modern wooden structure, in traditional Romanian style.

Within the citadel, the Act of Unification between Romania and Transylvania was signed in the ornate marble **Unification Hall** (Tues–Sun 10am–5pm; €1) on December 1, 1918, as the Austro-Hungarian Empire commenced its death throes; built in 1898–1900, it served as the officers' mess until 1968. Facing the hall, a military accommodation block (1853) houses the exhaustive **Museum of Unification** (Muzeul al Unirii; same hours and ticket), which embodies the credo that Romania's history has been a long search for national unity and glorifies the Wallachian prince **Michael the Brave**, who united Wallachia, Transylvania and Moldavia, and made Alba briefly capital of Romania in 1599–1600. In a fit of pique, the Magyars demolished his Coronation Church in 1713, so, unsurprisingly, the Romanians built a vast new **Orthodox Cathedral** in 1921, in which King Ferdinand and Queen Marie were crowned the next year. The neo-Brâncovenesc cloister through which you enter belies the medieval style of the cathedral, filled with neo-Byzantine frescoes, including portraits of Michael and his wife, Stanca.

The Catholic **St Michael's Cathedral** on the south side of Strada Mihai Viteazul testifies to the Hungarian connection. The foundations of the eleventh-century church have been preserved, as has a superb Maiestas carving above a blind door in the south aisle. What you see now was mostly built between 1247 and 1256, in late Romanesque style, with the Gothic choir added in the fourteenth and fifteenth centuries; of the later accretions, the most notable are the Renaissance László and Váraday chapels, built in 1512 and 1524 respectively. The **tomb of Hunyadi**, the greatest of Transylvania's warlords (see p.386), is the middle one of the three to the right of the west door; a century after his death, the tomb was vandalized by the Turks, still bitter at their defeats at his hands. Having been neglected for much of the twentieth century, the cathedral has recently been restored; if it's closed, ask for the key at the Bishop's Palace, flanking the gate to the new town. To the south of the Catholic cathedral stands the former **Princely Palace**, where the Transylvanian Diets met between 1542 and 1690. Leaving the citadel to the west, you'll come to the modern **Cetate quarter**, where the liveliest bars and restaurants can be found, as well as the Artists' Union Gallery on Bulevardul 1 Decembrie 1918.

Eating and drinking

In addition to the hotel **restaurants**, the popular *Pizzeria-Spaghettaria Roberta* is 100m north of Calea Moților on Strada Tudor Vladimirescu, and also has a branch on B-dul Transilvaniei, Cetate; *Erol*, in the pedestrian subway under Calea Moților by the market, is pleasant enough, serving reasonable pizza. There's decent Chinese food in the place at Str. Morii 5. The aptly named *Fast Food* is at Str. Parcului 4. For **drinking**, there are many new *terasas* on the lively pedestrianised Bulevardul Transilvaniei, including the two-storey *Blue Hours* and the *Terasa Dakota* opposite it.

Around Alba Iulia

Many of the towns around Alba Iulia bear witness to the centuries of Hungarian rule, including **Teiuș** and **Aiud**, which have a pleasant ambience, while **Blaj** is of historical interest as the cradle of Romanian Nationalism only. The area is easily visited on public transport: there are buses more or less hourly from Alba Iulia heading into the Apuseni highlands and good train links to Teiuș, Blaj, and Aiud.

Teiuș

Fifteen kilometres north along the main DN1 from Alba Iulia, through the wine country where white Fetească and sparkling Spumos are produced, is the small town of **TEIUȘ** (Tövis), a rail junction on the main Cluj–Sighișoara line. Few travellers leave the station for the fifteen-minute walk to the centre, although the town has an amenable village-like atmosphere and there are several **churches** that make the effort worthwhile. You'll also find the simple and friendly *Mini-Hotel* (☎0258/852 231; ❶), which has five rooms (two en suite) and a **bar-restaurant**; turning right on the main road, then immediately left on the Râmeț road and left again (behind the BCR bank and ATM), brings you to the more pretentious *Hotel-restaurant Perla* (☎0258/851 900; ❷), which has satellite TV but doesn't serve breakfast.

Blaj

Twenty-five kilometres east of Teiuş on the DN14b to Sighişoara, the small town of **BLAJ** stands at the junction of the main Sighişoara–Cluj rail line and the branch to Sovata and Praid (see p.195). Blaj's main claim to fame is its historical status as the ark of Romanian Nationalism, though it is now rundown; the town still produces good wine, however – notably the dry white Feteasca Regală – and Bergenbier is brewed here. The centre lies about 1km east of the train station (where buses also pull in); heading east past through communist-era blocs you'll come to Strada Republicii, the main drag, with the **History Museum** (Tues–Fri 8am–4pm, Sat & Sun 10am–2pm) to the right in Avram Iancu park. In addition to temporary art shows upstairs, the museum covers Blaj's history as headquarters of the **Uniate Church** (see box below) and that of the many intellectuals who taught here at the end of the eighteenth century and beginning of the nineteenth; they are also remembered by numerous plaques around town.

Continuing east on Strada Republicii you'll come to the hotel, and on Piaţa 1848 behind it, the Uniate (or Greco–Catholic) **cathedral**, which was built in

---

The Uniate Church

In 1596, the Austrian government persuaded the Orthodox Church in Galicia (now southern Poland and Ukraine) to accept the authority and protection of the Vatican, hoping to detach them from eastern, and above all Russian, influences and to tie them more firmly to the western fold. Thus was born the **Uniate Church**, also known as the Catholic Church of the Eastern Rite, or the Greco-Catholic Church. However, the new Church failed to attract most Romanian Orthodox believers, and was further marginalized when Romania's Orthodox Church gained autonomy in the 1920s. Even so, its leading figures exercised great influence. At the end of the eighteenth century, the **Transylvanian School** (Şcoala Ardeleana), a group of clerics and teachers in Blaj, played a key role in making Romanian a literary language, revitalizing Romanian culture and instilling a sense of nationhood into the Romanian people. The Uniate Church stood for independence of thought and self-reliance, as opposed to the more hierarchical and conformist Orthodox Church, so the communist regime called its million-plus adherents "agents of imperialism" and forcibly merged them with the Orthodox Church. Uniates remained a harassed and often imprisoned minority, with no status under the 1948 and subsequent constitutions (although these recognized the existence of fourteen other denominations or "cults"), until the overthrow of communism.

The Uniates accept four key points of Catholic doctrine: the Filioque clause in the creed (according to which the Holy Spirit proceeds from the Father and the Son, as opposed to the Orthodox doctrine by which the Holy Spirit proceeds only from the Father); the use of wafers instead of bread in the mass; the doctrine of Purgatory (unknown in the East); and, above all, the supremacy of the pope. All the other points of difference – the marriage of priests, a bearded clergy, the cult of icons, different vestments and rituals – remain identical to Orthodox practice.

In certain areas, such as Maramureş, there is now a considerable revival in the fortunes of the Uniate Church, although hopes that it can again revitalize the country as it did around 1800 under the Transylvanian School appear misplaced. The Iliescu government has also supported, and been supported by, the Orthodox Church, and the Uniates have found it a long hard struggle to reclaim even their buildings.

1749–79, the first Baroque building in Transylvania. To its south is the school where classes were held in the Romanian language from 1754; the great botanist Alexandru Borza (1887–1971) taught here. East of the town centre is the **Field of Liberty**, a famous rallying point in 1848 and 1868 for tens of thousands of Romanians protesting against Hungary's demands to reincorporate Transylvania within the "lands of Stephen".

The sole **hotel** in town is the central *Târnavele* (☎0258/710 255, ⓕ714 246; ❷), at B-dul Republicii 1, which has twin rooms only.

Aiud

Back on the DN1 (E81), 11km north of Teiuş, is **AIUD** (Nagyenyed), an attractive town despite the grim reputation of its prison, which was used to hold Soviet spies during World War II, and Iron Guardists after the communist takeover. The town's centre has one of the oldest **fortresses** in Transylvania, dating back to 1302, and still boasting a full ring of walls and eight towers. It shelters two Hungarian churches (the first Lutheran and built in the late nineteenth-century on a medieval groundplan, the second Calvinist and dating from the early fifteenth century) and a **History Museum** (Tues–Fri 9am–5pm, Sat & Sun 9am–1pm); there's a display of stuffed animals at the **Natural Sciences Museum** (Tues–Sun 10am–5pm) upstairs in the Bethlen College across the road. Behind the fortress, the landmark, turn-of-the-century **Industrial School** rises up like a huge Renaissance palace.

From the **train station**, it's a fifteen-minute walk to the centre – head up Strada Coşbuc, just to the left of the station, and after the stadium turn left to pass the Conti Internet café and turn right up Strada Iuliu Maniu to the market, the road continues as Strada Trandafirilor to Strada Băilor. Alternatively, you can turn left after the stadium to pass the prison and the **bus station** on Strada Băilor (hidden behind an ugly new church). There's a pleasant **youth hostel**, the *Casa Helvetica* (☎0744/635 655, ⓔoffice@aiud.apulum.ro; ❶), at Str. Gheorghe Doja 53A, rather hidden away behind the petrol station at the northern entrance to town. The best **restaurant** is the *Luk*, Str. Librtăţii 9, by the market.

Orăştie, Deva and Hunedoara

South of Alba Iulia, in the mountains between Timişoara and Sibiu, are a number of **Dacian citadels**, six of which were placed on UNESCO's World Heritage List in 1999; the most interesting, Sarmizegetusa, is accessible from **Orăştie**, a quiet town 38km southwest of Sebeş on the main road and rail line west towards Timişoara and Arad. There are also two striking medieval structures in this part of Transylvania: the ruined fortress on the **Hill of the Djinn**, overlooking **Deva**, and the huge, practically undamaged, Gothic castle of the Corvin family at **Hunedoara**. Deva lies west beyond Orăştie on the main road and rail lines, while Hunedoara is accessible by rail from **Simeria** on that same line, or by bus from Deva. The Dacian citadels, however, are further off the beaten track and you'll have to walk or hitch to reach them.

Orăştie and around

ORĂŞTIE, first recorded in 1224 as the Saxon *stuhl* of Broos, is a pleasant small town in which to break a journey along the Mureş valley. From the **train station**, 3km west of the town, trains are met by buses for the town centre (buses to the station depart from stops along the DN7 and are less predictable – roughly half-hourly – so you'll need to allow a bit of leeway). Heading into town, buses turn right at the Piaţa Europea roundabout; get off here, cross the main road and follow Strada Armatei south to Piaţa Victoriei – marked by a 1930s Orthodox cathedral – and the main street, Strada Bălcescu. The town **museum** (Tues–Sun 9am–5pm), at Piaţa Aurel Vlaicu 1, whose exhibits include Dacian relics, is off Strada Bălcescu to the right, as is the old **citadel**, immediately south, with large German Evangelical and Hungarian Reformed churches crammed close together.

The main **hotel** in town is the *Mini-Hotel Jorja*, Str. Bălcescu 30 (℡0254/241 574, ℻247 470; ❷), a good private guesthouse which offers a sauna, Internet, table tennis and secure parking, as well as non-stop hot water. There's also the *Sura*, a **restaurant** with rooms at Str. Stadionului 1A, off Bălcescu, and beds at the *Complex Riviera* truckstop as you enter town from the east. There are also half a dozen cabins (❶) attached to the *Hanul Margareta* restaurant, just over 1km west of town on the DN7.

Cetatea Costeşti and Sarmizegetusa

Cetatea Costeşti, the first of the Dacian citadels, is south of Orăştie along the Grădiştie valley. Several buses a day cover the 20km to the village of Costeşti, but from there you'll have to continue on foot for about 1km to the *Popas Salcâmul* campsite and *Costeşti* cabana (❶), then a further 3km west to the citadel – cross the river at the bridge and turn right past the sign to the citadel, then left at the junction and sharp left at the farm to reach the three rows of earthworks, grazed by cows and surrounded by birch and cherry trees.

The largest citadel, **Sarmizegetusa**, lies deeper into the mountains and you'll have to walk or hitch without your own transport; continue south from Costeşti along the valley road through the hamlet of **Grădiştea de Munte** and travel a further 8km over the roughest stretch of the road to Sarmizegetusa. Situated 1200m above sea level and covering an area of 3.5 hectares, it was the Dacian capital from the first century BC to 106 AD, though it requires some imagination now to conjure up a picture of its grandeur from the weathered walls and stumps of pillars that remain. That said, it's clear that Sarmizegetusa was divided into two distinct quarters: the citadel, used as a refuge during times of war; and the sacred area, dominated by the great sanctuary, a stone circle containing a horseshoe of wooden columns where ritual sacrifices were performed. The Romans, shrewd imperialists as they were, rebuilt Sarmizegetusa after its capture in 106 AD, stationed a detachment of the IV Legion here and appropriated the shrines, rededicating them to members of their pantheon. The Roman capital was southwest of here, near the modern town of Sarmizegetusa – and took its name from the Dacian citadel.

Deva

The capital of Hunedoara county, **DEVA**, 30km west of Orăştie, lies on the east side of a **citadel** built in the thirteenth century and transformed into one of Transylvania's strongest fortifications on the orders of the warlord, Hunyadi, in the fifteenth century. It crowns a volcanic hill in the shape of a truncated cone – supposedly the result of a stupendous battle between the djinns (spirits) of the Retezat mountains and of the plain, hence the nickname **Hill of the Djinn**. Despite the mason charged with building it reputedly immuring his wife in its walls in order to guarantee his creation's indestructability, the citadel was destroyed in 1849 when the magazine blew

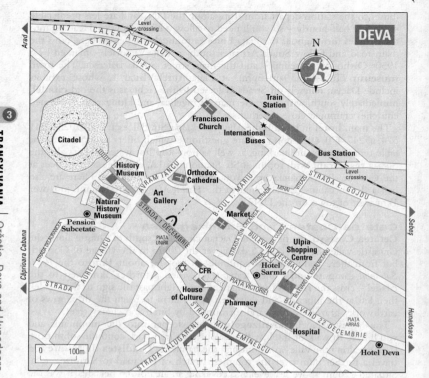

up, leaving only the ramparts and barracks standing. Until the funicular is completed, it's a stiff 184–metre climb; at the top you're rewarded with expansive **views** over the Mureş valley.

In the park at the bottom of the hill – beneath the Hollywood-style "Deva" sign on the citadel – is the Magna Curia palace, rebuilt in 1621 by Voivode Gábor Bethlen, under whom Deva was briefly capital of Transylvania. Since 1882, it has housed a **History Museum** displaying archaeological finds from the Orăştie mountains; it's closed for long-term restoration, but you can at least see some Roman stonework languishing in the long grass outside. The adjacent building houses a better-than-average **Natural History Museum** (Tues–Sun 9am–5pm) and there's a tiny art gallery in the prefecture opposite, on the corner of Strada Avram Iancu. Heading down this street, you'll come to the Orthodox **cathedral of St Nicolae**, dating from 1893. To the north, on Strada Progesului, is the Franciscan church. Alternatively, head east to the modern centre via the pedestrianized Strada 1 Decembrie, passing the country's only Ecological University in the former *Hanul Mare*, the inn where Alexandru Ioan Cuza slept on his way into exile in 1866.

Practicalities

All **trains** on the main line from Arad stop at Deva, making it a good place to pick up services to Budapest or the further corners of Romania; from the

The Festival of the Călușari

Around the second week of January, Deva hosts the colourful **Festival of the Călușari** (Călușerul Transilvănean). Ensembles from Wallachia and southern Transylvania perform the intricate dances and rituals originally devised to ensure good harvests and dispel the Rusalii – the spirits of departed friends or relations, who, according to Romanian folklore, would take possession of the living should any of the taboos associated with the Week of Rusalii (following Whitsun) be violated. The rite was also intended to promote fertility, and in the old days the dancers (all male) were accompanied by a mute who wore a huge red phallus beneath his robes and muttered lewd invocations. Under communism, such antics were discouraged and the mute carried a more innocuous wand covered in rabbit fur. Contact the Cultural Inspectorate in Deva (Str. 1 Decembrie 28; ☎0254/213 966) to confirm the exact dates of this and other festivals in Hunedoara county.

station, the town centre is just five minutes south along Bulevardul Iuliu Maniu. From the well-run **bus station**, next to the **train station**, five services a day head for the Apuseni mountains, while buses leave frequently for Hunedoara, Simeria and Orăștie. Maxitaxis for Călan and Simeria wait to the right of the train station, and international buses stop in front: buy tickets for Amad Turistik at Plus-Com, Piața Gării 2 (☎0254/211 411), or for Eurolines, at Str. Iuliu Maniu Bloc J (☎0254/234 220, ✉deva@eurolines.ro) or Nexus Travel, B-dul Decebal 4A (☎0254/214 543, ✉nexustravel@rdslink.ro); for AtlasSib, phone or fax 0254/231 519. Make **train bookings** at the CFR agency at Str. 1 Decembrie, Bloc A (Mon–Fri 8am–8pm).

There are only a few **hotels** in town, all overpriced; the best are the *Hotel Deva* at Str. 22 Decembrie 110 (☎0254/225 920/1, ⓕ226 183; ❻) and *Hotel Sarmis* at Piața Victoriei 3 (☎0254/214 730, ⓕ213 173; ❻); the only **guesthouse** is the *Pensiunea Subcetate*, Str. Delavrancea 6 (☎0254/212 535; ❹), which has a lovely garden. As well as those in the hotels, the best **restaurants** are *Casa Rustica* on Bulevardul 22 Decembrie, *Tata* at B-dul Decebal bloc 5 (west of Strada Kogălniceanu), the Franco-Romanian *Capriccio* at Strada Dorobanților 28, the *Pizzeria Marco Polo* on Strada 1 Decembrie, bloc A; *Pizzeria Veneția* on Iuliu Maniu (between Bulevardul Decebal and Strada 1 Decembrie) and the *Roata* across the road. The *Green House Club*, at Str. Eminescu 16, is a pleasant place for a **drink**.

There's an exchange office at the Ulpia shopping centre on Bulevardul 22 Decembrie. At the Ulpia centre, the Artima **supermarket** is good, although there's better fresh fruit and meat in the **market**. For **information**, ACR is at B-dul 22 Decembrie 253 (well to the east). **Internet** access is available at Industrial Software, opposite the *Hotel Sarmis*.

Hunedoara

HUNEDOARA (Vajdahunyad/Eisenmarkt), 16km south of Deva, would be dismissed as an ugly, smoggy, industrial town were it not also the site of **Corvin Castle** (Tues–Sun 9am–5pm), the greatest fortress in Romania. The travel writer Patrick Leigh Fermor found its appearance "so fantastic and theatrical that, at first glance, it looks totally unreal". It's moated to a depth of 30m and approached by a narrow bridge upheld by tall stone piers, terminating beneath a mighty barbican, its roof bristling with spikes, over-looked by multitudes of towers. Founded during the fourteenth century and rebuilt in 1453 by Iancu de Hunedoara, with a Renaissance-style wing added by his son, Mátyás Corvinus, and Baroque additions by Gabriel Bethlen in the seventeenth century, it was extensively and tastefully restored in 1965–70. Within, the castle is an extravaganza of galleries, spiral stairways and Gothic vaulting, with an impregnable donjon and a Knights' Hall with rose-coloured marble pillars.

The castle's **museum** relates the achievements of **Iancu de Hunedoara**, the warlord known in Hungarian as János Hunyadi. Legend has it that Hunyadi was the illegitimate son of King Sigismund, who gave the castle to Hunyadi's nominal father, Voicu, a Romanian noble, in 1409. Hunyadi, the "White Knight", rose largely by his own efforts, winning victory after victory against the Turks, and devastatingly routing them beneath the walls of Belgrade in 1456. Appointed voivode of Transylvania in 1441, Hunyadi later became regent of Hungary and a kingmaker (responsible for the overthrow of Vlad Dracul and the coronation of the Impaler, see p.421), while his own son, Mátyás Corvinus, rose to be one of Hungary's greatest kings.

The reserves of iron ore in the hills to the west of Hunedoara were known in Roman times; they were exploited on an industrial scale from 1884 and then after World War II, when the communists deliberately built a huge and ugly steel plant right in front of the castle.

Practicalities

Buses between Deva and Hunedoara run every twenty minutes; you pay on board. There are also **trains** from Simeria and five minibuses a day from Haţeg, forty-five minutes to the south (look out for the four huge gypsy palaces on entering Hunedoara from Călan). From the **train** and **bus stations**, it's a twenty-minute walk south to the castle: turn right onto the main road, Bulevardul Republicii, and then right again onto Bulevardul Libertăţii, passing the town hall and Ghelari church, until you reach a bridge on the right; cross this and follow the signs for the remaining five-minute walk to the castle.

Once you've seen the castle there's no reason to remain in Hunedoara; if you do get stuck, the *Rusca* **hotel** at B-dul Dacia 10 (℡0254/712 002, Ⓦwww.hotelrusca.ro; ❸), is just five minutes south of the station, on the left; or there's the private *Termorep* at Str. Ştefan cel Mare 1 (℡0254/712 449, Ⓕ712 050; ❹), well south of the centre, near the market. There are other accommodation options at the popular resort of **Lake Teliuc**, an artificial body of water 7km southwest of Hunedoara where lies the *Cinciş* **campsite** – though note that the only washing facilities are the lake itself.

Haţeg and around

Twenty kilometres southeast of Hunedoara is **HAŢEG**, the gateway to Transylvania's greatest Roman remains and one of the most convenient approaches to the Retezat mountains. In addition to the ruins, you'll find a number of interesting **Romanesque churches** in the surrounding area, all of which can, with a little difficulty, be reached by local buses from the terminal at Str. Caragiale 14, off Strada Mihai Viteazul by the market. For **accommodation**, the only hotel in town is the small *Belvedere* (℡0254/777 604; ❶–❺), at the Abator bus stop, a kilometre south on Strada Progesului, the Petroşani road; this is served by buses to Subcetate. The *Hanul Bucura*, at the northern entrance to town, has no accommodation, but its **restaurant** has great views across the town to the Retezat mountains.

The Romanesque churches

Fifteen kilometres northwest of Hațeg is **Prislop Monastery** – near Silvașu de Sus, at the head of the Silvașului valley in the foothills of the Poiana Ruscă mountains. Founded in 1400, this is one of the oldest convents in Romania but is remarkably little known and very tranquil, and the nuns are happy for you to go in and look around. It lies just off the direct road from Hunedoara to Hațeg, but most traffic goes via **Călan**, on both the rail line and the DN66 (E79) south from Simeria, which seems, at first sight, to be little more than an ugly town with a recently closed steelworks; however, there is a more pleasant spa (dating from Roman times) across the river to the east, with the lovely twelfth-century **church of Streisângeorgiu** on its southern fringe, with frescoes dating from 1313. A couple of kilometres south of Călan (beyond the Hunedoara turning), a similar church at **Strei** dates from the thirteenth century and has fine fourteenth-century frescoes.

Three kilometres south of Hațeg (an easy stroll from where the Subcetate bus turns off the main road) is **SÂNTĂ MĂRIA-ORLEA** (Oraljaboldogfalva), site of another late thirteenth-century church, which marks the transition from the Romanesque to Gothic style and has a fine collection of fourteenth-century frescoes; from the tower, there's a great **view** of the Retezat range. An eighteenth-century mansion in the village is now a **hotel**, the *Castell Sânta Maria-Orlea* (☎0254/777 768, ℻772 200; ❸), which provides an adequate stopover.

Twelve kilometres west of Hațeg, in **DENSUȘ**, a very strange little church has been cannibalized from the mausoleum of a fourth-century Roman army officer – most of what you see dates from the early thirteenth century, with frescoes from 1443. Ask at no. 15 on the main road, east of the statue of the etymologist Ovid Densușianu, for someone to let you in.

Roman Sarmizegetusa

SARMIZEGETUSA, 15km southwest of Hațeg, is the site of one of the key Roman settlements. Today, the town's fame still derives from the **Roman ruins** east of the centre, whose excavated portions are only part of the original municipality. You can see the remains of the forum, the palace of the Augustales, and the elliptical brick and stone amphitheatre. Start by visiting the **museum** (Tues–Sun 9am–5.30pm) across the road from the ruins, which avoids mentioning the likelihood that most of the Roman colonists believed to have interbred with the Dacians to create the ancestors of today's Romanians were actually of Greek or Semitic origin.

You can get here on the daily Hațeg–Reșița **bus** or on the twice-daily service (weekdays only) from Deva to Zeicani. The town has a recently refurbished **motel** (☎0254/777 360; ❷), the *Pensiunea Ulpia Traiana*, on the main street (☎0254/762 153), and a couple of other homestays, and there are three cabins (❶) at the bar by the entrance to the ruins.

The Iron Gate of Transylvania

It's only about 6km from Sarmizegetusa to Zeicani at the entrance to the **Iron Gate of Transylvania** (Poarta de Fier a Transilvanei), a narrow pass 700m above sea level. A monumental mace erected near the village commemorates the defeat of 80,000 Turks by 15,000 Transylvanians under the command of Hunyadi in 1442. Further up the pass, in 106 AD, the Dacians had their final clash with the Romans; as recorded by Roman scribes, this battle was a disaster for the Dacians – their forces were crushed, and their ruler Decebal

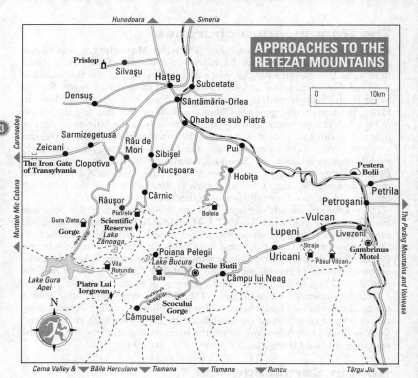

committed suicide rather than be ignominiously paraded through the streets of Rome. The pass itself is 10km long, and accessible by road (the DN68); minimal rail services resume at the mining village of Băuțar on the far side.

The Retezat mountains

Road and rail routes southeast from Hațeg skim the northern reaches of the **Retezat mountains**. Access is slightly harder here than in the other Transylvanian mountain ranges, though whereas in the Făgăraș or Piatra Craiului you find yourself for the most part following a ridge walk, with little opportunity to step aside and view the summits from a distance, here you'll find yourself surrounded by well-defined peaks, often reflected in clear alpine lakes. There is a large network of **hiking routes**, so you'll meet fewer walkers and have a better chance of seeing **wildlife** such as chamois and eagles. Note that the northwestern part of the massif is a scientific reserve (Ceaușescu treated it as a private hunting ground) and entry is restricted.

The **Retezat National Park** (☎0254/218 829, ⓦwww.retezat.ro) itself was set up in 1935, becoming a UNESCO Biosphere Reserve in 1980. To enter, you need a permit (€2 for a week plus a tent fee of €1 per night) available from an entry post (see opposite) or from a patrol; you'll be given a rubbish bag and a ticket with a basic map – it's worth buying a more detailed one in advance. **Entry posts** are at Râu de Morii, Cârnic and Câmpu lui Neag; boards here and elsewhere give **information** in English and German on the trails and the park's dozen camping sites. **Guides** can be booked through the National Park, or through New Horizons, an American-led charity in Lupeni (℡0254/563 117, Ⓦwww.new-horizons.ro).

Approaches to the Retezat

There are three main **approaches** to the Retezat: from Râu de Mori, a bus ride from Hațeg and on the west side of the massif; from various points along the Subcetate to Petroșani road and rail line to the northeast; and from the West Jiu valley to the south.

From Râu de Mori (where you can stay in the *Mara* or *Turbopin* pensions), it's at least a three-hour walk south along the Râul Mare valley (passing the *Pensiunea Dumbrăvița* after 5km and the *Pensiunea Anita* 2km further on) to the *Gura Zlata* cabana (see below) and campsite, from where you can strike out for the high peaks; continuing south you'll come to Lake Gura Apei; beyond its eastern end, 5km from Gura Zlata, is Ceaușescu's former Vila Rotonda.

Hiking in the Retezat

From Gura Zlata

Some popular hikes start from *Gura Zlata* cabana (❶), south of Sarmizegetusa along the Râul Mare valley. A succession of coloured symbols mark successive phases of the trail east from here to the *Pietrele* cabana (❶), going by way of Lake Zănoaga (campsite), Lake Tăul Portii and the Bucura Saddle. This is a nine- to ten-hour hike, which is closed in winter. The road through Gura Zlata continues 12km south to the Lake Gura Apei, from whose western extremity well-equipped hikers can follow a trail west across the mountains to the *Muntele Mic* cabana (❶) in the vicinity of Caransebeș, or south to Băile Herculane; allow two days for each. Heading east along the reservoir and up the Lăpușnic valley takes you to either the Buta cabana (❶) or the Bucura valley in four hours.

From Câmpu lui Neag

Also leading to the cabana at Buta are two of the most popular trails from Câmpu lui Neag and the *Cheile Butii* hotel in the south of the region. Red crosses mark the quickest route to the cabana (6–7hr), which runs through a fir forest and up to the La Fete sheepfold, offering great **views** of the "karst cathedrals" en route. Red triangles indicate the longer trail (10–12hr) to the cabana, which goes via the strange formations of the Scocului gorge, and the plateau of Piatră lui Iorgovan, where you can sometimes spot chamois. A forestry road continues southwest over the watershed from the Jiu valley into the Cerna valley, and on towards **Băile Herculane**, a good two days' walk (see p.342); another path, marked with blue triangles, heads south to **Tismana** in roughly six hours (see p.118).

Buta lies in the **Little Retezat**, the limestone ridge south of the great glacial trough of the Lăpușnic valley, which has an almost Mediterranean flora and fauna. However, the best hikes take you into the crystalline **Great Retezat** to the north, past serried peaks and alpine lakes. There are two trails into the Great Retezat from Buta; the first, marked by blue stripes, follows a switchback path to the **Pietrele cabana** (❶; 7hr), dropping into the Lăpușnic valley, and leading up past the wonderful lakes of the Bucura valley before coming down from a pass of 2206m past the Gențiana club's hut; the second, marked by red stripes then blue triangles, follows a trail to the **Stâne de Râu cabana** (❶), by way of the Bărbat springs and the Ciumfu waterfall (9hr; forbidden during winter).

From the northeast, tracks and roads lead from villages along the rail line between Subcetate and Petroşani. From Ohaba de sub Piatră, it's 18km (a five-hour walk, following blue stripes then blue triangles) to the *Pietrele* cabana (●) and campsite. The 2pm bus from Haţeg follows the route via Sălaşu de Sus (where there are guesthouses) as far as Nucşoara, 7km short of the cabana, and summer services, which meet trains at Ohaba, go a few kilometres further to Cârnic; alternatively, an information board at the Ohaba station gives phone numbers for taxis. Two-thirds of the park's visitors arrive this way, so the trail and cabana both get quite crowded. Some hikers therefore prefer to start from either the *Complex Turistic Râuşor* (a two-hour hike from Râu de Mori, following red triangles; with a motel, a guesthouse, camping and a basic skidrag), or the campsite at Pui, east of Ohaba, hiking for six and a half hours up a steep and winding mountain road (marked with red stripes) to the cabanas at Baleia (16km; now being rebuilt) and Stâne de Râu (6km further) – see box on p.191 for hikes beyond these points.

The final approach to the mountains is **from the mining towns of the West Jiu valley** to the east, but these are grim places and there's little accommodation.

From Petroşani to Voineasa

The largest of the mining towns is **PETROŞANI**, served by trains between Simeria and Târgu Jiu; these are desperately slow, and you may prefer to travel by maxitaxi. The only reason to stop here is to stock up on food before hiking in the Retezat mountains and most people head straight on to the cabanas above **Vulcan** and **Lupeni** in the West Jiu valley by train, bus or frequent maxitaxis from here. From Lupeni, buses continue every two hours up the valley to **Câmpu Lui Neag**, starting point for some good hikes into the mountains (see box on p.191 for hikes from here). In summer, the buses continue about 3km further west to the excellent *Cheile Butii* **hotel** (☎0722/210 278; ❷); there are also guesthouses here.

From Petroşani, the main road and railway – the latter built by political prisoners in the late 1940s – follow the Jiu valley south to **Târgu Jiu**, cutting through a scenic cleft between the Vâlcan and Parâng mountains and passing **Lainici**, whose motel (☎0253/463 502, ℻214 010; ❷) stands near a fine eighteenth-century monastery with a striking new church. A newly paved road, the DN7A, heads 83km east from Petroşani to **Voineasa**, passing the decent *Gropa Seaca* cabana (☎0254/542 246, 0744/136 555; ●) at km18; this is very rustic and peaceful, and marks the start of a fabulous day-hike into the Parâng range.

The Székely Land and the eastern Carpathians

In the ethnic patchwork of Transylvania, the eastern Carpathians are traditionally the home of the **Székely**, a people closely related to the Magyars who speak a distinctive Hungarian dialect and cherish a special historical identity.

For a long time it was believed that they were the descendants of Attila's Huns, who had entered the Carpathian basin in the fifth century. However, most modern historians and ethnographers believe that the Székely either attached themselves to the Magyars during the latter's long migration from the banks of the Don, or are simply the descendants of early Hungarians who pushed ever further east into Transylvania. Whatever the truth of their origins, the Székely feel closely akin to the Magyars who, in turn, regard them as somehow embodying the finest aspects of the ancient Magyar race, while also being rather primeval – noble savages, perhaps. Today, their traditional costume is close to that of the Romanian peasants, the chief difference being that Székely men tuck their white shirts in while Romanians wear them untucked and belted.

For visitors, the chief attractions of the region are likely to be the **Székely culture** and the scenery. Religion plays an important part in Székely life, as shown by the fervour displayed at the **Whitsun pilgrimage to Miercurea Ciuc**, the continuing existence of Székely mystics, and the prevalence of **walled churches** (less grimly fortified than the Saxon ones). Traditional Székely **architecture** is well represented throughout the Székely Land (Székelyföld); it is epitomized by tiny hilltop chapels and blue-painted houses with carved fences and gateways, incorporating a dovecote above, the best examples of which can be found in Corund. The **landscape** gets increasingly dramatic as you move through the Harghita mountains, particularly around the Tuşnad defile and St Anne's Lake to the south, and Lacu Roşu and the Bicaz gorges just before the borders of Moldavia.

Into the Székely Land

From Sighişoara and **Odorheiu Secuiesc**, the region's western capital, you can either head east to **Miercurea Ciuc**, the capital of the eastern Székely Land, or take a shorter loop to **Târgu Mureş** via the spa town of **Sovata Băi**. It's possible to make the approach from Braşov by rail; after passing the showpiece Saxon villages of **Hărman** and **Prejmer** (see p.157), the route follows the Olt and Mureş valleys through **Sfântu Gheorghe**, **Miercurea Ciuc** and **Gheorgheni**, looping around to Târgu Mureş.

Odorheiu Secuiesc

ODORHEIU SECUIESC (Székelyudvarhely) lies more or less 50km from Sighişoara, Miercurea Ciuc and Sovata; it's an unusually prosperous town thanks to textile companies producing 1.5 million men's suits per year, as well as the furniture and leather industries (factory outlets can add a whole new dimension to visits here). The town hosts a series of crafts, food and beer **festivals** throughout the spring and summer, while the excellent Szejke festival is held out at the spa of the same name, 4km north by the Sovata road, usually on the first Sunday of June, when folk dance groups put on displays to a picnicking audience. There's also a rock festival at Szejke on the fourth weekend of July.

Arrival and information

The **bus and train stations** are about a kilometre north of the town centre; trains stop first at Odorhei Sud halt (actually on the road north to Sovata), which is nearer the centre. Turning left out of the bus station on Strada

Târgului and then right onto Strada Bethlen (with the main train station to the left), you'll come in a couple of minutes to Strada Tompa László, which leads south to the citadel. For **information** visit TourInfo, Piaţa Primăriei 1 (Mon–Fri 8am–8pm; ☎0266/217 427, ⓦwww.tourinfo.ro); Robert Roth of Herr Travel, Str. Kossuth 43 (☎0722/201 997, ⓦwww.guide2romania.ro), offers **walking tours** of the town.

The **Internet** café at Str. Petőfi 17 also serves as a bar (8am–midnight), and the *Korona* itself has Internet service (10am–11pm), as has the *Tea Pub* at Str. Kossuth 20. Note that you can use Hungarian forints in some establishments.

Accommodation

The best **hotel** is the *Târnava* (the *Küküllo* to Magyars) at Piaţa Primariei 16 (☎0266/213 963, ⓦwww.kukullo.ro; ❼), which has comfortable rooms, a good restaurant, gym and sauna facilities, while the good *Sport-Hotel Akarat* (☎0266/211 377; ❷) lies beyond it on Strada Parcului. There's also a plethora of fairly luxurious pensions on the outskirts of town, and a few in the centre: try the *Lilla Panzió*, Str. Tompa 23 (☎0266/212 531; ❺); *Korona Panzió*, Piaţa Primăriei 12 (☎0266/217 227, ⓦwww.speednet.ro/korona; ❹); and *Maestro Panzió*, Piaţa Primariei 3 (☎0266/215 600, ⓔmaestro@udv.topnet.ro; ❷). **Hostel** accommodation is available in July and August in schools, for instance at Budvár 8A (☎0266/218 428, ⓔbanyai@udv.nextro.ro) and Rákoczi 17 (☎0266/218 060, ⓔmail.rda@rda.org.soroscj.ro). For **camping** there's *Camping Calypso* at the end of Strada Parcului, as well as wild camping 4km north at Szejke.

The Town

The centre of town is made up by two squares, **Piaţa Primăriei** (Városháza tér) and **Piaţa Márton Arón**, where three churches stand in a row: to the west, the former Franciscan monastery (1730–79); on the island between the two squares, the Reformed church (1780–81); and on the hill beyond, the Catholic church of Sf Miklós (1787–93), set between the Jesuits' building of 1651 and the huge Tamasy Aron Gymnasium or high school, established in 1593 and now in a Secession building dating from 1911–12. From Piaţa Primariei, Strada Cetăţii leads to the fifteenth- and sixteenth-century **citadel**; since 1891 this has housed an agricultural college, but you can go inside to stroll along the walls.

On the Sighişoara road, at Str. Kossuth 29, the **museum** (Tues–Fri 9am–4.30pm, Sat & Sun 9am–1pm) has a fine ethnographic collection, with ceramics and Székely funerary posts, which may hark back to the days when a Magyar warrior was buried with his spear thrust into the grave. Used only by Calvinists and Unitarians, these bear carvings of the tools of the deceased's trade and a ring for each decade of life; a man's post is topped with a star and a woman's with a tulip. Two kilometres further down the same road is the **Jesus chapel**, one of the oldest buildings in the area, built in the thirteenth century, with a coffered ceiling – a distinguishing feature of Hungarian churches – fitted in 1667.

Eating and drinking

The top **restaurants** in town are the *Pethö*, at Str Rákóczi 21; the *Jungle*, in the park behind the Casa de Cultura, which serves excellent pizza and has dark Ciuc beer on draught; and the restaurant of the *Târnava* hotel, with good vegetarian options; the *Korona* also has good food. Across the bridge from the bus station at Vasar tér 12, the *Irish Pub* (noon–3am, dancing from 11pm) has a good cellar and *terasa*, and serves the best fish in town. Near the train station at Str. Szabok 43, *Pizza Diablo* is excellent; *Pizza 21* at the junction of Bethlen Gabor and Eötvös József, near the Poliklinika, is also reasonable. *Lehel*, Str. Kossuth 56, is a great Székely pastry shop. The best **bars** can be found in the Casa de Cultura and at the *Korona*.

Around Odorheiu Secuiesc

The Unitarian village of **DÂRJIU** (Székelyderz), 17km southwest of the town, has a particularly fine fortified church, now on UNESCO's World Heritage List, with frescoes that date from 1419. As in some Saxon villages, ham and grain are still stored inside the church walls, a tradition dating back to the time when there was risk of siege. The key to the church is held next door, and the priest offers accommodation.

MUGENI (Bögöz) village, 9km west of Odorheiu by road and rail, has a fine fourteenth-century church with wonderful frescoes and a coffered ceiling. Continuing west from here will eventually bring you to Sighişoara, passing on the way the larger village of **CRISTURU SECUIESC** (Székelykeresztúr), whose excellent **museum** (Tues–Fri 10am–5pm, Sat & Sun 10am–noon) on the elongated square tells the story of the ceramic industry, established here since 1590, in addition to a natural history display. Through-buses stop in the main square, but those terminating here arrive at the bus terminal, which, like the train station, is ten minutes' walk east of the centre.

East of Odorheiu Secuiesc, en route to Miercurea Ciuc, are several little resorts with low-key accommodation, which are good options for breaking your journey. Passing through Satu Mare (Marefalva), you'll come to **BĂILE HOMOROD** (Homoródfürdő), which has hot springs that you can bathe in and the good *Lobogo* **pension** (℡0266/247 545, Ⓦwww.topnet.ro /homorodfurdo; ❷). A little further on, **VLĂHIȚA** (Szentegyházasfalu) also has mineral springs, as well as a campsite and guesthouses. About 13km beyond Vlăhiṭa, at the *Brădet* cabana (❶), a turning to the north leads up to **HARGHITA BĂI** (Hargita-fürdó), located in the beautiful, thickly forested Harghita mountains, renowned for their wildlife. Here you'll find the isolated *Hotel Ozon* (℡0266/124 770; ❷) and a cabana (❶). There are two buses a day from Miercurea Ciuc rail station, or it's under an hour's walk from the *Brădet* cabana. In the village of **SUBCETATE** (Zeteváralja), on a road that loses itself in the Harghita mountains northeast of Odorheiu, the village priest (at no. 96) has set up a good rural tourism infrastructure; a decent guesthouse is *Balász Panzió* at no. 60 (℡0744/644 812, Ⓔbalaszpanzio@pont.ro).

Corund, Praid and Sovata Băi

CORUND (Korond), 25km north of Odorheiu, is famed for its green and brown **pottery**, as well as the cobalt blue introduced by the Germans in the eighteenth century: you'll see it for sale everywhere, but for the best choice poke around the town's backstreet workshops or visit the colourful **market** held every year on the weekend closest to August 10.

For a complete change of atmosphere, push on to **PRAID** (Parajd), a small but popular holiday centre 12km to the north where there's a visitable salt mine. It's served by local buses from both Odorheiu and Sovata and by the rail branch from Blaj; the helpful **tourist office** at Str. Principală 211 (daily: mid-May to mid-Sept 8am–6pm; rest of year 8am–3pm; ℡0266/240 272, Ⓦwww.praid.ro), can arrange **accommodation** in private rooms (❶). There's also a fairly standard **motel** just north of the tourist office at Str. Principală 221

(☎0266/240 272; ❷), which offers cheaper beds to youth hostellers, as well as the basic *Hotel Omega* (☎0266/240 088; ❶) on the same road at no. 141. The fine *Casa Telegdy* **restaurant** is just north of the centre, and serves up mid-priced Székely-influenced food.

Seven kilometres further north by road and rail is **SOVATA** (Szováta), with **SOVATA BĂI** 1km to the east, a **bathing resort**, surrounded by beautiful forests, on the shore of Lacul Ursu (Medvető), where a surface layer of fresh water, a metre deep, acts as an insulator keeping the lower, saltwater at a constant temperature of 30–40°C year round; it rains a lot here, in short showers, but bathing is still pleasant. Its mineral waters are supposedly particularly effective for infertility. The resort's most distinctive feature is the array of wooden buildings that line the main street, Strada Trandafirilor: huge, extravagantly balconied villas and twee Hansel and Gretel churches.

Sovata Băi's **bus station** is on Strada Trandafirilor. The best of the **hotels** are the new *Danubius*, Str, Trandafirilor 82 (☎0265/570 151, ✇www.danubiusgroup .com; ❻) and the *Făget* (same address and contacts; ❹); both are supposedly three-star, despite the price difference. The *Villa Klein*, Str. Trandafirilor 81 (☎0265/577 686, ☏411 457; ❹), is a good guesthouse. Continuing east along the same road, a left turning just beyond a strikingly modernist Catholic chapel, takes you onto Strada Tivoli and brings you in about ten minutes to the excellent *Tivoli* hotel (☎0265/578 493, ☏570 493; ❺ half-board), surrounded by woods with deer foraging outside the windows. Strada Tivoli continues to Lacul Tineretului (Lake of Youth), a five-minute walk, where you can rent pedalos from the kiosks serving snacks. Another 700m along Strada Trandafirilor, you'll come to the *Stâna de Vale* **campsite** and, a couple of kilometres further still, the excellent *Edelweiss* hotel (☎0265/577 758, ✇www.digicomm.ro/edelweiss; ❼). In Sovata, the *Ursul Negru* hotel is at Str. Principală 152 (☎0265/570 987, ☏570 828; ❶), with hot water between 5pm and 8pm only, and there's also a new **campsite** at Str. Principală 129, which has plenty of tent space but, unusually, no cabins.

Sfântu Gheorghe

SFÂNTU GHEORGHE (Sepsi-Szentgyörgy), 30km northeast of Braşov, is a drab industrial town but following Ceauşescu's demise it has become the heart of the Székely cultural revival. The highlight is the **County Museum** (Tues–Fri 9am–4pm, Sat 9am–1pm, Sun 9am–2pm) at Str. Kós Károly 10, south of the centre; take bus #1 to the central park and walk south along Strada Kós Károly. Built in 1910 to the design of **Kós Károly** (see box opposite), it covers the archaeology, history and ethnography of the area, focusing on the revolution of 1848–49 (see p.389).

The museum lies to the south of the town centre, which is focused on the **Piaţa Libertăţii**, with a technical college designed by Kós and (behind the statue of Mihai Viteazul) the Casa de Cultură to the west, and the **Arcaded House**, the oldest building in town (1820–21), to the east. At the north end of the square, the **Art Gallery** (Tues–Fri 9am–4pm, Sat & Sun 10am–2pm) is in a big mustard-yellow block with a tower, built in 1870 as a department store and now hosting temporary art shows. North of the square, beyond the *Bodoc* hotel, Strada Kossuth leads past a Kós Károly house (no. 19) to the cobbled Strada Şoimului and the old town, with a fine fifteenth-century walled Reformat **church** at the top of Piaţa Kalvíny. In its cemetery, behind a Székely beamgate raised in 1981, you'll find stone versions of traditional wooden Székely graveposts.

Kós Károly

Kós Károly (1883–1977) was the leading architect of the Hungarian National Romantic school, which derived its inspiration from the village architecture of Transylvania and Finland. The Transylvanian style is reflected in the wooden roofs, gables and balconies of his buildings, while the Finnish influence appears in the stone bases and trapezoidal door frames. Fine examples of Kós's work can be seen in Sfântu Gheorghe and Cluj (notably the Cock Church), as well as in Budapest.

After the separation of Transylvania from Hungary, Kós, a native of Timişoara, was one of the few Hungarian intellectuals to accept the new situation, choosing to remain in Cluj (and in his country home just north of Huedin) and to play a leading role in Hungarian society in Transylvania. While continuing to work as an architect, he also travelled around Transylvania, recording the most characteristic buildings (of all ethnic groups) in delightful linocuts; these were published in 1929 by the Transylvanian Artists' Guild (co-founded by Kós himself), with Kós's own text outlining the historical influences on Transylvanian architecture. In 1989, an English translation of the book, *Transylvania*, was published by Szépirodalmi Könyvkiadó in Budapest, although the Hungarian edition is well worth having just for the linocuts.

Practicalities

Both the **train** and **bus stations** are 2km east of the centre; follow Strada 1 Decembrie 1918 to reach Piaţa Libertăţii. The best **hotel** is the *Park*, behind the techncal college at Str. Gábor Áron 12 (☎0267/311 058, ⓕ311 307; ❹), which even has non-smoking rooms. Also good are two small private hotels: the *Korona* (☎0267/351 164; ❶) opposite the station, which also sells good maps of the town; and the *Consic* (☎0267/326 984; ❷) at B-dul Bălan 31 – take bus #5 from the station, or walk north from the BTT office at the junction of Bulevardul Bălan and Strada 1 Decembrie 1918. Sfântu Gheorghe's BTT branch (☎ & ⓕ0267/351 902) is particularly active in agrotourism, arranging **homestays** in nearby spas and villages; this is also the place to book long-distance bus tickets and flights.

The choice **place to eat** in town is the restaurant of the *Hotel Park*; otherwise there are plenty of pizza places, of which the *Restaurant Tribel* (actually a cafeteria) at Str. 1 Decembrie 1918 no. 2 is best.

The **post offices** are on Strada 1 Decembrie 1918, in the early-twentieth-century Hotel Hungaria, and by the train station. **Internet** access is available at Internet Klub, Str. Ciucului 47 and in the Casa de Cultură. The town holds a **festival** on Saint George's day, April 23.

Covasna and around

Trains east from Sfântu Gheorghe to Târgu Secuiesc and Breţcu pass close to **COVASNA** (Kovászna), 30km away, although the DN11 (E574) lies well to the north. The "spa of the thousand springs", or Valea Zânelor (Fairies' Valley), east of here, is popular with walkers, and from here there's easy access to the Vrancea and Penteleu mountains. The main attraction is an amazing inclined plane, built in 1886 as part of Romania's first narrow-gauge **forestry rail line**, a UNESCO World Heritage Monument, where wagons of timber were lowered down a 1232-metre slope, before continuing to the main-line transfer sidings in Covasna.

From the **train station**, buses take you the 3km to the modern centre of town, and then continue 5km to the hospital in Valea Zânelor. The **bus**

station is behind the market at Str. Ştefan cel Mare 48, just east of the road to the station; **train tickets** can be booked at Str. Libertăţii 24.

For access to the mountains, the best **place to stay** is the *Hotel Bradul* (℡0267/340 081, ℻340 030; ❹), an excellent modern hotel opposite the hospital; otherwise try the *Turist* (℡0267/340 573, ℻340 632; ❶) at Str. Gării 2, a small, friendly place with limited facilities. There are also plenty of guesthouses, such as the *Lux* at Str. Ştefan cel Mare 106. A little further up the valley is a **campsite** (℡0267/340 401), which has cabins (❶), tent space, and proper toilets (only accessed when the restaurant is open).

Around Covasna

TÂRGU SECUIESC (Kezdivásárhely), half an hour beyond Covasna by train, is something of a backwater – it's a stronghold of Székely culture, with little Romanian spoken – but it was a major trading centre in medieval times and the first Székely town to be granted a charter in 1427 (its Romanian name means Székely Market); people still flock to its Thursday **market** today. Through buses from Braşov stop on the ring road, Strada Fabricilor, just north of the **bus station**. From the train and bus stations, it's about a ten-minute walk north along Strada Gării to the central Piaţa Gábor Arón, lined with nineteenth-century merchants' houses, one of which, at Curtea 10, contains the **Museum of the Guilds** (Tues–Fri 9am–4pm, Sat 9am–1pm, Sun 9am–2pm). In addition to the history of the guilds, there are temporary art shows and a surprisingly good display of costumed dolls. If you're looking for somewhere **to stay**, the *Hotel Oituz* (℡0267/363 798; ❷), opposite the museum at Piaţa Gábor Arón 9, is small and friendly, with shared bathrooms and limited hot water. The *Hotel Fortyogo*, Str. Fortyogo 14 (℡0267/362 663; ❸), is more comfortable, though a couple of kilometres out of town to the east. The *Restaurant Bujdosó*, by the park at the southern end of Curtea 33, serves Székely specialities, such as goulash and *kohlrabi*.

In the other direction, 10km down the Braşov road, it's well worth a detour to take a look at the **Bod Peter Museum of Székely life and culture** (daily 8am–late) at the northern end of the village of **CERNAT DE JOS** (Alsócsernáton); to get there, take the asphalt road signposted to Cernat de Sus, and fork left about 100m beyond the church – the museum is almost a kilometre along this road, at no. 330. A number of village houses have been moved here and there are excellent collections of wooden implements, decorated wooden dowry chests, and ceramics; unfortunately, information is only in Hungarian. Five **buses** run from Târgu Secuiesc to Cernat de Sus on weekdays; the last one returns at 1.30pm, but if you want to stay over, the museum has a couple of **rooms** (❶).

Băile Tuşnad and St Anne's Lake

To the north of Sfântu Gheorghe, the River Olt has carved the beautiful **Tuşnad defile**, at the far end of which is **BĂILE TUŞNAD** (Tusnádfürdó), a bathing resort set amid larch and fir woods, with a campsite, the *Popas Turistic Univers* (℡0266/335 087; May–Sept), offering bungalows (❶), easily spotted just south of the train station.

The main road, Strada Oltului, heads south from the Petrom garage near the train station to Univers Tourist (8am–8.30pm daily; ℡0266/335 415, ✉universtourist@kabelkon.ro), where **information** is available, as well as **accommodation** in villas (❶–❹) and at the *Lacul Sf. Ana* cabana (see opposite), and excursions. A Ştrand, with bathing in mesothermal waters, (9am–7pm from early May; €1) operates opposite the Casa de Cultură, which houses temporary exhibitions. Further down Strada Oltului are a library and an Ecotourism Information Centre, and the *Hotel Tuşnad* (☎0266/335 202, ℻335 108; ❹), which has **Internet** service. North of the station, the new guesthouses are concentrated on Strada Apor, including *Panzió Csomad* at no. 17 and *Panzió Iris* at no. 22 (a grander place with a **restaurant**; ☎0266/335 586; ❷).

South of town, from the village of Bixad, a road leads east to **St Anne's Lake** (Lacu Sf Ana), a two-hour walk from Băile Tuşnad following blue dot markings. Set in a crater on Mount Ciumatu, the lake is the only intact volcanic lake in Europe and is run by an NGO that charges a fee to visit; note that the Univers Tourist agency (see opposite) runs an excursion to the lake at 3pm daily. It's spectacularly twee and is the site of a fervent **festival** on St Anne's day (July 26). The *Lacul Sfânta Ana* cabana is set on the east rim of the crater, near the rare Tinovul Mohuş peat bog (in a secondary crater, with glacial relicts such as *Drosera* insectivorous plants). A few kilometres beyond, on the Târgu Secuiesc road, the tiny spa of **BĂILE BALVANYOS** (Bálványos-füred) makes a good stop, with both cabana-type accommodation (❶), pensions (❷), and the upmarket *Hotel Carpaţi* (☎0267/360 700, 021/231 7071, ℮balvanyos @bestwesternhotels.ro; ❼), built as a sanatorium in 1938 and now part of the Best Western chain.

Miercurea Ciuc

The industrial city of **MIERCUREA CIUC** (Csíksereda/Szeklerburg), 100km north of Braşov, is capital of Harghita county. Its city centre, with the windswept Piaţa Libertăţii at its heart, was extensively rebuilt in communist concrete, a situation made worse by a rash of ugly modern churches, and aside from the **Mikó citadel**, south of the centre, and the adjacent 1890s Law Courts and City Hall, there is little of architectural interest here. The citadel itself was built in 1611–21 then rebuilt in 1716 and now contains an excellent county **museum** (Tue–Sun 9am–5pm), with exhibits on Székely churches. Two kilometres further south in the suburb of Jigodin (Zsögödfürdő) the **Nagy Imre Gallery** (daily except Tues 9am–5pm) displays a rotating selection of the forceful paintings of Székely artist Nagy Imre (1893–1976); his former home, at the rear of the gallery, contains local textiles and Corund ceramics, as well as photos of the artist. Near the rail and bus stations, the Roman Catholic **church** on Strada Florilor was built in 1751–58 in a simple Baroque style; behind it, the utterly weird Millennium Templom, also Catholic, is a vision of what the Magyar nomads might have built a millennium ago if they'd had modern materials.

The city's only other attraction is the great **Székely pilgrimage to Şumuleu**, well worth the trip if you're looking for a flavour of the Székely culture. It takes place on Whit Sunday at Şumuleu (Csiksomlyó), a Franciscan monastery 2km northeast of the city (buses #11, #21, #40, #41, #42 from the station forecourt towards Păuleni and Şoimeni). Largely rebuilt in 1804, the complex was founded in 1442 by Iancu de Hunedoara in thanks for the Székely victory at Marasszentimre; the festival, however, commemorates the 1567 victory of Catholic Székely over János Sigismund Báthori's, who was attempting to impose Calvinism on them. At least 200,000 black-clad pilgrims attend, singing hymns and queuing up to touch the wooden statue of the Virgin in the sanctuary, before processing on to the three small chapels on the nearby hill top. From here, there's a good **view** of the plain, dotted with Székely villages.

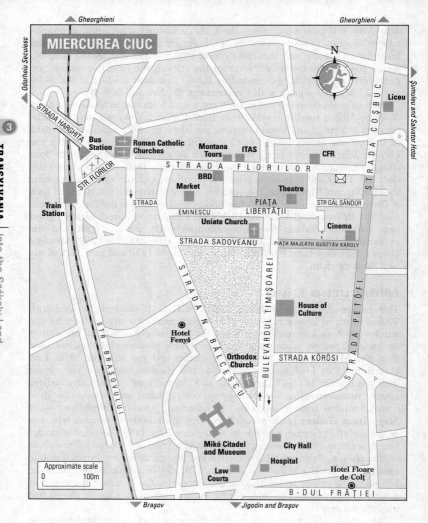

Practicalities

Miercurea Ciuc's **bus** and **train stations** are both west of the centre, south of the Odorheiu road; Ciceu station, one stop north, is the junction for the rail line across the Eastern Carpathians to Adjud. Trains between Cluj and Moldavia stop here without passing through Miercurea Ciuc; if there's no connecting train, take bus #22 (roughly hourly). Long-distance bus tickets can be bought from Montana Tours, Str. Florilor 26B (☎ & ⓕ0266/317 122; Mon–Fri 8am–6pm, Sat 9am–1pm), and ITAS, Str. Florilor 26A (Mon–Fri 8am–4pm, Sat 8am–noon). For **tourist information**, there's a CFR office at Strada Florilor 12 (☎0266/317007; ⓦwww.hargitatourism.ro); see also ⓦhttp://clmc.topnet.ro/tourinform. Several places offer exchange facilities, and there are supermarkets on the south side of Strada Florilor, plus a market at the rear. **Internet** access is available at Petőfi 3 (24hrs) and Petőfi 36; the **post office** is at Str. Florilor 5.

The most upmarket **hotel** is the *Fenyő* at Str. Bălcescu 11 (☎0266/311 493, ℮reserve@hunguest-fenyo.ro; ➏), with great service, a gym, sauna and massage. The town's real bargain, though, is the excellent *Hotel Floare de Colţ*, at B-dul Frătiei 7 (☎0266/372 068, ℉312 533; ➋). The *Salvator* (☎0266/372 126, ℮tanhaz@kabelkan.ro; ➎) is very snug, and conveniently situated next to the Şumuleu monastery at Str. Szék 147. There is also a **campsite** in Băile Jigodin, 2km south on the main road and served by buses #10 and #11; you can walk there by following the blue-dot hiking markings.

In addition to the **restaurant** in the *Hotel Fenyő*, there's the *Meteor* at the west end of Strada Gál Sándor, and some pleasant places on the pedestrianized stretch of Strada Petőfi, such as *New York Pizza* and *Renegade Pub & Pizza*, and just north, the *Két Gobé* at the junction of Stradas Coşbuc and Florilor; the excellent Sütike bakery is also on Petőfi. For **drinking**, there's the *Hockey Klub* and *Rodeo Saloon* on Petőfi, *Bobi-Com* on Bălcescu at the junction with Eminescu, and the *Western Pub* on Strada Harghita, on the way to the bus station.

The Upper Mureş valley

From Miercurea Ciuc, a semicircular route, by both road and rail, crosses a low pass from the Olt valley to the Mureş valley and curves around to the great Hungarian city of **Târgu Mureş**. It's a leisurely route taking in the tranquil Lacu Roşu, the untamed Căliman mountains and a plethora of attractive villages, including Gurghiu and Hodac, both of which hold renowned **festivals**. Travelling by train, you may need to change at Deda for Târgu Mureş; with your own wheels you can take a shortcut via Sovata, but there are next to no buses on this route.

Gheorgheni and around

GHEORGHENI (Gyergyószentmiklós) is jumping-off point for **Lacu Roşu** (see p.202). **Trains** arriving at Gheorgheni are met by buses to spare passengers the twenty-minute hike east into the town centre. Getting back to the station is not so easy, and you'll probably end up having to walk or take a taxi. The **bus station** is immediately south of the train station, but you can also board eastbound buses on Bulevardul Lacu Roşu, just north of the centre; the only bus west on the DN13B leaves at 6.45am (except Wed & Fri) for Sovata and Târgu Mureş.

The road from the station meets the DN12 at a well-conserved synagogue and continues east as Bulevardul Lacu Roşu; one block south is the triangular Piaţa Libertăţii, ringed with tatty buildings redolent of the Austro-Hungarian era. To the north of the square, the pedestrianized Strada Miron Cristea leads to Bulevardul Lacu Roşu and the splendid high school, completed in 1915; Strada Márton Arón leads east from the square past the Catholic church to Piaţa Petőfi and the **museum** (Tues–Fri 9am–4pm, Sat & Sun 9am–1pm), on the far side of the square at Strada Rácóczi 1. Housed in a former Armenian merchants' inn, it contains some fascinating artefacts, including weatherboards carved with shamanistic motifs brought by the Magyars from Asia.

Practicalities

The town's **tourist office** is on the south side of the square, with ATMs nearby and on the north side; **Internet** service and public toilets are off the square's southwestern corner, and the **post office** is on the west side, with the Calvinist church. The best **restaurant** is the *Mukátli* (℡0266/365 477), halfway to the station; other options are the *Sárkány* Chinese restaurant on Strada Gabór Aron just south of the square, and the pizzeria at the *Hotel Astoria*.

There are three simple **hotels** in Gheorgheni, none of which offer breakfast; at Piaţa Libertăţii 17, the *Szilagyi* (℡0266/367 591; ❷) has en-suite rooms with between two and six beds and is relatively over-priced; at the south end of Strada Doua Poduri (opposite the Catholic church) the *Astoria* (℡0266/363 698, ❶) has simpler en-suite rooms above a pizzeria. The *SportHotel Avântul* (℡0266/361 270; ❶) at Str. Stadionului 11, off Strada Bălcescu (the Topliţa road), has rooms with shared showers. There's also a **campsite** 4km east of town on the Lacu Roşu road, near the newish *Motel Patru* (℡ & ℻0266/364 213; ❷).

Lacu Roşu

Lacu Roşu, or the **Red Lake** (Gyilkostó in Hungarian or Murderers' Lake), lies in a small depression 25km east of Gheorgheni. It was formed in 1838 when a landslide dammed the River Bicaz, and the tips of a few pines still protrude from the water, which is rich in trout. Surrounded by lovely scenery and blessed by a yearly average of 1800 hours of sunshine, this is an ideal (and busy) stopover if you're crossing the Carpathians into Moldavia through the wild Bicaz gorges (p.255). The area is a national park, and the **Eco-Info-Center** (Tues–Sun 10am–6pm), on the main road near the lake at the western end of the resort, offers information on walks.

At km26, in the centre of the resort, a track crosses a bridge to the north and climbs to the simple *Bucur* **hotel** (℡0266/362 949; ❷). The more atmospheric *Casa Ranova* (℡0266/364 226; ❷) is right by the lake (next to the boat rental shack), and there are also guesthouses such as the *Capra Neagrǎ* (℡0740 /455 515), *Combucur* (℡0266/364 049) and *Turist* (℡0745/601 113). The **campsite**, with cabins, is at the eastern end of the resort, although nobody seems to mind if you just pitch tent anywhere.

Lăzarea

Six kilometres north of Gheorgheni on the DN12 (one stop by train), the village of **LĂZAREA** (Szárhegy) is worth a visit to see **Lazăr Castle**, situated just below the Franciscan monastery whose white tower is visible from the station and passing trains. The fifteenth-century castle's fine Renaissance hall and frescoed facade are being gradually restored by artists who hold a summer camp here each year. The **castle gallery** (Tues–Sun 9am–5pm) exhibits the work of artists attending the camp, and there is also now a well-stocked sculpture park, open all year, in the castle grounds. The OVR office (℡ & ℻0266/164 191) can provide information about their work as well as details of **homestay** schemes in the area.

Topliţa and the Căliman mountains

The train line continues north for a further 30km from Lăzarea to **TOPLIŢA** (Maroshéviz), a third-rate spa and logging town whose only real sights of interest are two wooden churches – the church of Sf Ilie, 1km north on the main road, built in 1847 and moved here in 1910, and the Doamnei Church in a lovely nunnery 10km further on, dating from 1658 – and a covered bridge south of town. A road runs through the eastern Carpathians from Topliţa into Moldavia, served by buses to Borsec, Poiana Largului and Târgu Neamţ.

From Topliţa, the road and rail routes head west along the Mureş valley, which is lined with various places to stay, such as the *Şoimilor* cabana (❶) 2km west of the Stânceni Neagră train halt, 16km west of Topliţa; the *Doi Brazi* motel (❷) in Sălard, a further 9km west and 3km west of Lunca Bradului station; and a homestay in Androneasa (Str. Principală 160; ❶), a further 6km west of Sălard. The wild, unpopulated **Căliman mountains** rise steeply to the north of this narrow, rugged defile, in which retreating German soldiers made a vain attempt to ambush the Red Army in 1944. Today, the Căliman range – the main volcanic zone of the Carpathians – is a paradise for hikers. The best route in is probably from Răstoliţa, 30km west of Topliţa. There's plenty of road traffic as far as the new dam at Secu, from where paths head northeast to the volcanic peaks and the settlements in the huge crater beyond, leading ultimately to Vatra Dornei in Moldavia (see p.287).

South to Târgu Mureş

From Topliţa roads and railtracks lead to Deda (the junction for Beclean and Cluj), and then south towards Târgu Mureş. **BRÂNCOVENEŞTI** (Marosvécs), 13km south of Deda and served by slow trains only, was founded on a Roman site and has the fine Kemény **castle** (visible across the river from the train) dating from the fourteenth century and best known for housing handicapped children judged too sick or traumatized to recover during Ceauşescu's regime.

REGHIN (Szászrégen/Sächsisch Reen), 10km beyond Brâncoveneşti, is ringed by factories, including an amazingly successful violin factory, located here because of the wealth of the very grainy curly sycamore (also known as flamed maple) in the Gurghiu valley. The main reason to stop here though, is to make bus connections to Gurghiu and Hodac from immediately outside the train station, so there's little reason to venture into town, 1.5km west.

GURGHIU, 14km east, and **HODAC**, 8km further are traditional shepherding communities. Gurghiu is known for its **Girl Fair** (Târgul de fete) on the second Sunday of May, similar to that of Muntele Găina (see box on p.225). At Hodac, 7km beyond Gurghiu, there's a **Measurement of the Milk** festival (see p.229) on the first Saturday of May, while the second Sunday in June sees the **Buying Back of the Wives Festival**, reaffirming the economic underpinnings of matrimony. To guard against a wasted journey, check when these are going on at the Cultural Inspectorate of the prefecture in Târgu Mureş (see below). During the festivals, special **buses** are laid on from Reghin; at other times, both villages can be reached by buses bound for Dulcea and Toaca, while Gurghiu is also served by buses to Glăjărie and Orşova.

Târgu Mureş

TÂRGU MUREŞ is still at heart **Marosvásárhely**, one of the great Magyar cities of Transylvania, although the Magyar influence has been diluted by recent Romanian and Gypsy immigration. The city was briefly notorious as a centre of ethnic tension, with riots in 1990, but is more reputably known as a centre of learning – its university is small, but both the medical and drama schools are renowned nationally. The city suffers from heavy pollution generated at the

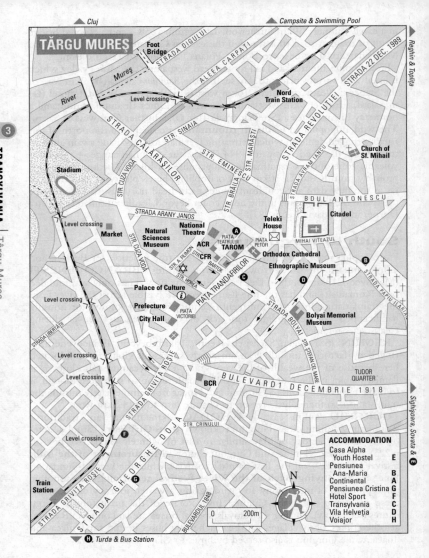

ACCOMMODATION

Casa Alpha Youth Hostel	E
Pensiunea Ana-Maria	B
Continental	A
Pensiunea Cristina	G
Hotel Sport	F
Transylvania	C
Vila Helveţia	D
Voiajor	H

chemical plant by the main road and rail line to the southwest of town – it's liable to be an unpleasant experience entering or leaving town along this route.

Arrival and information

Târgu Mureş is on a secondary line between Razboieni and Deda and is served by several fast **trains** a day, with extra services in the summer; however, connections south are poor, and you're best off taking a bus or maxitaxi to Sighişoara, 55km south, and catching a train from there. The **bus station** is at Str. Gheorghe Doja 52; note that some services to Cluj leave from the Autogara

Eurotur, B-dul 1 Decembrie 1918 no. 168, in the Tudor quarter. It's a twenty-minute walk north from the bus station to the city centre (bus #2, #4, #16, #17, #18 or #22, or maxitaxis) – turn right along Strada Gheorghe Doja, past the train station and on to Piaţa Victoriei and Piaţa Trandafirilor.

There's a decent city **map** outside the train station and another by the Minorite tower; the travel agency at Piaţa Trandafirilor 31 will change travellers' cheques and sells bus tickets. You can get some **information** at ⓦwww.tirgumures.ro, ⓦwww.muresonline.ro or ⓦwww.muresinfo.ro.

Internet access is available at Electro-Orizont (9am–11pm), behind the Ethnographic Museum at Piaţa Teatrului 11, Internet Club Europe (10am–midnight) at Trandafirilor 43, behind the *Leo* restaurant, and Explorer Internet Club, Horea 31. The **post office** is at Str. Revoluţiei 2 (Mon–Fri 7am–8pm, Sat 8am–1pm).

Accommodation

The bus station seems an odd location for the slick new *Voiajor* (Str Gheorghe Doja 143; ☎0265/250 750, ⓦwww.voiajor.ro; ⑤), with cable TV, minibar and data ports. Turning left out of the main train station, it takes under five minutes to reach the *Sport* **hotel** at Str. Griviţa Roşie 31 (☎0265/231 913, ⓕ266 797; ❶); most rooms have a half-share of a bathroom and the restaurant is poor, but it is easily the cheapest place in town and is handy for the bus and train stations. At Piaţa Teatrului 6, the *Continental* (☎0265/250 416, ⓔcontims@netsoft.ro; ❼) has modern fittings, a casino, cable TV and data ports, and even some non-smoking rooms. The *Transylvania*, at Piaţa Trandafirilor 46 (☎0265/265 616, ⓕ266 028; ❷) is a cheaper option, with both en-suite and shared-bath rooms and lots of faded red velvet. Three excellent new private places are the Swiss-owned *Vila Helveţia*, Str. Borsos Tamás 13 (☎0265/216 954; ❼); *Pensiunea Ana-Maria*, Str. Papiu Ilarian 17 (☎ & ⓕ0265/464 410; ⑤); and *Pensiunea Cristina*, near the train station at Str. Piatra de Moara 1A (☎0265/266 490, ⓔpensiunea.cristina@muresonline.ro; ⑤). All are clean, friendly and well managed.

The official **youth hostel** is the *Casa Alpha*, Alleea Vrancea 1 (☎0265/257 057, ⓔalfa@orizont.net; ❸); take maxitaxi #30B or #43 east along Bulevardul 1 Decembrie 1918 to the bridge. There's **camping** at the *Ştrand* on the river at the north end of Aleea Carpaţi, with a large boating lake and a café on a fake paddle steamer (take bus or maxitaxi #14 or #26 or walk from Târgu Mureş Nord train station), and at the *Stejeriş* motel (☎0265/233 509; ❷), 7km along the Sighişoara road.

The Town

The central squares of **Piaţa Victoriei** and **Piaţa Trandafirilor** are lined with fine Secession-style edifices, of which the most grandiose are the adjacent Prefecture and Palace of Culture, dating from 1907 and 1913 respectively and typical of an era when a self-consciously "Hungarian" style of architecture reflected Budapest's policy of "Magyarizing" Transylvania.

The Prefecture's rooftops blaze with polychromatic tiling, while the most stunning feature of the **Palace of Culture** (Tues–Fri 9am–4pm, Sat & Sun 9am–1pm) is its interior, where gloomy corridors are relieved by rich floral wallpaper and stained glass, and 50kg of gilding. One flight up the right-hand staircase is the most spectacular room of all, the **Hall of Mirrors** (Sala de Oglinzi), with stained-glass windows illustrating local myths. Another flight up, in the **history section** (same hours), look out for the careworn face of

György Dózsa (see p.336). Two flights up the left-hand staircase, a door gives you a free glimpse from the gods of the city's concert hall; the huge organ is often used for recitals. Another floor up is the museum's **art section** (same hours), focusing on the Hungarian Revival of the late nineteenth and early twentieth centuries. Outside, on Strada Enescu, a gallery houses free shows by local artists (Tues–Fri 9am–4pm, Sat & Sun 9am–1pm); the ticket office for concerts and plays is also here.

The **Natural Sciences Museum** (Tues–Fri 9am–4pm, Sat 9am–2pm, Sun 9am–1pm), largely dioramas of stuffed beasts, is northwest of the Palace of Culture at Str. Horea 24. Heading here from Piaţa Trandafirilor, you'll see the city's synagogue, all rose windows and domes, to the right on Strada Aurel Filimon. The colourful **ethnographic section** (same hours) is two blocks north of the Palace of Culture at Piaţa Trandafirilor 11 in the Toldalagy House, a fine Baroque pile built in 1759–62. Beside it, stands a tower raised in 1735 – all that remains of the Minorite (Franciscan) monastery – stands at the entrance to the concrete plaza of Piaţa Teatrului, with its undistinguished modern sculptures.

The neo-Byzantine **Orthodox Cathedral** (1925–34) marks the northern end of Piaţa Trandafirilor. The Romanian riposte to the imperialistic Magyar administrative buildings dominating the southern end of the square, it pushes aside the more modest Baroque church of the Jesuits (1728-64) on its eastern flank; for good measure, the new masters added a statue of Avram Iancu, on the cathedral's southern side, not to mention the Greek-Catholic Catedral Mică, or Little Cathedral (1926–36), at the south end.

Just northeast of the cathedral is Piaţa Petőfi, then Piaţa Bernardy György, dominated by the **citadel**, whose walls shelter the Calvinist church built for the Dominicans in 1430 and later used by the Transylvanian Diet; there's a small history display in a gate tower (built in 1613). Two blocks east of the citadel, along Bulevardul Antonescu, Strada Şaguna heads north to the **wooden church** of Sf Mihail (1793–94). Set in a large cemetery, the church has a shingled onion-dome and a beautifully decorated interior and is a virtual shrine to the national poet, Eminescu, who slept in the porch in 1866 because there was no room at the inn.

Despite its long-standing role as a garrison town, Târgu Mureş also takes pride in its intellectual tradition; the mathematicians **Farkas Bolyai** (1775–1856) and his son **János** (1802–60), founders of non-Euclidean geometry, receive their due in the **Bolyai Memorial Museum** at Str. Bolyai 17 (Tues–Fri 10am–6pm, Sat & Sun 10am–1pm), east from Piaţa Trandafirilor beyond a high school built in 1909 in the Hungarian Art Nouveau (flippantly known as Art Noodle) style. The museum also houses a hundred paintings by the Székely artist Nagy Imre as well as Târgu Mureş's greatest treasure, the **Teleki–Bolyai library**. The Teleki collection, consisting of 40,000 volumes, was built up by Count Samuel Teleki, and with the later addition of the Bolyai collection it now includes many ancient medical and scientific texts, as well as the works of the philosophers of the French Enlightenment.

Eating and drinking

Piaţa Trandafirilor is the place to find **food**, either in the supermarket at no. 42 or in the several snack bars and restaurants that line the square, notably the *Leo* at no. 44 or the cafeteria-like *LactoBar Balada* at no. 5, both of which serve a similar selection of traditional Romanian dishes; *Panda Pui* at no. 15 has basic fast food; *Piccolo Italia*, Str. Poştei 12 (Mon–Sat 1–11pm) is the best Italian place in town, in a pleasant cellar; *Pizzerie Venezia*, nearby at the corner of Strada Revoluţiei and Piaţa Petőfi, is better inside than out, with a bar upstairs.

Along Strada Bolyai there are various small **cafés and bars**, including *China Blue* and *Kebab*, both at no. 10, plus a good one in the court of the Patronatul Naţional Român at no. 18 (look for the Guinness sign), and its cellar. Others to try include the *Crama* at Str. Horea 6, and the *Doina & Jeno* between Piaţa Teatrului and Strada Bartok. Bars on Piaţa Trandafirilor, such as *Downtown* (no. 25) and *New York Casino Bar* (no. 44) are more youth-oriented.

Of the traditional *cofetăries*, the *Teatrului*, under the CFR agency, has a fume-free terrace, and the *Lido*, at Piaţa Trandafirilor 49, is attractive, set in a good Secession building. More modern cafés include the *Café Tutun* (until 4am daily) at Str. Bolyai 12, and the *Eifel* next door. Excellent doughnuts (*gogoşi* or *langoş*) are served till 10pm at the rear of the Cinema Arte on the south side of Piaţa Trandafirilor, with another counter selling *covrigi ardeleneşti* (Transylvanian bread rings) close by.

Listings

Bus tickets AtlasSib ⊤ & Ⓕ 0265/268 296; Intertours (see below); Total Tours, Piaţa Trandafirilor 24 ⊤ 0265/269 343, Ⓔ total-t @orizont.net.
Flights TAROM, Piaţa Trandafirilor 7 ⊤ 0265/236 200, Ⓕ 250 170; and Intertours, Str. Bartok 1 ⊤ 0265/264 011, Ⓔ office@intertours.ro.

Tour operators Transair Corbet, Piaţa Trandafirilor 43 (⊤ 0265/268 463, Ⓔ travel@corbet-transair.ro) offer tours, car rental and activities such as horse-riding and bear-watching; and Total Tours (see above) offer parapente, mountainbiking, rafting and skiing.
Train tickets CFR, Piaţa Teatrului 1.

Cluj and northern Transylvania

Cluj was the great Hungarian capital of Transylvania and remains a natural gateway to the region, just six hours from Budapest by train. There is more buzz to its café life than in other towns, maybe due to the seventy thousand students resident here, and shops also seem better stocked than elsewhere.

The area surrounding Cluj, particularly the **Transylvanian Heath** to the east, harbours some of the richest, most varied **folk music** in Europe. Weekends are the best time to investigate villages such as **Sic**, **Cojocna**, **Rimetea** and **Izvoru Crişului**, where almost every street has its own band and there are rich pickings to be had at spring and summer festivals. Cluj is also a natural base for visiting the **Apuseni massif**, with its wide green pastures, easy walking and caving opportunities, particularly on the **Padiş plateau**.

To the north of the Apuseni is **Sălaj county**, a rural backwater scattered with quaint wooden churches. Further east, the historic town of **Bistriţa**, once centre of an isolated Saxon community (and today more widely known for its Dracula connections), still guards the routes into Maramureş and northern Moldavia.

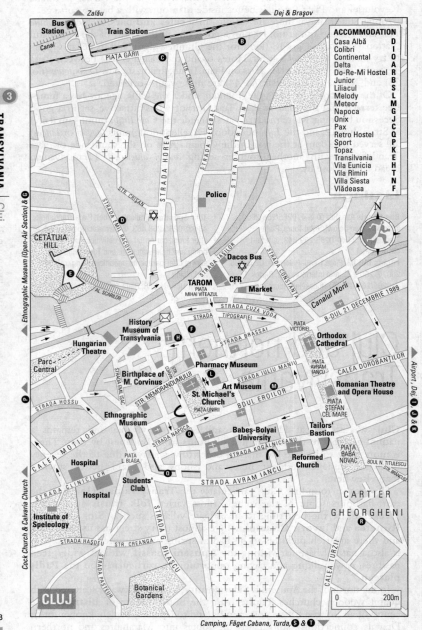

Zalău

Dej & Braşov

Bus Station A

Train Station

Canal

PIATA GARII

C

B

STR. CRAIOVA

STRADA DECEBAL

STRADA TRAIAN

STRADA HOREA

STR. CRISAN

ACCOMMODATION

Casa Albă	D
Colibri	I
Continental	O
Delta	A
Do-Re-Mi Hostel	R
Junior	B
Liliacul	S
Melody	L
Meteor	M
Napoca	G
Onix	J
Pax	C
Retro Hostel	Q
Sport	P
Topaz	K
Transilvania	E
Vila Eunicia	H
Vila Rimini	T
Villa Siesta	N
Vlădeasa	F

STRADA EMIL BACOVITA

Police

D

CETĂTUIA HILL

E

AL. SCARILOR

STRADA IASILOR

STRADA CONSTANTA

Dacos Bus

CFR

TAROM
PIATA MIHAI VITEAZUL

Market

Canalul Morii

B-DUL 21 DECEMBRIE 1989

STRADA CUZA VODA

STRADA TIPOGRAFIEI

History Museum of Transylvania

H

F

STRADA BRASSAI

PIATA VICTORIEI

Orthodox Cathedral

N

Hungarian Theatre

Parc Central

P

STRADA EMIL ISAC

Birthplace of M. Corvinus

STR. MEMORANDUMULUI

STR. CRISAN

Pharmacy Museum

L

Art Museum

M

St. Michael's Church

PIATA UNIRII

STRADA IULIU MANIU

BDUL EROILOR

PIATA AVRAM IANCU

CALEA DOROBANTILOR

Romanian Theatre and Opera House

PIATA STEFAN CEL MARE

Ethnographic Museum

N

STRADA NAPOCA

O

Babeş-Bolyai University

STRADA KOGALNICEANU

Tailors' Bastion

PIATA BABA NOVAC

BDUL N. TITULESCU

STR. BRANCUSI

CALEA MOTILOR

PIATA L. BLAGA

Hospital

STRADA CLINICILOR

Hospital

Students' Club

Q

Reformed Church

STRADA AVRAM IANCU

CARTIER

GHEORGHENI

R

Institute of Speleology

STRADA HASDEU

STR. CREANGA

STRADA G. BILASCU

STRADA PASTEUR

Botanical Gardens

CALEA TURZII

CLUJ

0   200m

N

Airport, Dej, 1, J & K

Ethnographic Museum (Open-Air Section) & G

Cock Church & Calvaria Church

Camping, Făget Cabana, Turda, S & T

Cluj

With its cupolas, Baroque and Secession outcroppings and weathered *fin-de-siècle* backstreets, downtown **CLUJ** (sometimes known by its full name of Cluj-Napoca; Klausenburg to the Germans and Kolozsvár to the Hungarians) looks every inch the Hungarian provincial capital it once was. The town was founded by Germans in the twelfth century for the Hungarian King Geza, on the site of a Roman Municipium, and the modern-day Magyars – now less than a fifth of the city's population – still regret its decline, fondly recalling the Magyar *belle époque*, when Cluj's café society and literary reputation surpassed all other Balkan cities. For most Romanians, however, Kolozsvár was the city of the Hungarian landlords until its restoration to the national patrimony in 1920; they consider Ceaușescu's addition of Napoca to its name in 1974 as recognition that their Dacian forebears settled here 1850 years ago, long before the Magyars entered Transylvania. It's rightly said that Romanians live in Cluj and Hungarians still live in Koloszvár, with separate schools, theatre and opera, and little trust between the communities. Cluj is also the birthplace of the

Gheorghe Funar

Gheorghe Funar, the "Mad Mayor" of Cluj from 1992 to 2004 and former leader of the Romanian National Unity Party, is notorious for his anti-Hungarian stance, and you'll see plenty of evidence of this around the city. Park benches and litter bins are painted red, yellow and blue, the colours of the Romanian flag. In 1994, the central Piața Libertății was renamed **Piața Unirii**, as "Unification" implies the union of Transylvania with the rest of Romania, and thus its removal from Hungary. Similarly, the lettering on the statue of Mátyás Corvinus, on Piața Unirii, which used to read *Hungarorum Matthias Rex*, now reads only *Matthias Rex*, and is flanked by six Romanian flags. In 1994, an archaeological dig (which revealed nothing of importance and is now full of weeds) was begun in front of the statue, and would have provided a pretext for removing it altogether if the government had not intervened. Additionally, Funar raised an absurdly expensive statue of Avram Iancu, leader of the 1848 revolt against the Hungarians, and a guillotine-like monument to the Romanians imprisoned for protesting in the 1892 *Memorandum* against Hungarian chauvinism, as well as plaques to mark the city's first Romanian-language school (1853) and its first Romanian mayor (1919). He even objected to a Bartók concert because the words would be sung in Hungarian.

Having again failed in the 1996 presidential election, Funar lost the leadership of the Romanian National Unity Party (which then more or less vanished), his reputation further damaged by a scandal concerning two million lei worth of calls from his private office to foreign sex lines (when two million lei was actually worth something). His anti-Hungarian campaign in Cluj continued, however – in 1999, he hung a banner outside the new Hungarian consulate on Piața Unirii reading "This is the seat of the Hungarian spy in Romania" – and in June 2000 he stood for mayor as a member of Romania Mare, now Romania's main nationalist party (although his election leaflets failed to mention any party affiliation). He was re-elected in a second round of voting, despite the best efforts of an unusually united opposition; he then got into a dispute with the city's Local Council, even barring members from meeting at City Hall for a while. A former economics lecturer, Funar was said to manage the city's budget well, though some of it went to companies owned by family members, and he continued to waste money on statues of notable Romanians. His last schemes were a full-size replica of *Trajan's Column* planned for Cluj's Piața Unirii, and a "Museum of Pains" to remember the victims of Horthyist (Hungarian fascist) dictatorship. In June 2004, he was finally voted out.

△ Wooden door detail, Cluj Village Museum

Unitarian creed and its centre in Romania, further adding to the multiethnic, multifaith cocktail.

Under communism, Cluj was industrialized and grew to over 330,000 inhabitants, becoming Transylvania's largest city, but it retained something of the langour and raffish undercurrents that had characterized the city in former times, as well as a reputation for being anti-Ceauşescu. Now, Cluj has a rabidly nationalist mayor, **Gheorghe Funar** (see box on p.209).

Arrival and information

From Cluj's **train station**, it takes about twenty minutes to walk down Strada Horea, across the Little Someş river, where the road becomes Strada Regele Ferdinand (until recently Strada Gheorghe Doja), and into the spacious **Piaţa Unirii**, the focus of the city's life. Across the road from the station, trolley buses #3, #4 and #9 stop on their loop route into the centre, going south on Strada Traian and returning along Strada Horea. The **bus station** is just across the tracks to the north of the train station (bus #31 or #42). Dacos Buses has a terminal (shared with AtlasSib and Sibiu's TransMixt) north of the market at Strada Iaşilor and an office at Str. Voiteşti 1-3, bl. D ap. 22 (☎ & ℱ 0264/534 584, 0744/551 902). The **airport** (ⓦ www.airportcluj.ro) is 5km east of the city at Calea Traian Vuia 149, connected by bus #8 to Piaţa Mihai Viteazul, node of the city's public transport system, in the centre just east of Strada Regele Ferdinand. A taxi to the centre costs under €1, if the road is clear, and certainly no more than €4 – check the price before getting in. The terminal, built in 1969, has been modernised but has no carousel; just wait in the hall until your bags appear.

Cluj's buses, trolley buses and trams provide frequent and reliable **city transport**, though stops are often far apart; buy tickets at kiosks (€0.50 for two rides). The most reliable taxis are operated by Pritax, Diesel, Pro Rapid, Terra and Nova.

There's no **tourist office** yet, although the city is obliged to open one soon. An excellent **map** of Cluj (including public transport routes) is published by Top-o-Gráf/Freytag & Berndt and can be found, among other places, in a cramped news kiosk at Piaţa Unirii 23. The local free **listings magazines** are *Zile şi Nopţi* (ⓦ www.zilesinopti.ro) and *Şapte Seri* (ⓦ www.sapteseri.ro), published weekly, while the English-language *Cluj What, Where, When* appears quarterly. The **websites** ⓦ www.cjnet.ro, ⓦ www.recognos.ro/new/cluj4all2 /home.php and ⓦ www.clujnapoca.ro are also worth a look.

Accommodation

Cluj has a wide range of **hotel** accommodation with welcome city comforts, but prices do tend to be higher than in most other towns in Romania. Thanks to its large student population, the city can also offer plenty of cheaper rooms over the summer in vacant student accommodation.

Hotels

Casa Albă Str. E. Racoviţa 22 ☎ 0264/534 556, ℱ 432 277. A very quiet, stopover in a small villa, with secure parking. ➒

Colibri Str. Între Lacuri 57 ☎ 0264/547 064, ℱ 418 641. A newish private pension by a lake a couple of kilometres east of the centre; the very helpful owners provide free transfers from Cluj town centre and the airport and all kinds of refreshments at all times. ➎

Continental Str. Napoca 1 ☎ 0264/591 441, ℮ conticj@cluj.astral.ro. A once-grand establishment and still the most atmospheric hotel in the centre. Rooms with baths are twice the price of those without. This is also an official HI hostel, but to stay here on those terms (€11 per person, breakfast included) you have to apply to the Continental travel agency next door (☎0264/593 977, ✉reservation@continentalcj.ro; Mon–Fri 10am–6pm). ④–⑦.

Delta in the bus station ☎0264/409 659. Basic but bearable four-bed rooms; rebuilt in 2003. ①

Junior Str. Căii Ferate 12 ☎0264/432 028. Twin, double and triple rooms in a new bar-with-hotel-attached just east of the train station. ②

Liliacul Calea Turzii 251A ☎ & ✆0264/438 129. A new hotel out of town on the DN1; the well-appointed rooms come with private bathrooms and cable TV, and there are also some more basic cabins. ②–⑤

Melody Piaţa Unirii 29 ☎0264/597 465, ⓦwww.hcm.ro. Also known as the *Central*, with friendly staff, reasonable rooms, and showgirls in the basement club. ③

Meteor Str Eroilor 29 ☎0264/591 060, ⓦwww.hotelmeteor.ro. A new hotel in a very central location (set back from the street), with satellite TV, gym, parking and buffet breakfast. ④

Napoca Str. Octavian Goga 1 ☎0264/580 715, ✆585 627. Good modern hotel with restaurant and MTV, across the river from the Parc Central (bus #27 from the station). ⑥

Onix Str. Albini 12 ☎0264/414 076, ⓦwww.hotelonix.ro. East of the centre (trolleys #2, #3, #25; bus #33); some rooms are considerably more expensive than others, with jacuzzi and PCs with free Internet access in every room. Sauna, massage and hairdresser also available; the nightclub's "erotic show" is nightly. ④–⑦

Pax Piaţa Gării 1 ☎0264/432 927. Small, gloomy and overpriced, but handy for the train station.

With only 12 rooms – none with private bathrooms – it fills up fast. ③

Sport Str. Coşbuc 15 ☎0264/593 921, ✆595 859. Not a traditional sport hotel, but a good hotel well renovated; bus #30 from Piaţa Unirii. ⑤

Topaz Str. Septimiu Albini 10 ☎0264/414 021, ✉topaz@rdslink.ro. A business-like modern place, immediately south of the *Onix*; now a Best Western. ⑥

Transilvania Str. Călăraşilor 1 ☎0264/432 071, ✉office@turismtransilvania.ro. Originally the *Belvedere* (until it was realized that it was the Belvedere Treaty that gave Northern Transylvania to Hungary), this luxurious modern place has an indoor pool, sauna, gym and parking, and overlooks the town from Cetăţuia hill. Main access by foot (up dilapidated steps, not safe at night), or by taxi – nearest bus is #37/38, stopping not too far north at Str. Gruia. ⑥

Vila Eunicia Str. Zola 2 ☎0264/413 950, ✉vilaeuniciamail@yahoo.com. A new central guesthouse with cable TV and Internet connections, and free parking; no restaurant. ⑤

Vila Rimini Str. Cometei 20A ☎0264/438 028, ⓦwww.rimini.ro. New four-star palace with rococo plaster mouldings, off the Turda road. Internet facilities available. ⑨

Villa Siesta Str. Şincai 6 ☎0264/595 582. A decent mid-range place, with air-conditioning, hairdriers, cable TV and radio; should soon have a restaurant. ⑥

Vlădeasa Str. Regele Ferdinand 20 ☎0264/594 429. A budget favourite, simple but friendly; good breakfast, but the restaurant is closed Sat evening and all Sun. ③

Camping, cabanas and hostels

The **Făget campsite** (open May–Oct; ☎0264/596 227; ①) is 4km south along the DN1 and a further 1.5km off the main road towards Turda (turn off at km472.5, by the *Liliacul* hotel); bus #40A goes there from Aleea Învaţatorului, on the south side of Piaţa Ştefan cel Mare, every hour or two in season, or failing that take any of the frequent buses for Feleacu and Turda to the *Liliacul* and then walk the remaining 1.5km. The site's facilities include cabins, a restaurant and bar, and non-stop hot water; there's also plenty of space for tents and caravans. Next to the campsite is the *Silva* (☎0264/438 470, 0722/228 158), a nice private bar-restaurant (recommended for its tripe soup) with three two-bed cabins (①) attached. There's also plenty of good woodland for camping wild.

About fifteen minutes' walk beyond the campsite is the *Făget* **cabana** (☎0264/596 880; ①); there are others at Cheile Baciului – take the train or buses #31 or #42 west on the DN1F to *Calea Baciului* (☎0264/435 454; ①), and at Făget-Izvor turn left onto Strada Primăverii at the Mănăştur roundabout, and then after a kilometre or so turn left at a signed turning, from where it's a futher kilometre to the cabana (☎0264/562 991; ①).

Cluj's main **hostel** is the very pleasant *Retro*, Str. Potaissa 13 (✆0264/450 452, ⓦwww.retro.ro; ❷), which has dorm beds and two-and three-bed rooms. In July and August, you could also try the *Do-re-mi*, Str. Braşov 2 (✆0264/586 616, ⓔdoremi@hihostels-romania.ro; check-in 9am–1pm, 6–10pm; ❶), near the Turda road (bus #3 to Piaţa Ciprariu), so-called because it's home to music students from mid–September to the end of June. It has three-bunk dorms, with the showers down the corridor, and cooking facilities; English is spoken. These are official HI youth hostels, as is the *Hotel Continental* (see p.211).

North of the river

Unlike almost every other Romanian city of comparable size, Cluj has no Civic Centre; it has thus avoided a widespread demolition of its old central zone, which remains largely unspoilt within the line of the city walls. The walls themselves have now been almost entirely demolished, although the remains of a fifteenth-century **citadel** still surround the *Transilvania* hotel on Cetăţuia Hill, north of the river. The Securitate used the hotel as its power base, and twelve people were supposedly gunned down on the steps in the 1989 revolution. The plinth of the massive cross, raised here by the Uniate Church in 1993–97 (replacing one demolished in 1948), is the best place to **view** the city. Behind the hotel is a tower that looks something like a dock for airships but was in fact built for testing parachutes.

The direct route from the train station to the city centre runs to the east of the citadel along Strada Horea, passing the Mughal-style Neologue **synagogue** (built in 1886, sacked by the Legionaries in 1927 and demolished in 1944, and rebuilt in 1951) and crossing the river to Piaţa Mihai Viteazul, dominated by a large statue of Michael the Brave, and a new eternal flame. To the east of the square and the market, a disused synagogue at Str. Croitorilor 13 now houses the university's new Centres for Jewish Studies, Holocaust Studies, Gender Studies and the like; it's a plain building, almost like a Methodist chapel.

Piaţa Unirii

Piaţa Unirii, surrounded by shops and restaurants, is the centre of the city; it's dominated by **St Michael's Cathedral**, built between 1349 and 1487 in the German Gothic style of the Saxons who then ruled unchallenged over the city. Dwarfing the congregation in the nave, mighty pillars curve into austerely bare vaulting. To this great hall-church the Hungarian aristocracy later added a sacristy – the door of which (dated 1528) encapsulates the Italian Renaissance style introduced under Mátyás Corvinus – a wooden Baroque pulpit, and a massive tapering nineteenth-century bell tower.

To the south of the cathedral, a clumsy but imposing equestrian **statue of Mátyás Corvinus** (raised in 1902) tramples the crescent banner of the Turks underfoot. His formidable Black Army kept the Kingdom of Hungary safe from banditry and foreign invasion for much of his reign (1458–90), but just 36 years later the nation was more or less wiped off the map at the battle of Mohács. A popular lament that justice departed with his death highlights Mátyás's political and military achievements, but the leader's reputation derives equally from his Renaissance attributes, for which his wife **Beatrix of Naples** should share the credit. By introducing him to the Renaissance culture of Italy and selecting foreign architects and craftsmen, and humanists like Bonfini to chronicle events and speeches, Beatrix was a catalyst for Hungary's own fifteenth-century Renaissance, and she personally commissioned many volumes in the Corvin library.

Beyond the statue, the **Hotel Continental**, in the southwestern corner of the square, stands out in the array of late nineteenth-century buildings: built in 1895 in an eclectic style combining Renaissance, Classical and Baroque elements, it later served as the German military headquarters in Transylvania at the end of World War II. Across the road, the University Bookshop is another fine building, bearing two plaques to those killed on 21 and 22 December 1989.

On the northern side of the square, on the corner of Strada Regele Ferdinand, is the Hintz House, which served as Cluj's first apothecary, opening in 1573 and finally closing in 1949. Inside, the **Pharmacy Museum** (Mon–Fri 10am–4pm), displays ancient prescriptions and implements; a Museum of Speleology (caving) is being built at the rear, at Str. Puşcariu 10. East of the cathedral, at Piaţa Unirii 30, stands the **Art Museum** (Wed–Sun noon–7pm), which, alongside its counterpart in Bucharest (see p.66), offers the best survey of Romanian art in the country. It is housed in the Baroque Bánffy Palace, built in 1774–91 to the design of Johann Eberhardt Blaumann for the Bánffy family. The collection is dominated by works of the largely French-influenced artists of the nineteenth and twentieth centuries, with pieces by Theodor Aman (1831–91) and Romania's best-known painter, Nicolae Grigorescu (1838–1907) – both of whom were influenced by the Barbizon group and the Impressionists – and Theodor Pallady (1871–1956), who spent several decades in Paris and was clearly inspired by Matisse. However, there's nothing by Brâncuşi, and there's virtually no abstract or truly modern art. In summertime, there's an open-air bar in the courtyard, and concerts performed by anyone from a Moldavian Gypsy brass band to the Cluj Philharmonic.

North of Piaţa Unirii

From the northwest corner of Piaţa Unirii, Strada Matei Corvin leads to the small fifteenth-century mansion at no. 6, now an art college, where Hungary's greatest king was born in 1440. Mátyás Corvinus was the son of Iancu de Hunedoara, and thus a Romanian, as a plaque added by Funar (see p.209) in 1999 makes clear (however, Magyar myth makes his father the illegitimate son of the Hungarian King Sigismund, and this was virtually a place of pilgrimage for Hungarians in Hapsburg days). Continuing north, Strada Corvin leads into Piaţa Muzeului, where Roman ruins have recently been excavated (and covered again) in the centre. Just to the left of the square, at Str. Daicovici 2, is the **History Museum of Transylvania** (Tues–Sun 10am–4pm; Ⓦwww .museum.utcluj.ro). On the first floor, strange skulls and mammoth tusks are succeeded by arrow- and spearheads, charting progress from the Neolithic and Bronze Ages to the rise of the Dacian civilization, which reached its peak between the second century BC and the first century AD; a reconstruction of Sarmizegetusa, the Dacians' highland citadel, is included in models and pictures. On the floor above, the story continues up to World War I, but this is a fairly standard display, with information in Romanian only.

At the east end of the square, the **Franciscan church** was built after the Tatar attack in the thirteenth century and handed over to the Domincan order by Iancu de Hunedoara in 1455; it was transferred to the Franciscans in 1725 and subsequently rebuilt in the Baroque style. Adjoining the church to the north, a fine Gothic house is home to a music school, and there are more Roman foundations opposite this. By the river, to the north, the Tranzit art centre

(fairly inactive in summer) has taken over a former synagogue at the rear of S'
Bariţiu 18. To the west is the city's park, with pedalos on a lake and a casino
its far end; near the river, the Academy of Visual Arts occupies an orange building with a few statues outside.

The university area

From Piaţa Unirii, Strada Napoca leads west to the **Students' Club** and the
old library on Piaţa Blaga, and Strada Universităţii heads south past the
Baroque church of the Piarist Order (1718–24) to the **Babeş–Bolyai
University**. Since its foundation in 1581, as a Jesuit Academy, the university
has produced scholars of the calibre of Edmund Bordeaux Székely (translator
of the Dead Sea Scrolls), but has also served as an instrument of cultural oppression. Long denied an education in their own language, the Romanians
promptly banned teaching in Hungarian once they took over in 1919, only to
hurriedly evacuate students and staff when Hitler gave northern Transylvania
back to Hungary in 1940. After liberation, separate universities were created to
provide education in the mother tongues of the two main communities, and
for a while it seemed that inequality was a thing of the past. However, in 1959
the authorities decreed a shotgun merger, enforced by a then little-known
cadre called Nicolae Ceauşescu, which led to the suicide of the Bolyai's
pro-rector, and, more predictably, a rapid decline in its Hungarian-language
teaching. This and a similar running down of primary and secondary schooling convinced many Magyars that the state was bent on "de-culturizing" them.
In 1997, it was decided to demerge the university, but this time it has found a
genuinely multicultural vocation, with teaching in both languages as well as the
first Jewish Studies courses in Romania. The **University Museum** at Str.
Brătianu 22 (Mon, Fri 11am–3pm, Thurs 10am–2pm, Tues & Wed noon–4pm),
lays out its complex history.

Outside the university's main door stand statues of Samuil Micu, Gheorghe
Şincai and Petru Maior, the leaders of the **School of Transylvania** (Şcoala
Ardeleana) whose philological and historical researches in Blaj fuelled the
Romanian cultural resurgence of the nineteenth century and the resistance to
Magyarization. They inspired the "generation of 1848", including Avram
Iancu, who lived as a student in 1841–44 at Str. Avram Iancu 17; nearby, flower
and coffin shops mark out the gate of the **cemetery** at no. 26 (March–Oct
6.30am–7.30pm; Nov–Feb 8am–5.30pm); the cave scientist Emil Racoviţa and
his family lie on the left as you go up to the graves of Kós Károly (see box on
p.197) and the writer Emil Isac, both on the right. Cutting across below
Károly's final resting place to the next avenue east, you'll find the grand grave
of the composer Nicolae Bretan at the junction, and the dramatist Szentgyörgy
István (1842–1931) on the right just below.

At Str. Bilaşcu (formerly Republicii) 42, just south of the university, are the
Botanical Gardens (daily 9am–7pm), the largest in southeastern Europe, with
more than 10,000 species. They contain a museum and herbarium, greenhouses
(to 6pm) with desert and tropical plants including Amazon waterlilies two
metres across, and a small Japanese garden. The gardens attract 600,000 visitors
a year, including newlyweds seeking the perfect backdrop for their photos.

East to Piaţa Ştefan cel Mare

The tree-lined Strada Kogălniceanu runs east from the university to the
Calvinists' **Reformed church**, built in 1486–1516 for Mátyás Corvinus, with
a pulpit added in 1646. Outside the church stands a copy of the statue of

St George and the Dragon in Prague's Hradčany castle – one of the world's most famous equestrian statues – made in 1373 by the masters Martón and György of Kolozsvár (Martin and George of Cluj). The church's interior is plain late Gothic stonework above the stalls and wooden panels, decorated with the coats of arms of all the leading Hungarian families of Transylvania. The ornate organ (1766) in the gallery, added in 1912, above the west door, is used for recitals. If the church is closed, the key is available at Str. Kogălniceanu 21.

Just east of the church is the restored fifteenth-century **Tailors' Bastion** (Turnul Croitorilor) on Piaţa Baba Novac, supposedly containing a branch of the History Museum (see p.214), but this is always closed. North of the bastion is an elongated square; its southern end, Piaţa Ştefan cel Mare, is dominated by the yellow and white facade of the **Romanian National Theatre and Opera House**, built in 1906 by the ubiquitous Viennese theatre architects Fellner and Helmer. On its north side, in Piaţa Avram Iancu, is the notorious statue of Avram Iancu commissioned by Funar (see box on p.209). The huge and startling **Orthodox Cathedral** (6am–8pm, closed 1–5pm Mon & Sat) looms beyond the statue; although built in 1921–33, the cathedral looks as if it fell through a time warp from Justinian's Constantinople. It was raised to celebrate the Romanians' triumph in Transylvania, and the neo-Byzantine stone facade hides a concrete structure. Inside, the gold mosaic Virgin and Child in the apse, above the silver iconostasis, bears the ugly heavy-handedness characteristic of the 1950s, when Socialist Realism was the prescribed mode.

From here, the most direct route back to the centre is along Bulevardul Eroilor, at the east end of which is Funar's *Memorandum* monument, commonly known as *The Guillotine*. At B-dul Eroilor 10 you'll see the Greco-Catholic cathedral of the Transfiguration, a Baroque pile built for the Minorites in 1775–79; other fine buildings are the Cinema Victoria (at the east end of the street) and nos. 42 and 49. Alternatively, you can take Bulevardul 21 Decembrie 1989, starting by the fine Secession prefecture and passing Unitarian and Evangelical churches, both Baroque, to end up at the Pharmacy Museum (see p.214).

West of Piaţa Unirii

The city's main east–west axis runs across the northern edge of Piaţa Unirii – to the east of the square as Bulevardul 21 Decembrie 1989 and westwards as

Strada Memorandumului. At Str. Memorandumului 21, the palace where the Transylvanian Diet met in 1790–91 (and where the 1894 trial of the Memorandumists was held), now houses the main branch of the **Ethnographic Museum** (closed for renovation in 2004, normally Tues–Sun 9am–5pm), containing what is probably Romania's finest collection of traditional carpets and folk costumes – from the dark herringbone patterns of the Pădureni region to the bold yellow, black and red stripes typical of Maramureş costumes. While blouses and leggings might be predominantly black or white, women's apron-skirts, and the waistcoats worn by both sexes for special occasions, are brilliantly coloured. Peacock feathers serve in the Năsăud area as fans or plumes, and the love of complicated designs spills over onto cups, masks, distaffs (used as an application for marriage), and linked spoons (used as a charm against divorce). The museum also has an excellent **open-air section** (Tues–Sun 9am–4pm) to the northwest of town on the Hoia hill, with peasant houses and three wooden churches from the surrounding areas; it's a thirty-minute walk from the centre, or you can take bus #27 from the station or #30 from Piaţa Unirii to Strada Haţeg (Cartier Grigorescu), and then head ten minutes north from there up Strada Tăietura Turcului.

Strada Memorandumului continues west from the museum to the splendidly towered city hall, where it becomes Calea Moţilor. At no. 84 is the **Cock Church**, a beautiful Calvinist church built in 1913 by Kós Károly (see box on p.197), who designed everything down to the light fittings, all with a cock motif symbolizing St Peter's threefold denial of Christ before cockscrow; ask for the key at the parish office behind the church. The architectural conservation group Utilitas is accommodated in Kós's first house, built for his parents at Str. Breaza 14, north of the train station. Further west is the **Mănăştur** quarter, the oldest part of Cluj, although you wouldn't know it from the serried ranks of 1980s apartment blocks – the best **views** are from the Calea Mănăştur flyover, where you can see ancient earthworks to the south and a relatively modern shrine and belfry atop them. Behind these is the **Calvaria church**, built by the Magyars in the twelfth century and rebuilt by the Benedictines in 1466; it's a Gothic hall-church, simple but surprisingly high, recently restored and with a new belfry.

Eating

The best **restaurants** in Cluj serve **Transylvanian** food, with a heavy Hungarian influence – notably the *Red House*, south of the centre at Str. Brâncuşi 114 (☎0264/442 186); the *Matei Corvin* at Str. Matei Corvin 3 (☎0264/597 496; to 11pm); and *The Feast*, Str. Einstein 9. *Agape*, Str. Iuliu Maniu 6 (☎0264/406 523) is more Hungarian, with a self-service cafeteria (Mon–Fri 11am–9pm) on the ground floor and six salons (noon–midnight) upstairs, as well as a *panzió*. More Romanian fare is on offer at the *Roata*, Str. Alex. Ciura 6A, off Str. Isac (☎0264/592 022), which is meat-heavy but unkitschy; *Hubertus* at B-dul 21 Decembrie no. 22 (☎0264/596 743; noon–11pm) which has occasional live music; the *Vărzărie*, at B-dul Eroilor 35 (9am–9pm), which serves the local speciality, *varza clujeana* (cabbage baked with mince, rice and sour cream); and the *Luciana*, B-dul Eroilor 51 (until 11pm), where there's a menu of the day for under €2. The best of the hotel restaurants, again serving typical Romanian fare, is the *Continental* (see p.211), with its splendid décor.

Of the rash of Italian and pseudo-**Italian** joints that's taking over the city, the nicest are the *Rex* at Str. Bolyai 9 (☎0264/596 430), and *Napoca Cincisprezece* at Str. Napoca 15 (☏0264/590 655; til 10pm); nearby at Str. Napoca 6, the *Yasmina* is a cheap and informal **Middle Eastern** place, open daily till late, and next to it *Speedy* and *Acapulco* are Oriental fast food places. The best **pizza** in Cluj is at the *New Croco*, Str. Babeş 12 (☏0264/590 213; to 11pm); **takeaways** can be had at *Marty Caffé*, Calea Moţilor 58 (☏0264/431 863) and *Marty Caffé II*, Str. Babeş 39 (☏0264/591 212). There's very good **Chinese** food at *Shanghai*, Str. Brâncuşi 98 (☏0264/409 905; noon–midnight) and *Hao Yi*, Str. Piteşti 11 (☏0264/430 298), while *Kokoro*, Str. Grigorescu 34 (☏0264/420581) – the only **Japanese** place in Transylvania – serves authentic and inexpensive dishes. **Greek** food is available at *Akropolis*, Calea Moţilor 40 (☏0744/549 700).

For **fast food**, the *Hungry Bunny*, Piaţa Unirii 12 (till at least midnight), offers such delights such as *pizza a la kebab*; there are two *placintarie* and giros places on Str. Bolyai, just off Bulevardul Eroilor, and studenty fastfood joints and bars on Str. Piezişă, an attractively tumble-down lane on the far side of the Strada Clinicilor university campus. VelPitar and Paniro are private chains of good **bakeries** with outlets on all the main streets.

Cafés and bars

To sample some of Cluj's **café** life, head for *Crema* at Piaţa Unirii 25 – a pleasant place to relax and watch the world go by, with a yuppy clientele; next door, *Flowers* is a tea house, like the smoke-free *Café Amadeus Mozart* at Str. Hossu (formerly Pavlov) 7. Classier places include the *Escorial*, an excellent cellar bar-restaurant with quiet music at Piaţa Unirii 23; *Bulgakov*, Str. Klein 17; *Club 30 Plus*, Str. Avram Iancu 29; and *Insomnia*, Str. Iuliu Maniu 4. Others include the *Roland Garros* with a riverside balcony, at Str. Horea 2, and the nearby *River* and *Samus*. Studenty bars can be found on Strada Napoca, including the *Cin-Cin* at no. 7, serving hot wine (*vin fiert*) in winter; there's also the *Tineretului* at Str. Universităţii 3, and the *Croco* student bar on Piaţa Blaga. There are relatively few **beer gardens** (*gradinas*) in central Cluj: the *Terasa Muzeu*, in the court of the Art Museum at Piaţa Unirii 17, has a nice setting but a limited choice of beers; the *Etno*, in the courtyard of the Ethnographic Museum at Str. Memorandumului 21, is similar. There are also nice places along Strada Hossu in the gardens of the Art School at no. 23 and *Club Italia* at no. 27. Cluj's actors hang out till midnight at the *Art Club*, Piaţa Ştefan cel Mare 14.

Entertainment

For late-night **music**, the *Diesel Jazz Bar*, in the cellars of Piaţa Unirii 17 (☏0264/598 441), is trendy but has terrible service, while the *Music Pub* at Str. Horea 5 (☏0264/432 517), another smokey cellar, is patronized largely by Hungarian students and has somewhat alternative music. The hottest new **club** (with its own underground parking) is *H2O*, Calea Turzii 203A (☏0264/406 344); others include the *Negro*, Str. Observatorului 34; *Atlantic* in the Mănăştur Cinema, Str. Bucegi; and *Wake-Up*, Str. Pasteur 77. Cluj also has a good range of **cinemas**, including the Republicii on Piaţa Mihai Viteazul (cheap entry on Mon); Arta-Eurimages, Str. Universităţii 3 (cheap on Tues); Victoria, B-dul Eroilor 51 (cheap on Wed); and Favorit, Str. Horea 6 (cheap on Thurs). The **Transylvania International Film Festival** takes place in Cluj in the last week of May.

Tickets for the Romanian **theatre** (mid-Sept to late June) can be bought next door to the *Art Club* (see above). Tickets for the State Philharmonic can be booked at Str. Kogălniceanu (Mon–Fri 11am–5pm).

Shopping

Cluj's main **department store**, the Central, is at Str. Regele Ferdinand 22, opposite the post office. Sora, 21 Decembrie 1989 no. 5, is a shopping arcade with a **supermarket** in the basement. There's also a Billa supermarket on Calea Floreştilor in Manǎstur, and a Metro hypermarket beyond it on the western edge of the city. The AgroFlip delicatessen on Piaţa Mihai Viteazul has a fair choice of imported goods and is open until 10pm (6pm on Saturday), with a smaller branch at B-dul Eroilor 17; also on Piaţa Mihai Viteazul at no. 8, the Napolact shop sells its own dairy products and other foods. **Outdoor gear** can be found at Polartek Sports, Str. Universitǎţii 8, Atta, Str. Moţilor 32, and Trakking and Sport House, both at Str. Dacia 1. Ziare, Str. Regele Ferdinand 1, and a kiosk at Piaţa Unirii 12 stock **magazines** such as *Newsweek* and *The Economist*. For English-language **books**, try the university bookstore at the corner of Piaţa Unirii and Str. Universitǎţii, which also has good dictionaries and books on Romanian ethnography and arts, and some French, German and Hungarian-language titles. Gaudeamus, Str. Iuliu Maniu 3, has books and maps in English; English Club, Str. Avram Iancu 29, just sells English dictionaries and childrens' books.

Piaţa Mihai Viteazul: a daily food **market**, and on Thursdays a craft market selling wood carvings and embroidery from the Apuseni highlands and the Transylvanian Heath.

Listings

Airlines TAROM, Piaţa Mihai Viteazul 11 ☎0264/432 669; Carpatair, at the airport ☎0264/416 016, ✆cluj-napoca@carpatair.ro; Happy Tour, Str. Horea 2 ☎0264/433 933; ✆cluj@happytour.ro; Lufthansa, at Str. Horea 1 ☎0264/433 124, ⊕www.aerotravel.ro.

Banks and exchange There are plenty of Bancomat cash machines, including at Piaţa Unirii 5, 17, 23 & 31, Piaţa Blaga, Piaţa Mihai Viteazul, Str. Regele Ferdinand 7 & 33, and B-dul Eroilor 36, as well as three opposite the rail station and at the airport. BCR, at Str. Bariţiu 10, also cashes travellers' cheques.

Car rental Avis, at *Hotel Victoria*, B-dul 21 Decembrie 1918 no. 54 ☎0264/439 403, 433 124 and at the airport ☎0723/260 105; Europcar c/o Jet-Tour at airport; Hertz c/o Calibra, Piaţa Unirii 11, book in advance on ☎021/337 2910, ✆office@hertz.eunet.ro; PanTravel (see below); Rodna Rentacar ☎0745/636 063, ⊕www .rodna-trans.ro; TopCar, Clinicilor 33 ☎0264/450 500, ✆450 709.

Consulate US Embassy Information Office, Str. Universitǎţii 7 ☎0264/593 815, ✆office .usembassy@cluj.astral.ro.

Internet access Bull-Net Club, at Dacos bus terminal; Cezar, Str. Horea 26; Club Internet, Str. Bariţiu 2 & B-dul Eroilor 37; Codec, Str. Iuliu Maniu 2; Computer Zone, Str. Cuza Vodǎ 40; DNT Club, Str. Iuliu Maniu 4; GoldNet, Str. Bolyai 4; KetNet,

Str. Raţiu 4; Kiro, Str. Bolyai 1; Millenium, Piaţa Mihai Viteazul 39 & Str. Şaguna 15 ; Net Zone, Piaţa Muzeului 5; Supernet, Str. Iuliu Maniu 1; Total Net, Str. Isac 2; Virtual World, B-dul Eroilor 37.

International bus tickets Amad Turistik, Str. Titulescu 4 ☎ & ✆0264/414 483; AtlasSib, Piaţa Mihai Viteazul 11, bloc D, ap. 1, Str. Voiteşti 3 ☎0264/433 432, ✆432 833; Avetour, Str. Şincai 2 & B-dul 21 Decembrie 1989 no. 8 ☎0264/596 257; Axis Travel, B-dul Eroilor 47; Bohoris Express, in *Hotel Napoca* ☎0264/580 715; Calibra, Piaţa Unirii 11 t0264/590 808, ✆calibra@mail.dntcj.ro; Eurolines, in *Hotel Victoria*, B-dul 21 Decembrie 1989 no. 54 ☎ & ✆0264/431 961, ✆cluj@eurolines.ro; Mihu-Reisen, c/o Napoca Tours, in *Hotel Napoca* ☎0264/580 927, ✆420 020, and c/o Unifix-Tour, Str. Poştei 5 ☎0264/430 425; Ognivia c/o Denarius (see above; TransEuropa, B-dul Eroilor 10 ☎0264/590 090; Kameleon Trans, Str. S. Micu 6 ☎0264/591 697; Optimus, Str. Gen. Grigorescu 12 ☎0264/584 966, ✆optimus@idilis.ro; Tihanyi Travel, Str. S. Micu 6 ☎0264/439 385, ⊕www.foltnet.hu/tihanyi; TransEuropa, B-dul Eroilor 10 ☎0264/211 296, ✆office@transeuropa.ro; Transervice, c/o Napoca Tours (see above).

Libraries British Library, Str. Arany Janos 11; American Library, Deutsches Institut & French Cultural Centre, Str. Brǎtianu 22; American Cultural Centre, Str. Iuliu Maniu 22.

Pharmacy The weekend rota is posted in the southeast corner of Piaţa Unirii; Cynara, Calea Floreşti 75 ☎0264/426 272 is open 24hr. Sensiblu, Str. Clinicilor 8 (8am–10pm) is a good modern place by a hospital. For medicinal plants, try Hypericum, Str. Horea 4, or B-dul Eroilor 7; you can find traditional Chinese medicines at Piaţa Unirii 2.

Police Str. Decebal 28 ☎112.

Post office Str. Regele Ferdinand 33. Mon–Fri 7am–8.30pm, Sat 7am–1pm.

Telephone office Directly behind the post office and also on the south side of Piaţa Unirii. Daily 7am–10pm.

Train tickets Agenţia CFR at Piaţa Mihai Viteazul 20. Mon–Fri 7am–6pm.

Travel agents and tour operators Agenţia Km 0, Str. Regele Ferdinand 20 ☎0264/591 114, ℻596 557; Agrotrip, Str. Regele Ferdinand 29/6 ☎ & f0264/406 363, ℮office@agrotrip.ro; Air Transilvania, Piaţa Ştefan cel Mare 14 ☎0264/593 245, ℻594 963; Eximtur, Str. Şguna 34 ☎ & f0264/592 475, ℮travel @eximtur.ro; Marshal Turism, Piaţa Mihai Viteazul 9A ☎0264/434 038, ⓦwww.marshal.ro; Pan Travel, Str. Grozăvescu 13 ☎ & f0264/420 516, ⓦwww.pantravel.ro; Student Travel, Str. Avram Iancu 32 ☎0269/592 885, ℮info@studenttravel.ro; Travel Linea Blu, B-dul 1 Decembrie 1918 no. 54 ☎0264/591 037, ℮lineablu@cluj.astral.ro; Unita, Piaţa Unirii 10.

The Apuseni mountains

The **Apuseni mountains** are bordered to the south by the Arieş valley and to the north by the Crişul Repede valley, enabling public transport to reach a variety of access points into the range. From Turda, the **Arieş valley** runs west, between the Apuseni massif to the north, and various smaller ranges such as the Trascău and Metaliferi (Metal Bearing) mountains to the south. The DN75 follows the valley as far as Câmpeni – capital of the **Moţi high-landers** – where one road heads west into the Bihor, and another runs south to Brad and Alba. Having successfully resisted the Roman conquest, the Moţi moved from the valleys into the hills in the eighteenth century when the Hapsburgs attempted to conscript them into the army, and they now live all year round at up to 1400m, some of the highest settlements in Romania, in scattered groups of high-roofed, thatched cottages. **Buses** run east along the valley to Turda and on to Cluj in the early morning and return west more or less hourly through the afternoon; there are also plenty of services from Alba Iulia to Câmpeni. Along the **Crişul Repede valley**, most Accelerat trains stop only at Huedin, Ciucea and Aleşd, but the less frequent Personal services give opportunities for exploration by stopping at every hamlet along the line.

A **national park**, first proposed in 1924, is at last being created in the mountains – despite opposition from the forestry and other industries – but uranium mines, which actually make large losses, remain open as the government dare not close them down due to the jobs (and votes) at stake, and Europe's largest opencast gold mine is now being planned beneath Roşia Montana (see p.225), despite the massive environmental impact.

Turda

TURDA (Torda) lies 30km south of Cluj along the main DN1 (€60/81). Thanks to salt mining, this was once one of the wealthiest towns in the country. The modern Turda, with its 58,000 mainly Magyar inhabitants, is ringed by filthy factories, but beyond these is still a surprisingly elegant centre. The main reasons to come here, however, are to visit the spectacular **Turda gorge**, 8km to the west, and to explore the Arieş valley beyond, in the foothills of the Apuseni mountains.

On the broad main street, Piaţa Republicii, stand two Gothic churches: the lower one, built between 1387 and 1437, is Calvinist, and the upper one is Roman Catholic (built in 1478–1504 and rebuilt in 1822 after a fire), with a Baroque interior and façade. It housed meetings of the Transylvanian Diet, including the promulgation of the 1568 **Edict of Turda**, which recognized the equality of four faiths – Calvinist, Lutheran, Roman Catholic and Unitarian – in Transylvania at a time when religious wars were all the rage in Europe. However, it merely tolerated Orthodoxy, the religion of the Vlachs, and contributed to the ethnic and religious discrimination against them. Christianity has a long history in Turda – fifth-century Christian tombs have been found among Roman remains, and these can be seen in the **museum** in the fifteenth-century Voivodal Palace (closed for renovation at the time of writing) at B-dul Haşdeu 2, behind the Calvinist church. The **salt mine**, or *salina*, at the northern edge of town at Strada Salinelor 54 (☎0264/311 690; daily 9am–5pm, last entry 3.30pm; €1) is worth a visit. Take bus #10 or #42 or walk for fifteen minutes along Strada Avram Iancu (which becomes Strada Mureşanu after the hospital) to a lovely leafy park shading another attractive Calvinist church to the east. From here, Strada Basarabiei heads past the north side of the church and (as Strada Tunel) to the mine, where a three-hundred-metre-long tunnel leads to huge hangar-like chambers, gradually excavated over 250 years, with stout wooden staircases leading ever further downwards.

Practicalities

Turda is well served by **buses** from Cluj, picking up at Piaţa Ştefan cel Mare, and by **maxitaxis** from Piaţa Ştefan cel Mare at Strada Brătianu, which drop off at the TransArieş kiosk north of the Catholic church. Longer-distance services stop at the new Autogara Sens Vest (☎0264/315 799; Mon–Fri 6.30am–9pm, Sat & Sun 6.30–9am & 1–7.30pm) below the town centre near Piaţa Romana, the roundabout where the DN75 (the Arieş valley road) leaves town. **Trains** stop at the town of Câmpia Turzii, 9km east; from the station; take bus #20 to Piaţa Republicii. There's just one central hotel in Turda itself, the *Potaissa*, at Piaţa Republicii 6 (☎0264/311 691, ☏311 771; ❸). The cheaper *Arieşul* (☎0264/316 844, ☏311 124; ❷) and *Bradul* (☎0264/315 029; ❷) lie just beyond the town's salt baths (take the Ştrand bus, #15) and the simple *Imperial* (☎0745/259 194; ❷), at no. 65A in Tureni, on the road to Cluj. The *Potaissa* has a **restaurant**, or there's the *Pizzeria Dana* at Piaţa Romană, as well as coffee shops around Piaţa Republicii. The Matrix **Internet** centre is at Piaţa Republicii 16.

The Turda gorge

The impressive **Turda gorge** (Cheile Turzii) is a two-hour walk from town, following red and blue cross markings west from Piaţa Romană. Catching a bus towards Corneşti and Moldoveneşti will take you part of the way – get off at the turning 2km beyond Mihai Viteazu (where there's a small Gothic church and a restaurant-pension) and continue north on foot for 5km. Either way, you'll end up at the cabana (❶) and campsite just before the gorge itself. From here, a footpath, marked with red stripes and crosses, heads north up the gorge, overshadowed by three-hundred-metre-high cliffs containing caves formerly used as hideouts by outlaws. The unique microclimate provides a habitat for plant species otherwise found only on the shores of the Mediterranean or in Central Asia; there are more than a thousand here, as well as 111 bird species,

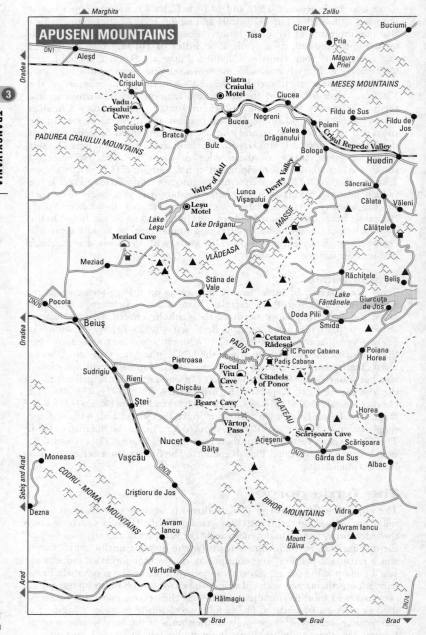

APUSENI MOUNTAINS

▲ Marghita   ▲ Zalău

DN1
Oradea ◄
Aleşd
Vadu
Crişului
Vadu
Crişului
Cave
Şuncuiuş   Bratca

PADUREA CRAIULUI MOUNTAINS

Bulz

Tusa   Cizer
Pria   Buciumi
*Măgura
Priei*

MESEŞ MOUNTAINS

Piatra
Craiului
Motel
Bucea   Ciucea
Negreni
Valea
Drăganului
Poieni
Fildu de Sus
Fildu de
Jos

Crişul Repede Valley

Bologa   Huedin

Valley of Hell

Lunca
Vişagului   *Devil's Valley*   Sâncraiu
Călata   Văleni
Călăţele

Leşu
Motel

*Lake
Leşu*   *Lake Drăganu*   *MASSIF*

Meziad Cave

Meziad

VLĂDEASA

Stâna de
Vale

Răchiţele   Beliş

*Lake
Fântânele*   Giurcuţa
de Jos

DN76
Pocola

Beiuş

Doda Pilii
Smida

Poiana
Horea

Pietroasa

PADIS

**Cetatea
Rădesei**

IC Ponor Cabana
Padiş Cabana

Sudrigiu
Rieni
Chişcău

Ştei

**Focul
Viu
Cave**

**Citadels
of Ponor**

Bears' Cave

PLATEAU

Horea

**Vârtop
Pass**   **Scărişoara Cave**

Nucet   Băiţa

Arieşeni   DN75
Scărişoara

Gârda de Sus   Albac

Moneasa

Vaşcău   *CODRU-MOMA MOUNTAINS*

Dezna

Cristioru de Jos

Avram
Iancu

BIHOR MOUNTAINS

Vidra

Avram
Iancu

*Mount
Găina*

Vârfurile

Hălmagiu

Arad ◄   Oradea ◄   Sebiş and Arad ◄

DN76

DN74

▼ Brad   ▼ Brad   ▼ Brad

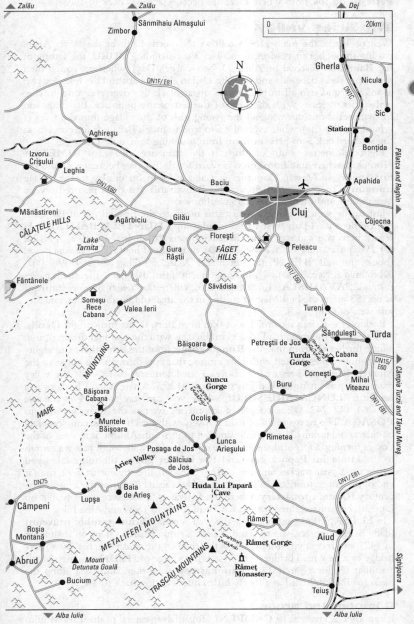

Pălatca and Reghin ►

Câmpia Turzii and Târgu Mureș ►

Sighișoara ►

including golden eagles and rock vultures. After around 3km, the path ends at **Petreştii de Jos**, from where there are occasional buses back to Turda.

The Arieş valley

West of Turda, the main DN75 follows the north bank of the River Arieş, passing through a succession of small villages including **BURU**, the setting of the **Babaluda festival** on April 23 (St George's Day), when six young men dress up: two as Babaluda and his wife, clad in cherry bark and birch leaves; two as soldiers; and two all in black, who smear black dye over everyone, forcing evil spirits to leave. With the help of the rest of the populace, Babaluda and his wife set about throwing all the young girls of the village into the river (a typical fertility rite), while everyone also tries to touch Babaluda for good luck; the soldiers' task is to prevent them from touching him, unless they pay.

Eight kilometres south of Buru is the attractive village of **RIMETEA** (Torockó), where traditional dress is worn for festivals on February 22 and the first Sunday of March. Costumes can also be seen on display in the village **museum** (Tues–Sun 9am–5pm). The Transylvania Trust has restored several houses here and there are several guesthouses.

Just to the west of Buru, a road turns north to the tiny village of Băişoara, from where it's 14km west to the single-slope **MUNTELE BĂIŞORII** ski resort; here, you can stay at the *Băişoara* cabana (T0264/314 569, F311 124; ❶), *Pensiunea Mini* (T0264/595 285; ❷), or the good new *BTT Băişoara* hostel (book through BTT, Piaţa Ştefan cel Mare 5, Cluj; T0264/598 067, Ebttcluj@zortec.ro; ❶). Continuing north from Băişoara, the road passes through **SĂVĂDISLA** (Turdaszentlászló), where the *Tamás Bistro* **restaurant** at no.153 offers the best Magyar cuisine in the area, and finishes at Luna de Sus, just west of Cluj.

Back on the Arieş valley road, it's 14km from Buru to the turn-off for **Ocoliş**, 4km north of the main road (don't confuse this with the Ocolişel turning), and, a little further up from that, the **Runcu gorge**; from the latter, there's an eight- to ten-hour hike, marked with blue crosses, that cuts through the gorge to the Muntele Băişorii ski resort (see above). Four kilometres past Ocoliş, the valley road runs past an unmarked junction at km126.5, where a road leads over a bridge to **LUNCA ARIEŞULUI**, where you can stay at the *Vila Ramona* (T0264/147 742; ❶); a couple of kilometres west is the turning north to **POŞAGA**. The next stretch of road is lovely, with beech woods, conglomerate boulders, and at km121.5 a small waterfall to its south. Almost 5km west of the Posaga turning, a footbridge signals the start of a day-walk south past watermills to the **Huda lui Papară cave** and **the Râmeţ gorge**; the route takes you either on a goat track along the cliff, or through the stream itself. At the far end of the gorge, tourists can stay in the *Râmeţ* cabana (❶), near the fourteenth-century **Râmeţ monastery**; where the festival of St Ghelasie is celebrated on June 30. From here, three buses a day head south to Teiuş and Alba Iulia.

In **LUPŞA**, 75km west of Turda, the well-regarded **ethnographic museum** (daily 8am–noon & 2–6pm) stands below a stone church raised on its hillock in 1421 and recently restored. Across the river to the south, reached by a footbridge or a new road bridge 1km west, is the village of **Hădărău**, which boasts a similar Gothic church. **Lupşa monastery** is another 2km west along the main road at km90; it has a lovely little church dating back to 1429.

Câmpeni and around

It's another 12km west to **CÂMPENI** (Topánfalva), capital of the Ţara Moţilor and a possible base for forays into the mountains. The town is well served by buses, which arrive at the station just east of the centre beyond the market. The best hotel is the *Hanul Moților* (☎0258/771 824; ❷), which has a *crama* and pizzeria; it's just north of the awful *Tulnic* hotel at Piaţa Avram Iancu 1. The town's **Avram Iancu Museum**, in his old headquarters by the river on the corner of Strada Revoluției 1848, is decrepit but functional, though opening times are erratic. There's a good supermarket opposite, and two simple **restaurants** and a **post office** on the semi-pedestrianised square west of the *Tulnic*.

From Câmpeni, the DN74A leads 10km south to Abrud, passing on the way a turning for **ROŞIA MONTANĂ**, 7km to the east. Transylvania was a major source of gold throughout history, with the Dacians the first to dig here, then the Romans; others followed more or less continuously and in the 1970s, Ceauşescu's open-cast mining here demolished the entire Cetate massif. Now there are plans to create Europe's largest open-cast gold mine beneath Roşia Montana, which is to be largely demolished, along with its attractive Baroque houses and historic mining tunnels; a campaign against the project is gathering momentum. Roman lamps, tombstones and wax tablets recording operational details can be seen in the **museum** at the mine, 2km before the village beside the Orlea hill.

From here, there's a one-hour walk (marked by red triangles) south to **ABRUD**. The old town, whose Baroque buildings incorporate stones from earlier Roman structures and are liberally adorned with plaques commemorating the many notables who visited when Abrud was the Moţi capital, is tatty but far more attractive than Câmpeni. From Piaţa Eroilor, the centre of the old town, there are buses to **BUCIUM POIENI**, 13km east and the centre of a *comuna* of six small mining villages; there's a Belgian-owned hostel here, and it's also the starting point for an hour's climb to two basalt towers known as the **Detunata**.

Gârda de Sus and around

From here, the DN75 continues another 15km through a gorge to **GÂRDA DE SUS**, a pretty village with a part-wooden church built in 1792, with naïve paintings inside; accommodation is available at the *Mama Uţa* pension–restaurant–camping (☎0258/627 901; ❷). More notably, it is the starting point for several excellent hikes, the most popular of which, marked with blue stripes, begins near the **campsite** and leads north through the Ordâncuşa gorges, past a mill and into a forest, ending after three hours at the village of **GHEŢARI**. This is named after the **Scărişoara ice cave** (Peştera gheţarul; daily 9am–5pm), a few minutes west of the village; filled with 70,000 cubic metres of ice, 15m thick, it has preserved evidence of climatic changes over the last 4000 years. At the back of the main chamber is the "church", so called because of its pillar formations.

Marked walking routes in this area link the cave with **Albac** and Horea's birthplace in **Fericet**, where a festival occurs in mid-August the village of **Horea** itself (reached by three buses a day from Câmpeni).

The Padiş plateau

The **Padiş plateau** (Plateul Padiş) is in the heart of a classic karst area, with streams vanishing underground and reappearing unexpectedly, and dips and hollows everywhere, all promising access to the huge cave and river systems that lie beneath the plateau. There are two or three buses from Monday to Friday (but none at weekends) departing Huedin for Răchiţele and Poiana Horea, from where it's an easy day's hike to the *Padiş* cabana (☎0788/561 223; ❶), which lies at the crossroads of the plateau and is the focal point for the Apuseni region's trails. Note that the *Padiş* has an open-air disco; a quieter (and cleaner) place to stay is the *Varişoaia* cabana (☎0788/601 815; ❶), about 2km northwest on the road towards Stâna de Vale.

Homestays are available in Răchiţele (bookable through Green Mountain Holidays – see p.227), while further south, 3km from Lake Fântânele in the village of **DODA PILII**, is the excellent (and aptly named) *Hotel Rustic* (☎0788/591 890; ❻ half-board), with trout fishing available. The comfortable new *Agroturism IC Ponor* cabana (☎0744/272 465, 0740/450 829, ✉agroturism_icponor@yahoo.com), with eight biggish *casuţe*, is at IC Ponor, two hours walk up the road from Padiş towards Răchiţele.

Hikes on the plateau

Of the various **trails** starting from the *Padiş* cabana, the most popular, marked with blue dots, is a three-hour hike south to the underground complex of **Cetăţile Ponorului** (Citadels of Ponor), where the Ponor stream flows through a series of sinkholes up to 150m deep. There's a good camping spot en route at Glavoi, a one-hour walk away, and the *Cetaţile Ponor* cabana (✉padis@email.ro; ❶) is just beyond Glavoi. A trail from the third hollow of the Ponor Citadels (marked by yellow dots) leads for 2km to the **Focul Viu** ice cave, and then (marked with red stripes) back to *Padiş*. Alternatively, you could head south from Ponor to Arieşeni (see p.329) in three hours following red triangles, or west from Focul Viu to Pietroasa (see p.328) in two-and-a-half hours, following yellow dots and triangles.

North of the *Padiş* cabana, you can hike to the **Cetatea Rădesei** cave; follow red stripes along a track to the forestry road and head north. Ten minutes beyond the Vărăşoaia pass, take another path (red dots) to the right to the citadel itself. Here you follow the stream through a cave – slightly spooky but quite safe, although a flashlight helps – and follow the overground route back (marked by red dots) to see the various skylights from above.

Other hikes simply follow forestry roads, west to Pietroasa (marked by blue crosses), east to Răchiţele or Poiana Horea (unmarked), or northwest to **Stâna**

de Vale (red stripes). This last route continues from Vărăşoaia, climbing to the Cumpănatelu saddle (1640m) and eventually turning right off the main ridge to descend through the forest to the resort (see p.328). Unlike most trails in the area, this six-hour walk is quite safe in winter.

The *Padiş* is also a five-hour hike southeast of Scărişoara (see opposite) along a marked track.

The Crişul Repede valley

From Cluj, the DN1 (E60) heads west along the verdant **Crişul valley**, shadowed for much of the way by the railway line. Ten trains a day run west to Oradea; buses are less frequent. **Cyclists** can take two lovely back roads through the valley that run parallel to the main DN1 to the south: from Leghia to Bologa, and from Bucea to Tileagd.

You'll find a rich choice of accommodation and camping options along or just off this route, including in **Gilău**, **Gura Răştii** (where the *Lui Pui* cabana offers hiking, kayaking, mountain-biking and tennis), **Valea Ierii** and **Izvoru Crişului** (Körösfő). Essentially one big bazaar selling Magyar arts and crafts, this last village has a seventeenth-century walled Calvinist church with an eighteenth-century painted ceiling, but is most important as the location of Green Mountain Holidays (☎0264/257 142, ⓦwww .greenmountainholidays.ro), a Belgian-run company that provides free information, sells maps, and arranges homestays and trips (including riding and walking tours with baggage transfers) throughout the Apuseni; it's at Str. Principală 305 but is likely to move to the east end of the village, where they'll have rooms.

The culture of the Kalotaszeg

The area immediately west of Cluj is known to Hungarians as **Kalotaszeg** and, since the great Hungarian Millennium Exhibition of 1896, it has been revered as the region where authentic Magyar culture has survived uncorrupted. It's common to see local people selling handicrafts by the roadside here – particularly to Hungarian tourists on pilgrimages to the wellsprings of Magyar culture.

The local **embroidery** is particularly famous, usually consisting of stylized leaves and flowers, in one bold colour (usually bright red) on a white background; the style is known as *írásos*, meaning "drawn" or "written", because the designs are drawn onto the cloth (traditionally with a mixture of milk and soot) before being stitched. The Calvinist churches of these villages are noted for their **coffered ceilings**, made up of square panels (known as "cassettes"), beautifully painted in the eighteenth century, along with the pews and galleries, in a naïve style similar to the embroidery. The architects of the National Romantic school, led by Kós Károly (see p.197), were strongly influenced by Transylvanian village architecture, as well as by that of the Finns, the Magyars' only ancestral relations.

The composers **Béla Bartók and Zoltán Kodály** amassed fine collections of Transylvanian handicrafts, and Bartók's assortment of carved furniture from Izvoru Crişului (Körösfő) can be seen in his home in Budapest. The composers' main project, however, was to collect the **folk music** of Transylvania. Starting in 1907, they managed to record and catalogue thousands of melodies, despite local suspicion of the "monster" (the apparatus for recording onto phonograph cylinders). Through the project, they discovered a rich vein of inspiration for their own compositions; Bartók declared that a genuine peasant melody was "quite as much a masterpiece in miniature as a Bach fugue or a Mozart sonata".

Huedin and Sâncraiu

HUEDIN (Bánffyhunyad), to the north of the Apuseni range and 46km west of Cluj, is a small town with a largely systematized centre; the chief reason for stopping here is to pick up buses to the surrounding valleys. Huedin's **train and bus stations** are just east and west respectively of the Zimbor road's level crossing, a five-minute walk north of the town centre. Most of the surrounding villages are served by two or three buses a day during the week, but the service is virtually nonexistent at weekends.

There's a good range of coffee shops in Huedin, but the town's only **hotel** is the *Motel Montana* (℡0264/253 090; ❷) at the eastern edge of town. **Homestays** are a better option, with at least two dozen (❶) available just on the main street of **SÂNCRAIU** (Kalotaszentkirály), known for its strong Magyar folklore and its thirteenth-century church, just 6km south; Green Mountain Holidays (see p.227) can arrange bookings and transfers, and bikes can be rented here.

Around Huedin

From Huedin, a minor road heads 9km south to the village of **Călata** (Nagykalota), where on Sundays the Magyar population still wear their home-made **folk costumes**, and on to the nearby village of **Călățele** (Kiskalota), where you'll see carved wooden homesteads. Sixteen kilometres beyond (connected to Huedin by three buses on weekdays) is **BELIŞ** (Jósikafalva), a village moved (along with its lovely wood church) from the valley when the artificial Lake Fântânele was created; there's now a small lakeside resort comprising two identical two-star hotels (both ℡0264/354 183), and a handful of homestays (bookable through Antrec, in Cluj). Hostel accommodation is also available at the *Popas Turistic Brădeţ* (May–Sept only; ℡0264/147 206; ❶); there's no campsite, but the hotels will allow you to pitch a tent.

MĂNĂSTIRENI (Magyargyerőmonostor) lies to the southeast of Huedin, on a minor road south from the DN1. The village has a lovely thirteenth-century walled Calvinist church whose gallery, pews and ceiling were beautifully painted in the eighteenth century; homestays can be arranged through Green Mountain Holidays (see p.227). Just west of here is **Văleni** (Magyarvalkó), where many of the houses have decorated mouldings. Another thirteenth-century Calvinist church here has a wonderful hilltop setting and a collection of carved wooden graveposts, more typical of the Székely Land.

In the valleys to the north of Huedin there are half a dozen villages with striking **wooden churches** – examples of the Gothic-inspired ones that once reared above peasant settlements from the Tisa to the Carpathians. The most spectacular, and the nearest to Huedin, towers over **Fildu de Sus** (Felsőfüld), a small village reached by a ten-kilometre track west from Fildu de Jos (Alsófüld) on the Huedin–Zalău road. Built in 1727, the church was painted in 1860, with scenes of Daniel in the den with some wonderful grinning lions. Two buses a day run from Huedin to Fildu de Sus, and the Huedin–Zalău bus passes through Fildu de Jos.

Ciucea and Bologa

Twenty kilometres west of Huedin, by road and rail, is the village of **CIUCEA** (Csucsa). Midway along the route lies **BOLOGA**, whose ruined fourteenth-century castle can be seen from the road and railway. There's a small but faded **hotel**, the *Romanţa* (℡0264/251 585; ❶) by the road and train halt. At the east end of the village is a **museum** (Tues–Sun 10am–5pm) dedicated to the poet and politician **Octavian Goga**, prime minister in 1937 for six chaotic weeks.

The Measurement of the Milk Festival

The practice of shepherds spending summer in the high pastures protecting the flocks from bears and wolves, and making cheeses for the community's winter sustenance has given rise to **Measurement of the Milk Festivals** (Măşurisul Laptelui), of which the best known is held by the villages around Ciucea on the slopes of Măgura Priei, the highest ridge in the Meseş range. At dawn on the first Sunday in May, the flocks are brought to a glade outside the village, where the "measurement" takes place. The she-goats are milked by women and the ewes by shepherds – the yield of each family's animals is measured to determine the quota of cheese that they will receive during that season. The ritual is followed by much feasting and dancing.

Măgura Priei is only ten kilometres or so north of Ciucea. During the festival, there are buses from Huedin to the event; at other times, a daily bus runs from Ciucea to Zalău via Cizer.

This house belonged to the wife of **Endre Ady**, the great figure of early modernist poetry in Hungary, who lived here until 1917; Goga bought it after his death in 1919 and had a sixteenth-century **wooden church** from Gălpâia brought here in order to preserve it. Later still, Goga's own mausoleum was built in the grounds. In Ciucea, the *Pension Caprioarea* on the main street (T0264/259 059; ❷) is good value.

Valea Drăganului and Valea Iadului

Two dramatically named valleys run south into the Apuseni mountains on either side of Ciucea, meeting at Stâna de Vale. To the east, the **Valea Drăganului** (Devil's Valley) runs from the train halt and tourist complex of the same name, passing through Lunca Vişagului, from where you can follow the forestry road south past a reservoir before tracing the track marked with blue crosses west to Stâna de Vale (see p.328). The road down the **Valea Iadului** (Valley of Hell) turns off the DN1 at the Piatra Craiului train station, by the wooden church of Bucea, and just east of the *Munţi Piatra Craiului* motel (T0259/341 756; ❷). Civilization ends after 25km, at the *Leşu* motel (❷), by the artificial lake of the same name; it's another 20km, past the Iadolina waterfall, to Stâna de Vale.

Northern Transylvania

The two counties of Sălaj and Bistriţa-Năsăud, covering the swath of ranges from the Apuseni mountains to the Eastern Carpathians, are historically referred to as **Northern Transylvania**. If you're travelling from Cluj to Maramureş, or eastwards over the Carpathians into Moldavia, road and rail routes are fast and direct, but it's well worth considering detours in this little-visited region. To the west, the chief attraction is the idyllic rural scenery of unspoilt Sălaj county, with its many old wooden churches.

Trains into Maramureş run via Jibou to Baia Mare, about two hours from Dej. The quickest road north is the DN1C to Baia Mare. Trains from Cluj into Moldavia run via Năsăud and the Ilva valley to Vatra Dornei and past several of the painted monasteries (see p.276). The DN17 heads east from Dej to Bistriţa and through the Bârgău valley to Vatra Dornei. Bistriţa and Năsăud, 22km apart, are linked by frequent buses, so it's easy to hop from one route to the other.

Bonţida, Gherla and Sic

From Cluj, both the DN1C (E576) and a rail line head north to nearby Gherla and Dej, passing **BONŢIDA** (Bonchida), site of a great Baroque palace (open daily; €0.50), visible from the road and railway. Its last owner was Miklos Banffy, a diplomat who was sent in 1944 to make peace with the advancing Red Army; in revenge, the retreating Germans virtually destroyed the palace. In 1999, the World Monuments Fund placed Bonţida on its list of the world's 100 most endangered monuments, and a Built Heritage Training Centre has since been established here, whereby craftsmen and architects will be trained while rebuilding the palace. A three-and-a-half-kilometre walk through the village brings you to its gateway; there's a café here (Tues–Fri 9–11am & 2–7pm, Sat & Sun 10am–7pm).

GHERLA (Szamosujvár/Neuschloss) has been a centre of Armenian settlement since 1672; carved Armenian family crests are still visible over many doorways, but the population is now assimilated with the local Hungarians. From the train station, it's three minutes west along Strada Avram Iancu to the Piaţa Libertăţii. The lurid green Baroque Armeno–Catholic **cathedral**, built between 1748 and 1798, stands on the square's south side; its greatest treasure is a painting of the *Descent from the Cross* by Rubens, which can be seen in a small chapel to the left of the choir (you may have to ask to see it). There's a pleasant park across the DN1C from the square; just to the northeast, at Str. Mihai Viteazul 6, the town **museum** (Mon-Fri 8am-3pm) houses its collection of Armenian manuscripts and icons on glass behind the superb gateway of a seminary, built in 1859. The only **hotel**, the *Vlamar*, is 15 minutes' walk south at Str. Clujului 4 (℡0264/243 173; ➋).

One of the best villages to hear traditional music in this area is **SIC** (Szék), 20km southeast of Gherla, with which it is linked by bus (7 daily). Sic spreads over several hills, with a number of churches and municipal buildings testifying to its former importance as a centre of salt mining. There's a high proportion of Magyars here, who wear costumes the like of which have long disappeared into museums – the men in narrow-brimmed, tall straw hats and blue waistcoats and the women in leather waistcoats and black headscarves embroidered with flowers, blouses and red pleated skirts. Every street in Sic seems to have its own band (normally consisting of just three musicians – on violin, viola and double bass), typically playing traditional ancient Magyar and Romanian melodies woven in with Gypsy riffs.

Dej

DEJ, 46km north of Cluj, lies at the junction of the two branches of the Someş river and the routes from Cluj to Maramureş and Bucovina. The town centre is a good kilometre to the north of the main train station, Dej Călători (bus #2, #3, #8 or #9); the bus station is almost as far on the other side of town – to reach the centre, take the path left across the rail line, cross the main road before the Peco station to Strada Pintea Viteazul and the footbridge across the Someş river to Strada Aleco Russo, and go through the park, heading for the spire of the **Reformed Church**, dominating Piaţa Bobâlna at the heart of the town. The **Municipal Museum** (Tues–Sun 9am–3pm) is at Piaţa Bobâlna 2, has good coverage of the neaby salt mines that drove the medieval economy here. At the **Military Museum** (Tues–Fri 8am–4pm), just south at Str. Petru Rareş 1, exhibits range from the Roman to the communist periods.

Dej has two **hotels**: the *Someş*, a decent enough 1970s tower block at Piaţa Mărăşeşti 1 (t0264/220 308, ℗216 982; ➌); and the better *Parc-Rex*, by the river at Str. Aleco Russo 9 (☎0264/213 799, Ⓕ211 325; ❸), which has good-sized rooms with private bath and cable TV, though be aware that it hosts strip-tease shows. There's an **Internet café** by the local bus terminal on Piaţa 16 Februarie, at Strada Titulescu, just east of the centre.

Zalău and around

ZALĂU, 23km west of Jibou, is little more than a small country town with a large industrial fringe grafted on since World War II, though the county **museum** at Str. Pieţei 9 (Tues–Sun 10am–6pm) has a good archaeological display, the best **hotel**, just to the north of the museum, is the *Meseş* (☎0260/661 050, Ⓕ613 093; ❻). There's a **restaurant** in the inside, as well as the *Restaurant Meseş* just below it; otherwise there's excellent pizza at *Champion* at the foot of Strada Gheorghe Doja. The **bus station** is about twenty minutes' walk north of the centre at Str. Mihai Viteazul 54, and the **train station** is a further thirty minutes north, at the south end of the village of Crişeni; buses #1 and #2 and maxitaxis link them both to the centre, taking about fifteen minutes from the train station. The town **festival** takes place on the Saturday nearest August 1.

Around Zalău

The Roman settlement of **Porolissum**, 12km east of Zalău, immediately south of the village of Moigrad (reached by bus #8 from Zalău's *autogară* and occasional buses to Jac), was founded in AD 106 to defend the northernmost limit of Roman Dacia, and grew to have a population of 25,000. The settlement's Praetorian Gate has been rebuilt, and you can still see the remains of the walls of the upper *castrum*; don't miss the **amphitheatre**, over the edge of the hill to the south, the largest public building known in Roman Dacia.

A couple of buses a day run south from Zalău to **Buciumi**, an old Romanian settlement noted for its local costumes and choral and flute music, which celebrates its festival on August 15, the Assumption of the Virgin. Rising to the west of Buciumi are the Meseş hills – rugged highlands that host the **Shepherds' Festival** (Măgura Priei) on the first Sunday of May.

The Vienna Diktat

On August 30, 1940, Hitler, needing Hungarian support in his new offensive against the Soviet Union, forced Romania to cede 43,492 square kilometres and 2.6 million people in northern Transylvania to Hungary in the **Vienna Diktat** (or Belvedere Treaty). The new border ran south of Cluj, Târgu Mureş and Sfântu Gheorghe and then more or less followed the watershed of the eastern Carpathians north to the border of what is now Ukrainian Transcarpathia. The border is still a living memory in these areas, and locals will be able to show you the earthworks that used to mark it.

Over 10,000 Romanians, mostly members of the educated classes, such as civil servants, teachers, lawyers and priests, were expelled in cattle trucks, some at just two hours' notice, and others after being subjected to mock executions. Atrocities were committed in the appropriated region by the Horthyist police, with 89 killed in the village of Treznea and 157 in Ip, both in Sălaj county, a pattern of cruelty that was repeated after the more extreme Sztójay Döme government took power in Budapest in March 1944 and the Hungarians, Hitler's last allies, retreated before the Red Army.

Năsăud and the Someş Mare valley

Twenty-five kilometres east of Dej lies the small town of **Beclean** (Bethlen), at the junction of routes north into Maramureş; this is the ancestral seat of the Bethlen family, which provided several distinguished governors of Transylvania. The road and rail routes to Vatra Dornei and Suceava in Moldavia also divide here, drivers heading southeast to Bistriţa while the train runs further north via Năsăud.

From **Salva**, 24km northeast of Beclean, road and rail routes head north to Maramureş; 9km along this road is the village of **COŞBUC**, named after its most famous son, **George Coşbuc** (1866–1918), poet and activist for Romanian cultural revival. His simple family home is now a **museum** (Tues–Sun 9am–5pm). **NĂSĂUD** (Nussdorf), 6km east of Salva, is at the heart of a region where villagers still wear their traditional embroidered waistcoats and blouses, and hats decorated with peacock feathers. A selection of these is on display in the **museum** at Str. Granicerilor 25. The sole **accommodation** in town is with Ancuţa Nistor of Transylvania Travel, Str. Valea Caselor 22a (ⓦ www.transylvaniatravel.from.ro; ❹), who offers student reductions and tours. Just 5km south of town along the Bistriţa road is the birthplace of **Liviu Rebreanu** (1885–1944), whose novels *Ion, Uprising* and *The Forest of the Hanged* give a panoramic view of Romanian society before World War I.

The Someş Mare valley

Twenty kilometres east of Năsăud lies Ilva Mică, the junction of a minor branch line that provides access to the shabby spa town of **SÂNGEORZ-BĂI**, a good starting point for hikes north into the Rodna mountains (see p.316). The refurbished *Vila Lotus* on Strada Izvoarelor provides the best value **accommodation**; otherwise, there's the large but rather impersonal *Hebe*, Str. Izvoarelor 94 (☎0263/370 228, ⓕ370 035; ❷), and guesthouses such as *Pensiunea Bradul* on Strada Someş (☎0263/370 441). The branch line ends at the mining town of **Rodna Veche**, where you can see the ruins of a tenth-century fort and a thirteenth-century church; buses then continue the 7km to **ŞANŢ**. This attractive village of wooden houses with open verandas and shingled roofs is noted for its elaborate wedding celebrations, lasting all weekend. **Homestays** are available here – at *Pensuine Grapini* (Str. Morii 65; ☎0263/379 124), where there's a kitchen, cable TV and Internet access, and *Pensiune Nechiţa* (☎0263/379 019).

The main railway line to Vatra Dornei runs to the south of the branch line up the Ilva valley. **LEŞU**, eight minutes up the line from Ilva Mică – from the stop, it's a four-kilometre walk east up the valley to the village – is home to one of the best festivals in the region, the **Rhapsody of the Trişcaşi Festival**, held on the first Sunday of September and bringing together pipers from three counties.

It's another 25km to **LUNCA ILVEI**, the last settlement before the pass into Moldavia Three kilometres east of the village centre and station there's the British-run Ştefan cel Mare **horse-riding** centre, at Str. Bolovan 340 (☎ & ⓕ0263/378 470, ⓦ www.riding-holidays.ro); day-rides are available, and offers tours from April to the end of October, as well as en-suite **accomodation** (❷–❸). There's a youth hostel (for groups only; book via Pantravel on ☎0264/420 516, ⓔ mail@pantravel.ro; ❶) at the west end of the village, a cabana nearby and several homestays.

Bistrița and the Bârgău valley

BISTRIȚA (Bistritz), 40km east of Beclean, and the forested Bârgău valley beyond, are the setting for much of Bram Stoker's *Dracula*; his Dracula's castle lies in the Bârgău valley and it was in Bistrița that Jonathan Harker received the first hints that something was amiss.

Remains of Neolithic settlements have been found near Bistrița, although the earliest records of the town coincide with the arrival of Saxon settlers, who built fine churches in many villages (less fortress-like than those further south). The bulk of the Saxon population left after World War II.

Arrival and information

Trains run from Cluj via Beclean to Bistrița Nord, but you may have to change trains at Sărățel, just southwest of Bistrița on the Dej–Brașov line. Just north of the junction is the small village of **Sărata**; from here, bus #10 will take you to Bistrița. The busy and well-run **bus station** is also a major hub for maxitaxis.

The CFR office (Mon–Fri 8am–5pm) is located right by the Coroana tourist agency at the top of Bulevardul Republicii; Tarom (Ⓣ & Ⓕ 0263/216 465; 8am–3pm) is at the *Coroana de Aur* hotel. The **Tourist Information Centre** is in the Casa de Cultura at Str. Albert Berger 10 (Mon–Fri 9am–5pm; Ⓣ0263/219 919, Ⓔcit@elcom.ro); it gives free information (including maps) and can arrange all sorts of outdoor activities. The free listings magazine *Șapte Seri* (Ⓦwww.sapteseri.ro) appears every two weeks.

The County's Folk Tradition Centre (Ⓣ0263/212 023), in Ceaușescu's former villa on Piața Petru Rareș by Bulevardul 1 Decembrie, has a gallery and will be able to confirm the dates of **festivals** at Leșu and the Bârgău villages;

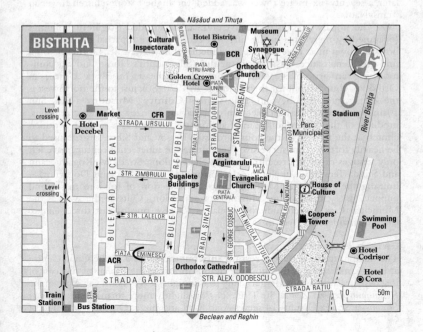

▲ Năsăud and Tihuța

▼ Beclean and Reghin

Bistriţa's own **International Folklore Festival** is held in the second week of August. The Union of Plastic Artists also has a gallery at Piaţa Centrală 24 (closed Mon).

Accommodation

There are several **hotels** in town, the most interesting to Dracula fans being the *Coroana de Aur* (Golden Crown) at Piaţa Petru Rareş 4 (☎0263/232 470, ⓦwww.coroanadeaur.bn.ro; ⑤), named after the inn where Jonathan Harker was warned not to travel on St George's Day. Much better – and cheaper – are the town's lower profile hotels: the *Codrişor* at Str. Codrişor 28 (☎0263/231 803, 227 352, ⓔcoroana@bistrita.ro; ③) has good service, and Hostelling International members can stay for €10, without breakfast. The *Cora* next door at Str. Codrişor 23 (☎ 0263/221 231, ⓕ227 782; ③) is not the most attractive but is friendly enough. More central are the *Bistriţa* at Str. Petru Rareş 2 (☎0263/231 154, ⓦwww.hotel-bistrita.ro; ③), and the *Decebal* at Str. Cuza Vodă 9 (☎0263/212 568, ⓕ233 541; ②), with clean but slightly cramped rooms.

The Town

From the train and bus stations, it's about ten minutes' walk to the centre; heading southeast on Strada Gării you'll pass a typically hideous Centru Civic, but as you turn northeast onto Strada Şincai you enter a more attractive townscape, with pedestrian alleys linking mostly north–south streets. The main square, **Piaţa Centrală**, is dominated by a great Saxon Evangelical **church** (Mon–Sat 9am–2pm, Sun 1–4pm, service 10am). Built in the Gothic style in the fourteenth century, the church was given Renaissance features in 1559–63, by Petrus Italus da Lugano, who introduced the style to Moldavia. A few decades later, a seventy-six-metre tower was added, the highest stone church tower in Transylvania.

On the northwest side of Piaţa Centrală, the arcaded **Şugălete** buildings (occupied by merchants in the fifteenth century) give a partial impression of how the town must have looked in its medieval heyday. At Str. Dornei 5 you'll find the Renaissance **Casa Argintarului** (Silversmith's House), now accommodating an art college, and continuing northeast, on Piaţa Unirii, an Orthodox church, built for the Minorites in 1270–80; just to the northwest is the synagogue and beyond that is the **County Museum** (Tues–Sun 10am–6pm), which has a collection of Thracian bronzeware, Celtic artefacts, products of the Saxon guilds, mills and presses, as well as a smallish wooden church at the far end of the courtyard. Like Braşov and Sibiu, Bistriţa used to be heavily fortified, but successive fires during the nineteenth century have left only vestiges of the fourteenth-century citadel along Strada M. Kogălniceanu and Strada Teodoroiu, including the **Coopers' Tower** (Turnul Dogarilor) – housing the Galeria de Măşti şi Papuşi, a collection of folklore masks and puppets (ask at the County Museum for admission). Outside the walls is the Municipal Park, which ludicrously claims to have one of just three *Gingko biloba* or maidenhair trees in Europe.

Eating and drinking

The main hotels have decent **restaurants**, but the *Venezia*, in the Civic Centre at Piaţa Eminescu 3, is the most prestigious in town. The *Primavera*, just east of Piaţa Centrală on Strada Berger (daily to midnight) serves good value pizza; the *Restaurant-pizzeria Zodiac*, Str. Titulescu 7, is slightly more formal; and the *Four Seasons* at Strada Ursului 14 serves Arab food and pizza. On the south side of the Casa de Cultura, the *Crama Veche* serves the best Romanian food in Bistriţa and the *Corrida en Sol* has a large pleasant terrace, open to midnight. For a snack, you can't beat the great *plăcinte* (pies) with cheese, cabbage, apple or plum sold from a hatch at Str. Şincai 37. There are a couple of nice **bars** in medieval basements, *Any Time* (Piaţa Centrală 1) and *Iris* (Str. Rebreanu 2). *Metropolis*, at Piaţa Eminescu 1 (☏0263/236 301, ⓦwww.metropolis.com.ro; 10pm–6am), is the biggest and most sophisticated **club** in Transylvania, with dancefloors on two levels, as well as bars, pizza and videogames.

Listings

Bus tickets C&I, Calea Moldovei 17 ☏0263/213 621, ⓔci_bistrita@topsoft.ro; Amad Turistik,Str. Mureşanu 3 ap. 3 ☏ & ⓕ0263/212 171; AtlasSib B-dul Decebal 11 ☏ & ⓕ 0263/233 659; Agenţia de Turism Coroana, Piaţa Petru Rareş 7A ☏0263/212 056, ⓦwww.draculatransylvania.ro; PasTur, Piaţa Centrală 39; and Pannonia Trans ☏0263/340 734.

Car rental Teo Astrabis Rentacar, Str. Şincai 1 ☏0744/912 208.
Internet access ClubNet, Strada Ursului, just east of Bulevardul Decebal (under the external staircase).
Tours See Agenţia de Turism Coroana, above.
Train tickets See Agenţia de Turism Coroana, above

The Bârgău valley

Four buses a day head east up the valley to Vatra Dornei in Moldavia (see p.287). Trains follow this route only as far as Prundu Bârgăului, from where it's another 60km to Vatra Dornei, including the 1200-metre Tihuţa Pass, crossed by two daily buses. The scenery of the Bârgău valley is dramatic, with huge hills draped in forests of fir trees, and villages appearing as living monuments to a way of life unchanged for centuries; the Saxon ceramics, woodcarvings and folk dress displayed in the Casa Sasească (Saxon House) museum of **LIVEZELE**, 8km from Bistriţa (local bus #3 and maxitaxis), are part of everyday life in other villages further up the valley – the museum is at Str. Dorolea 152, near the Lutheran church on the main square, and the key is kept by the curator at Str. Dorolea 197 (☏0263/270 109). In **JOSENII BÂRGĂULUI**, 8km beyond Livezele, black pottery is manufactured and old fulling mills and cottages remain in use. **PRUNDU BÂRGĂULUI**, 6km east of Josenii, is the venue for the Raftsmen's Festival on the last weekend of March, when unmarried men crown their usual attire of sheepskin jackets with a small hat buried beneath a plume of peacock feathers.

One kilometre on from Prundu Bârgăului is **TIHA BÂRGĂULUI**, occasional host to the interesting **Festival of Regele Brazilor** (King of the Fir Trees). This is an opportunity to hear the traditional songs, and the part-improvised lamentations (*bochet*) of relatives and friends of the deceased, an account of the deceased's deeds in this life; if the festival runs at all, it's on the third Sunday of June. The *Motel Cora* is at the west end of Tiha Bârgăului, and at km97 (35km from Bistriţa, beyond Mureşeni Bârgăului) is the *Bradului* cabana, where you can camp. Climbing steadily eastwards, the DN17 (E576) reaches the scattered settlement of **Piatra Fântânele** and at km108 the *Hotel Castel Dracula* (☏0263/265 192, ⓔdraculaland@logitec.ro; ⑤), where staff delight in hiding in a coffin from which they try and scare guests. Note that the map of hiking trails outside is incorrect; some trails don't exist, while some that do aren't shown. There are cabanas offering *camere de inchiriat* (private rooms) in the village; the *Pension Bubulea* (book ahead, ☏0263/238 563), behind the hotel on a short-cut to the Dornişoara road, is recommended, particularly for its cooking.

Just beyond, at km 113, lies the **Tihuţa pass**, which may be blocked by snow for a day or two between late October and mid–May. Although the country is relatively densely settled near the main road, the surrounding mountains harbour more **bears** than in any other part of Europe, as well as red deer, boars and **wolves**; the **view** from the pass of the green "crests" of Bucovina to the northeast and the volcanic Căliman mountains to the southeast is marvellous.

Travel details

Trains

Alba Iulia to: Arad (5 daily; 2hr 45min–3hr 45min); Braşov (3 daily; 3hr 15min–3hr 35min); Cluj (8 daily; 1hr 45min–2hr 40min); Deva (8 daily; 1hr 5min–1hr 30min); Hunedoara (1 daily; 1hr 55min); Sibiu (4 daily; 1hr 45min–2hr 30min); Sighişoara (3 daily; 1hr 30min–1hr 50min); Târgu Mureş (3 daily; 1hr 30min–3hr); Timişoara (4 daily; 4hr 35min–5hr).

Bistriţa to: Cluj (3 daily; 3hr); Sărăţel (13 daily; 15min).

Braşov to: Bucharest (23 daily; 2hr 30min–4hr 45min) Cluj (5–7 daily; 4hr 30min–6hr 15min); Deva (5 daily; 4hr 15min–5hr 30min); Făgăraş (11 daily; 55min–1hr 45min); Galaţi (daily; 4hr 55min); Miercurea Ciuc (12 daily; 1hr 30min–2hr 30min); Sfântu Gheorghe (15 daily; 30–55min); Sibiu (9 daily; 2hr 5min–3hr 35min); Sighişoara (16 daily; 1hr 35min–2hr 20min); Târgu Mureş (4 daily; 5hr 15min–7hr 45min); Zarneşti (5 daily)

Cluj to: Bistriţa (3 daily; 2hr 45min–3hr); Deva (3 daily; 3hr 15min–3hr 30min); Miercurea Ciuc (1 daily; 4hr 30min); Oradea (12 daily; 2hr 15min–4hr 50min); Sfântu Gheorghe (1 daily; 5hr 40min); Sibiu (2 daily; 3hr 35min); Sighişoara (5–8 daily; 2hr 50min–3hr 25min); Târgu Mureş (1 daily; 2hr 20min).

Făgăraş to: Braşov (10-11 daily; 55min–1hr 35min); Sibiu (10–11 daily; 1hr 10min–2hr 10min).

Hunedoara to: Simeria (9 daily; 35min).

Miercurea Ciuc to: Baia Mare (1 daily; 7hr 30min); Braşov (11–12 daily; 1hr 35min–2hr 40min); Dej (2–3 daily; 4hr 05min–5hr); Gheorgheni (9–10 daily; 55min–1hr 20min); Sighet (1 daily; 8hr 20min); Suceava (1 daily; 6hr 20min).

Petroşani to: Cluj (1 daily; 5hr 30min); Craiova (7–8 daily; 2hr 40min–4hr 10min); Deva (7–8 daily; 1hr 50min–2hr 50min); Simeria (10–11 daily; 1hr 35min–2hr 30min); Târgu Jiu (8–9 daily; 1hr–1hr 30min).

Sibiu to: Arad (1–2 daily; 4hr 35min–5hr); Cluj (2 daily; 3hr 35min); Copşa Mică (6 daily; 47min–1hr

20min); Deva (4–5 daily; 2hr 20min–2hr 45min); Mediaş (4 daily; 1hr 20min–1hr 35min); Sighisoara (daily; 1hr 24min); Timişoara (3 daily; 5hr 15min–6hr 5min).

Sighişoara to: Alba Iulia (3 daily; 1hr 35min–1hr 45min); Braşov (14–16 daily; 1hr 40min–2hr 40min); Cluj (6–8 daily; 2hr 55min–3hr 20min); Sibiu (daily);

Târgu Mureş to: Cluj (2 daily; 2hr 10min–2hr 20min); Deda (9–10 daily; 1hr–1hr 30min); Deva (1 daily; 3hr 40min); Razboieni (11 daily; 1hr–1hr 45min).

Zalău to: Jibou (8 daily; 40min).

Buses & maxitaxis

Abrud to: Alba Iulia (7 daily); Câmpeni (10 daily); Cluj (3 daily); Oradea (1 daily).

Alba Iulia to: Aiud (3 daily); Blaj (5 daily); Bucharest (4 daily); Câmpeni (7 daily): Cluj (11 daily); Deva (2 daily); Oradea (2 daily); Sebeş (32 daily); Sibiu (2–4 daily); Târgu Jiu (2 daily); Târgu Mureş (2 daily); Timisoara (4 daily).

Bistriţa to: Baia Mare (2 daily); Braşov (5 daily); Cluj/Oradea (4 daily); Borşa (1 daily); Năsăud (8–11 daily); Rodna (4 Mon–Fri, 2 Sat); Sibiu (3 daily); Sighişoara (4 daily); Suceava (5 daily); Târgu Mureş (9 daily); Vatra Dornei (6 daily).

Braşov (Autogară 1) to: Agnita (1 daily); Bacău (7 daily); Bistriţa (5 daily); Bucharest (2 hourly); Buzău (4 daily); Câmpulung Muscel (2 daily); Constanţa (1 daily); Făgăraş (1 daily); Gheorgheni (2 daily); Iaşi (1 daily); Odorheiu Secuiesc (1 daily); Piatra Neamţ (1 daily); Piteşti (1 daily); Prejmer (7 Mon-Fri, 3 Sat, 2 Sun); Sibiu (2 daily); Târgovişte (2 daily); Târgu Mureş (6 daily); Târgu Neamţ (1 daily); Târgu Secuiesc (10 daily).

Braşov (Autogară 2) to: Bran (24 Mon–Fri, 12 Sat/Sun); Câmpulung Muscel (4 daily); Curtea de Argeş/Râmnicu Vâlcea (1 daily); Piteşti (2 daily); Zărneşti (hourly Mon–Fri, 8 Sat, 2 Sun).

Braşov (Autogară 3) to: Bacău (3 daily); Buzău (1 daily); Hărman (6 Mon–Fri); Iaşi (1 daily); Prejmer (7 Mon-Fri, 2 Sat/Sun).

Câmpeni to: Abrud (10 daily); Alba Iulia (7 daily); Arad (1 daily); Arieşeni (4 daily); Brad (4 daily); Bucharest (1 daily); Cluj (4 daily); Deva (2 daily); Oradea (2 daily); Sebeş (1 daily); Timişoara (2 daily).

Cluj to: Abrud (3 daily); Alba Iulia (11 daily); Baia Mare (2 daily); Bistriţa (4 daily); Braşov (1 daily); Bucharest (1 daily); Câmpeni (4 daily); Cojocna (3 daily); Deva (2 daily); Gheorgheni (3 Mon–Fri); Huedin (2 daily); Hunedoara (6 daily); Oradea (4 daily); Piatra Neamţ (Tues, Thurs & Sat); Râmnicu Vâlcea (5 daily); Reghin (1–4 daily); Satu Mare (1 daily); Sibiu (8 daily); Sighet (2 daily); Târgu Jiu (2 daily); Târgu Lăpuş (2 daily); Târgu Mureş (2 daily); Turda (15 daily); Zalău (7 daily; & maxitaxis from station).

Covasna to: Sfântu Gheorghe (3–4 daily); Târgu Secuiesc (4 daily).

Deva to: Brad (14 Mon-Fri, 8 Sat/Sun); Câmpeni (2 daily); Cluj (2 daily); Hunedoara (3 hourly); Oradea (2 daily); Sarmizegetusa (2 Mon-Fri); Sibiu (3 daily); Târgu Mureş (1 daily); Timişoara (7 daily).

Gheorgheni to: Braşov (2 daily); Cluj (3 daily); Lacu Roşu (3 daily); Odorheiu Secuiesc (1 daily); Piatra Neamţ (3 daily); Târgu Mureş (3 daily); Târgu Neamţ (1 daily).

Haţeg to: Cluj (2 daily); Densuş (2 daily); Hunedoara (5 daily); Reşiţa (1 daily); Sarmizegetusa (3 Mon-Fri, 1 Sat/Sun); Timişoara (1 daily); Târgu Jiu (2 daily).

Hunedoara to: Cinciş (7-9 daily); Cluj (6 daily); Craiova (1 daily); Deva (3 hourly); Drobeta-Turnu Severin (1 daily); Haţeg (2 daily).

Mediaş to: Agnita (1–3 daily); Făgăraş (1 Mon–Fri); Sibiu (4 daily); Târgu Mureş (7 Mon-Fri, 4 Sat, 2 Sun).

Miercurea Ciuc to: Băile Tuşnad (4 daily); Braşov (2 daily); Frumoasa (11 Mon-Fri, 4 Sat/Sun); Odorheiu Secuiesc (5–7 daily); Piatra Neamţ (2 daily); Sovata (3 daily); Târgu Mureş (3 daily); Târgu Neamţ (1 daily); Târgu Secuiesc (2–3 daily).

Odorheiu Secuiesc to: Braşov (1 daily); Covasna/Târgu Secuiesc (1 daily); Gheorgheni (1 daily); Miercurea Ciuc (2 daily); Praid (10 daily); Sf. Gheorghe (1 daily); Sighişoara (1 daily); Sovata/Târgu Mureş (5 daily).

Reghin to: Bistriţa (1 daily); Cluj (1–4 daily); Hodac (17 daily); Sighişoara (1 daily); Sovata (2 daily); Târgu Neamţ (1 daily); Vatra Dornei (1 daily).

Sfântu Gheorghe to: Braşov (2 daily); Bucharest (1 daily); Covasna (3 Mon–Fri, 1 Sat/Sun), Odorheiu Secuiesc (1 daily); Piatra Neamţ (2 daily); Târgu Neamţ (1 daily); Târgu Secuiesc (2 daily).

Sebeş to: Alba Iulia (2 hourly); Câmpeni (1 daily); Cluj (8 daily); Sibiu (12 daily); Timişoara (2 daily).

Sibiu to: Agnita (4 daily); Bistrita (3 daily); Braşov (4 daily); Bucharest (4 daily); Cisnădie (30 Mon–Fri, 10 Sat/Sun); Cluj (8 daily); Constanţa (1 daily in summer); Curtea de Argeş (1 daily); Deva (4 daily); Galaţi (2 daily); Gura Râului (10 Mon–Fri, 2 Sat/Sun); Mediaş (3–5 daily); Oradea (1 daily); Păltiniş (3 daily); Râmnicu Vâlcea (7 daily); Sighişoara (8 daily); Slimnic (3 daily); Târgu Jiu (1 daily); Târgu Mureş (7 daily); Timişoara (2 daily).

Sighişoara to: Agnita (3 daily); Bistriţa (3 daily); Braşov (1 daily); Făgăraş (1 daily); Odorheiu Secuiesc (1 daily); Sibiu (8 daily); Sovata (1 daily); Târgu Mureş (7–9 daily).

Sovata to: Cluj (1 daily); Miercurea Ciuc (3 daily); Odorheiu Secuiesc (5 daily); Reghin (2 daily); Sighişoara (1 daily); Târgu Mureş (6–10 daily).

Târgu Mureş to: Alba Iulia (2 daily); Bistriţa (9 daily); Braşov (6 daily); Cluj (2 daily); Deva/Timişoara (1 daily); Făgăraş (1 daily); Mediaş (7 Mon–Fri, 4 Sat, 2 Sun); Miercurea Ciuc (3 daily); Odorheiu Secuiesc (5 daily); Piatra Neamţ (1 daily); Sibiu (7 daily); Sighişoara (7–9 daily); Sovata (6–10 daily); Târgu Neamţ (1 daily); Vatra Dornei (1 daily).

Târgu Secuiesc to: Bacău (5 daily); Covasna (4 daily); Miercurea Ciuc (2-3 daily).

Zalău to: Baia Mare (1 daily); Cluj (5–6 daily); Huedin (1 daily); Jibou (3 daily); Oradea (2 daily); Şimleu-Silvanei (4 daily); Timişoara (2 daily).

Planes

Cluj to: Bucharest (Tarom; 3 Mon-Sat, 2 Sun); Timişoara (Carpatair; 1 daily).
Sibiu to: Timişoara (Carpatair; 1 daily Mon–Sat).
Târgu Mureş to: Bucharest (Tarom: 2 weekly).

International trains

Braşov to: Budapest, Hungary (4 daily; 10hr 30min–13hr); Prague, Czech Republic (1 daily; 22hr 30min); Vienna, Austria (1 daily; 15hr 30min); Krakow, Poland (1 daily; 22hr).
Cluj to: Budapest (2 daily; 5hr 30min–7hr 10min).
Deva to: Budapest (3 daily; 5hr 30min–7hr 10min); Prague (1 daily; 17hr); Vienna (1 daily; 9hr 30min); Krakow (1 daily; 17hr).
Miercurea Ciuc to: Budapest (1 daily; 12hr 50min).
Sighişoara to: Budapest (3 daily; 8hr 30min–9hr30 min); Krakow (1 daily; 19hr 30min); Prague (1 daily; 18hr 30min); Vienna (1 daily; 12hr).

International buses

Braşov to: Budapest (Tues, Thurs & Fri); Chişinău, Moldova (Mon–Fri); Germany (several daily); Istanbul, Turkey (Thurs & Sun).

Cluj to: Athens, Greece (2 weekly); Budapest (2 daily); Germany (1 daily); Thessaloniki, Greece (2 weekly).

Deva to: Germany (several daily).

Gheorgheni to: Budapest (1 daily).

Miercurea Ciuc to: Budapest (2 daily).

Odorheiu Secuiesc to: Budapest (2 daily).

Reghin to: Budapest (Thurs & Sun).

Sebeş to: Germany (several daily).

Sfântu Gheorghe to: Budapest (1 daily).

Sibiu to: Germany (several daily).

Sighişoara to: Budapest (1 Mon & Fri); Germany (daily).

Târgu Mureş to: Budapest (1 daily).

Moldavia

CHAPTER 4

Highlights

* **Ghimeş** An isolated Hungarian enclave perched on the old Hapsburg-Ottoman border, this quiet village is surrounded by rolling green hills. See p.246

* **Agapia Monastery** This picture-perfect convent, where 300 nuns live in trim cottages, is one of the spiritual centres of the Romanian Orthodox Church. See p.251

* **The Neculai Popa Museum** A delightful collection of folk sculpture and other curiosities, set in the rugged village of Tărpeşti, south of Târgu Neamţ. See p.252

* **The Ceaulău massif** Bucovina is the most forested region of Romania, and the hills and rock formations that make up the massif offer wilderness on an impressive scale. See p.253

* **Iaşi** In spite of Ceauşescu's best efforts to crush its spirit, the old Moldavian capital is full of surprises; Iaşi's vibrant restaurant scene is especially impressive. See p.255

* **Casa Buburuzan, Humor** A standout among the dozens of hospitable Bucovina pensions; guests are served lavish traditional meals made from local products. See p.280

* **The Ladder of Virtue, Suceviţa Monastery** This splendid, richly detailed ensemble is just one of the unforgettable frescoes of Bucovina's Painted Monasteries. See p.281

△ Working horses, Bucovina

4

Moldavia

For travellers, Moldavia gets more interesting the further north you go, and the difficulty of some journeys can, perversely, add to the attraction of your final destination. This is particularly true of the jewels in the Moldavian crown, the **Painted Monasteries of southern Bucovina**. Secluded in valleys near the Ukrainian border, their medieval frescoes of redemption and damnation blaze in polychromatic splendour at the misty, fir-clad hills – Voroneţ and Suceviţa boast peerless examples of the Last Judgement and the Ladder of Virtue, Moldoviţa is famous for its fresco of the Siege of Constantinople, while Humor has a quiet charm. The unpainted Putna Monastery, final resting place of Ştefan cel Mare, draws visitors interested in Romanian history. Though all are more or less accessible from Bucovina's regional capital, **Suceava**, many visitors opt for ONT tours from Bucharest, although it's far less expensive to make your own way to Suceava and book a tour there (see p.268).

As in Wallachia, most towns and cities have been marred by hideous concrete apartment blocks and factories; only **Iaşi** holds any great appeal, having retained numerous churches and monasteries from its heyday as the Moldavian capital, and with a charm that puts Bucharest to shame. In contrast to the new-town developments, the countryside looks fantastic, with picturesque villages dwarfed by the flanks of the Carpathians. Just over halfway to Suceava, Neamţ county contains the eclectic **Neculai Popa Museum**, Moldavia's largest **convents** – Agapia and Văratec – and the weirdly shaped **Ceahlău massif**, a paradise for hikers and climbers. While backwaters such as **Ghimeş** in the Magyar-speaking **Csángó region** are worth investigating if you're interested in rural life, there are also numerous local **festivals** (see box on p.272). The main festivals are at Ilişeşti (July), Durău (August), Iaşi (October) and Odobeşti (November).

Moldavia's complex **history** is best understood in relation to the cities of Iaşi and Suceava, the former capitals of the region, and you'll find more details under the individual city accounts. Moldavia used to be twice its present size, having at various times included Bessarabia (the land beyond the River Prut) and Northern Bucovina (on the edge of the Carpathians). Both territories were annexed by Stalin in 1940, severing cultural and family ties; these have revived since the fall of communism, especially between Moldavia and the former Bessarabia – now the sovereign Republic of Moldova.

Motorists heading north along the DN2 should note that although the road is designated on maps as Euro-route 85, it's actually a country road where horse-drawn wagons without lights are a major hazard at night.

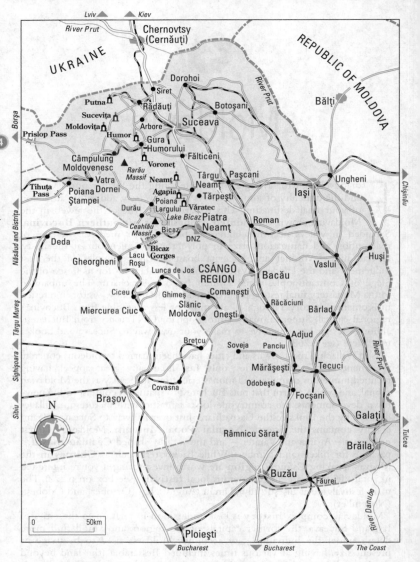

Brăila and Galaţi

Lying well off the main route through Moldavia, close to the region's south-eastern border and the Danube Delta, **Brăila** and **Galaţi** are seldom visited by tourists, and only then while en route to or from Tulcea, the Delta capital. Both were once ports where the Orient and Occident colluded in exporting Romania's agricultural wealth; now they are backwaters and monuments to economic failure. Brăila's docks are almost moribund – though its old town has retained more nineteenth century architecture than most other Romanian cities – while Galaţi is blighted by bankrupt industries. There are no bridges across the Danube in the vicinity, and now that ferries and hydrofoils have ceased operating the only way to get to Galaţi from Tulcea is by bus (5 daily; 2hr) or maxitaxi (5 daily; 1hr 15min), both incorporating a short ferry crossing at Galaţi. Both Brăila and Galaţi are linked to Bucharest by fast trains.

Brăila

BRĂILA has the air of a restful, pleasantly gone-to-seed Danubian town about it, laid out in concentric streets radiating from the port esplanade. As the region's principal harbour, Brăila shipped the harvests of the Bărăgan Plain to the rest of Europe in the nineteenth century, creating huge fortunes for a few landlords who built elegant villas here, using members of the local Gypsy population – at the time, the largest of any town in Europe – as domestic slaves. The villas have long crumbled while the Gypsies remain; the vestiges of wealth and splendour give the place a romantic, even bohemian, feel.

The old town, rebuilt in the 1830s after suffering heavy damage in the Russo-Turkish war of 1828–1829, is centred on **Piaţa Traian**, a leafy square on which stands the **Church of the Archangel Michael**, built as a mosque by the Turks, probably in the eighteenth century; its freestanding belfry was added later. Sepia photos of Brăila in its heyday appear in the **History Museum** (Tue–Sun 9am–5pm), at Piaţa Traian 3.

From the far side of Piaţa Traian, the lively axis of Calea Călăraşilor leads towards the **Centru Civic**, passing villas housing restaurants and banks, as well as a large **Greek Orthodox church** built by the community that dominated the shipping business before World War I.

From the bottom of Piaţa Traian, Strada Imperator Traian leads to the dismal **waterfront** with its mournful array of rusting freighters and patrol boats; when Ceauşescu visited here, they even had to paint the grass green.

Practicalities

Brăila's **bus station** is about 200m left of the train station, on Strada Siret. Maxitaxis to and from Galaţi call at the intersection of Bulevardul Dorobanţi and Calea Galaţi, 1km north of the centre. From outside the **train station**, take maxitaxi #4, or walk 1km down Strada E. Grigorescu to Bulevardul A.I. Cuza; bear right as far as Strada Eminescu, the pedestrianized street which leads left to Piaţa Traian, centre of the old town. There's an **Internet** café on Calea Galaţi, just off Piaţa Traian, and the most convenient **supermarket**, Plus, is at Calea Călăraşilor 104.

The best **place to stay** is the nondescript but recently renovated *Hotel Sport* (☏0239/611 346; ❸), at Str. D. Bolintineanu 4, which has clean and modern en-suite rooms. It's down the first turning to the right off Calea Galaţi, leading from Piaţa Traian. Standards are a bit higher at the more expensive *Traian* (☏0239/614 685, ☏612 685; ❹), a dull high-rise with English-speaking staff at Piaţa Traian 4. Of the **places to eat**, *LMS*, a pizzeria-restaurant on Calea Galaţi, is the most stylish in the centre, while the *Old City Café*, at Calea Călăraşilor 14, has good food, a pleasant terrace and an English menu. Most of the best **bars** are also found along this road.

Galaţi

GALAŢI, 30km north of Brăila by road and rail, grew up as a port at the confluence of the River Danube and Moldavia's inland waterways, the Siret and the Prut. In Bram Stoker's *Dracula*, Jonathan Harker and Godalming come here to catch a steamer up the Siret and Bistriţa rivers, heading for Dracula's castle at the Bârgău Pass. Galaţi swelled to its present size during the 1960s, when Romania's largest **steelworks** were constructed here. For Gheorghiu-Dej and Ceauşescu, this enterprise was the prerequisite for Romania's emergence as a fully industrialized nation, and a symbolic and concrete assertion of independence from the Warsaw Pact, which preferred Romania to remain a largely agricultural country.

Probably your own reason for visiting here will be to make a bus or maxitaxi **connection** to Tulcea. The town was badly bombed in 1944 and rebuilt as a series of numbingly identical apartment buildings. There is little to see, but Galaţi is a reasonably large town, with plenty of shops, hotels and restaurants, most found along the main avenue, Strada Brăilei.

Practicalities

Buses to or from Tulcea call not in Galaţi proper, but at the small ferry terminal in the village of I.C. Brătianu on the other side of the Danube. Regular ferries shuttle both foot passengers and cars across to Galaţi, a fifteen-minute ride. The final ferry sails around 8pm, just after the last bus from Tulcea arrives. Once you've disembarked at the small terminal on the Galaţi side, 3km south of town, take a taxi into the centre (going the other direction, ask the driver to take you to the *debarcader*). Galaţi's **train station** – adjacent to the **bus station** – lies 1km northeast of the town centre on Strada Gării. Maxitaxis to Brăila (much faster than trains) are to be found south of the centre; take local maxitaxi #19 to the last stop.

If you need **to stay**, try the *Sport*, at Str. A.I. Cuza 76 (℡0236/414 098, ℱ415 672; ❸), which is convenient for the train station, or the *Dunărea*, at Str. Brăilei 101 (℡0236/418 041, ℱ464 312; ❹). Of the more expensive places, the *Galaţi*, Str. Domnească 1 (℡0236/460 040, ℱ464 312; ❺), is a good choice, with modern facilities and friendly, competent staff.

From Buzău to Bacău

The main routes northeast from Bucharest through Moldavia, the DN2 and the Bucharest–Suceava train line, are a miserable advertisement for the region, as one hideously modernized town succeeds another without even the sight of the Carpathians to lift your spirits until you're halfway to Suceava. There's little reason to stop along the way unless for a detour into the wine-growing or Csángó regions of the Subcarpathians.

That said, you might consider visiting **BUZĂU**, 128km from Bucharest on the southern border of Moldavia, if you're around on the last Sunday in June, when it holds its kitsch Drăgaica **festival**; once widespread in rural Romania, this Midsummer Day's custom required young girls wearing crowns and hoods to go singing and dancing into the fields to verify the readiness of the wheat for harvesting.

FOCŞANI, 70km further north, is an unattractive town, but has buses and trains to the **wine-growing regions** of Panciu and Odobeşti, and further into the hills of Vrancea county, just west of the main routes north. **MĂRĂŞEŞTI** rail junction, 20km north of Focşani, is remembered for a savage battle in the summer of 1917, when German forces advancing on Iaşi were halted by Romanian troops, determined to preserve the last unoccupied region of their country. At **Panciu** they make sparkling wines, while **Odobeşti** produces the yellow wine that was Ceauşescu's favourite tipple. Odobeşti is also noted for its **festivals**; the grape harvest is celebrated in late September, and on the third Sunday of November the shepherds of Vrancea county gather to entertain each other with performances on alpine horns and pan-pipes. Pension **accommodation** in Panciu, Odobeşti and elsewhere can be booked through the Vrancea County Antrec office (☎0237/673 049 or 0722 491 665, ✉ vrancea@antrec.ro), located about 50km northwest of Focşani, in the village of Vidra. The spa of **Soveja** is a base for visiting the hills to the west, with a museum and monastery (founded in 1645), as well as the *Zboina* hotel (☎0237/636 021; ❸).

The Csángó region

The name "Csángó" is thought to derive from the Hungarian for "wanderer", referring to those Székely who fled here from religious persecution in Transylvania during the fifteenth century, to be joined by others escaping military conscription in the seventeenth and eighteenth centuries. There is evidence that Hungarians have been present in this area for even longer than that, however; the true origin of the Csángó remains a subject of contentious debate. Once, there were some forty **Csángó villages** in Moldavia, a few as far east as present-day Ukraine, but today their community has contracted into a hard core of about five thousand people living between Adjud and Bacău, and in **Ghimeş** at the upper end of the Trotuş (Tatros) valley. Most rural Csángó are fervently religious and fiercely conservative, retaining a distinctive folk costume and dialect; their music is harsher and sadder than that of their Magyar kinsfolk in Transylvania, although their dances are almost indistinguishable from those of their Romanian neighbours.

Mutual suspicions and memories of earlier injustices and uprisings made this a sensitive area in communist times. While allowing them to farm and raise sheep outside the collectives, the Party tried to dilute the Csángó and stifle their culture by settling Romanians in new industrial towns like Oneşti. Things are a lot freer now, and the idyllic upper valley is frequently visited during the summer by tour groups from Budapest, as well as a few independent travellers. Tourist infrastructure in Ghimeş has developed apace, though shops are still very basic and there are no ATMs – bring what supplies and money you're going to need with you.

Adjud is the junction on the main Bucharest–Suceava line for the branch line west to Oneşti, Ghimeş and Transylvania. However, if you're coming to Ghimeş from the north, rather than riding all the way down to Adjud it may be quicker to disembark at Bacău, catch a bus to Comăneşti (the last one leaves at 5pm), and wait there for the next train up the valley. The first major stop after Adjud is **Oneşti** (Onyest); dominated by the chemical industry, it is notable only as the birthplace of Nadia Comaneci (now a resident of Norman, Oklahoma). From here or from **Târgu Ocna** (Aknavásar), a small spa 12km to the west that boasts the largest underground sanatorium in Europe, you can reach the larger spa of **SLĂNIC MOLDOVA** (Szlanikfürdő) which lies 20km southeast of Târgu Ocna.

Ghimeş

The quiet charm that is the real attraction of the beautiful Trotuş valley, however, only begins to reveal itself on the far side of Comaneşti (Cománfalva), a coal-mining settlement that is also the junction for the

MOLDAVIA | From Buzău to Bacău

decrepit oil town of Moineşti, birthplace of Dada founder Tristan Tzara. Beyond Comaneşti, industry is present only in the form of a few small-scale timber mills, and trains call at one picturesque village after another before finally reaching **Ghimeş** (Ghimeş-Făget or Gyimesbükk), the largest and most rewarding of the Csángó settlements, and the only one that can be visited with any ease. The rail line continues on to Miercurea Ciuc in Transylvania, and daily trains to and from Braşov and Timişoara make this an attractive stopping point en route to Neamţ County, Iaşi or Suceava.

Nearly all of Ghimeş's residents are Hungarian, though there is a small Gypsy population, which, unusually, is totally integrated into village life. This helps to account for the strong musical tradition, most in evidence at the **winter fair** held annually on January 20–21. Ghimeş' appeal lies in its tranquil setting, but the town does have a few modest sights. It's principal monument, at least for those who wish to contemplate the injustices of Trianon, the post-World War I treaty under which Hungary was forced to cede Transylvania to Romania, is the nineteenth-century customs house that marked the old border of Transylvania and Moldavia and, earlier, the Hapsburg and Ottoman empires. It's just off the main road, 1.5km east of the station. The staircase behind the house leads up a small hill to the insubstantial ruins of **Rákóczi Castle**, built in 1626 by prince Gábor Bethlen – more than the ruins, though, it's the **view** of the Trotuş valley from here that makes the effort worthwhile. This is also the beginning of the path that leads up the ridge of Papoj mountain (1271m). The area's remoteness makes it an excellent place for **hiking**, and a series of little-used trails, including several longer routes into Transylvania, is delineated on the 1:60,000 DIMAP map of the area, sold at Deáky Panzió (see below). The village itself, divided in two by the Trotuş River, is also a pleasant and inviting place to take a walk – its houses are neat and colourful, with many boasting intricately carved eaves and flower gardens, and its streets are enlivened by the various farm animals wandering about. Opposite the train station, the **Gyimesi Házimúseum** (daily in summer 10am–2pm) displays rural memorabilia. The main church, rebuilt in 1976, is 200m up from the station, but more interesting, and a good place to picnic, is the small wooden chapel that overlooks the town from a hilltop meadow on the far side of the river. Reaching it entails scaling a few fences, but nobody seems to mind. Immediately east of Ghimeş, 2km from the old customs house, is the down-at-heel Romanian logging town of Palanca. Going the other direction, near the head of the valley, Lunca de Jos (Gyimesközéplok) and Lunca de Sus (Gyimesfelsőlok) stand on the borders with Transylvania.

Practicalities

Ghimeş's handful of commercial establishments are all in the centre of town, opposite the surprisingly vast nineteenth-century **train station**. There is a small **motel** (☎0234/385 765; ●) 200m up the main road from the station, but the better option by far is to stay at *Deáky Panzió* (☎0234/385 621, ⓔdeakyandras@xnet.ro; ●–●; open May–Sept), an attractive, comfortable **pension** situated on a converted farm next to the river and run by the village doctor. Turn left on leaving the station and follow the main road downhill for about 1km, past the post office and on past the clinic named András Deáky until you see the sign for *Deáky Panzió* on your right. The proprietor speaks only Hungarian, Romanian and German, but his wife is able to communicate in English. Accommodation ranges from rooms with bath to small but pleasant bungalows; it's advisable to book ahead, especially if arriving late. Food and wine here, all of which comes from local farms, is excellent and very reasonably priced; the communal dining room encourages conversation. If you stay for a few days, your visit is likely to coincide with that of one of the frequent groups of Hungarian tourists that come for dinner and an evening of wine, dancing and **Csángó and Gypsy music**. The singing, especially, is hauntingly beautiful, if a little overtly patriotic at times. The only place to eat, other than the pension, is a **restaurant** opposite the train station, with good food, slow service and a Hungarian/Romanian menu.

Bacău

BACĂU, 60km north of Adjud along the main rail and road routes to Suceava, is a large industrial town with good transport services, but little else to recommend it. To reach the centre from the **train station**, head east for fifteen minutes up Strada Eminescu, to the right of the department store across the road, which eventually leads to the *Hotel Moldova*, the massive high-rise that looms ominously over the town centre. The two main axes, Bălcescu and Unirii, converge here, while the **bus terminal** is ten minutes' walk east along Strada Unirii.

Most facilities in town are on Strada Bălcescu. The ACR tourist agency at no. 14 (Mon–Fri 9am–4pm) sells maps of Bacău County; **information** can be got from CFR at no. 12 (Mon–Fri 8am–8pm). The local Antrec representative, and director of Bacău's British Center, (℡0234/570 826 or 0744/584 176, Ⓔatrix@rdslink.ro) is well informed about rural tourism in Bacău county and can arrange pension and homestay accommodation in the Csángó region and elsewhere. Her office, at Mihai Viteazu 12 Bl. 2, is on the far side of the block of flats behind the Casa Culturii on Strada Bălcescu.

There's plenty of **accommodation** on offer, but none of it is good value, especially as there's no reason to stay. The best choice is the *Dumbrava* (℡ & Ⓕ0234/513 302; Ⓢ) at Str. Dumbrava Roşie 2, a clean, modern place with a fridge in every room. The only budget option, the *Central*, at Str. Nicolae Bălcescu 6 (℡0234/134 837), was closed for renovation at the time of writing. *Ciao*, opposite the Bacovia Theatre on Strada Bălcescu, is the best of a sad lot of **restaurants**.

Neamţ county

Neamţ county lies to the northwest of Bacău and is the best-known attraction between Bucharest and the old Moldavian capitals of Iaşi and Suceava. Although its towns – **Piatra Neamţ** and **Târgu Neamţ** – are nothing special, they serve as bases for the historic monasteries of **Neamţ**, **Agapia** and **Văratec**, set in wooded foothills that turn gloriously red and gold in autumn, and the delightful collection of naïve art and folk costumes at the **Neculai Popa Museum** in Tărpeşti. Further to the northwest rises the **Ceahlău massif**, whose magnificent views and bizarrely weathered outcrops make this one of the most dramatic hiking spots in Romania.

On arriving, you'll be faced with the question of where to base yourself. The pensions around Agapia are best if you're travelling by car, but can be somewhat isolated if you're not. Of the towns, Târgu Neamţ is closer to the sights and runs a few more buses than Piatra Neamţ, but the county seat, the latter, is livelier and offers a far better choice of places to stay and eat. The two are 40km apart and are linked by hourly **buses**, all but two of which run via Coşere and Sacalauşeşti, the respective turn-offs for Văratec and Agapia. On

Sundays, there are fewer services to the monasteries and none to Durău, the jumping-off point for the Ceahlău massif.

Piatra Neamţ

Sixty kilometres northwest of Bǎcau by road and rail, where the River Bistriţa emerges into the Cracau basin, lies **PIATRA NEAMŢ**. Hemmed in by the Carpathian foothills, it is one of Romania's oldest settlements, inhabited by a string of Neolithic and Bronze Age cultures, and the Dacians, whose citadel has been excavated on a nearby hilltop. The town was first recorded in Roman times as Petrodava, and in 1453 under the name of Piatra lui Craciun (Christmas Rock); its present title may refer to the German (Neamţ) merchants who once traded here, or derive from the old Romanian word for an extended family or nation – Neam. As one of Moldavia's earliest industrial centres, the town later played a major role in the general strike of 1919, and was one of the few places where the communists were able to sabotage production during World War II. That said, Piatra has little to attract visitors beyond a medieval church and a better-than-average collection of prehistoric relics in its history museum.

Arrival, information and accommodation

From the **train and bus stations**, it's a ten-minute walk up the tree-lined Bulevardul Republicii to the central Piaţa Ştefan cel Mare. CFR (Mon–Fri 8am–8pm) has an **information** office nearby at the northern end of Strada Eminescu. Tavernet is an unusually pleasant **Internet café** (daily 9am–11pm) in the basement of Teatrul Tinterului at Piaţa Ştefan cel Mare 5. Piatra Neamţ's only 24-hour **pharmacy** is in the Mioriţa Complex, opposite the *Central Hotel*. The friendly, English-speaking staff at Neamţ County's Antrec office (☏0233/234 204, ✉neamt@antrec.ro; Mon–Fri 9am–6pm), up the stairs on the left side of the house at Str. Ştefan cel Mare 17, are knowledgeable about accommodation and sights and may be able to arrange a car with driver for the area's day-trips.

Piatra Neamţ's three **hotels** all have private bathrooms and include breakfast, but are otherwise fairly uninspiring: the best of the lot is the *Central*, at Piaţa Petrodavna 1 (☏0233/216 230, ✉centralsecretariat@csc.ro; ❺), a recently renovated high-rise with modern comforts and a good but lifeless restaurant. *Ceahlău*, in the centre of town at Piaţa Ştefan cel Mare 3 (☏0233/219 990, ✉hotel_ceahlau_01@yahoo.com; ❺), has seen better days, though the rooms are decent enough and the twelfth-floor bar has good views and a pool table; alternatively, there's the *Bulevard* at B-dul Republicii 38–40 (☏0233/235 010 or 235 020, ✆218 111; ❹), with dull but clean rooms with bath. Next door is the three-room *Pension Elis*, at B-dul Republicii 40 (☏0233/217 940; ❷), which is unwelcoming but not quite as bad as it looks from the outside. Accommodation at several other pensions near the centre (❷), can be arranged through the Antrec office (see above). If you can't find a room in town, try *Pensiunea Nora* (☏0233/237 737; ❷), 2km west of the centre at Str. Petru Movilă 162A. There's also a **campsite**, the *Strand*, on Aleea Tineretului, a wooded summer-only site with cabins (❶); to get there, head 1km west along Strada Bistriţei until you reach the footbridge.

The Town

Today, Piatra Neamţ features every style of communist architecture, from dismal low-rises to the pseudo-malls that mushroomed in the 1980s. What's left

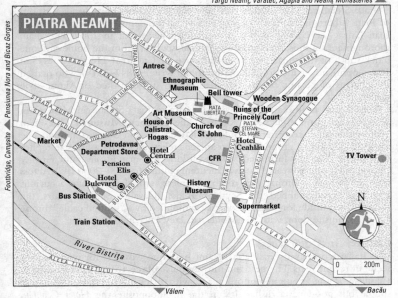

of the old town is clustered around **Piaţa Libertăţii**. The spireless **Church of St John** originally formed part of a Princely Court, of which only vestiges remain. Erected by Stephen the Great in 1497–98, hard on the heels of his seminal church at Neamţ Monastery, it set a pattern for Moldavian church architecture thereafter. The upper part is girdled by niches outlined in coloured brick, probably intended to hold saintly images. Beside the door, a votive inscription by his son Bogdan the One-Eyed presages a host of tacky modern paintings of Stephen inside, where a dusty case of valuables justifies a small entry charge. A sturdy Gothic **bell tower** with a witch's hat brim, constructed in 1499, stands on the northwest side of the church. West of the bell tower, in a building that combines folk architecture with Art Nouveau, is the **Ethnographic Museum** (Tues–Sun 10am–6pm), and beside that is a Brâncoveanu-style mansion, with ceramic studs echoing those on the church, which houses the **Art Museum** (Tues–Sun 10am–6pm) showing work by local painters. On the northeastern side of the square, some vaulted **ruins of the Princely Court** have been laid bare by a shaft dug into the slope below the Petru Rareş Liceu, but it's hard to see much through the gate, which is kept locked; ask at the museums for entry.

Northeast of the Princely Court, on Strada Dimitrie Ernica, is the eighteenth-century **Baal Shem Tov Wooden Synagogue**. Baal Shem Tov, the founder of Hasidism, was for a short time supposed to have lived close to Piatra Neamţ, occasionally visiting the town to pray here. This building is completely surrounded by other buildings and were it not for the stone tablets on the roof you would have no idea of its existence. It's generally locked, but there are signs that the site may soon receive funding for restoration from the World Monuments Fund Jewish Heritage Grant Program. Next door is the late nineteenth-century white stone **Temple Synagogue**, which contains frescoes representing Jerusalem and the Holy Land.

Strada Ştefan cel Mare, dotted with several attractive old villas, heads west out of Piaţa Libertăţii; Elena Cuza, the widow of the deposed leader, Alexandru Ioan Cuza (see p.388), lived at no. 55 until her death in 1909. The main thoroughfare south is Bulevardul Republicii; set back from the boulevard, one block south of the square, is the small **house of Calistrat Hogas** (Tues–Sun 10am–6pm), now a memorial museum to the writer (1847–1918), who praised the charms of Neamţ county when the town still consisted of Alpine-style chalets.

A small road heads east from Piaţa Libertăţii to Piaţa Ştefan cel Mare, from where Strada Eminescu heads south to the **History Museum** (Tues–Sun 10am–6pm on the corner of Bulevardul Decebal and Strada Chimiei. The museum devotes its ground floor to ancient relics; including a life-size replica of a Stone Age hut furnished with wolfskins and grindstones, and fertility charms and pottery created by the Cucuteni culture (c.3000–2000 BC). Across the corridor are a Bronze Age tomb, complete with skeleton, and a curious Iron Age figure dubbed the Scythian Rider (Cavalier Scit). Upstairs, the Romanian aptitude for woodcarving is exemplified by a "knitted cable" throne and an exquisite door, with the Moldavian crest entwined in foliage.

Eating and drinking

The Italian community in Piatra Neamţ has done wonders for its restaurant scene in recent years. The best and most popular **place to eat** in the centre is *Cavallino Rosso*, an unpretentious place with brick-oven pizzas and a few simple but good pasta dishes. It's in the mall opposite the *Hotel Ceahlău*. *Restaurant Cozla*, a few doors down, is a reasonable, if staid, Romanian joint. Around 1km west of the centre at Str. Burebista 65, is the more upscale *Villa Italia*, which has fine *bruschetta* and an extensive wine list. *Tequila Bowling*, next to the *Strand* campsite, is the best **place to drink**; in addition to occasional specials on Tequila shots, there's a good restaurant here, and a disco on Saturday nights. The terrace at the *Hotel Ceahlău* is also popular, with live music most nights in the summer. For dessert, more or less authentic *gelato* is on offer at *Patti Paris*, opposite the *Hotel Central*. Supermarket Cosmos, opposite the History Museum at Piaţa Mihail Kogălniceanu 3, is a good shop to stock up at before heading out on a day-trip; nearby, at Str. Mihail Kogălniceanu 4, Crama Tohani is a smart little wine shop.

Văratec and Agapia

The rolling countryside west of the road between Piatra and Târgu Neamţ provides an idyllic setting for Romania's largest convents: **Văratec**, with 280 nuns and **Agapia**, with 300. Each comprises a walled convent and a village, up the road from an agricultural village of the same name. The nuns live in cosy houses with pale blue, fretted eaves and glassed-in verandas. Note that taking photos within the convents is not allowed.

You can get to the convents by **bus** from Piatra Neamţ; services normally wait thirty minutes before starting back. Transportation between the convents is provided by three daily buses to Văratec from Târgu Neamţ, all of which call first at Agapia. These buses, however, are among the most decrepit in Romania, and as the landscape is so lovely you may prefer to walk from one to the other you're staying in Piatra Neamţ and miss the last bus back (which is all too likely if you don't get an early start), walk or hitch the 5km back to the main road, where the final buses between Târgu Neamţ and Piatra Neamţ come through at about 6pm.

Văratec Monastery and around

Hedgerows, alive with sparrows and wagtails, line the narrow road winding through Văratec to the pretty nuns' village and **Văratec Monastery**, its white-washed walls and balconies enclosing a lovely garden shaded by cedars. The novices inhabit two-storey buildings named after saints, while the older nuns live in cottages, next to a **museum of icons** (Tues–Sun 10am–6pm), and an **embroidery school** established by Queen Marie in 1934. It's an odd but not unfitting site for the **grave of Veronica Micle**, the poet loved by Eminescu, who couldn't afford to marry her after the death of her despised husband (see box p.262).

Văratec was founded in the eighteenth century, around a church that no longer exists; the site of its altar is marked by a pond with a statue of an angel. The present **church**, built in 1808, is plain and simple, culminating in two bell-shaped domes and six chimneys. To cope with the harsh winters, the nuns have sensibly installed stoves in the narthex, which is barely separated from the nave by a pair of columns.

In fine weather, it's an agreeable **walk from Văratec to Agapia**; the seven-kilometre trail through the woods takes one and a half hours, starting by house no. 219, back down the road from Văratec Monastery. It's also possible to walk along the road connecting the two convents (from Văratec, walk about 1km back towards the main road, then turn left). The road passes through the pretty village of Filioara, where you'll find the finest of the local agrotouristic pensions, the Antrec-affiliated *Pensiunea Alina* (☎0233/244 861; ❹ including dinner and breakfast), a friendly place with dark wood furniture and excellent meals. Another trail from Văratec, marked by blue dots, leads west to **Sihla hermitage** (2hr), built into the cliffs near the cave of St Teodora, and hidden by strange outcrops.

A backroad (1 bus a day) connects Sihla to the **Sihistria and Secu hermitages**, and continues to the main road between Târgu Neamț and the Ceahlău Massif, 2km west of the turn-off for Neamț Monastery (see p.253).

Agapia Monastery and around

Agapia Monastery actually consists of two convents a few kilometres apart; most visitors are content to visit only the main complex of **Agapia din Vale** (Agapia in the Valley), at the end of a muddy village of houses with covered steps. The walls and gate tower aim to conceal rather than to protect; inside is a whitewashed enclosure around a cheerful garden. At prayer times, one of the nuns beats an insistent rhythm on a wooden *toaca*; another plays the panpipes, followed by a medley of bells, some deep and slow, others high and fast. The monastery **church** was built in 1644–47 by Prince Basil the Wolf's brother, Gavril Coci. Its helmet-shaped cupola, covered in green shingles, mimics that of the gate tower. After restoration, the interior (obscured by scaffolding at the time of writing) was repainted in 1858–1860 by Nicolae Grigorescu, the country's foremost painter at the time; he returned to stay at Agapia from 1901–02. Off to the right is a **museum** of icons and vestments from the seventeenth and eighteenth centuries (daily 10am–7pm). Downhill by the Topolnița stream stands a wooden church with three shingled domes and a modern gate tower. For a snack, try the fine bakery stall at the entrance to the convent; further down the road a restaurant, *Cerbul Carpatin*, serves typical Romanian fare.

The older **Agapia din Deal** (Agapia on the Hill) or Agapia Veche (Old Agapia) is a smaller, more tranquil convent, high up a wooded slope about half an hour's walk from Agapia din Vale; ten minutes out, turn right at the unmarked junction. Another trail from the main monastery leads to Văratec (see above). Several **pensions** have sprung up around Agapia in the last few years. *Casa Timofte* (☎0233/244 663; ❶), halfway between the main road and the convent, is simple but clean; nearby, *Pensiunea Andreea* (☎0233/244 760, @pens_andreea@yahoo.com; ❷), with a small shop and a garish restaurant attached, is modern enough but far from realizing its pretensions to glamour. One more option, back on the main road 1km south of the Agapia turnoff, is the pleasant *Pensiunea Lacramioara*, (☎0233/247 012; ❷). During the summer, it's also possible to stay in Agapia's Theological Seminary (❶), 100m down from the convent.

Tărpeşti

Two daily buses from Piatra Neamţ to Târgu Neamţ trace a leisurely semicircle along backroads east of the main route, first taking in the village of **Războieni**, where there is a spireless church (built by Stephen the Great in memory of the soldiers who died here in a 1476 battle with the Ottomans), and then, about 10km southeast of Târgu Neamţ, passing the turn-off to the ramshackle village of **TĂRPEŞTI**, home of the delightful **Neculai Popa Museum** (daily 9am–7pm; ⬤npopamuseum.netfirms.com). Set in Popa's own yard, the museum's diverse works are displayed with care and wit. The main building is devoted to Popa's folk art collections, including paintings by naïve Romanian artists, an unusually good set of icons, and old Moldavian handicrafts such as thick leather belts and painted trousseaux. The colourful masks and folk costumes on display in the second building, many made by Popa's wife Elena, are occasionally used in children's pageants recounting legends such as that of Iancu Jianu, an eighteenth-century forest bandit known as the Robin Hood of Wallachia; performances featuring village children can be arranged with advance notice. In good weather, Popa can be seen in the sculpture garden using a timeworn chisel to fashion a new totem pole or menhir. His son is now the caretaker of the museum, and gives tours in Romanian and French, and there is also a gallery where folk art and icons are sold.

From the Tărpeşti turn-off, it's a pleasant but unshaded 3km walk to the village, where signs will direct you to the museum; alternatively, Tărpeşti (still shown on some maps and signs as Tărpeşti) is served by two direct buses from Târgu Neamţ. There is no accommodation here, and trade is limited to a few basic shops that double as taverns.

Târgu Neamţ

TÂRGU NEAMŢ (German Market) is smaller and duller than Piatra, making it a less attractive stopover. Neither of the two museums in town – the **house of Veronica Micle** and the **Historical and Ethnographic Museum** (both Tues–Sun 10am–6pm), facing each other on Strada Ştefan cel Mare – is of any great interest, but the town's saving grace is the Neamţ **citadel** (Tues–Sun 10am–6pm), Moldavia's finest ruined castle. Visible from the road to Neamţ Monastery, but far more impressive at close quarters, the citadel is a kilometre west along Strada Ştefan cel Mare and then ten minutes north up an asphalt path equipped like a motorway with street lights and crash barriers. Founded by Petru I Muşat in 1359, it was beefed up by Stephen just in time to withstand a siege by the Turkish sultan Mohammed II in 1496. Later, it was partly demolished on the orders of the Turks, but again saw service in 1691 in the war between Moldavia and Poland. The approach to the citadel is over a long, curving **wooden bridge** raised on pillars high above a moat; the final stretch was originally designed to flip enemies down into an oubliette. Within the **bailey**, a warren of roofless chambers that used to be an arsenal, courthouse and baths, surrounds a deep well, ringed by battlements that survey the Neamţ valley for miles around.

Practicalities

Târgu's **bus station** is a few minutes from the centre on Strada Cuza Vodă, and the **train station** is a further fifteen minutes east on the same road. The best **hotel** in town is the three-star *Trust Doina* at Str. Mihail Kogălniceanu (☎0233/790 272, ⓦwww.trustdoina.ro; ❹), a new and modern place behind the main church on Bulevardul Ştefan cel Mare. If you have a car, another option is the *Staţiunea Oglinzi* (☎0233/663 590; ❷), a balneo-therapeutical resort with an excellent restaurant 4km north of town on the Suceava road. The only decent **place to eat** in Târgu Neamţ proper is the restaurant at the *Trust Doina*. If you're heading to Iaşi by car, consider stopping 15km east of Târgu Neamţ at *Hanul Ancuţei* (☎0233/742 600, ⓔnusa@gavis.ro; ❸), an excellent if slightly kitsch roadside restaurant, which also has a few comfortable rooms.

Neamţ Monastery

The twelfth-century **Neamţ Monastery**, 12km northwest of Târgu Neamţ, is the oldest in Moldavia and is the region's chief centre of Orthodox culture; it is also the largest men's monastery in Romania, with seventy monks and dozens of seminary students. The original hermitage, founded by Petru I Muşat, was rebuilt in the early fifteenth century by Alexander the Good, with fortifications that protected Neamţ from the Turks and a printing house that spread its influence throughout Moldavia. The new church, founded here by Stephen the Great in 1497 to celebrate a victory over the Poles, became a prototype for Moldavian churches throughout the next century, and its school of miniaturists and illuminators led the field.

Outwardly, Neamţ resembles a fortress, with high stone walls and its one remaining octagonal corner tower (there used to be four). On the inside of the gate tower, a painted Eye of the Saviour sternly regards the monks' cells with their verandas wreathed in red and green ivy, and the seminary students in black tunics milling around the garden. The sweeping roof of Stephen's church overhangs blind arches inset with lozenges and glazed bricks, on a long and otherwise bare facade. Its trefoil windows barely illuminate the interior, where pilgrims kneel amid the smell of mothballs and candlewax. At the back of the compound is a smaller church dating from 1826, containing frescoes of the Nativity and the Resurrection.

Outside the monastery stands a large onion-domed **pavilion** for Aghiastmatar, the "Blessing of the water", to be taken home in bottles for use in times of illness.

The monastery can be reached by three daily **buses** from Târgu Neamţ; you could also catch one of the frequent services along the main road and walk the remaining 4km to the monastery. There are **rooms** (❷) and a summer **campsite** with huts (❶) at the *Hanul Branişte*, 3km east of the turning to Neamţ monastery.

The Ceahlău massif

West of Târgu Neamţ, 60km beyond the turning to Neamţ monastery, looms the **Ceahlău massif**. Aptly designated on local maps as a *zona abrupt*, it rises above neighbouring ranges in eroded crags whose fantastic shapes were anthropomorphized in folk tales and inspired Eminescu's poem, *The Ghosts*. The Dacians believed that Ceahlău was the abode of their supreme deity, Zamolxis, and that the gods transformed the daughter of Decebal into the Dochia peak. The massif is composed of Cretaceous sediments – especially conglomerates, which form pillar-like outcrops – and covered with stratified belts of beech, fir and spruce, with dwarf pine and juniper above 1700m. Its **wildlife** includes chamois, lynx, capercaillie, bears and boars, and the majestic Carpathian stag. Ceahlău's isolation is emphasized by the huge, artificial **Lake Bicaz** (Lacul Izvoru Muntelei) that half-encircles its foothills. A hydroelectric dam, built in 1950, rises at the southern end, 3km from the village of **BICAZ**, which is accessible by bus and train from Piatra Neamţ. During summer, there are **boat trips** from the dam to the Pârâul Mare landing stage below Ceahlău itself. Bicaz's **history museum** (Tues–Sun 10am–6pm) has a display on the building of the dam.

There are two basic **hotels** in Bicaz, the *Bicaz* (☎0233/671 122; ❸) and the *Lebada* (☎0233/671 036; ❸); whilst midway between the dam and the village of Potoci you'll find *Motel Cristina* (☎0233/671 456; ❷), where there are good **cabins** (❶). The *Bicaz Baraj* cabana (❶) stands right below the dam. Further up the lake is the village of **CEAHLĂU**, where there is a ruined seventeenth-century churchyard. There are also several pensions here, including *Elisabeta* (❶), an inexpensive place with traditional décor. At the northern end of the reservoir, the route from Târgu Neamţ to Durău and Transylvania, and the mountain road north to Vatra Dornei, converge at **POIANA LARGULUI**, where it's feasible to **change buses** if you're prepared to wait a few hours. In **Fărcaşa**, 10km out of Poiana Largului on the Vatra Dornei road, there's a fine, eighteenth-century wooden church, and a small motel, the *Orizont* (☎0233/267 111, ✉orizont@ambra.ro; ❸), which has a 24hr restaurant. The **campsite** in Poiana Largului is awful, but there's a decent one, *Popas Petru Vodă*, at the Argel Pass, 12km uphill towards Târgu Neamţ.

Hiking above Durău

The main base for **hiking** in the massif is **DURĂU**, on its northwestern side, which can be reached by bus from Piatra Neamţ or Târgu Neamţ. Durău's major draw is the **Ceahlău Feast**, on the second Sunday in August, an opportunity for shepherds to parade their finery and an attraction for many tourists. It also boasts a small **hermitage** built in 1830–3. The three-star *Bradul* (☎ & ☎0233/256 501; ❺) is the finest and best value of Durău's four hotels. There are also two central **campsites**, as well as a dozen or so **pensions**, of which *Gabriela* (☎0233/256 652; ❸) and *Dalia* (☎0233/256 504; ❸) are above average. Bikes can be rented at the *Bistriţa* hotel. From December to March, **skiing** replaces hiking as the main activity in the resort.

From the town, it's a forty-five-minute walk to the *Fântânele* cabana (1220m; ☎0744/186 360; ❷), on the steep, red-striped trail starting at the end of the road. A two-hour route (marked by blue crosses, then red crosses and finally yellow triangles) also runs there via the lovely **Duruitoarea cascade**, 2km from town, which falls a total of 25m in two stages. From *Fântânele*, the red-striped route (2hr) ascends within sight of the Panaghia rocks and Toaca peak to a plateau with glorious views and, in a further two hours, to the *Dochia* cabana (1750m; 0723/469 271; ❶). The route then continues south via several massive **rock pillars**, passing Ocolaşu Mare – at 1907m, the massif's highest peak – on its way to Poiana Maicilor, where the red-striped route turns downstream to the *Izvoru Muntelui* cabana and the Bicaz road, while another, less frequented trail marked with blue crosses runs on to Neagra village, on the road to the **Bicaz gorges**. Both routes take about two hours from Dochia.

Into Transylvania and north to Vatra Dornei

To the north and south of the massif, narrow valleys enable two routes **into Transylvania**. The northern one crosses the 1112-metre-high Borsec pass beyond the alpine spa of Borsec, before descending to Topliţa, in the upper Mureş valley. It's a scenic journey, and there are plenty of buses westwards from Borsec to Topliţa (see p.202). A better route runs through the **Bicaz gorges** (Cheile Bicazului), 25km upriver from Bicaz, past the lovely village of **BICAZ ARDELEAN**, which has a wooden church dating from 1829. Sheer limestone cliffs rise as high as 300m above the river, pressing so close around the Gâtul Iadului (Neck of Hell) that the road is hewn directly into the rockface. The *Cheile Bicazului* cabana, amid the gorges, marks the start of several **hiking** trails, and a longer one ascends from Lacu Roşu (see p.202) to the *Piatra Singuratică* (*Lonely Rock*) cabana. **Buses** from Piatra Neamţ, Târgu Neamţ and Bicaz travel this way en route to Gheorgheni (see p.201).

Alternatively, you can head north by bus from Târgu Neamţ via Poiana Largului to **Vatra Dornei** (see p.287). The 136-kilometre journey takes four hours following the River Bistriţa through a narrow, twisting valley hemmed in by fir-covered peaks. About 20km before Vatra Dornei, you'll see the well-signposted *Zugreni* cabana, across the river, from where a trail leads to the heart of the Rarău massif (see p.286).

Iaşi

IAŞI in the northeast of the region, is the cultural capital of Moldavia and by far its nicest city, the only one where you're likely to want to stay a while. Its university, theatre and resident orchestra rival those of Bucharest – which was merely a crude market town when Iaşi became a princely seat – and give it an air of sophistication enhanced by a large contingent of foreign students. Cementing its place in the nation's heart, Romanians associate Iaşi with the poet Eminescu, Moldavians esteem it as the burial place of St Paraschiva, and for several million smokers it's the home of Carpaţi, the country's cheapest brand of cigarettes.

Despite lying east of the main route northwards through Moldavia, Iaşi is accessible by direct **trains** from Bucharest, Cluj and several other major cities across the country, by **buses** and **maxitaxis** from most towns in Moldavia and by **flights** with Tarom and Angel Airlines (both Mon–Fri) from Bucharest. Carpatair operates flights to Timişoara, in the Banat (daily except Sun).

Some history

Iaşi's ascendancy dates from the sixteenth century, when the Moldavian princes (*hospodars*) gave up the practice of maintaining courts in several towns, and settled permanently in Iaşi. This coincided with Moldavia's gradual decline into a Turkish satellite, ruled by despots who endowed Iaşi with churches and monasteries to trumpet their earthly glory and ensure their eternal salvation. **Basil the Wolf** (Vasile Lupu, 1634–53) promulgated a penal code whereby rapists were raped and arsonists burned alive; he also founded a printing press and school, which led to the flowering of Moldavian literature during the brief reign, in 1710–11, of the enlightened **Dimitrie Cantemir**.

After Cantemir's death, Moldavia fell under the control of **Greek Phanariots**, originally from the Phanar district of Constantinople (Fener in modern Istanbul), who administered the region on behalf of the Ottoman

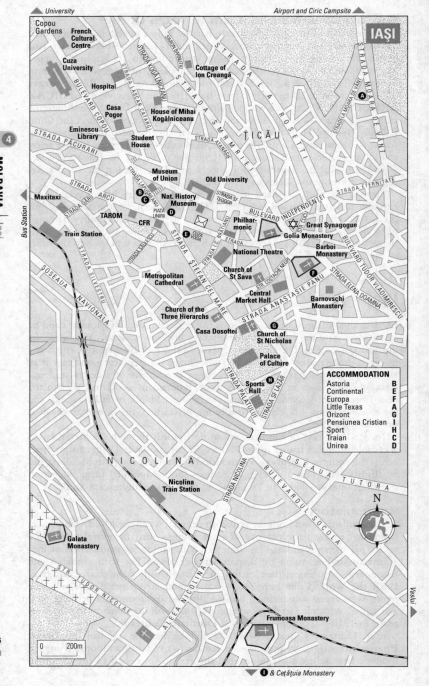

Copou Gardens

French Cultural Centre

Cuza University

Hospital

Casa Pogor

Eminescu Library

STRADA LASCAR CATARGI

STRADA KOGĂLNICEANU

SIMION BARNUTIU

STRADA A L A. ROSETTI

STRADA A SMÂRJE

STRADA MOARA DE VÂNT

STRADA MOARA DE VÂNT

Cottage of Ion Creangă

House of Mihai Kogălniceanu

Student House

BULEVARD COPOU

STRADA PĂCURARI

ŢICĂU

STRADA AŢANASIE

STRADA ETERNITATE

Maxitaxi

STRADA ARCU

STRADA GĂRII

TAROM

Museum of Union

Nat. History Museum

Old University

STRADA SF TEODOR

BULEVARD INDEPENDENTEI

STR TICĂU

B

C

CFR

PIATA UNIRII

D

CUZA VODĂ

E

Philharmonic

Great Synagogue

Golia Monastery

Train Station

SOSEAUA NATIONALA

STRADA SILVESTRU

STRADA SĂRĂRIEI

STRADA ŞTEFAN CEL MARE

STRADA I. C. BRĂTIANU

STRADA

National Theatre

Barboi Monastery

F

BULEVARD TUDOR VLADIMIRESCU

STR COSTACHE NEGRI

Church of St Sava

Metropolitan Cathedral

STRADA ELENA DOAMNA

Central Market Hall

Barnovschi Monastery

STRADA ANASTASIE PANU

Church of the Three Hierarchs

Casa Dosoftei

G

Church of St Nicholas

Palace of Culture

STRADA PALATULUI

STRADA SF LAZĂR

Sports Hall

H

ACCOMMODATION

Astoria	B
Continental	E
Europa	F
Little Texas	A
Orizont	G
Pensiunea Cristian	I
Sport	H
Traian	C
Unirea	D

NICOLINA

Nicolina Train Station

STRADA NICOLINA

BULEVARDUL SOCOLA

SOSEAUA TUTORA

N

Galata Monastery

STR. TUDOR NICOLAE

ALEEA NICOLINA

Frumoasa Monastery

Vaslui ▶

0   200m

▼ I & Cetăţuia Monastery

Moldavia and Iaşi have long been associated with the far right of Romanian politics. The most ardent member of Iaşi's League of Christian National Defence was **Corneliu Codreanu**, who went on, in the early 1930s, to found the Legion of the Archangel St Michael, better known as the **Iron Guard**. Wearing green shirts with bags of Romanian soil around their necks, the Legionari chased away village bailiffs to the delight of the peasantry, and murdered politicians deemed to be insufficiently nationalistic, until Marshal Antonescu jailed its leaders and Codreanu was shot "trying to escape". His followers fled to Berlin; when allowed back home, they helped carry out the Nazis' genocidal "Final Solution" in Romania.

After the war, the communists employed ex-Legionari as thugs against the socialists and the National Peasant Party, whom they regarded as their real enemies. Following the 1989 revolution, fascism has been making a comeback with the **România Mare** (Greater Romania) party of **Corneliu Vadim Tudor**, which ascribes all the nation's problems to a conspiracy of Jews, Magyars, Gypsies and everyone else who isn't a "pure" Romanian. Their headquarters in Iaşi is rather bizarrely shared with the Ecology Party.

Empire, chose and deposed the nominally ruling princes (of whom there were 36 between 1711 and 1821), and eventually usurped the throne for themselves. The boyars adopted Turkish dress and competed to win the favour of the Phanariots, who alone could recommend their promotion to the sultan. As Ottoman power weakened, this dismal saga was interrupted by the surprise election of Prince **Alexandru Ioan Cuza**, who clinched the unification of Moldavia and Wallachia in 1859 with the diplomatic support of France. In the new Romania, Cuza founded universities at Iaşi and Bucharest, introduced compulsory schooling for both sexes, and secularized monastic property, which at the time accounted for one fifth of Moldavia. Finally, his emancipation of the serfs so enraged landowners and military circles that in 1866 they overthrew Cuza and restored the status quo ante – but kept the union.

The latter half of the nineteenth century was a fertile time for intellectual life in Iaşi, where the Junimea literary circle attracted such talents as the poet **Mihai Eminescu** and the writer **Ion Creangă**, who, like the historian, **Nicolae Iorga**, both became national figures. This was also the heyday of Jewish culture in Iaşi, and in 1876 local impresario **Avrom Goldfadn** staged the world's first Yiddish theatre performance at the Pumul Verde (Green Tree) wine garden. The Junimea brand of nationalism was more romantic than chauvinist, but unwittingly paved the way for a deadlier version in the Greater Romania that was created to reward the Old Kingdom (Regat) for its sacrifices in World War I, when most of the country was occupied by the Germans, and the government was evacuated to Iaşi. With its borders enlarged to include Bessarabia and Bucovina, Moldavia inherited large minorities of non-Romanian-speaking Jews, Ukrainians and Gypsies, aggravating ethnic and class tensions in a region devastated by war.

During the 1920s, Iaşi became notorious for **anti-Semitism**, spearheaded by a professor whose League of Christian National Defence virtually closed the university to Jews, then over a third of the population, and later spawned the Iron Guard (see box above). Their chief scapegoat was **Magda Lupescu**, Carol II's locally born Jewish mistress, who was widely hated for amassing a fortune by shady speculations; in 1940, she fled abroad with Carol in a train stuffed with loot.

Arrival and accommodation

Arriving at Iaşi's main **train station** on Strada Silvestru, or the **maxitaxi station** across the street, you can either catch tram #3, #6 or #7 (buy a ticket from the driver or at one of the kiosks marked RATI), take a taxi, or walk to the central Piaţa Unirii in ten to fifteen minutes, past the ornamental tower up Strada Gării and right along Strada Arcu. Iaşi's **airport** is about 5km northeast of the centre; the only way to get there is by taxi. The **CFR** office is just down the road on Piaţa Unirii. The intercity **bus station** (℡0232/214 720) is behind the *Autocenter*, 1km past the train station on Şoseaua Moara de Foc; take tram #7. In general, **taxis** in Iaşi are metred and reliable, with most charging around €0.25/km; Delta Taxi (℡0232/222 222) and Go-Taxi (℡0232/279 444) are two good companies. There is no tourist information office.

Accommodation

Iaşi has some reasonable mid-range and upscale **hotels**, but the budget options, though central, are less appealing. You might find a bed in one of the many student dorms (*caminul de studenti*) located around the university on Bulevardul Copou, 1km northwest of the centre. **Camping Ciric**, by a lake 2km north of town, is only open over summer; buses run there hourly at weekends (and less frequently during the week) from Târgul Cocului, outside the Golia Monastery. There are also cabins (❷) here in a wooded setting, but the filthy toilets are a big deterrent. Antrec, at Str. Sf. Lazar 25 Bl. K4 (℡0232/216 227 or 0721/223 710, ✉iasi@antrec.ro), can arrange **homestay accommodation** outside the city.

Astoria Str. Lăpuşneanu 1 ℡0232/233 888, ✉reservation@hotelastoria.ro. A cheerful new place with comfortable beds, a/c and mini fridges. Next to the *Traian*. ❺

Continental Str. Cuza Vodă 4 ℡0232/211 846. Old-fashioned and dusty, with friendly, English-speaking staff but dodgy communal bathrooms that are not for the faint of heart. Note that room with bath actually means room with sink. ❷

Pensiunea Cristian Str. Cetăţuia 14A ℡0232/242 363, 🌐www.pensiunea-cristian.go.ro. Clean and friendly new pension with large rooms; a generous breakfast is included. Good value, but the drawback is the strange location, several kilometres south of the centre, with the Cetăţuia Monastery forest on one side and a disused tank-factory on the other. There's no public transportation here; a taxi costs about €1.50. ❸

Europa Str. Anastasie Panu 26 ℡0232/242 000, ℻242 002, 🌐www.hoteleuropa.ro. Lifeless, new four-star glass tower attached to Iaşi's World Trade Center; with conference facilities, high-speed Internet, room service and two restaurants. ❾

Little Texas Stradela Moara de Vânt 31 ℡ & ℻0232/272 545, 🌐www.littletexas.org. Out on the road towards the airport. No longer the only luxury option, but this small and gracious American-run hotel (actually a charity venture) is still a cut above the rest. Top-class facilities and furniture imported from the US; included is a typically hearty American breakfast in the superb restaurant (see p.264). ❼

Orizont Str. G. Ureche 27 ℡0232/256 070, ℻215 037. Small modern and decent-value hotel, with bar, coffee shop, restaurant, nightclub and an Internet café. Breakfast included. ❺

Sport Str. Sfântu Lazăr 76 ℡0232/232 800, ℻231 540. Five hundred metres downhill from the Palace of Culture. Better than the other budget options, with passable rooms and hot water, but usually booked by youth athletic groups in summer. ❷

Traian Piaţa Unirii 1 ℡0232/266 666, ℻212 187. Atmospheric establishment, designed by Eiffel in 1882, that's easily the most attractive building on Piaţa Unirii. All rooms elegantly furnished, with baths or showers. Friendly, very knowledgeable staff. Divided between two-star and four-star rooms at the time of writing, but everything slated to be four-star by the end of 2004. Breakfast included ❽

Unirea Piaţa Unirii 2 ℡0232/240 404, ℻212 864. Located on the main square, this large 1960s high-rise ought to be demolished but instead is being renovated. Friendly staff. Rooms with private baths; breakfast included. ❹

The Town

Many of the sights of Iași can be found on the streets radiating from **Piața Unirii**. To the north, Strada Lăpușneanu heads towards the university district of Copou and the residential district of Țicău. Heading east, Strada Cuza Vodă leads towards ancient monasteries and the sole remaining synagogue, while Bulevardul Ștefan cel Mare leads south towards the cathedral, the **Church of the Three Hierarchs**, easily the best known building in Iași, and the huge **Palace of Culture**, housing a range of museums. Beyond this lies the Nicolina quarter, where you'll find the hilltop monasteries.

Around Piața Unirii

Strada Lăpușneanu heads northeast from Piața Unirii to Cuza's old house at no. 14, which now houses the **Museum of Union** (Tues–Sun 10am–5pm), although at the time of writing this was closed for extensive renovation; among other exhibits normally on display is a coffee set emblazoned with an imperial "N", symbolizing Napoleon III's support for unification. The rather comic tale of Cuza's downfall in 1866 is glossed over. Bursting into his bedroom, soldiers found Cuza making love to the King of Serbia's daughter-in-law; when pressed to sign a decree of abdication, he objected, "But I haven't got a pen." "We have thought of that," they said, producing a pen and ink, whereupon Cuza complained of the lack of a table. "I will offer myself," said a colonel, presenting his back to forestall further procrastination, and so Cuza signed and went into exile. He died in Heidelberg in 1873.

South along Bulevardul Ștefan cel Mare

Iași's traditional interplay of civil and religious authority is symbolized by a parade of edifices along **Bulevardul Ștefan cel Mare și Sfânt**, (simply Ștefan cel Mare on most addresses) where florid public buildings face grandiose churches. Midway along the street, which is closed to traffic at weekends, the huge, colonnaded **Metropolitan Cathedral**, built in 1761 and still the largest Orthodox church in Romania, dominates the neighbouring Metropolitan's Palace and Theological College, and dwarfs worshippers with its cavernous interior, painted by Tattarescu. In 1641, Basil the Wolf spent the country's entire budget for the following year and a half to acquire the **relics of St Paraschiva** of Epivat (c.980–1050), which were moved to the cathedral in 1889. Venerated as the patron saint of Moldavia, households, harvests, traders and travellers, St Paraschiva seems to be a conflation of four Orthodox martyrs of that name. There are pilgrims here throughout the year (some crawling the last 100m or so), but on October 14 the cathedral overflows with thousands of worshippers who come to kneel before the blue and gold bier containing the relics. Immediately to the south stands the **Old Metropolitan Church of St George**, also raised in 1761; the pillars of its porch are carved with symbolic animal reliefs, in the post-Brâncoveanu style of Wallachia.

Across the road and east of an elegant park, is the French-eclectic style **National Theatre**, built by the Viennese architects Fellner and Helmer in the 1890s, with one of the most beautiful auditoriums in the country. The theatre is named after the company's founder, Vasile Alecsandri (1821–90) who, owing to a lack of plays in Romanian, had to write much of its initial repertory.

A few minutes further south along Bulevardul Ștefan cel Mare from the Church of St George, you arrive at the famous **Church of the Three Hierarchs** (daily 9am–noon & 3–5pm), its exterior carved all over with chevrons, meanders and rosettes as intricate as lace. When it was completed in

1639 – perhaps by the Armenian master-builder Ianache Etisi – Basil the Wolf had the exterior gilded, desiring it to surpass all other churches in splendour. Aside from its unique carvings, the church follows the classic Byzantine trilobate plan, with two octagonal drums mounted above the *naos* and *pronaos* in the Moldavian fashion. Over the following two centuries, the church was damaged by fire and six earthquakes, but was rebuilt by the French architect Lecomte de Noüy in 1882–87; the interior décor is wholly his and quite missable. The church houses the **sarcophagi** of Basil the Wolf, Dimitrie Cantemir and Alexandru Ioan Cuza. Since 1994, this has once more become a working monastery. The adjacent abbot's house, in which Basil the Wolf set up Moldavia's first printing press in 1644, contains a display of religious icons (officially Tues–Sun 10am–4pm; ask in the church if the door is locked).

From the Church of the Three Hierarchs, Strada Costache Negri heads east to the **Church of St Sava**, a contemporary, yet quite different building whose earth-coloured walls and red pantiles give it the look of an Andean village church. Its massive, squat bell tower is doubly impressive for being devoid of ornamentation.

The Palace of Culture and around

At the southern end of Ştefan cel Mare, an equestrian **statue of Stephen the Great** and a cross commemorating the martyrs of the revolution are over-shadowed by the stupendous **Palace of Culture** – a neo-Gothic pile built between 1905 and 1926 as a government centre, which now houses four of the city's **museums** (Tues–Sun 9am–5pm; €0.50 each). Its spired tower and pinnacled wings presage a vast lobby awash with mosaics, stained glass and armorial reliefs, dominated by a magnificent double staircase. You can admire the décor free of charge, but tickets are required for entry to the museums.

The corridor on the left of the lobby leads to the **Museum of Science and Technology**, displaying music boxes, symphoniums and orchestrions; the curators might be persuaded to demonstrate the ingenious Popper's Bianca, a kind of projector, which anticipated the cinema. To the right of the lobby, the **Moldavian History Museum** is strong on local archaeology. Upstairs, casts of antique statues line the way to an **Ethnographic Museum**, whose collection includes a small windmill, six-foot-long Moldavian alpine horns, hollow trunks used as beehives, and oil-presses the size of trees. The **Museum of Art**, which is divided into Romanian and European galleries, has no fewer than two-dozen paintings by Grigorescu, and a fine collection of post-1919 Colourist works, such as Pallady's *Nude on a Yellow Background*. Portraits of bearded boyars in Turkish fur hats, and scenes of Jewish life by Octav Băncila (1872–1944), give more local colour. In the European section, Ludovic Starski's *The City of Iaşi in 1842* presents an unrecognizable vision of church spires not hemmed in by concrete. There's also a *Pieta* by Murillo, and a Rubens, *Caesar Receiving Pompey's Head*. The vaulted Hall of Voivodes (*Sala Voievozilor*), containing the portraits of dozens of rulers, is used for temporary art shows.

Two much-restored relics of Iaşi's past stand between the Palace and the Centru Civic. The arcaded seventeenth-century **Casa Dosoftei** is a fitting home for the dull **Museum of Old Moldavian Literature** (Tues–Sun 9am–5pm) – it once housed a press that spread the words of the cleric and scholar Metropolitan Dosoftei, a statue of whom sits outside. The Phanariot policy of using Iaşi's presses to spread Greek as the language of Orthodox ritual had the unintended result of displacing the ossified Old Slavonic tongue from this position, clearing the way for intellectuals to agitate for the use of their own language, Romanian. Next door is the **Courtly Church of**

St Nicholas, the oldest building in Iaşi, erected by Stephen in 1491 but pulled down and rebuilt by Lecomte de Noüy in 1885–97; its svelte facade now masks a hermetic world of carved pews and gilded frescoes.

The Centru Civic and Golia Monastery

From the south end of Bulevardul Ştefan cel Mare, Strada Anastasie Panu leads east through the **Centru Civic**. Due to the array of administrative buildings that already existed on Ştefan cel Mare, the architects of Iaşi's Centru Civic wisely focused on consumer aspirations instead, hence the communist-era Moldova Magazin Universal, the more modern **Central Market Hall** midway along Strada Anastasie Panu, and the rounded Scala complex opposite. Further east, opposite the new World Trade Center and next to a open park, you can catch a glimpse of the former **Barnovschi Monastery**, founded by Prince Barnovschi in 1627; the monastery is now reduced to a pale buff church with a shingled porch and two onion-spires, flanked by a gate tower. The **Bărboi Monastery**, at the far end of the main road, has fared better. Housed in a walled garden with a tall neo-Byzantine gate tower, it still bears the name of its seventeenth-century founder, Urşu Barboi, although the monastery's Church of Peter and Paul, with an overhead gallery for the choir, was built in the 1840s by Dimitrie Sturza, who is buried in the pronaos.

North of the Centru Civic, protected by a thirty-metre-tall gate tower and rounded corner bastions, is the **Golia Monastery**, a peaceful haven in the heart of Iaşi, whose dozen monks enjoy a rose garden dotted with shrines. Founded in the 1560s by Chancellor Ion Golia, the monastery was rebuilt and fortified by Basil the Wolf, who began a new **Church of the Ascension** within the monastery's grounds, completed by his son Ştefăniţa in 1660. A striking mixture of Byzantine, Classical and Russian architecture (though the interior was filled with scaffolding at the time of writing), the church boasts of its associations with Tsarist Russia, having been visited by Peter the Great in 1711, and serving as the burial place for the **viscera of Prince Potemkin**, Catherine the Great's favourite. These were removed so that the rest of his body could be preserved and returned home after he died in 1791, after catching a fever in Iaşi and defying doctors' orders by wolfing huge meals, starting at breakfast with smoked goose and wine. He actually died across the border in present-day Moldova.

West along Bulevardul Independenţei

Bulevardul Independenţei, a drab thoroughfare linking the Golia Monastery with Strada Lăpuşneanu, has a few sights worth noting. Between an apartment building and a clump of kiosks near the start of the boulevard, you can see the Star of David atop the **Great Synagogue** – a sad misnomer for this low-domed edifice founded in 1671 and restored in the 1970s, shortly before most of its congregation left for Israel.

Midway along the boulevard, at no. 72, the **Natural History Museum** (Closed Aug; Tues, Thurs & Sat 9am–3pm, Wed & Fri 9am–4pm, Sun 10am–5pm) occupies the eighteenth-century Russet House, in whose Elephant Hall Cuza was elected Prince of Moldavia in 1859. At that time, the house belonged to the Society of Physicians and Naturalists, who had opened their collections to the public in 1834, making this one of the first such museums in Romania. Opposite stands the **Old University**, a Baroque pile that was constructed between 1795 and 1806 as the Callamachi family palace, and given to the university in 1860; it is now the centrepiece of the University of Medicine and Pharmacology. On the university's west side rises the spooky gate tower of the Sf Spiridion Monastery of 1786, which now houses a hospital; the monastery's old church contains the tomb of its founder, Grigore II Ghica, whose head was sent giftwrapped to the Sultan, for harbouring treasonous thoughts.

The boulevard finally leads to the **Independence Monument**, a statuesque woman striding forth ahead of billowing drapery, sculpted by Gabriela and Gheorghe Adoc in 1980. From here, you can head towards the university district or return to Piaţa Unirii via the shopping precinct behind the *Hotel Unirea*.

The university district

Copou, the university district, lies northwest of the centre, out along the boulevard of the same name, where trams (#1, #4, #8 and #13) rattle uphill with students hanging out of the doors. The foot of the hill is distinguished by a Stalinesque **Student House** to the right, with bas–reliefs of musical youths, alongside a small park overlooked by crumbling statues of Moldavian princes, and the colonnaded **Eminescu Library** to the left; working here as a librarian, Eminescu could nip across the road for meetings of the Junimea literary society (1863–85) in the **Casa Pogor**, just north of the Student House. Casa Pogor, which now houses the **Museum of Romanian Literature** (closed for renovation at the time of writing), belonged to Vasile Pogor, a co-founder of the Junimea society.

It's a few minutes' walk further uphill to **Cuza University**, an Empire-style edifice built in the 1890s, which acts as an umbrella for twenty-six faculties and eight research institutes of the Romanian Academy. Just to the north are the tranquil **Copou Gardens**, where Eminescu meditated under a favourite lime tree, now squat and ugly and boxed in by a low hedge. The park, with its many ponds, has an **exhibition centre** (Tues–Sun 10am–5pm) featuring a section on Eminescu.

Ţicău

Ţicău is a pretty, hilly, old residential quarter, east of the university area, where two memorial museums (Tues–Sun 10am–5pm) provide an excuse for a ramble. At no. 11 on the street that now bears his name, the **house of Mihail Kogălniceanu** commemorates the orator and journalist who was banned from lecturing for lambasting "oppression by an ignorant aristocracy", and who fled to Hapsburg Bucovina in 1848, but returned in the 1850s to help secure Cuza's election and serve as foreign minister. More entertaining is the **cottage of Ion Creangă** (Bojdeuca), at Str. Simion Bărnuţiu 11, which displays first

---

Mihai Eminescu

Mihai Eminescu, Romania's national poet, was born in 1850 in Botoşani, east of Suceava, and schooled in Cernăuţi, the capital of Hapsburg Bucovina. At the age of sixteen, he gave his surname, Eminovici, the characteristic Romanian ending *-escu* and became a prompter for a troupe of actors, until his parents packed him off to study law in Vienna and Berlin. Returning to Iaşi in 1874, he found a job as a librarian, joined the Junimea literary society, and had a tortured affair with Veronica Micle, a poet and wife of the university rector. After the rector's demise, Eminescu decided that he was too poor to marry her and took an editorial job in Bucharest to escape his grief. Overwork led to a mental breakdown in 1883, and from then on, until his death of syphilis six years later, periods of madness alternated with lucid intervals. He is best remembered for *Luceafărul* (*The Evening Star*), a 96-stanza ballad of love.

editions and prints of his works, including stills from films based on them. A defrocked priest and failed teacher, Creangă (1837–89) wrote *Recollections of Childhood* and fairy tales such as the *Giants of Irunica*, finally achieving critical success just before he died. From the cottage, you'll have a fine view of the vineyards and rolling hills that surround Iaşi.

The southern monasteries

A more ambitious way to stretch your legs is to visit the **monasteries** in the Nicolina district, south of the city centre, by the polluted stream of the same name. Catch bus #9 or a southbound maxitaxi downhill past the Palace of Culture and out along Strada Nicolina; cresting the flyover, you'll see the Cetăţuia and Galata monasteries on separate hill tops to the east and west, and a modern Roman Catholic church with a prow-like spire in the valley, which is where you should alight. From here, either follow Strada Tudor Nicolae west up the hill and past a cemetery, to reach Galata Monastery; or cross the main road, and head east through apartment buildings and across the tracks to find Frumoasa Monastery and the trail south to Cetăţuia. If you're intending to visit all three, it's best to see Cetăţuia first and work your way back to the others, as the hike to Cetăţuia requires the most effort.

The **Galata Monastery** stands on Miroslavei hill and is entered by a fortified gate tower. To the right of the gateway, beside a newer building in use today, are the ruins of the original monks' quarters and a Turkish bath. The monastery's church was built in 1579–84 to a typically Moldavian plan, with an enclosed porch and narthex preceding the nave. Its founder, Prince Petru Şchiopul, is buried in the nave with his daughter, Despina.

Frumoasa Monastery, on a low hillock surrounded by ruined walls, was derelict for decades, but after restoration is close to living up to its name, meaning "beautiful", once more. Largely built by the ill-fated Grigore II Ghica in 1726–33, Frumoasa differs from the other monasteries thanks to the ponderous form of Neoclassicism in favour when the complex was reconstructed in the early nineteenth century.

For Strada Cetăţuia, turn left out of the gate, at the far end of which you'll find a truck park with a road climbing to the summit of a hill. This is also accessible by a path, which is quicker, but a hard slog. Here, the "Citadel" or **Cetăţuia Monastery** seems remote from Iaşi; on misty days, the city is blotted out, and all you can see are moors. Its high walls conceal a harmonious ensemble of white stone buildings with rakish black roofs, interspersed by dwarf pines and centred on a church that's similar to the Church of the Three Hierarchs in town, but less richly carved. Prince Gheorghe Duca and his wife, who founded the monastery in 1669–72, are buried in the nave.

Eating, drinking and entertainment

Monasteries and museums notwithstanding, the best reason to visit Iaşi is its increasingly sophisticated restaurant scene. A number of stylish but affordable places offering Romanian interpretations of various world cuisines have opened recently, but there are also still plenty of staid, traditional establishments where you can try Moldavian cooking, as well as a few genuinely ethnic eateries. New places open fairly regularly; the free publication *Iaşi: What, Where, When* – available in the better hotels – carries details of the latest restaurant openings.

Fast food is available in the guise of the various joints dispensing pizza, spicy sausages (*mititei*) and other **snacks** along Bulevardul Ştefan cel Mare and in the university district. For a quick coffee or pastry, head for *Fast Food Amandina*, on

Piața Unirii. Additionally, there are a couple of kebab and falafel outfits on Strada Sfântu Teodor, near *Al-Rafidein* (see below). The best ice cream in town is in the *Gelateria Veneziana*, at the Iulius Mall. While many of the restaurants double as drinking spots, notably *GinGer Ale, Club Junimea* and *Casa Lavric*, there are also plenty of bars and summer-only terraces. In addition to the ones listed below, there are several flashy clubs 2km southeast of the centre, in the vicinity of the Iulius Mall. To get there, take tram #8, trolley-buses #42 or #43, or one of the maxitaxis marked *Tudor*.

Restaurants

Al-Rafidein Str. Sfântu Teodor 22. Unmarked, tiny Iraqi restaurant (look for the orange awning) on a small street just east of the old university building. Informal, with good meat dishes and salads. Daily 9am–midnight but sometimes closed in the afternoon.

Casa Alba Str. Lascăr Catargiu 16 bis. New Romanian restaurant in restored nineteenth-century house a few blocks northeast of Piața Eminescu. The food is basic but good; more striking is the modernist colour scheme. Daily noon–10pm.

Bamboo Chinese Str. Sfântu Teodor 26. Classy Chinese place that was closed for renovation at the time of writing.

Casa Bolta Rece Str. Rece 10. Legendary and still popular restaurant/wine garden that dates back well over a century. Decent traditional food and slightly kitsch peasant décor, with live folk music most evenings. Daily 8am–midnight.

La Cao Str. Arcu 8. Basic but pleasant Chinese restaurant. Daily noon–10pm.

Caraffa B-dul Tudor Vladimirescu, Iulius Mall. Mexican and Italian venture with the same owners as *GinGer Ale*. The food is up to scratch, but you may not wish to dine in a shopping mall. Daily noon–midnight.

Club Junimea Str. Vasile Pogor 4. Tuck into traditional Romanian food on the *Junimea's* summer terrace and indoor dining room, or sip on a beer down in the extraordinary wine cellar where Eminescu and his pals would drink during their literary meetings. Arrogant, slow service and relentless pop music, however, drive many away. Daily 10am–2am.

GinGer Ale Str. Săulescu 23 ☎0232/276 017. Tucked behind the CFR office on Piața Unirii, this is one of the best restaurants in the city, with a long and varied international menu (the risottos are especially good). Moderate to expensive, unless you come between noon and 4pm, when the entire menu (excluding drinks) is either half price (weekends) or 20 percent off (weekdays). Popular with expats. Daily 11am–1am.

Casa Lavric Str. Atanasie 21 ☎0232/229 960. Fashionable and slightly pretentious new restaurant serving surprisingly adventurous Romanian and international cuisine at reasonable prices. The *sarmale* are perfect; less traditional dishes are equally successful. Daily 11am–midnight.

Little Texas On the road towards the airport, attached to the hotel of the same name (see p.258). American establishment with impeccable service and exemplary Tex-Mex food (spice levels have been toned down to suit the Romanian palate); nachos are especially recommended, as is apple pie with vanilla ice cream. Choose between dining inside, amidst the more or less tasteful Wild West décor (smoking downstairs only), or on the fabulous terrace, which affords terrific views over the city. Well worth the €1 taxi ride. Daily 7am–11am.

Onyx Şos. Bucium 7. Elegant and upscale local favourite south of the centre, with well-prepared and stylishly presented European and Romanian cuisine. Daily 9am–midnight.

Rimini Str. Cuza Vodă 50. Cheap and agreeably informal Romanian place with simple but tasty food and friendly staff. Daily 11am–11pm.

Tosca Str. I.C. Brătianu 30. Straightforward, moderately priced Italian restaurant with a good selection of pasta dishes; convenient for the theatre. Daily 11am–10pm.

Traian Piața Unirii 1. Cavernous, empty holdover from the days when waiters eavesdropped for the Securitate. The food is decent; the prices remarkably low for such a posh place. Up for a complete renovation in the near future. Daily 11am–midnight.

Trei Sarmale Şos. Bucium 52 ☎0232/132 832. Ten minutes south of the centre by car or maxitaxi. Classic, vineyard-themed establishment, where staff in peasant costumes serve typical Romanian food. Standards have slipped a bit, but it's still a good place to eat. Daily 9am–2am.

La Valetta Str. Anastasie Panu, attached to the Central Market Hall. Clean and modern Italian place with above average pizza, strong espresso and floor-to-ceiling windows looking out over the vast concrete expanse of the Centru Civic. Daily 8am–11pm.

Bars, pubs and clubs

Corso Str. Lăpuşneanu 6. Massive, semicircular terrace bar that looks like an MTV dance set.
Club RS Str. Fătu 2. Bizarre, Greek-owned restaurant and nightclub with tone-deaf lounge singers.
Terasa Joker Str. Sfântu Sava 2. Simple and unpretentious, but very popular, summer beer garden located on a small street between the National Theatre and the Central Market Hall.
Old Time Café Str. Grigore Ureche 2. Near the *Hotel Orizont*. Home of Iaşi's best pool tables.

Quintas Str. Sf–ntu Sava 2. Pleasant, slightly louche café/bar in a lime-green Baroque mansion a few doors down from *Terasa Joker*. A good place for an afternoon drink or coffee; less agreeable Fri & Sat nights, when it's taken over by strutting teens.
Unirea Hotel Piaţa Unirii 2. There's a café-bar with a terrace on the thirteenth floor, the only place on the square from which you can't see the hotel itself.

Entertainment

Lovers of classical music should try to attend a performance of the **Moldavian Philharmonic**, the country's second orchestra after Bucharest. Its own venue was damaged in a recent fire, and performances are now held in the National Theatre on Bulevardul Ştefan cel Mare. Tickets are available at the National Theatre box office, or from the ticket agency (Agenţia Teatrală) at Ştefan cel Mare 8, near Piaţa Unirii.

Iaşi's big annual event is the **St Paraschiva festival week** (Sarbatorile Iaşului) on October 14, when people from all over Moldavia flood into town to pay homage to the saint buried in the Metropolitan Church. The **Festival of the Three Hierarchs** is celebrated on January 30, while traditional folklore festivals include the **Folk Music Festival** in mid-December, a **Festival of Winter Customs** on the first Sunday in January and a week-long **Ceramics Fair** (Târgul de Ceramica Cucuteni 5000) in mid-June.

Shopping

Iaşi has a decent variety of **shops**, including some of the best **bookstores** and **antique** retailers in the region. Galeriile Anticariat at Strada Lăpuşneanu 24 (daily 9am–8pm), selling antiques, icons and second-hand books in several languages, is easily the best shop of its kind in Moldavia, whilst the Galerile de Art at no. 7 is one of the few places where you can purchase genuine pieces of work by Iaşi's finest artists. There are outdoor bookstalls (daily 9am–7pm) lined along the same street while the Antiquarian bookshop, at Strada Cuza Vodă 15, is also worth a look, but the best place for new books in English is the small Librăria directly opposite the *Hotel Traian* on Piaţa Unirii. The Junimea bookshop, also on Piaţa Unirii, stocks a few **maps**.

Iaşi's outdoor **market** is behind the Central Market Hall, on Strada Costache Negri, in which you'll find Univers All (Mon–Sat 9am–9pm, Sun 10am–8pm), the most central of the modern **supermarkets**. The Gima Superstore (Mon–Sat 9am–11pm, Sun 9am–10pm), on the ground floor of the Iulius Mall, is another good choice. There's a smaller supermarket on Piaţa Unirii (Mon–Sat 7am–8pm), while two 24hr places can be found on Bulevardul Ştefan cel Mare.

Listings

Airport information ☏ 0232/278 510.
Car rental Icar Tours, in the Geleriile Comerciale at B-dul Ştefan cel Mare 1 (☏ 0232/216 319, ℱ 217 160, ℠ www.icar.ro), rents cars with or without drivers on a daily or weekly basis.

Flights Angel Airlines is at Str. Costache Negri 66 (☏ 0721/270 457, ℠ www.angelairlines.ro); a one-way ticket to Bucharest costs €68. The TAROM office is at Str. Arcu 3–5 (Mon–Fri 8am–6pm, Sat 8am–noon; ☏ 0232/267 768, ℱ 217 027).

Hospital On the corner of Str. L. Catargi and Str. G. Berthelot (☎0232/216 584).

Internet access There are good, 24hr Internet cafés on Str. Lăpuşneanu, opposite the *Galerile Anticariat*; on B-dul Ştefan cel Mare, opposite the Church of the Three Hierarchs; and inside the Hotel Orizont.

Libraries The British Council library is at Str. Păcurari 4 (☎0232/116 159; Mon, Tues & Thurs 1–7pm, Wed & Fri 9am–3pm, closed Aug).

Long distance buses Intertranscom (☎0232/588 557), located in the *Centrul Comercial Grand Orient*, opposite the train station, has maxitaxis to Piatra Neamţ, Târgu Neamţ and Suceava. Massaro Trans (☎0722/139 961), in the same building, has daily services to Bucharest via Bacău. Riedler Travel, near the Bărboi Monastery at Str. Costache Negri bl. C2 (☎0232/255 944, ✉riedler@euroweb.ro), runs a bus to Braşov every other day. Toros, 50m northwest of the train station on Şoseaua Moara de Foc (☎0232/276 339), has a daily bus to Istanbul.

Pharmacy There's a 24hr pharmacy at Piaţa Unirii 3, next to the Kodak shop and another on Str. Sfântu Lazar, next to the BCR on Str. Anastasie Panu.

Photography There are well-signposted Kodak outlets on B-dul Ştefan cel Mare and on the corner of Piaţa Unirii and B-dul Independenţei.

Post office Str. Cuza Vodă 3 (daily 8am–8pm). The Poste Restante service is unreliable.

Sports facilities The Strand athletic club, below the Palace of Culture on B-dul Ştefan cel Mare (daily 8am–7pm), has a swimming pool and tennis courts.

Train tickets The CFR office is at Piaţa Unirii 10 (☎0232/147 673; Mon–Fri 8am–8pm); upstairs, you can buy international tickets, including tickets for the overnight Prietenia to Chişinău in Republica Moldova, for which foreigners must already have a visa, obtainable from the Moldovan embassy in Bucharest (see p.87).

Suceava and around

When confronted with the belching factories sprawling across the river, it's difficult to imagine **SUCEAVA**, 150km northwest of Iaşi, as an old princely capital. The city's heyday more or less coincided with the reign of **Stephen the Great** (1457–1504), who warred ceaselessly against Moldavia's invaders – principally the Turks – and won all but two of the thirty-six battles he fought. This record prompted Pope Sixtus IV to dub him the "Athlete of Christ" – a rare accolade for a non-Catholic, which wasn't extended to Stephen's cousin Vlad the Impaler (see p.421), even though he massacred 45,000 of the infidel during one year alone.

While Stephen's successors, **Bogdan the One-Eyed** and **Petru Rareş**, maintained the tradition of endowing a church or monastery after every victory, they proved less successful against the Turks and Tatars, who ravaged Suceava several times. Eclipsed when Iaşi became the Moldavian capital in 1565, Suceava missed its last chance of glory in 1600, when **Michael the Brave** (Mihai Viteazul) completed his campaign to unite Wallachia, Moldavia and Transylvania by marching unopposed into Suceava's Princely Citadel. In terms of national pride, Suceava's nadir was the long period from 1775 to 1918, when the **Hapsburgs** ruled northern Moldavia from Czernowitz (Cernăuţi), although Suceava was able to prosper as a trading centre between the highland and lowland areas.

Under communism, this role was deemed backward and remedied by hasty **industrialization** – the consequences of which now blight the town. Its wood-processing and tanning plants have poisoned the Suceava River for miles, while the "Suceava Syndrome" of malformed babies has been linked to air pollution caused by the artificial fibres factory. The paper mill, one factory that has seen some success in recent years, is responsible for the noxious odours with which Suceava is too often enveloped.

For visitors, Suceava is primarily a base for **excursions to the Painted Monasteries** (see p.276), which are the only reason to spend much time here.

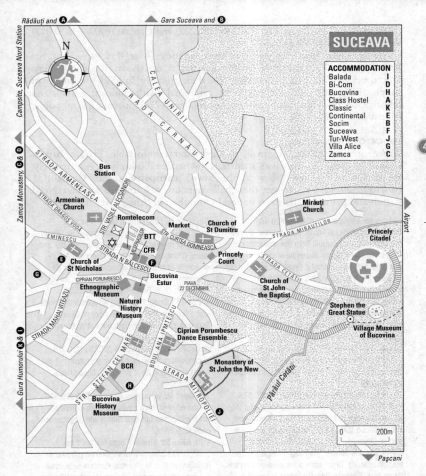

The town's own sights, many of which are dwarfed by apartment blocks, can be covered in a day.

Arrival, information and accommodation

Suceava Nord is the most useful of the town's three train stations, and the only one where every train stops. It wasn't designed to be a main station, though, and there is no tunnel connecting the platforms, so getting to or from your train often involves climbing through carriages on the intervening tracks. The **bus station** is just northwest of the town centre on Strada V. Alecsandri. Suceava's **airport**, 8km from town, is accessible only by taxi. There are still a few old public buses plying the city streets in a seeming endeavour to out-pollute the factories, but most locals have abandoned them for private **maxitaxis**. These follow three fixed routes, all stopping just east of the main square, Piaţa 22 Decembrie, between the Princely Court and the church of St John the Baptist. Maxitaxi #1 runs to and from Suceava Nord station, while #2 and #3 stop at Gara Suceava. Eurotaxi

(⊤0230/511 111), Canon Taxi (⊤0230/522 222) and Cristaxi (⊤0230/530 013) are respectable taxi companies.

The excellent Bucovina Estur **tourist agency** (Mon–Fri 9am–5pm, Sat 9am–2pm; ⊤0230/524 894, Ⓦwww.icar.ro), is on the west side of Piaţa Decembrie, at Str. Stefan cel Mare 24; their friendly English-speaking staff supply information on the city, offer car rental (with optional guide), and tailor-made tours of the monasteries (see box on p.276). Suceava has no public tourist information office.

Accommodation

There are a handful of small, modern and comfortable private **hotels** operating alongside Suceava's staid state-owned establishments. Alternatively, there's tent space and cabins at the town's **campsite**, at Str. Cernăuţi 1 (⊤0230/520 427; ❶); to get there, take maxitaxi #1 towards Suceava Nord station and get off at the Peco station before the rail bridge over the road.

Balada Str. Mitropoliei 3 ⊤0230/520 408, Ⓔbalada@balada.ro. Smart, private hotel, one of the best in town, downhill from the Monastery of St John the New. Some rooms have double beds and balconies plus cable TV. Breakfast included. ❻

Bi-Com Str. Narciselor 20 ⊤0230/216 881, Ⓦwww.geocities.com/bicom_hotel. Modern but rather gloomy private hotel in a quiet suburb. A 15min walk from the centre, or 5min from maxitaxi stop Maraşeşti. Some rooms have balconies. ❸

Bucovina B-dul A. Ipătescu 5 (⊤0230/217 048, Ⓕ520 250). Typical 1970s high-rise on the centre's southern fringe. A bit shabby, though all rooms have private bath and cable TV. Breakfast included. ❸

Class Hostel Str. Aurel Vlaicu 195 ⊤0230/525 213, Ⓦwww.classhostel.home.ro. New hostel literally on the edge of town; from the Suceava Nord station take a taxi (€1.50) or turn right and walk 15min. Clean and friendly, with two four-bed dorms and one double. Staff can arrange trips to the monasteries. Reservations necessary in winter. Camping is also possible. Breakfast is included. ❹

Classic Str. Universitatii 32 & 36 bis ⊤0230/510 000, Ⓦwww.classic.ro). Excellent new hotel in the university district, 700m east of the centre. The main wing has spotless modern rooms with a/c, while the annex, a few doors down, has smaller, good-value rooms that are just as well furnished. Breakfast extra. ❹–❻

Continental Arcaşul Str. Mihai Viteazul 4 ⊤0230/210 944, Ⓔarcasul@warpnet.ro. One of the better central hotels, with restaurant, bar and disco. Cheek by jowl with the fifteenth-century church of St Nicolas. Unrefurbished rooms ❹; otherwise ❼

Socim Str. Jean Bart 24 ⊤0230/516 901, Ⓕ257 133. Budget option in an apartment block just a few hundred metres in front of Gara Suceava. Clean and decent, but hot water is only at scheduled times. ❶

Suceava Str. N. Bălcescu 4 ⊤0230/521 079, Ⓔcentral@suceava.iiruc.ro. Very central, but not much else going for it. All rooms have private bathrooms. ❹

Tur-West Str. Humorului ⊤ & Ⓕ0230/526 626. On the edge of town down the Gura Humorului road, with small but nice rooms and a restaurant open till 9pm. ❹

Villa Alice Str. Simion Florea Marian 1 bis ⊤0230/522 254, Ⓔvillaalice2001@yahoo.com. Reliable pension in a central location with small but modern, clean and very comfortable rooms. One of the best-value places in town. Breakfast and laundry service extra. ❹

Zamca Str. Zamca ⊤0230/520 985, Ⓕ215 919. Private hotel overlooking the Zamca Monastery and a 10min walk from maxitaxi stop Maraşeşti. Modern and comfortable, with a lively outdoor bar and restaurant. ❹

The Town

Most of Suceava's sights relate to its past as a princely capital; the Princely Citadel and the Zamca Monastery are a good twenty minutes' walk east and west from the centre respectively, but most other sights are a short walk from the city's main square, **Piaţa 22 Decembrie**.

The **Princely Court** (Curtea Domnească), which amounts to very little more than ruins, is just north of Piaţa 22 Decembrie. To its northwest is the

Church of St Dumitru; built by Petru Rareş in 1534–35, it is typical of Moldavian churches of the period, with a double row of niche-bound saints on its facade, and coloured tiles ornamenting its drum. The interior frescoes, which date from the sixteenth to the nineteenth centuries, have recently been restored. The freestanding bell tower, added in 1561, bears the Moldavian crest (see box below). Five minutes' walk east along Strada Mirăuţilor from the Princely Court is **Mirăuţi Church**, the oldest in Suceava. Founded by Petru I Muşat, in about 1390, this was originally the Metropolitan cathedral, where the early princes of Moldavia were crowned. Its facade is decorated with blind arches and a sawtoothed cornice sandwiched between thick cable mouldings, while below the eaves are frescoes of saints, added at the end of the nineteenth century.

West from the Court along Strada Curtea Domnească will bring you to Suceava's **market**, which is busiest on Thursdays, when cartloads of peasants roll into town to sell their produce. Many wear traditional dress, such as fur-lined leather or sheepskin waistcoats, wrap-around skirts or white woollen pantaloons. Fine embroideries and crafts are exhibited in the **Ethnographic Museum** at Str. Ciprian Porumbescu 5 (Tues–Sun 10am–6pm), one block west of Piaţa 22 Decembrie via Strada Bălcescu. The museum is housed in a half-timbered building, the oldest civil edifice in Suceava county, which served as the court guesthouse during the seventeenth century.

The **Church of St John the Baptist**, built as his court chapel by Basil the Wolf in 1643, is just east of Piaţa 22 Decembrie, on the far side of the main Bulevardul Ana Ipătescu. At weekends, visitors may encounter funerals here, where the deceased is laid out in an open coffin, amid candles and loaves of bread, while a horse-drawn hearse waits outside. Corteges often parade around Piaţa 22 Decembrie, as do wedding parties – sometimes one follows another.

Strada Ştefan cel Mare runs parallel to Bulevardul Ana Ipătescu, south from Piaţa 22 Decembrie; the drab **Natural History Museum** (Tues–Sun 10am–6pm), at no. 23, is full of stuffed wildlife, and the **Bucovina History Museum** (Tues–Sun 10am–6pm), at no. 33, begins with an array of Neolithic shards, and works stolidly on through medieval times and the independence struggles. There's better coverage of World War II here than in most Romanian museums, plus there are some portraits by local artists. The main attraction is a life-size model of Stephen's throne room, occupied by richly costumed figures.

Midway between the Natural History Museum and the Bucovina History Museum, Strada Mitropoliei heads east to the **Monastery of St John the New** (Mănăsteria Sf Ioan cel Nou), which is readily identified by its colourful steeple, striped with blue, black and yellow chevrons. Started by Bogdan the

Prince Dragoş and the aurochs

Churches throughout Moldavia display the emblem of the medieval principality: an aurochs' head and a sun, moon and star. This symbolizes the legend of **Prince Dragoş**, who is said to have hunted a giant **aurochs** (the *zimbru* or European bison) all the way across the mountains from Poland, until he cornered it by a river and slew the beast after a fight lasting from dawn to dusk – hence the inclusion of the Sun, Moon and Morning Star in the emblem. Dragoş's favourite hunting dog, **Molda**, was killed in the fight, and the prince named the River Moldova in her honour, adopting the aurochs, the mightiest animal in the Carpathians, as his totem. The last wild aurochs in Romania was killed in 1852 near Borşa, although captive breeding populations survive.

One-Eyed in 1514 and finished by his son Ştefaniţa in 1522, its monumental **Church of St George** was intended to replace the Mirăuţi Church as Suceava's Metropolitan cathedral, so no expense was spared. The facade was once covered with frescoes like those of the Painted Monasteries of Bucovina, but only the *Tree of Jesse* and a fragment of the *Last Judgement* remain. The relics of St John the New rest here, to the right of the nave, and are taken on a grand procession through the city each year on June 24, the feast of St John the Baptist (the feast of Sânzâene). St John the New's martyrdom is depicted on the wall of a small chapel near the church. Arrested for preaching in Turkish-occupied Moldavia, he was dragged through the streets of Cetăţii Alba behind a horse, and slashed to death by enraged Muslims. The monastery, which serves as the headquarters of the Patriarchate of Suceava and Bucovina, has a pavilion for the blessing of holy water, which is stored in 230-litre drums, for the faithful to take away in bottles.

The Princely Citadel and the Village Museum of Bucovina

Suceava's most impressive monument is the **Princely Citadel** (Tues–Sun 10am–6pm), which overlooks the city from a hill to its east. Also known as the Throne Citadel of Moldavia (Cetatea de Scaun a Moldovei), it was built by Petru I Muşat (1375–91), who moved the Moldavian capital from Siret to Suceava; it was subsequently strengthened in the fifteenth century by Alexander the Good. Stephen the Great added the moat, curtain walls and bastions that enabled it to defy the artillery of Mohammed II, conqueror of Constantinople, in 1476. Although blown up in 1675, much of the three-storey keep and the outlying chambers remain; from the ramparts, there's a fine view over the city and to the Mirăuţi Church across the valley.

In a former pasture opposite the citadel, you'll find the **Village Museum of Bucovina** (March 15–Oct 15 Tues–Sun 9am–5pm), a work in progress currently displaying some two-dozen wooden buildings, all removed from Bucovina villages and reassembled on the site. A few, including a **tavern** from Roşu (near Vatra Dornei) and a **family house** from Şaru Dornei, have been furnished with colourful textiles, handmade furniture and housewares.

To reach the citadel and the museum, which are a twenty-minute walk from the centre, head east from Piaţa 22 Decembrie through the park and across the bridge into the woods, and follow the rather steep path uphill to the giant equestrian **statue of Stephen the Great**, unveiled in 1977; the bas-reliefs on the pedestal depict the battle of Vaslui against the Turks. From here, several paths lead up to the citadel. It is also possible to take a taxi (€2).

Zamca Monastery

Another, more neglected ruin, the Armenian **Zamca Monastery**, straddles a plateau on the northwest edge of town, twenty-five minutes' walk from the centre along Strada Armenească or a ten–minute ride from maxitaxi stop Maraşeşti. The Armenian diaspora had reached Moldavia by 1350, and Alexander the Good founded the Armenian bishopric of Suceava in 1401; in 1551, they fell foul of the Rareş family, leading to a pogrom, but in 1572 an Armenian actually became ruler of Moldavia. Founded in 1606 and later fortified with ramparts and a gate tower, the buildings combine Gothic and classical elements with oriental motifs and are the subject of a long and barely-funded restoration project, though the church is home to a few lovely **frescoes**. Nowadays, the moat is dry and the earthworks overgrown; much of the compound is planted with cabbages, belonging to a family squatting in the three-storey guesthouse where dignitaries were once accommodated. Though not much from a monumental standpoint, the site has a desolate grandeur, particularly at dusk.

Eating, drinking and entertainment

Though there are a few good **restaurants** in town, the selection is limited – if you want to sample Bucovina's indigenous cuisine, you'll be much better off in the villages around the monasteries. Worth seeking out is *Latino*, a stylish and affordable Italian place opposite the bus station at Str. Curtea Domnească 9 (℡0230/523 627; daily 10am–midnight). Both pastas and pizzas are superb, and the coffee is the best in Suceava; service here is professional and friendly. If there are no tables at *Latino*, also recommended for pizza is *B & B*, at Str. Eminescu 18B (don't be fooled by the "Pensiunea" sign; this is only a pizzeria). *Picollo Mondo*, an upscale Romanian eatery specializing in game, is at Str. Petru Rareş 21, just up from the bus station. The restaurant in the *Balada* hotel is another good choice for Romanian food, with tasty *sarmale*; of the other hotel restaurants, *Class* and *Zamca* are both passable, while the *Class Hostel* has a menu of interesting international dishes that can be prepared with a few hours notice.

There are several fastfood outlets around the centre. *Sempre Pizza*, run by Romanian Pentecostals, is a favourite with university students. It's near the Princely Court on Strada A. Ipătescu. *Markiz*, next to *Latino*, is a patisserie serving salads and sandwiches, as well as decent *baklava*. *Melibeea*, at the bottom of Piaţa Decembrie, has pretty good pastries but no coffee. Suceava's **nightlife** is scarce, though there are at least two somewhat atmospheric places to drink: *Underground Club*, next to the Catholic Church in the park between Strada Ştefan cel Mare and Bulevardul Ana Ipătescu, which has a subterranean bar and a pleasant summer terrace, and the *60's Club*, on Ştefan cel Mare, where there are pool tables and comfortable couches. There's a cinema at Str. Ştefan cel Mare 25. The excellent **Ciprian Porumbescu Dance Ensemble**, a folk dance troupe named after the Romanian composer, is based on Bulevardul Ana Ipătescu, beside the Invierea Domnului church. The ensemble is often away on tour, but is sure to appear at the **folklore festival** at Ilişeşti, in July (see box on p.272).

Listings

Books Librăria Casa Cartii, on the round-about at the top of Str. Bălcescu, has an English section with a few paperback classics, as well as Alan Ogden's sumptuous Bucovina photo album, *Revelations of Byzantium*.

Consulates Ukrainian Consulate, Str. Mihai Viteazu 48 (℡0230/520 167, ✉gc_ro@mfa.gov.ua). Tourist visas for most nationalities can be purchased within 1–2 days.

Flights Angel Airlines (℡0723/400 935) operates seven weekly flights to and from Bucharest (Mon & Wed–Fri; €78 each way). The Angel Airlines office is in the airport, but most of the travel agencies on Piaţa 22 Decembrie sell tickets. The TAROM office, at Str. Bălcescu 5 (℡0230/214 686; Mon–Fri 9am–5pm), sells tickets only for international flights out of Bucharest.

Hospital B-dul I Decembrie 1918 (℡0230/222 098).

Internet access Assist Internet on Piaţa Decembrie (open until 11pm).

Pharmacies Europharm on Str. Bălcescu (Mon–Fri 8am–9pm, Sat 8am–7pm, Sun 9am–3pm).

Post office On Str. Dimitrie Onciul, next to the synagogue (Mon–Fri 8am–7pm, Sat 8am–1pm).

Shopping and supermarkets There's a small, 24hr supermarket at the bottom of Str. Eminescu, next to the Modern Cinema, while the larger and much more modern Supermarket Premier is 300m up the street, at Str. Mărăşti 39A. A new shopping centre, Metro, was set to open just west of the centre on B-dul 1 Decembrie 1918.

Train tickets Seats on trains out of Suceava can be reserved a day in advance at the CFR at Str. Bălcescu 8 (Mon–Fri 7.30am–8pm). Note that the schedules posted at the stations and in the window of the CFR office are not necessarily accurate.

Dragomirna Monastery

The nearest of the Bucovina monasteries to Suceava is the (unpainted) Dragomirna convent, 4km beyond the village of **Mitocul Dragomirnei**, 12km north of town. As there is no public transport to the monastery, the only way to get there without taking a taxi is to hitch at the Dragomirna turnoff on the outskirts of Suceava. Plenty of locals do this, and you should at least be able to get to the village. Take maxitaxi #1 from the town centre to the first stop on the far side of the river, and then walk straight ahead on the main road, Strada G.A. Ghica; the turnoff is on the right, 50m past the train tracks. Rolling plains conceal the monastery from view until the last moment.

Massively walled like a fortress, the **Dragomirna Monastery** was founded in the early seventeenth century by Metropolitan Anastasie Crimca, who designed its **church**, which is dramatically proportioned at 42m high but only 9.6m wide. The church's octagonal tower, resting on two star-shaped pedestals, is carved with meanders and rosettes, like the Church of the Three Hierarchs in Iaşi. Standing outside the church are several pre-Christian tombs, brought here from the Black Sea coast, while Crimca himself is buried in the nave; his portrait is visible on the pillar to the left as you walk through. The star-vaulted nave is covered in frescoes.

The complex also contains a smaller church, living quarters for the nuns who farm much of the surrounding land, and a **museum** harbouring five of the surviving 26 manuscripts of the school of illuminators founded here by Crimca, who was himself a talented artist. One 1602 manuscript features Crimca's self-portrait, the earliest known of its kind by a Romanian. Also on display is an enormous candle first lit for the monastery's consecration in 1609. The defensive **walls** and towers were added in 1627 owing to the threat of foreign invasions; these were so frequent that wooden village churches were sometimes mounted on wheels so that they could be towed away to safety.

Accommodation in the convent is for women only, four of whom can stay at any given time. The lodgings are comfortable (but lacking hot water), and the ambience is tranquil. Opposite the convent, and open to both sexes, is a bungalow complex (❶) with a bar and **restaurant**.

Arbore and Solca

Though **ARBORE** is often grouped together with the Painted Monasteries by virtue of its external frescoes, it is in fact merely a village church. This quibble aside, however, its kinship in form and spirit is undeniable. Arbore lies about 35km northwest of Suceava, and getting there (and back) by **public transport** takes most of the day, and precludes carrying on to any of the other monasteries. Buses leave Suceava for Arbore on weekdays only at 6.30am and 6.30pm.

Opposite the cemetery on the road through Arbore stands the village **church** (May–Sept daily 9am–6pm; Oct–April call caretaker Alex Chifon ☏0740/154 213), built in 1503 by one of Stephen's generals, Luca Arbore, lord of the village. While its wooden stockade and stone bell tower are rustic enough, its frescoed walls and sweeping roof are as majestic as any monastic edifice. Like the Painted Monasteries, its murals, dating from 1541, follow iconic conventions inherited from Byzantium, which designated subjects for each wall, arranged in rows according to their hierarchical significance. This is obvious on the apses, where the angels and seraphim appear at the top; archangels and biblical saints below; then martyrs; and lastly a row of cultural propagators or military saints.

The best-preserved **frescoes** are found on the relatively sheltered south and west walls: the south wall has eight rows of scenes from Genesis and the lives of the saints, while the eaves and buttresses have protected half of the *Last Judgement* on the west wall, which consigns "heathens" awaiting hell to the top right-hand corner. In the courtyard lie two heavy, hollowed-out stone slabs used for mixing colours, after the walls had been rendered with charcoal and lamp-black. The most interesting part of the interior is the **iconostasis**. From a distance, the icons appear to have been removed; in fact, they have been so blackened by centuries of smoke and incense that only faint outlines of the original forms are visible.

If you're going to Arbore by car, consider stopping in the village of **Solca**, where there is a church dating from 1615, which due to its strategic location on the edge of the highlands, was fortified like a monastery and used as a garrison in times of crisis. The **church** is tall and heavily buttressed, with the characteristically Moldavian octagonal belfry on a double star-shaped base. A less worthwhile detour is to **Pǎrhǎuți**, midway between Suceava and Solca, where there is a small 1503 church, notable for its frescoed, two-level porch.

Cacica

The old salt mine of **CACICA** was founded in the late eighteenth century by Austrian emperor Franz Joseph II. The first miners to be settled here were Polish, and they named the village after wild ducks (*kaczki* in Polish) found nesting in nearby swamps. Workers of other nationalities followed, and by the mid-nineteenth century Cacica was known for its ethnic mix and nicknamed "little Austria". The Czechs, Germans and Slovenes who once laboured here are long gone, but there is still a sizable Polish community.

Moldavia's fortified monasteries

Moldavian fortified monasteries were usually sited at the head of a valley to form a defensive bottleneck against the Turks or Tatars. The exact spot was decided by shooting arrows from a nearby hill top; where the first one landed, a water source was dug and henceforth deemed holy; the second arrow determined the location of the altar; the third the belfry, and so on. After the monastery was finished, crosses were raised on the hill from where the arrows had been fired.

The old mine (daily 10am–4pm) is in the centre of town, adjacent to the modern mine. Inside, a moderately treacherous staircase descends to a large chamber 25m below the surface, where there is a chapel featuring salt reliefs. Stairs from the chapel open into the next cavern, which is adorned with biblical sculptures, also carved from salt. From here, a long hallway leads to a swimming pool and a tennis court. The rest of the more than 50km of underground passages are off limits to the public. The Cacica air is beneficial for those suffering from respiratory diseases. However, the salt vein here is mixed with clay and needs to be heated to the point of evaporation to crystallize: for many years, fuel oil was used in this process, and today a strong odor of petroleum acts as a deterrent to would-be convalescents.

The easiest way to visit Cacica is as part of a monastery tour, but several of the slow **trains** heading from Suceava to Gura Humorului follow a secondary route that stops 2km east of the town centre and the mine; a train leaves Suceava at 9.14am, arriving in Cacica around forty-five minutes later, while another in the opposite direction departs Cacica at noon.

Rădăuţi and around

The dreary, sun-baked market town of **RĂDĂUŢI** could be ignored but for its role in the local transport network as the junction for roads to Suceava, Putna and the Painted Monasteries of Suceviţa and Moldoviţa (see p.280). If you find yourself with a long wait between connections, there are a few sights of interest in the town centre, including the fourteenth-century **Bogdana Church**, opposite the round-about in the centre of town, which is the oldest stone church in Moldavia. A few blocks northwest, on the corner of Strada Republicii, the **Ethnographic Museum** (Tues–Sun 9am–5pm), has a fine collection of local costumes and artefacts. The museum also displays the local **black pottery** and houses a studio, which makes the painted ceramics of birds and flowers that are also typical of the region; items can be bought from their workshop.

On Thursdays and Fridays, the town hosts a **bazaar** attended by peasants from the surrounding villages. To add to the mayhem, there's also a car spares market on Fridays that draws people from all over Moldavia, making this the worst time to try to change buses or get a room in town.

Rădăuţi's **bus station** is 500m from the centre of town on the Suceviţa road. The **train station** is nearby; to get there from the bus station, walk towards the centre, then turn right. Note that the schedules posted at the bus and train stations are unreliable: confirm your departure at the ticket booth before setting off to explore the town. There are no taxis in Rădăuţi; if you get stuck, try calling Avram Mihai (☎0744/133 551), a local driver who speaks very basic French. If you need **accommodation**, the *Hotel Fast* (☎0230/560 060; ❹) within sight of the bus station at Str. Ştefan cel Mare 80, is the best in town, and has a decent bistro. A slightly cheaper alternative is the clean and comfortable *Casa Alba* (☎0230/561 783; ❸), next to the train station at Str. Gării 9. The restaurant here is a convenient place to while away a few hours, though the music is deafening. A budget option, the gloomy *Hotel Azur*, can be found on the opposite end of town, at Calea Cernăuţi 29 (☎ & ☎0230/564 718; ❶).

Southern Bucovina

The **Painted Monasteries of Southern Bucovina**, in the northwest corner of Moldavia, are rightfully acclaimed as masterpieces of art and architecture,

SOUTHERN BUCOVINA

Map labels:

Cernăuți, Mihăileni, UKRAINE, Brodina, Straja, Vicovu de Sus, Frătăuții Noi, Siret, Bâlca, Gălănești, Frătăuții Vechi, Vicovu de Jos, Voitinel, Horodnic, Dornești, Putna, Rădăuți, Grănicesti, Vârfu Câmpului, Zvoriștea, Ionașeni, Volovăț, Milisăuți, Dragomirna, Ciumârna Pass, Sucevița, Arbore, Mitocul Dragomirnei, Adâncata, Solca, Todirești, Pătrauți, Moldovița, Botoșana, Vatra Moldoviței, Poiana Micului, Cacica, Pârteștii de Jos, Scheia, Suceava, Ipotești, Frumosul, Humor, Ilișești, Stroiești, Bosanci, Vama, Gura Humorului, Păltinoasa, Drăgoiești, Horoniceni, Câmpulung Moldovenesc, Frasin, Voroneț, RARĂU MASSIF, PIETRELE DOAMNEI, Cornu Lucii, Fălticeni, Rarău Cabana, SLĂTIOARA SECULAR FOREST, Stulpicani, Mălini, Vatra Dornei, Dorohoi, Botoșani, Roman

steeped in history and perfectly in harmony with their surroundings. Founded in the fifteenth and sixteenth centuries, they were citadels of Orthodoxy in an era overshadowed by the threat of infidel invaders. **Grigore Roşca**, Metropolitan of Moldavia in the mid-fifteenth century, is credited with the idea of covering the churches' outer walls with paintings of biblical events and apocrypha, for the benefit of the illiterate faithful. These **frescoes**, billboards from the late medieval world, are essentially Byzantine, but infused with the vitality of the local folk art and mythology. Though little is known about the artists, their skills were such that the paintings are still fresh after 450 years' exposure. Remarkably, the layer of colour is only 0.25mm thick, in contrast to Italian frescoes, where the paint is absorbed deep into the plaster.

Perhaps the best of these are to be found at **Voroneţ**, whose *Last Judgement* surpasses any of the other examples of this subject, and **Sucevița**, with its unique *Ladder of Virtue* and splendid *Tree of Jesse*. **Moldovița** has a better all-round collection, though, and **Humor** has the most tranquil atmosphere of them all. Nearby **Putna Monastery**, though lacking the visual impact of the Painted Monasteries, is worth a visit for its rich historical associations.

The monasteries are scattered across a region divided by the imposing hills, or "crests", which branch off the Carpathians, and by the legacy of history. When the Hapsburgs annexed northern Moldavia in 1774, they called their new acquisition Bucovina, a Romanianized version of their description of this

Visiting the Painted Monasteries

Tours

Given that everyone comes to Southern Bucovina to visit the **Painted Monasteries**, public transport to them is limited, and it's not surprising that many visitors opt for organized **tours**, which can be arranged either in Suceava or (better) Gura Humorului. In **Suceava**, the Bucovina Estur tourist agency (see p.268) will provide a comfortable car with a driver for between €40 and €70, depending on the number of sights, and an additional €15 for an English-speaking guide. The fee is for the car, not per person. Bucovina Estur's staff are knowledgeable and charming, and it is one of the most reliable ways of making the tour, though with so much to see in one day you are likely to feel rushed. Alternatively, contact either Ciprian Slemcho (℡0744/292 588, ℯmonasterytour@yahoo.com) or Sorin Fodor (℡0745/248 119, ℯfosso@iname.com), both of whom are knowledgeable, independent guides. Another option, which may be a bit cheaper if you bargain well, is to hire a taxi driver for the day. You'll have more time to see the monasteries if you choose to stay in **Gura Humorului** (see opposite), where Vila Fabian (see opposite) run tours for between €35 and €50, and there are plenty of private taxis for hire. The higher tour prices for both Suceava and Gura Humorului include Putna Monastery, which is out of the way and thus more expensive to visit.

On your own

By making the trip independently, you'll be able to spend more time at each monastery and stay in Bucovina's charming **pensions**, many of which serve lavish, home-cooked meals. The route entails striking out by train from Suceava and following a circular route that requires some backtracking, although this can be avoided by hiking across the hills at certain points. The route can be done in reverse, but it's most convenient to head first to **Gura Humorului**, the jumping-off point for Voroneţ and Humor. From Gura Humorului, it's relatively easy to reach Vatra Moldoviţei, home of the Moldoviţa Monastery, by train. At this point, travel becomes more difficult; the road that leads from here to Suceviţa monastery is traversed only by one early morning bus, and light traffic makes hitching uncertain. The road continues (with a similar lack of transportation) from Suceviţa monastery to Rădăuţi, where you're likely to have a long wait for a train to Putna or back to Suceava. A good compromise is to make Gura Humorului your base, see Voroneţ and Humor on your own, and then either book a tour to the rest with Vila Fabian (see opposite) or commandeer a taxi for the day.

Though the monasteries have no set **visiting hours**, you can assume they'll be open daily from 9am to 5pm (8pm in summer). There is a modest **admission charge** (€1), which includes entrance to the **museums** attached to the monasteries, which are closed on Mondays, plus a surcharge (€3) for cameras or videos. As working convents or monasteries, they prohibit smoking and ask that visitors dress appropriately; a few robes are kept on hand for those who arrive in shorts. The small markets that have been set up outside the monastery entrances are among the best places in the country to buy **traditional handicrafts**.

beech-covered land (Büchenwald). Bucovina remained under Hapsburg rule until the end of World War I, when it was returned to Romania, only to be split in half in 1940 – the northern half being occupied by the Soviet Union and incorporated into the Ukraine, of which it is still a part today. Thus, Romanians speak of **Southern Bucovina** to describe what is actually the far north of Moldavia – implying that Bucovina might be reunited one day. Names aside, the scenery is wonderful, with misty valleys and rivers spilling down from rocky shoulders heaving up beneath a cloak of beech and fir. The woods are at their loveliest in May and autumn.

Gura Humorului

The monasteries of Voroneţ and Humor lie a few kilometres either side of **GURA HUMORULUI**, a small logging town accessible by bus or train from Suceava and Câmpulung that has more than enough facilities to make a satisfactory base. Unfortunately, the town's main street, Strada Ştefan cel Mare, is also northern Romania's principal thoroughfare and lorries come crashing through day and night.

The **bus and train stations** are adjacent to each other, a ten minutes' walk to the west of the town centre. Humor Monastery is serviced by maxitaxis that shuttle to and from Gura Humorului every half hour or so, but there are no services to Voroneţ. Both monasteries, however, are within walking distance of Gura Humorului; there are also plenty of taxis.

Near the edge of town on the road towards Voroneţ you'll find Gura Humorului's welcome **tourist information office** (☎0230/233 863), opposite the *Vila Fabian* pension (see below) and under the same management. The staff here can provide information on the region, arrange accommodation in Humor, Voroneţ and elsewhere, and organize monastery tours (see box opposite). **CFR** (Mon–Fri 8am–3pm) is near the **market**, west of the fork in the road at Piaţa Republicii, where there's a Raiffeisen Bank with an **ATM**. The **post office** is in a small commercial complex just east of the fork on Strada 9 Mai; there's an unpleasant **Internet café** nearby.

Gura Humorului's dominant landmark, and the finest large **hotel** in this part of Romania, is the new, 130-room *Best Western Bucovina* (☎0230/207 000, ⓦwww.bestwesternhotels.ro; ❽), which towers haughtily over Piaţa Republicii, the round-about marking the centre of town. Facilities include room service, sauna, jacuzzi and conference rooms, and the hotel has been popular with Romania's new business and leisure classes since opening in 2002. The best place to stay, however, is the *Casa Cristian*, just off the road to Humor at Str. Victoriei 26 (☎0230/230 864, ⑤232 987; ❼). A magnificent Austrian-style four-star pension with individually designed rooms, *Casa Cristian's* top-class facilities are complimented by gracious hospitality, a perfectly manicured garden and occasional concerts by internationally renowned classical musicians. Meals can also be arranged, but only with a few hours' notice. A good mid-range alternative is the clean and friendly *Vila Fabian*, out on the road towards Voroneţ at Str. Câmpului 30 (☎0230/232 387; ❹). The best budget option is *Pensiunea Renate* at Str. Ştefan cel Mare 43 bis (☎0230/235 039; ❷), which has clean rooms with shared bath, good laundry service and a downstairs bar. *Vila Simeria*, just off the river at Str. A. Ipătescu 19 (☎0230/230 746; ❷), is not as impressive but still adequate. Just across the street is *Vila Ramona* (☎0230/232 996, ⓦwww.ramona.ro; ❷) a comfortable place with unfriendly management. *Cazare Turişti*, at Str. Stefan cel Mare 48 (☎0740/493 376; ❶), is a self-styled three-room hostel that vibrates alarmingly when lorries pass in the night. The very sociable owner is likely to meet you at the train station. Alternatively, you may prefer to press on to the *Voroneţ* cabana (❶), which is open over the summer, near the bridge, 1km from Gura Humorului on the road to Voroneţ village.

The best **restaurant** in Gura Humorului, though you wouldn't know it from outside, is *Restaurantul Moldova* at Str. Ştefan cel Mare 16. The menu, which is translated into English, features a variety of delicious and inexpensive local specialties. The *sarmale* are good, as are *părjoale moldoveneşti* (lightly fried meatballs in a rich tomato sauce). The restaurant in the *Best Western*, in addition to offering reliable international cuisine, also has a few Moldavian dishes. Less interesting than either of the above choices is *Select*, above the post office on the corner of Strada 9 Mai. For self-catering, there are plenty of small supermarkets along Strada Ştefan cel Mare, all stocking more or less the same range of products.

Voroneţ Monastery

Ion Neculce's chronicle records that Stephen founded **Voroneţ Monastery** in 1488 to fulfil a pledge to the hermit Daniil, who had previously assured the despondent *hospodar* that, should he undertake a campaign against the Turks, he would be successful. The Turks were duly forced back across the Danube, and Voroneţ was erected in three months; chronologically, it comes between Putna and Neamţ monasteries. Its superb **frescoes** – added at the behest of Metropolitan Roşca in 1547–50 – have led to Voroneţ being dubbed the "Oriental Sistine Chapel", and put "Voroneţ blue" into the lexicon of art alongside Titian red and Veronese green. Obtained from lapis lazuli, this colour appears at its most intense on a rainy day, just before sunset.

The church was designed to be entered via a door in the southern wall, with a closed exonarthex replacing the usual open porch, thus creating an unbroken surface along the western wall. Here is painted a magnificent *Last Judgement*, probably the finest single composition among the Painted Monasteries. Fish-tailed bulls, unicorns and other zodiacal symbols form a frieze below the eaves, beneath which Christ sits in majesty above a chair symbolizing the "Toll Gates of the Air", where the deceased are judged and prayers for their souls counted. On either side are those in limbo, the Turks and Tatars destined for perdition. Beneath them, devils and angels push sinners into the flames, while two angels sound the last trump on alpine horns. In response, graves open and wild animals come bearing the limbs they have devoured – all except the deer (a symbol of innocence) and the elephant (no threat in Romania). Amusingly, there's a crush of righteous souls at the gates of the Garden of Eden.

Weather has damaged the frescoes along the north-facing wall, but you can still distinguish Adam and Eve (clothed in the Garden of Eden; naked and ashamed thereafter), the first childbirth, the discovery of fire and the invention of ploughing and writing. Also notice *Adam's Deed*, illustrating the myth that Adam made a pact with Satan. The south wall is covered by three compositions: comic-strip scenes from the lives of St Nicholas and St John on the buttress; a *Tree of Jesse*; and a register of saints and philosophers where Plato is depicted with a coffin-load of bones.

Inside, the walls and ceiling of the exonarthex are painted with martyrdoms and miracles. The second row from the bottom on the left depicts Elijah in his "chariot of fire", intent on zapping devils with his God-given powers. According to local folklore, God promptly had second thoughts and restricted Elijah's activities to his name day. On the right-hand sides of the gloomy narthex and star-vaulted sanctuary are the **tomb of Daniil** the hermit, and a fresco of Stephen, his wife Maria Voichita and their son Bogdan presenting the monastery to Christ. After 1786, the monastery was dissolved and the surrounding monks' cells disappeared; aside from its church, only the **bell tower** remains. More information about the iconography of the frescoes can be found in *The Sacred Monastery of Voroneţ*, a passionate and intelligent (though awkwardly translated) guide to the monastery by resident nun Elena Simionovici, on sale at the entrance for about €3.

Practicalities

A **taxi** from Gura Humorului to Voroneţ shouldn't cost more than €2, but on a fine day it's no hardship to walk the 4km; from the bus station, head left along the main road, Strada Ştefan cel Mare, for 750m to the clearly signposted turn-off. There's no chance of going astray on the valley road – at the fork, take the right-hand route to the monastery, entered by a gate near the cemetery. Be warned, however, that the number of tour buses heading for the monastery is on the rise. Although you're unlikely to be run over, the drivers are not happy to share the road, and many take revenge on the carless with gratuitous blasts of their horns. Of all the monasteries, Voroneţ is the most frequented by tourists and, being the smallest, can feel very crowded if you come at the wrong moment. Larger groups, however, rarely stay long; wait a bit and you may have the place to yourself.

If you want **to stay** overnight, there are a couple of very good options: in the village, the *Casa Elena* (℡0230/230 651, Ⓔ webmaster@casaelena.assist.ro; ⑤) comes complete with sauna and pool room, as well as an affordable but sophisticated **restaurant**. Across from *Casa Elena*, you'll find the simple and comfortable *Motel Voroneţ* (℡0230/232 542; ③), which also has a restaurant. Next to the monastery is another good choice, *Schanul Crizor* (0230/233 732; ②), a new pension with attractive wood furniture and a rustic dining room, while 3km on past the monastery, the *Vila Maria* (℡094/231 279; ①) is basic but wonderfully peaceful.

Humor Monastery

In another valley 6km north of Gura Humorului the tranquil wooden village of **MĂNĂSTIREA HUMOR** straggles towards its namesake, the sixteenth-century **Humor Monastery**.

Unlike the other complexes, Humor is protected by a wooden stockade rather than a stone rampart, and lacks a spire over the *naos* – indicating that it was founded by a boyar, in this case Teodor Bubuiog, Chancellor of Petru Rareş, who is buried here with his wife Anastasia. The **frescoes** were painted by Toma of Suceava; the prevailing hues are reddish brown (from oriental madder pigment), but rich blues and greens also appear.

The *Last Judgement* on the wall beneath the unusual open porch is similar to that at Voroneţ, with the significant difference that the Devil is portrayed as the Scarlet Woman, though this patch is now so faint that you can't actually tell. Such misogyny had its counterpart in the peasant conception of hell – said to be a cavern upheld by seven old women who had surpassed Satan in wickedness during their lifetimes. Since the women are mortal, the legend goes, the Devil (Dracul) must constantly search the world for replacements – and he never fails to find them. The *Tree of Jesse* along the northern wall has been virtually effaced by weathering, but restorers are busy touching up the *Hymn to the Virgin* on the south front. As at Voroneţ, this depicts her miraculous intervention at the siege of Constantinople by the Persians – although the enemy has been changed into Turks for propaganda purposes. Morale may have been stiffened, but neither murals nor the stone watch-tower added by Basil the Wolf could save Humor from marauding Turks, and the monastery was eventually declared derelict in the eighteenth century. It is now a small convent – the villagers use another church, on a nearby hillock.

Twelve kilometres further up the Humor valley, three **trails to Suceviţa Monastery** have their starting point at the long, strung-out village of **Poiana Micului**; the easiest one (marked by blue stripes) follows a forestry track and takes about five hours.

Practicalities

Maxitaxis leave for Humor from Gura Humorului's Piaţa Republicii, next to the *Best Western*. Note that the number of *babushki* waiting for a seat often outstrips supply, and the ride can be very crowded and uncomfortable. By contrast, the walk is pleasant, and there's little danger here of a bus chasing you into a ditch.

Tiny Humor has some excellent **pensions** clustered around the centre of town. The best of these are *Casa Buburuzan*, which is opposite the monastery (℡0745/849 832, Ⓦwww.geocities.com/cbuburuzan; ❹), and *La Maison du Bucovine* (℡0744/373 931; ❹), around the left side of the stockade. Both belong to Romania's agrotourism network, and prices include half board. The generous meals at *Casa Buburuzan*, which are prepared entirely from local products, are especially recommended. The nearby *Vila Andreea* (℡0744/558 629; ❸) has clean en-suite doubles. *Casa Gheorgiţa*, 150m north of the monastery (℡0744/793 485; ❶), is a cheaper option, and the upstairs rooms provide a lovely panorama of the valley. It's also possible to **camp** here. Another choice, also north of the monastery, is *Casa Ancuţa* (℡0744/638 749; ❶), which has ten clean rooms with shared bath and serves delicious meals. French is spoken at all of the above places; owners' children are likely to speak English. There aren't any restaurants in town, but the pensions can prepare meals if you call in advance. If you don't want to walk back, wait for a maxitaxi at the bench just below the fork in the road. If a local picks you up, the price for a ride back to Gura Humorului should be about €0.50.

Moldoviţa Monastery and Vatra Moldoviţei

Approaching from Gura Humorului, you'll come upon the **Moldoviţa Monastery** shortly after entering the village of **VATRA MOLDOVIŢEI**. The monastery is a smaller complex than Suceviţa but equally well defended, its ivy-clad walls enclosing white stone buildings with lustrous black-shingled roofs. It was founded in 1532 by Stephen's illegitimate son, Petru Rareş, during whose reign the Turks finally compelled Moldavia to pay tribute and acknowledge Ottoman suzerainty. The monastery's **frescoes** were painted by Toma of Suceava in 1537, at a time when Petru Rareş still hoped to resist the Turks, despite the inexorability of their advance since the fall of Constantinople in 1453.

To raise morale, the Turkish siege was conflated with an earlier, failed attempt by the Persians in 626. A delightfully revisionist *Siege of Constantinople* along the bottom of the south wall depicts Christians routing the infidel with arrows and cannons, and miraculous icons being paraded around the ramparts. Illustrated above this is the *Hymn to the Virgin*, composed by Metropolitan Sergius in thanksgiving for her intervention, while further along is a lovely *Tree of Jesse*, with dozens of figures entwined in foliage. All the compositions are set on an intense blue background.

The open porch contains a fine *Last Judgement*, showing a crowd of dignitaries growing agitated as a demon drags one of their number, said to be Herod, towards the fires below, where Satan sits on a scaly creature – defaced with oddly formal nineteenth-century German graffiti. Within the church, saints and martyrs are decapitated en masse around the narthex and the nave, whose doorway bears an expressive *Mary with Jesus*. Also notice the charming mural of Petru Rareş, with his wife and sons, dutifully presenting the monastery to Jesus, on the right as you enter the nave.

Nuns' cells line one side of the compound, while in the northwest corner rises an imposing two-storey *clisarniţa*, a guesthouse for passing dignitaries, with a circular tower. Built in 1612, this contains a **museum** of monastic treasures (Tues–Sun 10am–6pm) including a silver-chased Evangelistry presented by

Catherine the Great and the wooden throne of Petru Rareș, a bust of whom has been erected outside.

There are no other important sights here, but of all the monastery villages Vatra Moldoviței is the most isolated and picturesque. It's also the highest, and the air here feels cleaner than elsewhere in Bucovina. Shepherds' trails in the surrounding hills offer ample opportunities for **walking**, with the added incentive of a view of the monastery from above.

Practicalities

Vatra Moldoviței can be reached by a limited number of **bus and train services**, none of which make it feasible to continue on to the Sucevița Monastery in the same day. Even hitching is likely to take a while, as there's not much traffic over the Ciumârna Pass, which separates the two monasteries. This is a very scenic route, with a viewpoint at the pass over the low, parallel Obcinele Bucovinei ridges.

Trains to Vatra Moldoviței leave from Vama (see below), heading up a branch line that runs through Vatra Moldoviței's main street, en route, confusingly, to Moldovița proper. It is Vatra Moldoviței that is the monastery town. Trains depart from Vama at 7.13am, 3.35pm and 11.26pm; the fourteen-kilometre trip takes 35 minutes. There's also a decrepit bus that leaves Vama at about 8:20pm and passes through Vatra Moldoviței on the way to the obscure hamlet of Argel. Trains going back to Vama pass through Vatra Moldoviței at 12.25pm and 7.15pm. The one daily bus that crosses the Ciumârna Pass leaves Vatra Moldoviței at 7.45am, reaching Sucevița Monastery at 8.30am. Going in the other direction, a bus leaves Rădăuți at noon, reaching Vatra Moldoviței about an hour later.

The best **accommodation** in Vatra Moldoviței is the charming *Vila Crizantema*, a few doors down from the monastery at Str. Mănăstirii 204 (☎ & ℱ0230/336 116; ❷), an attractive and comfortable pension with small but well-furnished en-suite doubles. Meals here are simple but delicious, and the friendly owners (they speak French; their children speak English) have information about fishing and trips to local handicraft studios. The other choice is *Vila Lulu* (☎0230/336 440; ❷), a chalet-style pension/campground that's popular with Romanian families and has a bar, swimming pool, tennis court and trout pond, as well as the only restaurant in the area. It's 1.5km north of Moldovița Monastery on the road to Sucevița. Some villagers also rent rooms on request; ask the nuns at the monastery if you're interested. For self-catering, there are a few small but decent shops on the main street.

VAMA, the next village west of Gura Humorului on the Suceava–Câmpulung line and the jumping-off point for Vatra Moldoviței, offers more opportunities for sleeping. It's pretty enough, but feels less remote and tranquil than Vatra Moldoviței. If you need to stay, try *La Gorita*, near the centre of town at Str. Victoriei 5 (☎0230/239 185; ❷), a new place with **Internet access** and a collection of old agricultural implements. In the hills overlooking Vama, *Casa Lucretia* (☎0230/314 929, ⓦ www.casa-lucretia.ro; ❹) is a superb, isolated pension with huge rooms at affordable prices.

Sucevița Monastery

Sucevița Monastery – the last and grandest of the monastic complexes to be built – owes nothing to Stephen or his heirs; it is a monument to the feudal prince Ieremia Movilă, his brother and successor Simion, and his widow, Elisabeta, who poisoned Simion so that her own sons might inherit the throne.

△ Nuns painting eggs outside Suceviţa Monastery

The family first founded the village church in 1581, followed by the monastery church in 1584, and its walls, towers and belfry in stages thereafter. The fortified church's massive, whitewashed walls and steep grey roofs radiate an air of grandeur; its **frescoes** – painted in 1596 by two brothers – offset brilliant reds and blues with an undercoat of emerald green.

Entering the monastery, you're confronted by a glorious *Ladder of Virtue* covering the northern wall, which has been somewhat protected from erosion by the building's colossal eaves. Flights of angels assist the righteous to paradise, while sinners fall through the rungs into the arms of a grinning demon. The message is reiterated in the *Last Judgement* beneath the porch – reputedly left unfinished because the artist fell to his death from the scaffolding – where angels sound the last trump and smite heathens with swords, Turks and Jews can be seen lamenting, and the Devil gloats in the bottom right-hand corner. Outside the porch, you'll see the two-headed Beast of the Apocalypse, and angels pouring rivers of fire and treading the grapes of wrath. The iron ox-collar hanging by the doorway is beaten to summon the monks to prayer.

The *Tree of Jesse* on the south wall symbolizes the continuity between the Old and the New Testament, being a literal depiction of the prophecy in Isaiah that the Messiah will spring "from the stem of Jesse". This lush composition on a dark blue background amounts to a biblical Who's Who, with an ancestral tree of prophets culminating in the Holy Family. *The Veil* represents Mary as a Byzantine empress, beneath a red veil held by angels, while the *Hymn to the Virgin* is illustrated with Italianate buildings and people in oriental dress. Alongside is a frieze of ancient philosophers clad in Byzantine cloaks; Plato bears a coffin and a pile of bones on his head, in tribute to his meditations on life and death.

Inside the narthex, the lives of the saints end with them being burnt, boiled, dismembered or decapitated – a gory catalogue relieved by rams, suns and other zodiacal symbols. As usual, the frescoes in the nave are blackened by candle smoke, but you can still discern a votive picture of Elisabeta and her children on the wall to the right. Ironically, her ambitions for them came to naught as she died in a Sultan's harem – "by God's will", a chronicler noted sanctimoniously. Iremia and Simion are buried nearby, in marble tombs carved with floral motifs.

Sucevița's **museum**, inside the east wall in what was once the council chamber, displays a collection of richly-coloured tapestries, including sixteenth-century tomb covers featuring the portraits of founder Ieremia Movilă and his brother Simion, as well as illuminated manuscripts bound in silver, icons, and an ancient wooden lectern. By climbing the **hill** behind the village church's graveyard, you can see the complex as a whole, and appreciate its magnificent setting at the foot of the surrounding hills, carpeted with firs and lush pastures. The **trail to Humor** starts next to the *Hotel Memory*. It's not well-marked, but heading southeast from here it should take about five hours to reach **Poiana Marului**, 12km north of Humor along a logging road that's busy enough to make hitching feasible.

Practicalities

Sucevița lies midway between Moldovița Monastery, to the west beyond the Ciumârna Pass, and Rădăuti, 17km to the east. One daily bus, the Câmpulung to Rădăuti service, traverses this route, stopping in Sucevița at 8.30am. In the other direction, the Câmpulung-bound bus leaves Rădăuti at noon, passing through Sucevița about thirty minutes later.

There are plenty of **places to stay** in Sucevița, with most of the options to be found south of the monastery, along the main road. The most luxurious option is the *Plai de Dor* (☎0230/417 400, ℻417 200, ⓦwww.plaidedor.ro; ❼), a new establishment with pool and sauna 2.5km south of the monastery. Much more fun is the *Popasul Turistic Bucovina* (0230/417 000, ⓦwww.popas.ro), 700m further south, which has rooms in two delightful wood-panelled houses (❹), as well as excellent bungalows (❸) and camping; it also has a homely restaurant offering high-quality food. Of the numerous pensions here, the best value is the modest but comfortable *Elena* (☎0740/060 835; ❷), about 1km from the monastery. Rooms are also available at the *Han Sucevița* (☎0230/563 824; ❸), a clean if dull motel 500m north of the monastery towards Rădăuți; this also has a decent **restaurant**.

Putna Monastery

Putna Monastery lacks the external murals of the Painted Monasteries, but as the first of the great religious monuments of Southern Bucovina and the burial place of Stephen the Great, it is rich in historical associations and is as important to Romanian patriots as to Orthodox faithful. The slow train ride past meandering rivers and fir-clad hills whets your appetite for **PUTNA** village, a wonderful jigsaw of wooden houses with carved gables and shingled roofs. Head uphill from the station to reach the main road, and bear left for the monastery, which is at the end of a tree-lined drive, 1km further on.

In 1466, Stephen chose the site of **Putna Monastery** by firing an arrow from the steep hill that now bears a white cross (see box on p.273). The monastery was rebuilt after it burnt down in 1480, ravaged by war in the seventeenth century and repaired in the eighteenth, only to be damaged by an earthquake and restored again in 1902. Its walls and bell tower were plainly intended for defence; in these less troubled times, they emphasize Putna's status as a patriotic reliquary. The statue of Eminescu inside the entrance identifies the national poet with Moldavia's national hero, and commemorates the speech he gave here in August 1871, on the occasion of the monastery's quadricentennial: "Let us make Putna the Jerusalem of the Romanian people, and let us also make Stephen's grave the altar of our national conscience".

The **church** itself is plain and strong, its facade defined by cable mouldings, blind arcades and trefoil windows, while the interior follows the usual configuration of three chambers: the sanctuary, containing the altar and iconostasis at its eastern end; the nave; and the narthex, just inside the porch – although at Putna the porch has also been enclosed to form an exonarthex. Prince Bogdan the One-Eyed, the wife of Petru Rareș, and Stephen's daughter and nephew are buried in the narthex, which is separated from the nave by two thick, cable-moulded columns. Here, a graceful arch and a hanging votive lamp distinguish the **tomb of Stephen the Great** from those of his two wives, both called Maria. Unusually for an Orthodox church, the interior is unpainted, but illuminated by stained-glass windows.

Outside stand three **bells**, the largest of which, cast in 1484, was only used to herald events such as royal deaths, and was last rung in 1918, when it could be heard as far away as Suceava. Hidden from the communists for almost fifty years, it only came to light after the 1989 revolution. The middle bell traditionally served for everyday use, while the end one was the gift of an archimandrite who repaired its sixteenth-century precursor. At the rear of the yard stands a fifteenth-century tower, originally used as a treasury; the monks' cells along the wall date from 1856. The **museum** (Tues–Sun 10am–5pm) displays a wealth of icons, antique embroidery and illuminated manuscripts, as well as a fourteenth-century carved chest, which once held the relics of St John the New. Uphill and slightly to the east of the monastery, there's a curious hollowed-out rock with a door and window, reputedly once the **cell of Daniil the Hermit** – a monk who was indirectly responsible for the foundation of Voroneţ Monastery (see p.278). The **wooden church** (Biserica de Lemn) back along the main road is supposed to have been raised by Dragoş, and moved to its present location by Stephen.

Practicalities

Putna is accessible by **train** from Suceava via Rădăuţi, but services on this route are few and usually very crowded. The best **place to stay** is *Pensiunea Isidora* (☎0740/776 017; ❷), on the left as you walk from the station to the monastery, has simple, clean rooms. Otherwise, try the good-value pensions *Corola* (☎0230/414 188; ❶) or *Aga* (0230/414 223; ❶). Closer to the monastery, there is a summer **campsite** with huts; there are plans to build a new guesthouse here. The *Bucovina* restaurant, in the middle of town, is the sole place to eat. There are no bus services through Putna, so travelling on to the Painted Monasteries entails catching a train to Rădăuţi or Suceava, and then a bus from there. Alternatively, you could **hike to Suceviţa Monastery** in about three hours. Pick up the route (marked by blue crosses) from Putna station and follow the main valley for about an hour. Ignore the turn-off to the left near a hut and a bridge, but take the next turning on the right, cross another bridge and carry on round to the left, which will bring you out at a forestry hut, Canton Silvic 13. From here, stick to the track up to another forestry hut, Strulinoasa Sud, which deteriorates into a pony trail as it approaches the watershed, but improves once it descends into an open valley. You should reach the monastery about an hour and half after crossing the watershed.

Câmpulung Moldovenesc and Vatra Dornei

Câmpulung Moldovenesc and **Vatra Dornei**, to the west of the Painted Monasteries, are chiefly of interest as bases for **hiking** in the Rarău and Giumalău massifs, and as way-stations en route to Transylvania or Maramureş; Vatra Dornei also serves as a springboard for reaching several **festivals** just across the Carpathians. There's less reason to come out of season – particularly once the snow arrives, a month or two earlier than in the lowlands. Both towns are situated along the main train line from Suceava to Cluj.

Câmpulung Moldovenesc

CÂMPULUNG MOLDOVENESC is a logging town with a concrete centre and some old wooden houses in the backstreets. Being strung out along the valley, it has two **train stations** – don't alight at Câmpulung Est unless you want to hike straight off up Rarău. To reach the centre from Câmpulung Moldovenesc station, bear left, then right, and left along Calea Transilvaniei, the main street, which becomes Calea Bucovinei.

The **Museum of Wooden Art** (Tues–Sun 9am–5pm) on the corner at Calea Transilvaniei 10 displays alpine horns, fiddles and throne-like chairs, as well as a few modern sculptures, all beautifully carved. There are also black and white photos of peasant life, with captions in English. The museum stands beside a pseudo-medieval **church** with a multicoloured mosaic roof, behind which you'll find the market with a small **Ukrainian bazaar**, and the bus station. Câmpulung also boasts the late Professor Tugui's vast **collection of wooden spoons**, a bizarre delight that's said to be the only one of its kind in Europe, just west of the centre Str. Gheorghe Popovici 1. Look for the numerous colourful plates affixed to the exterior.

One early morning **bus** runs daily to Rădăuţi via Vatra Moldoviţei (for Moldoviţa monastery) and Suceviţa monastery; there are also regular services to Iaşi and Piatra Neamţ. Most buses and trains leave in the morning or early afternoon, and it can be difficult to get out of town later in the day; check schedules early. The best hotel in Câmpulung Moldovenesc is the new, three-star *Eden* (☎0230/314 733, ⓦwww.hotel-eden.ro; ❺), with pool, sauna and fitness facilities, at Calea Bucovinei 148, on the edge of town near the Câmpulung Est station. More conveniently located is the high-rise *Zimbrul*, a clean, warm hotel at Calea Bucovinei 1–3 (☎0230/314 356, ⓕ314 358; ❺). To reach the smaller, private *Hotel Minion* (☎ & ⓕ0230/314 694; ❹), walk past the *Zimbrul* and turn left at the post office. It's 300m north of here, at Str. D. Cantemir 26B, and has boxy rooms with decent bathrooms and cable TV. A good budget option is the clean and pleasant *Vila Sf. Gheorghe* (☎0230/311 050; ❷), at Str. Bradului 8. Continue past the *Hotel Minion* and turn left when Strada D. Cantemir comes to an end. The top **restaurant** is at the *Minion*, while the *Taverna Pizzeria*, at Calea Bucovinei 2, is well above the Romanian average. The *El Toro Pub*, opposite the museum at Calea Transilvaniei 27, is a good place for a drink. There's an **Internet café** at the same address, hidden inside a copy shop – look for the sign that says *Pro Vogue*.

The Rarău tourist agency (Mon–Fri 8am–4pm, ☎0230/314 358, ⓔrarau-turism@sv.ro) inside *Hotel Zimbrul*, has information about hiking, caving and mountain accommodation. The **CFR** office (Mon–Fri 9am–3pm) is on the other side of square from the *Zimbrul*, next to an abandoned synagogue. A hundred metres further on, across from the post office, is the main square – don't miss the impressively kitsch bronze **statue of Prince Dragoş and the aurochs** (see box on p.269), locked in mortal combat.

The Rarău massif

The **Rarău massif** to the south of Câmpulung is a popular **hiking** spot, with its dense spruce forests harbouring lynx, bears, roebuck and other **wildlife**. Most visitors base themselves at the *Rarău* cabana (❶), 14km and three to four hours' walk up the road from Câmpulung Est station. Reservations can be made through the Rarău tourist agency in Câmpulung. From the cabana, a four-hour trail marked by red triangles leads past the **Pietrele Doamnei** ("Princess's Rocks"), three huge Mesozoic limestone towers, to reach the ancient **Slătioara Secular forest** of fifty-metre-high firsand spruces. Another route (red-striped) runs southwest from *Rarău* to the *Giumalău* cabana (3–4hr), from where you can hike on to Vatra Dornei via the Obcina Mică peak (5–6hr). None of these trails is feasible in winter.

The road **to Vatra Dornei** crosses the Mestecăniş Pass (1096m), by way of two villages with Ukrainian-style **wooden churches**, to enter the Bistriţa valley at the Iacobeni pass. The *Mestecăniş* cabana (❶) is here, 8km east of the large village of Iacobeni, the site of a murder by poison recounted in Gregor von Rezzori's *The Snows of Yesteryear*, and where trains usually halt after emerging from a tunnel below the pass. Accommodation is available in Iacobeni at the *Roşan* cabana (☎0722/786 519; ❶).

Vatra Dornei

The logging town of **VATRA DORNEI** has been a spa since Hapsburg times, and has dabbled in skiing and other outdoor activities since the 1970s. The skiing facilities, in particular, have developed in recent years, and though the slopes themselves are not challenging, Vatra Dornei is an increasingly popular winter destination for Romanians and Ukrainians, and is rich in hotels and pensions, if not sights. Across the river from Vatra Dornei Băi train station (more useful than the Vatra Dornei station, east of the centre), you can spot the ochre and white Baroque casino, once the focal point for visitors but now derelict and awaiting investment for renovation. Behind this is the spa's park, home to a few squirrels, a mineral spring housed in a mock-Gothic chapel, a neo-Byzantine church and a seedy restaurant. Turning left at the casino and keeping parallel to the river, you'll come to a junction: to the right is Strada Unirii (the Piatra Neamţ road), with a small **Museum of Natural Science and Hunting** (Tues–Sun 10am–6pm) at no. 3. The **Ethnographic Museum** (Tues–Sun 10am–6pm) is back in the town proper, on Strada Eminescu.

Practicalities

Vatra Dornei's **bus station** and **market** are both 200m east of the casino. The excellent **tourist information office**, across from Vatra Dornei Băi station at Str Gării 2 (℡0230/372 767; Mon–Fri 9am–5pm), has town **maps** with hotels and pensions marked, as well as a map of area **hiking trails**. One of these (21–22hr), to the Rotunda Pass in the Rodna mountains (marked by blue stripes), begins at the Băi station, runs left along Strada Eminescu past an abandoned Moorish-style synagogue, and leaves town past a self-styled motel (actually a bar full of hunting trophies), and a **campsite** (Str. Runc 6, ℡0230/371 829), where cabins (❶) are available in summer; you'll need your own camping gear for this hike as there are no cabanas along the route. Another trail, rather shorter at about thirteen hours and with more dramatic scenery and a choice of mountain cabanas, heads east from the Băi station to Giumalău, Rarău and Câmpulung Moldovenesc (blue then red stripes). Of the two **chairlifts** in town, only the one at the top of Strada Negreşti is open year-round (daily 10am–5pm but sometimes closed from 1–3pm; €1 each way). From Strada Republicii, walk up Strada G. Cosbuc or Strada Negreşti, following the *telescaun* signs. The lift takes twenty-five minutes to ascend to the peak of Dealul Negrii (1300m), where ravens circle over alpine meadows. Bring provisions; the café at the top of the lift is frequently closed. The other, shorter chairlift, located behind *Hotel Bradul*, operates only in winter. There's also an Olympic cross-country ski centre near the campsite.

Most of Vatra Dornei's **accommodation** is located on the spa side of the river. Just west of the casino, the *Hotel Carol* (℡0230/374 690, ✉hotelcaroldorna@yahoo.com; ❻), at Str. Republicii 3, has the best rooms in town, and its obliging staff can arrange spa treatments and other activities; the nearby *Hotel Maestro* at Str. Republicii 1 (℡ & ℻0230/375 288; ❺), with smaller rooms, has a sauna, a jacuzzi and a fine restaurant. The Italian-themed *Hotel Musetti*, at Str. Republicii 19 (℡ & ℻0230/375 379; ❸) is a friendly and comfortable mid-range option. There are a dozen or more **pensions** in Vatra Dornei (all ❶), many located in the maze of unmarked sidestreets on either side of the spa's park. *Monica* (℡0230/375 154), 100m west of the park at Str. Alunis 5, has garishly furnished doubles and triples, and a yard full of chickens. *Robert*, on the other side of the park, offers humbler rooms, but with cleaner baths and the additional option of table tennis. Alternatively, **Antrec**, at Str. Runc 2 (℡0230/371 306, ⓦwww.biosan.ro), has its regional office here and can help you find homestay accommodation. One excellent agrotourism pension, easily accessible only if you're travelling by car, is *Poiana* (℡0745/809 234; ❷), located in the mountain village of Poiana Negri, 15km southwest of Vatra Dornei.

Of the hotel **restaurants**, the one in the *Carol* is the nicest, while those in the *Maestro* and *Bucovina* serve as decent alternatives. Another restaurant worth seeking out is the *Camy Lact* on Strada Cosbuc, which also has a small shop where local cheeses are sold. *Les Amis*, just before the bridge at Str. Luceafarului 15, has average fare and blaring music, though there is an English menu. Two doors down, you'll find an **Internet café**/stationery shop, and around the corner, opposite the train station, there is a 24-hour supermarket.

Routes to Maramureş and Transylvania

From Vatra Dornei, you can head southeast towards **Neamţ county**, northwest into **Maramureş**, or west into **Transylvania**. Seven buses a day follow the scenic Bistriţa valley down to Poiana Largului, at the northern end of Lake Bicaz and in the vicinity of the Ceahlău massif (see p.253); three of them carry on to Piatra or to Târgu Neamţ.

The route to Maramureş heads up the valley past such lovely villages as **CIOCANEŞTI**, where the houses are perched on hillocks, and **BOTOS**, which has a new **wooden church** in the Ukrainian style: very broad and square, with one large and four small cupolas. A Dutch-owned **pension** and campsite is set to open further up the road here in summer 2004. There's a **hotel** (❷) with cabins north of **CÂRLIBABA**, 8km before the road forks towards the Rotunda Pass into Transylvania, and the **Prislop Pass** into Maramureş, where the **Horă at Prislop Festival** occurs on the second Sunday in August. One bus daily (at 1.30pm) crosses the mountains to the Vişeu Valley in Maramureş, while three others run as far as Cârlibaba, from where you could probably hitch over the pass. Heading north instead of west from Cârlibaba, a pot-holed road that dead-ends at the Ukrainian border passes through tiny Moldova Suliţa, from where it's 7km up a dirt path to the **Lucina Stud**, where the famous Hutzul horses, used for cavalry in Austrian times, are bred. It's possible to ride here for around €10 per hour.

Of the three routes into Transylvania, the most dramatic is via the **Tihuţa Pass** – otherwise known as the Bârgău Pass, where Bram Stoker located Dracula's castle. Along the way, you'll find accommodation in **POIANA ŞTAMPEI**, at the *Vila din Carpati* (℡0230/379 312; ❺), located high up beside the main road. There are also a few **pensions** here. Three buses a day from Vatra Dornei run through the pass en route to Bistriţa. Travelling **by train**, you'll take a more northerly route via Ilva Mică; the Leşu Ilvei halt, one stop before Ilva Mică, is within walking distance of Leşu (see p.232). The third route, only possible if you're driving, crosses the 1271-metre-high **Rotunda Pass**, which is prone to blizzards.

Travel details

Trains

Adjud to: Braşov (2 daily; 4hr 45min); Ciceu (8 daily; 2hr 45min–4hr); Galaţi (2 daily; 2hr 30min–4hr); Ghimeş (10 daily; 1hr 45min–2hr 45min); Suceava (10 daily; 3hr–4hr 15min); Târgu Mureş (1 daily; 6hr 30min).

Bacău to: Bicaz (5 daily; 1hr 45min–2hr 30min); Iaşi (3 daily; 2hr 15min–3hr 15min); Piatra Neamţ (9 daily; 1hr–1hr 45min); Suceava (12 daily; 1hr 45min–3hr).

Galaţi to: Braşov (1 daily; 5hr 15min); Bucharest (5 daily; 3hr 30min–6hr); Constanţa (2 daily; 4hr–5hr 45min); Iaşi (1 daily; 4hr 15min); Mărăşeşti (5 daily; 2hr–3hr); Oradea (1 daily; 17hr); Suceava (2 daily; 7hr–10hr 30min); Târgu Mureş (1 daily; 9hr).

Ghimeş to: Adjud (8 daily; 1hr 45 min–3hr 15min); Braşov (1 daily; 3hr); Ciceu (8 daily; 1hr); Galaţi (1 daily; 4hr 30min); Miercurea Ciuc (4 daily; 1hr–1hr 15min); Suceava (1 nightly; 5hr); Târgu Mureş (1 daily; 4hr 30min); Timişoara (1 daily; 12hr)

Gura Humorului to: Câmpulung Moldovenesc (9 daily; 50min); Suceava (10 daily; 45min–1hr 15min); Vama (9 daily; 20min); Vatra Dornei (7 daily; 2hr).

Iaşi to: Braşov (1 daily; 7hr 30min); Bucharest (6 daily; 5hr 45min–7hr); Cluj (4 daily; 9hr 30min); Constanţa (1 daily; 7hr 30min); Suceava (5 daily; 1hr 45min–3hr); Timişoara (2 daily; 16hr–17hr).

Mărăşeşti to: Iaşi (4 daily; 3hr 30min–5hr 30min); Panciu (4 daily; 30min); Suceava (6 daily; 3hr 30min–5hr).

Paşcani to: Bacău (22 daily; 1hr–2hr); Iaşi (13 daily; 1hr–1hr 30min); Suceava (21 daily; 50min–1hr 15min); Târgu Neamţ (4 daily; 45min).

Piatra Neamţ to: Bacău (9 daily; 1hr–1hr 45min); Bicaz (2 daily; 25–45min); Bucharest (2 daily; 6hr).

Suceava to: Bucharest (8 daily; 7hr); Cacica (5 daily; 45min); Câmpulung Moldovenesc (9 daily; 1hr 45min–2hr 15min); Cluj (4 daily; 7hr); Iaşi (5 daily; 1hr 45min–3hr); Putna (2 daily; 2hr 30min); Rădăuţi (3 daily; 1hr 15min); Timişoara (3 daily; 13hr 30min–14hr 30min); Vama (9 daily; 1hr 15min–1hr 45min); Vatra Dornei (6 daily; 2hr 30min–3hr 30min).

Vama to: Moldoviţa (3 daily; 45min).

Vatra Dornei to: Cluj (4 daily; 4hr); Iaşi (4 daily; 5hr–7hr); Ilva Mica (7 daily; 1hr 30min–2hr); Suceava (7 daily; 2hr 30min–3hr 30min).

Buses and maxitaxis

Bacău to: Adjud (1 daily); Braşov (5 daily); Comăneşti (7 daily); Iaşi (4 daily); Oneşti (2 daily); Piatra Neamţ (1 daily); Târgu Neamţ (1 daily); Vatra Dornei (2 daily).

Brăila to: Constanţa (1 daily); Focşani (2 daily); Tulcea (2 daily).

Galaţi to: Focşani (2 daily); Iaşi (1 daily).

Gura Humorului to: Arbore (1 daily); Câmpulung (1 daily); Iaşi (1 daily); Piatra Neamţ (2 daily); Solca (1 daily); Suceava (9 daily); Vatra Dornei (4 daily).

Iaşi to: Bacău (3 daily); Braşov (1 daily); Câmpulung Moldovenesc (1 daily); Comăneşti (1 daily); Galaţi (1 daily); Gura Humorului (1 daily); Oneşti (1 daily); Piatra Neamţ (2 daily); Rădăuţi (1 daily); Târgu Neamţ (3 daily); Tulcea (1 daily); Vatra Dornei (1 daily).

Piatra Neamţ to: Agapia (2 daily); Braşov (2 daily); Câmpulung Moldovenesc (1 daily); Comăneşti (1 daily); Durău (Mon–Sat 2 daily); Galaţi (1 daily); Gheorgheni (1 daily); Gura Humorului (1 daily); Iaşi (7 daily); Oneşti (1 daily); Suceava (2 daily); Târgu Neamţ (11 daily); Topliţa (1 daily); Vatra Dornei (2 daily).

Suceava to: Bistriţa (3 daily); Braşov (1 daily); Bucharest (3–6 daily); Câmpulung Moldovenesc (up to 9 daily); Cluj (1 daily); Constanţa (2 daily); Gura Humorului (13 daily); Iaşi (5 daily); Piatra Neamţ (2 daily); Rădăuţi (up to 6 daily); Solca (2 daily); Târgu Neamţ (3 daily); Vatra Dornei (5 daily).

Târgu Neamţ to: Agapia (up to 5 daily); Bacău (1 daily); Braşov (1 daily); Câmpulung Moldovenesc (1 daily); Durău (2 daily); Gura Humorului (1 daily); Iaşi (2 daily); Neamţ Monastery (3 daily); Piatra Neamţ (12 daily); Rădăuţi (2 daily); Sihistria (1 daily); Suceava (2 daily); Târgu Mureş (1 daily); Văratec (3 daily); Vatra Dornei (1 daily).

Vatra Dornei to: Bacău (1 daily); Bistriţa (1 daily); Cârlibaba (3 daily); Gura Humorului (3 daily); Iaşi (1 daily); Piatra Neamţ (3 daily); Poiana Largului (4 daily); Suceava (5 daily); Târgu Neamţ (3 daily); Vişeu (1 daily).

Planes

Iaşi to: Bucharest (Tues, Thurs 3 daily; Mon, Wed, Fri 2 daily)

Suceava to: Bucharest (Mon, Wed–Fri 1 daily).

International trains

Iaşi (Nicolina) to: Chişinău, Moldova (2 daily; 5hr 30min–6hr 30min).
Suceava Nord to: Cernăuţi, Ukraine (1 daily; 5hr 30min); Kiev, Ukraine (1 daily; 23hr 30min); Moscow, Russia (1 daily; 39hr); Sofia, Bulgaria (1 daily; 20hr).

International buses

Bacău to: Chişinău, Moldova (1 daily).
Iaşi to: Bălţi, Moldova (2 daily); Chişinău, Moldova (3 daily); Istanbul, Turkey (1 daily).
Suceava to: Cernăuţi, Ukraine (5 daily); Chişinău, Moldova (1 daily); Balţi, Moldova (1 daily); Przemyśl, Poland (via Ukraine; 1 daily); Istanbul, Turkey (1 daily); Athens, Greece (4 weekly).

MOLDAVIA | Travel details

Maramureş

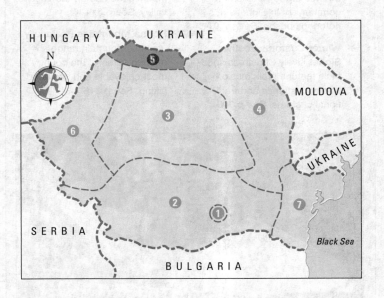

CHAPTER 5

Highlights

✱ **Wooden churches** With their magnificent spires, wooden churches such as the finely crafted structure at Șurdești, are an integral part of the Maramureș landscape. See p.301

✱ **Prison Museum, Sighet** Illuminating and moving tributes to the victims of communism in Sighet's notorious prison. See p.307

✱ **Winter Customs Festival, Sighet** Lively Christmas spectacle featuring folk music, wacky costumes and traditional customs. See p.308

✱ **Merry Cemetery, Săpânța** Exuberantly coloured and beautifully crafted wooden headstones in one of Romania's most unusual attractions. See p.309

✱ **Logging train, Vișeu de Sus** Jump aboard the early morning logging train for a picturesque ride up the Vaser valley. See p.314

✱ **Rodna Mountains** Beautifully unspoilt mountain range offering some of the country's most enjoyable and secluded hiking. See p.316

△ Traditional weaving

5

Maramureş

omania has been described as a country with one foot in the industrial future and the other in the Middle Ages – still an accurate enough
characterization of **Maramureş**, crammed up against the borders with
Hungary and Ukraine and little changed since Dacian times. Within
30km of the heavily industrialized town of Baia Mare, thickly forested mountains and rough roads maintain scores of villages in a state of almost medieval
isolation, amid a landscape of rounded hills with clumps of oak and beech and
scattered flocks of sheep.

The historic county of Maramureş lies to the north of the Gutâi pass; in
1968, this was merged with parts of Someş and Satu Mare counties to
form present-day Maramureş, though for convenience we also include in this
chapter the town of Satu Mare and the Oaş region, both in Satu Mare county.

Sitting roughly in the centre of the region, **Baia Mare**, the capital of
Maramureş, makes a good base from which to explore the county's **villages**,
which are the main reason for visiting the area: the majority of buildings are
made of wood by skilled craftsmen, with carvings decorating the eaves, doorways and windows of the houses that line each main street. Every family shares
a compound – fenced with timber, brush or latticework, and entered via a
beamed gateway (*poarta*), the size of which indicates the family's status and
prosperity – with its livestock, and produces virtually everything that they
wear, use and eat. Nowhere else in Europe do **folk costumes** persist so
strongly, the men wearing tiny *clop* straw hats and medieval rawhide galoshes
(*opinchi*) or archaic felt boots bound with thongs, and the women weaving
boldly striped *catriniţa* aprons with cloth from the water-powered fulling mills,
and embroidering intricate designs on the wide-sleeved cotton blouses worn
by both sexes – most conspicuously during markets and **festivals**, when the
villages are ablaze with colour. On Sunday afternoons people promenade, and
there may be a public dance, either in the street or on a purpose-built wooden
platform. Just as folk costume endures, so villagers have retained their traditional **religion** (a mixture of pagan beliefs and the Uniate rite), myths and
codes of behaviour.

Most interesting of all is the marvellous **woodwork** of Maramureş: the
village compound gateways, many elaborately carved with symbols such as the
Tree of Life, sun, rope and snake, continue to be produced today, and are only
surpassed in their intricacy by the *biserici de lemn* or **wooden churches**, mostly
built during the eighteenth century when this Gothic-inspired architecture
reached its height. Originally founded upon huge blocks of wood rather than
stone, they rear up into fairy-tale spires or crouch beneath humpbacked roofs,
and are generally sited on the highest ground in the village to escape seasonal

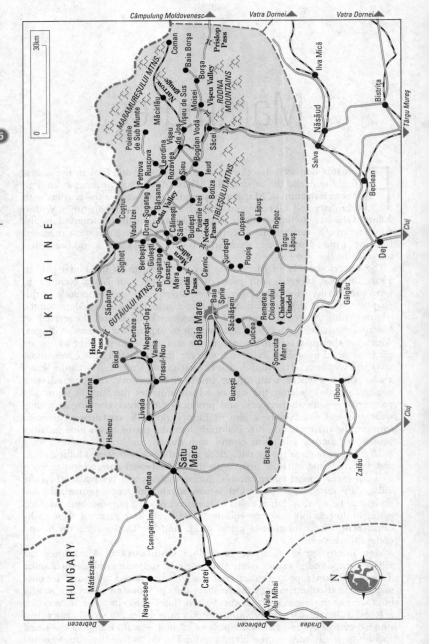

Câmpulung Moldovenesc   Vatra Dornei   Vatra Dornei

30km

0

Coman

Baia Borşa   Prislop Pass

Borşa

Ilva Mică

Vişeu Valley

Moisei   RODNA

MOUNTAINS   Bistriţa

Măcirlău   Vişeu de Sus

Vişeu   Bogdan Vodă

de Jos

Săcel   Năsăud   Târgu Mureş

Poienile

de Sub Munte

MARAMUREŞULUI MTNS.

Petrova   Leordina   Şieu

Ruscova   Rozavlea   Ieud

Botiza   Salva

Coştiui   Cosău Valley   Poienile Izei   Cupşeni   Beclean

Vadu Izei   Ocna-Şugatag   Neteda   Lăpuş

Budeşti   Pass   Rogoz

Sârbi   Surdeşti   Plopiş   Târgu

TIBLEŞULUI MTNS.   Lăpuş   Cluj

Sighet   Berbeşti   Cavnic

Giuleşti   Mara   Dej

Sat-Şugatag   Valley

Desești   Gutâi   Gâlgău

Săpânţa   Mara   Pass   Baia

GUTÂIULUI MTNS.   Sprie   Remetea

Certeze   Săcălăşeni   Chioarului

Huta   Negreşti-Oaş   Culcea   Citadel

Pass   Vama   Baia Mare   Şomcuta

Bixad   Oraşul-Nou   Mare   Jibou

U K R A I N E

Cămărzana   Livada   Buzeşti

Halmeu   Bicaz   Zalău

Satu   Cluj

Mare

Petea

Csengersima

Mátészalka   HUNGARY   N

Nagyecsed   Carei

Valea

lui Mihai

Oradea   Debrecen   Debrecen   Debrecen

floods. Whilst many wooden churches are in a poor state, around twenty of the most valuable have been restored in recent years, eight of which are on UNESCO's World Heritage list.

It's particularly worth making the effort to see the towering wooden church at **Şurdeşti**, the beautiful church paintings at **Bârsana**, **Rogoz** and **Deseşti**, the frescoes and icons of **Călineşti** and **Budeşti**, the superb prison museum in **Sighet** and the quirky "Merry Cemetery" at **Săpânţa**. Further afield in the Iza Valley, the visions of hell painted inside the church at **Poienile Izei** are the most striking images you'll see in Maramureş, while the frescoes at **Ieud** are the most famous. Maramureş also offers hiking in the peaceful **Rodna mountains** on the borders with Moldavia and Ukraine.

Without your own transport, however, getting around the region is tricky: **public transport** is patchy, and what buses and trains that do exist are few and far between. The alternatives are cycling – which is a great way to see the region, especially given the short distances between villages – or hitching, though be prepared for intermittent lifts or short rides in the back of carts or vans. **Hotel** accommodation is generally limited to towns, but there are **homestay schemes** in many villages; otherwise, come prepared to camp wild, and bring plenty of food supplies. If you get really stuck in a village, ask the priest (*popă* or *preot*) for advice, and try to repay any hospitality with gifts (tea and coffee are ideal).

Baia Mare

Lying to the south of the Gutâi and Igniş mountains, **BAIA MARE** is Romania's largest non-ferrous metals centre. Mining mania has waxed and waned here since the fourteenth century when, under its Magyar name of Nagybánya, it was the Hungarian monarchs' chief source of gold. The main reason for staying here is to prepare for forays into the surrounding country-side, but the town has an attractive, if fairly dilapidated, old core and a couple of museums to pass the time, the best of which is the **Village Museum**.

Arrival and information

The **train** and **bus stations** lie some 2km west of town on Strada Gării. The best source of **information** is the Mara Holiday agency (℡0262/226 656, Ⓔagentie@hotelmara.ro) inside the *Mara* hotel; they can also organize horse-back excursions and caving trips. Otherwise, there's the Mara agency just off Piaţa Libertăţii at Str. Culturii 1, which sells a good **map** of the region, essential if you're planning to tour the villages. For information on village **festivals**, contact the Cultural Inspectorate in the prefecture at Str. Şincai 46 (℡0262/212 042).

The **CFR** office is at Str. Victoriei 57 (Mon–Fri 7am–7pm; ℡0262/221 613) and the **TAROM** office is at B-dul Bucureşti 5 (Mon–Fri 8am–6pm; ℡0262/221 624). There's 24hr **Internet** access at Internet Checker, next to the *Dali Café* (see p.298) on Strada 22 Decembrie.

Accommodation

Baia Mare has a good selection of **hotels**, most of them affordable, but if you don't fancy staying here contact the Mara Holiday agency (see above) who'll be able to arrange **homestays** in local villages. In addition, there's a **cabana**, the *Apa Sărata* (*Salty Water*), 7km west of town on the Satu Mare road, reached by city buses #6, #7, #13 and #29, and another, the *Firiza* cabana, at Firiza dam, 10km north of town and served by bus #18 six times a day. The nearest **campsite** is also here, attached to the *Caprioara* guesthouse (☎0262/222 099).

Baza Turistica Mara ☎0262/217 123. Down an alley on the south side of Piața Revoluției, between a pharmacy and Constructiv Group, the *Baza Turistica Mara* has dorm beds with basin and toilet but shared showers. ❶

București Str. Culturii 3 ☎0262/215 311. A dingy, run-down hotel stuck somewhere in the 70s, but offering cheap rooms with or without showers. ❷–❸

Carpați Str. Minerva 16 ☎0262/214 812, ⓦwww.hotelcarpati.ro. A pricey little hotel with modestly sized rooms and small bathrooms – it's worth paying the slight extra or the better rooms – but in a nice location by the river. ❻

Mara B-dul Unirii 11 ☎0262/226 660, ⓦwww.hotelmara.ro. This big, white cumbersome building to the southwest of the centre conceals the most comfortable rooms in town. ❻

Maramureș Str. Șincai 37a ☎0262/216 555. Reasonable, if somewhat dull, the *Maramureș* is frequented in the main by businessmen and foreign groups. ❺

Minion Str. Malinului 22a ☎0262/276 056. A small private hotel with swimming pool and sauna, but it's all rather tacky in style. ❺

Sport B-dul Unirii 14a, but actually one block west on Strada Transilvaniei ☎0262/226 869. A classic (ie very basic and very cheap) sport hotel intended for visiting teams but open to all. Plenty of space, unless there's a big tournament on. ❶

The Town

The core of the **old town** centres on Piața Libertății, a small, scruffy square lined with crumbling sixteenth- to eighteenth-century houses. At no. 18, the

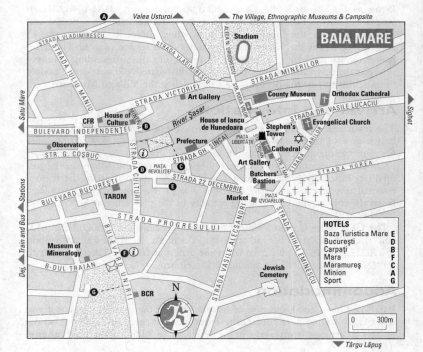

▼ *Târgu Lăpuș*

The Nagybănya (or Baia Mare) School was responsible for transforming Hungarian art at the close of the nineteenth century. Its founder was **Simon Hollósy** (1857–1918), born of Armenian stock in Sighet and trained in Munich, where he was influenced by the refined naturalism of Jules Bastien-Lepage, and in 1886 set up his own school there. From 1896, he brought his students to a summer school in Baia Mare, where he painted *en plein air* for the first time. An exhibition in 1897 of the school's paintings was seen as marking the start of a new era in Hungarian art and the school became known as the "Hungarian Barbizon", although the area's motifs and colours were more similar to those of Provence.

In 1902, Hollósy suffered a creative crisis, and the leadership of the school was taken over by **Károly Ferenczy**; tuition fees were abolished, and the embittered and jealous Hollósy left to set up a rival school in Técső, now the Ukrainian town of Tyachiv, just downstream of Sighet. Ferenczy suffered a similar crisis in 1910, and did little work thereafter. Of the second generation of artists, the most gifted was Cavnic-born Jenő Maticska (1885–1906). After his untimely death, Béla Czóbel, Csába Vilmos Perlrott, Sándor Ziffer and others revolted against creeping stagnation; their 1906 exhibition, influenced by German Expressionism and by Cézanne and Matisse, again marked the start of a new era in Hungarian art. After World War I the school was opened to both Hungarian and Romanian students – up to 150 a year – but interest in it faded away in the 1930s and the school closed its doors.

Other renowned artists associated with the school include Eugen Pascu (1895–1948), Tibor Boromisza (1880–1960), János Krizsán (1886–1948) and Krizsán's wife Antónia Csikos (1887–1987).

thick-walled Casa Elisabeta was the **house of Iancu de Hunedoara**, fifteenth-century Regent of Hungary, and now houses temporary art and local history exhibitions (Tues–Sun 10am–4pm). To the south of the square rises the fifteenth-century, fifty-metre-high **Stephen's Tower**, all that remains of a twin-naved cathedral that burnt down in 1769; the adjacent Baroque pile, built by the Jesuits in 1717–20, subsequently became the town's cathedral. Behind the cathedral at Str. 1 Mai 8, the **Art Gallery** (Tues–Sun 10am–4pm) contains eighteenth- and nineteenth-century paintings on wood and glass, and a number of canvases by artists of the **Nagybánya School** (see box above). Much of the work is now in Budapest, however, and the stuff here is attributed to the "Baia Mare School" – a sly piece of Romanian revisionism. There's more art on show north of the river at Str. Victoriei 21, where temporary exhibitions (same hours) are held in an old villa that housed the Nagybănya School in 1910–12.

The **Reformat church** of 1809 at the junction of Strada Monetăriei and Strada Podul Viilor, just north of Piața Libertății, is a landmark that appears in many works of the Nagybănya School. Nearby, housed in the old mint building at Str. Monetăriei 1, is the **County Museum** (Mon–Fri 8am–4pm, Sat & Sun 10am–2pm), whose permanent mining and minting exhibition is undergoing extensive renovation – in the meantime, there's an impressive collection of clay vessels and sixteenth- to nineteenth-century religious books. The **Museum of Mineralogy,** towards the stations at B-dul Traian 8 (Tues–Sun 9am–5pm), displays a myriad variety of rocks, crystals and ore deposits extracted from the region's mines.

Running east from Piața Libertății, Strada Dr Vasile Lucaciu has some interesting old buildings whose cellars are entered from the street. At the early twentieth-century Orthodox Cathedral, head south along Strada Olarilor (which follows the line of the old city walls) to reach Piața Izvoarelor, where the fifteenth-century **Butchers' Bastion** (Bastionul Măcelarilor) overlooks the market place in which the Robin Hood-style outlaw Pintea Viteazul (Pintea the Brave) was shot in 1703.

Baia Mare's main attraction is its open-air **Village Museum** (Tues–Sun 10am–5pm), ten minutes' walk north of the town on Florilor hill, and although not as well maintained as many of the country's other open-air venues, it has an eye-catching collection. There are over a hundred examples of peasant houses, wine presses, watermills and other structures from the surrounding region, but in particular look out for the wooden church – raised in 1630 in the village of Chechiş, just south of Baia Mare – and, close by, the homestead from Berbeşti, featuring a fine carved gate with the Tree of Life motif. The **Ethnographic Museum** (Tues–Sun 10am–5pm), on nearby Strada Dealul Florilor, offers a neatly presented array of agricultural and viticultural implements, ceramics, textile and garments.

Eating, drinking and entertainment

Of the few **restaurants** in town, the best is the anonymous looking *Inside*, at Str. Cloşca 11, a classy little place offering terrific Romanian cuisine, good wines and a convivial atmosphere. The bright and breezy *Pizza H*, at B-dul Bucureşti 6, is a better than average pizzeria which also dabbles in pasta and chicken dishes, while other possibilities include the rather old-fashioned *Select* at Str. Progesului 54, the *Bulevard* at B-dul Bucureşti 26a, and the *Dealul Florilor*, just east of the Village Museum, which gives fine views over the city. The restaurant in the *Mara* hotel is also perfectly agreeable, and very reasonably priced.

For **drinking**, try the traditional *Butoiasul cu Bere* at Str. Şincai 13 or the colourful and relaxing *Cafe Dali* across from the *Bucureşti* hotel on the south side of Piaţa Revoluţiei.

The town's key festival is the week-long **Chestnut Festival** (Sărbătoarea Castenelor) at the end of September/beginning of October, which, appropriately enough, celebrates the chestnut season with exhibitions and a riotous beer festival.

Southern Maramureş

The area to the south of Baia Mare was part of Someş county until it was dismembered in the 1968 reforms. The southwestern corner of the present Maramureş county, beyond the River Someş, is known as **Codrul**; the area immediately south of Baia Mare is **Chioarul**; and further east is **Lăpuş**. Whilst the landscape of southern Maramureş is not as dramatic as that in the north, it is unremittingly lovely, and you could easily spend a couple of days pottering around the region's fine wooden churches, at settlements such as **Baia Sprie**, **Şurdeşti** and **Plopiş**. Folk costumes here are similar to those of Maramureş proper, although the tall straw hats are unique to the region.

Codrul and Chioarul

The most accessible village in Codrul is **BUZEŞTI**, 30km west of Baia Mare, with a wooden church built in 1739, the bulbous steeple of which bears witness to the penetration of Baroque influences into this area, while the four corner pinnacles echo the Gothic towers of both Transylvania and Hungary. Much more remote, in the far western extremity of the county (though served by two or three

There is a strong tradition of building **wooden churches** right across Eastern Europe, from northern Russia to the Adriatic, but in terms of both quality and quantity the richest examples are in Maramureş. From 1278, the Orthodox Romanians were forbidden by their Catholic Hungarian overlords to build churches in stone, and so used wood to ape Gothic developments.

In general, the walls are built of blockwork (squared-off logs laid horizontally) with intricate joints, cantilevered out in places to form brackets or consoles, which support the eaves. However, in Maramureş Western techniques such as raftering and timber framing have enabled the development of the high roofs and steeples that are characteristic of the area, rather than the tent roofs or stepped cupolas used further north. Following the **standard Orthodox ground plan**, the main roof covers the narthex and naos and a lower one the sanctuary; the naos usually has a barrel vault, while the narthex has a low-planked ceiling under the tower, its weight transmitted by rafters to the walls and thus avoiding the need for pillars. The main roof is always shingled and in many cases double, allowing clerestory windows high in the nave walls, while the lower roof is sometimes extended at the west end to form a porch (exonarthex or *pridvor*).

Most of the Maramureş churches were rebuilt after the last Tatar raid in 1717, acquiring large porches and tall towers, often with four corner-pinnacles, clearly derived from the masonry architecture of the Transylvanian cities. Inside, almost every church has a choir gallery above the west part of the naos; always a later addition, as shown by the way it is superimposed on the **wall paintings**. These extraordinary works of art were produced by local artists in the eighteenth and early nineteenth centuries, combining the icon tradition with pagan motifs and topical propaganda. They broadly follow the standard Orthodox layout, with the *Incarnation* and *Eucharist* in the sanctuary (for the priest's edification), the *Last Judgement* and moralistic parables such as the *Wise and Foolish Virgins* in the narthex (where the women stand), and the *Passion* in the naos; the treatment of the last, however, changed in the nineteenth century as the Uniate Church gained in strength, with more emphasis on the *Ascension* and the *Evangelists*.

Sixteenth-century **icons** (such as those found in Budeşti) show a northern Moldavian influence; the seventeenth-century Moisei school was the first to show the imprint of the Renaissance, and from the late eighteenth century, Baroque influences were added. The first of the major painters was **Alexandru Ponehalski**, who worked from the 1750s to the 1770s in Călineşti and Budeşti, in a naive post-Byzantine style with blocks of colour in black outlines. From 1767 to the 1780s, **Radu Munteanu** worked around his native Lăpuş and in Botiza, Glod and Deseşti, painting in a freer and more imaginative manner. A far more Baroque style developed in the first decade of the nineteenth century, with **Toader Hodor** and **Ion Plohod** working in Bârsana, Corneşti, Văleni, Năneşti and Rozavlea.

Since 1989, there has been a **renaissance of the Uniate or Greco-Catholic faith**, repressed under communism and forcibly merged with the Romanian Orthodox Church: many parishes have reverted to Greco-Catholicism, reclaiming their churches; in others, one church is now Orthodox and the other Uniate; while in some villages the congregations have even agreed to share one building. Many villages have started to build large, new churches, making it more likely that you'll find the wooden churches locked up – even on a Sunday. Finding the key-holder can be problematic, but ask around long enough and someone is likely to help out. Remember that people **dress conservatively** here, and the wearing of shorts, particularly for visiting churches, is not appropriate.

buses a day from Baia Mare), is **BICAZ**, whose Orthodox church and wall paintings both date from the early eighteenth century. As in Buzeşti, a new church has been built here and the old one is disused, though it has been recently repaired.

Many of the villages of Chioarul have old churches, but the most interesting is at **SĂCĂLĂŞENI**, just 10km south of Baia Mare. Rebuilt at the end of the seventeenth century, the church originally dates from 1442, with a carved doorway and paintings from 1865. There's a good **motel** here: the simple, but clean and modern *Moara Veche* at no. 137 (☎0262/289 353; ❷), which has two- three- and four-bed rooms. Just 2km to the southwest, in **CULCEA**, is an early eighteenth-century wooden church with plastered walls – it's hidden away on a small elevation just beyond the ugly modern church. Continuing south for a further 5km, you'll come to the larger village of **REMETEA CHIOARULUI**, which also has a fine church, dating from 1800 – to gain entry, pop across to the neighbouring modern church, where the caretaker should have the key. The village is also the starting point for the three-hour return trip south through the gorge of the River Lăpuş to the ruins of the sixteenth- to eighteenth-century Chioarului citadel (6km each way). Ten kilometres further south of Remetea, on the DN1C, is **ŞOMCUTA MARE**, where choirs and bands assemble for the Stejarul **festival** on the first or third Sunday of July – check with the Mara Holiday agency (see p.295) in Baia Mare. Five buses a day run from Baia Mare to Şomcuta Mare, via Săcălăşeni and Remetea.

Lăpuş

Sitting in the centre of the Lăpuş area is the small, non-descript town of **TÂRGU LĂPUŞ**, served by seven buses a day from Baia Mare and home to a couple of pensions and numerous houses offering **private rooms**, should you wish to make the town your base. Buses from the station, (5min walk east of the centre across the bridge) visit the surrounding villages, many of which boast fine wooden churches. The best examples are the two in **ROGOZ**, 5km east of Târgu Lăpuş, which despite the arrival of a large modern church, remain well maintained: the Uniate church, built around 1695 in Suciu de Sus and moved here in 1893, stands within the grounds of the Orthodox church, built of elm some time between 1661 and 1701. The latter is unique thanks to its naturalistic horse-head consoles, which support the roof at the west end, and its asymmetric roof, which has a larger overhang to the north to shelter a table where paupers were fed by the parish. Some of the paintings by Radu Munteanu were painted over in the 1830s, but even so this remains one of the most beautifully decorated churches in Maramureş: look out for a *Last Judgement*, to the left inside the door, and the *Creation* and the *Good Samaritan*, on the naos ceiling. There are four buses a day from Baia Mare, heading for Băiuţ or Grosii Tibleşului, as well as local services from Târgu Lăpuş. Băiuţ buses also pass through **LĂPUŞ**, 7km east of Rogoz, which boasts a village museum and a seventeenth-century wooden church with carved and painted walls. The oldest murals in the church date from the early eighteenth century, and its icons include the first works of Radu Munteanu (see box on p.299). **CUPŞENI**, 11km north of Rogoz (just one bus a day from Târgu Lăpuş), is one of the most idyllic villages in the region and home to some of its best carpenters. Here, the upper church, built in 1600, has a fine tower, but badly damaged paintings, and the tiny lower church, moved here from Peteritea in 1847 by the Uniates, was beautifully painted in 1848 by Radu Munteanu.

Baia Sprie, Şurdeşti and Plopiş

The small town of **BAIA SPRIE** lies 10km east of Baie Mare along the Sighet road (served by city buses #8 and #21), and like most Romanian mining towns, it is highly multiethnic, as reflected by its multiplicity of churches. On

Piaţa Libertăţii, just north of the modern centre (at the Şurdeşti junction), you'll find the massive Neoclassical Roman Catholic church (1846–58) and Calvinist church; down a lane to the right is the wooden-roofed Orthodox church, built in 1793. From Baia Sprie, you can detour off the main road to reach some classic Maramureş villages, on the fringes of the Chioar district.

The magnificent Uniate wooden church at **ŞURDEŞTI**, 10km south of Baia Sprie, stands just beyond the village on a hill overlooking a stream. Built in the early eighteenth century, the church is clad in thousands of oak shingles, and boasts a forty-five-metre-high tower, three times the length of the church itself, which was the tallest wooden structure in Europe until the new monastery at Bârsana (see p.312) topped it; you can climb up into the tower and roof space from the porch for excellent views of the surrounding countryside. Inside the church, which someone from the painted house near the stream will unlock for you, there are remarkable wall paintings dating from 1810, and also some interesting late eighteenth-century icons.

PLOPIŞ, a kilometre or so south across the fields, has a similar, though slightly smaller, church, built between 1798 and 1805, which features four corner turrets on its spire, a characteristic of many wooden churches here and in the Erdehát region of Hungary. If you continue north along the minor road, it eventually leads through the mining town of Cavnic, over the **Neteda Pass** (1039m) and down to **Budeşti** (see p.305); there are five buses a day from Baia Mare to Cavnic via Şurdeşti, of which one continues to Budeşti and Sighet; otherwise, you'll have to hitch.

Northern Maramureş

The historic county of Maramureş – and the heart of Maramureş proper – lies north of Baia Sprie, beyond the Gutâi Pass. Here, you'll find idyllic rolling countryside, still farmed in the traditional manner, together with some of the finest **churches** in the region, set in picturesque villages where customs have remained virtually unchanged for centuries. The main town is **Sighet**, worth stopping off at for a couple of splendid museums, and a good place to base yourself for visiting the villages.

The Mara valley

Four kilometres northeast of Baia Sprie, a road breaks off the main DN18 up to the Mogoşa ski complex, 3km east, where there's accommodation at the simple *Mogoşa* cabana (☎0262/260 800; ❷), and the very comfortable *Şuior* hotel (☎0262/262 080; ❹), which also has sporting facilities. Back on the main DN18, the road zigzags up to the 987-metre-high **Gutâi Pass**, at the top of which is the *Hanul lui Pintea*, a basic restaurant, where you can also stock up on provisions in the adjacent food shop. There follows a fifteen-kilometre-long winding descent into the Mara valley, past the splendidly carved houses and gateways of **Mara** village. One kilometre beyond Mara, the village of **DESEŞTI** conceals a lovely wooden church, hidden among some trees to the left, above the road and the trackbed of an old forestry rail line now used as a cycle path. Built in 1770, the church has a fine example of the "double roof" or clerestory style that enabled the builders to construct windows high up inside the nave to increase the illumination. Nevertheless, it's dark inside and even with candles you'll find it hard to pick out the marvellous **wall paintings**. Executed by Radu Munteanu in 1780, the

△ Geese outside a wooden gate, Maramureş

paintings seem more primitive and less stylized than the frescoes in the Moldavian monasteries which were painted some two hundred years earlier. Boldly coloured in red, yellow and white, the figures of saints and martyrs are contrasted with shady-looking groups of Jews, Turks, Germans, Tatars and Franks. The frescoes also include folk-style geometric and floral motifs, while the inscriptions are in the Cyrillic alphabet – Old Church Slavonic remained the liturgical language of Romanian Orthodoxy until the nineteenth century.

The next church is 2km along the road, in the village of **HĂRNICEŞTI**, also dating from 1770 and housing some fine icons; in 1942, the apse was widened, and in 1952 the porch was added, so that now the tower seems disproportionately short. The museum house here is supposedly the only remaining nineteenth-century noble home in Maramureş. The church stands just north of the junction of a back road east towards Ocna Şugatag and Budeşti; two buses a day from Baia Mare to Ocna Şugatag take this road via **HOTENI**, 3km east of Hărniceşti, known for its Tânjaua **festival**, held on the first or second Sunday of May – check with the Mara Holiday agency (see p.295) in Baia Mare. As in many of the villages of the Mara valley, this is a celebration of the First Ploughman, a fertility rite that dates back at least to Roman times. In the ritual, a dozen youths adorn bulls and lead them to the house of the chosen First Ploughman, the hardest-working farmer in the village, for him to plough the first field of the season, before dunking him into a stream or pool and commencing the feasting and dancing.

Continuing a couple of kilometres further along the main road towards Sighet brings you to **SAT-ŞUGATAG**, site of another church, though this one is located, unusually, on a flat piece of land beside the road. Accessed via a finely carved wooden gate, this beautifully compact church was built in 1642, and features a twisted rope motif just below the eaves. The graveyard contains beautiful stout wooden crosses and the village itself has some quite picturesque cottages. A minor road heads off from here to Ocna Şugatag, Călineşti, Sârbi and Budeşti, with another right turn 2km north leading to **MĂNĂSTIREA GIULEŞTI**, a tiny village with a tiny church, founded in 1653 and now shared by Orthodox and Uniate congregations; it boasts fine paintings from 1653 and 1783, as well as late eighteenth-century icons by Alexandru Ponehalski.

The main road continues northwards to **GIULEŞTI**, one of the main villages in the Mara valley, which has a stone church and, like many of these villages, an ancient **watermill**: its two mill wheels grind wheat and corn, with the miller traditionally taking one cupful of each hopper-load. Everything is made of wood, right down to the little channels siphoning off water to lubricate the spindles of the wheels, and the whole set-up doubles as a fulling mill, its large wooden mallets beating the cloth clean.

Further north, on the edge of **BERBEŞTI**, a 300-year-old carved wooden crucifix (*troiţa*), adorned with four mourning figures and symbols of the sun and moon, stands beside the road, a throwback to the time when travel was considered a hazardous undertaking; no journeys were made on a Tuesday, deemed an unlucky day, and it was believed that after sundown ghosts and vampires (*strigoi*) roamed the highways, seeking victims. From Berbeşti, the DN18 continues to Vadu Izei, the mouth of the Iza valley (see p.312), and beyond to Sighet (see p.305).

The Cosău valley

At Fereşti, 2km southeast of Berbeşti, a minor road turns off to the right and leads up the **Cosău valley** – the most interesting of all in Maramureş – to

The **Cult of the Dead**, central to Romanian culture, is particularly well developed in Maramureş, where the rituals are fixed and elaborate; if anything is omitted, it's believed that the soul will return as a ghost or even a vampire. There are several phases that cover the separation from the world of the living, preparation for the journey, and entry into the other world. A dying person asks forgiveness of his family and neighbours, who must obey his last wishes. Black flags are hung outside the house where the deceased lies for three days, a period during which the church bells are rung thrice daily, neighbours pay their respects and women (but not men) lament the deceased in improvised rhyming couplets.

When the priest arrives at the house on the third day, the wailing and lamenting reach a climax before he blesses a bucketful of water, extinguishes a candle in it, and consecrates the house with a cross left etched on the wall for a year. The coffin is carried by six married male relatives or friends, stopping for prayers (the priest being paid for each stop) at crossroads, bridges and any other feature along the way, and then at the church for absolution. The funeral itself is relatively swift, with everyone present throwing soil into the grave and being given a small loaf with a candle and a red-painted egg, as at Easter; these must also be given to passers-by, including tourists (if you're ever offered one, be aware it would give great offence if you refused it). The knot-shaped loaves or *colaci* bear the inscription NI KA ("Jesus Christ is victorious"), which is stamped in the dough by a widow or some other "clean woman" using a special seal called a *pecetar*. The seal's handle, usually wooden, is often elaborately carved with motifs such as the Endless Column, the Tree of Life, wolf's teeth or a crucifix.

Three days later there is another *pomană* or memorial meal, when bread is again given to all present; after nine days, nine widows spend the day fasting and praying around the deceased's shirt; six weeks and then six months after the funeral, the absolution is repeated with another meal, as the dead must be given food and drink, and after a year a feast is given for all the family's dead. Mourning lasts for one year, during which time the close family may not attend weddings or dances and women wear black. As elsewhere in Romania, *şergare* (embroidered napkins) are hung over icons in the church or over plates on house walls in memory of the dead. The Uniates also remember their dead on All Souls' Day.

Marriage is seen as essential in Maramureş, so much so that if a person of marriageable age (in fact from eight years old, the age of first confession) dies unmarried, a **Marriage of the Dead** (Nunta Mortului) is held. A black flag is carried, while the deceased and a bridesmaid or best man (and, in the case of a man, a stand-in bride) dress in wedding costume, although everyone else wears mourning garb.

several picturesque villages where traditional costume is still worn; the villages can also be approached from the south over the Neteda Pass (see p.301); from the west, using the road via Hoteni; or from Bârsana, to the east.

Across the river from Fereşti is small, tranquil **CORNEŞTI**, where there's an early eighteenth-century church and another **watermill**, which also serves as a laundry. Here, women beat clothes with carved wooden laundry bats beside the river, often improvising songs and verses as they work, using a distinctive local technique called singing "with knots", in which the voice is modulated by tapping the glottis while the singer doesn't breathe for lengthy periods.

Continuing south you come to three villages about 4km apart, with two **wooden churches** apiece. At sprawling **CĂLINEŞTI**, the beautiful Susani (upper) or Băndreni church, high above the road just north of the junction, was built and painted in the 1780s. Its companion, the Josani (lower) or Caieni church, built in 1663, is one of the loveliest in Maramureş, with its huge nineteenth-century porch and beautiful internal paintings by Ponehalski. It's best reached by a path across the fields next to house no. 385, on the road east to Bârsana. **SÂRBI** has two small and unassuming wooden churches – the Susani to the north, built in 1667, with icons by Radu Munteanu, and the Josani, to the south, built in 1703 – and some fine watermills, while 4km further south is **BUDEŞTI**, a large village but one of the least spoilt in Maramureş, with even its new houses largely built in the traditional style. The Josani church stands in the centre of the village by a memorial to the dead of the 1989 revolution; the church was built in 1643 and contains a chain-mail coat of the outlaw Pintea the Brave (see p.298). Its frescoes are amongst Alexandru Ponehalski's finest works, especially the *Last Judgement*. The upper church, dating from 1586, has particularly fine paintings from the 1760s, also by Ponehalski, and has been gradually extended westwards, so that the tower is now almost central. From here, there's a particularly fine ten-kilometre walk through idyllic countryside to Hoteni (see p.303) via **BREB**, a small village with a particularly lovely and tranquil wooden church dating from 1531 hidden away in the valley. Budeşti can be reached by four **buses** a day from Sighet, taking the high road via **OCNA ŞUGATAG** (also known as Ocna Maramureşului), a former salt-mining centre that is now a small spa, with a smart and very good-value **hotel**, the *Salina* (☎0272/374 362; ❸), and some adjoining two- and four-bed huts (❶). It's also one of the few villages hereabouts with any amenities, including a bank and some shops.

Standing at the junction of the roads along the Iza and Mara valleys, **VADU IZEI** has a well-developed rural **homestay scheme** (❷). The scheme also operates in Botiza (see p.312) and Ieud (see p.313), but you can book for all three villages at Vadu Izei's Agro-Tur office (June–Aug daily 9am–9pm, Sept–May Mon–Fri 9am–4pm; ☎0262/330 171, ⓦwww.vaduizei.ovr.ro), located next to the library in a small wooden hut at no. 161. They can also arrange local excursions – walking, cycling (there are also bikes for hire) and tours of the wooden churches – as well as visits to local *artisanat* (carpet-makers, basket-weavers, wood carvers and icon painters) workshops. The office manager, Ioan Berlean, is himself one of the region's most renowned glass icon painters. Vadu Izei is known as the workplace of Gheorghe Borodi (1917–91), who carved monumental **gateways** erected by Maramureş families as symbols of nobility; as most claimed to be *nemeşi* or nobles, there's no shortage of gateways. A good time to be here is mid-July for the Maramuzical **festival** of folk fiddle playing.

Sighet

Sighetu Marmaţiei, or **SIGHET** as it's generally known, stands just a few kilometres from the Ukrainian border and has the air of a frontier town. When the territory to the north – now Ukraine – was called Ruthenia, Sighet was a famous smuggling centre. Today, it's a peaceful modern town with around 45,000 inhabitants, where you can see residents of the surrounding villages in local costume, especially on the first Monday of the month, when the livestock market takes place. The key attractions are the superb **Prison museum** – one of Romania's best museums – and the **memorial house** dedicated to holocaust survivor Elie Weisel. The town is also famed for its **winter carnival** (see box on p.308), when many of the participants wear extraordinary shamanistic costumes and masks; unfortunately, though, few foreign visitors are around to witness this on December 27.

The Town

From the train and bus stations, it's a ten-minute walk south down Strada Iuliu Maniu to the **Reformat church**, a fourteenth-century structure rebuilt on an unusual ground plan. The town centre extends to the east of here and comprises two one-way streets, both of which change their names, and are linked by several squares, so it can be hard to make sense of addresses.

Immediately east of the Reformat church is the **Curtea Veche**, the Baroque county hall of 1690–91, now housing a restaurant and shops. Beyond here is Piaţa Libertăţii, with the **Roman Catholic church**, built by the Piarist order in 1730–34, on its northern side. On the east side of the square is the **Maramureş Ethnographic Museum** (Tues–Sun 10am–6pm), featuring a better than average collection of local pottery and woodwork – including some beautifully carved gates and gateposts typical of the region – as well as a selection of costumes and masks worn by participants during the town's Winter

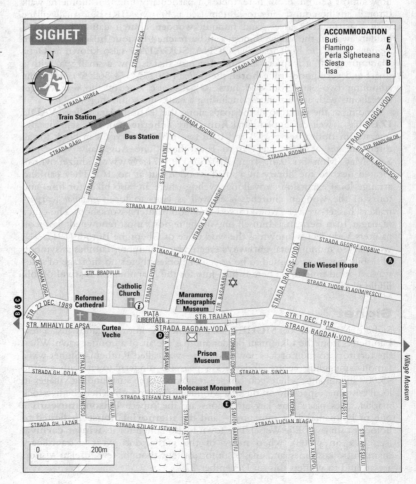

The prison of the ministers

Sighet prison operated from 1898 until 1977, and in that time achieved a notoriety gained by few others. Its nadir was between 1950 and 1955, when political prisoners (former government ministers, generals, academics and bishops) were held here so that they could be "protected" by the Red Army or rapidly spirited away into the Soviet Union if the communist regime was threatened. The prison's 72 cells held 180 members of the pre-war establishment, at least two-thirds of them aged over sixty; they were appallingly treated and, not surprisingly, many died. The most important figure to perish in Sighet prison was **Iuliu Maniu**, regarded as the greatest living Romanian when he was arrested in 1947 (at the age of 73) and now seen as a secular martyr – the only uncorrupt politician of the pre-war period, organizer of the 1944 coup, and notably reluctant to pursue revenge against Transylvania's Hungarians after the war.

The leading Hungarian victim was **Arón Márton**, Roman Catholic bishop of Alba Iulia, who opposed the persecution of the Jews in 1944 and of the Uniates in 1949, and was imprisoned from 1950 to 1955, surviving until 1980. Others who died in Sighet included two of the three members of the Brătianu family imprisoned here – Dinu, president of the National Liberal Party and Finance Minister 1933–34, and Gheorghe, historian and second-division politician – as well as Mihail Manoilescu, theoretician of Romanian fascism, and Foreign Minister in 1940. Their graves can be seen in the Cearda cemetery, just off the main road to the west of town.

Carnival (see box on p.308). The museum's **Natural Sciences** section (same hours), at Piaţa Libertăţii 16 on the west side of the Roman Catholic church, is dull by comparison, mainly stuffed with hunting trophies.

On Strada Coposu, to the south of the Ethnographic Museum, stands the town's former **prison** (see box above), which opened in 1997 as the **Memorial Museum of the Victims of Communism and of the Resistance** (Tues–Sun: May–Oct 9.30am–6.30pm, plus Mon in July & Aug; Nov–April 10am–4pm). The prison has retained many of its original fixtures and fittings including the cells, some two dozen of which have been converted into exhibition spaces, with themes pertaining to the communist era. In addition to memorials to Iuliu Maniu and Gheorghe Brătianu, the prison's two most famous inmates, there are displays on collectivization, forced labour on the Danube–Black Sea Canal, the deportations to the Bărăgan, and the demolition of the heart of Bucharest during the 1980s. There's also fascinating coverage of the feared Securitate, and another cell stuffed with Ceauşescu-oriented memorabilia (amusingly entitled 'Communist Kitsch'), featuring paintings and busts, and photos of the Romanian leader lording it with world dignitaries such as Castro and Nixon.

In the courtyard to the rear of the museum is an underground memorial hall, the walls of which are carved with the names of some 8,000 people detained in Romanian prisons during the communist period, and a dozen or so bronze statues, depicting figures in various states of pose.

Turning right one block down Strada Barnuţiu brings you to a **monument** to the 38,000 Maramureş Jews rounded up by the Hungarian gendarmerie and deported in 1944. The community's nineteenth-century synagogue survives, and can be found on the far side of Piaţa Libertăţii at Strada Basarabia 10. One block east at Strada Tudor Vladimirescu 1, at the corner of Strada Dragoş Vodă, is a plain house that was the childhood home of **Elie Wiesel**, Auschwitz survivor and winner of the 1986 Nobel Peace Prize for his work in helping to understand and remember the Holocaust. It's now an impressive memorial house (Mon–Fri 9am–3pm), complete with books, furniture and religious items donated by local Jewish families, as well as pictures of Wiesel's many visits to Sighet, including his last return in 2002 to open the house.

Situated on Dobăieş hill on the town's eastern outskirts, the **Village Museum** (Tues–Sun 10am–6pm) presents dozens of houses, farm buildings and churches collected from the Iza Valley – worth viewing if you're intending to give the real thing a miss. If you don't fancy walking (30min), take bus #1 to the bridge and School no. 5, then walk northeast for five minutes up Strada Muzeului.

Practicalities

The **train and bus stations** are located north of town on Strada Gării, from where it's a fifteen-minute walk south along Strada Iuliu Maniu to the centre. Trains depart regularly to Vişeu de Jos, most continuing to Salva and Beclean, the junctions for trains to Suceava, Cluj and Braşov, while there are good, if sporadic, bus connections to the surrounding villages, with many often departing in the early morning. There's a small **tourist office** (Mon–Fri 8am–4pm, Sat 9am–1pm; ☏0262/514 319) next to the church on the north side of Piaţa Libertăţii, which can distribute basic info and maps.

Sighet has a good stock of reasonably priced **hotels**, though none particularly excel: the most central is the run-down and rather gaudy *Tisa*, at Piaţa Libertăţii 8 (☏0262/312 645, ⓕ315 484; ❸), while a couple of blocks behind it, at Str. Barnuţiu 6 (at the junction with Strada Ştefan cel Mare), the *Motel Buţi* (☏0262/311 035; ❸) is more impressive than it looks from the outside, with small, but modern rooms. Two blocks behind the **post office**, at the southeastern end of the central squares, the *Motel Flamingo*, Str. Coşbuc 36 (☏0262/317 197, ⓦwww.sighetumarmatiei.alphanet.ro; ❸), has comfortable rooms, though it can get quite loud with the downstairs bar. A little way out of town, on the road to Săpânţa, there's the *Perla Sigheteana* motel at Str. Avram Iancu 65 (☏0262/310 613, ⓦwww.sighetumarmatiei.alphanet.ro; ❸), which also has a pool, sauna and gym, and, 300m further along at no. 42, the marginally more enticing *Siesta* motel (☏0262/311 468, ⓔoffice@siesta.mm.ro; ❸). To the west of town, Strada Eminescu leads in ten minutes to the Grădina Morii park and a footbridge over the river to Solovan hill, where you can easily **camp** wild.

Winter Customs Festival

Held in Sighet on December 27, the annual **Winter Customs Festival** (Festivalul Datinilor de Iarna) is a vibrant display of music, and winter costumes and customs, all combined to depict the dual influences of ancient pagan and Christian beliefs. The festival is heralded by brightly decorated horses galloping down the main street. Upon the arrival of the official party, the parade begins with up to fifty groups from villages all over Maramures, Bucovina, Transylvania and Ukraine slowly making their way down the street to present their song or skit to the mayor.

Thereafter, the rather mishmash play is enacted thus: soldiers arrive to tell King Herod about the rumour of a saviour, while bears roll around the ground to raise the earth spirits. Meanwhile, horsemen are called to find the infant child and men bearing heavy iron cowbells arrive to drive away the evil spirits – represented by multi-coloured, animist style dracus. Present throughout is the clapping wooden goat (*capra*), warding off evil spirits to ensure that spring will return. In the afternoon, a full-length concert takes place both on the streets and in a nearby theatre, which lasts until early evening when more impromptu celebrations take over.

There are precious few options for **eating out** in Sighet. Other than the hotel restaurants, the best of which is the *Flamingo*'s, you could try your luck at *Curtea Veche*, Str. Mihalyi de Apşa 2, which serves solid Romanian fare, or the *Interbijoux* pizzeria across the road at Str. Mihalyi de Apşa 1 (next to the painter Simon Hollósy's birthplace). The *Patiseria Adrada*, by the post office, serves fine French-style pastries.

Săpânţa and the Oaş depression

Sixteen kilometres northwest of Sighet, and served by five buses a day, **SĂPÂNŢA** has achieved a star on every tourist map, thanks to the work of the woodcarver Stan Ion Pătraş (1909–77). Its **Merry Cemetery** (Cimitir Vesel) features beautifully worked, colourfully painted wooden headstones carved with portraits of the deceased or scenes from their lives, chosen by relatives and inscribed with witty limericks (in Romanian) composed by Pătraş as he saw fit. Some are terse – "who sought money to amass, could not Death escape, alas!" – while a surprising number recall violent deaths, like that of the villager killed by a "bloody Hungarian" during the last war, or a mother's final message to her son: "Griga, may you pardoned be, even though you did stab me." Pătraş himself is buried directly in front of the church entrance, his headstone marked by two white doves either side of his carved portrait. Following Pătraş' death, the funerary masterwork was continued by his two apprentices, Turda Toader and Vasile Stan, though all the headstones are now carved and painted by Pop Dumitru Tincu, whom you may be lucky enough to see going about his work in the cemetery. You can find more of Pătraş' artistry in his old house, a modest wooden cottage located some 300m behind the cemetery along the dusty road (it's signposted). The barn where he worked is adorned with some spectacularly colourful fixtures and fittings, as well as what must be the only wood-carved portraits of Nicolae and Elena Ceauşescu in existence. The village is also known for the traditional *cergi* or woollen blankets and is now lined with handicraft stalls and rather too accustomed to busloads of tourists making a stop for half an hour and then rushing on.

There's a smattering of **accommodation** in Săpânţă, including four basic rooms in the unnamed pension (☎0262/372 137; ❸) directly opposite the cemetery at no. 656, and OVR **homestays**, available through Traian Telaptean (☎0262/318 498, ⓕ330 171). There's a simple **campsite** (☎0262/372 228), with a handful of two-bed huts (❶), 2.5km south of the cemetery on the main road.

The Oaş depression

Beyond Săpânţa, the road turns south towards Satu Mare, winding up to enter the **Huta Pass** (587m) to enter the **Oaş depression**. Oaş is sometimes billed as "undiscovered Maramureş", but most of the local men now work or trade abroad, so that the roads are lined with new bungalows and imported Audis, and traditional costume is little worn except in the remotest villages such as Cămărzana, and at festivals. The shepherds of this region assemble on the first or second Sunday of May for the **festival of Sâmbra Oilor**, when the milk yield of each family's sheep is measured. Whether this process – known as Ruptul Sterpelor – occurs in May (as here) or early July (as it does further south), the participants dress for the occasion in waist-length sheepskin jackets (*cojoc*) covered in embroidery and tassels, or fluffy woollen overcoats called *guba*, and heartily consume fiery Maramureş *horincă* (plum brandy) and sweet whey cheese.

NEGREŞTI-OAŞ, some 35km southwest of Săpânţa, is the largest settlement in the region. Here, the **Oaş Museum** (Mon–Fri 8am–3pm), at Strada Victoriei 17, just north of the centre, has a good display on local ethnography, and a small open-air exhibit of half a dozen blue-painted houses and a wooden church on Strada Livezilor, to the south beyond the bridge. Negreşti's **festival** is on September 1. In addition to local buses, the village can be reached by trains on the Satu Mare–Bixad line: get off at the Negreşti halt, rather than at the station, which is a couple of kilometres west of town.

Accommodation is available in Negreşti at the gloomy *Oşanul* hotel, 400m south of the museum at Str.Victoriei 89 (☎0261/854 162, ⨏851 163; ❷). The other hotels in Oaş are the *Valea-Măriei* (☎0261/850 750; ❷), 5km north of Vama, and the *Călineşti* (☎0261/851 400; ❷) in Călineşti-Oaş, by a reservoir 15km west of Negreşti.

Satu Mare

When the diplomats at Versailles signed the Treaty of Trianon, they drew an arbitrary line across the old Hungarian county of Szabolcs-Szatmár and left its capital Szatmárnémeti in Romanian hands. Renamed **SATU MARE** and shorn of its traditional links with the Great Plain, the town lost its original function as a trading post along the River Someş, shipping salt from Ocna Dejului downstream to Vásárosnamény on the River Tisza, but retained a sizeable Hungarian population. Although there's really very little of interest to detain you here, it's a useful place to break up a journey en route to or from Oradea or Hungary.

The town

The centre of town is Piaţa Libertăţii, a pleasant green space and a minor haven from the grinding traffic. Heading one block north from the square along Strada Ştefan cel Mare, lined with some interesting if tatty turn-of-the-century buildings, you'll come to the Reformat **"Church with Chains"**, a long and relatively low Baroque church built at the turn of the nineteenth century in the middle of Piaţa Pacii. A few paces south of the church is the **fire tower**, a slender 45-metre-high red-brick structure raised in 1904 and resembling a Turkish minaret. Some 500m east of here, along Bulevardul Traian at Piaţa Vasile Lucaciu 21, the **Historical and Ethnographic Museum** (Tues–Sun 9am–5pm) features ethnographic and archaeological exhibitions: the former contains the standard rural implements and folk costumes, as well as some brightly coloured ceramics from Hollóháza and Vama in Hungary, while the beautifully presented archaeological section features fine Daco-Roman remains, clay vessels and grave goods, including some intricate jewellery. Back on Piaţa Libertăţii, at no. 21, the town **Art Gallery** (same hours) features the work of local artist Aurel Popp (1879–1960), who produced sun-bathed post-Impressionist views of Baie Sprie, and much darker images depicting World War I and the death of capitalism. To the south of Piaţa Libertăţii down by the river, is the **Centru Civic**, a typically ghastly 1980s concrete development where you'll find a small department store and the prefecture, a striking modern tower.

Practicalities

The **bus** and **train stations** are 1km east of the centre on Strada Griviţei (a continuation of Bulevardul Traian, which runs east from Piaţa Libertăţii), and are connected to town by trolley buses and maxitaxis. Bus #9 links the **airport**

Petea (Border)

SATU MARE

0   100m

STRADA WOLFENBÜTTEL

Market

PIATA EROILOR
REVOLUTIEI

Old Hospital

STR. IOAN SLAVICI

STR. IOAN SLAVICI

STR. IOAN SLAVICI

STRADA CARDINAL IULIU HOSSU

STR. COSBUC

STRADA GEORGE COSBUC

STR. COSBUC

Church with
Chains

STR. IULIU MANIU

STRADA STEFAN CEL MARE

STRADA MILENIULUI

STRADA MIHAI VITEAZUL

PIATA
PACII

Fire Tower

PIATA
LIBERTĂTII

Roman
Catholic Cathedral

STRADA 1 DECEMBRIE 1918

Department Store

TAROM   CFR

BCR

House of
Culture   Prefectura

Art Gallery

STR. LAZAR

STRADA A.I. CUZA

STRADA CODRULUI

STRADA DECEBAL

STRADA MIRCEA CEL BATRIN

STRADA VASILE LUCACIU

STRADA CORVINULUI

BULEVARD TRAIAN

PIATA

Historical and
Ethnographic Museum

Orthodox
Cathedral

STRADA CORVINULUI

STRADA AVRAM IANCU

Bus Station

Train Station

STRADA GRIVITEI

STRADA BOTIZULUI

Level
crossing

STRADA STRANDULUI

STRADA H. COANDĂ

N

Campsite

River Somes

Cluj & Baia Mare

F & Oradea

ACCOMMODATION	
Aurora	E
Casblanca	B
Dacia	C
Dana	F
Sport	A
Villa Bódi	D

with Piaţa Libertăţii; tickets for flights to Bucharest can be bought at the **TAROM** office (Mon–Fri 8am–6pm; ℡0261/712 795), next door to the **CFR** office (Mon–Thurs 9am–5pm, Fri 9am–4pm; ℡0261/721 202) at Piaţa 25 Octombrie 9. Either of the *Aurora* or *Dacia* hotels (see below) can provide limited **tourist information**.

There's plenty of accommodation in Satu Mare: by far the best of the cluster of **hotels** on Piaţa Libertăţii is the Hungarian-run *Villa Bódi* (℡0261/710 861, ✆www.villabodi.ro; ❸) at no. 5, which has beautifully furnished rooms complete with wood-panelled flooring. The alternatives on this square are the Secession-style *Dacia* (℡0261/714 276, ℻715 774; ❹), a few paces along at no. 8, and the ugly *Aurora* (℡0261/714 946, ✆www.aurora-sm.ro; ❺) at no.11, both of which are friendly and functional enough. Cheaper options are the *Casablanca* (℡0261/768 188, ℻768 204; ❷), opposite the train station, which has perfectly fine rooms (including triples), though the downstairs bar is very noisy; and the *Sport* at Str. Mileniului 25 (℡0261/712 959, ℻711 604; ❷), a reasonable, if predictably unspectacular place. For somewhere more peaceful, there's the brand new hotel *Dana* (℡0261/768 465, ✆www.dana-hotel.ro; ❹), 2km south of town out on the road to Oradea at Drum Carei 128. Satu Mare's **campsite** is fifteen minutes' walk southeast of the centre by the River Someş on Strada Ştrandului.

With a dearth of **places to eat**, your best bet is the oddly named but perfectly reasonable *Complex Transylvania* on the corner of B-dul Train and B-dul Dr Vasile Lucaciu – it's a bit plastic looking but the menu is substantial and the service is good; there's also a bar and **Internet** access here. For coffee and cakes, try *Elit*, an enjoyable patisserie next to the Art Gallery on the south side of Piaţa Libertăţii. For **drinking**, there's a *Bierkeller*, courtesy of the town's Swabian (German) minority, at Piaţa Lucaciu 9 (Mon–Fri 9am–5pm, Sun 9am–2pm).

The Iza valley

Some of the loveliest villages and wooden churches in Maramureş are situated in the **Iza valley**, which extends for roughly 60km from Sighet to the Rodna mountains, which form the frontier with Moldavia. Most of the villages along the Iza and in the side valleys are served by a daily bus service from Sighet, and there are several buses to Vişeu de Sus and Borşa, most following the DJ186 along the Iza valley, some following the DN18 along the Rona and Vişeu valleys.

Bârsana and Rozavlea

The church at **BÂRSANA**, 19km southeast of Sighet on the DJ186, is small and neat and perfectly positioned atop a hillock to the west of the village centre. The florid **paintings**, among the best in Maramureş, date from 1720, soon after the church's construction, and 1806. Hodor Toador and Ion Plohod were responsible for the later set of paintings, with icons on wood by the former artist – the narthex is adorned with saints and processional images, while the naos is painted with Old and New Testament scenes, each in its own decorative medallion. Look in particular for the images of angels covered in eyes. Four kilometres east of the village stands **Bârsana Monastery**, a large monastic complex comprising several wooden buildings, all constructed in the local style, including the wooden church which, unusually, has a pentagonal *pridvor* and two apses, as well as a 56-metre steeple – higher even than the one at Şurdeşti (see p.301). The original sixteenth-century church was confiscated by the Austrians in 1791 and handed over to the Greek–Catholic Cernoc Monastery, before being returned to the Orthodox church in 1993, the year most of the buildings here were built.

Being a border region, Maramureş remained vulnerable to attacks by nomadic tribes until the eighteenth century, and the wooden church at **ROZAVLEA**, 20km further along the valley, was one of many rebuilt after the last Tatar invasion in 1717 and painted by Ion Plohod. Its magnificent double roof was recently restored and is now weathering nicely. There are homestays in Şieu, 2km east; look out for signs advertising rooms.

Botiza and Poienile Izei

BOTIZA, 15km south of Rozavlea, is one of the most comprehensive centres for **agrotourism** in the area, with a few competing networks. The best is the Asociaţia Agroturistică Botiza (AAB), based near the church at no. 742 (T & F0262/334 233), while rooms can also be booked through Agro-Tur (see p.305) in Vadu Izei or the Mara Holiday agency (see p.295) in Baia Mare. There are also comfortable private rooms at no. 743 (T0262/334 207; ❷), whose owner, Victoria Berbecaru, is renowned locally for her craftwork, notably carpet making. The wooden church, beautifully located on a hillside, with a view down the valley to the peaks of Ukraine, was built at the turn of the eighteenth century in Vişeu de Jos and moved here two hundred years later. Beyond a handful of blackened frescoes of the apostles and some floral motifs, there's little to see inside, but if you want to have a look, contact no.743 for the key. Several mineral springs are located along the road to Poienile Izei, notably a sulphurous well at a ruined spa by the bridge about a kilometre from the village centre.

From the northern edge of Botiza, an execrable sidetrack leads 6km into the hills to the village of **POIENILE IZEI** (The Meadows of the Iza), famous for its old wooden church filled with nightmarish **paintings of hell**. The red walls depict dozens of sinners being tortured by demons (*draci*) with goat-like heads and clawed feet, while beneath them, processions of more sinners are driven into the mouth of hell – an enormous bird's head with fiery nostrils. These pictures constitute an illustrated rulebook too terrifying to disobey, whose message is still understood by the villagers. Within the paintings, a huge pair of bellows is used to inflict punishment for farting in church, while a woman guilty of burning the priest's robes while ironing them is herself pressed with a hot iron. Women violating traditional morality face torments in the afterlife: adultresses are courted by loathsome demons and a woman who aborted children is forced to eat them. These hell scenes presumably formed the nasty part of a huge *Day of Judgement* in the narthex, which has half disappeared. Opposite are paintings of gardens and distant cityscapes in a sort of Gothic Book of Hours style, executed around 1793–4. Murals in the nave are badly damaged and soot-blackened, but from the balcony you can recognize *Adam and Eve*, *The Fall*, and episodes from the lives of Christ and John the Baptist. If the church is locked, anyone in the house above the new church will unlock it for you.

Ieud and beyond

Back in the Iza valley, a turn-off about 6km east along the valley road at Gura Ieudului leads upstream to the village of **IEUD**, 3km south. Lanes fenced with lattices run between the houses, clustered within their courtyards, and during summer the air is full of the scent of lady's mantle, a plant mixed with elder and wormwood to make "face water" for the complexion; it was once used for baths to invigorate weak children. Divorce is virtually unknown in this religious and traditional village; about fifty of Ieud's women are "heroine mothers", having borne fourteen children each, and almost half the population of 5000 is of school age. It was Ieud artisans, supervised by the master carpenter Ion Țâplea, who restored Manuc's Inn in Bucharest (see p.75), and master carpenter Gavrila Hotico is currently building new wooden churches all over Maramureş and beyond; the tradition of woodworking has been maintained since the superb Orthodox **Church on the Hill** was first raised here in 1364. Supposedly the oldest church in Maramureş (though largely rebuilt in the eighteenth century), with a double roof and tiny windows, it once housed the Ieud Codex (now in the Romanian Academy in Bucharest), the earliest known document in the Romanian language. It has perhaps the best-known paintings of any Maramureş church, executed by Alexandru Ponehalski in 1782; look out for Abraham, Isaac and Jacob welcoming people in their arms, in the pronaos. Ask opposite at the Textile-Incaltimente shop for the church key, and don't miss the ingenious removable ratchet used to open the bolt in the main door. No less splendid is the Uniate **lower church** (the Val or Şes church), built in 1718 and featuring an immensely high and quite magnificent roofline, though, unusually, no porch; there are few wall paintings left, but the icons on glass and the iconostasis are of great artistic worth. **Homestay** accommodation is available in the village: if you haven't already booked it in Vadu Izei, contact Dumitru Chindriş at no. 233 (☎0262/336 100).

BOGDAN VODĂ, 1km further along the valley road from Gura Ieudului, is one of the valley's main villages, located on the road leading to Moldavia and with long-standing ties to that region. The village was known as Cuhea until the late 1960s, when it was renamed in honour of the local voivode, Bogdan, who left supposedly to hunt bison (see p.385), but ended up founding the

Moldavian state in 1359. The influence of Stephen and other Moldavian rulers has imparted a semi-Byzantine style to the frescoes inside Bogdan Vodă's church, though the building materials used in 1722 were typical of eastern Maramureş – thick fir beams rather than the stone used at Putna and other Moldavian monasteries, or the oak of western Maramureş. Unfortunately, the church is now dwarfed by a huge modern successor erected far too close to it.

From Bogdan Vodă, a rough road leads to Vişeu de Jos in the next valley north (see below), while the main road continues east to **DRAGOMIREŞTI**, whose original village church stands in Bucharest's Village Museum (see p.79); a new Uniate wooden church was completed in 2000 just west of village centre. Half a dozen houses offer homestays here; look out for the signs. The next village you come to is **SĂLIŞTEA DE SUS**, 4km east, which boasts two old wooden churches, one built in 1680 and the other in 1722 – the latter painted by Radu Munteanu in 1775. The road passes the *Iza* cabana at the Iza rail halt and ends at **SĂCEL**, known for its unglazed red ceramics, from where the DN17C heads north to Moisei or south to Salva and Bistriţa.

The Vişeu valley and the Rodna mountains

The railway east from Sighet follows the River Tisza (which marks the Ukrainian frontier) for 25 kilometres before heading up the beautiful **Vişeu valley**; the DN18 runs just to the south of the railway, and local buses from Sighet terminate at the tiny spa of **COŞTIUI**, 22km from Sighet, which has a motel and *căsuţe*. Road and rail routes finally converge at **PETROVA** 16km further on. About 7km south of Petrova, at **Leordina**, a rough sideroad runs north following the River Ruscova into an enclave of Huţul or Ruthenian people, the archetypal inhabitants of the Carpathians, who speak a dialect of Ukrainian incorporating many Romanian words. The centre of the area is the village of **POIENILE DE SUB MUNTE**, where there's a Ukrainian-style wooden church dating from 1788. Back in the Vişeu valley, trains continue 10km east from Leordina to **VIŞEU DE JOS**, where most turn south, passing through Săcel and Salva en route to Beclean; passenger trains no longer run up the branch line from Vişeu de Jos to the alpine resort of Borşa, but there's a good bus connection as far as Vişeu de Sus, and less frequent buses on to Borşa.

The next village along from Vişeu de Jos is **VIŞEU DE SUS**, a large settlement with several useful services, and the starting point for the logging train up the steep Vaser Valley (see below). There's a small **tourist office** (Mon–Sat 9am–5pm; ☎0262/352 285) on the corner of Strada 22 Decembrie and Strada Libertăţii, which can organise private rooms here and in the surrounding area. Otherwise, both the *Hotel Brad* (☎0262/352 999; ❸), at the junction of Strada 22 Decembrie and Strada Iuliu Maniu, and the *Hotel Gabriela* (☎0262/354 526; ❸), about 1km east of town on the road to Moisei at Str. Randunelelor 1, are perfectly decent places. Across the river to the north, by Strada Republicii, the market stands on the edge of the **Zipser quarter**, formerly a sizeable community of German foresters, but which now has largely evaporated. A wooden church, newly built by the Uniate congregation, stands on Strada 22 Decembrie, the main road, next door to the post office.

Moving on towards Borşa, **buses** depart from the dusty yard about 300m south of the tourist office at the bottom of Strada Libertăţii. Plans are afoot for a dedicated steam engine to transport visitors up into the mountains, but in the meantime it's possible to catch the **logging train** (Mon–Sat 6am or 7am; €5 return), which chugs up the picturesque **Vaser valley**, leaving from the yard about 1.5km north of the centre on Strada A.I. Cuza. Usually hauled by a small diesel engine, the train carries lumberjacks (*butinarii*) the 41km up to their camps at Coman, near the Ukrainian border, and at about 3pm begins the journey back down again. Note, though, that these departure times can be a little erratic, so make sure you get there in plenty of time; it's also worth checking on the running of the train with the tourist office in Vişeu de Sus (see opposite). Along the route, you'll see bears and deer drinking from the river, unperturbed by the trains and loggers, while in the mountain forests live stags, elusive lynxes, and wolves. The River Vaser, rich in trout and umber, descends rapidly through the fifty-kilometre-long valley, and its whirling waters have begun to attract **kayaking** enthusiasts to logging settlements like **MĂCIRLĂU**, the start of a very rugged trail over the Jupania ridge of the Maramureş mountains to the mining centre of Baia Borşa, just to the north of Borşa.

Back in the main Vişeu valley, twelve kilometres beyond Vişeu de Sus, the straggling village of **MOISEI** lies beneath the foothills of the Rodna massif, whose peaks are often still snowy while fruit is ripening in the village's orchards. Though today it seems tranquil, within living memory Moisei suffered a tragedy that's become a symbol of atrocity and martyred innocence throughout Romania: in October 1944, retreating Hungarian troops machine-gunned 29 villagers and set Moisei ablaze – a massacre commemorated by a circle of twelve stone figures by sculptor Vida Geza, with faces modelled on two of the victims and on the masks that are worn during festivals in Maramureş. The memorial is 5km east of the centre, opposite a small museum at km141. Today, Moisei's peaceful existence is exemplified by its womenfolk – spinning wool as they walk down the lane, or working in the fields with their babies nearby, hung in cradles from trees. A couple of kilometres along a side valley south of the village stands a **monastery**, scene of a major pilgrimage on August 15, the Feast of the Assumption. **Accommodation** in Moisei is limited to the pleasant *Motel Lido* (☎0262/347 622; ❷), just east of the village centre on the road to Borşa.

Most of the valley's amenities, including several **hotels**, lie in **BORŞA**, a grubby little town 5km east of Moisei: at the entrance to the village is the clean and tidy *Pension Rominvest* (☎0745/275 910; ❷), while the more centrally located *Pension Rodna* (☎0262/344 122; ❶), down an alley opposite Str. Libertăţii 197, has ordinary but good-value rooms. Otherwise, there's the rustic *Perla Maramureşului*, opposite the hospital at Str. Victoriei 37 (☎0262/342 539; ❷), and the bright new hotel *Mihali*, some 300m beyond the *Perla* at Str. Victoriei 65 (☎0742/797 599; ❸). Naturally, there's also a wooden church here, rebuilt in 1718 and hidden away north of Strada Libertăţii, west of the centre.

It's roughly 10km (14 buses a day) from Borşa to the small **Borşa Complex ski resort** (beginners and intermediates only), where there's also a plentiful supply of accommodation, most of which is open year-round: the best of the **hotels** here are the *Focus* (☎0262/344 038; ❸), just up to the left of the chair-lift, and the slightly less attractive *Cerbul* (☎0262/344 199; ❸). There are also a couple of friendly little cabanas in the resort, both with two- to five-bed rooms: the *Casa Ursu* (☎0262/343 270; ❶), 100m down from the *Cerbul*, and the *Casa Lucian*, at Str. Cascada 6 (about a kilometre up the track to the water-fall; ☎0262/343 663; ❶). A new wooden church has been built in the resort in traditional style, except for its massive stone plinth. From Borşa Complex, a hairpin road heads up to the Prislop Pass – 2km away as the crow flies, but closer to 10km by road on this tightly twisting route. **Buses** to and from Borşa usually set off and terminate either at Baia Borşa, 6km north, or at the Borşa Complex ski resort; there are four buses a day from Baia Mare via the Iza valley, and one each from Bistriţa and Vatra Dornei.

Hiking in the Rodna mountains

The Rodnas are one of Romania's best **hiking** areas, largely because you're sure to have them virtually to yourself. The easiest way into the mountains is either by the chairlift from the Borşa Complex (you may have to wait until a dozen or so people have gathered) or from the 1416m **Prislop Pass**; from the pass you can head either north into the Maramureş mountains, wild and largely unvisited, although scarred by mining and forestry, or south into the Rodnas. Following red triangles, then blue stripes, it should take you two hours at most to reach the main crest at the Gârgălău saddle, from where you can follow red stripes east to the Rotunda Pass and ultimately to Vatra Dornei (see p.287), or west into the highest part of the massif. The route west will get you to La Cruce in four and a half hours, from where you can turn right to follow blue stripes up to the weather station on the summit of **Mount Pietrosul** (2303m), ninety minutes away. There are great views in all directions, particularly deep into Ukraine to the north. Borşa is 1600m below, and it takes another two and a half hours to get back there.

Apart from camping, the only place to sleep in the mountains is the *Puzdrele* **cabana** – two to three hours' trek from the hamlet of Poiana Borşa, following the route marked by blue triangles, which continues to the main ridge in another couple of hours. With a map, you can hike on south and down towards the Someş Mare valley and Năsăud (see p.232) in two days, camping wild en route.

Routes on to Moldavia and Transylvania

Just before the Prislop Pass, 12km east of Borşa and linking Maramureş with **Moldavia**, you'll see a monument marking the site where the last Tatar raid was finally driven off in 1717. At the pass, close to the Hanul Prislop bar, the **Horă at Prislop festival** takes place every year on the nearest Sunday to August 1, attracting thousands of participants and spectators. On the far side of the pass, the road runs down the lovely Bistriţa Aurie Valley to Câmpulung Moldovenesc (see p.285), from where you can reach Suceava and several of the Painted Monasteries by rail. A daily bus runs from Vişeu to Vatra Dornei; you can change either there or at Iacobeni for trains to Câmpulung Moldovenesc. Travelling to **Transylvania**, four trains a day link Vişeu de Jos with Salva, 61km to the south and a junction on the busier line from Cluj to Vatra Dornei and Suceava; there's also a daily bus from Borşa to Bistriţa.

Travel details

Trains

Baia Mare to: Beclean (1–2 daily; 3hr); Braşov (3–4 daily; 8hr–9hr 30min); Bucharest (2 daily; 10hr–12hr); Cluj (3 daily; 3hr 10min–6hr 10min); Dej (8 daily; 2hr 15min–4hr); Satu Mare (8–11 daily; 1hr 20min–2hr 20min); Timişoara (1 daily; 9hr).

Satu Mare to: Baia Mare (8–11 daily; 1hr 20min–2hr); Braşov (1–2 daily; 9hr 45min–11hr 10min); Bucharest (1 daily; 11hr); Cluj (2 daily; 4hr 30min); Negreşti-Oaş (4 daily; 1hr 40min–2hr); Oradea (6 daily; 2hr 30min–3hr 50min); Timişoara (1 daily; 7hr 45min).

Sighet to: Beclean (3–4 daily; 5hr 15min–6hr); Braşov (1 daily; 12hr 30min); Bucharest (1 daily; 12hr 45min); Cluj (2 daily; 6hr 45min–7hr 25min); Salva (4–5 daily; 4hr 40min–5hr 15min); Timişoara (1 daily; 14hr 45min); Vişeu de Jos (6–7 daily; 2hr–2hr 40min).

Buses

Baia Mare to: Bicaz (4 daily); Borşa (4 daily); Cavnic (4–5 daily); Cluj (4 daily); Negreşti-Oaş (3 daily); Oradea (1 daily); Satu Mare (3 daily); Sighet (5–7 daily); Târgu Lăpuş (7–8 daily); Vişeu (2–3 daily); Zalău (2 daily).

Borşa to: Baia Mare (4 daily); Bistriţa (1 daily); Sighet (3 daily).

Satu Mare to: Baia Mare (1 daily); Cluj (2 daily); Negreşti-Oaş (1 daily); Oradea (hourly); Sighet (1 daily).

Sighet to: Baia Mare (7 daily); Borşa (2 daily); Botiza (1 daily); Budeşti (4 daily); Ieud (1 daily); Satu Mare (2 daily); Săpânţa (5 daily); Târgu Lapus (1 daily); Vişeu (2 daily).

Târgu Lăpuş to: Baie Mare (7 daily); Băiuţ (2 daily); Cluj (1 daily); Cupşeni (1 daily); Sighet (1 daily).

Viseu to: Baia Mare (2–3 daily); Borşa (4 daily Mon–Fri); Botiza (1 daily); Sighet (3 daily Mon–Fri).

Planes

Baia Mare to: Bucharest (7 weekly).
Satu Mare to: Bucharest (5 weekly).

International buses

Baia Mare to: Budapest, Hungary (Tues & Fri).
Satu Mare to: Budapest (1 daily Mon–Sat).

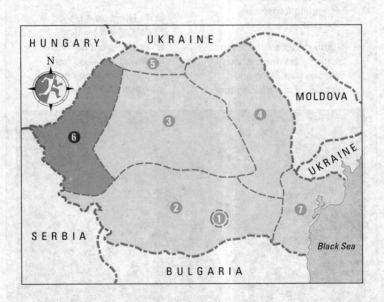

The Banat

CHAPTER 6

Highlights

* **Oradea** Charming town rampant with Secessionist architecture and located close to a couple of small spa resorts. See p.321

* **Chişcău and Meziad Caves** Take a tour through these atmospheric caves, featuring stunning stalactite and stalagmite formations. See p.327

* **Stâna de Vale** Attractive alpine resort, from where you can partake in any number of hikes along the western spur of the Apuseni mountains. See p.328

* **Timişoara** Birthplace of the 1989 revolution, this vibrant, engaging city is characterized by colourful squares, green parks and a lively nightlife scene. See p.335

* **Băile Herculane** Elegant Hapsburg-era buildings and bathing opportunities aplenty in this once fashionable nineteenth-century spa resort. See p.342

△ Orthodox Cathedral, Timişoara

6

The Banat

The **Banat** (Bánság) is the historical term for the western marches of Romania between the Timiş and Mureş rivers, but it has also come to include the Crişana, which encompasses the northwestern most part of the region between the Apuseni massif and the Hungarian border. The Banat has much in common with Hungary's Great Plain and Serbia's Vojvodina region, with its largely featureless scenery, great rivers, historical sites and an intermingling of different ethnic groups. The frontiers were finally settled according to the principle of national self-determination at the Versailles conference of 1918–20, to which each country's delegates brought reams of demographic maps and statistics to support their claims. During the communist era, policies towards ethnic minorities were comparatively fair until the 1960s, when an increasingly hard line began to cause a haemorrhaging of the population in the Banat region, particularly of ethnic Magyars. In both 1988 and 1989, around 80,000 left, as liberalization gained apace in Hungary but things went downhill fast in Romania. The Schwab Germans, who originally settled in this area when the marshes were drained and colonized after the expulsion of the Turks, have now almost all emigrated to Germany. Nevertheless, many villages of Slovaks, Serbs, Magyars and other minority groups remain here.

Its key attractions are the cities of **Oradea**, **Arad** and **Timişoara**, partly on their own merits, but also because each town dominates a route between Transylvania and Hungary or Serbia, and provides access to most other places of interest in the region. Timişoara, in particular, is hugely enjoyable, and the city not to miss should you make a beeline for just one place in the region. Away from the cities, there are rural temptations aplenty, such as the western ranges of the **Apuseni mountains**, with their stalactite caves and wooden churches, and the spas at **Băile Herculane** and **Băile Felix**; moreover, there are some terrific **festivals** to be experienced in the smaller villages.

Transport links with major towns in Transylvania, such as Cluj and Sibiu, as well as major cities across the border in Hungary (Debrecen and Szeged) and Serbia (Belgrade), are excellent.

Oradea and around

Situated on the banks of the River Crişul Repede, the congenial city of **ORADEA** is the capital of Crişana. The city is located close to the site of Biharea – the capital of the Vlach voivode, Menumorut, who resisted

Hungarian claims on the region during the tenth century. Founded around a monastery, the medieval town of Nagyvarad (as the Magyars still call it) prospered during the reign of **Mátyás Corvinus**, who was raised at the Bishop's Palace here, and later acquired a mammoth Vauban-style citadel and the wealth of stately Neoclassical, Baroque and Secession piles which constitute Oradea's most characteristic feature today. Aside from serving as a useful place to break-up a journey en route to or from Hungary, Oradea is just a short bus ride away from the spas at **Băile Felix** and **Băile 1 Mai.**

Arrival and information

From the **train station** on Piaţa Bucureşti, trams #1 and #4 run south along Calea Republicii towards the town centre (those with black numbers run from the station and those with red numbers run to it), past the Crişul department store and southeast along Strada Gen. Magheru. To reach the town centre proper, get off the tram at the department store stop and continue on foot along Strada Republicii. The **bus station**, southeast of the centre at Str. Războieni 81, is immediately adjacent to the Oradea Est train halt, from where it's a twenty-minute walk into town (or take bus #13). The **airport** is on the southern edge of Oradea, on the Arad road; flights are met by buses for the town centre, while buses for the airport leave from the TAROM office (see below) seventy minutes before each flight.

Information can be obtained from the Turist Centre agency, located inside the *Astoria* hotel at Str. Teatrului 1 (℡0259/407 285, ✉agentie@turist center.ro); they also arrange visits to the Chişcău and Meziad caves (see p.327), though there needs to be a minimum of five people for excursions to run. The **CFR office** is at Calea Republicii 2 (Mon–Fri 7am–7pm); and the **TAROM office** at Piaţa Regele Ferdinand 2 (℡0259/231 918; Mon–Fri 8am–6pm). There's **Internet access** at the Internet Club, Str. A. Edy 2 (daily 10am–2am).

Accommodation

Oradea has a decent selection of **hotels**, most of which tend to be either budget or high-end, with little in between; you could also try chasing up a **dorm bed** from the County Youth and Sport Office at Str. Vulcan 11 (℡0259/414 254). Otherwise, there are many possibilities in **Băile Felix** and **Băile 1 Mai**, two resorts located a short distance southeast of town (see p.327). The latter also has a **campsite**.

Astoria Str. Teatrului 1 ℡ & ℱ0259/130 508. A pleasant Secession building with a range of very cheap one- to three-bed rooms, with or without baths or showers. ❶–❷
Hotel Atrium Str. Republicii 38 ℡0259/414 421, ✉hotelatrium@xnet.ro. Exceptional new hotel designed within a large atrium, with windows facing towards an airy, indoor courtyard; the rooms are very stylish while the bathrooms come with fabulous little corner tubs. Home to a quality restaurant too (see p.326). ❼
Continental Aleea Ştrandului 1 ℡0259 /418 655, ⓦwww.continentalhotels.ro. Part of the Romanian *Continental* group, this thoroughly modern and efficient hotel is frequented almost exclusively by businessmen and tour groups; there's a decent restaurant here, too (see p.326). ❻
Elite Parcul I.C. Bratianu 26 ℡0259/476 251, ⓦwww.hotelelite.ro. A more expensive option than the *Continental*, but with a touch more class; facilities include private parking, Internet access, sauna and jacuzzi, not to mention an enchanting little restaurant. Airport transfers and car rental also available. ❾
Gala Str. Bogdan Petriceicu Haşdeu 20 ℡ & ℱ0259/467 177. Cracking-value luxury hotel with comfortable, ultra-stylish rooms; facilities include sauna, massage, private parking and an inviting cellar bar. ❽
Parc Strada Republicii 5 ℡0259/411 699, ℱ418 410. Another pleasant, if slightly shabby,

Secession building on the city's main pedestrianized street. The rooms – singles, doubles and triples with and without shower facilities – are perfectly clean and spacious, though. ④–⑤

Vulturul Negru Str. Independenţei 1 ☎0259/135 417. Housed in an extraordinary building, straight out of the pages of a cold-war thriller, the *Black Eagle* is possibly the country's grottiest hotel – yet it's traditionally the first stop in Romania for backpackers. Single, twin and triple rooms, some with shower. ①–②

The City

Oradea's sights are concentrated in two main areas to the north and south of town. In the large leafy park just west of the train station on Strada Şirul Canonicilor stands the **Roman Catholic Cathedral**, built by countless serfs

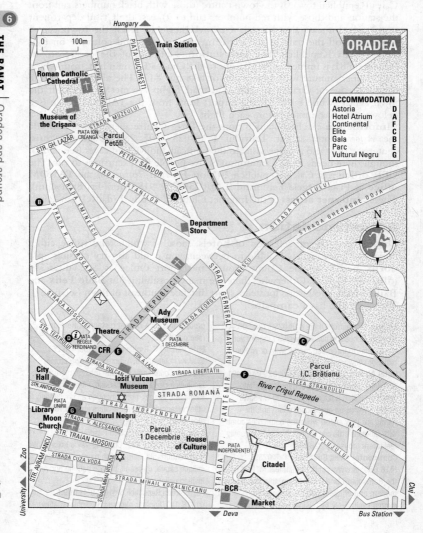

between 1752 and 1780, and reputedly the largest Baroque building in Romania. Unattractive from the outside, its interior is decorated with gold leaf and marble and accommodates a huge organ – see posters for details of one of the regular concerts held here. The serfs' labour was also doubtless exploited to construct the vast U-shaped **Bishop's Palace** adjacent to the cathedral; built by Franz Anton Hillebrandt in 1762–77, the vast three-floored building was modelled on Lucas von Hildebrandt's Belvedere Palace in Vienna. It's now home to the **Museum of the Crişana** (Tues, Thurs & Sat 10am–3pm; Wed, Fri & Sun 10am–6pm), which contains fairly standard history, natural history and ethnographic displays, as well as a good selection of nineteenth- and twentieth-century art.

Heading south towards the river, Calea Republicii becomes a pedestrianized promenade, lined with shops, cafés, fast-food joints and many ostentatious Secession buildings in various states of decay. It eventually opens onto **Piaţa Regele Ferdinand**, dominated by the State Theatre, opened in 1900, a typically pompous design by the Viennese duo, Helmer and Fellner, but now in dire need of a spruce up.

Just to the east of Strada Republicii are two small memorial houses: the lovely, custard-coloured Muller building (Wed, Fri & Sat 10am–2pm & 4–6pm; Tues, Thurs & Sun 10am–3pm) in the centre of the tiny Traian Park commemorates the celebrated Magyar poet **Endre Ady** who lived in Oradea for four years and, unusually for his era, opposed Hungarian chauvinism towards the Romanians; formerly a society café where Ady and his pals would gather for evenings of drinks and bonhomie, it now keeps a handful of personal effects and Ady-era furnishings, including a neatly arranged editorial suite complete with beautiful oak bureau – to the rear is a cool, shaded terrace café and basement bar (see p.326). The other memorial house, at Str. Vulcan 16, remembers **Iosif Vulcan**, who lived here between 1880 and 1906 and edited the literary magazine *Familia*, in which Mihai Eminescu (see p.262) made his debut in 1866.

Piaţa Unirii and around

Crossing the Crişul Repede from Piaţa Regele Ferdinand brings you to **Piaţa Unirii**, a vast open space which, aside from the nondescript Catholic church half-blocking the square's north side, is replete with fanciful Secessionist buildings. The former **City Hall** in the northwestern corner is a monumental restatement of well-worn classical themes to which the architects added a fun touch: chimes that play the March of Avram Iancu every hour, though it actually sounds more like some dodgy national anthem. Given that the Austro-Hungarians were still in control when the building was raised in 1902–03, it seems odd that they allowed this commemoration of Iancu, a Romanian revolutionary whose agitation inspired the protest on the "Field of Liberty" at Blaj in 1848 (see p.183), and who then took to the hills with a guerrilla band, harassing Magyar troops and landlords and urging the serfs to revolt. Standing just south of City Hall is the **City Library** (1905), a more spectacular piece of architecture spotted with all manner of protrusions and jutting towers.

Facing these across Piaţa Unirii is the splendidly named **Vulturul Negru** (Black Eagle), an ornate Secession-style edifice dating from 1908. Running through it is an arcade, devoid of life but retaining its beautiful stained-glass roof connecting three neighbouring streets. Part of the complex is occupied by a hotel of the same name (see p.324) that could have sprung from the pages of a Graham Greene thriller – an ill-lit labyrinth of rooms and corridors inhabited by brooding staff and a furtive clientele. To the south of the hotel,

Oradea's main Orthodox church, built in 1792, marks the stylistic transition from Baroque to Neoclassical; it is better known as the **Moon Church** after the large sphere mounted beneath its clock, which rotates to indicate the lunar phases over a period of 28 days. There are also no fewer than three imposing **synagogues** nearby, testament to Oradea's role as a major Jewish settlement prior to World War II: on Strada Independenţei near the Vulturul Negru; just east of Piaţa Unirii, at Str. Mihai Viteazul 2; and just west on Piaţa Rahovei. In December 1927, Codreanu's League of the Archangel Michael, soon to become the Iron Guard (see box on p.257), held a congress here – they wrecked four synagogues before leaving.

To the east of Piaţa Unirii rises the imposing bulk of Oradea's **citadel**, a Renaissance stronghold enlarged during the eighteenth century by Italian disciples of the Swiss military architect Vauban. Pentagonal in shape, with bastions guarding each corner, the citadel used to be additionally protected by a moat filled with warm water from the River Peţea, which runs around the southern edge of the town. Although the external walls seem very dilapidated, the citadel now houses the university's art faculty and an assortment of companies.

Heading south from the Piaţa, Strada Avram Iancu becomes Calea Armatei Române, with a Military Museum (Wed–Sun 10am–4pm) on the left at no. 24 – containing a dusty collection of costumes, weaponry and medals through the ages – and the university on the right. Opposite the museum is a wooden church, built in Letca in 1760 and moved here in 1991 to serve as the theological faculty's chapel; with its new porch and radiators, and freshly-smelling pine pews, it no longer has the authentic atmosphere of a village church, but it is usually open and you can climb up into the tower. Returning north, Strada Matei Basarab leads to the zoo (daily: summer 10am–7pm; rest of year 8am–4pm), as depressing an advertisement for a zoo as you could possibly imagine.

Eating, drinking and entertainment

There's little choice in town when it comes to **eating**, though Oradea does possess one of Romania's few vegetarian restaurants, the delightful Cris, secreted away at Str. G Enescu 30 (closed Sat). Otherwise, the Piccola (opposite the Continental hotel) is a smoky little cellar restaurant serving more straightforward Romanian fare, or there's the slightly more pleasant Mignon, just off Strada Republicii at Str. R. Ciorogariu 1. Beyond here, you could try the smart, and not too expensive, restaurants in the Atrium, Continental, and Elite hotels, all of which have accomplished international menus, though the Atrium and Elite are a touch more characterful. The Unic **supermarket** on Str. Eminescu (Mon–Fri 7am–7pm, Sat 8am–2pm) is a good place to stock up before moving on.

The town has a smattering of fairly lively **drinking** venues; the most popular spots are The Bridge, a large, atmospheric riverside pub at the southern end of the bridge linking Strada Libertăţii and Strada Independenţiei, the Lion café, next to the Vulturul Negru hotel on Strada Independenţei, and the cool Chanson café in the basement of the Endre Ady memorial house (see p.325); it also has live music on selected weekdays. Kelly's, at the corner of Strada Republicii and Strada Moscovei, is a poor imitation of an Irish pub, but it has a pleasant enough terrace and also serves a limited bar menu. Otherwise, a wander up and down Strada Republicii will yield a café every fifty yards or so. The town's **Philharmonic Orchestra**, housed at Piaţa 1 Decembrie 10 (tickets from Str. Republicii 6), is well regarded, while children might enjoy performances at the **Puppet Theatre**, Str. Alecsandri 9, part of the Vulturul Negru arcade on Piaţa Unirii.

Băile Felix and Băile 1 Mai

Located within easy reach of Oradea are the **spa towns** of Băile Felix and
Băile 1 Mai. Neither is especially attractive, but they're enjoyable places to
spend an afternoon relaxing; treatments (available at the town's hotels) include
healing mud baths, either in sapropelic fossil gunge or the local peat bog, and
dips in pools fed by the warm and slightly radioactive River Pețea, in which
the **thermal lotus**, otherwise found only in the Nile Delta, has survived since
the Tertiary Period.

Just 8km southeast of Oradea along the DN76, is **BĂILE FELIX**, a small,
compact town whose atmospheric residential core has been almost totally
subsumed by an ugly jumble of concrete high-rise hotels. Its central attractions
are a large **thermal pool** (8am–6pm) surrounded by mock-rustic buildings,
and a park containing a **wooden church**. Most of the resort's dozen or so
hotels are bland and not particularly good value, though there are one or two
bargains to be had: the best of the upper end places is the *Termal* (☎0259/318
214, ⓕ318 478; ➐), which has pool, sauna and solarium, and of the mid-range
places, the *Bungalow Monaco* complex (☎0722/239 105; ➌), which has
spacious, a/c rooms with TV and fridge. Reasonable-value two-stars include
the *Lotus* (☎0259/318 361, ⓕ318 399; ➍) and *Nufărul* (☎0259/318 142,
ⓕ319 172; ➍), while the cheapest of the lot is the very basic *Felix* (☎0259/318
421, ⓕ318 422; ➋). You'll also find many houses in the residential area
advertising private rooms (*cazare* or *camera*). The resort is served by tram #4
from Oradea's train station or bus #12 from the Moon Church to the Nufarul
terminal on the outskirts of Oradea, and then bus #l4; alternatively, six trains a
day head for Felix.

The much smaller and less developed spa of **BĂILE 1 MAI** (Ântâi Mai) is
reached by bus #15 from Nufarul, turning off the DN76 just before Băile
Felix. There's some great-value accommodation here, mostly in the form of
some excellent **pensions**; two of the best are *Catalin* at no. 15a (☎0259/319
848; ➌), and, a few paces along at no. 87, *Chrisland* (☎0259/319 048; ➌).
Opposite here, there's a small **campsite** with two-bed huts (May to
mid-Oct; ➊).

The western Apuseni mountains

The **Apuseni mountains** lie predominantly in Transylvania (see p.220), but a
few attractions along its **western approaches** are within easy reach of
Oradea. Most are close to the DN76, but trains to Beiuş and Vaşcău now take
a very roundabout route, following the main Arad line through **SALONTA**,
birthplace of the Hungarian poet Arany Janos (1817–82), who is remembered
in a museum (Tues–Sun 10am–4pm) in the seventeenth-century tower on the
main square.

Beiuş and the caves

The small town of **BEIUŞ**, 55km southeast of Oradea, is the main jumping-
off point for the impressive stalactite **caves of Meziad and Chişcău**,
excursions (€20) to which are organized by the Turist Centre agency in
Oradea (see p.323). Otherwise, **buses** run twice daily (Mon–Sat) from the
station on the southern edge of town to the village of **MEZIAD**, 10km
northeast of Beiuş. The famous Meziad cave, with its huge entrance arch, is a
further 3km beyond the village. The cave was first explored in 1859, and in the
1960s a road was built to it, enabling some 25,000 visitors a year to come here
until its popularity was usurped by the opening of the even more spectacular

cave at Chişcău (see below) in 1980. Guides shepherd parties around the caves, commenting on the stalactites and other features of this warren, whose total length is almost 5km; hour-long tours (daily 9am–6pm) start as soon as there are enough people.

There are also bus services (twice daily Mon–Sat) between Beiuş and **CHIŞCĂU**, some 25km to the southwest, where in 1975 local quarry workers accidentally discovered a cave containing dozens of Neolithic bear skeletons – hence, it's name **"Bears' Cave"** (Peştera Urşilor). Unlike other caves in Romania, this one is atmospherically lit, making the one-hour guided tour (Tues–Sun 9am–6pm; €1.50) an experience not to be missed. The rock formations of the 488-metre-long upper gallery – shaped like castles, wraiths and beasts – are accompanied by the sound of water crashing into subterranean pools.

In summer, buses run the 38km from Beiuş to **STÂNA DE VALE**, a modest alpine resort, where an excellent two-star **hotel**, the *Iadolina* (☎0259/322 583; ⑨), **cabins** and a **campsite** serve the hiking fraternity in summer and skiers in winter. There's a long ski season here, with the resort's three **pistes** usually open from November to April, and lessons available for beginners. From the resort, it's about five hours' walk to the *Padiş* cabana (see opposite), taking a path marked with red stripes that runs via the Poieni peak, the Cumpănăţelu saddle and the Vărăşoaia clearing. Experienced hikers might prefer the more challenging trail to Meziad (6–8hr, marked by blue triangles; not recommended in winter or bad weather); with many twists and turns around karstic features, this follows the ridge above the Iad valley, surmounting the Piatra Tisei peak before descending to the *Meziad* cabana (❶) below.

East into the mountains

Buses run from Beiuş to **PIETROASA**, a picturesque village on the upper reaches of the River Crişul Pietros, where water-powered sawmills remain operational and the older residents still wear traditional Bihor costume. Each year, on a Sunday in August, the villagers troop 8km north up the Aleu valley for the **festival** of Bulciugul de Valea Aleu. The forest road, which leads up to the Padiş plateau near the Citadels of Ponor (see p.226), can be covered on foot

Dr Petru Groza

A delegate at the Assembly of Alba Iulia in 1918, **Dr Petru Groza** (1884–1958) was an important politician before and after World War II. With the Communist Party banned since 1924, it was he who, in 1933, founded the agrarian party known as the Ploughmen's Front, which was actually a cover for the communists; as a prosperous lawyer and landowner, Groza was well camouflaged. He was imposed as prime minister of the coalition government in 1945 – after communist agents-provocateurs had gunned down communist demonstrators to discredit the democratic parties then leading the government – and organized elections in 1946 to establish the communists in power. The people voted overwhelmingly against them but to no avail: the result was falsified, and in mid-1947 the remaining leaders of the democratic parties were arrested.

Groza tried to moderate the nationalism of the Communist Party leader Gheorghiu-Dej; however, on December 30, 1947, he visited King Mihai with Gheorghiu-Dej to force the king's abdication. As an internationalist Groza sought reconciliation with Hungary, and his dismissal in 1952, along with Ana Pauker's Hungarian acolyte Vasile Luka, was a harbinger of the regime's crackdown on Romania's Magyar minority.

or by car – there are no bus services beyond Pietroasa – and the hiking trail to the *Padiş* cabana, marked with blue crosses, follows the road for the most part, with a path diverging south after about 5km (marked by yellow triangles) to the Focul Viu cave, near Ponor. If you do plan to do any extensive hiking in the mountains, arm yourself with the 1:200,000 *Munţii Apuşeni* **map**.

About 3km south of the turning to Pietroasa is **RIENI**, worth a look for its **wooden church**, just west of the village, by the train halt. Built in 1753, the church is now slightly run down, with lots of woodpecker damage, but is interesting for its doorway and its spire, typical of this area. However, the best part of the journey to Scarişoara comes once you leave the DN76 and the rail line beyond the grimy industrial town of **Ştei** – known as Dr Petru Groza under communism – and head eastwards along the sinuous DN75, where the scenery becomes more dramatic. The village of **BĂIŢA**, 10km east along the DN75, has several caves nearby and holds a lively **fair** on the last Sunday in September. On the far side of the Vârtop Pass (1160m) lie **Arieşeni** and **Gârda de Sus**, southern entry points to Padiş (see p.226).

The branch line from Oradea terminates at **Vaşcău**, but the DN76 continues through the mountains for 32km until it joins the Arad–Brad road and rail line at the village of **Vârfurile**. En route, just south of Criştioru de Jos, a rough track leaves the main road and leads 30km east into Transylvania to the village of **Avram Iancu** below **Mount Găina**, where the famous Girl Fair occurs every year (see p.225). There are several more festivals in the villages around Vârfurile, but these are easier to approach from Arad (see below).

Arad and around

One of the oldest towns in the Banat, **ARAD** is an appealing city, chock-full of impressive Habsburg-era buildings, but dominated above all by its eighteenth-century citadel. Although not as vibrant, and with fewer sights than either Oradea or Timişoara, its position on the main road and rail routes between these two cities, as well as its status as a major rail junction for international connections, makes it a convenient place to stop off for an afternoon's discovery; moreover, it's a good base from which to strike out towards many of the nearby **villages** in the foothills of the Apuseni mountains.

Arrival and information

The **train and bus stations** lie 500m apart in the north of the city on Piaţa Gării and Calea Aurel Vlaicu respectively; take tram #1, #2 or #3 for the city centre. All trains from Timişoara halt in the southern suburb of Arad Nou, from where trams #3 and #5 head into the centre. Arad's tiny **airport** (☎0257/254 440) is about 3km west of town, though you'll have to rely on taxis to get there as there's no public transport – check with the tourist office (see below) for taxi companies.

The town's **tourist office** – a rarity in Romania – located opposite the *Continental* hotel at B-dul Revoluţiei 84–86 (April–Sept Mon–Fri 9am–7pm, Sat 9am–2pm; Oct–March Mon–Fri 9am–3pm; ☎0257/270 277). Another good source of **information** is the Sirius travel agency at B-dul Revoluţiei 55 (Mon–Fri 8am–8pm, Sat 9.30am–1.30pm; ☎0257/255 545, ⓦwww .siriustravel.ro), a friendly little office that can also arrange **homestays** in the region. Both the **TAROM** (Mon–Fri 7am–7pm, Sat 9am–2pm; ☎0257/211 777) and **CFR** offices (Mon–Fri 8am–8pm) are at the southern end of

Bulevardul Revoluției at Str. Unirii 1. The main **post office** is at B-dul Revoluției 46–48 (Mon–Fri 7am–8pm, Sat 8am–1pm) and there's **Internet** access at a smoky little dive just off Piaţa Avram Iancu on Strada Tribunul Dobra.

Accommodation

There's plenty of accommodation in town, with a good stock of **hotels** and **pensions** both in the centre and the suburbs. There are also two reasonable **motels** within reach of the city: the *Hanul de la Răscruce* (☎0257/237 963; ➋), 7km west of town along the Nădlac road, and the *Vinga* (☎0257/460 630; ➋), located in the village of the same name some 20km south of Arad on the road to Timişoara. If you're looking for something a bit more rural, call in at the Sirius agency (see p.329), who can help arrange **homestay accommodation** outside Arad.

Ardealul B-dul Revoluţiei 98 ☎0257/280 840, ⓕ281 845. Arad's most characterful hotel is a former coaching inn where Brahms, Liszt, Johann Strauss and Casals all once performed. The grand, spiralling staircase rather belies the faded, soul-less rooms (triples and quads available, too), but it's cheap and there's a hearty breakfast included. ➋–➍

Best Western Central Str. Horia 8 ☎0257 /256 636, ⓔcentral@inext.ro. This modern, central hotel has a range of well-furnished but dull rooms; the welcoming staff, however, makes this one of the better places to stay. ➎–➐

Continental B-dul Revoluţiei 79–81 ☎0257/281 700, ⓦwww.continentalhotels.ro. The town's most expensive hotel is much like all the others in the *Continental* chain, a slick but rather characterless place predominantly aimed at foreign business-men. ➐

Pension Olymp Str. Vrancei 36 ☎0257/279 443. A sweet little pension out in the eastern suburbs with fifteen clean and inviting rooms (including three-bed rooms), all with TV and bath; laundry facilities, too. Bus #5 or #7. ➎

Parc B-dul Gen. Dragalina 25 ☎0257/280 820, ⓔparc@inext.ro. Good, central location on the Mureş River bank, but a fairly ordinary place with tired-looking rooms. ➏

Hotel President Calea Timisorii 164 ☎0257 /278 804, ⓦwww.hotel-president.ro. This classy place, 2km south of town, across the river and out on the road to Timişoara, has neat, colourful and airy rooms; there's a decent restaurant here, too. Bus #3 or #5. ➐

Pension Roberto Str. C. Brâncoveanu 5 ☎0257/289 014, ⓦwww.hotelroberto.ro. Reasonable place in a dull but safe area 1km west of the bus station, with large rooms with and with-out shower. Take any bus heading north from the train station and alight at the second stop; it's just off Str.Cocorilor. ➋–➌

Pension XeMar Calea Timisorii 13 ☎0257/287 485, ⓔxemarpens@yahoo.com. Simple but homely little pension south of town near the *President*. ➌

The town

Spearing southwards from the train station is **Bulevardul Revoluţiei**, a long, tree-lined avenue, bisected by a continual stream of trams which rattle up and down its central strip. Of the many impressive buildings lining the boulevard, the standout is the brilliant white **City Hall** (1876) at no. 75, in front of which is a commemorative plaque listing the names of all those who died during the 1989 revolution; opposite, in the middle of the road, is a simple monument to the same martyrs. Closing off the streets' southern end is the **State Theatre**, dating from 1874, while close by is the massive turn-of-the-century **Roman Catholic church**, with an impressive domed entrance hall.

Immediately behind the theatre is **Piaţa Avram Iancu**, a large green square fringed by numerous two- and three-storey Secessionist buildings, many adorned with interesting stucco work and motifs. East of the square, at Str. Gh. Lazăr 2, is the **Old Theatre**, built in 1817 and now in need of extensive renovation – it was here that Eminescu and many famous actors worked –

Map labels:

▲ A & Nădlac   ▲ Curtici   ▲ Oradea

ARAD

ACCOMMODATION

Ardealul	F
Best Western Central	C
Continental	D
Pension Olymp	B
Parc	E
Hotel President	G
Roberto	A
Pension XeMar	H

Bus Station
CALEA AUREL VLAICU
Train Station
BCR
STR. PENES CORCANUL
STRADA PETRU
BAREŞ
STRADA LACULUI
PIATA CAIUS IACOB
PIATA REVOLUTIEI
CALEA IULIU MANIU
STRADA ANTONESCU
STRADA TUDOR VLADIMIRESCU
STRADA GENERAL MILEA
Department Store
Policlinic
STRADA GEORGE COSBUC
PIATA MIHAI VITEAZU
STR CRISAN
Market
River Mureş
Airport
STR.GHEORGHE DIMA
Art Gallery
C
STRADA HORIA
City Hall
PIATA GEORGE ENESCU
Pontoon Bridge (Pedestrian)
N
BULEVARD REVOLUTIEI
B-DUL DECEBAL
D
i
Roman Catholic Church
STRADA LUCIAN BLAGA
STR. 1 DECEMBRIE 1918
Palace of Culture
CFR
STRADA MIHAI EMINESCU
F
TAROM
E
STR. GENERAL DRAGALINA
Citadel
State Theatre
STRADA V. GOLDIŞ
PIATA AVRAM IANCU
Old Theatre
STRADA N. BĂLCESCU
Market
Orthodox Cathedral
PIATA PLEVNEI
PIATA VECHE
River Mureş
Serbian Orthodox Church
0   200m
Lipova & Deva ►
B. Lipova & Deva ►

▼ G, H & Timişoara

while, to the west, is the main **market** and the Baroque Romanian Orthodox cathedral (1865). The jumble of dusty streets south of the square once comprised Old Arad, and was also home to a large Serb minority, as evinced by the **Serbian Orthodox church** on Piaţa Sărbească.

Commanding a loop of the River Mureş, Arad's huge **citadel** faces the town on the west bank. A six-pointed star with ramparts and bastions angled to provide overlapping fields of fire, it was the "state of the art" in fortifications when it was constructed, in the style of Vauban, between 1762 and 1783. The Turks, against whom it was ostensibly raised, had already been pushed out of the Pannonian basin in 1718, but its underground casemates provided the Habsburgs with a ready-made prison following the suppression of the 1848 revolution. It remains a barracks to this day, and can only be admired from a distance. After 1718, the Habsburgs drained the marshy southern Banat, an area known as the Partium, and colonized it with Swabians, Slovaks, Serbs and Romanians, excluding Magyars so as to facilitate the assimilation of this strategic region into their empire. But despite this, Arad's population rose up against Habsburg rule several times in 1848–49; the revolt was finally crushed with the help of Tsarist Russia, and the Habsburgs made an example of the ringleaders by executing thirteen generals, mostly Hungarian, outside the fortress walls.

The executions feature prominently in the **County History Museum** (Tues–Sun 9am–5pm) housed within the eclectic **Palace of Culture** (1913) behind the City Hall on Piaţa George Enescu; there are also decent archeo-logical and ethnographical displays here, though the absence of English captions will leave you none the wiser as to what you're looking at. The palace is also home to an interminably dull **Natural Sciences Museum** (same times) and to Arad's Philharmonic Orchestra. On the opposite side of B-dul Revoluţiei, in the library building at Str. Gheorghe Popa 2, you'll find the **Art Gallery** (Tues–Sun 10am–5.30pm), which features furniture from the seventeenth century on, as well as the odd painting by the likes of Grigorescu and Aman.

Eating and drinking

The best **restaurant** in Arad is the *Mozart House*, a cosy little bistro just off B-dul Revoluţiei at Str. Lucian Blaga 7, whose Romanian and international food is a cut above anything else in town, as are the elegant, candlelit surrounds – you even get piano recitals while you eat. Other options include the *Lake Grove* restaurant, opposite the new church on Piaţa Caius Iacob, which has a large terrace overlooking an artificial lake; and the *International* at B-dul Revoluţiei 24, which houses both a brasserie and a classier restaurant, the latter offering particularly good-value set menus. There are simpler dishes – pizza, spaghetti and pancakes – to be had at *Coccodrillo*, B-dul Revoluţiei 44. Across the road at no. 51, *Libelula* is a busy café/patisserie, where you can also indulge in the town's best ice cream. The liveliest **drinking** spot in town is *Wings*, an energetic cellar pub on the south side of Piaţa Avram Iancu, whilst the Neptun Strand Park, across the bridge by the citadel, is rammed with bars and cafés during the summer months.

The **markets** in Piaţa Catedralei and Piaţa Mihai Viteazu sell bread, cheese and seasonal fruit and veg, while imported foodstuffs can be found at the Mini-Maxi Plus deli (Mon–Fri 7am–10pm, Sat 8am–6pm) at B-dul Revoluţiei 80 and at the supermarket at no. 26.

West of Arad

The area to the west of the Arad–Timişoara route is the quintessence of the Banat, once marshy plains drained after the expulsion of the Turks and settled with a patchwork of diverse ethnic groups, some of whom still remain. One of the largest towns here is **SÂNNICOLAU MARE** (Nagyszentmiklós), where you can visit the birthplace of the Hungarian composer Béla Bartók (1881–1945). The town is just as well known for the Nagyszentmiklós Hoard, the largest known find of ancient gold; 23 ten-kilogramme vessels, believed to be made in the late eighth or ninth century and buried at the time of the Magyar invasion of 896, were found here in 1799 and removed to Vienna, where they still reside in the Imperial collection.

Moving on into Hungary and Germany

Arad, like Oradea, 117km to the north, lies just inside the border from Hungary. The crossing at Nădlac on the E68, some 50km away, is now mainly frequented by trucks; **cars** and buses are encouraged to use a new, quieter route off the DN7 (E68) to Turnu, 17km from Arad, to Battonya in Hungary. Travelling **by train**, you'll cross over from Curtici, 12km to the north of Arad, to Lőkösháza just inside Hungary. All international **bus services** to Budapest and most of those to Germany run from the train station forecourt in Arad. Tickets for Budapest can usually be bought on the bus, but you may need to buy your ticket to Germany in advance from one of the following companies: Atlassib Reisen (B-dul Revoluţiei 35; ☎0257/252 727); Touring (B-dul Revoluţiei 39–41; ☎0257/250 397); Andronic (Calea Victoriei 104; ☎0257/222 105).

Northeast of Arad

From Arad, it's possible to reach a number of villages noted for their **festivals**, either by road, or by branch rail lines. The formerly Schwab village of **SÂNTANA**, 7km east of the Arad–Oradea highway (a 35min journey by train from Arad towards Oradea or Brad, then a 15min walk to the centre), hosts the Sărbătoarea Iorgovanului festival in late May. Although nowadays little more than an excuse for dancing, music and dressing up in traditional costumes, the festival originated as a parish fair, like the one on February 1 at **PÂNCOTA**, 15km east and another thirty minutes by train towards Brad. Twenty kilometres northeast of Pâncota is **INEU**, where there's nothing except an abandoned castle, which once held one of Romania's notorious orphanages, but a further eighteen kilometres to the east lies the village of **Bârsa**, noted for its pottery and its fete, Sărbătoarea Druştelor, held on the first Sunday in April.

Continuing southeast towards Brad, you'll come to **Vârfurile** at the junction with the DN76 from Oradea. Just west, a minor road runs 6km north to the small village of **AVRAM IANCU** (not to be confused with the other village of the same name just over the mountains), where people from thirty mountain villages gather for the mountain **festival** Tăcaşele, on the second Sunday of June. Besides being an occasion for trading and socializing, this large fair provides a chance for musicians to play together, and the festival is an excellent time to hear *cetera* (fiddles), *nai* (pan-pipes) and *buciume* or *tulnic* (alpine horns). The connection between new life and stirring lust probably underlies a good many spring festivals, and it is one that the delightfully named **Kiss Fair** (Târgul Sărutului) at **HĂLMAGIU**, 10km and two stops by train to the south of Vârfurile, acknowledges. Traditionally, the event enabled young men and women to cast around for a spouse while their elders discuss the fecundity of livestock and crops; the festival takes place in March, but the exact date varies from year to year so check with the tourist office in Arad (see p.329) first. Continuing towards Transylvania, trains terminate at **Brad**, but around a dozen buses a day plug the 32km gap to Deva; there are also daily services to Cluj, Oradea and Timişoara.

From Bârsa, another road branches off to the east, through the villages of Sebiş and Dezna, and up to **MONEASA**, a small spa resort in the Codru-Moma mountains. There's a fair amount of **accommodation** here, including the very average *Hotel Moneasa* (☎0257/313 151; ❸–❹), which has a thermal pool (€2) and various treatments; the similarly unspectacular *Hotel Parc* (☎0257/313 231; ❸); and opposite the *Parc*, the colourful *Vila Ana* pension (☎0257/499 737; ❻), which has four sumptuous rooms, a pool, sauna and jacuzzi. Cheaper alternatives are the *Dallas* cabana (☎0257/313 202; ❶), serenely located beneath the wooded slopes to the north of the village, and the many private rooms advertised all around. Just two buses a day make the journey from here to Arad, and there are also local buses to Sebiş train station.

East of Arad

In 1934, the travel writer Patrick Leigh Fermor walked from Arad into Transylvania, staying with Magyar aristocrats whose dusty mansions and diminished bands of retainers spoke eloquently of the decline in their fortunes since the Trianon Treaty. Nowadays, you're more likely to make the journey by road or train, but be warned that rapid services stop at few places of interest. Passing through **SÂMBĂTENI**, 17km east of Arad, you'll see huge Gypsy palaces with colonnaded and pedimented fronts, built with the proceeds of sanction-busting trade with former Yugoslavia. **GHIOROC**, just off the DN7, 22km from Arad but reached by trams as well as local trains from the city, serves as a jumping-off point for the **Zărand Mountains**; there's a chalet 500m away, from which you can make the three-hour hike (marked with blue stripes) to the *Căsoia* cabana (❶).

Radna and Lipova

RADNA, 35km from Arad, is the first major stop on the DN7 towards Transylvania. Here, Leigh Fermor played skittles with a Franciscan monk, until "we were both in a muck-sweat when the bell for vespers put an end to play". The great Abbey of Maria-Radna is now a hospital, but the echoing church is open, and the corridor to its left, lined with sacred hearts and images of bloody crashes in which Mary supposedly helped make things less bloody, opens onto the abbey's courtyard. The Abbey is an old pilgrimage site, where many churches were built, only to be destroyed by the Turks. The Baroque edifice of the current church was begun in 1756, but only consecrated in 1820; behind it, steps lead up to shrines and the Stations of the Cross in the oak woods.

Radna station, served by slow trains from both Arad and Timişoara, is actually nearer to **LIPOVA**, a dusty, but quaint little town on the south bank of the Mureş. Its main sight is the lovely fifteenth-century **Orthodox Church of the Annunciation**, with its classical facade and a rather eccentric spire; these features belie the interior, which dates from 1338 and contains the most important **murals** in the Banat – in a pure Byzantine style, though painted in the early fifteenth century. Fragments of old murals are also visible on the exterior of the north wall. The church served as a mosque from 1552 to 1718, and was then rebuilt in 1732 in the Baroque style. Ask at the parish house, immediately north, for access. The town **museum** (Tues–Sun 9am–5pm), on the main street at Str. Bălcescu 21 and identified by casts of Trajan's Column over the door and two cast-iron lanterns either side, holds a painting apiece by Grigorescu and Aman, as well as bits of sculpture and furniture. Unlikely as it is that you'll need to stay here, the *Faleza* pension at Str. P Maior 13 (☎0257/561 702), is a perfectly respectable place northeast of town on the banks of the Mureş. Four kilometres south of town, and reached by eight buses a day from Radna station, is the spa of **Lipova Băile**; the pool aside (€2), there's little here save for some two-bed huts (☎0257/563 139; ❷) and a campsite, a restaurant and terrace bar. There's also the *Bistro* **campsite**, west of Radna on the DN7, just beyond the service station.

The Mureş defile

Just a couple of kilometres beyond Lipova lies the ruined castle of Şoimoş. Built in the thirteenth century, and beefed up by Iancu de Hunedoara and his son Mátyás Corvinus in the fifteenth century, it guards the entry to the **Mureş defile** between the Zărand and Poiana Ruscă mountains. At the narrowest point of the defile is **SĂVÂRŞIN**, which hosts fairs on January 30 and November 27; the *Săvârşin* hotel (℡0257/557 322; ❷) offers simple rooms. Slow trains make half a dozen more stop, notably at **ZAM**, which marks the frontier with Transylvania, before they reach **ILIA**, scene of fairs on July 1 and March 25. If you want to break the journey, there's a hotel (❶) on the main road to the east of the centre, and in **LESNIC**, 10km east, there are several homestays (contact Dorinel Ilea, no. 174; phone ahead on ℡0254/623 160). From here, the railway and the DN7 continue eastward towards Deva, Cluj and Sibiu, a route described more or less in reverse order in the Transylvania chapter. Alternatively, you can head southwest across the Poiana Ruscă range towards Lugoj (see p.340), on the DN68A or the secondary railway (three fast and five slow trains daily).

Timişoara

An engaging and, in parts, enchanting city, **TIMIŞOARA** has long been the most prosperous and advanced of the cities of the Banat, claiming to be the first place in Romania to have a public water supply, the first in Europe to have electric street lighting, and one of the first in the world to have horse-drawn trams. It still boasts Romania's premier technical university.

From the fourteenth century onwards, Timişoara functioned as the capital of the Banat, playing a crucial role during the 1514 uprising and Hunyadi's campaigns against the Turks, who in 1552 conquered the town, from where they ruled the surrounding area until 1716. The Habsburgs who ejected them proved to be relatively benign masters over the next two centuries, the period when Temeschwar, as they called it, acquired many of its current features. These days, Timişoara is best known as the **birthplace of the 1989 revolution**, and still sees itself as the only true guardian of the revolution's spirit, swiftly hijacked by the neo-communists of Bucharest.

Close to the borders with Serbia and Hungary, and with an airport operating regular scheduled international flights, Timişoara is also a major hub for travel.

Arrival and information

From the city's main **train station**, Timişoara Nord, it's an easy fifteen-minute walk east to the centre along Bulevardul Republicii (or trolley buses #11, #14 and #18). The hectic and grubby **bus station** is across the canal from the train station and one block west, at Str. Reşiţa 54, next to the largest of Timişoara's markets. Timişoara **airport** is 12km east of the city; no public transport serves the airport, but there is an airport taxi (€6) – avoid the rip-off regular taxis. All TAROM flights are met by TAROM buses (free), which drop passengers outside their office at B-dul Revoluţiei 3–5 (see listings on p.340).

The city's new **tourist office** is hidden away in the Bazaar courtyard, opposite the Bega shopping centre at Str. Proclamaţia de la Timişoara 5 (Mon–Sat 10am–8pm, Sun 10am–2pm; ℡0256/437 973); as well as a basic city centre **map**, they should also have copies of the useful English-language listings magazine, *Timişoara What, Where, When*.

Accommodation

There is, unfortunately, almost nothing in the way of budget accommodation in Timişoara, and despite a very healthy stock of hotels scattered around town, most are optimistically aimed at the business traveller. There's a good year-round **campsite** (℡0256/208 925, ℻225 596), with cabins (❷–❹) sleeping two- to four-people, on Aleea Pădurea Verde, 4km east of the city in the Green Forest. Take trolley bus #11, which terminates just beyond the 24-hour PECO filling stations on Calea Dorobanţilor (the DN6), opposite the campsite.

Banatul B-dul Republicii 5 ℡0256/491 903, ℻490 130. Wonderfully convenient for both the train station and the centre, this completely renovated good-value hotel is now a slick and modern place. ❹

Central Str. Lenau 6 ℡0256/490 091, ⓦwww.hotel-central.ro. Simple but clean, modern rooms, a great central location and extremely welcoming staff. ❹

Club Senator Calea Lugojului 7 ℡0256/225 463, ⓦwww.hotelclubsenator.ro). This bright and breezy three-star hotel, 6km east of town on the road towards the airport, has a swimming pool, sauna and smart restaurant. ❺

Continental B-dul Revoluţiei 3 ℡0256/494 144, ⓦwww.hotelcontinental.ro. The former Securitate hotel, now used predominantly by businessmen and tour groups. Not surprisingly, it's overpriced. ❼

Eurohotel Str. Mehadia 5 ℡0256/201 251, ⓦwww.eurohotelsite.com. High-standard hotel with plush, a/c rooms, although its location is somewhat out of sync amongst a jumble of apartment blocks; it's a 15min walk east of the centre across the canal. ❻

Nord B-dul Gen. Dragalina 47 ℡0256/497 504, ℻491 621. Cheerless, but better than average station hotel, and the cheapest place going. ❹

Perla I, II (and **IV**), and **III** Str. Oltul 11 ℡0256/195 202, Str. Turgheniev 9 (℡0256 /195 203), Str. Paltinis 14 (℡0256/197 858, all ⓦwww.hotelperla.dnttm.ro). Four uniformly excellent hotels; modern, chic and supremely comfortable. ❹–❺

Silva B-dul V. Babeş 25 ℡ & ℻0256/201 406. One of the city's best small hotels, just around the corner from *Perla I*; with comfortable, bright, and very spacious rooms. ❺

Solaris Str. Daliei 7 ℡0256/294 619. Very pleasant nine-room hotel near the *Eurohotel*, with big square rooms, huge beds and ultra-modern furniture. No twins. ❺

Timişoara Str. 1 Mai no. 2 ℡0256/198 856, ⓦwww.hoteltimisoara.ro. In a plum location overlooking Piaţa Victoriei, this reasonable hotel offers dowdy two-star rooms and much better three-star rooms, which are well worth paying that little bit extra for. ❻

The City

Timişoara originally grew up around a Magyar fortress in the marshes between the Timiş and Bega rivers, the draining of which created the **Bega Canal**, which now separates the old town, to the north, from the newer quarters. North of the canal, the city centre is a network of carefully planned streets and squares radiating from **Piaţa Libertăţii**, which boasts a substantial Baroque pile on its north side; originally built as the **Town Hall** in 1734 and now used as the university's music faculty, it stands on the site of the Turkish baths. The square was the setting for the particularly gruesome execution of György Dózsa (Gheorghe Doja), leader of the peasant uprising that swept across Hungary and Transylvania in 1514; an iron throne and crown for the "King of the Serfs" were both heated until red-hot, then Dózsa was seated and "crowned" before his body was torn asunder by pincers. Some of his followers were starved, compelled to watch his torture and then force-fed parts of the charred corpse, before themselves being executed, while others were hanged above the gates of Oradea, Alba Iulia and Buda as a deterrent.

To the south of Piaţa Libertăţii, the **Museum of the Banat** (Tues–Sun 10am–5pm) occupies the fourteenth-century castle raised for the Hungarian monarch Charles Robert, extended by Hunyadi in the fifteenth century. Alas,

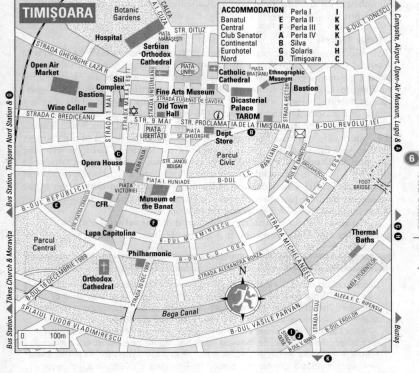

no effort has been spared to make the voluminous display of historical exhibits as dull as could possibly be, and you're best off giving this a miss.

A few paces to the west of the museum is **Piaţa Victoriei**, a wide, pedestrianized boulevard flanked on either side by shops and cafés and sliced down the middle by an attractive strip of greenery. It was here, in December 1989, that the **revolution** in Romania first took hold, as demonstrators came out in force and the tanks rolled in for what turned out to be a series of bloody and tragic battles. There's now little sign of those events, save for the odd memorial or pockmarked building, such as the one above *McDonalds* at the square's northern end. Just across from here is the charmless-looking Opera House, and at the square's southern end, near the Bega Canal, is the monumental **Romanian Orthodox Cathedral**, constructed between 1936 and 1946 after the signing of the Treaty of Trianon. The cathedral, whose architectural style blends neo-Byzantine and Moldavian elements, houses a fine collection of eighteenth-century Banat icons in its basement, but it is best known as the site where many of the protesters killed in the 1989 uprising were gunned down; there are memorials and candles to the victims outside. With its 83-metre-high middle dome (Pantocrator), it's quite a startling sight, especially at night when it's lit up.

Beyond the cathedral, across the canal, is **Tokes Reformed Church**, where Lászlo Tökes ignited the 1989 revolution (see box on p.338). There is now a plaque on the plain apartment building at Str. Timotei Ciprariu 1 (left off Bulevardul 16 Decembrie 1989), where his eviction took place – Tökes's church was on the first floor and its stained-glass windows can just about be seen from the street.

Piaţa Unirii

Two blocks north and east of Piaţa Libertăţii is the vast **Piaţa Unirii**, a splendid traffic-free showpiece of Baroque urban design lined with delightful yellow, green and red buildings. At the heart of the square is the Holy Trinity, or **Plague Column**, a stone-carved column depicting a number of plague-ridden victims, which was raised in 1740 following a particularly virulent attack of the Black Death in 1738–39. On opposing sides of the square are two monumental cathedrals: the **Roman Catholic Cathedral**, which stands along the eastern side, was built between 1736 and 1754 to the design of the younger Fischer von Erlach and is a fine example of the Viennese Baroque style; the **Serbian Orthodox Cathedral** was built, ironically enough, at the same time (1744–48), with its beautiful religious paintings completed by the local artist Constantin Daniel. The **Museum of Fine Arts**, on the southeast corner of the square, normally displays work by minor Italian, German and Flemish masters, but is presently closed for extensive renovation.

To the east of Piaţa Unirii, the huge but dull **Dicasterial Palace** (1754), a complex of 450 rooms built for the Habsburg bureaucracy of the

Lászlo Tökeş and the Revolution of 1989

Despite doubts about the authenticity of the events of **December 1989** in Bucharest (see p.64), Timişoara's popular uprising is still regarded as the catalyst of the revolution. The spark was lit to the southwest of the centre, when crowds gathered to prevent the internal exile of the Reformat pastor **Lászlo Tökeş**.

Pastor Lăszlo Tőkés comes from a distinguished dynasty of Reformed (Calvinist) churchmen. Born in 1952, he followed his father into the priesthood, but was soon in trouble for teaching Hungarian culture and history to his parishioners in Dej; after two years without a job, he was posted to Timişoara in 1986. Here, he became increasingly outspoken in his criticism of the government and the church authorities, while stressing that he spoke not only for Hungarians but also for the equally oppressed Romanians. In particular, he protested against the systematization programme, denouncing it on Hungarian television in July 1989. This led to an increasingly vicious campaign against him by the local Securitate, who spread slanderous rumours about him, smashed his windows and harassed his family and friends, culminating in the murder in September 1989 of one of the church elders.

Lăszlo Papp, Bishop of Oradea, a government placeman, agreed that he should be transferred to the tiny village of Mineu, north of Zalău, but he refused to leave his parish and resisted legal moves to evict him. Being officially deemed unemployed, he lost his ration book, but his parishioners brought him food despite continuing harassment. Eventually, he was removed to Mineu on December 17, and stayed there until the 22nd; the fact that it took so long for a police state to shift him, and that the eviction was so clearly signalled and then delayed for a day or two, is cited as evidence that plotters against Ceauşescu were deliberately trying to incite an uprising. After the removal of Tökes, **riots** erupted on the streets of Timişoara, culminating in Ceauşescu's order for the army to open fire on protesters.

The new National Salvation Front (FSN) tried to co-opt Tőkés onto its council, along with other dissidents, but he soon asserted his independence; appropriately, in March 1990 he took over the job of Bishop Papp, who fled to France. Romanian nationalists have always accused him of being an agent of the Hungarian government and of the CIA, and he continues to be a hardliner, pushing for autonomy for the Magyar-dominated areas.

nineteenth century, is worth a look for its sheer bulk. One block west, on the corner of Strada Eugeniu de Savoya and Strada Augustin Pacha, a plaque marks the house in which Cuza apparently spent his last two nights in Romania on his way to exile (see p.388) – as the Banat was not part of Romania until 1918, he was presumably under the impression that he was already in exile.

In 1868, the municipality purchased the redundant citadel from the Habsburg government, and demolished all but two sections, loosely known as the **Bastions**, to the west and east of Piaţa Unirii. Today, the western section contains a market and wine cellar, both called Timişoara 700, in honour of the city's 700th anniversary in 1969, and to the east, the entrance at Str. Hector 2 admits you to a beer and wine bar; just to the west of here, at Str. Popa Şapcă 4, is the **Ethnographic Museum** (Tues–Sun 10am–5pm), where there are some nicely presented displays of textiles and folk costumes, icons on glass, and beautifully-carved staffs and musical instruments. Disappointingly, though, there's very little mention of the region's ethnic diversity, or of the 40,000 Serbs exiled to the Dobrogea in 1951, which radically altered the Banat's ethnic make-up. The museum also has an **open-air section** about 5km east of town, where old Banat homesteads and workshops have been reassembled in the **Pădurea Verde** (Green Forest) – take trolley bus #11.

Eating, drinking and entertainment

Timişoara has a decent selection of quality **restaurants** scattered around town, and there's no shortage of **drinking** venues either, particularly down by the canal, and, during term-time, around the lively student area – principally Aleea Studenţilor. The best spot for a daytime drink is Piaţa Unirii, where you can take your pick from numerous outdoor cafés; although slightly out of the way, *Café Olli*, next door to *Da Toni's* pizzeria near the student quarter, is worth venturing to for its fabulous **ice cream**. The town's best **bar** is *Club 30*, a groovy jazz club at the southern end of Piaţa Victoriei, which usually has live music on Thursdays. Other places worth a visit are *Café Colt*, at Str. Ungureanu 9, a vibrant, two-floored café-cum-bar open round the clock; and *The Note*, an atmospheric bar at Str. Fagului 22 (closed Mon), which occasionally puts on live music. If you're looking for somewhere to **dance**, then head for *Discoland*, or the *Paladino Club*, located side-by-side on Piaţa I. Huniade, by the Opera House. In summer, make a beeline for the canal-side cafés behind the Orthodox cathedral, or the Rozelor Park, to the east, where regular open-air concerts and events are staged.

The city's main concert venue is the **Opera House** on Piaţa Victoriei, which also houses two theatres that stage plays in German and Hungarian, while the Banat Philharmonic gives occasional concerts at B-dul C.D. Loga 2. If you're around in early May, be sure to check out the Timişoara Muzicală festival.

Restaurants

Da Toni Str. Daliei 14. Genuinely excellent, and extremely popular, pizzeria, located near the student quarter, just behind the Petrom station off B-dul Eroilor.

Dinar Str. Turgheniev 10. Typically lively Serbian restaurant in the south of town, opposite the *Perla II/IV* hotel, serving Serb specialities such as *cevapi* (minced meat rolls) and *sarma* (cabbage leaves

wrapped around rice and meat). Vegetarians need not bother.

Grizzly Str. Ungureanu 7. Sumptuous food and generous portions in comfortable surroundings. Downstairs bar and café make this an ideal place to pop in any time of the day.

Harold's Aleea Studenţilor 17. A touch of class amidst the fast-food joints dominating the student quarter, this neat place offers Chinese, Mexican

and Romanian food and is also one of the best restaurants in town for vegetarians.
Maestro Str. Janos Bolyai 3. Stylish establishment with prodigious international menu. Choose between the cosy indoor atmosphere or the convivial outdoor terrace. Live music most nights.

Mioritic Str. Cluj 26. Characterful litte restaurant decked out with traditional Romanian ornaments and textiles, and serving some of the best (and most inexpensive) Romanian food in town – worth sampling is the *tochitură haiducească* (outlaw's stew). Located ten-minutes' walk south of the canal.

Listings

Airlines TAROM, B-dul Revoluţiei 3–5 (☎0256/490 150; Mon–Fri 7am–7pm, Sat 7am–1pm); Carpatair, Timişoara airport (☎0256/202 701).
Car rental All the following have offices at the airport: Avis (☎0256/203 234); Europcar (☎0256/194 074); Hertz (☎0256/220 552).
Hospital Str. Gheorghe Dima.
International buses Services to Germany are run by: Eurolines Touring inside the *Banatul* hotel (☎ & ℻0256/490 931); Atlassib, at B-dul Republicii 1 (☎ & ℻0256/201 040) and at Gară Est (☎ & ℻0256/226 486); and Priamus, B-dul 16 Decembrie 1989 (☎ & ℻0256/190 202). There are also services running to Istanbul (Oz Murat; ☎0256/497 868) and Athens (Bocheris Express Travel; ☎ & ℻0256/436 283).
Internet access The following are all open 24hr: Computer Club, Str. Aurelianus 19; Internet

Bastion, Str. Hector 2; Internet Café, Str. Medicinei 1; Internet Club, Str. Lucian Blaga 2.
Libraries British Council, Str. Paris 1 (Mon, Tues & Thurs 1pm–7pm; Wed & Fri 9am–3pm), has Internet access and week-old newspapers.
Post office B-dul Revoluţiei 2 (Mon–Fri 7am–8pm, Sat 7am–1pm) and Str. P. Craiului (Mon–Fri 8am–7pm).
Pharmacy Vlad, B-dul 16 Decembrie no. 53 (24hr).
Shopping The Bega Shopping Complex (Mon–Fri 9am–9pm, Sat 9am–7pm) next to the *Continental* hotel has a good supermarket, while Stil, on Str. Mărăşeşti, is another well-stocked supermarket (open 24hr). Librărie Noi, at Str. Hector 2–4 (Mon–Fri 9am–8pm, Sat 10am–6pm, Sun 11am–5pm), has the best stock of English-language books and a particularly good arts section.
Train tickets The CFR office is just off Piaţa Victoriei at Str. Macicsilor 3 (☎0256/220 534; Mon–Fri 8am–8pm).

The Timiş valley

The main rail line and the DN6 follow the River Timiş southeast from Timişoara towards Băile Herculane and Wallachia, passing through the small Habsburg towns of **Lugoj** and **Caransebeş**. From Caransebeş, there is easy access into the mountains, either west into the Semenic massif, or east to Muntele Mic, Ţarcu, Godeanu and, ultimately, to the Retezat range.

Lugoj

LUGOJ, 63km east of Timişoara, is notable as the birthplace of several Romanian musicians, including the operatic tenor Traian Grozăvescu (1895–1927), and the composers Tiberiu Brediceanu (1877–1968) and Ion Vidu (1836–1931). Its non-Romanian sons are less likely to be remembered by plaques, but Béla Ferenc Blasko (1882–1956) immortalized his birthplace's Hungarian name when he became Béla Lugosi, Hollywood's most famous Dracula and its nearest thing yet to a genuinely Transylvanian Count.

From the **train station** on Splaiul Gării, exit left and head up Strada Al. Mocioni – which becomes pedestrianized beyond the Hotel *Timiş* – towards the junction of Strada Bălcescu and the River Timiş. Here, you'll find the dusty old town **museum** (Tues–Sun 9am–5pm), which has displays of weapons, ceramics and local costumes. Continue east across the Iron Bridge to the **Uniate Cathedral** on Piaţa Republicii, which has some fine neo-Byzantine paintings.

Nearby, on Piaţa Victoriei, is the **Orthodox Church of the Assumption**, a hall-church built between 1759 and 1766 by the younger Fischer von Erlach, which is one of the most important Baroque buildings of the Banat. The fifteenth-century tower of the church of St Nicholas stands next door.

There are three **hotels** in Lugoj, two of which are on Strada Al. Mocioni: the *Timiş*, 200m up from the train station at no. 20 (☎0256/355 045, ℻350 671; ❸), is a quiet, pleasant place with large clean rooms; while the good-value *Dacia* at no. 7 (☎0256/352 740, ℻350 671; ❸), a hotel of sorts since 1835, has individually (and tastefully) designed rooms. The third, and best, is the sleek *Tivoli*, across the bridge at Str. A. Popovici 3 (☎0256/359 567, ⓦwww.hoteltivoli.ro; ❹), which has a/c, designer-furnished rooms. Its classy restaurant is also the best **place to eat** in town. In addition to these places, there's the very cheap but perfectly acceptable *Tirol*, 3km out along the road to Făget and Deva (the DN68A) at Str. Salcâmului 15 (☎0256/353 832, ℻354 183; ❷), and reached by bus #7. The **CFR** office (Mon–Fri 8am–4pm) is just down from the *Dacia* hotel.

Caransebeş and the Muntele Mic

CARANSEBEŞ lies beneath the mountains at the confluence of the Timiş and Sebeş rivers, around which gypsies of the Zlatari tribe used to pan for gold. Having served as the Banat's judicial centre during the Middle Ages and commanding communications through the Eastern Gate, Caransebeş inevitably became a Habsburg garrison town – hence, the outcrops of *belle époque* buildings among the prefabricated structures of the socialist era. There's little to occupy you here today, other than the **County Museum of Ethnography and the Border Regiment** (Mon–Sat 10am–4pm), housed in the eighteenth-century barracks on Piaţa Dragolina, and featuring some impressive local artefacts from central and south Banat, but you may well be passing through or need to stay the night if you're heading for the mountains.

The main **train station** is located well north of town, from where maxitaxis will take you into the centre; otherwise, it's a good thirty-minute walk. Some local services also stop 2km further south at the Caransebeş halt, west of the centre. Most trains from Caransebeş run north to Timişoara, or south to Orşova and Turnu Severin on the Danube (see p.119), but there are also branch services west to Reşiţa (see p.343). The **bus terminal** is on Splaiul Sebeşului, south of the River Sebeş; for the town centre, cross the bridge and turn right at the spiky neo-Gothic synagogue.

There are three **places to stay** in Caransebeş, all of which are located on or just off the main road leading from the main train station to the centre of town: the best is the modern hotel *Gea* at Str. Crişan 1a (☎0255/511 637; ❸), while the *Tibiscum*, at Str. Dolmei 1 (☎0255/511 255; ❷), also has an area in which to pitch your tent. To reach the *Tibiscum* take the steps to the west from the south end of the rail bridge. A cheaper, and more convenient, alternative is the *Vila Natalia* (☎0255/517 645; ❷), 300m from the train station as you exit to your right.

Borlova and the Muntele Mic

BORLOVA, 13km from Caransebeş, is noted for its embroideries and peasant weddings, and holds a Measurement of the Milk **festival**, around April 23 every year. Most visitors, however, pass straight through en route to the **Muntele Mic** (Little Mountain) resort. You can hitch a ride to the resort on the staff bus or make the ten-kilometre walk from Borlova, followed by a chairlift ride. Thanks to the heavy snowfalls in the area, you can **ski** here from late autumn until late spring; there are also good **hiking** trails for the summer months. The resort's one hotel is the *Sebeş* (❸), but there's also a selection of less expensive villas and chalets. You can walk north to the Muntele Mic itself in an hour, or south to the weather station (2190m) atop Mount Ţarcu in three hours. Outside the winter months, suitably equipped hikers can take trails from here heading eastwards towards Lake Gura Apei and the Retezat mountains in four hours (following red stripes), or southwards to Godeanu and the Cerna valley in six hours (red dots) – be prepared for an overnight expedition (a tent is essential). From Muntele Mic, there's also a route (following blue stripes) to Poiana Mărului, to the east, from where three buses a day head back to Caransebeş via Oţelu Roşu.

The Cerna valley

Continuing south by road or rail from Caransebeş, you pass through the **Poarta Orientalis** or Eastern Gate of Transylvania before reaching **Băile Herculane** and its spa at the bottom of the **Cerna valley**. The middle and upper reaches of the valley itself are still much as Patrick Leigh Fermor described them when he travelled through the region in the 1930s: "a wilderness of green moss and grey creepers with ivy-clad water-mills rotting along the banks and streams tumbling through the shadows [illuminated by] shafts of lemon-coloured light". Among the butterflies and birds that proliferate here are bright blue rollers, which the Romanians call *dumbrăveancă*, "one who loves oakwoods".

Băile Herculane and around

BĂILE HERCULANE gets its name from the Roman legend that Hercules cured the wounds inflicted by the Hydra by bathing here, and the nine springs, with their varied mineral content and temperature (38–60C), are used to treat a wide range of disorders. During the nineteenth century, royal patronage made Herkulesbad, as it was then known, one of Europe's most fashionable watering holes. Today, Băile Herculane is split between the old spa area, centred around elegant Piaţa Hercules, and the ugly modern satellite spa of **PECINIŞCA**, 2km towards the train station and dominated by half a dozen or so grim high-rise hotels.

Other than wallowing in the renowned **Apollo Baths**, Băile Herculane's chief attraction is its surroundings – statuesque limestone peaks clothed in lush vegetation and riddled with caves. You can bathe in the **Seven Hot Springs** (Şapte Izvoare Calde) about 35 minutes' walk upstream, just beyond the Cerna rapids, while another two hours hiking will bring you to the white **Gisella's Cross**, from where there are magnificent views. From here, an unmarked path leads you in thirty minutes to a forest of black pines, dotted with boulders, and a spectacular 300-metre precipice. Other paths provide access to the vaporous **Steam Cave** on Ciorci hill (1hr 30min), the **Outlaws' Cave** where Stone Age tribes once sheltered (30min), and the **Mount Domogled nature reserve**, which has trees and flowers of Mediterranean origin and more than 1300 varieties of butterfly (4hr).

It's roughly 40km from Băile Herculane to the watershed of the River Cerna, on a forestry road that continues to Câmpuşel and the Jiu valley. A path marked with red stripes runs parallel along the ridge to the north to Piatra lui Iorgovan in the **Retezat mountains** (see p.190) – allow one or two days.

Practicalities

From Băile Herculane's lovely turn-of-the-century **train station**, 5km from the spa, maxitaxis run every half-hour to Piaţa Hercules. A stack of **hotels** offer a good range of accommodation both here and in Pecinişca: the best-value places in the old spa area are the gloriously cheap and crumbling *Apollo* (☎0255/560 688, ⓕ560 454; ❷), and the *Cerna* (☎0255/560 436, ⓕ560 440; ❷), both as basic as they come, with hot water available for limited periods each day. Beyond the *Apollo*, where the road narrows, is the Hotel *Roman* (☎0255/560 390, ⓕ560 454; ❺), the best place to get any tourist **information** and location for the **Imperial Roman Baths** (daily 8am–6pm).

None of the big and unsightly hotels in Pecinişca differ much from each other, but they're all pretty cheap, and there should be plenty of availability. The one exception is the pleasantly isolated *Pension El Plazza* (☎0255/560 768, ⓔelplazza@baile-herculane.ro; ❸), located about 1km from the train station, just off the main road across the bridge; this terrific-value place has large, homely rooms, a swimming pool and play area for kids.

There are also numerous houses along Pecinişca's main street advertising private rooms. There are a couple of **campsites** here, the best of which is *Camping Hercules* (☎0255 523 458), about 800m north of the train station along the DN6 to Timişoara: this excellent little site also has a handful of rooms available, as well as a good **restaurant**. The other site is the *Flora* (☎0255/560 929), just north of the new part of the resort, which also has some very basic huts (❶).

Reşiţa and the Semenic range

People have been beating iron into shape around **REŞIŢA**, 40km southwest of Caransebeş, since Dacian times. The foundry can trace its history back to 1771, and steam locomotives were manufactured here from 1872 until 1964; if you're entering from Timişoara on Bulevardul Revoluţiei din Decembrie, you'll pass a rusting collection of **locomotives** outside the Reşiţa Nouă train halt. The iron works, and the ropeway across town, are still active, but the town has a depressed feel about it: the county **History Museum** resides at Str. Republicii 10, but has yet to open due to lack of funds, while the bus service to Văliug, starting point for excursions into the Semenic mountains, has ceased to operate. A private bus may run on summer weekends, but otherwise you'll have to hitch or take a taxi. However, the town does stage a couple of festivals: local steelworkers take pride of place in the **Spring Parade** (Alaiul Primăverii), normally held during the first week in April, while there's also the **Bârzava Song Festival** in August. At other times you may as well continue straight on to the mountains.

Arriving at the town's **bus station** on Strada Traian Lalescu, walk west past the post office and theatre, over the footbridge and under the ropeway, and you'll come to the town's central square, Piaţa 1 Decembrie 1918. Arriving by **train**, get off at Reşiţa Sud station, just across from Piaţa 1 Decembrie 1918, as opposed to the Nord stop.

The *Semenic*, an ugly squat **hotel**, stands on Piaţa 1 Decembrie 1918 (☎0255/213 481; ❸–❹), though it's cheaper to stay outside town at Semenic or Crivaia (see p.344) or at one of the three **cabanas**, the *Constructorul*, *Splendid* or *Turist* (all ❶), 13km east on Lake Secu. If you're planning to do some hiking, Reşiţa is the last chance before the Semenic mountains to stock up on food; just east of the Sud train station there's a good **market**, as well as a **supermarket** (Mon–Fri 6am–8pm, Sat 6am–2pm & Sun 8am–noon).

Into the Semenic mountains

From Văliug, 12km southeast of Reşita, one road leads 3km south to **CRIVAIA**, a good base for hikes, where there are bungalows and a **campsite**, while another leads up to **SEMENIC**, also accessible by chairlift from Văliug, which has chalet-style **accommodation** and two hotels, the *Central* (T 0255/214 450; ③) and *Gozna* (T 0255/223 599; ③). **Skiing** is possible here from November to April – pistes are graded from very easy to difficult.

Although the massif is lower and less rugged than others in the Carpathians, it still offers the chance of good **hiking**. One of the most popular treks is west from Semenic through Crivaia to the Comarnic Cave and on to the **Caraşului Gorges** (10–11 hours; blue stripe markings). Situated just before the eastern entrance to the gorges, the **Comarnic Cave** is the Banat's largest grotto, with a spectacular array of rock "veils" and calcite crystals distributed around its four hundred metres of galleries on two levels (guided tours daily until 3pm). The gorges themselves are extremely wild and muddy and harbour several more caves, of which Popovăţ (also open for tours) to the south is the most impressive. If you don't fancy hiking here from Semenic or Crivaia, the gorges can also be entered near **CARAŞOVA**, a village 16km south of Reşiţa on the main road. However, they may be impassable in part thanks to occasional flooding, in which case you should follow the blue stripes onwards from Comarnic to the hamlet of **PROLAZ**, and pick up the route through the gorges there.

Travel details

Trains

Arad to: Baia Mare (1 daily; 6hr 30min); Brad (5 daily; 4hr 30min–5hr); Braşov (6 daily; 6hr–7hr 45min); Bucharest (6 daily; 8hr 30min–10hr 15min); Deva (12 daily; 2hr–3hr 15min); Hălmagiu (5 daily; 4hr); Oradea (6 daily; 1hr 30min–2hr 30min); Radna (12 daily; 30–45min); Sânnicolau Mare (5 daily; 2hr); Sântana (10 daily; 25–40min); Satu Mare (1 daily; 4hr 30min); Sebiş (5 daily; 2hr 30min); Sibiu (1 daily; 5hr); Sighişoara (3 daily; 4hr); Timişoara (14 daily; 50min–1hr 15min); Vârfurile (5 daily; 3hr 30min).
Caransebeş to: Băile Herculane (12 daily; 1hr 15min–2hr); Bucharest (7 daily; 7hr–9hr 30min); Drobeta-Turnu Severin (8 daily; 2hr–3hr); Lugoj (14 daily; 30min–1hr); Orşova (9 daily; 1hr 30min–2hr 15min); Reşiţa (7 daily; 50min–1hr 15min); Timişoara (14 daily; 1hr 15min–2hr 30min).
Oradea to: Arad (6 daily; 1hr 45min–3hr); Baia Mare (2 daily; 3hr 30min); Beiuş (2 daily; 3hr 45min); Bucharest (2 daily; 10hr–11hr); Ciucea (6 daily; 1hr 15min–2hr 45min); Cluj (10 daily; 2hr 30min–4hr 30min); Iaşi (1 daily; 11hr 45min); Satu Mare (5 daily; 2hr–3hr); Ştei (2 daily; 4hr 45min);

Suceava (1 daily; 9hr 30min); Târgu Mureş (1 daily; 4hr 45min); Timişoara (2 daily; 3hr–4hr 15min).
Timişoara to: Arad (15 daily; 50min–1hr 15min); Bucharest (7 daily; 7hr 30min–10hr 30min); Buziaş (8 daily; 40min–1hr); Caransebeş (13 daily; 1hr 15min–2hr 30min); Lugoj (13 daily; 45min–1hr 30min); Oradea (3 daily; 2hr 45min–3hr 30min); Reşiţa (6 daily; 2hr 30min); Sânnicolau Mare (4 daily; 2hr).

Buses and maxitaxis

Arad to: Abrud (2 daily); Câmpeni (1 daily); Lipova (4 daily); Moneasa (2 daily); Oradea (9 daily); Satu Mare (3 daily); Timişoara (9 daily).
Băile Herculane to: Orşova (Mon–Fri 1 daily).
Caransebeş to: Borlova (7 daily).
Oradea to: Alba Iulia (1 daily); Arad (9 daily); Cluj (4 daily); Deva (2 daily); Sighet (1 daily); Târgu Lăpuş (1 daily); Timişoara (9 daily).
Reşiţa to: Caransebeş (1 daily); Deva (Mon–Sat 1 daily); Lugoj (1 daily); Târgu Jiu (1 daily); Timişoara (3 daily).
Timişoara to: Anina (1 daily); Arad (8 daily); Câmpeni (1 daily); Lipova (3 daily); Lugoj (1 daily); Moneasa (1 daily); Oradea (8 daily); Reşiţa (3 daily); Sibiu (2 daily); Târgu Jiu (1 daily).

Planes

Arad to: Bucharest (10 weekly).
Oradea to: Bucharest (12 weekly).
Timişoara to: Bucharest (24 weekly); Cluj (3 weekly); Iaşi (2 weekly).

International trains

Arad to: Budapest, Hungary (7 daily; 4hr 30min–5hr 15min); Prague, Czech Republic (1 daily; 15hr); Vienna (1 daily; 10hr).
Oradea to: Budapest (2 daily; 4hr 30min).

Timişoara to: Belgrade, Sebia (1 daily; 3hr 45min); Budapest (2 daily; 6hr 15min).

International buses

Arad to: Baja, Békéscaba, Budapest and Szeged, all Hungary (1 daily).
Oradea to: Budapest (1 daily); Debrecen, Hungary (1 daily); Kecskemet, Hungary (1 daily).
Timişoara to: Békéscaba (Tues & Fri 1 daily); Budapest (1 daily); Istanbul, Turkey (1 daily); Pancevo, Serbia (2 daily); Szeged (Tues & Fri 1 daily).

THE BANAT | Travel details

7

The Delta and the
coast

* **Birdlife in the Delta** Even visitors without a special interest in winged fauna will be taken aback by the diversity of birdlife on view in the Danube Delta. See p.351

* **Sfântu Gheorghe** This cluster of brightly painted houses of mud and reed, a short walk from the Black Sea, is one of the prettiest of the Delta's fishing villages and a perfect base for exploring the surrounding wetlands. See p.359

* **Fresh fish** All over the Delta, meals consist of the day's haul: carp, pike or catfish, usually served with juicy tomatoes from local gardens. See p.361

* **Halmyris** The ancient Roman city of Halmyris is an archaeological work in progress that recently saw the discovery of the remains of legendary martyrs Epictet and Astion. See p.362

* **Constanţa** Romania's principal port and second largest city is rich in historical associations, and offers an attractive mix of places to stay and eat. See p.366

* **Mamaia** The epicentre of Black Sea tourism and home to the finest hotels outside Bucharest, Mamaia is, for better or for worse, a showpiece for the aspirations of post-communist Romania. See p.372

* **Vama Veche** The most charming and untouched of Romania's Black Sea resorts also has the best bars and nightlife. See p.378

△ Pelicans taking flight in the Danube Delta

The Delta and the coast

Nearly three thousand kilometres downstream from the Black Forest, the **Danube Delta** is a vast network of reeds and shifting land clinging to the far eastern side of Romania. Rich in **wildlife**, the Delta provides a unique habitat for over three hundred species of bird, many of which are found nowhere else in Europe. Most visitors head for the main arm (*braţul*) of the Danube that flows from the Delta capital of **Tulcea** down to **Crişan** and **Sulina**, and it can feel very crowded in July and August; the southern arm, which terminates at the fishing village of **Sfântu Gheorghe**, is an attractive alternative. To really appreciate the diversity of bird life, however, you'll have to pay one of the local fishermen to row or motor you into the backwaters and lakes; travel in the Delta can be time-consuming, so if you're seriously bent on bird watching, be prepared to spend at least a week here.

Further south, Romania's **Black Sea coast** is blessed with abundant sunshine, warm water and sandy beaches, and numerous Roman remains, but due to the popularity of summer resorts such as **Mamaia**, **Neptun** and **Venus** it's best to book a package holiday from home (see Basics), or head to one of the prettier former fishing villages near the Bulgarian border; **Doi Mai** is quiet and family-oriented, while **Vama Veche** grows more fashionable by the year. There are fewer tourists in the coastal city of **Constanţa**, but better restaurants, and lots of sights in the old quarter around the seaport.

Transport to the region is fairly simple. **Train** services to Constanţa are fairly fast and frequent, but very overcrowded in season, when many services are extended to Mangalia. In addition, quick (but cramped) **maxitaxis** regularly run between Bucharest and Constanţa, and between Constanţa's train station and the various resorts. **Driving** from Bucharest will be made easier by a new toll motorway; work proceeds slowly, but there are signs that patches of the new road will be complete by 2006.

The Danube Delta

Every year, the River Danube dumps forty million tonnes of alluvium into the **Danube Delta** (Delta Dunării), the youngest, least stable landscape in Europe. Near **Tulcea**, the river splits into three branches (named after their respective ports, Chilia, Sulina and Sfântu Gheorghe), dividing the Delta into more than 4000 square kilometres of reeds and marsh, half of which is flooded in spring and autumn. The **grinduri**, tongues of accumulated silt supporting oak trees, willows and poplars, account for the five percent of the Delta that remains permanently above the water. Over time, the distinction between these and the **plaur** (floating reed islands) is a fine one, since flooding continually splits, merges and often destroys these patches of land, making any detailed map of

The Lipovani

Descendants of the Old Believers who left Russia around 1772 to avoid religious persecution, the **Lipovani** (identified by their blond hair, beards and blue eyes) were once dispersed all over the Delta but are now found only at Periprava, Mila 23, Mahmudia, Letea, and two villages on Lake Razim – Jurilovca and Sarichioi.

Adapting to their environment, the Lipovani became skilled **fishermen** and gardeners, speaking a Russian dialect among themselves but equally fluent in Romanian. Since you're likely to rely on Lipovani boatmen to guide you through the confusing side channels (*gârla*), be prepared for their fundamentalist abhorrence of the "Devil's weed", tobacco; their consumption of vodka, however, is legendary.

the delta outdated almost as soon as it's drawn. Although fishing communities have lived here for centuries, it's an inhospitable environment for humans: a Siberian wind howls all winter long, while in summer the area is inundated with mosquitoes.

Yet it's a paradise for wildlife, and after years of environmental neglect culminating in Ceauşescu's plan to drain the Delta for agricultural use, it was declared a **Biosphere Reserve** in 1990, with over 500 square kilometres strictly protected, and a UNESCO World Heritage Site the following year. The area is particularly important for **birds**, which pass through during the spring and autumn migrations, or come from Siberia to winter here or from Africa to breed in summer. Besides herons, glossy ibis, golden eagles, avocets, shelduck and other Mediterranean breeds, the Delta is visited by

Delta tours

Travel agencies mostly offer packages to **floating hotels** in the heart of the Delta, though their tours generally stick to the main axes, from which most of the wildlife has been scared off. In Tulcea, ATBAD at Str. Babadag 11 (☏0240/514 114, ⓦwww.atbad.ro) has two nights full board in its three-star floating hotel for €150 per person, including transfers, while Simpa Tourism at *Hotel Delta*, Str. Isaccei 2 (☏040/515 753, ⓦwww.simpaturism.ro) charges €64 to €94 per person (including boat transfers) for two nights at its *Cormoran Complex* in Uzlina. ATBAD also runs its own holiday village at Lake Roşu, south of Sulina, reached by boat from its pontoon near the Art Museum (May–Oct every 5 days; €25 return); two-star/three-star accommodation costs €30/€50 per person, per day. These options offer high standards of accommodation, but are isolated from the Delta's fascinating village life. Most travel agencies in Constanţa can organize Delta tours, but only for groups of five or more.

If you want to travel **independently** around the Delta, you'll need a **permit** but you can make all the necessary arrangements in Tulcea (see box on p.355) or, for the southern arm, Murighiol. ATBAD and Simpa Turism (see above) offer day-trips to Crişan, Mila 23 and the other canals from €30 per person, as do Amatour, on the waterfront opposite the *Hotel Delta* (☏0240/518 894), Europolis SA, in the *Hotel Europolis*, Str. Păcii 20, (☏0240/512 443), and Danubius, at B-dul Ferdinand 36 in Constanţa (☏0241/615 836, ⓦwww.danubius.ro). Alternatively, there are smaller and less formal outfits along the Tulcea waterfront, which charge from €10 to €50 per group per hour, depending on the size of the boat. **Pensions** in Murighiol can also arrange various excursions.

reed buntings, white-tailed eagles and various European songbirds; whooper swans, arctic grebes and half-snipes from Siberia; saker falcons from Mongolia; egrets, mute swans and mandarin ducks from China; and its remoter lakes support Europe's largest pelican colonies. The best time to see birds is from May to early June, the latter being the wettest month of the year. The Delta is also home to otters, mink, boars, wolves and other **animals**. At night, streets in the Delta villages are alive with frogs, beetles and the abundant nocturnal hawk moths. Stocks of fish such as carp and pike have gradually improved since intensive fertilizer use desecrated them in the mid-1980s, although sturgeon, the most lucrative of all, have largely vanished.

Tulcea

Clustered around the south bank of a bend in the Danube, **TULCEA** has been tagged the "Threshold of the Delta" ever since ancient Greek traders established a **port** here. Its maritime significance was slight until the closing stages of the period of Ottoman domination (1420–1878), when other powers suddenly perceived it as commercially and strategically important. Nowadays, the outskirts of the town are heavily industrialized, and the port is too shallow for large modern freighters, but it's still the chief access point for passenger vessels entering the Delta – though without the decent restaurants and transport links you might expect. The uninspiring town centre has enough attractions to fill a day, but your time will be better spent in the Delta; it's worth arriving early enough to catch one of the ferries that depart at 1.30pm. Tulcea is busiest in August and December, when its regular **festivals** take place: the International Folk Festival of the Danubian Countries, held in odd-numbered years, and an annual winter carnival.

Arrival, information and accommodation

Tulcea's gleaming new **train station** is on the western edge of town, and it's an easy walk from there along the waterfront to Piața Republicii, passing the **bus station** and the NAVROM **ferry terminal** and office on the way. Tulcea is linked to Bucharest and Constanța by train, but it's a slow journey down to the junction at Medgidia. Regular **maxitaxis** serve both cities between 7am and 7pm. Since the closure of the hydrofoil to Galați in Moldavia, you're now limited to taking a maxitaxi or a (slower and bumpier) local bus to I.C. Brătianu, across the Danube from Galați. There are four buses and six maxitaxis a day for Galați, and two buses and four maxitaxis for Brăila, all of which leave from the bus station, save the daily Istanbul service, which calls in front of the sports hall on Strada Isaccei.

The **Danube Delta Biosphere Reserve Administration** (ARBDD; Mon—Fri 8am–4pm; ☎0240/518 924, ⓦwww.ddbra.ro), on the waterfront just east of the bus station, functions as the region's **tourist information office**, and can provide information on accommodation and trips in the Delta, as well as issue entry permits and fishing and licenses. Most **travel agencies** are concerned with Delta trips (see box on p.351); some also sell international bus and plane tickets. The all-night pharmacy is Farmacia 29, at Str. Babadag 4. **Internet** access is to be had at Future Games at Str. Isaccei 12. Further down, at Str. Isaccei 20, is a bookstore selling Delta maps and a few English-language novels.

Accommodation

Tulcea has several decent **hotels** spread across town or you might find a **floating hotel** (*ponton dormitory*) moored alongside the promenade; look for the one owned by Amatour (☎0240/518 894; ❸) opposite the *Delta* hotel – facilities are basic but the atmosphere compensates. Tulcea's Antrec office (☎0240/511 279 or 0721/092 150 evenings and weekends, ⓦwww .deltaturism.ro), on the ground floor of the ARBDD building, can make reservations for **homestay** and **pension** accommodation in the Delta.

Delta Str. Isaccei 2 ☎0240/514 720, ☎516 260. Functional but pricey three-star on Piaţa Republicii. Crisp service and a lively, stylish lobby provide an air of sophistication, but the rooms themselves aren't much better than those at the *Europolis*. Breakfast included. ❼

Europolis Str. Păcii 20 (☎0240/512 443, ⓦwww.europolis.ro). Bland, respectable two-star on the far side of the Piaţa Civică. ❹

Han Trei Stele Str. Carpaţi 16 ☎0240/516 764. On the right as you ascend the steps behind the Ukrainian market, this pleasantly chaotic but less than sanitary budget option has non-stop hot water via a hose pipe. ❶

Rex Str. Toamnei 1 ☎0240/511 351, ☎511 354. New four-star hotel, just past the synagogue on Str. Babadag, with a/c, conference rooms and pleasant staff; breakfast included. ❽

The Town

Tulcea is centred around Piaţa Republicii, northeast of which, on the corner of Strada A. Sahia and Strada 9 Mai, is the town's main attraction, the **Art Museum** (Tues–Sun: July–Oct 9am–5pm; Nov–June 8am–4pm), built by Ismail Pasha in 1870; its fine collection of paintings includes Impressionistic female nudes by Pallady, Delta landscapes by Sirbu and Stavrov, and a selection of Surrealist and avant-garde works. You'll also see Igolesco's *Balchik*, a depiction of the thriving artistic community in southern Dobrogea, a village so loved by Queen Marie that she asked for her heart to be buried there. When the area was handed over to Bulgaria, the queen's heart was brought back in a casket that now rests in the National History Museum in Bucharest (see p.69). From Strada 9 Mai, Strada 14 Noiembrie heads north

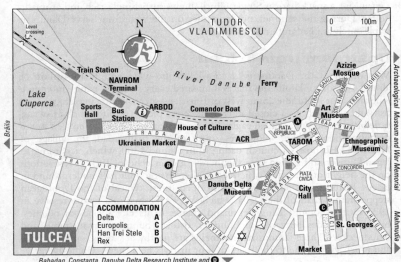

to the nondescript nineteenth-century Azizie Mosque; having been fairly inconspicuous under communism, the local Turkish women are now much more visible, dressed in bright colours and baggy trousers. Beyond the mosque, Strada Gloriei runs through a pretty area of small white houses with gardens, ending at the Parcul Monumentului Independenţei, where you'll find the town's **Roman remains**, an **obelisk** to the dead of the 1877–78 war, and the **Archaeological Museum** (Tues–Sun 10am–5pm), noted for its collection of Roman, Greek, Byzantine and medieval coins.

Back in the centre, the **Ethnographic Museum** at Str. 9 Mai 2 (Tues–Sun: June–Sept 10am–6pm, Oct–May 8am–4pm) has displays on the varied groups inhabiting the region. On the far side of the systematized Piaţa Civică is the **Museum of the Danube Delta**, Str. Progresului 32 (Tues–Sun 9am–5pm); equipped with multilingual guides and captions, it has a fascinating geological display showing the formation of the Delta. The museum's lower level also houses a modest aquarium featuring local aquatic species. Back on the waterfront, at the dock opposite the ACR office, **ferries** shuttle across the river to the suburb of **Tudor Vladimirescu** (every 15min from dawn to dusk), where there's a sandy bank for sunbathing.

Eating and drinking

The main **market**, good for buying snacks and provisions for trips into the Delta, is just south of the centre down Strada Păcii, beyond St George's, one of the town's several barn-like churches built under Turkish occupation. At Str. Isaccei 16, there's a bakery with excellent cheese pastries. The supermarket on Str. Unirii 2 has Tulcea's best selection of imported foods, as well as decent bread and fruit. The finest **restaurant** in town is the *Select*, on Strada Păcii, opposite the *Egreta* hotel; take your pick from a varied menu, presented in six languages. The restaurant in the *Comandor Boat* has a basic menu and a good wine list, although the cabin tends to fill up with smoke. A more conventional choice is the reasonably priced *Central*, on Str. Babadag 3. The classiest **place for a drink** is the bar in the *Hotel Delta*; the floor-to-ceiling windows looking out on the Danube are perfect for watching the resident bird life. *Union Visa*, a snack bar on Strada Unirii, brews surprisingly rich and aromatic coffee. During the summer, outdoor cafés on the waterfront serve Danubian staples such as beer and grilled sausages.

Upstream from Tulcea

West of Tulcea, the Danube is up to a kilometre wide, with a **floodplain** of almost 100 square kilometres that is inundated every spring as nature intended. The area near Rotundu, 25km west of Tulcea, is especially rich in plankton and fish, and although it's a closed reserve there are plenty of birds, such as swans, little bittern and white-tailed eagles (Romania's largest raptor) to be seen in the neighbourhood. Three kilometres south of the main road, the village of **NICULIŢEL** boasts a church dating from around 1300, which, according to legend, was found buried by a shepherd – a clear echo of Turkish restrictions on the height of churches, which led to them being built half-underground in places. Inland from here is a beautiful open forest, typical of the Dobrogean steppes rather than of the Delta, which was established as a nature reserve in 1927 by the botanist King Ferdinand, thanks to its rare species of peonies; bird life includes buzzards, nightingales, ortolan buntings, tawny pipits and woodpeckers. Three famous **monasteries** are nearby, at Cocoş (built in 1833, and much visited due to the relics of four martyrs held there), Chilic-Dere

To enter the **Danube Delta Biosphere Reserve (RBDD)**, you need a **permit**, which gains you access to everywhere except the strictly protected reserves. If you're taking a tour, this will be handled by the tour company; independent travellers can get permits from the ARBDD and travel agencies and hotels in Tulcea for a basic price of less than a euro, with supplementary charges for boating and fishing. Organized tours cost about twenty times as much, and are limited to seven fixed routes. If you're planning to explore beyond these, take a compass and a detailed **map** – the green Olimp map (available in Tulcea at the bookstore at Str. Isaccei 20 and at the *Europolis* hotel), which has English text and shows the strictly protected zones, and the Amco Delta map (available in Bucharest) are the best. The boat rental kiosk in Murighiol also sells good maps.

Camping is prohibited except in Murighiol, Crişan and on the shore of Lake Roşu, but the regulations are laxly enforced. There are **hotels** only in Sulina and Murighiol, but good **pensions** can be found virtually everywhere, at least between May and September, when most of them close for the season. If these are full – and in July and August they might be – you should be able to find bed and breakfast accommodation in a **private home**, though this will likely be without hot water. Alternatively, try one of the agencies in Tulcea, particularly Simpa Turism and ATBAD (see box on p.351), who both have their own hotels in the Delta. Wherever you end up staying, expect generous fish dinners and lovely tomato salads. The shops in Sulina sell a respectable variety of foodstuffs; elsewhere, the selection can be very limited – finding still water can be especially difficult. Before you set off, it's worth buying **essential supplies** like canned food, fruit and cheese in Tulcea; candles and plenty of mosquito repellent are also vital. Most Delta villages have a bakery, but fresh bread sells quickly – locals tend to start queuing when there's a batch in the oven.

There are currently five weekly NAVROM **ferries** to Sulina (departing Tulcea Mon–Fri; returning Tue–Fri and Sun), and four to Sfântu Gheorghe and Periprava (in both cases departing Tulcea Mon and Wed–Fri; returning Tue, Thu, Fri and Sun). All leave Tulcea at 1.30pm, or a bit later if there's a crowd. Ferries return early: from Sulina at 7am, from Periprava at 5am and from Sfântu Gheorghe at 6am. The ticket office (open sailing days only 9am–1.30pm) is on the waterfront; **tickets** (€4 one-way) can only be bought on the day you're travelling, up to two hours before departure. The ferries are lumbering vessels crammed with people and piled high with dinghies, rods and camping gear; it's worth avoiding the cabins, where the air is poisonous Note that projecting empty beer cans and cigarette ends from the deck into the Danube is a holiday ritual here.

Hydrofoils are run by AFDJ, whose vessels are moored next to the NAVROM ferries. They operate daily services throughout the year to Sulina (departing 2pm, returning 7am; 1hr 30min), but don't expect a view; the hydrofoils are swift, businesslike craft with opaque windows. Tickets (€6), available on the vessel, sell out early.

(1840, where there's a wooden windmill), and Saon, just north of the main road. It's possible to sleep at these monasteries, and the monks may even feed you.

Into the Delta

The following sections cover each arm of the Delta in turn, starting from Tulcea, and then the Lake Razim region. If you just want to take a trip down to the sea and back, **Sfântu Gheorghe** is probably the best choice; it's prettier than Sulina, has a more tranquil beach, and is within easy reach of several good

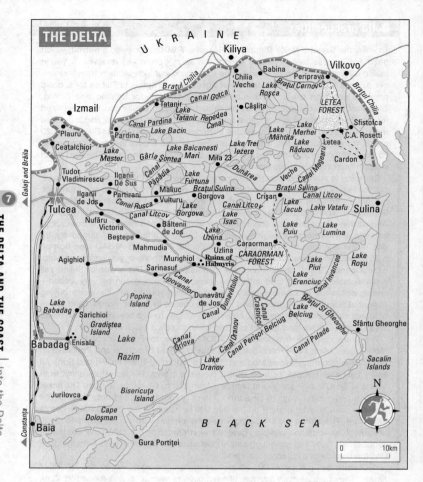

THE DELTA

bird-watching spots. **Sulina** is more crowded and built up, but richer in historical associations. Of the numerous ancient ruins in the vicinity of the Delta, the Roman city of **Halmyris**, near Murighiol, is rewarding and easily accessible.

Brațul Chilia

The **Chilia arm** of the river (Brațul Chilia), which branches off upstream from Tulcea and marks the border with Ukraine, carries over half of the Danube's water, but very little tourist traffic, mainly because boats will only carry you as far as the largely Lipovani village of **PERIPRAVA** (100km from Tulcea but still 30km from the Black Sea), where there's a total lack of tourist facilities. In the days when the entire Delta was part of Moldavia, **CHILIA VECHE**, 35km from Periprava, was merely a suburb of Chilia (now Ukrainian Kiliya) across the river. When the town repelled a Turkish invasion in 1476, Chilia was just 5km from the coast – today, it's 40km away. **Lake Roşca**, roughly 10km south of Babina on the Cernovca tributary between Chilia Veche and Periprava, is one of the larger strictly protected reserves, harbouring geese, egrets, storks and Europe's largest **white pelican colony**. Immediately to the east is Periprava, south of which lies the **Pădurea Letea**, a forest of oaks tangled with lianas, now a haven for falcons, white-tailed eagles, boar and wildcats. Surrounding the forest are **sand dunes** inhabited by tortoises and lizards. One way of seeing a little of this route is to travel as far as **Ceatalchioi**, 20km from Tulcea, where the reeds (*stuf*) that are used to build Delta houses are gathered by hand. Not far beyond Ceatalchioi (due north as the river flows), boats pass **Izmail**, the main Ukrainian city in the Delta, whose bloody recapture from the Turks in 1790 is described in Byron's *Don Juan*.

Braţul Sulina

Between 1862 and 1902, the **Sulina arm** (Braţul Sulina) was shortened from 84km to 63km by the digging of long straight sections. Constant dredging and groynes running 10km out to sea still enable 7000-tonne freighters to take this route from Tulcea; with the additional tourist traffic, this is the busiest and least serene of the Danube's branches. However, it has a tourist infrastructure and several settlements that offer a fair chance of renting boats to visit a variety of wildlife habitats. The journey from Tulcea to Sulina takes an hour and a half by hydrofoil or four hours by ferry. Travellers who come equipped to explore the Delta by **canoe** will face turbulence from the wakes of passing ships on the main waterway, but **beyond Ilganii de Sus** you can escape into calmer backwaters leading to the inland lakes. Sulina itself has seen something of a revitalization in recent years and is now the Delta's most popular tourist destination. It's also the most built up, and the only one with streets and cars. There are a few interesting sights in Sulina, but the fishing villages along the way make much better bases for seeing wildlife and exploring the wetlands.

Maliuc

Fishermen in **MALIUC**, on the left bank of the river 24km from Tulcea, can row you to see the pelicans and marsh terns nesting on **Lake Furtuna**. The reeds in this area provide a home for great-crested grebes, the solitary red-necked grebes, bearded reedlings – which nest in piles of cut reeds – and herons and little egrets, which favour nesting in overhanging willow trees. Maliuc has a **campsite** (❶) and the *Salcia* **hotel** (❹). From Lake Meşter or the Păpădia channel, **canoeists** can try following the Gârla Şontea to reach the original Dunărea Veche branch of the river near Mila 23 (see p.358); be warned, though, that submerged roots and aquatic plants may block the way. Nearby **Lake Gorgova** hosts a large colony of glossy ibis, and has a small cabana (❶).

Crişan, Mila 23 and around

CRIŞAN, a fishing settlement that consists of a single dirt path, lined with houses and straggling along the south bank of the shoreline for 7km, is the main tourist centre in this part of the Delta, and a good place to see the region's most common bird species; the ditch that runs behind the houses shelters herons, egrets and other waders, and you're likely to find hoopoes, rollers and goldfinches in the brushland at the west end of the village. Pelicans glide high overhead in long formations throughout the day, making their way from Lake

Merhei to Lake Iacob. Across the river at Mila 13, there is a **monument** (marking the distance from the sea in nautical miles), unveiled by Carol I in 1894 to inaugurate the new short-cut sections. Also on the north bank, before Mila 14, is an EcoInfoCentre, a good source of **information** on all areas of the Biosphere Reserve, with an excellent viewing tower. Ferries stop on the south bank, in the centre of town; both the best shop and the bakery are opposite the ferry pier. Accommodation is available at a moderately luxurious **hotel**, the *Lebăda* (☎0240/543 778; ❼), on the north bank, and at several good **pensions**, the finest of which is the *Pensiunea Nufărul* (☎0240/519 214, ❸), a professionally run establishment a few hundred metres east of the ferry landing, which can arrange day-trips to more remote parts of the Delta. In the other direction, 500m west of the landing, the *Hotel Delia* (☎0240/547 018; ❷) is larger, with comfortable rooms, permanent hot water and a good laundry service. *Oprişan* (☎0240/547 034; ❷), 200m east of the ferry landing, is also recommended. Private homestays are cheaper (usually ❶) and often serve more generous fish dinners, but facilities can be basic. Crişan's **campsite** (❶) is at the far west end of the village.

Boats meet the ferry (but not the hydrofoil) to take you across to the north bank, and continue on to **Mila 23**, 10km north on the "old" branch of the Danube; this is the starting point for excursions to most of the surrounding lakes. Mila 23 is a large village of reed cottages (rebuilt after a flood in the 1960s), where the men fish and the women tend to gardens of vegetables, plums, pears, grapes and quinces, and look after the poultry, pigs and beehives. The only pension is *Valodea* (❷), but many of the villagers rent out rooms. Golden orioles – which nest high in deciduous trees – and bladder frogs are widespread around here.

South of Crişan, the forest of **Pădurea Caraorman**, now a strict reserve, is the best area of dunes in the Delta, striped with unusual linear forests of ancient oaks, poplar, ash and willow and protecting wildlife such as ural owls, white-tailed eagles, wildcats, boars and wolves. The dyke that runs south from Crişan leads to a dead end; to get to the forest, catch the boat that connects with ferries at Crişan to take passengers to the predominantly Ukrainian village of **CARAORMAN**, where you can stay at two pensions, *Grindul Verde* (☎0722/732 076, Ⓦwww.caraorman.ro; ❷), which has English-speaking staff, and the slightly upmarket *Purda* (❷), which is affiliated with Antrec in Tulcea (see p. 353). Under Ceauşescu, there were plans to remove the dunes en masse until the 1989 revolution intervened; half-a-dozen skeletal apartment blocks are all that remain of the project.

Three remote and very different villages lie to the north of Crişan, on the south side of the Letea forest: **LETEA**, a village of Lipovani/Ukrainian fisherfolk, where there's a rangers' house and bird-watching tower; neighbouring C.A. **ROSETTI**, home to Romanian cattle breeders and the Delta's last windmill; and **SFISTOFCA**, an even smaller Lipovani village. You may get a room in these villages on the spot, but it's best to check with the ARBDD in Tulcea (see p.352) before setting out. The Letea forest, just north of Rosetti and Letea, is strictly off-limits, but the Sfistofca forest, to the south, is almost as good, a maze of trees up to two hundred years old, tangled with lianas and orchids.

Sulina

Ever since it was recorded as a port by a Byzantine scribe in 950, **SULINA** has depended on shipping. Genoese vessels used to call here during the fourteenth century, while throughout the period of Ottoman power it was not so much a trading port as a nest of pirates who preyed on shipping in the Black Sea. From

1856, Sulina was the headquarters of the International Danube Commission, established after the Crimean War to regulate free passage along the waterway, and in 1900 it became a free port. Within a decade, however, larger vessels and worldwide recession had emptied Sulina, so that by 1940 the writer John Lehmann found "a hopeless, sinking feeling" in a place where "people get stranded, feel themselves abandoned by civilization, take to drink, and waste into a half-animal existence". The state has tried to sustain Sulina, an economically futile endeavour: expensive annual dredging is required to enable even small-capacity ships to enter, while larger freighters can now bypass the Delta altogether by taking the Danube–Black Sea Canal. Today, tourism is succeeding where trade has failed, and, drawn by the long sandy beach 2km from the port, a small but growing contingent of Romanians has discovered Sulina as an alternative to the more established resorts further south.

A bit of the ambience of the golden days survives in the nineteenth-century houses along the waterfront, as well as at the **Old Lighthouse** (Mon–Fri 4–8pm), built in 1802, and the **cemetery** between the town and the sea, which provides an evocative record of all the nationalities who lived and died here in its days as a free port. Greeks dominated business, but there was also a large British contingent, now resting beneath suitably dignified Victorian tombstones in the Anglican plot, directly behind the chapel. Like so much of the Delta, the cemetery is full of birds; this is one of the best places to find hoopoes, and you're also likely to see cuckoos and orioles here. The lighthouse is two blocks south of the ferry landing; the cemetery is 500m further to the southeast. From the cemetery, it's a one-kilometre walk to the litter-strewn **beach** (minivans also run this route). Back in the centre of town, there's a good **visitor centre** on the promenade near the harbour, which can supply practical information on the area. Also look for two **churches** from the nineteenth century: the Greek Church of Saint Nicholas is on the waterfront, while the Russian church is near the west end of town.

There are a number of **pensions** in Sulina, many of which send touts to meet the ferries. The most exclusive place to stay is the three-star *Casa Coral* (☏0240/543 777; ❹), a new establishment on the waterfront with smart rooms and a restaurant attached. Shabbier, but much more atmospheric, is the *Hotel Jean Bart* (0240/543 128; ❸); the fish restaurant here is the **best place to eat**. Around the corner from the *Jean Bart* is *Pensiunea Velcu* (☏0240/543 403; ❷), which is associated with Antrec, and a few blocks further in is the modest but friendly *Pensiunea Ana* (☏0230/543 252; ❶), at Str. IV no. 144. At the beach, there's a **campsite** with cabanas (❶) and rooms (❷). There are a few bars in Sulina, but the principal evening activity is strolling on the promenade, where the supermarkets do a brisk trade in ice cream.

Braţul Sfântu Gheorghe

The Delta's oldest, most winding arm, the Braţul Sfântu Gheorghe, is the least used by freighters and fishing boats; it carries a fair amount of tourist traffic and, unlike other parts of the Delta, some of its settlements can be reached by bus from Tulcea. If you plan to visit these, it's easiest to go direct to Sfântu Gheorghe, then by boat to Murighiol, from where you can make a boat trip to the fishing village of Uzlina or visit the ruins of Halmyris. There's plenty of parking in Murighiol; if you're driving into the Delta, it's best to leave your car there rather than in Tulcea.

SFÂNTU GHEORGHE, 75km downriver from Murighiol, is a small village of brightly painted Lipovani cottages that has subsisted on fishing since

△ A fisherman sorts through the day's catch, the Danube Delta

the fourteenth century. Most prized are **sturgeon**, whose eggs, *icre neagre* or black caviar, once drew thousands of Romanian tourists here on shopping trips. The catch is not what it used to be, though you still might find some caviar if you come in late August or early September. The reed and mud houses, most of which support colonies of swallows, are the main attraction of the village itself, but most tourists come for the relatively untouched beach or to make trips into the surrounding marshes. A large tractor, one of the two or three motorized land vehicles in the village, carries tourists to and from the beach in a trailer, departing every hour or so from the centre – the schedule should be posted on one of the information boards near the main square.

There are no hotels or restaurants in Sfântu Gheorghe. The one first-rate **pension** in town, the *Mareea* (℡0744/306 384, ⓦwww.mareea.go.ro; ❻ with half board), has attractively furnished air-conditioned rooms, and the meals are superb – if not caviar, there's at least a chance of finding sturgeon on the menu. The owner, who speaks English well, can arrange fishing and bird-watching excursions. Less exclusive, and without air-conditioning but with hot water, is the five-room *Pensiunea Sperante*, at Str. I no. 30 (℡0744/621 892; ❹ with half-board). Locals know it as *casa galben*, the yellow house. Dora Dumitru has a summer home (℡0240/540 219; ❸ with half board) one block north of the *Sperante*, with four bedrooms and an enclosed, mosquito-free dining room. She makes excellent salads, and prepares fish in a mouth-watering variety of ways. She speaks French; her daughters, who are sometimes around, speak English. Other villagers with private rooms will meet your ferry; the only alternative is to camp wild, which is officially forbidden. Sfântu Gheorghe's shops, sparsely stocked and with relatively high prices, are in the centre, as is the bakery. There's also a bar, and, on Friday and Saturday nights, a disco. More entertainment is sometimes provided by a band of local fisherman, who play a mix of Beatles covers and traditional songs in the town's bar.

During July and August, the tractor makes occasional day excursions to Sulina (1hr 30mins) – look for a sign in the town centre or ask around if you're interested. Otherwise, From Sfântu Gheorghe, you can take **boat trips**, either north to Lake **Roşu**, or south, down the Gârla de Mijloc canal to **Lesser Sacalin Island** (Insula Sacalinu Mic) at the river's mouth, which is inhabited by all three species of marsh tern, stilts, ibis and other waders, as well as goosanders, red-breasted geese, and goldeneyes. This is one of the oldest parts of the Delta and a strictly protected reserve, so boats are not allowed to moor: to get to the beach on the island, you'll have to wade through the ankle-deep mud at the canal's end. Depending on the wind, the trip takes an hour or more; the motor boat is faster but, at €10 per hour, at least twice as expensive. Look for kingfishers along the way. Further south still is Greater Sacalin Island (Insula Sacalinu Mare), while to the west, on Lake Lejai and near the Crasnicol sand bank, is the remote area where the Delta's 70–80 pairs of dalmation pelicans breed. The trip to Lake Roşu is longer than that to Lesser Sacalin Island, but you're likely to see white pelicans on the lake. There's an isolated **campsite** on the canal between Roşu and Puiu lakes. Also located here is the ATBAD-run Roşu Complex, with a three-star **hotel** (❾) and two-star **bungalows** (❼), a **restaurant** and a **disco**. To see the most birds, boat trips should be taken as early as possible; note that fishermen can be unreliable on the mornings after the disco.

Murighiol, Uzlina and Halmyris

Returning towards Tulcea, the main settlement en route is **MURIGHIOL**, which, though connected to the outside world by road as well as canal, still has some of the isolated feeling of an interior Delta village. Murighiol has its natural attractions – namely black-winged stilts, red- and black-necked grebe, Kentish plover, avocets, and red-crested pochards, and Romania's only colony of Mediterranean gulls, all nesting around the late-freezing salt lakes (Sărături Murighiol) nearby, but the principal reason to come here is to visit the ruin at Halmyris or the fishing village of Uzlina. Seven buses and maxitaxis a day run to and from Tulcea, on a circular route via either Mahmudia or Sarinasuf. Be warned that the buses don't go anywhere near the ferry landing, which is 5km from the centre of town – if you're on your way to or from Sfântu Gheorge, you'll have to walk or hitch. Arriving by bus from Tulcea, you'll be dropped off in the centre of Murighiol, next to the shell of an abandoned Centru Civic; from here, walk downhill past the two or three main shops, beyond which you will see pensions on either side of the street, including, on your left, *Pensiunea Riviera* (℡0240/545 910; ❶), which is open year-round. The owner can arrange four-hour Delta trips from €40 for up to six people. For more **accommodation**, continue down the main road, turning left just before Murighiol's last house, and follow the dirt path over a barren field. On the other side of the field is the excellent *Motel Halmiiris* (℡0744/300 957; ❸), one of the cheapest three-star hotels in Romania. Nearby is the larger *Complex Turistic Pelican* (℡0240/545 877), which has a hotel (❸), chalets (❷) and a **campsite**. Between the *Halmiiris* and the *Pelican* is a boat-rental kiosk affiliated with Simpa Turism; the staff here can arrange day-trips or transportation to the *Cormoran Complex* at Lake Uzlina (see box on p.351). For ferries to Sfântu Gheorge, follow the forested road that begins next to the *Halmiiris*; the ferry landing, where there's also a large car park, is 1.5km further on.

Several hundred metres east of the *Motel Halmiiris* lies its namesake, the ruined Roman city of **HALMYRIS**. One of the most important ancient sites in Romania, Halmyris was continuously inhabited from the sixth century BC to the seventh century AD, when a combination of marauding barbarians, climatic changes and dwindling imperial support occasioned its demise. Originally a small seafront fort – in ancient times, a Danube channel met the Black Sea only a few hundred metres to the east – it grew in size and importance until it became the permanent home to vexilations of Roman legions and a station for the Danube fleet *Classis Flavia Moesica*, serving as a stopping point on the road that connected the major Roman settlements of the Delta.

Today, Halmyris is best known for the **tomb of Epictet and Astion**, two Christians from Asia Minor who were tortured and executed here on July 8, 290, after refusing to renounce Christianity; thus becoming the earliest Romanian martyrs (and earning a place on the Romanian Orthodox calendar). One of their judges was said to have been converted by the resolve with which Epictet and Astion met their fates, and to have secretly buried their remains, which were then kept hidden until the conversion of Constantine, when they were interred in Halmyris's **basilica**. The principal details of the story were the stuff of legend until 2001, when excavators discovered a **crypt** containing two skeletons beneath the basilica's altar, along with a **fresco** (currently under restoration) bearing the name "Astion".

In addition to the basilica and the crypt, the two-hectare site also features extensive remains of an L-shaped private **bathhouse**. The Western Gate, which dates from the sixth century AD, was constructed largely of stones carved with honorary inscriptions that had in earlier times adorned the homes of the town's more prominent citizens. Much of Halmyris, as well as the surrounding cornfields which were once its harbour, remains unexcavated (digging only began here in 1981), and the best reason to visit is not for the ruins themselves, or the tombs of Epictet and Astion, but for the chance to see an ancient city still in the process of being uncovered.

Murighiol is also the jumping-off point for the tiny fishing village of **UZLINA**, the site of the scientific centre of the Biosphere Reserve and the Cousteau Foundation, and an **EcoInfoCenter** in what was Ceauşescu's lodge. North of Uzlina, the Isac and Uzlina lakes are home to a protected **pelican colony**, which you can see from a respectful distance. Heading downstream, the new channel is edged by high levees, but the meanders of the old channel are tree-lined and populated by deer, boar, foxes, water snakes, black ibis and egrets. **Lake Belciug**, roughly halfway back towards Sfântu Gheorghe, is one of those least affected by algal blooms and deoxygenation, and retains the submerged vegetation once typical of the Delta, as well as a colony of glossy ibis.

Around Lake Razim

South of the Delta proper, **Lake Razim** is separated from the Black Sea by two long, tongue-like *grinds*. It's a good spot for bird-watchers, particularly in November and December, when the western shoreline is invaded by a million white-fronted and red-breasted geese from arctic Russia, which stay here, or around Istria further to the south, until the reed beds freeze. In the north of the lake, Popina island is now a closed reserve. Like other parts of the Delta, however, Razim has been adversely affected by development: the western shores were empoldered in 1969 for fish farming, and in 1974 a sluice at Gura Portiţei cut the lake off from the sea, causing it to fill with fresh water, which has led to frequent algal blooms, deoxygenation, and a steady decline in fish yields and biodiversity.

Babadag, Enisala, Jurilovca, and Gura Portiţei

From Tulcea, the DN22 and the rail line head south to **BABADAG**, home to the sixteenth-century **Ali Ghazi Mosque**, Romania's oldest. There's a visible Turkish minority here, present since 1263, but the mosque is now disused. Just down the street, though, in the Casa Panaghia Expoziţie de Artă Orientală, is a small but engaging **museum** (Tue–Sun 10am–6pm), which displays the folk art of the Dobrogean Turks, including embroidered robes and copper vessels. Maxitaxis running between Tulcea and Constanţa, as well as the less frequent services to Enisala and Jurilovca, call at the **bus station** across the street from the mosque. Babadag's only hotel, the *Dumbrava* (☎0240/561 302; ❷), five minutes to the north of the bus station, is only useful if you find yourself stranded here.

A quiet village of reed cottages, **ENISALA** lies 8km east of Babadag. In the centre of town, a traditional peasant home (Gospodăria Tărănească) has been preserved as a **museum** (Tue–Sun 10am–6pm) displaying colourful tapestries, painted carts and a wealth of implements. About 1km north, overlooking the lake, is the **ruined Heracleia citadel**, built by Genoese merchants late in the thirteenth century at the behest of the Byzantine emperor. Taken by Sultan Mehmet I in 1417, it was held by the Ottomans until they abandoned it around the sixteenth century. This area is one of Europe's prime bird-watching sites, thanks to a mix of habitats: a vast area of reedbeds along the shoreline, stretching back to open land and the Babadag forest. You're likely to spot white-fronted and red-breasted geese, terns, waders, pelicans, herons and warblers. If you're coming from Tulcea, watch the left side of the road: shortly before passing the citadel, you'll see an apiary that supports a sizeable colony of bee-eaters. Three of the daily maxitaxis from Tulcea take a pot-holed backroad, passing through Enisala en route to Babadag.

The tiny fishing village of **JURILOVCA**, 17km further down the coast and served by two daily buses from Tulcea, is of interest mainly for its access to Lake Razim's outer rim, but there is a small **Ethnographic Museum**, which bears witness to the village's population of Romanians, Lipovani and a few Muslim Turks and Tatars: unlike Transylvania, the Delta has never really been noted for ethnic rivalry, since all groups are relatively recent colonists. Around 5km east of Jurilovca, on Cape Doloşman, lie the remains of the second- to sixth-century Greek citadel of Arganum, which faces **Bisericuţa Island**, itself the site of some medieval ruins. From Jurilovca, three boats (departing 9am, 2pm and 6pm; €3) run daily to **GURA PORTIŢEI**, on a spit of land between Lake Razim and the sea. Before 1989, this was one of the few remote corners of Romania where it was possible to escape the Securitate for a week or two; today, it consists of a few Lipovani reed huts and a new **resort** (April–Oct; T0724/214 224, Wwww.guraportitei.ro) with a three-star **hotel** (○) and **bungalows** (○). The hotel rooms are air-conditioned and have private baths; bungalows have shared showers with hot water. Activities include volleyball, tennis, and fishing, as well as bird-watching excursions to the **Periteaşca-Leahova reserve**, just north, where 20,000 red-breasted geese (half the world population) spend the winter. Heading back onto the main DN22, the next village south of Jurilovca is **BAIA**, better known as **Hamangia**, site of Romania's most famous Neolithic finds.

Istria

Heading south from Babadag towards Mamaia, you'll pass through **ISTRIA**. Eight kilometres east of the village, on the shores of Lake Sinoe, is the **ruined Greek city of Histria** with its shattered temples to diverse deities. The ruins (Wed–Sun: July–Aug 8am–8pm, Sept–June 9am–5pm) cover a fairly small area, despite the fact that this was long the most important of the ancient Greek settlements along the coast. It was founded in 657 BC, though none of the remains date from earlier than 300 BC. Istria's decline began soon after that, but it was inhabited until early in the seventh century AD, when the port was smothered in silt and the town abandoned after attacks by Avar-Slavic tribes. There's a **museum** (same hours as the ruins) near the entrance to the site. Today, this strictly protected zone is one of Europe's best areas for bird-watching, with over 200 species making an appearance in the winter months. Near the ruins is a **campsite** with chalets (○); there's another site just south along the road to Năvodari at **NUNTAŞI**. Four maxitaxis a day run from Constanţa to Istria village; the Istria train stop is on the DN22, too far west to be of use.

The coast

Romania's **Black Sea coast** (the *litoral*) holds the promise of white beaches, dazzling water and an average of ten to twelve hours of sunshine a day between May and October. Under communism, one and a half million people flocked to the resorts during the season, but the number of visitors has since halved. Travelling from the Delta, your first stop on the coast will almost certainly be

Constanţa, a relaxed seaport-cum-riviera town, dotted with Turkish, Byzantine and Roman remains, which has always seemed to keep a discreet distance from the surrounding resorts.

Unless you're planning on staying in one of the five-star hotels in **Mamaia**, the region's hotspot, the best option is to take a **package tour** (see Basics, p.11), which guarantees you a room, minimizes extraneous hassles, and tends to work out cheaper than doing it independently. Otherwise, travel agencies in most towns on the coast offer rooms in bungalows or basic hotels. Though not as isolated as they once were, **Doi Mai** and the stylish **Vama Veche**, just a few miles from the Bulgarian border offer an escape from the crowds.

The Dobrogea and the Danube–Black Sea Canal

The overland approaches to Constanţa cross one part or another of the bleak northern **Dobrogea**, a poor area where donkeys still haul metal-wheeled carts. While there's no reason to break your journey here, the changes wrought over the last forty years certainly merit some explanation. Driving on the DN2A, you'll cross the Danube at **Giurgeni** and see orchards and fields planted on what used to be pestilential marshland; this transformation is nothing compared to the great works further to the south, starting at Cernavodă, where the rail line crosses the Danube on what was, at 4088m, Europe's longest bridge when it opened in 1895. A road bridge was added in 1987, linking the DN3A and the DN22C to provide the most direct road route to Constanţa, parallel to the rail line and the **Danube–Black Sea Canal**.

Cernavodă and the canal

CERNAVODĂ, whose name rather ominously translates as "Black Water", was chosen in the late 1970s to be the site of Romania's first nuclear power station (problems with welding have meant that only one of the five reactors has so far come into service) but it's more well known as the western entrance

---

The Canal of Death

Work on the **Danube–Black Sea Canal** started in 1949 when the Communist Party launched its "hero project", and soon writers like Petru Dumitriu (who made his name with a book on the canal, *Dustless Highway*) were waxing lyrical about the transformation of humble peasants into class-conscious proletarians through the camaraderie of the construction site. But, as Dumitriu acknowledged after his defection in 1960, the Canalul Mortii (Canal of Death), as it came to be known, claimed the lives of around 50,000 workers, the bulk of whom were there under duress – **forced labour** was permitted from 1950, with six-month sentences doled out without trial by the Ministry of the Interior. Those "convicted" included Uniate priests, peasants who resisted collectivization, and people caught trying to flee abroad.

In 1953, after years of untold suffering, it was realized that the chosen route through the Canara Hills towards Năvodari, north of Constanţa was impossible and the project was abandoned. Work on a new route resumed in 1973, this time with better conditions, and the canal was successfully pushed eastwards to join the sea at Agigea, south of Constanţa.

to the **Danube–Black Sea Canal**. Opened to shipping in 1984, the canal put Cernavodă a mere 60km from the Black Sea, offering obvious savings in fuel and time. However, realizing a profit on such a huge investment remains dependent on European economic revival and on the success of the Rhein–Main and Nürnberg–Regensburg canals. Charlemagne's vision of a 3000-kilometre-long waterway linking Rotterdam with the Black Sea finally came to fruition in 1993, although environmental protests in Bavaria and soaring costs had stalled the final stage of the project for ten years.

Along the canal

Most trains through the Dobrogea stop at the town of **MEDGIDIA** (the junction for Tulcea and Negru Vodă, the crossing-point to Bulgaria) on the canal, 24km east of Cernavodă, while slow trains also halt at the canal-side town of **BASARABI** and its eastern suburb of **MURFATLAR**, which gives its name to the surrounding wine-growing region. Three million bottles a year are produced here, seventy percent white, although the full fruity reds are more distinctive. Note that visits here are only possible on an organized tour.

Adamclisi and crossing into Bulgaria

Just north of the DN3 and the village of **ADAMCLISI** stands an arresting marble structure, a reconstruction of the **Tropaeum Traiani** (Tues–Sun 10am–6pm) that was erected here in 109 AD to celebrate Trajan's conquest of the Dacians, every facet reflecting unabashed militarism, not least the dedication to Mars Ultor. The trophy-statue – an armoured, faceless warrior – gazes over the plateau from a height of 30m. Carved around the side of its 32-metre base are 49 bas-reliefs or **metopes** portraying the Roman campaign. Each of the six groups of metopes comprises a marching scene, a battle, and a tableau representing victory over the enemy, an arrangement identical to the one that underlies scenes XXXVI–XLII of Trajan's Column in Rome a copy of which is in Bucharest's National History Museum (see p.69). Around the statue are **ruins** of buildings once inhabited by the legionary garrison or serving religious or funerary purposes. **Buses** run from Cernavodă and Medgidia (heading for Băneasa and Ostrov), and five daily maxitaxis from Constanţa stop here on their way to Oltina; it may also be possible to take a private tour from Constanţa or Mamaia (see p.372).

Into Bulgaria

Sixty kilometres west of Adamclisi along the DN3 is the small border town of **OSTROV**, where you can cross over to the Bulgarian town of **Silistra**. Although the **Vama Veche crossing** (see p.378) is more suitable if you're driving down the coast to Varna, it's also possible to enter Bulgaria from **NEGRU VODĂ** at the south end of the DN38, a crossing that's used by three local trains a day from Medgidia. All three crossings are open 24 hours a day; if you need a visa, make sure you get it either before leaving home or in Bucharest (see Listings, p.87). The duty-free shops at the borders accept dollars and euros only.

Constanţa

Most visitors first encounter the Black Sea coast at **CONSTANŢA**, a busy riviera town and Romania's principal port. Its ancient precursor, Tomis, was

Map labels:

Airport, Sat de Vacanță, ⓘ & ▲▲ Ⓐ   ▲ Mamaia & Ⓑ

Tulcea, Mamaia ▲

CONSTANȚA

BLACK SEA

Hospital

BULEVARD TOMIS

STRADA MIRCEA CEL BĂTRÂN

Beach

Ⓒ

Ⓓ

BULEVARD MAMAIA

STRADA MIHAI VITEAZU

STRADA TRASCAIETULUI (?)

Theatre

Ⓔ

TAROM

STR. MIRCEA CEL BĂTRÂN

Art Museum

Church of the Transfiguration

STRADA D. UICA

STRADA STEFAN CEL MARE

Market

Danubius

BULEVARD TOMIS

Geamia Hunchiar Mosque

STR. V. ALECSANDRI

Ⓖ

Ethnographic Museum

Ruins of Tomis

Tomis Harbour

ⓘ

BULEVARD FERDINAND

STRADA TRAIAN

Museum of the Romanian Navy

ALEEA V. CANARACHE

CFR

Tourist Port

Bucharest ◄

Archaeological Museum

PIAȚA-STRADA REMUS OPREANU

Roman Mosaic

Mahmudiye Mosque

Genoese Lighthouse ▲

Cathedral
Ion Jalea Collection

ⓘ

Casino

BCR

Mangalia ▲ Train Station ▲ & Ⓗ

ACCOMMODATION

Capri	C
Dali	D
Florentina	H
Guci	E
Casa Harghita	A
Intim	I
New Safari	G
Royal	B
Sport	F

0 _____ 500m

N

7

THE DELTA AND THE COAST | Constanța

---

supposedly founded by survivors of a battle with the Argonauts, following the capture of the Golden Fleece; centuries later, the great Latin poet Ovid was exiled here for nine years until his death in 17 AD. These days, the town is an attractive mix of Greco-Roman remains, Turkish mosques and crisp modern boulevards, home to several interesting **museums** and a lively restaurant scene. Since the collapse of COMECON and the imposition of sanctions on Yugoslavia in 1992, the economy has become more export-oriented and the port is booming once more.

Arrival and information

Constanța is served by **Mihail Kogălniceanu airport**, 25km northwest of town, from where it's a half-hour journey into the centre. The **train station** and *Autogară Sud*, the **bus station** serving destinations south of town, are 2km west of the centre; the train station has a 24-hour left-luggage service. Maxitaxis and private buses leave for the resorts (*stațiuni*) south of Constanța from a parking lot just south of the train station.

From the train station, take **trolley bus** #40 or #41 along Bulevardul Ferdinand to the centre, where both services swing north: #40 continues to the southern fringe of Mamaia, while #41 runs all the way through the resort.

Bus #32 takes a different route to Mamaia, passing the Autogară Nord, which serves destinations north along the coast, including Tulcea. Tickets, each good for two rides within Constanţa or one if you're going all the way to Mamaia, are available from most kiosks. Note that inspectors are especially vigilant here; the fine for riding without a ticket is 500,000 lei. If you're going to Mamaia, remember to cancel both ends of your ticket. General Taxi (☎0241/617 844) and Mondial Taxi (☎0241/693 333) are trustworthy **taxi** companies.

Constanţa's **tourist information** office, Info Litoral, is at Str. Traian 36, Bl. C1, Sc. C, Apt. 31 (Mon–Fri 9am–4pm; ☎0241/555 000, ⓦwww.infolitoral .ro); its friendly, English-speaking staff have good, free maps and can provide useful information on the Black Sea coast, book hotel accommodation and arrange excursions. From the station, it's two stops on a trolley bus; get off at Republica and turn right between the flats – the office is in a regular apartment block. For excursions outside the region, it's best to book through Mamaia's tourist information office (see p.372).

Accommodation

The number of **hotels** in Constanţa has grown as the port has flourished in recent years, though there are still only a few budget options. If you're looking for something less expensive, take bus #32 or tram #100 from the station towards Mamaia, and get off at the far end of Lake Tăbăcărie, where you'll find Constanţa's Sat de Vacanţă, a fairground with several pensions. Be warned that it can be very noisy and crowded here during the summer. Otherwise, locals with **private rooms** sometimes wait by the train station, holding signs reading *cazare*.

Capri Str. Mircea cel Bătrân 109 ☎0241/553 090, ⓔcapri_hotel@yahoo.com. Competent new establishment with indoor swimming pool and jacuzzi, a/c rooms and underground parking. Breakfast included. ❽

Casa Harghita Sat Vacanţă ☎0241/513 738. The best of the pensions in the fairground, the *Casa Harghita* also has a good restaurant. ❸

Dali Str. Smărdan 6A ☎0241/619 717, ⓦwww.hotel-dali.ro. New, four-star hotel with pastel façade and spacious, comfortable rooms, including some with a sea view. Well-run and often full. ❾

Florentina Str. I. C. Brătianu 24 ☎0241/512 535, ⓕ510 202. Turn left out of the train station, and left again when you reach Strada I. C. Brătianu. Excellent-value hotel 250m north of the railway station offering spacious, clean rooms, all with bath and refrigerator and hot water until midnight. ❷

Guci Str. Răscoala din 1907 no. 23 ☎0241/695 500, fax 638 426. Classy central hotel with first-

rate facilities – a/c rooms, sauna, jacuzzi, and a rooftop Mexican restaurant. ❾

Intim Str. N. Titulescu 9 ☎0241/617 814, fax 618 285, ⓔhotelintim@yahoo.com. An old hotel, with badly fading décor, on one of the most desolate streets in the old town, but retaining a feeling of tradition; this was once the *Hotel d'Angleterre*, where Eminescu stayed in 1882. ❺

New Safari Str. Karatzali 1 ☎0241/555 571. The best value place in the centre, this new, seven-room pension overlooking the harbour has comfortable, Mediterranean-style rooms. ❹

Royal B-dul Mamaia 191 ☎0241/542 690, ⓔoffice@hotelroyal.ro. North of town, on the road to Mamaia. One of the finest hotels in Constanţa; attractively furnished, with international papers on sale in the lobby. ❾

Sport Str. Cuza Vodă 2 ☎0241/617 558. All rooms in this clean and busy hotel have bathroom and cable TV. There's also a restaurant and bar; the terrace has a pleasant sea view but suffers from stultifying disco music. ❹

The Town

The oldest area of Constanţa, centred on **Piaţa Ovidiu**, stands on a headland between what is now the tourist port and the huge area of the modern docks to the south and west home to the excellent Archaeological and National

History Museum. Walking up the shore from the tourist port, you'll find Constanţa's passable **beach**, and to the north, beyond the remains of the walls of ancient Tomis, the modern **commercial area**, along boulevards Ferdinand and Tomis. Further north, nearing the resort of Mamaia, are various sights designed to appeal to children (but in fact, likely to frighten them), including a funfair and planetarium.

Around boulevards Ferdinand and Tomis

The pivotal point of the new town is the junction of **Bulevardul Ferdinand and Bulevardul Tomis**. Here, you'll find an archaeological park displaying sections of ancient walls, serried amphorae and other **ruins of Tomis**. Tomis was settled by Greeks from Miletus in the sixth century BC as an annex to Histria, which it later superseded before being incorporated within the Roman empire at the beginning of the Christian era. The most prominent remains are those of the defensive wall created in the third and fourth centuries and the Butchers' Tower, raised in the sixth century by Byzantine colonists who revived the city and renamed it Tomis to honour Constantine.

South of the archaeological park, Strada Traian overlooks the commercial *portul maritim*, and provides an appropriate setting for the **Museum of the Romanian Navy** at no. 53 (Tues–Sun 10am–6pm). Despite its name, the museum includes models of Greek triremes that sailed long before Romania existed, and photographs recording the unexpected visit of the battleship *Potemkin*, whose mutinous sailors disembarked at Constanţa in July 1905 and scattered. Little is said about the role of Romania's own navy during the last war, when it supported the occupation of Odessa and aided the Nazi fleet.

Back on Bulevardul Tomis, north of Bulevardul Ferdinand, the **Art Museum** at no. 84 (Wed–Sun: July & Aug 9am–8pm, Sept–June 9am–5pm) has some interesting canvases by Iosif Iser, Ştefan Dumitrescu and other painters of the Dobrogean landscape. Much of the top floor is devoted to the abstract artist Ion Gheorgiu; his paintings are less engaging than the collections of seashells, beetles and primitive icons decorating his *atelier*, which is preserved intact. South of here, at no. 32, the **Ethnographic Museum** (Wed–Sun: July & Aug 9am–7.30pm; Sept–June 9am–5pm) has a fine display of colourful Dobrogean rugs, pewter vessels and eighteenth- and nineteenth-century Lipovani and Greek icons. The museum stands almost opposite the **Geamia Hunchiar**, a small mosque built in 1869, surmounting a tangle of dingy coffee houses, kebab and pizza joints. Watch out for **thieves** here, typically idle teens who will ask you for the time – just keep walking, and you shouldn't have any problems. A couple of blocks east, at Str. Mircea cel Bătrân 36, is the **Church of the Transfiguration**, dating from 1865, when the Greek community finally got permission from the Ottoman rulers to build it.

Piaţa Ovidiu

At the southern end of Bulevardul Tomis, **Piaţa Ovidiu**, the central square of the old quarter, is dominated by a mournful statue of Ovid, exiled here from Rome by Emperor Augustus in 8 AD. Marooned in backwater Tomis, the poet spent his last years unsuccessfully petitioning emperors for his return, and composing his melancholy *Tristia*:

Rain cannot pit it, sunlight fails in burning
this snow. One drift succeeds another here.
The north wind hardens it, making it eternal;
it spreads in drifts through all the bitter year.

On the southern side of the square, Constanţa's **Archaeological and National History Museum** (Wed–Sun: July–Aug 9am–8pm, Sept–June 9am–5pm) has an excellent collection of statues of deities, including – in the first room on the left – the extraordinary **Glykon Serpent**, a unique creation about the size of a squatting toddler, with an antelope's head, human hair and eyes, and a gracefully coiled serpentine body ending in a lion's tail, which dates from the second or third century BC. Upstairs are mammoth tusks and menhirs, while the top floor is devoted to more recent history.

Outside the museum, a modern structure encloses extensive fragments of fine **Roman mosaic**, more than 600 metres squared, that was discovered 5m below street level in 1959; it may have once graced the upper hall of the Roman baths, whose outer walls can be seen from Aleea Canarache.

South of Piaţa Ovidiu

From **Piaţa Ovidiu**, it's a short walk south to the **Mahmudiye Mosque** (daily 9.30am–5.30pm; closed Fri), whose fifty-metre-high minaret spikes the skyline and offers a great **view** of the town and harbour. Built in 1910, it's the seat of the Mufti, the spiritual head of Romania's 55,000 Muslims (Turks and Tatars by origin), who live along the coast of the Dobrogea. South from the mosque along Strada Muzeelor is the fancy **Orthodox Cathedral** of St Peter and St Paul, an early (1884) neo-Byzantine design by Ion Mincu and, at the street's end, opposite more ruins of ancient Tomis, the **Ion Jalea collection of sculptures** (Wed–Sun: July–Aug 10am–6pm, Sept–June 9am–5pm), an assortment of conventional and academic sculptures.

On the **waterfront**, the former **Casino** stands on a jutting promenade. Originally erected as a pavilion for Queen Elisabeta (Carmen Sylva) in 1904, it is now a restaurant. During a visit in 1914 by the Russian Imperial family, it was the venue for a disastrous gala performance that ended in smashed scenery and broken limbs; the Russians sailed away less than a day later, Grand Duchess Olga having refused the proposed marriage to Prince Carol, and thus sealing her fate at the hands of the Bolsheviks three years later. Just beyond, you can see the so-called **Genoese Lighthouse**, erected in 1860 in memory of the thirteenth- and fourteenth-century mariners who tried to revive the port.

The beach and Lake Tăbăcăriei

Visitors with children or a low tolerance for provincial museums often head straight for the **beach** behind the art museum, spread beneath a terraced cliff north of the *port turistic*, or the park at **Lake Tăbăcăriei**, between Constanţa and Mamaia: from the train station, trolley buses #40 and #41 run along Bulevardul Mamaia, to the east of the park, while bus #32 and tram #100 head up Bulevardul Alexandru Lapuşneanu to the **fairground** (Sat de Vacanţă) on the west side of the lake. Buses #40 and #41 pass a more than usually depressing dolphinarium and a **planetarium** (daily: July–Aug 9am–8pm, Sept–June 9am–4pm) at the southeastern corner of the park. From the nearby Tăbăcăriei Wharf, a **miniature train** carries children around the lake, which due to algal bloom has taken on a toxic-looking hue of green. On the other side, the Sat de Vacanţă is a lively holiday area where vendors hawk sausages and other fried perishables. Just to the north, at the entrance to Mamaia, is the noisy **Luna Park** (Parc Distracţii), with various decrepit rides and games. There's a bowling alley here, and an **ice-skating** rink on the edge of the Pioneers' Park.

Eating, drinking and entertainment

The number of worthwhile **restaurants** in Constanţa continues to grow; you'll find variety enough here to rival any Romanian city outside of Bucharest. In addition, several energetic **bars** along Bulevardul Tomis, have buoyed up the drinking scene. The town's **theatre**, at Str. Mircea cel Bătrân 97, puts on plays and music events; buy tickets at the agency at B-dul Tomis 97.

Restaurants

Casa Ana B-dul Tomis 17. The best restaurant in the area, this smart establishment in the old town has a very good meat-based menu and a pleasant ambience of jazz and rock. Daily 10am–10pm.

China Restaurant Str. Zorelelor 67. Excellent Chinese-run place with an extensive menu, also offering free delivery. Daily noon–10pm.

Guci On the top floor of the *Guci* hotel, Str. Răscoalei din 1907 no. 23 (℡0241/695 500). This little-known Romanian/Mexican restaurant is a delight; exemplary food and service. Daily 10am–1am.

Irish Pub Str. Ştefan cel Mare 1. Upscale pub serving Irish beers and expertly prepared meals. Fine terrace with lovely views across the port makes this an ideal early-evening drinking venue. Open 11am–1pm.

La Arcade Str. Ecaterina Varga 17. Simple but pleasant Romanian restaurant two blocks south of the art museum. Daily 9am–11pm.

La Pizza Str. Răscoalei din 1907 no. 15. Central branch of popular local chain. Decent pizza, pasta and espresso; excellent gelato. Daily 9am–11pm.

Lokanta Unmarked Turkish restaurant attached to the bus station. Good *pide*, *lahmacun* and kebabs; all the Istanbul bus drivers eat here. Open 24hr.

Marco Polo Str. Mircea cel Bătrân 103 ℡0722/230 976. The best of Constanţa's myriad pizzerias. Also does fine pasta and salads. Daily 10am–1.30am.

New West B-dul Tomis 78. Pricey Lebanese-owned establishment with *hookahs* and fine Middle Eastern food. Daily 8am–midnight.

New Safari Str. Karatzali 1. Seafood restaurant perched on a cliff over the beach. The view from the terrace is the best in Constanţa, and the food is almost as good. Daily 8am–midnight.

On Plonge Tomis harbour. Lovely harbour restaurant primarily serving up fish dishes; atmospheric terrace makes this an enjoyable place to dine. Usually crowded, and better than the nearby *Le Gavroche*. Daily 10am–1am.

Terasa Colonadelor Str. Traian 57. Beer garden serving up grilled sausages, as well as more adventurous dishes such as brain and testicles. Daily 9am–midnight.

Taverna El Greco Str. Decebal 18. Expensive establishment serving fine Greek cuisine. Daily noon–midnight.

Bars, Pubs and Clubs

Bourbon House Str. Puşkin 36. Not far from the intersection of Boulevards Tomis and Mamaia. Sophisticated bar with a long list of cocktails; music is a mix of house and R&B. The garden out back is ideal for an afternoon drink.

Cazino B-dul Elisabeta 2. Old-style communist set-up with a great view over the Black Sea from the terrace and a pool table in the bar.

City Flowers Café B-dul Tomis 55. American-style coffeehouse above a flower shop; slightly frumpy, but a welcome addition to the Constanţa café scene. Good coffee and several dozen teas.

Deep Club B-dul Tomis 129. Dark, recently refurbished cellar bar. Very popular.

Impala B-dul Tomis 122. Outdoor bar and dance club for the socially ambitious.

La Taclale B-dul Tomis 57. Unpretentious café/bar popular with artsy types. A good place to meet young English-speaking Romanians.

New Orleans B-dul Mamaia (at Str. Siretului). Massive, four-level disco with lots of fluorescent lights.

Listings

Air tickets TAROM is at Str. Ştefan cel Mare 15 (Mon–Fri 8am–6pm, Sat 9am–1pm; ℡ & ℡ 041/614 066). The branch of Danubius at Piaţa Ovidiu 11 (℡0241/619 039, ℡ticketing@danubius.ro) sells tickets for most major airlines.

Buses Özlem Tur (☎0241/662 626) runs the overnight bus to Istanbul, departing daily at 3pm; its office is behind the bus station.
Car rental Avis c/o TAROM ☎0241/616 733; Hertz c/o Paradis, B-dul Tomis 65, ☎0241/552 858, ⓔparadis@rdsct.ro; Budget c/o Latina, B-dul Ferdinand 71, ☎0241/639 713, ⓔlatina@latina.ro.
Consulates Turkey, B-dul Ferdinand 82 (Mon–Fri 9am–noon; ☎0241/611 135).
Internet access Planet Games, at the intersection of Strada Ştefan cel Mare and Strada Răscoalei din 1907, is open 24hr.
Market Str. Răscoalei din 1907, one block north of Bulevardul Ferdinand.
Pharmacy Europa, at Str. Ecaterina Varga 55, is open 24hr, as is Dumifarm, opposite the *McDonald's* on Strada Ştefan cel Mare.
Post office B-dul Tomis 79 (Mon–Fri 7am–7pm, Sat 7am–1pm).

Shopping Strada Ştefan cel Mare is the main shopping street – especially the pedestrianized stretch from Strada Răscoalei din 1907 to Strada Duca – with the Tomis Mall (Mon–Sat 9am–9pm, Sun 9am–6pm) opposite the Eminescu bookshop. The supermarket in the basement (same hours as the mall) is the best in the centre. Anticuariat, at Str. Mircea cel Bătrân 4 has used books in English and French. There is a 24hr supermarket at B-dul Tomis 55, and a Kodak photographic shop on Str. Ştefan cel Mare.
Train tickets The CFR office is at Str. Vasile Canarache 4 (☎0241/614 960; Mon–Fri 7am–7pm, Sat 7am–1pm), overlooking the new port. You need to book several days in advance in summer.
Travel agents Danubius, B-dul Ferdinand 36, ☎0240/615 838, ⓦwww.danubius.ro; Latina, B-dul Ferdinand 71, ☎0241/639 713, ⓔlatina@latina.ro; Simpa Turism, Str. Răscoala din 1907 no. 9, ☎0241/660 468, ⓦwww.simpaturism.ro.

Mamaia

MAMAIA, 6km north of Constanţa, is Romania's best-known coastal resort, and the place where the majority of package tourists end up. Legend has it that the gods created the **beach** to reunite a kidnapped princess with her daughter, who was abandoned on the seashore wailing "Mamaia, Mamaia!"; its fine, almost white sand, fringed with wild pear trees is the resort's greatest asset, especially since its gentle gradient and the absence of currents and strong tides make it particularly safe for children.

Arrival, information and accommodation

In summer, **trolley buses** #32 and #41 run from Constanţa's train station to the far end of Mamaia; out of season, you'll have to change from the #40 to the #47 at the Pescarie terminal, one stop south of the beginning of the resort. If you arrive without a room reservation, the Litoral SA **tourist office** (May–Sept daily 8am–9pm, Oct–April Mon–Fri 9am–5pm; ☎ & ⓕ0241/831 517), in the middle of the resort, is your best bet. The staff may also be able to arrange day-trips to the Danube Delta or Transylvania from €30, and half-day excursions to Histria, Adamclisi or the Murfatlar vineyards, starting at €15. Mamaia's **shopping centre**, where you'll find a small supermarket, a **post office** and a **pharmacy** (9am–9pm), is just south of the *Best Western Savoy*. There are 24hr **Internet** cafés in the *Hotel Parc*, at the southern end of the resort, and on the promenade near the **casino**.

Accommodation

Most of Mamaia's seventy-odd **hotels** (all but a handful of which are ageing concrete-block structures) are within 100m of the beach. With the exception of the *Best Western Savoy*, all of the four- and five-star hotels listed below are clustered together, several hundred metres north of the casino. At the far end of the resort is a very basic **campsite**, the *Turist*; from here, it's about 5km straight up the road (or take bus #23) to the equally crowded *Hanul Piraţilor* site.

Albatros ☎ 0241/831 381, ✉ office@albatross.ro. Reliable three-star hotel just north of the casino. ⑧

Best Western Savoy ☎ 0241/831 426, ⓦ www.savoyhotel.ro. A refurbished communist-era block at the northern end of Mamaia; with competent staff and a long list of amenities. ⑨

Club Scandinavia ☎ 0241/607 000, ⓦ www.clubscandinavia.ro. Directly opposite the *Rex* on the shore of Lake Siutghiol, the perfectly sleek and modern *Club Scandinavia* has been the pride of Romania's tourist establishment since opening its doors in June 2002; its first-class facilities include outdoor pool, tennis court, conference room and fitness suite. ⑨

Condor ☎ 0241/831 142, ⨍ 831 758. Three-star hotel in the centre of Mamaia offering rooms with bath and cable TV. ⑦

Delfin ☎ 0241/831 640. Basic place near the south end of the resort, opposite the entrance to Constanţa's Luna Park. ④

Flora ☎ 0241/831 059, ⨍ 831 887. Several hundred metres north of the *Delfin*, the *Flora* is a standout for the price and has a good restaurant serving traditional Romanian food. ⑥

Iaki ☎ 0241/831 025, ⓦ www.iaki.ro. A renovated 1960s construction, *Iaki* boasts indoor and outdoor pools and an excellent spa and gerontology clinic. International newspapers are available in the lobby. ⑨

Majestic ☎ & ⨍ 0241/831 981. Four-star hotel popular with German tour groups and featuring an outdoor pool and, out back, a small menagerie with rabbits and peacocks. ⑧

Mamaia ☎ 0241/831 100, ✉ mamaia@cta.ro. Small, sophisticated five-star hotel north of the casino. ⑨

Midia ☎ 0241/831 940. Mamaia's best budget hotel, the *Midia* has friendly staff and small but decent rooms without television. ②

Palm Beach ☎ 0241/607 900, ⨍ 607 909. The seventy-room *Palm Beach* is the largest and most welcoming of Mamaia's five-star hotels. ⑨

Rex ☎ 0241/831 595, ⨍ 0241/831 690. A stately pile built in 1936, the *Rex* is Mamaia's oldest and grandest hotel, the only one to achieve anything like grandeur. ⑨

Town

As late as the 1930s, Constanţa was, in the words of author Gregor von Rezzori, "an empty expanse, excepting two or three bathing huts and a wooden pier, of miles of golden sand and tiny pink shells"; a far cry from what you'll find here today. Ranged along a narrow spit of land between the Black Sea and Lake Siutghiol, the resort's main street curves away around the shore of the lake – the southern stretch of beachfront promenade is dominated by unappealing fast food stands and buffets, but beyond the casino, the resort is more peaceful and the hotels better.

Eating, drinking and entertainment

Though not on the same scale as Constanţa's cuisine, there are some good **restaurants** in Mamaia, especially those in the *Rex*, *Mamaia*, *Junona* and *Palm Beach* hotels, and the *Aquarium* (☎0241/831 868), an upscale seafood place near the *Flora* hotel whose menu features swordfish, sturgeon and Portugese carp. Unfortunately, dining in Mamaia is inevitably accompanied by blaring pop music. The best Italian food is in *La Fattoria* (☎0241/831 010), next to the *Majestic*. *Scapino*, on the promenade near the *Albatros*, is also good for pizza and pasta, while the nearby *China Restaurant* is the best of Mamaia's three Chinese establishments. There's also a summer-only Lebanese restaurant in the *Club Scandinavia*.

The best places to go for **dancing** and house music are the pricey *Motor Club*, next to the *Tomis* hotel, or *Club XXL*, near the casino; both are open late. Otherwise, there are downmarket outdoor **discos** in hotels such as the *Perla*, *Select* and *Delta*. Top **bars** include *Febaria*, adjacent to the *Club Scandinavia* hotel, and the *Note Beach Club*, on the beach just south of the casino. Alternatives consist of glitzy cabaret most nights at the *Melody* near the casino, or the Nunta la Romani (Wedding in Romania) folklore show at the *Majestic*.

Mamaia has ample **sporting facilities**, including waterskiing (€60 per hour), jet-skiing (€40), kayaking (€3) and surfing (€3). The finest equipment and facilities (and the highest prices) are at the *Nautica Blue Club*, attached to the *Club Scandinavia* hotel, but most package tours include all activities and equipment. Easily the best place in Mamaia to take **children** to is the gleaming new Aqua Magic waterpark (May–Sept 8am–8pm; €6 adults, €3 children, half price after 4pm), near the southern end of Mamaia.

Around Mamaia

From Mamaia, regular motorboat trips (departing hourly 10am–2pm; €3) run from the pier opposite the *Condor* hotel to **Ovid's Island** – where there's a suitably rustic restaurant, the *Insula Ovidiu* – at the northern end of **Lake Siutghiol**. Also known as Lake Mamaia, it was formed when a river's outlet silted up, and for many centuries it was a watering hole for herds of sheep and cows brought down from the Carpathians – hence, the name Siutghiol, meaning "Lake of Milk" in Turkish.

Buses #22 and #23 run to Năvodari, a beach town tarnished by a reeking petrochemical complex, beyond which a minor road heads north past Lake Nuntaşi and its **campsite** to the Greek ruins at Histria (see p.364).

Agigea to Vama Veche

Just south of Constanţa, the road and rail line cross the Danube–Black Sea Canal where it meets the coast at the **Agigea** port complex. Beyond this, the array of resorts extending to **Mangalia** is another facet of Romania's development over the last quarter century – modern complexes created where only scrubland or run-down villages existed before. Except for the fact that most are situated along a cliff top overlooking the beach, they are fairly similar to their prototype, Mamaia, to the north. The exceptions are **Mangalia**, which is not dependent on tourism and is thus more alive in the off season, and **Doi Mai** and **Vama Veche**, neither of which saw any development until after the fall of communism. From Constanţa, the resorts down to Mangalia are best reached by **maxitaxis** and **private buses**; these leave several times per hour, from early morning to around 8pm, from a spot 100m to the right of the railway station as you exit. For Doi Mai and Vama Veche, you'll have to change at Mangalia.

Eforie Nord, Eforie Sud and Lake Techirghiol

Trains, private buses, maxitaxis and buses #10, #11 and #12 run 14km south from Constanţa to **EFORIE NORD**. Founded in 1899 by Bucharest's Eforia hospital as a spa for convalescent patients, Eforie Nord extends along a cliff top above the rather narrow beach. The resort is, however, best known for the therapeutic **black mud** scooped from the shores of **Lake Techirghiol**, whose mineral-saturated waters gave the lake its name, derived from *tekir*, Turkish for "salt" or "bitter". **Baths** by the lake (a few minutes' walk south of the train station) specialize in treating rheumatic disorders and the after-effects of polio; while on the lake's single-sex nudist beaches, people plaster themselves with mud, wait until it cracks (happily exposing themselves to passing trains), and then jostle good humouredly beneath the showers.

The resort itself comprises two parallel streets, Bulevardul Tudor Vladimirescu, running along the cliff top, and Bulevardul Republicii, where you'll find the bus stops, shops and offices. As a spa, Eforie Nord has some fine **hotels** that are more likely to be open out of season than elsewhere, the *Europa* at B-dul. Republicii 13 (☎0241/741 710, ⓦwww.anahospitality.ro; ⑨), a towering, steel blue four-star hotel designed by two of Romania's best-known architects; its amenities include a swimming pool and one of the top spas in the country. Closer to the beach at B-dul. Tudor Vladimirescu 9 is the *Astoria* (☎0241/742 475, ⓦwww.anahospitality.ro; ⑨), a smaller and more compact facility under the same management as *Europa*. Tennis and bowling here cost €6 and €10 per hour respectively; guests at either hotel have access to a private section of the beach. *Decebal* (☎0241/ 742 977; ③), adjacent to the train station and run by Romanian Railways, is unfriendly but good value and open year-round, and offers twin rooms with hot water and TV. A popular budget choice is the *Cristal* (☎0241/742 828; ②), next to the bus stop. If you can't find a place to stay, Dispecerat Cazare at Str. Brizei 6 (☎0241/741 351), near the *Hermes* hotel, may be able to find you a vacancy.

The nicer of the resort's two **campsites** is the *Meduza*, just inland at the northern end of Bulevardul Vladimirescu. There are plenty of **restaurants** in Eforie Nord, including a mass of self-service places in the centre, near the bus stop. **For a drink**, walk north from the bus stop until you see *333*, a friendly Guinness-themed pub that also has good espresso.

From Eforie Nord, it's a pleasant two-kilometre trip around the lake to **TECHIRGHIOL** (terminus of bus #11), where you can stay at the *Baze de Tratament* at Str. Ovidiu 4 (☎0241/735 61; ②), a clean and friendly spa run by the Romanian Orthodox Church. Bizarrely, there's a wooden village church (moved here from Transylvania in 1951) in front of the spa.

Compared to its northern neighbour, **EFORIE SUD** can seem like a ghost town – most of the hotels are run-down or closed, and the quiet, tree-lined streets of the residential quarter are pleasantly dilapidated, but the beach itself is better than that in Eforie Nord. The best hotel here is the three-star *Edmond* (☎0241/748 522, ⓔcosy012003@yahoo.com; ⑤), a new establishment with sauna and jacuzzi 50m from the beach and just south of the centre of town at Str. Dezrobirii 24.

South to Mangalia

The resorts between Tuzla, 3km south of Eforie Sud, and Mangalia are best reached by maxitaxi and private bus, which drop you off on the main highway outside the resorts. Separate maxitaxis shuttle amongst the resorts themselves (between Neptun and Saturn), stopping wherever you flag them down. Express trains slow to a crawl between Constanța and Mangalia, taking an hour to cover 43km; from mid-June to mid-September extra services are laid on, providing an almost continuous service along the coast, with reservations required only west of Constanța.

Costinești

The 8km of beach immediately north of Mangalia is lined with the modern hotels that have grown up in the last three decades. The stretch of cliffs to their north is broken only by the former fishing village of **COSTINEȘTI**, now the site of Romania's principal International Youth Camp, with a fine sandy **beach** sheltered to the north by Cape Tuzla. There are several **hotels** here, including the new *Amiral Nord* (℡0241/734 944; ❺), next to the train station. Additionally, most of the villagers let their spare rooms during the summer; quality and prices (❶–❸) vary. Costineşti's premier restaurant is *Albert*, an excellent pizzeria at the north end of the lake. An **independent film festival** is held at the end of August – films are shown in Romanian with English subtitles.

Neptun and Olimp

Eight kilometres further south is **NEPTUN**, the most desirable of the Black Sea resorts. Fast trains stop only at the *halta* by the *Hotel Doina*, and resorts to the south are best reached by maxitaxis, which enter the resorts proper; if arriving from, or travelling to, Constanţa, note that it's a walk of nearly 3km from Neptun to the highway road. Neptun was built in 1960 between the Comorova forest and the sea, ensuring a lush setting for the artificial lakes and dispersed villas and the shopping centres, discos, sports facilities and hotels here are a cut above the Romanian average, as they are in the satellite resort of **OLIMP**, just north. Originally enclaves for the communist *nomenklatura*, today Neptun and Olimp are patronized by moderately well-to-do Romanian families and some Western tourists.

Most rooms are still assigned to those on package tours, however, so if you're hoping to find **accommodation** in high season it may be best to go through Rainbow Travel (℡0241/701 300, ✉anatravel@xnet.ro; 10am–10pm May–June and Sept, 24hr July–Aug), which is affiliated with many of the hotels; it's opposite Neptun's *Hotel Decebal*. The best hotels in Neptun-Olimp are the recently renovated *Majestic*, in the centre of Olimp (℡0241/701 030); the *Cocor*, in a secluded spot at the southern edge of Olimp (℡0241/701 042); the *Albert* (℡0241/731 514), which has a terrific restaurant, near the bottom of Neptun; and, on the northern fringe of Neptun, the *Doina* (℡0241/701 012, 🅕701 112), which is open from March to November thanks to its treatment centre. The **campsites** at the north and south ends of the resort, *Camping Olimp* and *Holiday Village Neptun*, each with bungalows (❷), are well above average. Eating out, try the chic but reasonably priced *Mediterraneo* **restaurant** (open year-round) in the centre of Neptun, or for Romanian cuisine *Calul Bălan*, further south. *Insula*, on the lake behind the *Neptun* hotel, specializes in fish. The swinging **discos** are *Why Not* and *Paparazzi*, in Neptun and Olimp respectively. For family entertainment, try the nightly folklore show at the *Rustic* restaurant in Neptun. The resort also has a **post office**, opposite the Commercial Complex.

Jupiter, Aurora, Venus and Saturn

The four resorts to the south of Neptun are more uniform, less lively and likely to have fewer hotels open outside July and August. The first resort, immediately abutting Neptun, is **JUPITER**, which rubs shoulders with the forest and has a gently sloping beach with fine sand. Centred on artificial Lake Tismana, this resort draws a younger crowd than most of the others, many of whom stay at the vast *Zodiac* **campsite** at the north end of the resort. Easily the best place to stay is *Sat Vacanta Liliacul*, a comfortable, new three-star bungalow complex in Jupiter's centre (℡0241/731 169, 🅕732 022; ❼). The cheaper *Violeta* (℡0241/713 115; ❸) is lively and well run. *Four Seasons* is the standout **restaurant**, while nightlife focuses on *Captain Mondy's*, which recently won an award for best **club** south of Constanţa; bartenders pour drinks in the flamboyant style of Tom Cruise á la *Cocktail*.

Imagine Mayan architects called upon to design Palm Beach and you'll get some idea of the pyramidal complexes that are the most striking feature of **AURORA**, the most recent resort, set on the cape of the same name southeast of Jupiter. Small and elegantly designed compared to the other resorts, Aurora has ten **hotels**, all two stars, save the three-star *California* (T0241/731 293, Wwww.californiahotel.panda.ro; ④). The *Cristal* (T0241/731 353) and *Topaz* (T0241/731 292) both have a few cheaper rooms (③) with shared showers.

There's a barely perceptible gap before you hit **VENUS** – broadly similar to Jupiter, but quieter and more family oriented. There are two excellent four-star hotels here, the hundred-room *Carmen* (T0241/731 608, Wwww.hotelcarmen.ro; ⑨), which has an indoor pool and is open all year, and the *Euro Orlando* (T0241/731 605, Wwww.orlando.ro; ⑧), open May–Sept. The *Dana* (T0241/731 638, F731 465; ⑥), Venus's sole three-star hotel, has a lovely terrace bar in the garden, while good two-star places include the *Felicia*, which has a pool and is sited right by the sea (T0241/731 607; ⑤), and the *Silvia* (T0241/731 188; ④), which is livelier and attracts a younger crowd. There's a **campsite at** the south end. *Calipso* is the best of the resort's **discos**. CFR shares its premises with the **post office** at the western end of the resort; to the south are a sulphurous **spa** and, just inland, stables where you can **hire horses** to explore the forest, inhabited by roe deer, grouse and pheasants.

A reed-fringed lake lies between Venus and **SATURN**, a high-rise resort with lots of low-rent, state-owned **hotels** – booked through the accommodation office (T0241/752 452, Wwww.saturnsa.ro).

Mangalia and beyond

The modern suburbs of **MANGALIA** are close to swallowing up Saturn, and in fact Mangalia's train station is nearer to Saturn than to the centre of town. As with Constanţa, Mangalia's appearance of modernity belies its ancient origin – the Greeks founded their city of Callatis here during the sixth century BC, when population pressure impelled them to colonize the Black Sea coast.

Heading south from the **train station** and turning left at the first roundabout, you'll reach the *Mangalia* hotel (T0241/752 052, Emangalia.turism@radiotel.ro; ⑥), a decent enough place with spa, disco and casino. Behind, in Parc Stadionului, are the **ruins of Callatis**, which include sarcophagi and the vestiges of a Christian basilica, and beyond, at Şos. Constanţei 19, is the dull **Archaeological Museum** (June–Sept daily 8am–8pm; Oct–May Tues–Sun 9am–5pm). Just south of the small town centre, on Strada Oituz, stands the **Sultan Esmahan Mosque**, built in 1590 and surrounded by a Muslim graveyard.

At Str. Teilor 6, just south in the town centre, rises the *Hotel President* (T0241/755 861, Wwww.hpresident.com; ⑧), which relies more on business conferences than bikinis and is easily the best **place to stay**, with all the faci-lities you'd expect of a four-star hotel, including gym, sauna and beauty centre. The *President* was built atop the southern boundary of ancient Callatis, and the extensive ruins that were uncovered during the hotel's construction in 1993–94 have been preserved elegantly underneath the hotel. Towards the harbour, there are three near-identical hotels to choose from (all ⑤) along Strada Teilor: the *Zenit* (T0241/751 645), *Astra* (T0241/751 673) and *Orion* (T0241/751 156). The one budget option is the modest *Pensiunea Oituz* (T0241/753 980; ②), west of the *President* at Str. Oituz 11. Mangalia's **campsite** is north of town – from the train station, turn left, then right after five minutes at the *Saturn* sign. The Constanţa County Antrec representative is located in Mangalia, at Str. George Murnu 13 bl. D sc. B ap. 21 (☎0241/759 473, Ⓔconstanta@antrec.ro), and can help you find **homestay accommodation** in Mangalia, Agigia and Eforie Sud. The best **restaurants** are the one in the *President* hotel (overlooking the hotel's archaeological site) and the *Café del Mar*, just across the street from the *President*, which has an ambitious menu and is open 24hr in the summer. The *Peach-Pit* patisserie, on Şos. Constanţei, is a cracking little place for a quick bite or to stock up on pastries.

Doi Mai and Vama Veche

The laid-back villages of Doi Mai and Vama Veche, traditionally the haunts of artists, intellectuals and non-conformists, lie near the border with Bulgaria, about 10km south along the coast from Mangalia. Though neither had a hotel until as recently as a couple of years ago, tourist facilities in both villages have grown rapidly since. Fortunately, the new developments have been planned with consideration for their surroundings and are on a reasonably modest scale. Doi Mai, in spite of its beach lying in the shadow of Mangalia's bright-yellow Daewoo container cranes, is peaceful and relaxed, and popular with families; Vama Veche has a better beach and, since its discovery by Bucharest cognoscenti, has acquired an air of bohemian sophistication not to be found elsewhere on the coast. The pace of change, however, is steady, and traditional donkey carts are unlikely to outnumber imported cars for much longer – the sooner you come, the better. Maxitaxis shuttle from Mangalia to the Bulgarian border every twenty minutes or so during the summer; out of season, bus #14 runs to both roughly every ninety minutes. There are no ATMs in either village, so bring what money you'll need with you.

Coming from Mangalia, you'll be dropped off at the intersection of Şoseaua Principala and Strada Scolii, **DOI MAI**'s two main streets. *Casa Margo* (☎0241/732 939; ❸), just up Şoseaua Principala, is a clean **pension** offering fourteen rooms with bath, television and refrigerator. *Casa Vizante*, closer to the beach at Str. Falezei 8 (☎0722/805 125; ❸) is smaller and quieter but equally comfortable. The *Hellios Inn*, a Greek-owned establishment on Strada Scolii (☎0241/619 744, Ⓦwww.hellios-inn.ro; ❸), has simple but attractive rooms, including some triples. There's an outdoor swimming pool here, as well as a pleasant courtyard and a rustic restaurant. It's also possible to find **private rooms** (❶–❷); look for signs reading *cazare*. There are several good seafood **restaurants** in Doi Mai, the best of which is *La Dinamo*, on the main street. Just north of the maxitaxi stop is the *Incognito* **disco**, which has **Internet** access. The Doi Mai–Vama Veche **Marine Reserve** begins just south of the Mangalia port and extends to the border. Loggerhead turtles can be seen here, as well as sea horses and three species of dolphin. **Diving** trips can be arranged through the staff at the *Hellios Inn*.

Under communism, **VAMA VECHE**, just short of the border with Bulgaria, was closed to all but staff of Cluj University or those who could claim some vague affiliation with it; it became a haven for non-conformists looking for an escape from the surveillance of the Securitate. In recent years, locals and investors have begun to capitalize on Vama Veche's counterculture reputation, and there's now an attractive assortment of **accommodation** on offer, ranging from three-star hotels and pensions to camping wild on the beach. There are still, however, plenty of chickens and sheep wandering about, and the Save Vama Veche organization (Ⓦwww.savevamaveche.home.ro) has thus far succeeded in keeping the ravages of mass tourism at an arm's length.

The finest **hotel** in Vama Veche is *Ca'Bianca* (☎0721/820 122, Ⓦwww.cabianca .rdsct.ro; ❻), while the nearby *Dini* (☎0744/553 672; ❺) and *Golden Sea*

(☎0722/215 827) are almost as good. Cheaper options include *Vila Madi* (☎0723/452 091; ❸), which has clean rooms without bath, *Lyana* (☎0744/671 213; ❸) and the Turkish-owned *Subacuatic* (☎0723/164 917; ❹). *Camping Vama Veche* (☎0745/629 157) has a ten-room motel (❸), bungalows (❷) and pitches. Bibi Vama Veche (May–Sept 8am–10pm, ☎0241/743 870, ⓦwww.vama -veche.com), a private **tourist office** in the centre of town, can help if you can't find a place to stay. **Camping** wild is easiest south of the main part of the beach.

Most of the hotels and pensions have **restaurants**. The one in the *Lyana* is especially recommended for its fish, while *Bibi Bistro* is cheaper but also quite good. Otherwise, try *La Frontier*, for decent pizza, or the kebab and baklava stand in front of the *Subacuatic* hotel. The small Bibi Market in the centre of town stocks just enough provisions for a beachfront picnic; there is also a book-stall with a few English classics next to the beach. Vama Veche's **nightlife** is without equal on the coast. The Mexican-themed *Club Zapata*, an outdoor disco with dance floor under a giant sombrero, is open until dawn, and some of the restaurants, especially the *Bibi Bistro* often have live music. Annual **events** include the BB Jazz and Blues Festival, held in the last week in August and featuring mostly Romanian jazz bands; and (usually a week earlier) Stufstock (ⓦwww.stufstock.ro), a music festival put on by Save Vama Veche.

Travel details

Trains

Constanţa to: Braşov (2–4 daily; 4hr 45min, summer 6hr 15min); Bucharest (8–18 daily; 2hr 15min–4hr 45min); Galaţi (2 daily; 3hr 50min–6hr); Mangalia (5–21 daily; 1hr–1hr 25min); Medgidia (15–21 daily; 24–55min); Suceava (1 daily; 8hr); Tulcea (1 daily; 4hr–4hr 30min).
Medgidia to: Babadag (5 daily; 1hr 50min–2hr 30min); Bucharest (10–11 daily; 2hr 15min–4hr); Mangalia (4–8 daily; 1hr 50min–2hr 30min, summer 1hr 45min); Negru Vodă (4 daily; 1hr 15min–1hr 25min); Tulcea (5 daily; 2hr 45min–3hr 15min).
Tulcea to: Bucharest (1–2 daily; 5hr 15min–6hr 50min); Constanţa (2 daily; 4hr–4hr 30min); Medgidia (4–5 daily; 2hr 45min–3hr 15min).

Buses and maxitaxis

Constanţa to: Brăila (3 daily); Braşov (1 daily); Bucharest (hourly); Costineşti (every 30min); Galaţi (10 daily); Hârşova (4 daily); Istria (4 daily); Mangalia (every 20min); Oltina (for Adamclisi, 5 daily); Suceava (2 daily); Techirghiol (every 20 min); Tulcea (every 30min).

Mangalia to: Doi Mai and Vama Veche (May–August every 20min, Sept–April every 90min).
Tulcea to: Brăila (6 daily); Bucharest (8 daily); Constanţa (every 30min); Enisala (2 daily); Focşani (1 daily); Galaţi (10 daily); Iaşi (1 daily); Jurilovca (2 daily); Mahmudia (3 daily); Murighiol (7 daily); Niculiţel (3 daily).

Ferries

Tulcea to: Periprava (4 weekly; 5hr 30min); Sf. Gheorghe (4 weekly; 3hr 30min); Sulina (5 weekly; 3hr 30min).

Hydrofoils

Tulcea to: Sulina (daily, 1hr 30min).

International trains

Constanţa to: Budapest, Hungary (1 daily; 16hr).

International buses

Constanţa to: Athens, Greece (Tues, Thurs & Sat, 1 daily); Chişinău, Moldova (Thurs & Sat, 1 daily); Istanbul, Turkey (1 daily).
Tulcea to: Istanbul (1 daily).

Contexts

Contexts

The historical framework

Although inhabited since prehistoric times, Romania only achieved statehood in the nineteenth century, and Transylvania, one third of its present territory, was acquired as recently as 1920. Hence, much of Romania's history is that of its disparate parts – Dobrogea, the Banat, Bessarabia, Maramureş and, above all, the principalities of Moldavia, Wallachia and Transylvania.

Greeks, Dacians and Romans

Despite the discovery of bones, weapons and implements within Carpathian caves, very little is known about the nomadic hunter-gatherers of the early **Stone Age**. With the retreat of the glaciers, humans seem to have established their first settlements in Dobrogea, where evidence suggests that a people known to archaeologists as the **Hamangia Culture** probably had a matriarchal society, worshipping fertility goddesses.

Other societies developed in the Bronze and Iron Ages, followed by Celts who arrived from Asia in the last millennium BC; meanwhile, during the sixth and seventh centuries BC, **Greek traders** established ports along the Black Sea coast, the ruins of which can still be seen at Istria (Histria), Constanţa (Tomis), Mangalia (Callatis) and other sites, but the interior remained virtually unknown to the Greeks until 512 BC, when the Persian emperor Darius attempted to expel the Scythians, another Asiatic people newly settled along the Danube. In 335 BC, Alexander the Great occupied Dobrogea and crossed the Danube, defeating the Getae but failing to subdue them.

The chronicler Herodotus had reported in the sixth century BC that of the numerous and disunited tribes of **Thracians** who inhabited the mountains on both sides of the Danube, the "bravest and most righteous" were those subsequently known as the "Geto-Dacians". The word "Thracians" is now taken as an umbrella term for the mix of original East Balkan and incoming central European tribes then occupying this area, including the Getae on the Danube, the Dacians to their north, the Thracians proper to the south, and the Illyrians in present-day Albania. Over the centuries, these related tribes gradually coalesced so that by the first century BC a single leader, Burebista (82–44 BC), ruled a short-lived **Dacian empire**, occupying the territory of modern-day Romania and beyond, the apex of which was the religious and political capital, **Sarmizegetusa**, located in the Orăştie mountains. Archaeological digs have revealed Dacian settlements from the Black Sea to Slovakia, and the sheer size of the kingdom contributed to its fragmentation after Burebista's demise.

A Roman colony

Before **Decebal** (87–106 AD) managed to reunite this kingdom, the lower reaches of the Danube had already been conquered by the **Romans**, who then began to expand northwards. Decebal immediately defeated a Roman army but was then driven back; a stalemate followed until two campaigns (in 101–2 and 105–6 AD) by the Emperor Trajan (98–117 AD) led to the conquest of

Dacia. Although the Apuseni mountains, Maramureş and Moldavia were never subdued, most regions fell under Roman rule, maintained by the building of roads linking the garrison posts and trading towns. For the **colonization of Dacia** (so rich and important that it was known as Dacia Felix or Happy Dacia), settlers were brought from imperial territories as far afield as Greece, Egypt and Persia. Later, the adoption of Christianity as the official religion led to its acceptance in Dacia, at least superficially; and under Hadrian, the region was divided into two provinces for easier administration. With increasing incursions by nomadic Asian tribes such as the Goths in the third century, however, the defence of Dacia became too costly, and in 271 AD, Emperor Aurelian withdrew Rome's presence from the region.

The Age of Migrations and Daco-Roman Continuity

The Romans' departure was followed by the arrival of nomadic peoples sweeping out of Asia and into western Europe during the **Age of Migrations**, including the Huns (4th and 5th centuries), Avars (6th century), Slavs (7th century) and Bulgars (7th century, along the coast en route to Bulgaria). The low-lying regions were greatly exposed to these invasions, whereas high mountains protected the area later to be called Transylvania, where excavations have yielded coins whose dates suggest that the settlements continued to trade with the empire despite Roman withdrawal; the Draco-Romanian Continuity theory holds that the Romanians are descendents of the Roman settlers and the indigenous Dacians, forming a hybrid culture, and Romanian philologists point to numerous words in their language derived from Latin. Yet while some Romanians boast loudly about their Roman heritage, many of the imperial settlers would have been not free Romans but former slaves and soldiers, many of them Greeks and Arabs.

The theory would be of academic interest only were it not entwined with the dispute, now centuries old, between the Magyars and Romanians over the **occupation of Transylvania**. By claiming this uninterrupted residence, Romanians assert their rightful ownership of Transylvania. Conversely, the Magyars (who had first passed through around 896 as just another Asiatic horde before settling Hungary) claim that their occupation, from about 997 to the thirteenth century, met little resistance, and that the indigenous people were of Slavic stock. According to some Magyar historians, **Vlachs** (Romanians) are first mentioned in Transylvania around 1222 as groups of nomadic pastoralists crossing the Carpathians, having wandered over the course of centuries from their original "homeland" in Macedonia and Illyria.

The medieval principalities

Whatever the indigenous population's identity, István I (Saint Stephen) and later monarchs of the Árpád dynasty, gradually extended Hungarian rule over **Transylvania**, using foreigners to bolster their own settlements. Besides subduing local Cumans, Bulgars and Vlachs, the colonists had to withstand frequent invasions by the **Tatars** (or Mongols), nomadic warriors who devastated much of Eastern Europe in 1241–42 and continued to wreak havoc over the next five centuries.

While the Teutonic Knights colonized the Bârsa Land (around Braşov) in 1211 but were evicted in 1225, other groups of Germans – subsequently known as **Saxons** – built up powerful market towns like Hermannstadt (Sibiu) and Kronstadt (Braşov), which were granted self-government as "seats" (Sedes, or Stühle). Another ethnic group, the **Székely**, acted as the vanguard of colonization, moving during the thirteenth century from settlements in the Bihor region to the eastern marches, where they too were allowed relative autonomy.

Hungarians, however, were either classed as plebs liable to all manner of taxes, or as nobles and thus tax-exempt. This group dominated **the feudal system**, being represented alongside the Saxon and Székely "nations" on the Diet that advised the principality's military and civil governor, the **Voivode**, who acted for the Hungarian king. Under the Árpád dynasty, Diets included Romanian-speaking Vlachs who, even then, may have constituted the majority of Transylvania's population. From the mid-fourteenth century onwards, however, Vlachs faced increasing **discrimination**, both social and political. Besides the mistrust sown by Bogdan Vodă's rebellion in Maramureş (see p.313), **religion** played an important part in this process. Whereas the Vlachs were Orthodox (barring a few apostate nobles), the other communities adhered to the Catholic Church.

Wallachia and Dobrogea

On the far side of the Carpathians, fully-fledged principalities emerged somewhat later. Chronicles attribute the foundation of **Wallachia** (Vlahia or the Ţara Românească) to Negru Vodă (the Black Prince), who made Câmpulung its first capital in 1290, though they may instead refer to his son Radu Negru (1310–52), usually credited as the first of the Basarab dynasty. The shift in Wallachia's capitals over the centuries – from Câmpulung in the highlands down to Curtea de Argeş and Târgovişte in the foothills and then Bucharest on the plain – expressed a cautious move from the safety of the mountains to the financial opportunities of the trade routes with Turkey. Oppression, anarchy and piety were commonplace: the tithes and labour squeezed from the enserfed masses allowed the landowning **boyars** to endow Orthodox churches and engineer coups against the ruling voivodes. Yet commerce was entirely in the hands of Germans, Poles, Greeks and Jews; and though lavishly bestowed, the Orthodox Church was subordinated to the Bulgarian and Byzantine patriarchates, in part a legacy of Bulgar rule during the eighth and ninth centuries, but also reflecting the tendency of Wallachia's rulers to look south for allies (soon to be wiped from the map for centuries) against Hungary.

Moldavia and Bessarabia

Attempts to enforce Hungarian rule in Maramureş provoked some of the indigenous population to follow **Bogdan Vodă** over the Carpathians in 1359 to the cradle of a new principality, **Moldavia**; but the process of occupying the hills and steppes beyond the Carpathians had begun centuries earlier. Groups of Romanian-speaking pastoralists and farmers gradually moved to the Dnestr where they encountered Ukrainians who named them Volokhi. The Moldavian capital shifted eastwards from Rădăuţi to Suceava, and then southwards to Iaşi. **Alexander the Good** (Alexandru cel Bun) may have gained his honorary title by ousting Turks from the eastern marches, though it could well have been bestowed by the Basarab family, whom he made feudal lords of the region, subsequently known as **Bessarabia**; or retrospectively by Moldavia's peasantry who suffered during the prolonged, violent anarchy that followed his death. Besides Tatar invasions and rebellious boyars, Moldavia faced threats from Hungary, Poland and the Turks.

Ottomans, Nationes and Phanariots

From the mid-fourteenth century, the fate of the Balkan countries was determined by the **Ottoman empire** of the Seljuk Turks, which spread inexorably northwards, finally subjugating Bulgaria in 1393. The Turks were briefly halted by **Mircea the Old** (Mircea cel Bătrân; 1386–1418) at the battle of Rovine in 1394, but subsequent defeats compelled Mircea to acknowledge Ottoman suzerainty in 1417. By surrendering the fertile **Dobrogea** region and paying tribute, outright occupation was avoided and Wallachia's ruling class retained their positions; but henceforth, both rulers and ruled were confronted with the alternatives of submission or resistance to an overwhelming force.

Even before the fall of Constantinople in 1453, Wallachia, Moldavia and Transylvania had become Christendom's front line of resistance to the Turks – and indeed, with Russia, the only Orthodox Christian land remaining free. Throughout the fifteenth century, the principalities' history is overshadowed by this struggle and the names of four remarkable military leaders. First was Transylvanian voivode **Iancu de Hunedoara** (János Hunyadi), who defeated the Turks near Alba Iulia and Sibiu in 1441–43 and lead multinational armies to victory at Niş and Belgrade. Iancu's son **Mátyás Corvinus** (1440–90, also known as Hunyadi Mátyás or Matei Corvin), Hungary's great Renaissance king, continued to resist the Turks, who were dislodged from southern Bessarabia by **Stephen the Great** (Ştefan cel Mare) of Moldavia and temporarily checked by the fortresses of Chilia and Cetatea Alba (now deep in Ukraine). However, their resurgence under Bajazid II, and peace treaties signed by the Turks with Poland, Hungary and Venice in the 1470s and 1480s presaged the demise of Moldavian independence, as was apparent to Stephen by the end of his embattled reign (1457–1504). Meanwhile, due to Wallachia's greater vulnerablity, its rulers generally preferred to pay off the Turks rather than resist them, **Vlad Ţepeş** (Vlad the Impaler – see p.421) being a notable exception from 1456 until his death in 1476.

In **Transylvania**, the least exposed region, the **Bobâlna peasant uprising** of 1437–38 rocked the feudal order. To safeguard their privileges, the Magyar nobility concluded a pact known as the **Union of Three Nations** with the Saxon and Székely leaders, whereby each of these three ethnic groups (Nationes) agreed to recognize and defend the rights of the others. As a consequence, the Vlachs were relegated to the position of "those who do not possess the right of citizenship... but are merely tolerated by grace", and they were effectively prohibited from holding public office or residing in Saxon and Magyar towns. The increasing exploitation of the Magyar peasantry led in 1514 to an uprising under György Dózsa (Gheorghe Doja), savagely repressed by governor **János Zápolyai** (Johann Zapolya, 1510–40), who imposed the onerous Werbrczy Code, or Tripartium, a feudal version of apartheid in 1517.

The crushing defeat of Hungary by Suleyman the Magnificent at **Mohács** (1526) and the Turkish occupation of Buda (1541) exacerbated the isolation of the principalities. Although the Hapsburg dynasty of Austria laid claim to what was left of Hungary after Mohács, Zápolyai won Ottoman support to maintain a precarious autonomy for Transylvania, even gaining control of Hungary east of the River Tisza (the Partium) in 1538. Successors such as István Báthori (1571–81, who was elected King of Poland from 1575 and drove back Ivan the Terrible), and Zsigmond Báthori (1581–97) were able to maintain this independence; in Moldavia, however, **Petru Rareş** could only hold his throne (1527–38 and 1541–56) by breathtaking duplicity and improvisations, while his successors plumbed even further depths.

Short-lived unification

Understandably, Romanian historiography has scant regard for such figures, and prefers to highlight the achievements of more successful leaders such as **Michael the Brave** (Mihai Viteazul, often known in Wallachia as Mihai Bravul). Crowned ruler of Wallachia in 1593, his triumph against the Turks in 1595 was followed by the overthrow of Andrew Báthori in Transylvania in 1599 and a lightning campaign across the Carpathians in 1600 to secure him the Moldavian throne. This opportunist and short-lived **union of the principalities** under one crown – which fragmented immediately following his murder in 1601 – has subsequently been presented as a triumph of Romanian nationalism, but it was only between 1604 and 1657 that Transylvania attained genuine independence from the Hapsburgs and Ottomans, although the region was rarely then at peace.

From the 1630s onwards, Moldavia and Wallachia avoided direct occupation as Turkish *pashaliks* by accepting Ottoman "advisers", known as **Phanariots**. In Moldavia, they encouraged the Orthodox church to abandon Old Slavonic as the language of the scriptures and ritual in favour of Greek, but this had the unintended result of stimulating a move towards the Romanian language. This presaged a minor cultural renaissance – particularly in the field of architecture – during a period of relative stability from 1633 to 1711 in Moldavia and 1714 in Wallachia. Thereafter, the Turks dispensed with native rulers and instead appointed Phanariot princes, who were purely concerned with plundering the principalities; their rapaciousness, combined with more than seventy changes of ruler in Moldavia and Wallachia until 1821, crippled both regions.

The struggle for independence and unification

The end of the siege of Vienna in 1683 precipitated **Hapsburg** control of Transylvania. As Catholics and imperialists, the Hapsburg monarchy persuaded the Orthodox clergy there to accept papal authority, and promised that Vlachs who joined the **Uniate Church** (see p.183) would be granted equality with the Nationes. Although this promise was retracted in 1701, Bishop Inocenţiu Micu and the intellectuals of the Transylvanian School agitated for equal rights and articulated the Vlachs' growing consciousness of being **Romanians**. Yet despite Joseph II's edict of religious toleration in 1781, his dissolution of the monasteries and embarkation upon the abolition of serfdom, it was too late to prevent the great peasant rebellion led by **Horea, Crişan** and **Cloşca** in 1784–85. Its crushing only stimulated efforts to attain liberation by constitutional means, however.

The gradual development of liberal and nationalist factions in **Moldavia and Wallachia** stemmed from a variety of causes, such as the ideals of the Romantic movement and the French Revolution gaining hold, the success of Serbian and Greek independence movements, and the emergence of capitalism in the principalities, showing that Turkish dominance and feudalism were in decline. The upshot was a major uprising against Phanariot rule in Wallachia in 1821, led by **Tudor Vladimirescu**. Although defeated, it persuaded the Turks that it was time for the end of Phanariot rule, and power was restored to native boyars in 1822.

The rise of Russia and World War I

As the power of the Ottomans declined, that of **Tsarist Russia** grew. Fired by imperialist and Pan-Slavist ideals and a fear of Hapsburg encroachment (manifest in 1774, when Austria annexed the region henceforth known as **Bucovina**), Russia presented itself in 1779 as the guardian of the Ottomans' Christian subjects, and expanded its territories towards the Balkans as well as into the Caucasus and Central Asia. In 1792, Russian forces reached the River Dnestr; one Russo–Turkish war led to the annexation of Bessarabia in 1812, and another to the Treaty of Adrianople (1829), by which Moldavia and Wallachia became Russian protectorates. The Tsarist governor **General Kiseleff** was in no sense a revolutionary, but he introduced liberal reforms and assemblies in both principalities, which remained in force after the Russians withdrew in 1834, having selected two rulers. Of these, Michael Sturdza in Moldavia was the more despotic but also the more energetic, levying heavy taxes to construct roads, dykes, hospitals and schools.

Given the boyars' dominance of the assemblies, economic development took precedence over the political and social reforms demanded by sections of the liberal bourgeoisie. The **democratic movement** – led by Nicolae Golescu, Ion Brătianu, Nicolae Bălcescu and Mihail Kogălniceanu – which emerged in Moldavia and Wallachia and campaigned for the unification of both principalities briefly came to power in 1848, the **Year of Revolutions** (see below).

Russia, now claiming to be "the gendarme of Europe", intervened militarily to restore the status quo, while the build up to the Crimean War saw Russia also occupying Moldavia and Wallachia and fighting the Turks along the Danube. The Congress of Paris, ending the war in 1856, reaffirmed Turkish rule (although with increased autonomy for the boyars), and the nationalist cause was thwarted until January 1859, when the assemblies of Moldavia and Wallachia circumvented the restrictions imposed to prevent their **unification** under a single ruler, **Alexander Ioan Cuza**, who embarked on a series of reforms, the most important of which were the **abolition of serfdom** and the expropriation of the huge monastic estates, enraging the landowning classes and other conservative elements. Under Cuza's replacement, **Prince Carol I**, Rumania declared its **independence** on May 9, 1877.

Events in **Transylvania** followed a different course during the nineteenth century with popular support for the 1848 revolution split along nationalist lines. Whereas the abolition of serfdom was universally welcomed by the peasantry, the Romanian population opposed the unification of Transylvania with Hungary, which Magyars of all classes greeted with enthusiasm; the Saxons were lukewarm on both issues. Following protest meetings at Blaj,

Avram Iancu formed Romanian guerrilla bands to oppose the Hungarians; belated attempts by Kossuth and Bălcescu to compromise on the issue of Romanian rights came too late to create a united front against the Tsarist armies which invaded Transylvania on behalf of the Hapsburgs. As in Hungary, the Hapsburgs introduced martial law and widespread repression in the aftermath of the revolution.

In 1867, the Ausgleich, or Compromise, established the Dual Monarchy of the Austro-Hungarian Empire and the region became part of Greater Hungary, ruled directly from Budapest, with a policy of **Magyarization** in Transylvania making Hungarian the official language; a barrage of laws were passed to further undermine Romanian culture (Bucovina and Maramureş remained under Austrian rule and avoided the worst of this). The cultural association **ASTRA**, founded in 1861, acted in its defence until the establishment of the **National Party** in 1881, which maintained close links with kindred groups across the Carpathians.

The influence of foreign capitalism increased enormously around the turn of the century, as Rumania's mineral wealth – particularly its oil – inspired competition among the great powers. While liberal and conservative politicians engaged in ritualistic parliamentary squabbles, however, nothing was done about the worsening impoverishment of the people. Peasant grievances exploded in the **răscoala** of 1907 – a nationwide uprising that was savagely crushed (with at least 10,000 deaths) and then followed by a series of ineffectual agrarian reforms.

Rumania's acquisition of territory south of the Danube in 1878 was one of the many bones of contention underlying the **Balkan Wars** that embroiled Rumania, Bulgaria, Serbia, Macedonia and Greece. Rumania sat out the first Balkan War (1912–13), but joined the alliance against Bulgaria in 1913, gaining the southern part of Dobrogea in the process. King Ferdinand, who succeeded Carol in 1914 was married to Princess Marie, granddaughter of both Queen Victoria and Tsar Alexander II; thus, when Rumania entered **World War I** in August 1916, it joined Great Britain, France and Russia and attacked the Austro-Hungarian forces in Transylvania. The disastrous campaign left it with an onerous peace treaty in May 1918, but by October, the disintegration of the Central Powers reversed this situation entirely, and Rumanian armies advanced into Transylvania, and then on into Hungary to overthrow the short-lived communist régime of Béla Kun in August 1919. On December 1, 1918, the Romanian assembly of Alba Iulia declared **Transylvania's union with Rumania** to scenes of wild acclaim. The Romanian population of Bessarabia, set free by the Russian Revolution, had already declared their union with Rumania in March 1918, followed in November by Bucovina. The **Treaty of Trianon** in 1920 upheld Rumania's gains and as a nation it doubled both in population and territory, while Hungary lost half of its populace and two-thirds of its land – the source of great resentment ever since.

Greater Romania

The country's enlarged territory was dignified by the adoption of the name **Greater Romania**, but the lives of the masses hardly improved. The expropriation of Hungarian estates in Transylvania affected not only the nobility, but smallholders as well; Hungarian employees were dismissed on a huge scale and

Romanian immigrants were brought in to replace them. Equally, the many peasants who expected to benefit from agrarian reform were rapidly disillusioned when speculators and boyars appropriated much of the land.

Romania was governed by the **National Liberal Party**, favoured by King Ferdinand but soon damaging the economy by pursuing nationalist and populist policies. On Ferdinand's death in 1927, it was dismissed and replaced by the **National Peasant Party**, led by **Iuliu Maniu**, which in 1928 won the only remotely fair election of this period. Despite a parliamentary majority and genuinely reforming policies, Maniu pursued conservative strategies, constrained by the world economic crisis of 1929, vested interests and entrenched corruption.

However, it was a bizarre moral issue that led to the government's eventual fall: in 1930, after a three-year regency, **Carol II** took the throne and at once broke a promise to put aside his divorced Jewish mistress, Magda Lupescu. The puritan Maniu resigned and the government fell apart. Carol then exploited the constitution of 1923, giving the king the right to dissolve parliament and call elections at will; a corrupt system soon developed whereby the government would fix elections by every means possible, only to be dismissed and replaced by the opposition when the king had tired of them. Between 1930 and 1940, there were no less than twenty-five separate governments, leading ultimately to the collapse of the political parties themselves. Strikes in the oil and rail industries in 1933 were put down by armed force; Carol set up his own "youth movement", and soon began routine phone-tapping by the **Siguranţa**, the Securitate's predecessor.

The Iron Guard and World War II

A **fascist movement** also established itself, particularly in Bessarabia, which had a long tradition of anti-Semitism. The main fascist party, taking much of the National Peasant Party's rural support, was the Legion of the Archangel Michael, founded in 1927; its green-shirted paramilitary wing, the **Iron Guard** (see box on p.257), extolled the soil, death, and a mystical form of Orthodoxy; it also fought street battles against Jews and followers of other political parties, and murdered four current and former prime ministers. In 1937, the anti-Semitic National League of Christian Defence was installed in power by the king, but the prime minister, the poet Octavian Goga, immediately insulted Lupescu and was dismissed in February 1938, just six weeks after taking power. This at last provoked Carol to ban all political parties (other than his own National Renaissance Front) and set up a royal dictatorship.

In February 1939, Germany demanded a monopoly of Romanian exports in return for a guarantee of its borders, and in March agreed an oil-for-arms deal. In April, Carol obtained feeble guarantees from Britain and France, but in August the equilibrium was shattered by the Nazi–Soviet Non-Aggression Pact. In June 1940, a Soviet ultimatum led to the annexation of Bessarabia and northern Bucovina, and, two months later, Hitler forced Carol to cede Northern Transylvania to Germany's ally Hungary, and southern Dobrogea to Bulgaria. On September 6, unable to maintain his position after giving away such huge portions of Romanian territory, Carol fled with Lupescu and his spoils, leaving his son **Mihai**, then nineteen years old, to take over the throne.

Mihai accepted the formation of a government led by Codreanu's successor Horia Sima and by **Marshal Ion Antonescu**, who styled himself Conducator ("leader", equivalent to Führer) but had little influence over the local legionary groups who unleashed an orgy of violence against Jews and liberals. To ensure himself a stable and productive ally, Hitler forced Antonescu to disarm the Iron Guard; this provoked an armed uprising (and the savage butchery of 124 Jews in Bucharest) in January 1941, only suppressed by the army after a fierce struggle.

Romania entered **World War II** in June 1941, joining the Nazi invasion of Russia with the objective of regaining Bessarabia and northern Bucovina. Romanian troops took Odessa and participated in the battles of Sevastopol and

The Holocaust in Romania

In 1939, Romania had the third greatest **Jewish population** in Europe after Poland and the Soviet Union. Most lived in Bessarabia, Bucovina and parts of northern Moldavia, notably around Dorohoi. In June 1940, Bessarabia and northern Bucovina were ceded to the Soviet Union, as demanded by Hitler, and at least fifty Jews were killed in Dorohoi by retreating Romanian troops. A year later troops carried out an awful pogrom in Iaşi, killing about 8000 Jews, leading the Germans to comment, "we always act scientifically... we use surgeons, not butchers." As the army advanced (with units of the German Einsatzgruppe D following), there were many more massacres; at least 33,000 Jews died in Bessarabia and Bucovina between June 22 and September 1, 1941, and, in fact, the worst single massacre of the Holocaust was committed by Romanians whilst they took Odessa.

Deportations to Transnistria, the conquered territory beyond the River Dnestr, began in earnest on September 16; around 150,000 Jews were taken, of whom 18,000 to 22,000 died in transit. Up to 90,000 more died from starvation, disease and general mistreatment. Between November 21 and 29, 1941, all 48,000 Jews held in the Bogdanovka camp in southern Transnistria were killed; another 18,000 were killed in the Dumanovka camp.

In July 1942, the Germans began to press hard for the Jews of Wallachia, Moldavia and southern Transylvania to be deported to the camps, following the 120,000 who were taken to Auschwitz from Hungarian-controlled Northern Transylvania. This was agreed but then refused after lobbying by neutral diplomats and the Papal Nuncio, although it was probably more due to the fact that the Jews were still vital to the functioning of the economy. In November 1942, it was decided that Romanian Jews in Germany should be sent to the German death camps.

When Romania was thinking of changing sides, the **World Jewish Congress** in Geneva proposed a plan to save 70,000 Romanian Jews, and possibly 1.3 million more in Eastern Europe, by paying the Romanian government twelve shillings per head to allow them to leave by ship for Palestine. This plan was blocked by opposition from anti-Semites in the US State Department and Britain, worried about the reaction of Arabs to further Jewish immigration to Palestine, as well as by the practical problems inherent in sending money to a Nazi ally. Thirteen ships did leave, with 13,000 refugees, but two sank (with 1,163 on board) and others were stopped by Turkey, under pressure from both Britain and Germany.

In 1944, Antonescu began a **limited repatriation** from the camps of Transnistria, bringing back 1500 in December 1943 and 1846 orphans by March 1944. He warned the Germans not to kill Jews as they retreated; nevertheless, a final thousand were killed in Tiraspol jail. On March 20, 1944, the Red Army reached the Dnestr, and the worst of the nightmare ended. In Antonescu's trial in May 1946 it was said, "if the Jews of Romania are still alive, they owe it to Marshal Antonescu", who claimed to have saved about 275,000 Jews by his policy of keeping them for extermination at home. Overall, between 264,900 and 470,000 Romanian Jews, and 36,000 Gypsies, died in the war; 428,000 Jews survived or returned alive. In 2003, a major row blew up with Israel when Iliescu appeared to claim that the Holocaust hadn't just affected the Jews.

Stalingrad, taking heavy casualties. Jews and Gypsies in Bessarabia, Bucovina and the Hungarian-controlled area of Transylvania were rounded up and deported for slave labour and then on to extermination camps. By 1943, however, the Red Army was advancing fast, and Antonescu began to look for a way to abandon Hitler and change sides. Opposition to the war mounted as the Russians drew nearer, and, as they crossed the border, a **royal/military coup** on August 23, 1944 overthrew the Antonescu regime – a date commemorated until 1989 as **Liberation Day**, although it took a further two months to clear the Germans from the country.

The People's Republic

While the Romanian army subordinated itself to Soviet command, the struggle to determine the state of **postwar Romania** was already under way, with the country firmly within the Soviet sphere but with Western powers maintaining observers in Bucharest to require a veneer of democratic process. The first government formed by King Mihai was a broad coalition, with **communists** only playing a minor role, but gradually they increased their influence. In March 1945, a new coalition was installed under the premiership of **Dr Petru Groza** (leader of the Ploughmen's Front); again, this included politicians from the pre-war parties, but the key posts were occupied by communists. The land reform of 1945 benefited millions of peasants at the expense of the Saxons and Swabians of Transylvania and the Banat, who had become the biggest landowners since the dispossession of the Magyars, while women voted for the first time in 1946, supposedly contributing to the election of another ostensibly balanced government. In fact, while virtually every device ever used to rig an election was brought into play, the takeover steamed on regardless.

Like Groza's first administration, this included leading capitalists and former Guardists, whom the communists initially wooed, since their first aim was to eliminate the left and centre parties, who were often forcibly merged with the Communists. On December 30, 1947, **King Mihai was forced to abdicate** and Romania was declared a **People's Republic**. Antonescu and up to 60,000 were executed after highly irregular trials in 1946 and 1947. Eighty thousand arrests followed in an effort to overcome peasant resistance to **collectivization** (a reversal of the earlier agrarian reform), with many more in 1948 in the campaign to "liquidate" the Uniate Church. The **nationalization** of industries, banks and utilities in June 1948 placed the main economic levers in the hands of the Communist Party, which openly declared its intention to reshape society on Stalinist lines. **Police terror** was used against real or potential opponents, with victims incarcerated in prisons or conscripted for reed-cutting in the Delta or work on the Danube–Black Sea Canal, the "Canal Mortii" (see p.365) that claimed over 100,000 lives.

The Communist Party itself was split by bitter conflicts between the Muscovites (those who had spent the war in Moscow, led by Ana Pauker and Vasile Luca) and the nationalists, themselves divided between the prison-communists and the secretariat-communists who had remained free and in hiding. In 1952, the prison-communists emerged victorious, under **Gheorghe Gheorghiu-Dej**, General Secretary of the party's Central Committee since 1948, who had retained Stalin's confidence largely because the secretariat group was too ideologically flexible, while Pauker and her group were simply too Jewish. She and 192,000 other members were purged from the Party, and Lucreţiu Pătrăşcanu (Minister of Justice 1944–48) was executed in 1954. Stalin had died in 1953, but Gheorghiu-Dej took great exception to reformist trends in the USSR, and stuck grimly to the Stalinist true faith, developing heavy industry and claiming the impossible growth rate of 13 percent per year.

The USSR, having annexed Bessarabia once more, had given parts of it to the Ukraine and created the puppet **Republic of Moldova** from the rest. Therefore, Gheorghiu-Dej's increasing refusal to follow the Moscow line was a great success domestically, tapping into a vein of popular nationalism; and by arresting the leadership of the left-wing Hungarian People's Alliance and establishing an "Autonomous Hungarian Region" in the Székely Land in 1952, he simultaneously decapitated the Magyar political organization in Transylvania while erecting a facade of minority rights.

In March 1965, Gheorghiu-Dej died, and was soon succeeded by **Nicolae Ceauşescu**, until then a little-known party hack, who was able, by 1969, to outmanoeuvre his rivals in the collective leadership and establish undisputed power.

The Ceauşescu era

There seems little doubt that for the first few years of his rule, **Ceauşescu** was genuinely popular: he encouraged a cultural thaw, put food and consumer goods into the shops, denounced security police excesses (blaming them on Gheorghiu-Dej), and above all condemned the Warsaw Pact invasion of Czechoslovakia in 1968. His independent **foreign policy** gained Romania the reputation of being the "maverick" state of the Eastern bloc building links with the West maintaining ties with countries with which the USSR had severed.

However, he soon reverted to tried and tested methods of control as his **economic failure** became obvious. Ceauşescu stuck throughout to the Stalinist belief in heavy industry, and during the 1970s, the country's **industrialization programme** absorbed thirty percent of GNP and $10.2billion in foreign loans. Living standards plummeted as all but a minimal amount of food was exported, and the population was obliged to work harder and harder for less and less. Amazingly, all the foreign debt was repaid by 1989, although there was no prospect of any improvement in living standards thereafter.

Ceauşescu was convinced that the key to industrial growth lay in building a larger workforce, and in 1966 banned abortions and contraception for any married woman under 40 with fewer than four children (in 1972, the limits were raised to 45 and five). In the 1980s, when his developing paranoia and personality cult put him increasingly out of touch, he introduced the **Baby Police** and compulsory gynaecological examinations; unmarried people and married couples without children were penalized by higher taxes. Ceauşescu also **discriminated against the minorities**: it became increasingly hard to get an education or to buy books in Hungarian or German, or to communicate with relatives abroad; and families were persuaded to give their children Romanian names.

The two million-plus Magyars (including the Székely and Csángós) bore the brunt of this chauvinism, causing a notable worsening of diplomatic relations

Ceauşescu's orphans

The result of Ceauşescu's scheme to increase the workforce was that many women had children that they could not possibly afford to bring up and these were abandoned in dire **state orphanages**, grossly under-staffed and underfunded. With desensitized staff and with no mental stimulation, it's not surprising that many orphans were diagnosed (at three years old) as mentally handicapped and left without education in "Institutes for the Irrecuperable".

The Western media was saturated with distressing images of these orphanages, and emergency aid and volunteers flooded into Romania. Today, relief agencies focus on long-term strategies with emphasis on training and helping the Romanians to help themselves. Some orphanages have been replaced by family-home-type units, and family support centres have opened in some towns. There are still blackspots – little aid of any kind has reached southern Wallachia, and most orphans are Gypsies and therefore not wanted. In 2001, the EU published a shocking report linking adoptions to the organ trade and child pornography, and a two-year moratorium was imposed on adoption, during which time some improvements were made.

The problem of unwanted children remains, and will do so until there is comprehensive family planning, now the object of a huge programme, but official funds for charities have dried up and donations are welcome.

Charity contacts

Everychild UK ☎020/7749 2468, 🖥www.everychild.org.uk

Cleaford Christian Trust UK ☎0845/124 9402, 🖥www.cleafordchristiantrust.org.uk, 🖥www.riac.org.uk

FARA UK ☎01328/821 444, 🖥www.faracharity.org.

Medical Support for Romania UK ☎01223/276 504, 🖥www.msr.org.uk

Partnership for Growth/Link Romania UK ☎01903/529 333, 🖥www.p4g.org

Peace Corps USA ☎1800/424 8580, 🖥www.peacecorps.org

Regional Environmental Centre Romania ☎021/314 0433, 📧rec@recromania.ro

Relief Fund for Romania UK ☎020/7733 7018, 🖥www.relieffundforromania.co.uk

Romanian Angel Appeal Romania ☎021/323 6868, 🖥www.raa.ro

World Vision UK UK ☎01908/841 000, 🖥www.worldvision.org.uk

with Hungary. Neither this, nor criticism of the treatment of the Gypsy population worried Ceauşescu, but he tried to keep on the right side of the German and Israeli governments, who purchased exit visas for ethnic Germans and Jews in Romania for substantial sums.

Abuses of human rights got worse through the 1980s, including the **systematization** programme for rural redevelopment and constant repression by the **Securitate** (secret police), which produced an atmosphere of ubiquitous fear and distrust even between family members, as up to one in four of the population was rumoured to be an informer. Increasingly, key posts were allocated to relatives of the Ceauşescus, while all other senior figures were rotated every few years between jobs to prevent anyone building up an independent powerbase.

In the **1980s**, everything went downhill rapidly, as the truth about the country's economic collapse was hidden from Ceauşescu by his subordinates. Absolutely everything was in short supply, but Ceauşescu and Elena pushed on with megalomaniac projects such as the Palace of the People in Bucharest, the Danube–Black Sea Canal (again) and the village systematization programme. Ceauşescu also made plain his opposition to *glasnost*.

The Revolution

By **1989**, the situation in Romania was so desperate that it seemed impossible for Ceauşescu not to bow to the wave of change that had swept over the whole of Eastern Europe. In December that year, events snowballed dramatically, with a series of strikes and riots culminating on December 20 with a mass demonstration of 100,000 people in Timişoara demanding Ceauşescu's resignation; despite his orders to fire, the army withdrew rather than launch into a massacre. The very next day, another crowd of 100,000, this time coralled into appearing by Ceauşescu's security forces as an intended show of support, gathered in Piaţa Republicii (now Piaţa Revoluţiei) in Bucharest to to hear him speak, but he was soon interrupted by heckling. The police and Securitate opened fire but were unable to clear the crowds from the city centre, partly because the Minister of Defence, **General Vasile Milea**, ordered the army not to shoot. On the morning of December 22, Ceauşescu had Milea shot, but this merely precipitated the defection of many army units to the side of the protestors. By noon, the crowds had broken into the Party's Central Committee building, and the Ceauşescus fled by helicopter from the roof. After going to their villa at Snagov and then on to a military airfield near Titu, they then hijacked a car before being arrested in Târgovişte. When the news of their capture proved insufficient to stop loyal Securitate units firing on the crowds, they were summarily tried and **executed** on Christmas Day.

Meanwhile, throughout the country's cities there was more street fighting, with army and police units changing sides; it's unclear at what point their leadership had decided to abandon Ceauşescu, but evidence suggests that it was earlier, rather than later. Nor is it clear at what stage the **National Salvation Front** (Frontul Salvării Naţionale or FSN), which emerged to take power from December 22, had been formed; supposedly shaped in the Central Committee building on the afternoon of December 22 by people who had gathered there independently, it was clear many of them were already in contact. The key figures were Party members who had been sidelined by Ceauşescu, and **Ion Iliescu** was soon named president; his prime minister was **Petre Roman**, an up-and-coming member of the younger generation of communists.

Around a thousand people died in the revolution and the "terrorist" phase that lasted until January 18, although, initially, both the new government and the Hungarian media published inflated death tolls of 10,000 or more.

Free Romania

It didn't take long after the Ceauşescus' execution for the FSN to consolidate its power; almost at once, it reversed its pledge not to run as a party in the elections in 1990, and it was evident that the former governing élite had no intention of leaving office. Further protests in Bucharest even saw the government shipping in around 10,000 miners to deal (violently) with the crowds, leaving seven dead and 296 injured. The reaction abroad was dismay, with the US suspending non-humanitarian aid and boycotting Iliescu's inauguration as president. At home, the nation went into shock, and it remained cowed for the next year while the economy collapsed.

In the meantime, in May, the FSN had easily won Romania's **first free election**, while Iliescu won the vote for president. The whole process was deemed fair enough by international observers, even though a million more votes were cast than were on the register, supposedly "due to the enthusiasm of the people for democracy". Most intellectuals soon took to referring to December 1989 as the "so-called revolution", and it was increasingly taken for granted that nothing much had changed.

Economic reform got under way slowly, but hardship was unavoidable as the country was rocked by its opening up to Western imports and by world recession. **Food rationing** had ended as soon as the FSN took power, along with a raft of prohibitions, and the government took care to empty the warehouses and fill the shops with groceries. Food subsidies were cut in November 1990, and the state-controlled **prices** increased steadily from then on. Imports rose by 48 percent in 1990, and exports fell by 42 percent (due in part to food being kept for home consumers), while **inflation** climbed from 65 percent in 1990, to almost 300 percent in 1993.

A **second general election** was held in 1992, after the adoption of a new constitution making the country a **presidential democracy**, in which the prime minister has little autonomy. Iliescu won the presidency, but a coalition government was installed that survived a succession of parliamentary votes of confidence and strikes by key groups of workers, managing for the most part to avoid inflationary wage rises. The need for aid and a fear of international isolation kept the government on a reformist course in 1993, Romania became the last Eastern Bloc state to join the Council of Europe and in January 1994, it was the first to sign the Partnership for Peace. The granting of Most Favoured Nation status by the USA in 1993 led to huge cuts in tariffs.

Particularly welcome (and rewarded by substantial loan assistance from the World Bank and IMF) was Iliescu's support for the tight **fiscal policies** of the National Bank's governor Mugur Isarescu, which halved inflation to 6 percent per month and allowed the leu to actually rise slightly against the dollar. The official exchange rate matched the black-market rate, and in 1995, taxes were cut to the lowest levels in Central or Eastern Europe.

Industry, the economy and unemployment continued to improve, with real wages rising 16 percent in 1995, but it wasn't enough to win Iliescu the 1996 general elections. Voters were alienated by a series of scandals and an education bill that required history, geography and civics to be taught in the Romanian language even in Hungarian-language schools.

Constantinescu's Romania

The 1996 election was won by the Democratic Convention of Romania (CDR), a coalition of four main parties and a dozen smaller ones. **Emil Constantinescu**, a professor of geology and former rector of Bucharest University, was elected president and appointed the youthful mayor of Bucharest, **Victor Ciorbea**, as prime minister. Their government was genuinely liberal-democratic and Western-oriented; its priorities were accelerated privatization, the slashing of the budget deficit and elimination of almost all price controls, introduction of a transparent tax system, and an attack on corruption. Before the elections they promised radical reforms with increased social protection; in the event, they found the economy had been abused even more than expected by Iliescu's attempts at re-election, and the result was the most radical "shock therapy" campaign anywhere in East Central Europe. In January 1997 alone, fuel and phone prices doubled, the cost of electricity rose five times, and rail fares rose by eighty percent, as subsidies were removed, so that real wages fell by twenty percent in that month; fuel prices rose by half again in February.

Other moves included a law providing for multilingual universities, leading to renewed friction with Hungary (who had pressured for separate Hungarian-only universities) and a law opening Securitate files (although the body set up to implement it soon suspended its activities in protest at the non-cooperation of the Romanian Information Service). Increasingly, however, the Constantinescu government was seen as failing to deliver, in particular in the war against corruption and in reforming and reviving the economy, and became particularly unpopular. Once Constantinescu announced that he would not seek re-election, the search was on for anyone who could stop Iliescu (now 70) returning to power.

The return of Iliescu – and the future

In the general elections of 2000, an angry electorate voted the presidency to Iliescu (who suddenly seemed relatively benign to the West), with **Adrian Nastase** becoming prime minister of a another coalition government, this one supposedly committed to continuing the move towards a market economy and integration with the West; although various scandals have led to resignations, the government proved remarkably stable, and in 2003 it was restructured with fewer ministries.

The earliest date for **entry to the European Union** is 2007, but this may be optimistic, given the many doubts, above all, about the elimination of corruption. A measure of free trade has been introduced with Bulgaria, Turkey and Macedonia, and NATO admitted Romania in 2004. Of the EU accession nations, Romania is the most enthusiastic, with over 74 percent of Romanians in favour of speedy entry; the country is already benefitting handsomely, with almost €250 million in EU grants received in 2003, and perhaps €1.2 billion per year after 2007. However, the EU is seriously concerned about Romania's ability to manage this level of funding in an accountable and non-politicized way. Already, almost a million Romanians are working (legally and illegally) abroad, mostly in Western Europe, with €2 billion in earnings transferred to Romania annually – yet they will not be free to work legally in EU countries until around 2014.

Minorities and religions

While Wallachia and Moldavia are largely monocultural, Transylvania has always been pluralistic and multi-ethnic. Although there is a specifically Transylvanian culture and sensibility common to all the races living there, there are still those who seek to make political capital by setting one race against another. For visitors, of course, this multi-ethnic mix is at the heart of Transylvania's charm. For an overview of the history of the **Magyars** (Hungarians) and **Germans** in Romania, refer to the "History" section of Contexts.

The Jews

Jews have been in Romania since Roman times, with more arriving in the eighth and ninth centuries after the collapse of the Jewish Khazar empire, and also in 1367 and in 1648 when they were expelled from Hungary and Poland. Most settled in Bessarabia and Bucovina, and prospered there; the community peaked around 1924, when it numbered 800,000. Romania was one of the few parts of the world where Jews were allowed to own land and form self-sufficient rural communities.

Although the Turks had treated Jews fairly, independent Romania increasingly regarded them as foreigners, and they began to emigrate, mostly to North America. In 1878, equal citizenship was forced on Romania by the great powers at the Congress of Berlin. The 1907 revolt was strongly anti-Semitic, and was followed by the rise of the Iron Guard and other nationalist parties; during **World War II**, the Jewish population was devastated (see box on p.391), leaving only 428,000 Jews in Romania by 1947.

In the new world of communism, the people were to be without ethnic distinction, and all national minorities' organizations were disbanded in 1953. However, Stalin was anti-Semitic and after the purging in 1952 of Romania's Jewish Foreign Minister, Ana Pauker, the climate turned against Romania's Jews again. Ceauşescu was happy to sell Jews to Israel for up to $3000 for each exit visa; at least 300,000 had left by 1989, and there remain only about 10,000 now.

The Gypsies

Gypsies or Roma left northern India in the tenth and eleventh centuries and arrived in Europe around 1407. Almost at once, many were enslaved, and in the sixteenth century came the first great period of **persecution**, a time of cruelty matched only by the Nazi holocaust. In Wallachia and Moldavia, Gypsies were divided into two main groups, the nomadic lăieţi and the enslaved vătraşi. In 1837, the politician Mihail Kogălniceanu, who campaigned on their behalf, wrote: "On the streets of the Iaşi of my youth, I saw human beings wearing chains on their arms and legs, others with iron clamps around their foreheads, and still others with metal collars about their necks. Cruel beatings and other punishments such as starvation, being hung in the snow or the frozen river, such was the fate of the wretched Gypsy."

Wallachia and Moldavia **freed their Gypsies** between 1837 and 1856. Many stayed on with their owners as paid employees, while others emigrated, reaching Germany in the early 1860s, France in 1867, Britain and the Netherlands in 1868, and North America by 1881. At least 20,000 were deported to Transnistria by Antonescu's regime during World War II, and a higher proportion died then than in any other European country. The communist regime forced them to settle on the edges of villages, jailing them if they refused. Today, Romania's Gypsies number between 550,000 and 2 million (of 8 million in Europe) – between 2 and 9 percent of the population – forming one of Europe's largest minorities. About 10 percent of them are still nomadic, spending the winter at permanent encampments; around 40 percent no longer speak Romany and consider themselves barely Roma.

There is increasing discrimination against Gypsies, seen as universal scapegoats, although they still earn respect as musicians. They receive very little international aid, and bigotry, particularly in employment, has inevitably pushed many into crime. Perhaps more alarming is the great rise in **crime against Gypsies**, often condoned at a local level by authorities; indeed, police sometimes mount raids to beat up Gypsies at random for general intimidation. Economically speaking, over sixty percent of those living in poverty in Romania are Roma but perhaps correspondingly, there has been a rise in ethnic consciousness among the Roma, and there are now five Romany newspapers.

Other minorities

Around 70,000 **Ukrainians** live in Maramureş and Bucovina, and 45,000 **Russians** (mostly Lipovani) in the Danube Delta, Dobrogea and Moldavia. Almost as many **Serbs** reside at the other end of the country, in the Banat, having fled from Turkish domination in the eighteenth and nineteenth centuries, and there are about 18,000 **Slovaks** in the same area, descendants of colonists brought into the region after the Turks had gone. Muslim descendants of the Turks and Tatars themselves still live on the Black Sea coast, around 23,000 of them, with 10,000 Bulgarians in the same area. In the thirteenth century, the **Armenian** diaspora reached Moldavia, and later moved on into Transylvania, settling in isolated but prosperous communities in towns such as Suceava, Brăila, Constanța, Dumbrăveni, Gheorgheni and Gherla; now, they number around 5000, almost totally assimilated, although their churches survive.

The **Aroumanians** are a group of ethnic Romanians who lived in Bulgaria and near Thessaloniki for many centuries as prosperous merchants with their own Romanian-language schools and culture; almost all returned to Romania between the World Wars, and they have virtually vanished as a recognizable culture, although their weaving (dark red geometrical patterns on a black background) can still be seen in museums.

Religion

The country's ethnic differences are reflected in its religions. The Romanian majority follows the **Romanian Orthodox** creed, which like the other

Orthodox Churches is a hierarchical body not given to free thought or questioning dogma or authority. Under Ceauşescu, the Church did everything it was asked to, and positively discouraged dissidence. In Transylvania, and particularly in Maramureş, many Romanians follow the **Uniate** creed (see p.216), which was regarded by the Communists as untrustworthy. Both churches are now resurgent.

The Hungarian population is divided more or less equally between the **Roman Catholic** and **Calvinist** (Reformat) faiths; the Calvinist Church was pretty much under the communist thumb, but the Catholic Church had the strength to resist and to keep its integrity. The Schwab and Landler Germans are also Roman Catholics, while the Saxons, Catholics when they arrived in Romania, later embraced the **Lutheran** faith, although a few are Seventh-Day Adventists. In addition, about 75,000 Hungarians, mainly around Cluj, Turda and Odorheiu Secuiesc, are **Unitarian** (see p.216), and since 1989, the Baptists and newer evangelical churches have been making great gains, mostly among people who are disoriented by change and the loss of certainty and stability in society.

Wildlife and environmental issues

Thanks to its antiquated agriculture and extensive areas of untouched native forest and wetland, Romania is uniquely important for wildlife in Europe. Whilst outside its borders, the image of the country is of industrial pollution, the reality is that its landscapes are considerably less polluted than much of present-day Western Europe. As you climb up into the hills, you enter a world where pesticides and fertilizers have never been used and where meadows are full of an amazing variety of birds and wild flowers – a landscape representative of Europe two or three centuries ago.

That said, the country has suffered, and there are numerous industrial plants that cause immense damage in their immediate neighbourhood. While the bulk of the damage was inflicted during the communist period, some of the worst offenders, such as Copşa Mică's carbon-black plant and the Valea Călugărească fertilizer plant (east of Ploieşti), were built in the capitalist period, while the Reşiţa and Hunedoara steelworks and the Zlatna copper smelter date back to the eighteenth century.

Habitat

One third of Romania is mountain, largely forested, and this is where most of the more interesting flora and fauna are to be found. One third of the country is hill and plateau, with a fair quantity of woodland remaining, and one third is plain, mostly intensively farmed.

The **Carpathian mountains** form an arc sweeping south from Ukraine and around Transylvania to end on the Danube at the Iron Gates. At lower levels (up to around 800m) the natural vegetation is forest oak and hornbeam, lime (especially lower down) and ash. Romania still has impressive stretches of this kind of forest which has largely disappeared in other parts of Europe. This altitude is still too low for the large carnivores, though wolves may have started to repopulate some areas. Even the hill farmland at this height – largely grazing and hay meadows with small-scale plots of crops – is comparatively rich in wildlife, however, with an abundance of butterflies, and birds such as red-backed shrike. Above 800m, beech becomes increasingly common, and at around 1400m, it forms an association with common silver fir and sycamore known as Carpathian Beech Forest (*Fagetum carpaticum*). Spruce is dominant above this, and above 1700m, comes the lower alpine zone, characterized by dwarf pine, juniper and low-growing goat willow, and then, from 1900m upwards, the higher alpine zone of grass, creeping shrubs, lichen, moss and ultimately bare rock.

Elsewhere, particularly on the **Transylvanian plateau**, there is much more oak and beech forest, although large areas have been cleared for grazing and small-scale arable farming. Until the twentieth century, large areas of eastern Romania – particularly southern Moldavia and Dobrogea – were covered by grassy steppes, the western end of the immensely fertile Chernozem or "black earth" belt that stretches east for 4000km to Novosibirsk in Russia.

The majority of this steppe went under the plough after World War II, though remnant areas can still be found, some (such as Cheia Dobrogea, 38km northwest of Constanţa), protected as nature reserves.

In the **southwest** of the country, near the Iron Gates of the Danube, the spectacular Cerna Valley is notable for its more Mediterranean climate, with Turkey and downy oaks, Banat pine and sun-loving plant species on the limestone rocks of the Mehedinţi, Cerna and Little Retezat massifs.

The **Danube Delta** is a unique habitat, described in detail on p.000. Formed from the massive quantity of sediments brought down the river, it is Europe's most extensive wetland and the world's largest continuous reedbed. It is a uniquely important breeding area for birds, as well as a wintering area and a key stepping-stone on one of the most important migration routes from northern Europe via the eastern Mediterranean to Africa.

Nature reserves have existed in Romania since the 1930s, and some 6.6 percent of the country is now protected. These reserves range from vast uninhabited areas to relatively modest, but still valuable sites, including caves, rocks and even individual trees. The first National Park was created in 1935 in the Retezat mountains (for a few years treated by Ceauşescu as a private hunting reserve). The core area of the Danube Delta received similar protection at much the same time. The Retezat and Rodna mountains and the Danube Delta have been named as part of UNESCO's worldwide network of Biosphere Reserves, and at least ten other national parks are yet to be designated. These include the Bicaz and Nera gorges, the Cerna valley, and the Apuseni, Piatra Craiului, and Căliman mountains.

Flora

The Romanian landscape has generally been less affected by man than that of Western Europe and the richness of wild flowers is one result. In springtime, the **mountain meadows** of Romania are a riot of wild flowers, 12 percent of which are endemic to the Carpathians. The timing of this varies with the altitude, so that any time from April to July you should be able to find spectacular scenes of clover, hawkweed, burdock, fritillary and ox-eye daisy covered in butterflies and, at higher levels, gentians, white false helleborine, globeflower and crocus. **Alpine plants** include campanulas, saxifrage, orchids, alpine buttercup, pinks and, in a few places, edelweiss. The **hay meadows** lying below the areas of mountain forest are also extremely rich in flowers.

In the warmer **southwest** of the country, the Cerna and Nera gorges are especial suntraps, with rarities such as *Allium obliquum*, *Aconitum fissurae*, *Hieracium tordanum* and various species of *Dianthus*, while there are other rare varieties of *Hieracium* in the Retezat Scientific Reservation, and orchids, lilies and *Carduus* varieties on the limestone of the Little Retezat, as well as a number of rarities in Turda Gorge in the Apuseni. One of the most accessible flower-rich sites is the wonderful Zănoaga Gorge in the Bucegi mountains.

The **Danube Delta** is home to at least 1600 plant species, which fall into three main categories. The floating islets (*plaur*) that occupy much of the Delta's area are largely composed of reeds (80 percent *Phragmites australis*), with mace reed, sedge, Dutch rush, yellow water-flag, water fern, water dock, water forget-me-not, water hemlock, and brook mint. In the still backwaters, wholly submerged waterweeds include water-milfoil, hornwort, and water-thyme;

while floating on the surface you'll find water plantain, arrowhead, duckweed, water soldier, white and yellow waterlily, frog bit, marsh thistle, and épi d'eau. The river banks are home to white willow and poplar, with isolated strands of alder and ash, while the more mature forests of Letea and Caraorman also contain oaks, elm, aspen and shrubs such as blackthorn, hawthorn and dog rose. The Romanian peony can be found in woodlands such as Babadag Forest, just to the south.

Birds

Europe's most important wetland, the **Danube Delta**, serves as a breeding area for summer visitors, a stopping-off point for migrants and a wintering-ground for wildfowl; permanent residents are relatively few. Dedicated birders time their visit to the area for two seasons – from the end of March to early June, and from late July to October – but the Delta and especially the more accessible lakes and reedbeds near the coast to the south are worth a visit with binoculars at any season. The Delta lies on the major migration route from east Africa via the Nile Delta, the eastern Mediterranean and the Bosphorus, northwards along the great river-systems of Russia all the way to the Arctic.

The **spring period**, especially May, is an excellent time to visit, with the rare breeding species – black-winged pratincole, pygmy cormorant, glossy ibis, white and Dalmatian pelicans, and warblers including paddyfield warbler – all arriving. The reedbeds are alive with the returned songbirds, of which audibly the most obvious is the very noisy great reed warbler. These are accompanied by large numbers of waders still on passage to wetlands far to the north, such as the curlew sandpiper, broad-billed and marsh sandpipers and little stints, as well as more common species such as green, curlew and wood sandpipers and vast teeming flocks of ruff. By this time, the great colonies – of herons (night, grey and squacco herons, great white and little egrets), and of both species of cormorant – are at a peak of activity; the lower Danube holds most of the world population of the endangered pygmy cormorant, which is common in and near the Delta. The wader breeding colonies are also very active, and you will find yourself being scolded loudly when near the nests of avocets and black-winged stilts.

High summer is no less rich in birds, this being a good time to see the first of the returning waders and the population of summer visitors is at a peak in the period immediately after breeding. This is an excellent time to see formation-flying white pelicans (and the rare Dalmatian pelican), as well as birds of prey such as the colonial red-footed falcon, lesser spotted eagle, marsh harrier and long-legged buzzard.

In **winter**, the number of visiting birds in the Delta area is reduced but still impressive. Main visitors include most of the European population of great white herons (or egrets), at times the entire world population of red-breasted geese (around 70,000 birds) and hundreds of thousands (rising to a peak of around a third of a million) white-fronted geese; there are significant populations of other wildfowl including the exotic-looking red-crested pochard, as well as the pintail, goldeneye, wigeon, teal, smew and red- and black-throated divers; just off the Black Sea shore the water can teem with wintering black-necked grebes, and rough-legged buzzards are a common sight on roadside wires in open country.

Inland from the coast, on the **inland plains**, some species indicative of steppe country still persist, such as short-toed and calandra larks (the largest European lark), while summer visitors include the exotic-looking hoopoe, lesser-spotted and booted eagles, red-footed falcons, European rollers, bee-eaters and lesser grey shrikes – the last three of these are common on roadside wires in Dobrogea and the lowlands.

Away from the Delta, the most worthwhile nature reserves are inevitably in the **mountains**; golden eagles are now rare, but ravens are common. On the tree line, black and three-toed woodpeckers can be found, together with ring ouzels in summer, while on the highest crags there are alpine accentors and wallcreepers, together with the common black redstart, water pipits and alpine swifts and, in some lower crags, crag martins and rock buntings. There are also birds usually associated with more northerly regions, such as shore larks and the rare dotterel (breeding only in the Cindrel mountains).

Mountain forests are home to the very shy capercaillie, as well as the (slightly easier to see) hazel grouse, and (in the north, around dwarf pine areas) black grouse. Restricted to the vast forests, mainly of spruce, is the shy nutcracker, as well as the crested tit, willow tit and coal tit, and the crossbill. The forests are also home to raptors, including buzzards, honey buzzards, sparrowhawks and goshawks, as well as a number of owl species, including the Ural owl, eagle owl, pygmy owl and Tengmalm's owl. The relatively healthy state of Romania's forests favours some birds that have declined in other extensive conifer forests (for example in Scandinavia) due to mismanagement and a paucity of rotting wood – a prime example is the white-backed woodpecker.

The extensive **lowland deciduous forests** of Romania harbour huge numbers of common European woodland birds – chaffinches, hawfinches, nuthatches, song thrushes, treecreepers and great, marsh and blue tits. Oak woods in this area are the domain of the middle-spotted woodpecker, joined in summer by nightingales, wood warblers, chiffchaffs and common redstarts.

Romania is also a refuge for the white stork, whose large nests are characteristically built in the heart of human habitations, on telephone poles and chimneys. The much rarer black stork also occurs, breeding in extensive areas of forest near water, for example along the Olt in southern Transylvania.

Animals

Romania has the most important national populations of large carnivore species – bear, wolf and lynx – in Europe. Having been protected under Ceauşescu for his own personal hunting, there are now five or six thousand **brown bear** in Romania, particularly in the eastern Carpathians. Although they do raid garbage bins on the outskirts of Braşov and in Poiana Braşov – as well as almost all mountain huts that are near or below the tree line – they are generally afraid of humans and will keep well clear unless you come between a female and her cubs in April or May. Whilst they will take prey as large as red deer (not to mention sheep, cattle and horses), they are by diet omnivorous, famously raiding wild bees' nests not only for honey but also for the larvae. In addition to this they will eat carrion, especially wolf-kill, large amounts of wild fruit (occasionally raiding apple orchards in hill villages), wasps' nests, and beech mast in autumn. Bears are hunted, but in a strictly controlled way, and the population is at a healthy level.

There is currently a population of around two thousand **wolves** in Romania, generally restricted to forests. Although they do regularly take sheep in grazing areas, wolves represent no danger at all to mankind. Their prey consists almost entirely of red deer, roe deer, occasionally boar and chamois, and the odd sheep. They are hunted, especially in winter, when their tracks can be followed in the snow. **Lynx** are fairly widespread (but very hard to spot) in hill forests and are the most specialized large predator of all (bear and wolf are both happy to scavenge); they take roe deer in forest areas and chamois above the tree line.

Red deer can be found in some lowland forests but the species is most widespread in spruce forest in hill areas. The mating cries of the stags can be heard echoing through the valleys in September and October, and it's sometimes possible to observe their ritual conflicts from a distance. Above the tree line in the Transylvanian Alps and the Rodna, the most visible mammal is the **chamois**, which can be seen grazing in flocks with a lone male perched on the skyline to keep watch. **Wild boar** are also very widespread, being found in the lower forests (including the Delta), and all the way up to and beyond the tree line in the mountains. They appear mostly at night, and can leave a clearing looking as if it has been badly ploughed when they have finished digging for roots. Weighing up to 200kg, almost as much as a red deer stag, they have a reputation for aggression when protecting their young in the springtime.

Other mammals include the European bison, which is kept in a semi-wild state in several different areas; the golden jackal, which is spreading from its stronghold in the south, especially in Dobrogea; the wild cat, which occurs commonly in lowland forests as well as up to the highest forests in the mountains; the red fox, which is even more widespread, from the forests of the Delta to the very highest mountain summits; and the badger, which is widespread but very uncommon. There are three species of polecat, all of them very shy, and in the mountain forests pine martens are common, as are beech martens in woods at a lower altitude.

The Danube Delta is one of the last refuges of the European mink (which continues to thrive there), and also home to enot (or raccoon dog), coypu and muskrat, all North American species that have escaped from fur farms in the former Soviet Union. European beaver (a native mammal) has recently been reintroduced in Transylvania. Most of the predator species (in which Romania is so rich) depend to a large extent on various rodent species for their prey; in steppe areas it is impossible to miss the charming European souslik, Romania's very own gopher, found especially in Dobrogea. Three kinds of hamster occur, including the endemic Romanian hamster, and hikers in the Făgăraş, Retezat, Rodna and a few other areas will provide encounters with the enchanting alpine marmot, living in colonies in the alpine zone, well above the tree line. In forest areas there are no fewer than four kinds of dormouse. Stoats and weasels are also widespread, as are bats.

The most frequently seen **amphibians** are the abundant little bombina toads: yellow-bellied toads in the hills and fire-bellied toads in the lowlands. More unusual amphibians include two species of spadefoot toad, the moor frog and the agile frog. The quite amazingly loud frog chorus of the Danube Delta and other lakes and reedbeds is formed by massed choirs of male marsh frogs. Newt fanciers find heaven in Romania's myriad ponds and watercourses; as well as the familiar warty, smooth and alpine newts there is the endemic Montandon's newt, restricted to the Eastern Carpathians. Fire salamanders with their vivid black and orange colouring are easily seen when wandering in the woods during or just after rain, while the exotic-looking green toad (with its trilling call) is frequently seen under village street lights in all areas as it hunts for bugs that are attracted by the light.

There is a healthy population of **snakes** – the commonest being the grass snake, found in the Danube Delta and up to some altitude in the mountains. In coastal areas is the more aquatic, fish-hunting dice snake; other non-venomous species include the smooth snake, four-lined snake and the impressively large whip snake. Europe's most venomous and fastest-moving snake, the horned viper, occurs near Băile Herculane, and the common viper (or adder) is more widespread, tending to be found in hill areas. The steppe viper (or Orsini's viper) survives in the Delta, for example in the woods north of Sfântu Gheorghe.

The warmer climate of the southern Banat and Dobrogea is especially suitable for **other reptiles** – not just snakes but also some fairly exotic-looking lizards, such as the Balkan green lizard, the green lizard and the Balkan wall lizard. More everyday lizard species, such as the sand lizard and viviparous lizard, are widespread. The aquatic European pond terrapin is common around the edge of lowland lakes and in the Danube Delta, and there are two species of tortoise: the rare Hermann's tortoise, found only in areas of the southwest such as the Cerna valley, and the more widespread spur-thighed tortoise, fairly common in woods in Dobrogea.

With little in the way of industry and an absence of fertilizers and pesticides in almost all hill areas, the river systems have impressive populations of **fish**. Grayling, for example, is much less rare in Carpathian hill streams than it has become in other areas of Europe. Six species of sturgeon occur in the Danube, and the picture for these is less rosy, the Iron Gates dam preventing the migration upstream of several species, with resulting hybridization. Rainbow trout have been less widely introduced than in western Europe, meaning that the native brown trout is much more common; the endemic Danube salmon or huchen is now very rare.

It is scarcely possible to avoid fish when in the Danube Delta; the common species caught are common carp, crucian carp, pike (especially in autumn), pike-perch or zander, and catfish or wels. In fact, the Delta is a remarkable place for fish, with catfish around two metres long being regularly caught and confirmed accounts of even larger specimens showing some interest in taking village women fetching water from channel banks. Sturgeon migrate through the Delta, as do Danube mackerel. Several fairly rare goby species also occur, especially in lakes and lagoons south of the Delta. Most of these species have declined to some extent due to pollution, over-fishing and eutrophication of the water due to algal blooms. For this reason, several areas of the Delta that are free from these problems have become strictly protected reserves, with great efforts made to preserve the water quality.

James Roberts, a true friend of Romania, who died far too young in 2002

The environment

Romania's mammoth increase in industrial output – particularly of steel and fertilizer – was achieved by a total disregard for any considerations other than maximizing production. Thus, industrial injuries are commonplace, while **energy consumption** is shockingly inefficient; **pollution** is calculated to affect 10 percent of the population (5 percent severely), and 20 percent of the country's territory. **Rubbish** too, is a developing problem, as Western-style packaging takes over.

The most polluted sites are Copşa Mică, Zlatna and Baia Mare, all of which produce acid rain and a cocktail of heavy metals that run straight into the water system. Toxic emissions are regularly above the legal maximum here, with life expectancy up to ten years below average. In **Baia Mare**, for example, the industrial zone was built upwind of the residential area, and in a valley subject to thermal inversions that trap the pollution. Almost as bad are the artificial fibre factories of **Brăila** and **Suceava**, and there are fertilizer and petrochemical plants in Arad, Dej, Făgăraş, Piteşti, Ploieşti and Târgu Mureş, all producing illegal levels of hydrocarbons and inorganic compounds. In **Bucharest**, total emissions have fallen by a third since 1989, due to industrial recession; however, in some industrial areas, ammonia levels are still nine times the legal limit and lead two hundred times the limit, but throughout the city, nitrous oxides and lead (in car fumes) and dust are the main problems.

Additionally, the use of **fertilizers**, **pesticides** and **insecticides** has caused problems, damaging 900,000 hectares of agricultural land and leaving 200,000 hectares totally unproductive; agricultural nitrates, too, entered the drinking water supply, putting millions of people at risk, and many of the country's rivers are now dead. Although fertilizer use has halved since 1989, this is due to cost rather than environmental awareness, and ecological disasters continue to occur. In January 2000, a dam at the Aurul goldmine near Baia Mare gave way, releasing water containing a hundred tonnes of cyanide, which made its way into Hungary, killing everything in the Someş and Tisa rivers – the situation wasn't helped when the chairman of Aurul's Australian owners claimed the fish had died of cold. In March that year, there was also a spill of sludge contaminated with heavy metals from a mine at Baia Borşa, which also made its way into the Tisa, precipitating demands for international efforts to clean up Romania's mines.

Furthermore, the damming of the Iron Gates and the dyking of the Danube flood plain has led to the **Danube's flow** through the Delta being reduced dramatically, leading to algal blooms and lower fish yields, and the Delta may die unless water flows can be sped up. Consequently, the **Black Sea** is one of the most polluted areas in the world – toxic wastes, over-fishing, and a one-fifth fall in freshwater inputs combining to disastrous affect. Surfeits of nutrients cause plankton blooms (red tides), leading to loss of light and dissolved oxygen, and thus decimating fish stocks.

For a brief period, Ceauşescu did take an interest in pollution problems, with several environmental protection laws passed, but as he became more obsessed with expanding industrial capacity, environmental data became increasingly secret. After the revolution, a new **ministry** was created with the aim of reducing pollution; two ecological parties were set up, and there's now an Environmental Protection Agency in each county.

Ceauşescu was also determined to have his own **nuclear power station** at Cernavodă, on the Danube. However, construction standards were so appalling that it had to be almost totally rebuilt. The reactor now produces ten percent of Romania's power, and a second reactor should be operational by 2007. Thirty percent of power comes from hydroelectric dams, a wind power project is to be developed in Constanţa harbour, and the Austrian government is sponsoring a scheme in Călimăneşti to provide domestic hot water from geothermal energy.

The protection of **historical monuments** was upheld until 1977, when the Historical Monuments Administration was disbanded for daring to oppose Ceaușescu's plans for Bucharest's Civic Centre. There was no effective protection from then until 1989, and many towns have simply been gutted. In 1990, the bureau was re-established but without financial support, and the required legislation got stuck in parliament. In 2001, a law was at last passed to end the demolition of listed buildings, but most conservation to date has been achieved with funding from the Church, or, in the case of **Saxon monuments**, from Germany. **Biertan**, the **Bucovina** and **Horez monasteries**, and a group of wooden **Maramureş churches** have all become UNESCO World Heritage sites.

Music

The Carpathian mountains trace a cultural fault line across Romania that separates Central Europe from the Balkans, sharply dividing the musical styles on either side. Of course such borders are rarely impermeable; the same language is spoken on either side and there is plenty of cultural and musical cross-fertilization. The many strands of Romanian music are extraordinarily varied and archaic, preserving almost archaeological layers of development, from the "medieval" music at the extremities in Ghimeş and Maramureş, to the "Renaissance" sounds of Mezőség and the more sophisticated music of Kalotaszeg.

Tours to study Romanian folk **dance** are organized by the Doina Foundation, Aarhuispad 22, 3067 PR Rotterdam, Netherlands (☏10/421 8622, ✉stichting.doina@hetnet.nl), which also helps organize an annual Balkan festival in Zetten and sells flutes, boots, costumes and icons.

Transylvania

With its age-old ethnic mix, Transylvania's music is extraordinary, with wild melodies and dances that are played all night, and is part of a distinctly

Classical music

Classical music was lavishly funded by the communist state and still has far less elitist connotations than in the West. Main cities have a philharmonic orchestra and/or an opera house, and tickets (available through the local Agenţia Teatrale) are very cheap. Additionally, the Saxon communities have maintained a Germanic tradition of singing chorales by Bach and his contemporaries.

Romanian classical music remains virtually synonymous with **George Enescu**, born near Dorohoi in 1881. His *Romanian Rhapsodies* were first performed in 1903 and remain his most popular works; his *Third Violin Sonata* is his best chamber work and also has a Romanian flavour. Later works also showed experimental features, such as the use of a musical saw in his masterpiece, the opera *Oedipe*, the most comprehensive treatment of the myth, covering Oedipus's entire life from birth to death. There is a good modern recording (1989) featuring José van Dam. Romania's greatest pianist was **Dinu Lipatti** (Enescu's godson), who died aged just 33 from leukaemia, in 1950. In his lifetime he was referred to as "God's chosen instrument". His recordings (just five CDs) have never been deleted, and one of them, made in Besançon just months before his death, is highly regarded. **Sergiu Ceilibidache** (1912–96) studied in Berlin and conducted the Berlin Philharmonic, the Swedish Radio Symphony Orchestra, the Stuttgart Radio Orchestra, and from 1980 the Munich Philharmonic, making his US debut only in 1984. Described as "transcendentally endowed", although not very interested in music outside the mainstream Germanic repertoire, he was also a perfectionist, demanding up to eighteen rehearsals for some concerts.

Perhaps the best-known contemporary Romanian musicians are soprano **Angela Gheorghiu** (born in 1965), and violinist Alex Bălanescu, founder of the **Bălanescu Quartet**, who has worked with David Byrne, Kraftwerk, Spiritualized, Gavin Bryars and Michael Nyman.

Transylvanian culture – the composers Bartók and Kodály found this the most fertile area for their folk-song collecting trips in the early twentieth century. Music serves a social function, and in some areas there are still regular weekly dances, but everywhere, music is played at weddings, sometimes at funerals and at other occasions, including when conscripts go off to the army, and around Christmas.

The Romanians and Hungarians share many melodies and dances and it takes a very experienced ear to tell the difference (and even then, a particular melody may be described as Hungarian in one village and Romanian in another just over the hill). The Romanian dances often have a slightly less regular rhythm than the Hungarian, but often the only difference between one tune and another is the language in which it is sung. There's even a unique recording of an old man from the village of Dimbău (Küküllődombó) singing a song with the first half of each line in Hungarian and the second half in Romanian.

The music of Transylvania sounds much less Balkan than that from over the Carpathians; it might seem wild and exotic, but it is recognizably part of a Central European tradition with added spice from its geographical location. The traditional ensemble is a **string trio** – a violin, viola (*contra*)and a double bass, plus in certain parts of Transylvania, a cimbalom. The *primás*, the first violinist, plays the melody and leads the musicians from one tune into another, while the *contra* and bass are the accompaniment and rhythm sections of the band. The *contra* has only three strings and a flat bridge so it only plays chords, and it's the deep sawing of the bass and the rhythmic spring of the *contra* that gives Transylvanian music its particular sound. Often an extra violin or *contra* is added to give more volume.

Wedding parties

Wedding parties last a couple of days and often take place in a specially constructed wedding "tent" built from wooden beams and tree fronds. The place is strung with ribbons and fir branches, tables are piled high with garish cakes and bottles of *ţuică*, and fresh courses are brought round at regular intervals. There's a space for dancing and on a platform is the band of musicians sawing and scraping away at battered old fiddles, and a bass making the most mesmerizing sound.

Wedding **customs** vary slightly from region to region but generally the band starts things off at the bride's or groom's house, accompanying the processions to the church and possibly playing for one of the real emotional high spots, the bride's farewell song (*cântecul miresei*) to her family and friends, and to her maiden life. While the marriage takes place within the church, the band plays for the young people, or those not invited to the feast, to dance to in the street outside. Once the couple come out of the church there's another procession to the wedding feast – either in the village hall or the wedding "tent" – where the musicians will play all night, alternating songs to accompany the feast with dances; there are even particular pieces for certain courses of the banquet.

Late in the evening comes the bride's dance (*jocul miresei*) when, in some villages, the guests dance with the bride in turn and offer money. Things usually wind down by dawn on Sunday; people wander off home or collapse in a field somewhere and then around lunchtime the music starts up again for another session until late in the evening.

With the trend towards larger and larger weddings, all sorts of **instruments** have started to find their ways into bands. Most common is the piano-accordion, which, like the *contra*, plays chords, though it lacks its rhythmic spring. Very often you can hear a clarinet or the slightly deeper and reedeer *taragot*, which sounds wonderful in the open air. Sadly, however, because young people have moved away to work in towns, they often demand the guitars, drums and electric keyboards of the urban groups – along with appalling amplification, which is increasingly brought in, too, by traditional acoustic bands. Some groups stick unswervingly to the traditional line-up, like the marvellous **Pălatca** band, recognized as one of the finest in Transylvania.

Gypsy bands

The band from Pălatca (Magyarpalatka), like most of the village musicians in Romania, are **Gypsies**. In the villages, Gypsy communities all tend to live along one particular street in the outskirts, often called Strada Muzicanţilor or Strada Lăutari – both meaning "Musicians' Street". Gypsy musicians will play for Romanian, Hungarian and Gypsy weddings alike and they know almost instinctively the repertoire required. Children often play alongside their parents from an early age and grow up with the music in their blood.

Playing music can earn good money; the best bands command handsome fees, plus the odd chicken and bottles of *ţuică*. It's also an indication of the value of music in this society that the musicians are not only well rewarded but also well respected. When the old *primás* of the Pălatca band died, all the people he had played for in the village came to pay their respects at his funeral.

It's difficult to highlight the best bands – there are dozens of them – but in addition to the Pălatca band, those of the following villages of central Transylvania are excellent (the names are given in their Romanian form with the Hungarian in brackets): Vaida–Cămăraş (Vajdakamarás), Suatu (Magyarszovát), Sopuru de Câmpie (Mezőszopor), Sângeorz-Băi (Oláhszentgyőrgy) and Sic (Szék), an almost totally Hungarian village and one of the great treasure houses of Hungarian music.

The Hungarians

The music of the Hungarian minority has made most impact outside of Transylvania, as the Hungarians consciously promoted the culture of their brethren in the region to highlight their suffering under Ceauşescu. Hungaroton, the state label, produced a large number of excellent recordings while Budapest-based groups such as **Muzsikás** and the **Ardealul Ensemble** have toured extensively and acted as ambassadors for the music.

Transylvania has always held a very special place in Hungarian culture as it preserves archaic traditions and medieval settlement patterns that have disappeared in Hungary itself. Under Ceauşescu's rule, the Hungarians were threatened, and there was a deliberate effort to wear their traditional costumes, sing their songs and play their music as a statement of identity, even protest. These days, national costume and dances are much more visible among the Hungarian minority than the majority Romanians (other than in Maramureş).

Regional styles

Within the overall Transylvanian musical language, there are hundreds of local dialects: the style of playing a particular dance can vary literally from village to village. But there are some broad musical regions where the styles are distinct and recognizable.

Bartók gathered much of his Romanian material in the area around **Hunedoara**. The area is still musically very rich though, strangely enough, a recent musical survey found that virtually the entire repertoire had changed. Further north is the area the Hungarians call **Kalotaszeg**, home to some of the most beautiful music in the region. This area lies along the main route from Cluj (Kolozsvár) to Hungary and Central Europe, and the influence of Western-style harmony shows itself in the sophisticated minor-key accompaniment – a development of the last twenty years. Kalotaszeg is famous for its men's dance, the *legényes*, and the slow *hajnali* songs performed in the early morning as a wedding feast dies down, which have a sad and melancholy character all their own. One of the best of all recordings of Transylvanian music includes both these forms, featuring the Gypsy *primás* **Sándor Fodor** from the village of Baciu (Kisbács), just west of Cluj. There is also some fine Romanian music in Sălaj county, in the north of this area, which can be heard in the villages or on a very fine Romanian recording of dances from Sălaj (*Jocuri Sălajene*) by a small ensemble from Zalău.

Probably the richest area for music is known to the Romanians as **Câmpia Transilvanei** and to the Hungarians as **Mezőség**. This is the Transylvanian Heath, north and east of Cluj – a poor, isolated region whose music preserves a much more primitive feel with strong major chords moving in idiosyncratic harmony.

Further east is the most densely populated Hungarian region, the **Székelyföld** (Székely Land). The Székelys, who speak a distinctive dialect of Hungarian, were the defenders of the eastern flanks of the Hungarian kingdom in the Middle Ages, when the Romanians, as landless peasants, counted for little. Rising up towards the Carpathians, their land becomes increasingly wild and mountainous, and the dance music is different once again, with eccentric ornamentation and very often a cimbalom in the band.

For Hungarian-speakers, the songs are fascinating as they preserve old-style elements that survive nowhere else. One village ballad about a terrible massacre of the Székelys by the Hapsburgs in 1764 (see p.192), often sung as if it had happened yesterday, recounts their flight over the Carpathians into Moldavia, where they preserved music and customs that are no longer found in the Székelyföld itself. During World War II, 14,000 Székelys were resettled in the south of Hungary. In those outer reaches, the string bands of Transylvania have given way to a solo violin or flute accompanying the dances.

Moldavia and Maramureş

Moldavia's music – with its archaic pipe and drum style – sounds wild and other-worldly, split across the divide between Transylvania and the Balkans. Hungarian records of the Csángós (the Hungarian occupants of this area) often feature music from the Ghimeş (Gyimes) valley, where you find peculiar duos of violin and *gardon* – a sort of double bass played by hitting its strings with a stick. The fiddle playing is highly ornamented and the rhythms complex and irregular, showing Oriental influence. The extraordinary Csángó singer **Ilona Nyisztor** from Oneşti (in Bacău county) has a growing reputation.

On the other side of Transylvania, sandwiched between Hungary, Ukraine and the Carpathians, are the regions of **Maramureş** and **Oaş**, both areas of distinctive regional character. Village costumes are worn for everyday life and the music includes magic songs and spells of incantation against sickness and the evil eye. You can still find Sunday afternoon village dances, and a *băută* or musical party can be arranged on the slightest pretext. From birth, through courtship and marriage to death, life has a musical accompaniment.

The music of Maramureş, while recognizably Transylvanian, sounds closer to that of Romanians beyond the Carpathians. As often happens in the highland regions of Romania, here the music is played predominantly by Romanians, not Gypsies. With an instrumental group of violin (*cetera*), guitar (*zongora*) and drum (*doba*), it has a fairly primitive sound, lacking beguiling harmonies and with a repeated chord on the *zongora* (often played vertically and back to front) as a drone. Hundreds of years ago, much of the music of Europe probably sounded something like this. A *zacala de baut* or drinking song is an instrumental piece during which people call out improvised couplets, usually men teasing women and vice versa; a *zacala de jucat* is a dance, of which the most popular are the *barbatesc* (men's dance), a circle dance for men with similar improvised lyrics, and the *învârtita*, a quick couple dance.

Wallachia

Most village bands in **Wallachia** comprise **Gypsies**: the group is generally named **Taraf** and then their village name. These musicians (*lautari*) are professionals who play a vital function in village life, yet their music sounds altogether different from that of their Transylvanian counterparts. The word *taraf* comes from the Arabic and suggests the more oriental flavour of this music. Songs are often preceded by an instrumental improvisation called *taksim*, another name borrowed from the Middle East.

The lead instrument is the fiddle, played in a highly ornamented style. The middle parts are taken by the *ţambal* (cimbalom), which fills out the harmony and adds a rippling to the texture. At the bottom is the double bass, ferociously plucked rather than bowed Transylvanian style. In the old days, you'd always find a *cobza* (lute) in such bands, but it has given way to the *ţambal*, guitar and accordion. The staple dances are the *hora*, *sârba* and *brâu* – all of which are danced in a circle.

In Romanian, the word *cânta* means both "to sing" and "to play an instrument", and the *lautari* of Wallachia usually do both. Whereas in Transylvania the bands play exclusively dance music, the musicians in the south of the country have an impressive repertoire of **epic songs and ballads** which they are called on to perform. These might be specific marriage songs or legendary tales like *Şarpele* (The Snake) or exploits of brigands. One of the tunes you hear played by *lautari* all over Romania is *Ciocârlia* (The Lark), which has also become a concert piece for the stage ensembles.

Considering the wealth of village musicians in Romania, it's significant that four of the few recordings available feature the same *taraf* from the village of **Clejani**, southwest of Bucharest (see p.000); it's a village of some five hundred Gypsies, almost all professional musicians, much in demand throughout the area – the recordings of the **Taraf of Haidouks** are extraordinary, packed full of truly virtuoso performances.

The doină

The **doină** is a free-form, semi-improvised ancient song tradition. With poetic texts of grief, bitterness, separation and longing, it might be called the Romanian blues. Very often, different texts are sung to the same melody, which may then take on a contrasting character. It is essentially private music, sung to one-self at moments of grief or reflection, although nowadays the songs are often performed by professional singers or in instrumental versions by Gypsy bands. Old *doinăs* of the traditional kind can still be found in Oltenia, between the Olt and Danube rivers in the south of the country.

Flutes and pipes

The pastoral way of life is fast disappearing and with it the traditional instrumental repertoire of the *fluier* (shepherd's flute). But there is one form – a sort of folk tone poem – that is still regularly played all over the country: **the shepherd who lost his sheep**. Referred to as early as the sixteenth century by the Hungarian poet Bálint Balassi, it begins with a sad, *doină*-like tune as the shepherd laments his lost flock. Then he sees his sheep in the distance and a merry dance tune takes over, only to return to the sad lament when he realizes it's just a group of stones. Finally the sheep are found and the whole thing ends with a lively dance in celebration.

For years, Romania's best-known musician on the international stage was **Gheorghe Zamfir**, composer of the soundtrack of *Picnic at Hanging Rock*. He plays *nai*, or **pan-pipes**, which have existed in Romania since ancient times. In the eighteenth century "Wallachian" musicians were renowned abroad and the typical ensemble consisted of violin, *nai* and *cobză*. But by the end of the next century, the *nai* had begun to disappear and after World War I only a handful of players were left. One of these was the legendary **Fanica Luca** (1894–1968), who taught Zamfir his traditional repertoire. Nowadays, Zamfir plays material from all over the place, often accompanied by the organ of Marcel Cellier; Radu Simion is another fine player.

The Banat

The Banat, Romania's western corner, is ethnically very mixed, with communities of Hungarians, Serbs, Slovaks, Germans and Gypsies living alongside the Romanians. Its music is fast, furious and a relatively new phenomenon, having absorbed a lot from the *novokomponovana* music of neighbouring Serbia. It's extremely popular, played all the time on the national radio and by Gypsy bands everywhere. Probably its attraction is its fast, modern, urban sound, with saxophones and frequently erotic lyrics. The Silex recording of the Taraf de Carancebeş (sic) is a great introduction to this virtuoso style.

The Ceauşescu legacy

Nicolae Ceauşescu's legacy even extends to some of the country's folk music, which was manipulated into a sort of "fakelore" to glorify the dictator and present the rich past of the Romanian peasantry. Huge sanitized displays called **Cântarea Romaniei** (Song of Romania) were held in regional centres around the country with thousands of peasants dressed up in costume bussed out to picturesque hillsides to sing and dance. This was shown on television every Sunday (indeed, programmes of this kind are still used to fill the odd half-hour gap in the TV schedule). The words of songs were often changed – removing anything deemed to be religious or that questioned the peasants' love of their labours, and replacing it with bland patriotic sentiments or hymns to peace.

This gave folklore a pretty bad name among the educated classes, though the peasants were hardly bothered by it. They just did what they were told for Cântarea Romaniei and got on with their real music in the villages. The fact is that traditional music still flourishes throughout Romania – probably more than anywhere else in Europe – not thanks to Ceauşescu, but despite him.

CONTEXTS | Music

Discography

Many of these recordings can be bought from Passion Music in the UK (☎01256/770 747; Ⓦwww.passion-music.co.uk); see also Ⓦwww.hungaroton .hu, Ⓦwww.fono.hu, Ⓦwww.etnofon.hu, Ⓦwww.crammed.be, Ⓦwww .dol.ro/producatori/muzica/Electrecord/Electrecord.htm and Ⓦwww.cdroots .com. You can hear selections of Romanian music at Ⓦwww.bbc.co .uk/radio3/world/guideromania.shtml.

General compilations

Romania: Musical Travelogue (Auvidis/Silex, France). An excellent disc with music from the Banat, Maramureş, and Wallachia, including good music by ethnic minorities and beautiful *cobză* playing by Dan Voinicu.

Romania: Wild Sounds from Transylvania, Wallachia & Moldavia (World Network,

Germany). The best overall anthology of Romanian music, with great ensembles including the Taraf de Haidouks and the Moldavian Fanfare Ciocărlia.

Village Music from Romania (AIMP/VDE-Gallo, Switzerland). A three-disc box of archival recordings of specialized interest made by the musicologist Constantin Brailoiu.

Transylvanian music

Romanian, Hungarian and Gypsy village bands, as well as *táncház* groups from Budapest.

Ardealul Ensemble *Gypsy Music From Transylvania* (Ethnophonie,

Romania). Instrumental music led by Emil Mihaiu, currently considered the best fiddler in Transylvania, with two Hungarian-speaking Roma. Excellent notes. Also Emil Mihaiu

Ensemble, *Romanian and Hungarian Music from Transylvania* (Ethnophonie).

Budatelke Band *Budatelke / Szászszantgyörgy* (Fonó, Hungary). The village band of Budatelke in northern Mezoség, playing mainly Romanian repertoire plus Hungarian, Gypsy and Saxon tracks.

Sándor Fodor *Hungarian Folk Music from Transylvania* (Hungaroton, Hungary). From the most respected Gypsy fiddler of the Kalotaszeg region, the energy and bite of this compelling disc of both Hungarian and Romanian music are fantastic. One of the essential Transylvanian records. Also *The Blues at Dawn* (Fonó, Hungary), a beautifully produced CD of the slow, melancholy *hajnali* (morning songs).

Béla Halmos *Aza szép piros hajnal* (Hungaroton, Hungary). One of the leading musicians of the Budapest *táncház* scene with a selection of music from various regions of Transylvania.

The Mácsingó Family *Báré – Magyarpalatka* (Fonó, Hungary). One of the important musical Gypsy families from the villages of Báré and Déva in central Transylvania. This may be too raw for some tastes - the bass saws, grates and often slides onto its notes and the lead fiddle is heavily ornamented, drawing energy and emotion out of every note – but it is the real thing.

Sandor Mate and band *Most jöttem Gyuláról, Gyulafehérvárról* (Periferic, Hungary). Some of the best Kolozsvar (Cluj) musicians playing instrumental tunes from the Szamos–Maros region.

Muzsikás *Máramaros* (Hannibal/ Ryko, UK). A fascinating CD from the top Hungarian *táncház* group joined by two veteran Gypsy musicians on fiddle and cimbalom to explore the lost Jewish repertory of Transylvania, distinguishable by the oriental-sounding augmented intervals in the melody. Also *Blues for Transylvania* and *Morning Star,* fine selections of Hungarian music from Transylvania and *The Bartók Album* (all Hannibal/Ryko, UK), recreating the music collected by Bartók.

Ökrös Ensemble *Transylvanian Portraits* (Koch, US). Comprehensive guide to the various styles of Transylvania by one of the best Budapest *táncház* groups. The fiddle playing of Csaba Ökrös on the last track is stunning.

Palatca Band *Magyarpalatka – Hungarian Folk Music from the Transylvanian Heath* (Hungaroton, Hungary). Probably the most celebrated band of central Transylvania, led by members of the Codoba family in the village of Magyarpalatka and typically comprising two fiddles, two *contras* and bass. A beautiful selection of traditional dance sets – one CD from the archives, the other by currently active musicians.

Katalin Szvorák, Márton Balogh, Márta Sebestyén and the Hegedos Ensemble *Tündérkert (Fairyland) - Hungarian and Romanian Folk Music from Transylvania* (Hungaroton, Hungary). Released in 1988 and something of a classic, a cross-section of the music to be heard in the various regions of Transylvania.

Szászcsávás Band *Folk Music from Transylvania* (Quintana/Harmonia Mundi, France). Szászcsávás (Ceuaş in Romanian) is a predominantly Hungarian village in the Kis-Küküllő region with one of the best Gypsy bands in the area. This is a great recording of a real village band with a wide dance repertoire, including Hungarian, Romanian, Saxon and Gypsy tunes.

Taraful Soporu de Cîmpie
(Buda/Musique du Monde, France)
Another fine Gypsy band from
Soporu in the Câmpia Transilvaniei.
Several sets of dance tunes and songs
sung by Vasile Soporan.

Várálmási Band *Várálmási Pici
Aladárés Bandája* (Fonó, Budapest).
One of the last old-time groups of
the Kalotaszeg region, whose *primás*
(leader) died shortly after the
recording in 1997. Includes a
bizarre Jewish tango.

Various *La Vraie Tradition de
Transylvanie* (Ocora, France). A
pioneering disc from the 1970s
that highlights real peasant music
from Maramures and Transylvania
when sanitized folklore was preva-
lent. It features some excellent
ensembles, bagpipes and a violin
with a horn, and from Maramures
there's a track from Gheorghe
Covaci, son of a fiddler Bartók
recorded in 1913.

Various *Magyarszovát – Búza* (Fonó,
Hungary). A double CD of

Hungarian music performed by
musicians and singers from two villages in Mezőség; dance sets and
many unaccompanied songs which
are, perhaps, more of an acquired
taste.

Various *Musiques de Transylvanie*
(Fonti Musicale, Belgium). One of
the best introductions to
Transylvanian music, featuring a
mainly Hungarian repertoire from
Kalotaszeg, Mezoség and Ghimes
plus Romanian dances from Bihor
and Moldavia.

Various *Romania – Music for Strings
from Transylvania* (Chant du Monde,
France). A great collection of dance
music played by village bands from
the Câmpia Transilvaniei, Maramureş
and Oaş. Excellent notes and photos,
too.

Various *Visa - Traditional Hungarian
Music from the Transylvanian Heath*
(Fonó, Hungary). From the Zoltán
Kallós Archive, recordings from
1964–65 and 1987, made in the
Mezoseg village of Visa.

Hungarian music from Ghimeş and Moldavia

Ilona Nyisztor *To The Fat Of The
Earth, To The Sun's Little Sister* (Fonó,
Hungary), *The Little Bird Has Gone
Away* and *Pusztinai Nagy Hegy Alatt
– Csángó Hungarian Songs from
Moldavia* (both Etnofon, Hungary).
Ilona Nyisztor sings Csángó songs
that were sung by her mother,
grandparents and great-
grandparents.

Mihály Halmágyi *Hungarian Music
from Gyimes* (Hungaroton, Hungary).
Halmágyi is a veteran Csángó violin
player from Ghimeş who plays a
five-stringed fiddle, producing
strange and wild music. A great
performance of "the shepherd
and his lost sheep", with running
commentary.

Various *Moldavia Csángómagyar
"Síposok" – Csango-Hungarian
Bagpipers of Moldavia* (Fonó,
Hungary). Field recordings
(1973–2001) of the unearthly
Csángó bagpipe music.

Various *Giving you Golden Rod –
Traditional ballads from Moldova* (Fonó,
Hungary). A two-CD set from the
extensive folk music collection of
Zoltán Kallós.

Zerkula Janos *Zerkula Janos keserve-
sei – Zerkula Janos's laments* (Fonó,
Hungary). Janos Zerkula and his
wife Regina Fiko are renowned
Csángó musicians from Ghimes; this
disc is packaged as a small book with
full notes and bilingual lyrics.

Maramureş

Ioan 'Popicu' Pop and Ensemble *Romanian, Ukrainian and Jewish Music from Maramureş* (Ethnophonie, Romania). Maramureş party music: the *hori* are occasional, widely accessible lyrical songs sung individually or in groups, with or without instrument accompaniment; The *zicali* (instrumental pieces) are performed on fiddles, guitars and drums.

Iza *Craciun in Maramureş* (*Christmas in Maramureş*); Buda/Musique du Monde, France). This Maramureş-based group led by *zongorǎ*-player Ioan Pop, with various fiddlers and drummer Ioan Petreuş, is trying to keep the traditional style intact. Excellent notes and translations.

Pitigoi Ensemble *Musiques de Mariage et de Fêtes Roumaines* (Arion, France). The best selection of the extraordinary music of Oaş, played by the Pitigoi brothers. Also a good selection of music from Maramureş and Bihor.

Popeluc *Blue Door* (Steel Carpet, UK). Maramureş dancing and drinking music (some recorded live at village bashes), with the odd Irish reel and English song too.

Various *Fiddle Music From Maramures* (Steel Carpet, UK). Real peasant fiddlers, recorded in their own homes in the Mara Valley.

Various *Musiques de Mariage de Maramureş* (Ocora, France). Maramureş wedding music, performed by three village bands.

Various *The Edge of the Forest: Romanian Music from Transylvania* (Music of the World, US). A collection of dances from Codru and Chioar (southern Maramureş), part of the central Transylvanian tradition, and a few tracks from Maramureş proper and Oaş.

Lowland music compilations

Romania: Wedding Music from Wallachia (Auvidis/Ethnic, France). A selection of songs and dance tunes from various bands including members of the Taraf de Haidouks and more urban repertoire from Ion Albeşteanu. The Music of the World disc (opposite) covers similar repertoire and is more attractive.

Taraf: Romanian Gypsy Music (Music of the World, US) A very good selection of tracks from various Wallachian Tarafuri including members of the Taraf de Haidouks. Mostly small ensembles of a couple of violins, *ţambal* and bass, with *cobzǎ* lute on a couple of tracks.

Specific artists

Ion Albeşteanu *The Districts of Yesteryears* (Buda/Musique du Monde, France). Albeşteanu, who died in 1998, was known as an expressive violinist and singer. Here he is accompanied by a good band with beautifully textured *ţambal*, accordion and fine *cobzǎ* playing. "At the Reed House", sung in an intimate "head voice" is quite beautiful. Good notes.

Fanfare Ciocǎrlia *Radio Paşcani* (Piranha, Germany). This brass band from the Moldavian village of Zece Prǎjini are perhaps the last representatives of a tradition. A frenetic romp, punchily recorded, with some fearsomely fast dance numbers, the pace occasionally breaks for a *doinǎ*.

Panseluța Feraru *Lăutar Songs from Bucharest* (Long Distance, France). A live recording by the veteran "restaurant singer" (indicating that she's a cut above other Gypsy singers), with great backing from a band led by husband Gheorghe Stephane.

Nicolae Gutsa *The Greatest Living Gypsy Voice* (Auvidis/Silex, France). Nicolae Gutsa is a very popular singer, performing traditional music in a contemporary style. Despite the absurd title, this is a great disc.

Trio Pandelescu *Trio Pandelescu* (Auvidis/Silex, France). Vasile Pandelescu is a virtuoso accordionist who played for many years with Gheorghe Zamfir. Recorded live with high-quality, intimate playing, delicate moments of real poetry, and all the requisite fire; including a couple of beautiful *tambal* solos by his son Costel.

Taraf de Carancebes *Musiciens du Banat* (Silex, France). A five-piece band of saxophone, trumpet, clarinet, accordion and bass. Some stunning virtuoso playing, explaining the popularity of the Banat style.

Taraf de Haidouks *Honourable Brigands, Magic Horses and Evil Eye*. Romania's most recorded Gypsy band allow you to trace the dynamic development of Gypsy music in Wallachia as new styles are absorbed without diluting the distinctive flavour of the *taraf*. *Honourable Brigands*, is the best starting point, while 2001's live set, *Band of Gypsies*, is probably their best-known recording in the West.

Maria Tanase Volumes 1, 2 & 3 (Electrecord, Romania). A versatile talent, Tanase distinguished herself as a stage and film actress, as an operetta singer, a music hall star, but mainly as the finest interpreter of Romanian folk-songs.

Other recordings

Dumitru Fărcaș & Marcel Cellier *The Art of the Romanian Taragot* (ARC Music Production, UK) and *Taragot et Orgue* (Pierre Verany Records, France). One of the leading players of the clarinet-like *taragot*, here with Zamfir's accompanist on church organ.

Toni Iordache *A Virtuoso of the Cimbalom 2* (Electrecord, Romania). One of the great virtuosi of the cimbalom (dulcimer), accompanied by small folk orchestras.

Luca Novac accompanied by the Orchestras of Radu Simion and Paraschiv Oprea *A Virtuoso of the Taragot* and **Petrica Pasca accompanied by the Rapsozii Zarandului Band** *Un Virtuose du Taragote* (both Electrecord, Romania). Luca Novac and Petrica Pasca are among the

numerous *taragot* virtuosi from the Banat.

Radu Simion *Pan pipe concert* (Electrecord, Romania). Radu Simion is one of the most gifted interpreters of the *nai* (pan pipe), here accompanied by various folk orchestras.

Gheorghe Zamfir *The Heart of Romania* (Pierre Verany, France). Born in Bucharest in 1941, *nai* player Zamfir must be Romania's most recorded musician, with albums of easy-listening arrangements of anything from Vivaldi to Andrew Lloyd Webber. Zamfir's music has little to do with the traditional music of Romania, but his arrangements of *doinas* and folktunes have an ethereal beauty.

Nightlosers *Sitting on top of the World, Plum Brandy Blues* (Genius

419

Enterprise Ltd, Bucharest).
Romanian "ethnoblues" – listen to
the leaf solo on "Stormy Monday".

Various *Roumanie: polyphonie vocale
des Aroumains* (Le Chant du Monde,
France). CNRS/Musée de l'Homme
recordings of the Romanians living in
Dobrogea, Bulgaria and elsewhere in
the Balkans. Hard-core ethnic stuff.

Various *YIKHES: Klezmer recordings
from 1907–1939* (Trikont,
Germany). Remastered 78s, including a couple of 1910 tracks by
Belf's Romanian Orchestra, virtually the only European Klezmer
band of the period to have been
recorded.

Simon Broughton

Dracula and vampires

Truth, legends and fiction swirl around the figure of Dracula like a cloak, and perceptions of him differ sharply. In Romania today, schoolbooks and historians extol him as a patriot and a champion of order in lawless times, while the outside world knows Dracula as the vampire count of a thousand cinematic fantasies derived from Bram Stoker's novel of 1897 – a spoof-figure or a ghoul.

The disparity in images is easily explained, for while vampires feature in native folklore, Romanians make no associations between them and the historical figure of Dracula, the Wallachian prince Vlad III, known in his homeland as Vlad Țepeș – **Vlad the Impaler**. During his lifetime (c.1431–76) Vlad achieved renown beyond Wallachia's borders as a successful fighter against the Turks and a ruthless ruler; his reputation for cruelty spread throughout Europe via the newly invented printing presses and the word of his political enemies – notably the Transylvanian Saxons. At this time, Vlad was not known as a vampire, although some charged that he was in league with the Devil – or (almost as bad) that he had converted to Catholicism.

The historical Dracula

He was not very tall, but very stocky and strong, with a cold and terrible appearance, a strong and aquiline nose, swollen nostrils, a thin reddish face in which very long eyelashes framed large wide-open green eyes; the bushy black eyebrows made them appear threatening. His face and chin were shaven, but for a moustache. The swollen temples increased the bulk of his head. A bull's neck connected his head to his body from which black curly locks hung on his wide-shouldered person.

Such was the papal legate's impression of **Vlad Țepeș** – then in his thirties and a prisoner at the court of Visegrád in Hungary. He had been born in Sighișoara and raised at Târgoviște after his father, Vlad Dracul, became Voivode of Wallachia in 1436. Young Vlad's privileged childhood effectively ended in 1442, when he and his brother Radu were sent by their father as hostages to Anatolia, to curry favour with the Turkish Sultan. Vlad Dracul incurred the enmity of Iancu de Hunedoara, prince of Transylvania, who arranged his murder in 1447; his sons were released by the Turks to be pawns in the struggle between their expanding empire, Iancu and the new ruler of Wallachia. The experience of five years of Turkish captivity and years of exile in Moldavia and Transylvania shaped Vlad's personality irrevocably, and educated him in guile and terrorism.

Seeking a vassal, Iancu helped Vlad to become **ruler of Wallachia** in 1456; but promptly died, leaving him dangerously exposed. Signing a defence pact and free trade agreement with the Saxons of Brașov, Vlad quickly decided that it was also prudent to pay an annual tribute of 10,000 gold ducats to the Sultan while he consolidated his power in Wallachia. For generations the boyar families had defied and frequently deposed their own rulers, including Vlad's father and his elder brother Mircea, whom they buried alive.

His method of law enforcement was simple: practically all crimes and individuals offending him were punished by death; and Vlad's customary means of execution was **impaling people**. Victims were bound spread-eagled while a stake was hammered up their rectum, and then were raised aloft and left to die in agony, for all to see. To test his subjects' honesty, Vlad disguised himself and moved among them; left coins in shops and over-compensated merchants who had been robbed; and slew all that failed the test. Foreigners reported the demise of theft, and Vlad symbolically placed a golden cup beside a lonely fountain for anyone to drink from and no one dared to take it away. On Easter Day in 1459, Vlad eliminated the potentially rebellious boyars en masse by inviting them and their families to dine at his palace; guards then entered and seized them, impaling many forthwith, while the remainder were marched off to labour at Poienari. In a similar vein, he invited Wallachia's disabled, unemployed and work-shy to feast with him at Târgoviște, and asked if they wished to be free of life's sufferings. Receiving an affirmative reply Vlad had them all burnt, justifying his action as a measure to ensure that none of his subjects should ever suffer from poverty or disability.

All this was but a ramp for Vlad's ambition to be the acknowledged ruler of a mighty power, which caused much feuding with the **Saxons** of Brașov, Sibiu and the Bârsa Land. It began in 1457, when he accused them of supporting claimants to his throne, and decided to end the Saxon merchants' practice of trading freely throughout Wallachia. When they persisted, Vlad led his army through the Red Tower Pass to burn Saxon villages, and had any of their people found inside Wallachia impaled. In 1460, Vlad annihilated the forces of his rival, Dan III, who invaded with the support of Brașov; and on this occasion dined in a garden among the impaled bodies of his enemies, using a holy icon as a dish, according to the *Chronicon Mellicense*. A month later, he attacked the Bârsa Land, and impaled hundreds of townsfolk on Sprenghi Hill within sight of Brașov's defenders before marching off to ravage the Făgăraș region.

At the same time, Vlad plotted to turn **against the Turks** and form alliances with his cousin Stephen of Moldavia, and the Hungarian monarchy. Having defaulted on payments of tribute for two years, and nailed the turbans of two emissaries to their heads when they refused to doff them, Vlad **declared war** by raiding Turkish garrisons from Vidin to Giurgiu. A massive army led by Sultan Mehmet II crossed the Danube into Wallachia in 1462, but found itself advancing through countryside denuded of inhabitants, food and water, "with the sun burning so that the armour of the ghazzis could well be used to cook kebabs". On the night of June 17, Vlad's army raided the Turkish camp inflicting heavy casualties, and a few days later the demoralized invaders approached Târgoviște only to recoil in horror. En route to the capital, Vlad had prepared a forest of stakes 1km by 3km wide, upon which 20,000 Turkish and Bulgarian captives were impaled. Shattered by their losses and these terror tactics, the Turks retreated in disorder.

Vlad's downfall has been attributed in part to the Saxons, who used every opportunity to support his enemies and defame him throughout Europe, after he had raised customs duties to pay for his army. Most likely, they forged the implausible "treason note" (in which Vlad purportedly offered to help the Sultan capture Transylvania) – the pretext for Mátyás Corvinus to order Vlad's arrest in November 1462, after a fresh Turkish attack had forced him to flee over the Făgăraș mountains from Poienari. Until 1475, he was a "guest" at Visegrád, where Mátyás would introduce him to Turkish ambassadors to disconcert them; Wallachia's throne was occupied by Vlad's pliable brother Radu "The Handsome", who had once served as the Sultan's catamite. Having married a relative of Mátyás, Vlad was released to continue the anti-Turkish struggle, spending a year in Sibiu (the townsfolk deeming it politic to be hospitable) and regaining his throne in 1476. His triumph was short-lived, however, for Radu offered the boyars an alternative to "rule by the stake" and a chance to placate the Turks, which they seized gratefully. In circumstances that remain unclear (some say that a servant was bribed to slay him), Vlad was betrayed by the boyars and killed. His head disappeared – supposedly sent to the Sultan as a present – while the Impaler's decapitated body was reputedly buried inside the church at Snagov Monastery, where it's said to remain today.

The lack of any inscription on Vlad's tomb and of any portraits of him in medieval church frescoes suggests that attempts were made for some time to erase the memory of Dracula in Romania, although he was remembered in the nineteenth century, and also in the Ceaușescu epoch, as a fighter for national independence and a wise lawmaker.

Vampires

Horrible though his deeds were, Vlad was not accused of **vampirism** during his lifetime. However, vampires were an integral part of folklore in Eastern and Southeastern Europe, known as *vámpír* in Hungarian and *strigoi* in Romanian. Details of their habits and characteristics vary from place to place, but in their essentials are fairly similar. A vampire is an **undead corpse**, animated by its spirit and with a body that fails to decay, no matter how long in the grave. Vampirism can be contagious, or people might occasionally be born as vampires, bearing stigmata such as a dark-coloured spot on the head or a rudimentary tail. However a vampire is usually created when a person dies and the soul is unable to enter heaven or hell. The reason may be that the person has died in a "state of sin" – by suicide, for example, or holding heretical beliefs – or because the soul has been prevented from leaving the body. Hanging was a form of death dreaded by Romanians, who believed that tying the neck "forces the soul down outward"; while the Orthodox custom of shrouding mirrors in the home of the deceased was intended to prevent the spirit from being "trapped" by seeing its reflection. As Catholicism and Orthodoxy competed for adherents in the wake of the Ottoman withdrawal from the Balkans, priests also claimed that the cemetery of the opposing church was unconsecrated land, thereby raising the fear of vampires rising from the grave.

Once created, a vampire is almost immortal, and becomes a menace to the living. In Romanian folklore, vampires frequently return to their former homes at night, where they must be propitiated with offerings of food and drink, and excluded by smearing garlic around the doors and windows. Should a new-born baby lie within, it must be guarded until it is christened, lest a vampire sneak in and transform it into another vampire. Two nights of the year are especially perilous: **April 23**, St George's Day (when, as Jonathan Harker was warned in Bram Stoker's novel, "all the evil things in the world will have full sway"), and **November 29**, the eve of St Andrew's Day. On the latter night, vampires rise with their coffins on their heads, lurk about their former homes, and then gather to fight each other with hempen whips at crossroads. Such places were considered to be unlucky, being infested by spirits called *Iele* (Man's enemies). In Gypsy folklore, vampires (*mulé*) also live at the exact moment of midday, when the sun casts no shadow. Gypsies must cease travelling, for at that instant *mulé* control the roads, trees and everything else. Interestingly, Gypsies only fear their own *mulé* – the ghosts and vampires of *gadjé* (non-Gypsies) are of no account.

The greatest danger was presented by **vampire epidemics**, which began in the seventeenth century, perhaps due to the influence of Gypsy folklore. Although in horror films and Bram Stoker's novel, vampires must bite their victims and suck blood to cause contagion, in Eastern European folklore, the vampire's look or touch can suffice. A classic account refers to the Austro-Hungarian village of Haidam in the 1720s. There, before witnesses, a man dead ten years returned as a vampire to his son's cottage, touched him on the shoulder and then departed. The man died the next morning. Alarmed by this report and others relating how long-dead villagers were returning to suck their children's blood, the local military commander ordered several graves to be exhumed, within which were found corpses showing no signs of decay. All were incinerated to ashes – one of the classic methods of exterminating vampires. Another epidemic occurred in the village of Medvegia near Belgrade, starting in 1727. A soldier claimed to have been attacked by a vampire while in Greece (where vampire legends also abound), and died upon his return home. Thereafter, many villagers swore they had seen him at night, or had dreamt about him, and ten weeks later complained of inexplicable weakness. The body was exhumed, was found to have blood in its mouth, and so had a stake driven through its heart. Despite this precaution, there was an outbreak of vampirism a few years later, and of the fourteen corpses examined by a medical commission in 1732, twelve were found to be "unmistakably in the vampire condition" (undecayed).

This was the catalyst for an explosion of interest across Europe, until Pope Benedict XIV and the Austrian and Prussian governments declared vampirism a fraud and made it a crime to dig up dead bodies. But in 1899, Romanian peasants in Caraşova dug up thirty corpses and tore them to pieces to stop a diphtheria epidemic, and in 1909, a Transylvanian castle was burned down by locals who believed that a vampire emanating from it was causing the deaths of their children. Only recently, in 1988, outside Niş in southern Serbia, a thirteen-year-old girl was killed by her family, who believed her to be a vampire.

Sceptics may dismiss vampires and vampirism entirely, but some of the related phenomena have rational or scientific explanations. The "return of the dead" can be explained by premature burial, which happened frequently in the past. Nor is the drinking of blood confined to legendary, supernatural creatures. Aside from the Masai tribe of Kenya – whose diet contains cattle blood mixed with milk – numerous examples can be found in the annals of criminology and psychopathology.

Bram Stoker's Dracula

During the eighteenth century, numerous well-publicized incidents of vampirism sparked a **vampire craze in Europe**, with both lurid accounts and learned essays produced in quantity. The first respectable **literary work** on a vampire theme was Goethe's *The Bride of Corinth* (1797), soon followed by Polidori's *The Vampyre*, which arose out of the same blood-curdling holiday on Lake Geneva in 1816 that produced Mary Shelley's *Frankenstein*. Other variations followed, by Kleist, E. T. A. Hoffmann, Mérimée, Gogol, Dumas, Baudelaire, and Sheridan Le Fanu, whose *Carmilla* features a lesbian vampire in Styria.

These fired the imagination of **Bram Stoker** (1847–1912), an Anglo-Irish civil servant who became manager to the great actor Sir Henry Irving in 1878 and wrote a few other novels, now being rediscovered. In 1890 he conceived the suitably *fin-de-siècle* idea of a vampire novel; initially it, too, was to be set in Styria, with an antihero called "Count Wampyr", but after detailed research in Whitby Public Library and the Reading Room of the British Museum, the setting moved east to Transylvania, and **Count Dracula** was born. Stoker's fictional Count was possibly influenced by the "Jack the Ripper" murders which happened a decade earlier in Whitechapel, where Stoker lived for a time while writing his book. Stoker delved deep into Romanian folklore, history and geography, and the book is a masterpiece in its mixture of fantasy and precise settings.

Other books on the same theme followed, but it was the advent of cinema and the horror film that has ensured the fame of Dracula. The silent *Nosferatu* (1922) is perhaps the greatest vampire film, followed by Béla Lugosi's 1931 *Dracula*, while Hammer's 1958 classic *Dracula* boasted the dream coupling of Christopher Lee as the Count and Peter Cushing as Van Helsing. The BBC's *Count Dracula* (1978) is the most faithful to Stoker's novel, while Coppola's camped-up *Bram Stoker's Dracula* (1992) confuses things by including the historic Vlad Țepeș in a prelude. There is also a fine tradition of spoofs such as *Love at First Bite* (1979), which opens with the communists expelling Dracula from his castle.

Books

The surge in interest in Eastern Europe since 1989, and the particularly dramatic nature of Romania's revolution and its problems since then, have led to several excellent writers visiting in quick succession. In addition, there is a wealth of nineteenth-century and early twentieth-century travellers' accounts, although many are out of print. Romanian literature is still under-represented in translation.

The **Center for Romanian Studies**, based in Iaşi, publishes many books on Romanian history and literature – for details contact their distributors, ISBS (920 NE 58th Ave, Portland, OR 97213, USA; ☎1800/944 6190, ⓦwww.isbs.com). Note that out of print titles are indicated as (o/p).

Specialized guides

Dave Gosney *Finding Birds in Romania*. This covers the Danube Delta only. Informative, but strangely it does not include a checklist of possible species.

James Roberts *Romania – a Birdwatching and Wildlife Guide*; and *The Mountains of Romania*. Detailed guides to the fauna and habitats of Romania, and information for hiking.

Travellers' tales

Many of the out-of-print accounts listed below may be found in secondhand bookshops or at Marijana Dworski Books, 21 Broad St, Hay-on-Wye HR3 5DB, UK (☎ & ℉01497/820 200, ⓦwww.dworski.demon.co.uk).

Recent accounts

Nick Crane *Clear Waters Rising*. A walk along the mountain spine of Europe, from Finisterre to Istanbul, including the entire length of the Carpathians – interesting contrasts between life in the mountains of Eastern and Western Europe.

Helena Drysdale *Looking for Gheorghe*. A search for a lost friend leads to unsavoury insights into life with the Securitate and finally to a hellish "mental hospital". The picture of Romanian life both before and after the revolution is spot-on.

Jason Goodwin *On Foot to the Golden Horn*. An engaging and well-informed writer walking from Gdansk to Istanbul in 1990 – almost half the book is, in fact, set in Transylvania. Very thoughtful, but it's annoyingly hard to work out which are the author's opinions and which those of the characters he meets.

Brian Hall *Stealing from a Deep Place*. Hall cycled through Hungary, Romania and Bulgaria in 1982 and produced a beautifully defined picture of the nonsense that communism had become.

Georgina Harding *In Another Europe*. Another cycle tour, this one in 1988. Slimmer than Hall's book but concentrating far more on Romania, with a more emotional response to Ceauşescu's follies.

Eva Hoffmann *Exit into History*. Not a patch on *Lost in Translation*, her superb account of being uprooted from Jewish Kraków to North America, but this tour of East-Central Europe in 1990 still yields seventy insightful pages on Romania.

Caroline Juler *Searching for Sarmizegetusa*. A captivating glimpse of traditional life and the pressures that are undermining it.

Andrew MacKenzie *Romanian Journey* and *Dracula Country* Both (o/p). *Romanian Journey*'s dollops of history, architectural description and bland travelese wouldn't be so bad if MacKenzie didn't also whitewash the Ceauşescu regime. *Dracula Country* is preferable, and assembles interesting facts about folklore and Vlad the Impaler.

Rory MacLean *Stalin's Nose*. With its wonderfully surreal humour, this is not exactly a factual account, but it is fundamentally serious about the effects of World War II and communism all over Eastern Europe.

Claudio Magris *Danube*. Full of scholarly anecdotes and subtle insights as Magris follows the Danube from source to sea.

Dervla Murphy *Transylvania and Beyond*. A serious, analytical book that tussles with the problems of immediately post-revolutionary Transylvania and its ethnic tensions in particular. Tellingly, she uses the Hungarian spelling "Rumania" throughout.

Peter O'Conner *Walking Good: Travels to Music in Hungary and Romania* (o/p). Another Irish fiddler in search of Gypsy music, forty years after Starkie (see p.428). O'Conner's quest took him to Slobozia, Cojocna and Făgăraş, staying with local people a few years before this became illegal. Entertaining.

Alan Ogden *Romania Revisited*. An anthology and bibliography of English travellers to Romania between 1602 and 1941, interwoven with the author's own journeys in 1998.

Julian Ross *Travels in an Unknown Country*. A summer-long horse-ride across Transylvania and, Moldavia, encountering the villages and people of a vanishing Romania.

Sophie Thurnham *Sophie's Journey*. Heart-warming story of work in the orphanages.

Giles Whittell *Lambada Country*. Another trip to Istanbul, at the same time as Jason Goodwin's. Less than a quarter of the book is on Romania, but it's interesting and informative, particularly on Magyar attitudes.

Older classics

Henry Baerlein (ed). *Romanian Scene* and *Romanian Oasis* (o/p). Two fine anthologies of travellers' tales in which most of the prewar authors listed below are featured.

Emily Gerard *The Land Beyond the Forest* (o/p). One of the classic nineteenth-century accounts of Transylvania – rambling, but highly informative on folk customs, superstitions, proverbs and the like.

Patrick Leigh Fermor *Between the Woods and the Water*. Transylvania provides the setting for the second volume in this unfolding, retrospective trilogy, based on Leigh Fermor's diaries for 1933–34, when he walked from Holland to Constantinople. His precocious zest for history and cultural diversity rose to the challenge of Transylvania's striking contrasts and obscurely turbulent past; the richness of his jewelled prose is impressive.

Lion Phillimore *In the Carpathians* (o/p). A fascinating account of a journey by horsecart through the Maramureş and Székelyföld just before World War I, by a proto-hippy who wants nothing more than to commune with the mountains and the trees.

Sacheverell Sitwell *Romanian Journey*. Motoring around, the Sitwells were both politely appalled, and vaguely charmed, by Romania; but most of all seem

to have been relieved that their gastronomic fortunes didn't suffer unduly.

Walter Starkie *Raggle Taggle* (o/p). After his exploits in Hungary, Starkie tramped down through Transylvania to Bucharest, where his encounters with Gypsies and lowlife are recounted in a florid but quite amusing style.

Teresa Stratilesco *From Carpathians to Pindus* (o/p). Covers the same ground as Gerard, with an equally sharp eye for quirky details.

Rosa G Waldeck *Athene Palace*. Eyewitness account of demi-mondaines and spies of all sides in wartime Bucharest.

History and politics

Mark Almond *The Rise and Fall of Nicolae and Elena Ceauşescu* (o/p). Very readable account by one of the best academics writing on Romania, though too kind to the sinister Silviu Brucan. Rather wayward footnotes and accents.

Dan Antal *Out of Romania*. An insider's version of the dreadful oppression under Ceauşescu and even worse disillusion after the revolution. Well enough told by a sympathetic character.

Ed Behr *Kiss the Hand You Cannot Bite*. A good, populist account of the Ceauşescus' rise and fall.

Burton Y Berry *Romanian Diaries 1944–47*; and **Donald Dunham** *Assignment: Bucharest*. The communist takeover of Romania, as seen by senior US diplomats.

Dennis Deletant *Ceauşescu and the Securitate: Coercion and Dissent in Romania 1965–89*; *Communist Terror*

in Romania: Gheorghiu-Dej and the Police State, 1948–1965; Romania under Communist Rule. Fascinating coverage of many hidden aspects of communist Romania.

Terence Elsberry *Marie of Romania*. A colourful biography of Queen Marie.

Mary Ellen Fischer *Nicolae Ceauşescu: A Study in Political Leadership*. Academic, detailed and readable description of the system created by Ceauşescu that was soon to drag him down.

Stephen. Fischer-Galaţi *Twentieth Century Rumania*. An easy read with good illustrations, basically sympathetic to many changes that happened under communism.

Vlad Georgescu *The Romanians: A History*. The best modern history in translation, although the importance of dissidents under Ceauşescu seems overstated. Georgescu, head of the Romanian Service of

Radio Free Europe, died in 1988, but an epilogue covers the events of 1989.

Nicolae Klepper *Romania: an Illustrated History*. Paperback history giving the standard view of the progress of the Romanian people towards nationhood.

Alan Ogden *Fortresses of Faith*. A history of the Saxon churches with fine black-and-white photos.

Ion Pacepa *Red Horizons*. A lurid, rambling "exposé" of the Ceauşescu regime, written by its former intelligence chief (who defected in 1978), describing disinformation and espionage abroad, corruption and perversions among the élite, and much else. Pacepa was deeply involved but reveals little about himself.

Prince Paul of Hohenzollern-Roumania *King Carol II: A Life of my Grandfather* (o/p). The nephew of King Mihai, Paul doesn't deny his grandfather's dreadful personal life, but attempts to rehabilitate him as a statesman placed in an impossible position.

Ioan Aurel Pop *Romanians and Romania – A Brief History*. Romanian history and civilization from the first century BC to the present.

Martyn Rady *Romania in Turmoil*. Wonderfully clear account of Ceauşescu's rise and fall, continuing to the end of 1991.

Nestor Ratesh *Romania: The Entangled Revolution*. A careful account of the revolution, laying out all the confusion that still surrounds it.

Ion Raţiu *Contemporary Romania*. A generally negative portrayal of the communist system by an émigré

who made a million in Britain and was to return after Ceauşescu's downfall to lead an opposition party.

George Schöpflin *The Hungarians of Rumania*. A careful presentation of the evidence on communist discrimination against the Magyars.

R. W. Seton-Watson *A History of the Roumanians*. Although it largely ignores social history and eschews atmospherics, and even the author admits his despair at the welter of dynastic details, it's still the classic work in English on Romanian history before 1920. Seton-Watson's *Roumania and the Great War* (1915) and *The Rise of Nationality in the Balkans* (1917) somewhat influenced British policy in favour of the Successor States, and for this reason he attracted great hostility in Hungary.

Christine Sutherland *Enchantress: Marthe Bibesco and her World*. A brilliant snapshot of both Romanian and French society and politics in the first half of the twentieth century, and of one of its most charismatic figures, Queen Marie's rival.

Lászlo Tökes *With God, for the People*. The autobiography of the man who lit the spark of the revolution and continues to be a thorn in the establishment's side, even as a bishop.

Kurt Treptow (ed) *A History of Romania*. From ancient times to the 1996 elections; with accompanying CD-ROM.

Richard Wurmbrand *In God's Underground*. The memoirs of a Lutheran priest who spent many years incarcerated at Jilava, Piteşti and other notorious prisons.

Folklore

David Buxton *Wooden Churches of Eastern Europe* (o/p). A learned and thorough tome.

Nicolae Klepper *Taste of Romania; its Cookery and Glimpses of its History, Folklore, Art and Poetry*. Cookery and cultural asides.

Gail Kligman *The Wedding of the Dead; Căluş: Symbolic Transformation in Romanian Ritual; The Politics of Duplicity – Controlling Reproduction in Ceauşescu's Romania*. The first is a wonderful book if you want to know everything about the anthropology and rituals of one Maramureş village, Ieud; the second is a slim but interesting anthropological study of the

Whitsun Căluş rite, which still lingers in parts of southern Romania; and the third is a similar study of Ceauşescu's efforts to boost the birth-rate.

Karsten D McNulty *Romanian Folk Art: a Guide to Living Traditions*. A paperback overview of Romania's many types of crafts, with colour photos.

Katherine Verdery *Transylvanian Villagers: Three Centuries of Political, Economic and Ethnic Change*. Based on field work west of Sebeş – a duller area than Maramureş, but therefore more broadly applicable than Kligman's book, though not as readable.

Dracula

Paul Barber *Vampires, Burial and Death: Folklore and Reality*. Proclaims itself as "a scholarly work on human decomposition and historical attitudes to it", which says it all.

Barbara Belford *Bram Stoker: A Biography of the Author of Dracula*. A more rigorous biography than Farson's, though marred by cold psychology.

Daniel Farson *The Man who wrote Dracula: A Biography of Bram Stoker*. Entertaining account of the life of the fictional Dracula's creator.

Radu Florescu & Raymond McNally *In Search of Dracula; Dracula: A Biography; Dracula, Prince of Many Faces, His Life and Times*. Founts of knowledge on the Impaler but overstating his connection with Dracula

Christopher Frayling *Vampyres*. Primarily a study of the vampire theme in literature and broader

culture, but also a near-definitive review of the phenomenon itself.

Clive Leatherdale *Dracula: The Novel and the Legend*. More concerned with the novel than with its Romanian background.

Elizabeth Miller *Reflections on Dracula; Sense & Nonsense*. A set of essays on Stoker's novel; and an entertaining debunking of many of the myths surrounding Stoker and his most famous book.

Nicolae Stoicescu *Vlad Ţepeş: Prince of Wallachia*. The standard Romanian biography of the Impaler, whom Stoicescu practically attempts to sanctify.

Bram Stoker *Dracula*. The Gothic horror original that launched a thousand movies. From a promising start with undertones of fetishism and menace in Dracula's Transylvanian castle, the tale degenerates into pathos before returning to Romania, and ending in a not too effective chase.

Kurt Treptow *Vlad III Dracula*. A balanced biography of the historical Vlad.

Romanian prose

Miklós Bánffy *They Were Counted, They Were Found Wanting* and *They Were Divided*. The *Transylvanian Trilogy*, written in the 1930s, is a tale of two Transylvanian cousins has been compared to Proust, Dostoevsky and Trollope. Also *The Phoenix Land*, a memoir of Hungary after the Trianon Treaty dismembered it.

Emil Cioran *On the Heights of Despair*. A key early work (1934, reissued in 1992) by this nihilist anti-philosopher.

Petru Dumitriu *The Family Jewels, The Prodigals* and *Incognito*. All (o/p). A literary prodigy lauded by the Party for his book *Dustless Highway*, Dumitriu fled Romania in 1960 and subsequently published two tales of dynastic ambition, followed by his masterpiece of moral and psychological exploration, *Incognito*, set against the backdrop of the war and the communist takeover.

Mircea Eliade *Shamanism; Youth without Youth; Fantastic Tales*. The first is the most interesting and informative example of the academic work for which he is internationally known. The latter two are fiction which don't quite match his reputation as a magical realist in the South American tradition, although this is partly due to the translation.

Norman Manea *On Clowns: The Dictator and the Artist*. Deported to the camps of Transnistria at the age of five, after the war Manea became an engineer and then an increasingly dissident writer, fleeing to the USA in 1986. This collection consists largely of over-intellectual musings on the nature of dictatorship and the subjected populace's complicity. See also his memoir *The Hooligan's Return* of 2003, which hinges on his anti-climactic first return to Romania in 1997.

Sándor Marai *Ember*. Much like Bánffy's *Transylvanian Trilogy*, this was written in 1942 and only rediscovered in the 1990s. Two old friends meet after 41 years in a Transylvanian castle and a tale of betrayal unfolds.

Herta Müller *The Passport; The Land of Green Plums*. Müller is a Schwab who left Romania in 1987. *The Passport* is a tale, in a distinctive staccato style, of the quest for permission to leave for Germany; *The Land of Green Plums* deals more with repression under Ceauşescu and is in a more accessible style.

Dumitru Popescu *The Royal Hunt*. One of seven volumes, this novel describes the way in which terror can overwhelm a community. Popescu is perhaps Romania's best-known contemporary novelist.

Liviu Rebreanu *Uprising; Ion; The Forest of the Hanged*. This trilogy comprises a panoramic picture of Romanian social life from the late nineteenth century to the First World War. *Uprising*, which deals with the 1907 peasant rebellion, shocked Romanian readers with its violent descriptions when it first appeared in 1933.

Elie Wiesel *Night*. Wiesel was born in Sighet in 1928 and was deported

CONTEXTS | Books

to Auschwitz, where his family died, in 1944. After the war, he pursued an academic career in the USA and was awarded the Nobel Peace Prize in 1986. This slim book opens in the ghetto of Sighet, but soon moves to the death camps.

Romanian poetry

George Bacovia *Plumb/Lead*. Along with Arghezi (none of whose work is available in translation), Bacovia is the leading prewar Romanian poet. Exquisitely melancholy.

Maria Banuş *Demon in Brackets*. Born in 1914, Banuş was a left-wing activist through the 1930s and 1940s, but her intimate lyricism remains popular today.

Lucian Blaga *Complete Poetical Works*. At last, one of Romania's finest and most popular poets available in English translation.

Ion Caraion *The Error of Being*. A leading poet of the older generation, who composed many of his poems in the camps of World War II.

Petru Cârdu *The Trapped Strawberry*. A Romanian-Yugoslav, Cârdu writes ironic poems in both Romanian and Serbo-Croat.

Nina Cassian *Call Yourself Alive? Cheerleader for a Funeral*. Savagely sensual and wickedly funny work from one of Romania's best poets.

Paul Celan *Selected Poems*. Romania's greatest poet – although all his work is in German – and one of the best of the twentieth century. Born in Bucovina in 1920, Celan survived the camps of Transnistria and emigrated to Paris, killing himself in 1970.

Mihai Eminescu *In Celebration of Mihai Eminescu*; *Selected Works of Ion Creangă and Mihai Eminescu*; *Poems and Prose of Mihai Eminescu*. The national poet – it's a scandal that there isn't a paperback in English of his greatest hits.

John Farleigh (ed) *When the Tunnels Meet*. A great idea – contemporary Romanian poems in versions by contemporary Irish poets, with a corresponding volume published in Romania: Dinescu, Sorescu and, most notably, Blandiana interpreted by Seamus Heaney.

Ioana Ieronim *The Triumph of the Water Witch*. Prose poems about the destruction of a Saxon community by Ceauşescu, written before 1989 and only published (and shortlisted for the Weidenfeld Prize) ten years later.

Jon Miloş *Through The Needle's Eye*. A Yugoslav-Romanian now living in Sweden, Miloş writes about universal social and environmental problems.

Oskar Pastior *Many Glove Compartments: selected poems*. A Saxon, Pastior spent five years in a Soviet labour camp after World War II, and has since been obsessed by themes of freedom and determinism.

Marin Sorescu *Let's Talk about the Weather; Selected Poems 1965–73; The Biggest Egg in the World; Censored Poems; The Bridge*. Hugely popular and respected both before 1989 (when his readings had to be held in football stadiums) and after (when he was briefly Minister of Culture), Sorescu died in 1996. His style is more ironic and accessible than that of many of his contemporaries.

Adam Sorkin (trans & ed) *Transylvanian Voices; City of Dreams and Whispers.* Anthologies of contemporary poets from Cluj and Iași respectively. Sorkin has also translated Magda Carneci, Ioan Flora, Saviana Stănescu and Daniela Crasnaru.

Nichita Stănescu *Bas-Relief with Heroe.* Stănescu died aged fifty in 1982, but his prolific work is still very influential.

Ion Stoica *As I Came to London one Midsummer's Day; Gates of the Moment.* A poet of the older generation, blending old and new influences.

Grete Tartler *Orient Express.* An excellent Schwab writer, translated by Fleur Adcock.

Liliana Ursu *The Sky Behind the Forest.* "Carnivorous and tender, majestic and human", a clear insight into her country and its people.

Brenda Walker (ed) *Anthology of Contemporary Romanian Poetry.* Features the work of Romania's two best living poets, Nina Cassian and Ana Blandiana.

Foreign prose

Paul Bailey *Kitty and Virgil.* A fine novel of survival in Ceaușescu's Romania and love found and lost in Britain.

Saul Bellow *The Dean's December.* The repression and poverty of Ceaușescu's Romania is contrasted with the hypocrisy and decadence of American society.

Olivia Manning *The Balkan Trilogy.* The TV screening of *The Fortunes of War* made Manning's epic story of thoroughly exasperating characters, widely known in Britain. The atmosphere of wartime Bucharest is well rendered, but as an extended study of human relationships, it's weakly constructed.

Bel Mooney *Cascades: The Voices of Silence.* A 13-year-old's experience of Ceaușescu's overthrow; written for the same age group, studying themes such as the individual and society.

Gregor von Rezzori *Memoirs of an Anti-Semite; The Snows of Yesteryear.* The first is an account of growing up in the largely Romanian city of Czernowitz (Cernăuți, now in Ukraine); the second is similar but more episodic.

Barbara Wilson *Trouble in Transylvania.* Inveterate traveller Cassandra Reilly goes to Sovata to investigate a murder, and gets the hots for most of the women she meets. Pretty strong on local colour in other respects.

Language

Language

Language

Romanian is basically a Romance language with a grammar similar to Latin. This familial resemblance makes it easy for anyone who speaks French, Italian or (to a lesser extent) Spanish to recognize words and phrases in Romanian, even though its vocabulary also contains words of Dacian, Slav, Greek and Turkish origin, with more recent additions from French, German and English.

German may be understood – if not spoken – in the areas of Transylvania and the Banat traditionally inhabited by Saxons and Swabians; and many educated Romanians have learned the language for professional reasons, although the tendency among students nowadays is increasingly towards English. Foreigners who can muster any scrap of Hungarian will find it appreciated in the Magyar enclaves of Transylvania, but its use elsewhere invites hassle rather than sympathy, which is even more the case with Russian – a language greeted with derision by almost everyone except the Lipovani communities of the Delta.

Romanian **nouns** have three genders – masculine, feminine and neuter. **Adjectives** (usually placed after the word they describe) and **pronouns** always "agree" with the gender of the noun. *Mai* and *cel mai* are generally used to make comparatives and superlatives: eg. *ieftin* (cheap); *mai ieftin* (cheaper), *cel mai ieftin* (the cheapest). In Romanian, **articles** are not always needed: the indefinite article "a" comes before the noun and is *un* for masculine and neuter words, *o* for feminine ones; the definite article "the" is added to the end of the noun: *-a* for feminine words, *-ul* or *-le* for masculine or neuter ones. The plural forms of nouns are slightly more complicated, but tend to end in *-i* or *-le*. **Verbs** are conjugated, so do not require pronouns such as "I" or "you", although these may be added for emphasis.

Pronunciation is likewise fairly straightforward. Words are usually, but not always, stressed on the syllable before last, and all letters are pronounced except for the terminal '–i'. However, certain letters change their sounds when combined with other ones. When speaking, Romanians tend to slur words together.

L

LANGUAGE

Elementary Hungarian

Yes	**Igen**	How much is it?	**Mennyibe kerül?**
No	**Nem**	Cheap	**Olcsó**
Please	**Kérem**	Expensive	**Drága**
Thanks	**Köszönöm**	Good	**Jó**
Hello	**Jó napot, servus, csokolom**	Bad	**Rossz**
		Open	**Nyitva**
		Closed	**Zárva**
Goodbye	**Viszontlá tásra**	Station	**Palyaudvar, vasú, allomas**
Cheers!	**Egeszegedre!**		
I don't understand	**Nem értem**	Hotel	**Szálloda**
Where is...?	**Hol van...?**	Restaurant	**Étterem**
When?	**Mikor?**	Bar?	**Pince**
Today	**Ma**	Bread	**Kenyér**
Tomorrow	**Holnap**	(No) meat	**(Nem) hús**

Elementary German

Yes	**Ja**	Tomorrow	**Morgen**
No	**Nein**	How much is it?	**Wieviel**
Please	**Bitte**		**kostet es?**
Thanks	**Danke**	Cheap	**Billig**
Hello	**Guten Tag,**	Expensive	**Teuer**
	Grüss Gott	Good	**Gut**
Goodbye	**Auf**	Bad	**Schlecht**
	Wiedersehen	Open	**Offen**
Cheers!	**Prost!**	Closed	**Geschlossen**
I don't understand	**Ich verstehe**	Station	**Bahnhof**
	nicht	Hotel	**Gasthaus**
Where is...?	**Wo ist...?**	Restaurant	**Restaurant**
When?	**Wann?**	Bread	**Brot**
Today	**Heute**	(No) meat	**(Kein) Fleisch**

A "o" sound as in done.

Â (or **Î**) is pronounced 'uh', midway between the O in lesson and the O in sort.

Ă "er" sound as in mother; the combinations AU and ĂU resemble the sounds in how and go.

C and **Ch** are hard, like "k" or as in country, except when C precedes E or I when it sounds like "ch".

E sounds as in ten; but at the start of a word it's pronounced as in year; while the combined EI sounds like bay or ray.

G is hard as in gust, except in the dipthong EG (like sledge), or preceding E or I when it is soft as in gesture; GHI is hard (as in gear).

I is as in feet; except for the vowel combinations IU as in you; IA as in yap; and IE as in yes.

J is like the "s" in pleasure.

K only occurs in imported words like kilometre.

O is as in soft; except for OI, which is like boy, and OA as in quark.

R is always rolled.

Ş is slurred as in shop.

Ţ is a "ts" sound as in bits.

U sounds like book or good; but UA is pronounced as in quark.

W occurs in such foreign words as whisky and western.

In addition to the language box above, see the specialist vocabularies for eating and drinking (pp.442–444) and hiking (p.40), and the glossary on the following pages.

Linguistic politics

The letter î replaced â when Stalin forced Romania to change the rules to make the language seem more Slavic in form, although a few exceptions such as România and Brâncuşi were allowed to survive. In 1994 the Romanian Academy decreed that î should revert to â, so that Tîrgu Mureş is officially Târgu Mureş, and Cîmpulung is now Câmpulung. As a rule, this does not apply where a word begins with Î.

The rules (to do with whether words have a Latin root, where in the word the letter falls, and whether it follows a prefix) are too complex for most Romanians to follow, and many old maps and signs are still in use; therefore you should be aware of the potential for confusion, for instance in words such as *vânători* (hunters).

LANGUAGE

Words and phrases

Basics and greetings

Yes, no, and	Da, nu, şi
Please, thank you	Vă rog, mulţumesc
Sorry, excuse me	Îmi pare rău, permiteţi-mi
Good, bad	Bun, rău
Do you speak English?	Vorbiţi englezeste?
I don't understand	Nu ânţeleg
Please speak slowly	Vă rog să vorbiţi mai rar
Please write it down	Scrieţi, vă rog
Say that again, please	Vreţi să repetaţi, vă rog
I, we, you	Eu, noi, dumneaca (tu is informal)
Hello	Salut
Good morning	Bună dimineaţă
Good day	Bună ziua (or Servus)
Good evening	Bună seară
Good night	Noapte bună
How are you?	Ce mai faceţi?
What's your name?	Cum vă numiţ?
Cheers!	Noroc! (literally Good Luck!)
Good, that's fine	Bun, minunat (De acord = it's agreed)
Goodbye	La revedere (or ciao, pa)
Bon voyage	Drum bun (literally "Good road")
Leave me alone!	Lăsaţi-ma ân pace!

Directions and accommodation

Where?/When?	Unde?/Când?
The nearest	Cel mai aproape
A (cheap) hotel	Un hotel (ieftin)
Campsite	Loc de campare, popas
Toilet	Toaletă, WC (pro-nounced vay-say-oo)
Is it far?	Este departe?
What bus must I take?	Ce autobuz trebuie sa iau?
Is there a footpath to...?	Există potecă spre...?
Right, left, straight on	Dreapta, stânga, dreapt ânainte
North, south, east, west	Nord, sud, est, vest
Have you a room?	Aveţi o cameră?
With, without	Cu, fără
Twin beds	Două paturi
Double bed	Un pat dublu
For one person (alone)	Pentru o persoană (singura)
Shower, bathroom	Duş, baie
There's no water	Nu curge apă
Hot, cold	Cald/fierbinte, frig/rece
How much per night?	Cât costa pentru o noapte?
Is breakfast included?	Micul dejun este inclus ân preţ?
Have you nothing cheaper?	Nu aveţi altceva mai ieftin?
Can you suggest another (a cheaper) hotel?	Puteni să-mi reco-mandaţi un alt hotel (un hotel mai ieftin)?

Signs

Arrival, departure	Sosire, plecare
Entrance, exit	Intrare, Ieşire
Vacant, occupied	Liber, ocupat
No vacancies	Nu mai sânt locuri
Open, closed	Deschis, ânchis
Admission free	Intrare gratuită
Ladies' (Gents') WC	WC femei (bărbaţi)
Waiting room	Sală de aşteptare
Operating, cancelled	Circulă, anulat

| No smoking | Fumatul oprit (Nefumatori) | No entry, danger | Intrare interzisa, pericol |

Requests and Buying

I want (should like)...	(Aş) vreau...	Same again, please	Încă un rând, vă rog
I don't want...	Nu vreau...	What's that?	Ce este acesta?
How much?	Cât costă?	Is it any good?	Merita?
A little (less)	(Mai) puţin	Bon appétit	Poftă bună
Is there...?	Există...?	Bill, receipt	Notă, chitanţă
Have you/do you sell...?	Aveţi...?	When will it be ready?	Când este gata?
Where can I buy...?	Unde pot să cumpăr...?	At once, we're in a hurry	Imediat, noi grăbim
Too expensive	Prea scump	What's the rate for the pound/dollar?	Care este cursul lirei sterling/ dolaruli?
What do you recommend?	Ce âmi recomandaţi?		
Waiter, waitress	Chelner, Chelneriţa	Will you refund my money?	Vă rog sa-mi daţi banii ânapoi?
It's finished	S-a terminat	Any letters for me?	Aveţi vreo scrisoare pentru mine?
Two glasses (bottles) of beer	Două pahare (sticle) de bere		

Getting around

Does this bus go to the train station?	Autobuzul acesta merge la gară?	I want to reserve a sleeper (couchette)	Vreau sa rezerva loc de vagon de dormit (cu cuşete)
Bus terminal	La autogară		
Beach	La plajă	I want to change my reservation to...	Aş vreau să schimba rezervă pentru...
Into the centre	În centru		
Does it stop at?	Opreşte la?	Is this the train for...?	Acesta este trenul de...?
Has the last bus gone?	A trecut ultimul autobuz?		
I (want to) go to...	(Vreau să) merg la...	Where do I change?	Unde schimb trenul?
Where are you going?	Unde mergeţi?	arrival time	sosire (sos.)
Stop here (at...)	Opriţi aici (la...)	departure times	plecare (pl.)
Is it a good road?	Drumul este bun?	Is there a boat from here to...?	Există curse de vapor de aici la...?
It isn't far	Nu este departe		
Crossroads	Intersecţie		
Bridge	Rascruce, pod	When does the next boat leave?	Când pleacă vaporul următor?
Which platform does the train to... leave from?	De la ce peron pleacă trenul către...?		
		Can I rent a (rowing) boat?	Pot să ânchiriez o barcă (cu vişie)?
When does the train leave?	Le ce ora pleacă trenul?	How much do you charge by the hour/for the day?	Cât costa ora/ziua?
Two seats for... (tomorrow)	Două locuri pentru... (mâine)		

Time and dates

What's the time?	Ce oră este?
It's early/late	Este devreme/târziu
This morning	Azi dimineaţă
Day, afternoon	Zi, după masă
Midday, midnight	Amiază, miezul nopţii
Evening, night	Seară, noapte
Week, month	Săptămână, lună
Today, yesterday (day after) tomorrow	Azi, astăzi, ieri (poi) mâine
Soon, never	Curând, niciodată
Everyday	În fiecare zi
Monday	Luni
Tuesday	Marţi
Wednesday	Miercuri
Thursday	Joi
Friday	Vineri
Saturday	Sâmbătă
Sunday	Minică
January	Ianuarie
February	Februarie
March	Martie
April	Aprilie
May	Mai
June	Iunie
July	Iulie
August	August
September	Septembrie
October	Octombrie
November	Noiembrie
December	Decembrie
New Year	Anul Nou
Easter	Paşte
Christmas	Crăciun

Numbers

Number	Romanian	Number	Romanian
0	zero	20	douăzece
1	un, una	21	douăzeci şi un(a)
2	doi, doua	30	treizeci
3	trei	40	patruzeci
4	patru	50	cincizeci
5	cinci	60	şaizeci
6	şase	70	şaptzeci
7	şapte	80	optzeci
8	opt	90	nouăzeci
9	nouă	100	o sută
10	zece	500	cinci sute
11	unsprezece	1000	o mie
12	doisprezece	first	ântâi
13	treisprezece	second	al doilea
14	paisprezece	1 kilo	un kilo
15	cincisprezece	a half	jumatăte
16	şaisprezece	a third	o treime
17	şaptsprezece	a quarter	un sfert
18	optsprezece	three- quarters	trei sferturi
19	nouăsprezece		

Food and drink glossary

Basic foods

brânză	cheese
iaurt	yoghurt
lapte	milk
omletă	omelette
orez	rice
oţet	vinegar
ouă	eggs
pâine or pîine	bread
piper	pepper
sandvici or tartină	sandwiches
sare	salt
smântână	sour cream
ulei	oil
unt	butter
zahăr	sugar

Soups (supe)

ciorbă	mixed soup, with sour cream
ciorbă de burtă	tripe soup
ciorbă de cartofi	potato soup
ciorbă de fasole	dried or green bean soup
ciorbă de miel	lamb broth
ciorbă de perişoare	soup with meatballs
ciorbă de peşte	fish soup
ciorbă ţăranească	soup with meat and mixed vegetables
supă	soup with one main component
supă de carne	consommá
supă de găină	chicken soup
supă de găluşti	dumpling soup
supă de roşii	tomato soup
supă cu tăiţei	noodle soup
supă de zarzavat	vegetable soup

Salads (salate)

salată de cartofi cu ceapă	potato and onion salad
salată de fasole verde	green bean salad
salată de icre de crap	carp roe salad
salată de roşii şi castraveţi	tomato and cucumber salad
salată de sfeclă roşie	beetroot salad
salată verde	lettuce salad

Meat and poultry (carne şi pasăre)

babic (ghiudem)	smoked (goat's meat) sausage
berbec/oaie	mutton
biftec	steak
chiftele	fried meatballs
crenwurst	hot dog
curcan	turkey
ficat	liver
gâscă	goose
ghiveci cu carne	meat and vegetable hotpot
miel	lamb
mititei	spicy sausages
parizer	mortadella-type sausage
(pastramă de) porc	(salted and smoked) pork
patricieni	sausages (skinless)
pui	chicken
raţă (pe varză)	duck (with sauerkraut)
rinichi	kidneys
salam	salami
slănină	bacon fat
şniţel panâ	wiener schnitzel
şuncă	ham
tocană de carne/de purcel	meat/pork stew
vacă	beef
varză acră cu costiţă afumată	sauerkraut with smoked pork chops

Vegetables (legume)

ardei (gras/iute)	(green/chilli) pepper
cartofi	potatoes
ceapă (verde)	(spring) onion
ciuperci	mushrooms

conopidă	cauliflower
dovlecei	courgettes/zucchini
dovleci	marrows
fasole (albă grasă/verde)	(broad/string) beans
ghiveci	mixed fried vegetables, sometimes eaten cold
gogoşari	red peppers
lăptucă	lettuce
mazăre verde	peas
morcovi	carrots
roşii	tomatoes
salată verde	green salad
sfeclă roşie	beetroot
spanac	spinach
usturoi	garlic
varză	cabbage
vinete	aubergine (eggplant)

Fish and seafood (peste)

cegă	sterlet
chiftele de peşte	fish cakes
crap	carp
icre negre	caviar
midii	mussels
nisetru	sturgeon
păstrăv	trout
scrumbie	herring
şalău	pike-perch
ton	tuna

Fruit (fructe)

caise	apricots
căpşune	strawberries
cireşe	cherries
fragă	wild strawberries
mere	apples
pepene galben	melon
pepene verde	watermelon
pere	pears
piersici	peaches
prune (uscate)	plums (prunes)
struguri	grapes
zmeură	raspberries

Desserts and sweets (dulciuri)

bomboane	sweets (candy)
clătită (cu rom)	pancake (with rum)
cozonac	brioche
dulceaţă	jam (served in a glass)
ecler	éclair
gogoşi or langoş	doughnut
halva	halva
ânghetată	ice cream
măr in foietaj	baked apple in pastry
mascotă	chocolate fudge cake
miere	honey
papanasi	cream doughnut
pască	easter cake
plăcintă cu brânză	cheese pie
plăcintă cu mere	apple pie
plăcintă cu vişine	cherry pie
prăjitură	cake
rahat	turkish delight
ruladă	sponge and jam roll
strudel cu mere	apple strudel

Drinks (băuturi)

apă minerală	mineral water
suc de fructe	fruit juice
cafea filtru	filter coffee
cafea mare cu lapte	large white coffee
cafea neagră cafea naturală	sweet black coffee or plain black coffee
cafea turcească	turkish coffee
o ceaşcă de ceai	a cup of tea
bere	beer
vin roşu (or alb)	red wine (or white)
şampanie	sparkling wine
sticlă	bottle (of beer)
ţuică	plum brandy
vodca	vodka
rom	rum

Common terms

| aveţiă... | do you have a... |
| Aş/am vrea | I/we would like |

cină	dinner	noroc!	cheers!
cu maioneză	with a mayonnaise sauce	pahar	a glass
		piure de	mashed
cu mujdei de usturoi	in a garlic sauce	poftă bună	enjoy your meal
dejun	lunch	prăjit	fried
fiert	boiled	prânz,	lunch
friptură	roast	pulpă de... la tavă	roast leg of ...
la grătar	grilled	rasol	poached
meniu or listă	menu	tare/moale	hard/soft boiled
micul dejun	breakfast	umplut	stuffed

Glossary

Alimentară food store.

Ardeal "forested land", the Romanian name for Transylvania.

Baie bath, spa (plural Băile; not to be confused with Baia or mine).

Biserică church; **Biseri de lemin** wooden churches.

Bivol buffalo, introduced from India by the Gypsies.

Boyar or Boier, feudal lord.

Bucium alpine horn used by shepherds, also known as a Tulnic.

Bulevardul (B-dul or Blvd.) boulevard.

Calea avenue.

Căluș traditional Whitsun fertility rite performed by Călușari in rural Wallachia and southwestern Transylvania.

Câmpulung (or Cîmpulung) meadow or long field, for which settlements like Câmpulung Moldovenesc are named.

Capră masked "Goat dance" to celebrate the New Year.

Casă house.

Cetate fortress or citadel.

CFR Romanian Railways

CHEI gorge.

Csángó Hungarian "Wanderers" from Transylvania.

Dacians earliest established inhabitants of Romania.

Deal hill.

Drum road; Drum Național highway.

Erdély the Magyar name for Transylvania.

FSN Frontul Salvării Național, the National Salvation Front set up as an umbrella front during the revolution and soon transformed into a new government.

Gadjé Roma (Gypsy) term for non-Gypsies.

Gradinița garden.

Grind raised area of accumulated silt in the Danube Delta.

Gură mouth.

Horă traditional village round dance.

Iconostasis literally "icon-bearer", decorated screen in an Orthodox (or Uniate) church containing tiers of icons that separates sanctuary from nave and priest from congregation during the Eucharist.

Județ county.

Lac lake.

Legion or Iron Guard, Romanian fascist movement, 1927–41.

Lipovani ethnic group living by fishing and gardening in the Danube Delta, descended from Russian "Old Believers".

Litoral the coast.

Magazin large store.

Magyars Hungarians, roughly two million of whom live in Romania, mainly in Transylvania.

Mănăstirea monastery or convent.

Maxitaxi minibus.

Moară mill.

Muntenia the eastern half of Wallachia, paradoxically not at all mountainous.

Nai pan-pipes.

Naos nave or central part of an Orthodox church, lying below the central cupola and in front of the iconostasis.

Narthex entrance hall of an Orthodox church, often decorated with frescoes.

Nations (or Nationes) historically, the privileged groups in Transylvania.

Nedeia village fair or festival characteristic of the mountain regions.

Oltenia the western half of Wallachia, flanking the River Olt.

Pădure woods.

Pas a mountain pass.

PCR Partidul Communist Roman – until 1989, the Romanian Communist Party. Since reconstituted as the Socialist Party of Labour (PSM).

Peștera cave.

Piaţa square; also a market.

Piatra stone or crag.

Plajă beach.

Plaur floating reed islands, characteristic of the Delta.

Pod bridge.

Poiana glade, meadow.

Popă (or **Preot**) Orthodox priest.

Poteca path.

Pronaos see Narthex.

Răscoala peasant rebellion; usually refers to the great uprising of 1907.

Râu river.

Regat the "Old Kingdom", as Moldavia and Wallachia were known after they united in 1859.

Rom or **Roma** Gypsies.

Sanctuar sanctuary or altar area of a church, behind the iconostasis.

Sat village.

Saxons name given to Germans who settled in Transylvania from the twelfth century onwards.

Schwaben (Swabians) name given to Germans who settled in Banat in the eighteenth century; others who moved to Transylvania at this time are known as Landler.

Securitate Communist security police, now reborn as the SRI or Romanian Information Service.

Siebenburgen Saxon name for Transylvania (literally, "seven towns").

Şoseaua (**Şos.**) long tree-lined avenue.

Stâna sheepfold.

Strada (**Str.**) street.

Székely Hungarian-speaking ethnic group inhabiting parts of eastern Transylvania known as the Székelyföld.

Ţara land, country (Romanian); Gypsy encampment.

Târg or **Tîrg**, market, fair or festival.

Vad ford.

Vale valley.

Vătaf leader of Căluşari dancers (Romanian); tribal chieftain (Gypsy).

Virf peak, mount.

Vlachs (or **Wallachs**) foreign name for the Romanians of Wallachia, Moldavia and Transylvania before the nineteenth century.

Voevod or **Voivode** Ruling prince of Transylvania or Wallachia.

Rough Guides
advertiser

...music & reference

Trinidad & Tobago

Africa & Middle East
Cape Town
Egypt
The Gambia
Jordan
Kenya
Marrakesh
 DIRECTIONS
Morocco
South Africa, Lesotho
 & Swaziland
Syria
Tanzania
Tunisia
West Africa
Zanzibar
Zimbabwe

Travel Theme guides
First-Time Around the
 World
First-Time Asia
First-Time Europe
First-Time Latin
 America
Skiing & Snowboarding
 in North America
Travel Online
Travel Health
Walks in London & SE
 England
Women Travel

Restaurant guides
French Hotels &
 Restaurants
London
New York
San Francisco

Maps
Algarve
Amsterdam
Andalucia & Costa del Sol
Argentina

Athens
Australia
Baja California
Barcelona
Berlin
Boston
Brittany
Brussels
Chicago
Crete
Croatia
Cuba
Cyprus
Czech Republic
Dominican Republic
Dubai & UAE
Dublin
Egypt
Florence & Siena
Frankfurt
Greece
Guatemala & Belize
Iceland
Ireland
Kenya
Lisbon
London
Los Angeles
Madrid
Mexico
Miami & Key West
Morocco
New York City
New Zealand
Northern Spain
Paris
Peru
Portugal
Prague
Rome
San Francisco
Sicily
South Africa
South India
Sri Lanka
Tenerife
Thailand

Toronto
Trinidad & Tobago
Tuscany
Venice
Washington DC
Yucatán Peninsula

**Dictionary
Phrasebooks**
Czech
Dutch
Egyptian Arabic
EuropeanLanguages
 (Czech, French, German,
 Greek, Italian,
 Portuguese, Spanish)
French
German
Greek
Hindi & Urdu
Hungarian
Indonesian
Italian
Japanese
Mandarin Chinese
Mexican Spanish
Polish
Portuguese
Russian
Spanish
Swahili
Thai
Turkish
Vietnamese

Music Guides
The Beatles
Bob Dylan
Cult Pop
Classical Music
Country Music
Elvis
Hip Hop
House
Irish Music
Jazz
Music USA

Opera
Reggae
Rock
Techno
World Music (2 vols)

History Guides
China
Egypt
England
France
India
Islam
Italy
Spain
USA

Reference Guides
Books for Teenagers
Children's Books, 0–5
Children's Books, 5–11
Cult Fiction
Cult Football
Cult Movies
Cult TV
Ethical Shopping
Formula 1
The iPod, iTunes &
 Music Online
The Internet
Internet Radio
James Bond
Kids' Movies
Lord of the Rings
Muhammed Ali
Man Utd
Personal Computers
Pregnancy & Birth
Shakespeare
Superheroes
Unexplained
 Phenomena
The Universe
Videogaming
Weather
Website Directory

449

Also! More than 120 Rough Guide music CDs are available from all good book
and record stores. Listen in at www.worldmusic.net

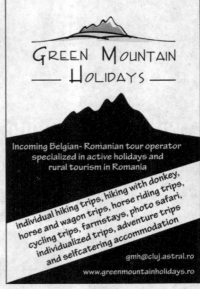

small print and

Index

A Rough Guide to Rough Guides

In the summer of 1981, Mark Ellingham, a recent graduate from Bristol University, was travelling round Greece and couldn't find a guidebook that really met his needs. On the one hand there were the student guides, insistent on saving every last cent, and on the other the heavyweight cultural tomes whose authors seemed to have spent more time in a research library than lounging away the afternoon at a taverna or on the beach.

In a bid to avoid getting a job, Mark and a small group of writers set about creating their own guidebook. It was a guide to Greece that aimed to combine a journalistic approach to description with a thoroughly practical approach to travellers' needs – a guide that would incorporate culture, history and contemporary insights with a critical edge, together with up-to-date, value-for-money listings. Back in London, Mark and the team finished their Rough Guide, as they called it, and talked Routledge into publishing the book.

That first *Rough Guide to Greece*, published in 1982, was a student scheme that became a publishing phenomenon. The immediate success of the book – with numerous reprints and a Thomas Cook prize shortlisting – spawned a series that rapidly covered dozens of destinations. Rough Guides had a ready market among low-budget backpackers, but soon also acquired a much broader and older readership that relished Rough Guides' wit and inquisitiveness as much as their enthusiastic, critical approach. Everyone wants value for money, but not at any price.

Rough Guides soon began supplementing the "rougher" information about hostels and low-budget listings with the kind of detail on restaurants and quality hotels that independent-minded visitors on any budget might expect, whether on business in New York or trekking in Thailand.

These days the guides – distributed worldwide by the Penguin group – offer recommendations from shoestring to luxury and cover more than 200 destinations around the globe, including almost every country in the Americas and Europe, more than half of Africa and most of Asia and Australasia. Our ever-growing team of authors and photographers is spread all over the world, particularly in Europe, the USA and Australia.

In 1994, we published the *Rough Guide to World Music* and *Rough Guide to Classical Music*; and a year later the *Rough Guide to the Internet*. All three books have become benchmark titles in their fields – which encouraged us to expand into other areas of publishing, mainly around popular culture. Rough Guides now publishes:

* Travel guides to more than 200 worldwide destinations
* Dictionary phrasebooks to 22 major languages
* History guides ranging from Ireland to Islam
* Maps printed on rip-proof and waterproof Polyart™ paper
* Music guides running the gamut from Opera to Elvis
* Restaurant guides to London, New York and San Francisco
* Reference books on topics as diverse as the Weather and Shakespeare
* Sports guides from Formula 1 to Man Utd
* Pop culture books from *Lord of the Rings* to Cult TV
* World Music CDs in association with World Music Network

Visit www.roughguides.com to see our latest publications.

SMALL PRINT

Rough Guide credits

Editor: Keith Drew
Layout: Ajay Verma
Cartography: Rajesh Chhibber and Manish Chandra
Picture research: Sharon Martins
Proofreaders: Madhulita Mohapatra and Rima Zaheer
Editorial: London Martin Dunford, Kate Berens, Helena Smith, Claire Saunders, Geoff Howard, Ruth Blackmore, Gavin Thomas, Polly Thomas, Richard Lim, Clifton Wilkinson, Alison Murchie, Fran Sandham, Sally Schafer, Alexander Mark Rogers, Karoline Densley, Andy Turner, Ella O'Donnell, Keith Drew, Andrew Lockett, Joe Staines, Duncan Clark, Peter Buckley, Matthew Milton; **New York** Andrew Rosenberg, Richard Koss, Hunter Slaton, Chris Barsanti, Steven Horak
Design & Pictures: London Simon Bracken, Dan May, Diana Jarvis, Mark Thomas, Jj Luck, Harriet Mills; **Delhi** Madhulita Mohapatra, Umesh Aggarwal, Ajay Verma, Jessica Subramanian

Production: Julia Bovis, John McKay, Sophie Hewat
Cartography: London Maxine Repath, Ed Wright, Katie Lloyd-Jones, Miles Irving; **Delhi** Manish Chandra, Rajesh Chhibber, Jai Prakash Mishra, Ashutosh Bharti, Rajesh Mishra, Animesh Pathak, Jasbir Sandhu, Karobi Gogoi
Cover art direction: Louise Boulton
Online: New York Jennifer Gold, Cree Lawson, Suzanne Welles, Benjamin Ross; **Delhi** Manik Chauhan, Narender Kumar, Shekhar Jha, Rakesh Kumar
Marketing & Publicity: London Richard Trillo, Niki Smith, David Wearn, Chloë Roberts, Demelza Dallow, Kristina Pentland; **New York** Geoff Colquitt, Megan Kennedy
Finance: Gary Singh
Manager India: Punita Singh
Series editor: Mark Ellingham
PA to Managing Director: Julie Sanderson
Managing Director: Kevin Fitzgerald

Publishing Information

This fourth edition published October 2004 by **Rough Guides Ltd**,
80 Strand, London WC2R 0RL.
345 Hudson St, 4th Floor,
New York, NY 10014, USA.
Distributed by the Penguin Group
Penguin Books Ltd,
80 Strand, London WC2R 0RL
Penguin Putnam, Inc.
375 Hudson Street, NY 10014, USA
Penguin Books Australia Ltd,
487 Maroondah Highway, PO Box 257,
Ringwood, Victoria 3134, Australia
Penguin Books Canada Ltd,
10 Alcorn Avenue, Toronto, Ontario,
Canada M4V 1E4
Penguin Books (NZ) Ltd,
182–190 Wairau Road, Auckland 10,
New Zealand
Typeset in Bembo and Helvetica to an original design by Henry Iles.

Printed in Italy by LegoPrint S.p.A

464pp includes index
A catalogue record for this book is available from the British Library.
ISBN 1-84353-326-X

The publishers and authors have done their best to ensure the accuracy and currency of all the information in **The Rough Guide to Romania**; however, they can accept no responsibility for any loss, injury, or inconvenience sustained by any traveller as a result of information or advice contained in the guide.

1 3 5 7 9 8 6 4 2

Help us update

We've gone to a lot of effort to ensure that the fourth edition of **The Rough Guide to Romania** is accurate and up to date. However, things change – places get "discovered", opening hours are notoriously fickle, restaurants and rooms raise prices or lower standards. If you feel we've got it wrong or left something out, we'd like to know, and if you can remember the address, the price, the time, the phone number, so much the better.

We'll credit all contributions, and send a copy of the next edition (or any other Rough Guide if you prefer) for the best letters. Everyone who writes to us and isn't already a subscriber will receive a copy of our full-colour thrice-yearly newsletter. Please mark letters: **"Rough Guide to Romania Update"** and send to: Rough Guides, 80 Strand, London WC2R 0RL, or Rough Guides, 4th Floor, 345 Hudson St, New York, NY 10014. Or send an email to **mail@roughguides.com**

Have your questions answered and tell others about your trip at **www.roughguides.atinfopop.com**

Acknowledgements

The authors would like to thank the following people:

Tim – Isolde, Julian Ross, Colin Shaw, Mike Morton, Dan Gaman, Alison Richardson, Cris Parau, Kristin Soper, Johan Pyfferoen, Tibor Kalnoky, Alex Popescu, Patrick Colquhoun, Alin Prunean, Christoph Promberger, Grig Opriţoiu, Dana and Brandi Bates, Andrei Mahalnischi, Mátyás Ildiko, Angus and Loredana Sutherland, Robert Roth, Doru Munteanu, William Blacker, Jessica Douglas-Home, Csilla Hegedus, Dave Baxter, all the wonderful Peace Corps volunteers, including Nik Crain, Kris Vagos, Kathy Tin, Jack Dougherty, Ian Harrison and Deborah Grayson, and my Rough Guides colleagues including Norm Longley, Geoff Howard and Keith Drew…. and Pat – who gives me space in which to work.

Norm – Keith, Tim and Thomas; Dan Gaman, Mike and Angie Morton and Camelia Bolte.

Thomas – Tim, Norm, Geoff, Daga, Seth Baker, Zenko Balint, Colby DeHoff, Marius Dumitroaei, Rodica Firoiu, Beatrice Grigoraş, Christiaan M. Johnson, Lucia Muj, Myrna Phelps, Ciprian Slemcho.

Readers' letters

Thank you to all those readers who took the trouble to write in with their comments and suggestions (apologies for any misspellings or omissions): Marc Paul de Boer, Lee Devrey, Dave Ellen, Robert H. MacDonald, Amy Marsh, Jo Nicel, Robin Oakley, Caspian Richards, H. H. Saffery, Rita Shaw, Sarah Tierney, Philip Tolhurst.

Photo credits

SMALL PRINT

Index

Map entries are in colour.

G

H

I

J

K

L

M

Map symbols

Maps are keyed by number in the index (see coloured text)

International boundary	Waterfall
Chapter division boundary	Synagogue
Motorway	Lighthouse
Major road	Fountain
Minor road	Statue
Pedestrianized road	Ruin
Road under construction	Monastery
Steps	Castle
Path	Tower
Railway	Airport
Glacier	Arch
River	Tourist office
Canal	Accommodation
Wall	Post office
Metro station	Bus stop
Park	Hospital
Place of interest	Building
Campsite	Church (town maps)
Museum (Village)	Christian cemetery
Cave	Jewish cemetery
Mountain range	Peak
Gorge	Beach
Mountain pass	Marsh/bog

Map symbols

Maps are listed in the full index using coloured text.

INDEX

International boundary	Waterfall
Chapter division boundary	Synagogue
Motorway	Lighthouse
Major road	Monument
Minor road	Refuge hut
Pedestrianized road	Ruin
Road under construction	Monastery
Steps	Castle
Path	Tower
Railway	Airport
Cable car	Arch
River	Tourist office
Canal	Accommodation
Wall	Post office
Metro station	Bus stop
Peak	Stadium
Place of interest	Building
Campsite	Church (town maps)
Museum (Village)	Christian cemetery
Cave	Jewish cemetery
Mountain range	Park
Gorge	Beach
Mountain pass	Marsh land